'The early yea[...]h its clear and accessible style[...]cher education. A range of well[...]ight to relevant and varied issu[...]larly input and practical approaches, including engaging tasks throughout, which will info[...]r's professional development in the early stages of teaching. This book should be at the top of every reading list for new teachers!'

Anna Lise Gordon, Academic Director and National Teaching Fellow, St Mary's University, UK

'*Learning to Teach in the Secondary School* has been the core text for the PGCE Secondary Course at the University of Worcester for a number of years. The contributors have a wealth of experience and expertise that helps trainees get to the root of issues in the secondary school, providing a foundation for further reading and discussion. The authors have the ability to separate the salient issues so that trainees can "question the given", offering intelligent opinion and thought. Readers can look practically, and rationally, at what constitutes effective teaching in the secondary classroom, proving that this is an excellent starting point for any new teacher. Every reference list I read cites this book, demonstrating it as a key text in teacher education. The 7th edition is a welcome update and will appeal massively to any professional who shares the ambition to make a difference in the classroom.'

Suzanne Lawson, Secondary PGCE Course Leader, University of Worcester, UK

'This book provides a useful and effective insight into being a teacher, and a pedagogical and practical understanding of the complexity of teaching. It successfully breaks down the various elements of the profession into sections, acknowledging that there might not be a template of a perfect teacher, but rather a series of skills, qualities and behaviours that inform and underpin effective teaching and learning.

With the changing landscape of ITE (initial teacher education) and the growth of school-led approaches, a comprehensive guide to support trainees across all aspects of their training (from what is a teacher and classroom behaviours to developing professional practice and securing a first post) is extremely valuable.'

Martin Husbands, Head of School Direct, Newman University, UK

'*Learning to Teach in the Secondary School*, Seventh Edition describes, analyses and reflects pertinently a trainee's experience in a Secondary school. It gives the Secondary trainee confidence by highlighting key foci; for example, professionalism, specific curriculum pedagogy, how to observe, and why teachers want to teach. Indeed, the edition "sells" the individualism of the teaching profession and why there is no other profession like it. This is also supported by relevant tasks for the trainee to engage with which explain and consolidate key concepts such as teacher reflection, mixing the practical with the theoretical learning theories.

The seventh edition is very accessible for all trainee teachers, full of useful advice on time management, how to manage work/life balance and how to be proactive in an ever evolving profession. Highly recommended.'

Alyson Midgley, Secondary Flexible PGCE Programme Leader, Edge Hill University, UK

'This book covers the key themes affecting secondary teacher education today. The authors offer a challenging rather than a descriptive account of contemporary issues affecting Initial Teacher Education. Trainee teachers are encouraged to think about their changing professional role and to explore broader conceptions of it; they are asked to engage with current issues surrounding pedagogic knowledge, its influences and determiners, and to reflect on their actions in response.

Trainee teachers following pre- or in-service routes into teaching will find the book a useful resource. It will appeal to trainee teachers following one of a number of routes into teaching, including university-based; School Direct; school-centred (SCITTs) and the Assessment-Only routes to QTS. Whilst offering many practical ideas and suggestions for use in everyday practice, it also makes the link between initial teacher education and on-going professional career development.

If not already included, the book will make a useful addition to programme reading lists.'

Val Butcher, Associate Dean and Head of Department,
Manchester Metropolitan University, UK

LEARNING TO TEACH IN THE SECONDARY SCHOOL

Learning to Teach in the Secondary School is the market-leading text for all undergraduate, postgraduate and school-based routes to qualified teacher status. It offers an in-depth and practical introduction to the knowledge, skills and understanding needed to become a confident and effective teacher. With a focus on evidence-based practice, the book includes a wealth of examples to demonstrate how to successfully apply theory to practice, and how to critically analyse your practice to maximise pupil learning.

This seventh edition is fully updated in light of the latest initiatives, evidence and research in the field, offering comprehensive coverage, unit by unit, of the key concepts and skills addressed on initial teacher education programmes in preparation for work in schools. The wide range of pedagogical features support both university-based work – including that up to Masters level – and school-based initial teacher education, and are designed to help you develop those qualities that lead to good practice and a successful future in education.

Written by expert practitioners, 36 essential units include:

- planning lessons, units of work and schemes of work
- adopting a positive approach to managing behaviour to support learning
- ways pupils learn
- motivating pupils
- assessment
- inclusion and special educational needs
- using ICT and digital technologies
- pupil grouping, progression and differentiation
- managing time, workload and stress
- getting your first teaching post.

With a variety of activities and tasks to help you to reflect on your own learning and performance, and a revised companion website with three brand new units, *Learning to Teach in the Secondary School* provides practical help and guidance for many of the situations and potential challenges you are faced with in school. Supported by the *Learning to Teach Subjects in the Secondary School* series, it is an essential purchase for every aspiring secondary school teacher.

Susan Capel is Professor of Physical Education at Brunel University, UK.

Marilyn Leask is Chair of the Education Futures Collaboration charity and was previously a teacher and Professor at Brunel University, UK and the University of Bedfordshire, UK.

Sarah Younie is Reader in Education, Innovation and Technology at De Montfort University, UK.

LEARNING TO TEACH SUBJECTS IN THE SECONDARY SCHOOL SERIES

Series Editors: Susan Capel and Marilyn Leask

Designed for all students learning to teach in secondary schools, including those on school-based initial teacher education programmes, the books in this series complement *Learning to Teach in the Secondary School* and its companion, *Starting to Teach in the Secondary School*. Each book in the series applies underpinning theory and evidence to address practical issues to support student teachers in school and in higher education institutions in learning how to teach a particular subject.

LEARNING TO TEACH IN THE SECONDARY SCHOOL

A companion to school experience

Seventh edition

Edited by
Susan Capel, Marilyn Leask and
Sarah Younie

Routledge
Taylor & Francis Group

LONDON AND NEW YORK

First published 2016
by Routledge
2 Park Square, Milton Park, Abingdon, Oxon OX14 4RN

and by Routledge
711 Third Avenue, New York, NY 10017

Routledge is an imprint of the Taylor & Francis Group, an informa business

British Library Cataloguing in Publication Data
A catalogue record for this book is available from the British Library

Library of Congress Cataloging in Publication Data
Names: Capel, Susan Anne, 1953- editor.
Title: Learning to teach in the secondary school : a companion to school experience / edited by Susan Capel, Marilyn Leask and Sarah Younie.
Description: Seventh edition. | New York : Routledge, 2016.
Identifiers: LCCN 2015035497| ISBN 9781138787698 (Hardback) | ISBN 9781138787704 (Paperback) | ISBN 9781315766232 (Ebook)
Subjects: LCSH: High school teaching - Handbooks, manuals, etc. | Classroom management - Handbooks, manuals, etc.
Classification: LCC LB1737.A3 L43 2016 | DDC 373.1102 - dc23
LC record available at http://lccn.loc.gov/2015035497

ISBN: 978-1-138-78769-8 (hbk)
ISBN: 978-1-138-78770-4 (pbk)
ISBN: 978-1-315-76623-2 (ebk)

Typeset in Interstate
by Florence Production Ltd, Stoodleigh, Devon, UK

Printed and bound in Great Britain by
TJ International Ltd, Padstow, Cornwall

CONTENTS

3 CLASSROOM INTERACTIONS AND MANAGING PUPILS 139

3.1 Communicating with pupils 141
PAULA ZWOZDIAK-MYERS AND SUSAN CAPEL

■ Verbal communication ■ Types of communication ■ Non-verbal communication ■ Presenting yourself effectively ■

3.2 Motivating pupils 160
MISIA GERVIS AND SUSAN CAPEL

■ What is motivation? ■ Theories of motivation ■ What motivates people? ■ Some specific factors that influence pupils' motivation to learn ■ Motivating individuals and the class as a whole ■

3.3 Managing classroom behaviour: adopting a positive approach 180
PHILIP GARNER

■ The current context: official advice and guidance ■ What is unacceptable behaviour? ■ Scoping the causal factors ■ Key principles of a behaviour for learning approach ■ Getting the simple things right! ■ Rights, responsibilities, routines and rules ■ Consequences ■

3.4 Primary-secondary transitions 200
DIVYA JINDAL-SNAPE

■ Conceptualisation of educational transition and its impact on planning and preparation ■ Issues related to primary-secondary transitions ■ Understanding transitions through theoretical perspectives ■ Examples of planning and preparation for primary-secondary transition ■ What seems to work for pupils? ■

4 MEETING INDIVIDUAL DIFFERENCES 215

4.1 Pupil grouping, progression and differentiation 217
ALEXANDRA TITCHMARSH

■ Grouping pupils across the school ■ Progression and differentiation ■ Case studies of pupils ■

4.2 Adolescence, health and well-being 235
CERI MAGILL AND BARBARA WALSH

■ About development and growth ■ Diet, health and well-being ■ Moving forward ■

4.3 Cognitive development 248
JUDY IRESON AND PAUL DAVIES

■ Differences between pupils ■ Developing cognitive abilities ■ Creative problem-solving ■ Measuring cognitive development and intelligence tests ■

COMPANION @ WEBSITE

ILLUSTRATIONS

Figures

Tables

■ TASKS

CONTRIBUTORS

Michael Allen is Senior Lecturer in Education at Kingston University, UK.

Sophy Bassett is Senior Lecturer and Admissions Tutor for the BA (Hons) Secondary Physical Education degree with QTS at the University of Bedfordshire, UK.

Anna Beck is a Lecturer in Teacher Professional Learning at the University of Strathclyde. Prior to this, she undertook a PhD in Teacher Education Policy at the University of Glasgow. Her research interests include public policy-making; network governance and policy networks; critical policy analysis; educational politics; teacher engagement and teacher professional learning.

Mark Bowler is Senior Lecturer and Course Coordinator for the BA (Hons) Secondary Physical Education degree with QTS at the University of Bedfordshire, UK.

Hazel Bryan is Professor of Education at the University of Gloucestershire, UK, having formerly been Head of Research and Knowledge Exchange in the Faculty of Education at Canterbury Christ Church University, UK.

Diana Burton leads Education Research at the University of Wolverhampton, UK, and was previously Pro-Vice Chancellor for Research and Academic Enhancement at Liverpool John Moores University, UK.

Susan Capel is Professor (Physical Education) in the Department of Life Sciences at Brunel University, London, UK.

Chris Carpenter is a Senior Lecturer in Secondary Education at Canterbury Christ Church University, UK.

Sue Collins has a background in primary science education and initial teacher training. She was subject leader for Education at Brunel University, London, UK, for two years and is now Visiting Research Associate at UCL Institute of Education.

Paul Davies is a Senior Lecturer in Science Education at University College London Institute of Education, University of London, UK. He has a background in biology education, taught in London schools for 10 years and is interested in informal learning in biology and how technology supports learning in science.

Philip Garner is Professor of Education at the University of Northampton, UK.

Misia Gervis is Senior Lecturer (Coaching and Performance/Sport Psychology) and Programme Development Coordinator in the Department of Life Sciences, College of Health and Life Sciences, Brunel University, London, UK.

David Grace taught for nearly 40 years in Inner London and Pembrokeshire, most as Head of Physics and Head of Science, until taking up his current position as PGCE Physics and Balanced Science Tutor at Aberystwyth University.

Andrew Green is Senior Lecturer in Education at Brunel University, London, UK.

Terry Haydn is Professor of Education at the School of Education and Lifelong Learning at the University of East Anglia, UK.

Graham Haydon retired as Reader in Philosophy of Education, at the Institute of Education, UCL, London, UK.

Ruth Heilbronn is a Senior Research Associate at the Institute of Education, UCL, London, UK.

Paul Howard-Jones is Professor in Neuroscience and Education at the University of Bristol, UK, publishing on issues of theory, policy and practice at the interface of these two fields. He is presently applying neuroimaging techniques and classroom-based research methods to understand more about the design and implementation of learning games in schools.

Judy Ireson is Emeritus Professor of Psychology in Education at the Institute of Education, UCL, London, UK.

Divya Jindal-Snape is Professor of Education, Inclusion and Life Transitions. She is the founder Director of the Transformative Change: Educational and Life Transitions (TCELT) Research Centre at the University of Dundee, UK. She has published extensively in the area of transitions and is also involved in designing creative educational resources to facilitate educational and life transitions.

Jeanne Keay is Pro Vice Chancellor at the University of the West of Scotland, UK.

Julia Lawrence is Head of School Partnerships in the Department of Teacher Education at the University of Hull, UK.

Marilyn Leask is co-Chair of MESH, the Mapping Educational Specialist knowHow initiative (www.meshguides.org) following a career in universities and government organisations as Teacher, Researcher and Professor of Education focused on research on pedagogic knowledge, digital technologies and evidence-informed practice.

Dawn Leslie has recently returned to secondary school teaching having previously held the position of Senior Lecturer in Education at Brunel University London, UK.

Susan Lewis is a Lecturer in Education at Aberystwyth University where she contributes to the PGCE science and to the CPD programmes.

Tony Liversidge is Assistant PGCE Secondary Programme Leader and Senior Lecturer in Science Education at Edge Hill University, UK.

Michelle Lowe is the Director of the Institute of Education at the University of Wolverhampton, UK.

Paul McFlynn is a lecturer in Education and PGCE post-primary Physical Education Course Director at the University of Ulster, UK.

Paul McQueen is a lecturer in Education and PGCE post-primary Music Course Director at the University of Ulster, UK.

Ceri Magill is Senior Lecturer in Physical Education and Sport Development at Liverpool John Moores University, UK.

John Moss is Dean of Education at Canterbury Christ Church University, UK.

Colette Murphy is Associate Professor in Education at Trinity College, University of Dublin, Ireland.

Debra Myhill is Director of the Centre for Research in Writing at the University of Exeter, and researches all aspects of writing and the teaching of writing. She is particularly interested in composing processes, both in children and adults; writers' linguistic choices and metalinguistic understanding; and the relationship between talk and writing.

Angela Newton is Principal Lecturer in Physical Education at the University of Bedfordshire, UK.

Nick Peacey taught in secondary schools and then managed provision for excluded pupils and those at risk of exclusion in Camden, Hackney and Islington. From 1990 to 2011, he was a member of staff at the Institute of Education, University of London, UK, responsible for a consortium of 40 LAs working on special education and directing government-commissioned national programmes in the same area, including the TDA Toolkit.

Andrea Raiker is an educational consultant, specialising in pedagogy and educational theory. She researches with academic colleagues in Finland, Kosovo, Italy and Slovenia.

Matti Rautiainen is Senior Lecturer in Pedagogy and Vice Head in the Department of Teacher Education at the University of Jyväskylä, Finland. His main research interests are education for democracy and teacher education.

Clyde Redfern is a Principal Lecturer and the Academic Group Leader (AGL) for Professional Practice and Policy Studies in Schools based in the School of Education at Staffordshire University, UK. He is the PGCE Primary and Secondary Awards Leader and Award Leader for the Design and Technology PGCE course.

Ana Redondo is Senior Lecturer and Subject Leader in Foreign Languages Education in Higher Education at the University of Bedfordshire, UK.

Antony Stockford is Senior Lecturer in PGCE Computer Science and Information Technology Education at the University of Bedfordshire, UK.

Stefanie Sullivan is Lecturer in Education at the Faculty of Social Science, School of Education, University of Nottingham, UK.

Alexandra Titchmarsh is Assistant Subject Leader for Geography at Tring School in Hertfordshire, UK.

Rob Toplis was Senior Lecturer in Secondary Science Education at Brunel University, London, UK. He is now an education consultant.

Barbara Walsh is a National Teaching Fellow and Director of the School, Sport Studies, Leisure and Nutrition at Liverpool John Moores University, UK.

Annabel Watson is Lecturer in Language Education and a member of the Centre for Research in Writing at the University of Exeter, UK. She teaches on Secondary English Initial Teacher Education programmes and her research interests centre on secondary students' writing development, particularly relating to linguistic and metalinguistic development and digital composition.

Carrie Winstanley is Principal Lecturer and Subject Leader for Education at the University of Roehampton, UK.

Bernadette Youens is Professor in Education at the School of Education, University of Nottingham, UK.

Sarah Younie is Reader in Education, Innovation and Technology at De Montfort University, UK, and also MA Programme Leader and supervises research students.

Paula Zwozdiak-Myers is a Lecturer in Education, Senior tutor, Programme Director for the EdD, and Programme Leader for the MA in Teaching at Brunel University, London, UK.

ACKNOWLEDGEMENTS

As we write this, the seventh edition of the book, we would like to start by thanking those who have contributed to the previous six editions.

First, we would like to thank Tony Turner for his vital contribution as editor throughout that time.

We would also like to thank all those people not cited as authors of units in the seventh edition but nevertheless whose work on units in the first six editions has contributed to the underpinning of units in the seventh edition.

Francoise Allen

Steve Bartlett

Rob Batho

Richard Bennett

Graham Butt

David Crook

Jon Davison

Jane Dowson

Susan Heightman

Margaret Jepson

David Lambert

Ralph Levinson

David Lines

Hilary Lowe

John McCormick

Catherine Moorhouse

Gill Nicholls

Norbert Pachler

David Pollak

Janet Pritchard

Jonathan Sharples

Roger Strangwick

Alexis Taylor

Allan Thurston

Keith Topping

Tony Turner

Gill Watson

Mike Watts

Margaret Whitehead

Barbara Wynn

Introduction

Susan Capel, Marilyn Leask and Sarah Younie

The book introduces the professional knowledge and skills required by teachers, including general principles of effective teaching. The book is backed up by subject-specific and practical texts (*Learning to Teach X Subject in the Secondary School* and *A Practical Guide to Teaching X Subject in the Secondary School*) in the *Learning to Teach in the Secondary School* series by the same editors and by *Readings for Learning to Teach in the Secondary School: A Companion to M Level Study*. This reader provides extension reading around key areas of professional knowledge underpinning teaching.

Teaching is a complex activity and is both an art and a science. In this book, we show that there are certain essential elements of teaching that you can master through practice and that help you become an effective teacher. An effective teacher is one who can integrate theory with practice, use evidence to underpin their professional judgement and use structured reflection to improve practice. An effective teacher is also comfortable in the presence of young people and is interested in them as individuals as well as learners. An effective teacher motivates and encourages pupils by planning interesting lessons, and links their teaching to the life experiences of pupils. Part of being effective is to respect your pupils and in turn earn their respect, not only through the skills mentioned, but by maintaining firm but fair discipline.

However, there is no one correct way of teaching, no one specific set of skills, techniques and procedures that you must master and apply mechanically. This is, in part, because your pupils are all different and each day brings a new context in which they operate. Every teacher is an individual and brings something of their own unique personality to the job and their interactions with pupils. We hope that this book helps you to develop skills, techniques and procedures, and provides you with an entry to ways of understanding what you do and see that you can bring together into an effective whole, which is appropriate for your individual personality and style and helps you to develop your personal philosophy of teaching and learning. We also hope that the text provides the stimulus for you to want to continue to learn and develop throughout your career as a teacher.

Developing your philosophy of teaching and learning

On your initial teacher education (ITE) programme, much of your time is spent in school. You can expect your ITE not merely to provide *training*, but also to introduce you to wider educational issues.

What we mean by this is that ITE is not an apprenticeship, but a step on the journey of personal development in which your teaching skills develop alongside an emerging understanding of the teaching and learning process and the education system in which it operates. This is a journey of discovery that begins on the first day of your ITE programme and may stop only when you retire. Teachers are expected to undertake further professional development throughout their career (many join their subject association to keep up to date (www.subjectassociation.org.uk/members_ links.aspx)). Thus, we use the term initial teacher *education* rather than initial teacher training throughout this book.

The school-based element of your ITE programme provides the opportunity to appreciate first-hand the complex, exciting and contradictory events of classroom interactions without the immediacy of having to teach all the time. It should allow you time, both in the classroom and the wider school, to make sense of experiences that demand explanations. Providing such explanations requires you to have a theory of teaching and learning.

By means of an organised ITE programme that provides for structured observation, practical experience and reflective activity suitably interwoven with theoretical inputs and evidence, you begin to develop your own theory of teaching and learning, which is embedded in your practice. Theoretical inputs and evidence to underpin practice can come from a range of sources, including tutors and teachers, lectures and print- and web-based resources. Theory also arises from practice, the better to inform and develop practice.

Everyone who teaches has a theory of how to teach effectively and of how pupils learn. The theory may be implicit in what the teacher does and teachers may not be able to tell you what their theory is. For example, a teacher who is a disciplinarian is likely to have a different theory about the conditions for learning than a teacher who is liberal in their teaching style. Likewise, some teachers may feel that they do not have a philosophy of education. What these teachers are really saying is that they have not examined their views, or cannot articulate them. What is your philosophy? For example, do you consider that your job is to transfer the knowledge of your subject to pupils? Or are you there to lead them through its main features? Are you 'filling empty vessels' or are you the guide on a 'voyage of discovery'? On the other hand, perhaps you are the potter, shaping and moulding pupils.

There are a number of different theories about teaching and learning. You need to be aware of what these are, reflect on them and consider how they help you to explain more fully what you are trying to do and why. Through the process of theorising about what you are doing, reflecting on a range of other theories as well as your own, and drawing on the evidence base, you understand your practice better and develop into a reflective practitioner, that is, a teacher who makes conscious decisions about teaching strategies to employ and who modifies their practice in the light of experiences. It is recognised that ITE only enables you to start developing your own personal understanding of the teaching and learning process. Hence, this process must continue throughout your career.

An articulated, conscious philosophy of teaching emerges only if a particular set of habits is developed, in particular the habit of reviewing your own teaching systematically. It is these habits that need to be developed from the start of your ITE programme. This is why we (as well as your ITE tutors) ask you to evaluate your own teaching, to keep a diary of your evaluations (reflective practice), a folder of your lesson plans and other material to develop a professional development portfolio (PDP) to record your development and carry that forward from your ITE programme to your first post. (This is a file where you record evidence of your practice and reflections on practice. Your ITE programme provider will advise you about how to keep these records.)

Many higher education institutions now expect student teachers to develop their PDP or equivalent as an e-portfolio. If you are learning to teach in England, you may be required to compile a self-evaluation tool, which includes reflection and evidence.

How to use this book

Structure of the book

The book is laid out so that elements of appropriate background information and theory, along with evidence from research and practice, introduce each topic. These are interwoven with tasks designed to help you identify key features of the topic.

A number of different enquiry methods are suggested for you to use to generate data; for example, reflecting on reading and observation or on an activity you are asked to carry out, asking questions, gathering data, discussing with a tutor or another student teacher. Some of the tasks involve you in activities that impinge on other people; for example, observing a teacher in the classroom, or asking for information. If a task requires you to do this, *you must first of all seek the permission of the person concerned*. Remember that you are a guest in school(s); you cannot walk into any teacher's classroom to observe. In addition, some information may be personal or sensitive, and you need to consider issues of confidentiality and professional behaviour in your enquiries and reporting.

 This text is written primarily for student teachers, but should also be valuable to teachers in their early years of teaching. An appendix on writing and reflection is included on the companion website to help you with the written assignments on your ITE programme. The text also provides advice for you in undertaking the kind of action research project that could lead to master's-level accreditation. A glossary of terms is also included at the back of the book to help you interpret the jargon of education.

We call schoolchildren *pupils* to avoid confusion with *students*, by which we mean people in further and higher education. We refer to those learning to teach as *student teachers*. The important staff in your life are those in your school and higher education institution; we have called all these people *tutors*. Your institution will have its own way of referring to staff.

Meeting the requirements of your ITE

The range and type of requirements (standards) you are expected to meet during your ITE programme are derived from those for all student teachers in the country in which you are learning to teach. The units in this book are designed to help you work towards meeting these requirements. Your tutors in school and in your institution help you meet the requirements for your ITE programme. At appropriate points in the text, you should relate the work directly to the specific requirements for your ITE programme.

  Many student teachers are on programmes that provide accreditation towards a master's degree, which can be completed through further research and study focused on the workplace in your early years of teaching. The content of this book, some of the tasks, Further reading and the reader, together with the extra materials on the website, are intended to support master's-level work within your ITE. In this book, we use the symbol shown on the left to denote tasks that can be designed to meet the requirements of master's-level work, but it is up to your tutors to design assignment titles that meet the requirements of the higher education institution with which you are registered. Once you have qualified as a teacher, master's-level and doctorate in education programmes are designed to support your further professional development through research, reflection and wider reading.

Reflective practice, evidence-informed practice and your professional development portfolio (PDP)

As you read through the book, undertake other readings, complete the tasks and undertake other activities as part of your ITE programme, we suggest you keep a professional development portfolio (PDP). You may want to keep a diary of reflective practice to record your reactions to, and reflections on, events, both good and bad, as a way of letting off steam! It enables you to analyse strengths and areas for development, hopes for the future, and elements of your emerging personal philosophy of teaching and learning. Developing the ability to critically appraise research about teaching is integral to many ITE programmes as teaching moves towards being a profession with a publically accessible knowledge base (see www.meshguides.org for background information).

Your PDP holds a selective record of your development as a teacher, your strengths as well as areas for further development, and is something that you continue to develop throughout your teaching career. It is likely that your institution has a set format for a PDP. If not, you should develop your own. You can use any format and include any evidence you think appropriate. However, to be truly beneficial, it should contain evidence beyond the minimum required for your ITE programme. This further evidence could include, for example, work of value to you, a response to significant events, extracts from your diary of reflective practice, good lesson plans, evaluations of lessons, teaching reports, observations on you made by teachers, outcomes of tasks undertaken, and assessed and non-assessed coursework.

At the end of your ITE programme, you can use your PDP to evaluate your learning and achievements. It is also used as the basis for completing applications for your first post, and to take to interview. It can form the basis of a personal statement describing aspects of your development as a teacher during your ITE programme. Your PDP could include teaching reports written by teachers, tutors and yourself. It can also help provide the basis of your continuing professional development (CPD) as it enables you to identify aspects of your work in need of development and thus targets for induction and CPD in your first post, first through your self-evaluation tool if you are learning to teach in England, then as part of the appraisal process you will be involved with as a teacher.

Ways you might like to use this book

With much (or all) of your ITE programme being delivered in school, you may have limited access to a library, to other student teachers with whom to discuss problems and issues at the end of the school day and, in some instances, limited access to a tutor to whom you can refer. There are likely to be times when you are faced with a problem in school that has not been addressed up to that point within your ITE programme and you need some help immediately; for example, before facing a class the next day or next week. This book is designed to help you address some of the issues or difficulties you are faced with during your ITE programme, by providing supporting knowledge interspersed with a range of tasks to enable you to link theory with practice.

The book may be useful in a number of ways. You may wish to use it alongside your ITE handbook, which outlines specific ITE requirements, agreed ways of working, roles and responsibilities. It is designed more for you to dip in and out of, to look up a specific problem or issue that you want to consider, rather than for you to read from cover to cover (although you may want to use it in both ways, of course). You can use it on your own as it provides background information and supporting theory along with evidence from research and practice about a range of issues you are likely to face during your ITE programme.

Using the tasks

Reflecting on an issue faced in school with greater understanding of evidence of what others have written and said about it, alongside undertaking some of the associated tasks, may help you to identify some potential solutions. The tasks can also be used for collaborative work with other student teachers or your tutors. Although you can complete many of the tasks individually, most tasks benefit from wider discussion, which we encourage you to do whenever possible. However, some tasks can be carried out only with other student teachers and/or with the support of a tutor. You should select those tasks that are appropriate to your circumstances.

Further reading

This book will not suffice alone; we have attempted to provide you with guidance to further reading by two methods: first, by references to print- and web-based material in the text, the details of which appear in the References; second, by Further reading and relevant websites at the end of each unit.

 There is much educational material on the Internet. Government, teaching council and subject association websites are useful. However, there are many others but do look at the evidence underpinning the advice on offer. Custom and practice in all professions is under scrutiny as expectations for professional practice to be evidence-based rise. Useful websites are listed in each unit in the book. The companion website for this text (www.routledge.com.cw.capel) includes further information and links to useful websites. It also contains several units, including 'Managing yourself and your workload' and 'Using research and evidence to inform your teaching', from the text *Starting to Teach in the Secondary School* (Capel *et al.* 2004), which support material in this text and were written specifically to support newly qualified teachers. We suggest you keep a record of useful websites in your PDP. Many of the contributors to this book are producing guidance based on research summaries to support your ongoing professional development (these are published via www.meshguides.org).

If you see each unit as potentially an open door leading to whole new worlds of thought about how societies can best educate their children, then you have achieved one of our goals: that is, to provide you with a guidebook on your journey of discovery about teaching and learning. Remember, teaching is about the contribution you make to your pupils, to their development and their learning, and to the well-being of society through the education of our young people.

Finally, we hope that you find the book useful, and of support in school. If you like it, tell others; if not, tell us.

Susan Capel, Marilyn Leask and Sarah Younie
March 2016

1 Becoming a teacher

The four units in this chapter explore the complexity and breadth of the teacher's role and the nature of teaching. To become an effective teacher, you need to supplement your *subject content knowledge* with *pedagogical knowledge* (about teaching and learning) and to develop your *professional knowledge, skills and judgement*; for example, about managing situations that arise with pupils, such as the one below in the poem called 'Late'.

> You're late, said miss
> The bell has gone,
> dinner numbers done
> and work begun.
> What have you got to say for yourself?
> Well, it's like this, miss
> me mum was sick,
> me dad fell down the stairs,
> the wheel fell off my bike
> and then we lost our Billy's snake
> behind the kitchen chairs. Earache
> struck down me grampy, me gran
> took quite a funny turn.
> Then on the way I met this man
> whose dog attacked me shin –
> look, miss you can see the blood
> it doesn't look too good,
> does it?
> Yes, yes sit down –
> and next time say you're sorry
> for disturbing all the class.
> Now get on with your story
> fast!
> Please miss, I've got nothing to write about.

(Judith Nicholls, 'Late', cited in Batchford 1992)

Ways of developing your professional knowledge, skills and judgement provide themes running throughout the book. Evidence about effective practice is becoming increasingly easy to access to support your development. In the UK, you can find a wealth of material on websites, including government-supported and subject association websites, to support you as a teacher.

Each unit in this chapter examines different facets of the work of student and experienced teachers. You are posed questions about your values and attitudes because these influence the type of teacher you become, the ethos of your school and the values and attitudes of pupils in your care.

Unit 1.1 is designed to give you an introduction into what teachers do. We look at teachers as individuals, before considering your role as a teacher, including wider aspects of the teacher's role – academic and pastoral roles and administration, as well as introducing the work in the classroom. We then consider professional knowledge for teaching generally, followed by specific consideration of one aspect of general pedagogic knowledge – aspects of managing the learning environment, as well as teacher language. Finally, we introduce classroom rights and responsibilities.

In Unit 1.2, we discuss your roles and responsibilities as student teachers. This is designed to support you in preparing for school experience and on school experience itself. Your professional relationships with those with whom you work are very important; hence, we look at working with staff and pupils on school experience (including your professional and subject tutors, the class teacher and the pupils themselves). We then consider the expectations that the tutors in school and higher education institution responsible for your initial teacher education have of you. The meaning of professionalism is discussed and the idea that you will have your own philosophy of teaching is introduced. Phases that mark your development as a teacher are identified. We suggest that as your own confidence and competence in managing the classroom grow, you can expect the focus of your work to move from your self-image and the mechanics of managing a lesson, to the learning taking place generally and, as you become more experienced, to the learning for the individual pupil.

Unit 1.3 provides advice for managing your workload and your time, both inside and outside the classroom. It then looks at potential causes of stress, ways of preventing stress and managing and coping with stress that you cannot prevent. The unit emphasises that approaches to managing your workload, time and stress are individual, but being successful in managing competing demands on your time gives you time to enjoy your work and have time for leisure. It then considers how you can build your resilience, which is what sustains and enables teachers to thrive rather than just survive in the profession.

Unit 1.4 focuses on using information and communications technology (ICT)/digital technologies for professional purposes. It gives a rationale for, and highlights the relevance of, using ICT. It also provides a framework for auditing your knowledge and understanding of ICT, which is important self-knowledge for enhancing your competence in using ICT. The unit 'walks you through' an example of using ICT – taking a video as part of a lesson – which is designed to show you how everyday technology (a mobile phone) can be used to enhance your pupils' learning. The unit then looks at pupils bringing their own devices to lessons. Finally, the unit focuses on your planning to teach using ICT resources.

1.1 What do teachers do?

Andrew Green and Marilyn Leask

Now, what I want is, Facts. Teach these boys and girls nothing but Facts. Facts alone are wanted in life. Plant nothing else, and root out everything else. You can only form the minds of reasoning animals upon Facts: nothing else will ever be of any service to them. This is the principle on which I bring up my own children, and this is the principle on which I bring up these children. Stick to Facts, sir!

(Thomas Gradgrind – Dickens, *Hard Times*)

Tell me, I will forget. Show me, I may remember. Involve me, and I will understand.

(old Chinese proverb)

Introduction

Your personal values, views of the purposes of education and of the role of the teacher in the development of the pupils are major influences on your development as a teacher. Education is probably the most powerful influence on the development of our society. The education that young people receive through schooling goes beyond knowledge about a body of academic subjects: it is built upon and shapes the values, rights and responsibilities that make our society distinctive. That is why the form and content of education are so often the focus of scrutiny and are so keenly contested, and why you need to be able to articulate and develop your personal philosophy of education. To develop your understanding, you may wish to join such debates, which are held through subject association networks, conferences and, to some extent, social media.

Everyone has an opinion of what teachers do. Often, these views are formed by personal experiences of school, and they are often idealised by the passage of time. The media, television, cinemas and literature also provide people with many and varied representations of teachers. What examples spring to your mind? Nobody entering the teaching profession does so as a blank canvas; everyone has experienced education, and this shapes their sense of what teachers are and do. Not all of these views are either valid or useful, however, and it is important to understand these in the context of the current school system, national education policies and the demands they place on teachers. In Units 5.3 and 7.1, you are invited to consider your personal stance on the aims, purposes and practices in education.

The two epigraphs at the beginning of the unit illustrate how different views of education and its functions can be; how differently societies and cultures construct the relationship between teachers and learners.

Teachers, pupils, parents, carers, politicians, local authorities (LAs)/councils, teachers' unions, professional subject associations and educational researchers may have very divergent views of what teachers should do and how they should do it. Each of these perspectives needs to be considered. What a parent may expect from you as a teacher, what their child may expect and what you as a teacher believe you should provide may differ significantly.

What teachers do, therefore, is complex. How to manage this without compromising either the needs of the individual pupil, the requirements of parents and carers, or your own professional integrity is the focus of this unit.

OBJECTIVES

At the end of this unit, you should be able to:

- describe your developing vision of yourself as a teacher and the values and ethical code/code of conduct that will guide your work;
- describe various aspects of a teacher's academic, pastoral and administrative roles;
- consider effective use of language as a teacher;
- understand the multifaceted nature of the knowledge required for effective teaching;
- explain how teachers can proactively manage the learning environment;
- explain the rights and responsibilities of teachers and learners within classrooms;
- demonstrate that your digital profile reflects the values and behaviours you aspire to as a teacher.

Check the requirements of your initial teacher education (ITE) programme to see which relate to this unit.

Teachers as individuals: your values and ethics

Teaching is a deeply personal activity. Pupils respond strongly to individual teachers. Think back to your own schooldays and the teachers you had. What do you remember about them? What did they do? Who are the teachers you most liked, and why? Which teachers did you least like, and why? Almost certainly the issues you identify are to do with personality (enthusiasm, intelligence, humour, eccentricity, conformity, efficiency, incompetence). Similarly, some of the first things *your* pupils will pick up on are your personality and your qualities. Parents and carers look at you as a person, but are also interested in a different set of issues: Are you likely to form supportive relationships with their child? Do you communicate with them regularly and clearly? Do they believe you're competent?

Your head of department and senior staff may apply another set of criteria: What skills and interests do you have that could be of benefit to the department or wider school curriculum?

What you do as a teacher, therefore, has to meet a complex set of demands, and your ITE programme should provide you with opportunities both to explore individually the kind of teacher you wish to be, and also to understand the context in which you are working and the demands this places upon you as a teacher to be professional and collegial. For further reading about professionalism, see Kizlik (2015); OECD TALIS (2015); the Brindley (2015) *Masterclass* texts; and Wragg (2004).

Your values and your ethical code

What ethical code will guide your practice as a teacher? Teaching Councils are organisations that deal with teacher professionalism, and adhering to an ethical code of practice is a condition of registration. See the United Kingdom (UK) Teaching Councils and Teachers' Standards websites (listed on page 595) and review the ethical codes that teachers who are members are required to adhere to. The General Teaching Council for Scotland (GTCS) also has a code of conduct for student teachers that touches on these issues: professionalism, responsibilities, competence, collegiality and working with stakeholders, equality and diversity (www.gtcs.org.uk/web/FILES/teacher-regulation/ student-teacher-code-0412.pdf). Task 1.1.1 asks you to consider several codes of conduct and adopt or draw up your own ethical code/code of conduct to guide you during your ITE programme and beyond into your teaching career.

 Task 1.1.1 Your code of professional conduct and ethics

Consider some of the professional codes of conduct on subject association and Teaching Council websites (see websites listed on page 595). Review the ethical codes that teachers are required to adhere to in different countries. The GTCS also has a code of conduct for student teachers, which provides a starting point (www.gtcs.org.uk/web/FILES/teacher-regulation/student-teacher-code-0412.pdf).

Discuss the outcomes with other student teachers and record your code of conduct in your professional development portfolio (PDP) or equivalent professional record file.

Your role as a teacher

 The teacher's job is first and foremost to ensure that pupils learn. To a large extent, *what* pupils should learn is determined through a published curriculum. The term hidden curriculum refers to what is learned outside the formal curriculum (see Unit 7.2). In England, there is a 'National Curriculum' – although many schools, for example free schools, independent schools and academies, are not subject to this. The companion website for this book (www.routledge.com.cw.capel) has units about the Welsh, Scottish and Irish curricula. *How* you teach, however (that is, the methods and materials used), is left to your professional judgement.

Task 1.1.2 now focuses on what you personally need to do to become a qualified teacher.

Task 1.1.2 Focusing on the teachers' standards

You need to be familiar with the Teachers' Standards for the country relevant to your ITE programme. These should be in your ITE programme handbook and other documentation provided by your ITE provider. Look at them now. What do they tell you about your role as a teacher? What do they mean to you at the beginning of your ITE programme? Do you feel they capture what you want to be as a teacher? Talk to your tutor about what achieving the standards might look like at the end of your programme.

Which aspects of these Teachers' Standards do you feel most prepared to meet? Which do you believe you need more help to meet? How do you see yourself developing your capability over your career as a teacher? You may find it useful to discuss these areas with an experienced teacher, thinking about how you can record evidence of your achievements and any areas where you may require additional support.

Store the information in your PDP.

You need to spend time observing experienced teachers, and you are unlikely to see two teachers the same (see Unit 2.1). Some of the teaching styles and strategies you see you will like and relate to; others may not seem as appropriate and comfortable (see Unit 5.3). These preferences and responses are important as you think about your own developing practice. Do not dismiss anything too quickly, however. Just because you do not like a particular approach or because a particular class does not respond well does not necessarily make the approach inappropriate. There is no single correct way to teach. Provided effective teaching and learning takes place, a range of approaches, from didactic (formal, heavy on content) to experiential (learning by doing), is appropriate – often in the same lesson (see Unit 5.3 on teaching styles and Unit 4.1 on ways to group pupils for learning). Using video to record your practice so you can analyse and improve this is recommended.

You also have responsibility for the pastoral and personal development of your pupils. In approaching this, you have an important role to play in supporting the school ethos by reinforcing school values, rules and routines; for example, behaviour, dress, mutual respect, the right to learn, and in encouraging pupils to develop self-discipline so that the school can function effectively and pupils can make the most of opportunities the school and their schooling offers.

Finally, you will need to develop efficient ways of dealing with administration (see Unit 1.3). Developing your information and communications technology (ICT) skills is essential in helping you prepare teaching materials, in recording and monitoring progress, and in keeping up to date with daily administrative tasks. Some teachers keep their pupil records electronically using spreadsheets, and schools normally have management information systems holding data used to monitor pupil performance and assessment. For advice in your subject area, see the subject-specific and practical texts in this *Learning to Teach in the Secondary School* series (see p. ii of this text).

So, your role as a teacher falls into distinct categories. You have responsibility for both the academic and the pastoral development of your pupils. Table 1.1.1 lists the main activities in each of these areas that you are expected to undertake.

Table 1.1.1 Some of the activities that teachers undertake in their academic and pastoral roles

The academic role	The pastoral role and spiritual and moral welfare
This encompasses a variety of activities, including: ■ subject teaching ■ lesson preparation ■ setting and marking of homework ■ monitoring pupil progress over time ■ assessing pupil progress in a variety of ways, including marking tests and exams ■ writing reports ■ working as part of a subject team ■ curriculum development and planning ■ undertaking visits, field courses ■ reporting to parents ■ planning and implementing school policies ■ extracurricular activities ■ being an examiner for public examination boards; for example, General Certificate of Secondary Education (GCSE)/General Certificate of Education (GCE)/Advanced (A) Level boards ■ keeping up to date (often through work with your subject association) (see www.subjectassociation.org.uk/members_links) ■ undertaking research in research active schools ■ supporting the professional development of other staff	These roles vary from school to school. They often include: ■ getting to know pupils as individuals ■ helping pupils with problems ■ being responsible for a form/tutor group ■ registering the class, following up absences ■ monitoring sanctions and rewards given to form members ■ reinforcing school rules and routines; for example, on behaviour ■ recording achievement ■ writing reports, ensuring records of achievement and/or profiles are up to date ■ working collegially as part of a pastoral team ■ teaching personal, social, health education (PSHE) and citizenship ■ house/year group activities (plays/sports) ■ liaising with parents and carers ■ ensuring school information is conveyed to parents via pupils ■ giving careers and subject guidance ■ extracurricular activities; for example, educational trips ■ taking part in a daily act of worship required by legislation ■ liaising with primary schools

Your role in raising attainment and improving life chances

Raising attainment is a collective endeavour involving all in the school working together. The connection between educational attainment and life chances is significant. Pupils obtaining the best grades have more choices, are able to access the top-ranking universities and employment, and so on. It is thus clearly desirable that pupils attain to the very best of their ability through their schooling. It is incumbent on you as a teacher to ensure that every pupil is given the very best opportunity to fulfil his or her potential, and great pressure is often applied to teachers. Pupil attainments are compared internationally and the results are of great interest and concern for governments (see Unit 7.4). However, where too much attention is paid to raising attainment without corresponding attention to developing learners' inquisitiveness and autonomy, instrumental practice can easily emerge. 'Spoon-feeding' and 'teaching to the test' may lead to improved attainment in headline examinations, but do little genuinely to enhance pupils' transferrable abilities as lifelong learners (see, for example, Volante 2004). For the teacher, the drive to ensure that pupils achieve the best possible results in their assessments must be tempered by the need to provide pupils with the resources they need to be independently functional members of society. This is where educational politics comes face-to-face with educational ethics. It is the pupils who emerge with the most robust independent abilities who are best placed to meet the increasingly challenging and uncertain demands of employability in the twenty-first-century world. Therefore, you need to think very carefully about how you respond to the needs of your pupils and the demands of your employers as you consider issues of raising attainment. Pupils' self-belief and motivation to learn are essential in providing foundations for successful learning, and there is no foundation for commonly held beliefs that intelligence is fixed (see Unit 5.6). You have responsibility for ensuring pupils themselves realise that they do have considerable capacity and can set high expectations of themselves. The poem 'The Average Child' highlights the damaging effect on learners of views that intelligence is fixed (see Table 1.1.2). Then complete Task 1.1.3.

Table 1.1.2 'The Average Child'

I don't cause teachers trouble, my grades have been okay.
I listen in my classes and I'm in school every day.
My parents think I'm average, my teachers think so too.
I wish I didn't know that cause there's lots I'd like to do.
I'd like to build a space rocket, I've a book that shows you how.
Or start a stamp collection, well no use trying now.
Cause since I've found I'm average, I'm just not smart enough you see,
I know there's nothing special that I should expect of me.
I'm part of that majority that hump part of the bell*,
Who'll just spend all his life in an average kind of hell.

* This refers to the bell shape of a 'normal distribution' curve.
Source: Buscemi (date unknown).

 Task 1.1.3 Motivating learners

Reflect on 'The Average Child' (Table 1.1.2). Think about its implications for your own teaching. In your classroom observations and evaluations, focus on an 'average child' for a number of sessions. Plan your interactions with a small group of these pupils so that you leave them feeling positive about learning and their capacities. Discuss your perceptions with other student teachers and record these in your PDP.

Teacher language

Language is clearly central to the process of teaching and learning. Whether you are communicating with pupils in the spoken or the written medium, it is essential that you think very carefully about your use of language. It is important to remember that language is used in the classroom for a variety of purposes:

- to give instructions;
- to impart information;
- to question;
- to develop relationships;
- to provide direction through the lesson, and so on.

An important issue to consider in relation to teacher language is the use of technical subject terminology. Every subject has its own vocabulary, and it is the subject teacher's responsibility to think about this. If science teachers wish their pupils to know how to spell and use the word 'photosynthesis' accurately, it is their job to teach this. Similarly, if you are a business studies teacher and wish your pupils to write reports, you need to equip them with the language tools to do so. Think very carefully about the language and the written forms of your subject. Are these in themselves useful and meaningful, or is it the concepts behind the words and forms that are more important? Think in detail about how and when to introduce subject-specific terminology and develop concise and accurate definitions that pupils are able to work with. Also be aware that terms have different meanings in different subject contexts. Take, for instance, the word 'depression':

- in geography, a depression is an area of low air pressure;
- in history, the Depression was a specific era of United States history in the late 1920s and the 1930s;
- in medicine, depression is a mental state;
- in English, it may be all of the above, or a hollow in the ground.

As a teacher, it is very important to think about how and when these different language modes are required, and how pupils will differentiate between them, whether encountered in the written or the spoken form. It is well worthwhile spending time exploring the range of your voice, so that you can develop appropriate varieties of tone and register for these different types of talk (see Unit 3.1). Which tone of voice will you adopt so that pupils know when you are giving instructions? How about when you are disciplining an individual or a class? Your tone of voice reinforces the purposes of language. Also, spend time thinking carefully about language formulas that might be useful, recording those used by experienced teachers whom you are observing and practising using them so as to build your professional toolkit. Such formulas include:

- I am not happy with . . .
- I want you to think carefully about . . .
- Either . . . or . . .
- I want you to make sure that . . .

Thinking through both what you want to say and how you want to say it will increase your confidence in the use of teacher language. Questions should be planned (see Unit 5.2). Transactional language (for example, instructions about how to move into groups) can be prepared ahead. Explanations are usually much clearer if you have thought them through in advance rather than trying to develop them on the spot in the classroom. Much of the language you will need to use is firmly within your control, and needs to be thought through in detail.

There are, of course, occasions when language needs to be spontaneous, such as when answering unexpected questions, or when dealing with behaviour that doesn't meet the standard you require. When managing such behaviours, it is very important to ensure that your language is clear, controlled and respectful – regardless of the language pupils may be using themselves and regardless of your own emotions. Behaviour management situations tend to arise unexpectedly but many behaviour management issues can be prevented by planning ahead and preparing possible responses (see Unit 3.3). The following questions will help you consider use of language in these situations; also, we suggest recording the techniques used by experienced teachers whom you are observing and practising using them. Such formulas include:

■   Is a verbal response necessary at all? Would silence or some non-verbal form of communication be more effective? Note stance, facial gestures, and arm and hand movements of experienced teachers.
■   Which tone of voice is best? A raised voice? A quiet voice? A sympathetic voice?
■   Should you speak in front of the whole class so all can hear – which may inflame a situation? Would it be more effective to speak to the individual or group of perpetrators quietly – saying perhaps "We can discuss this after the lesson"?
■   Should a response be immediate or would taking a moment to consider before speaking be more appropriate?

See the Behaviour2Learn website for detailed research-based advice (www.behaviour2learn. co.uk).

Think through and plan some language formulas that could be used in different situations. This will help you to behave in a calm, controlled and measured way. How and when, for example, might you use the following?

■   Either . . . or . . .
■   If you cannot calm down, then . . .
■   You know I do not like it when . . .
■   Are you refusing to . . .
■   Would it help if . . .
■   I think it would be better if . . .

Teacher language in all its forms needs to be very carefully considered, and is further explored in Unit 3.1, 'Communicating with pupils', and Unit 5.8, 'Creating a language-rich classroom'.

Finally, as this all makes clear, your voice is very important to you as a teacher, so you need to look after it. See if your ITE provider puts on sessions on voice projection and voice protection. Voice projection equipment designed for use in classrooms is also available should you need it.

The work in the classroom: the tip of the iceberg

On the surface, teaching may appear to be a relatively simple process – the view that teachers stand and talk to their classes and that the pupils automatically learn appears to be all too prevalent. (Ask friends and family what they think a teacher does.) The reality is somewhat different.

Classroom teaching is only the most visible part of teachers' work. The contents of this book introduce you to what we see as the invisible foundation of the teacher's work: *professional knowledge* (see Table 1.1.3) about teaching and learning and *professional judgement* about the routines, skills and strategies that support strong teaching. Effective teachers draw on these elements in their planning and preparation to ensure that there is *continuity* and *progression* in pupils' learning. Each lesson is planned as part of a sequence of learning experiences designed to build pupils' engagement with and understanding of the topics they are studying (see Unit 2.2).

The following analogy may help you understand what underpins your work in the classroom. Think of a lesson as being like an iceberg. The work in the classroom represents the tip of an iceberg (20-30 per cent). Supporting this tip, but hidden in the base (70-80 per cent), are the elements of teachers' professional expertise (see Figure 1.1.1). These elements include:

■ *planning* a sequence of lessons to ensure learning progresses;
■ *evaluation* of previous lessons;
■ *planning and preparation* for individual lessons;
■ *established routines and procedures* that ensure that the work of the class proceeds as planned;
■ *personality*, including the teacher's ability to capture and hold the interest of the class, to establish their authority;
■ *professional knowledge* such as subject content knowledge (SCK); pedagogic knowledge about effective teaching and learning; knowledge of learners; and knowledge about the educational context in which you work – local and national;
■ *professional judgement* built up over time through reflection on experience.

Throughout your ITE programme, you should expect to develop confidence and new levels of competence in all the areas in Figure 1.1.1.

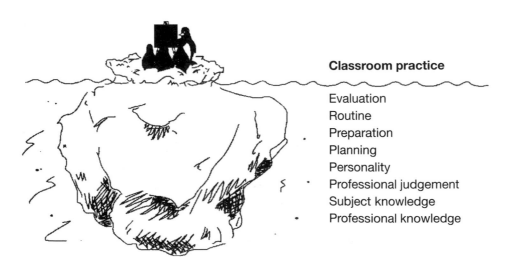

Classroom practice

Evaluation
Routine
Preparation
Planning
Personality
Professional judgement
Subject knowledge
Professional knowledge

Figure 1.1.1 The work in the classroom: the tip of the iceberg

Source: With kind permission of Simon Beer

Professional knowledge for teaching

This section gives an overview of the forms of knowledge you need for teaching.

Teaching requires you to transform the knowledge you possess into suitable tasks that lead to learning (sometimes called pedagogic knowledge). Knowing a lot about your subject does not automatically make you an effective teacher. Your professional knowledge comprises a number of different components.

The forms of knowledge teachers need have been described in different ways. Shulman (1986, 1987) identifies seven knowledge bases that form what he regards as the minimum knowledge for teaching. These are summarised in Table 1.1.3. This is a starting point for thinking about the forms of professional knowledge you may need to acquire.

Table 1.1.3 Forms of professional knowledge for teaching

---

1   *(Subject) content knowledge (SCK)*: the content that is to be taught. Schwab (1964) identifies two components of content knowledge:

- ▪ substantive: core concepts and skills in the subject;
- ▪ syntactic: the way these concepts and skills are structured and organised within the subject.

2   *General pedagogic knowledge (GPK)*: broad principles and strategies of classroom management and organisation that apply irrespective of the subject.

3   *Pedagogical content knowledge (PCK)*: knowledge of what makes for effective teaching and deep learning, providing the basis for teachers' selection, organisation and presentation of lesson content; that is, the integration of subject content and its related pedagogy. Grossman (1990) breaks PCK into four components:

- ▪ knowledge and beliefs about the *purposes* of teaching a subject at different levels;
- ▪ knowledge of pupils' understanding, *conceptions and misconceptions* of subject matter;
- ▪ knowledge of *curriculum* materials available for teaching a subject and knowledge of horizontal and vertical curricula for the subject;
- ▪ knowledge of *instructional strategies* and representations for teaching particular topics.

4   *Curriculum knowledge*: materials and programmes that serve as 'tools of the trade' for teachers.

5   *Knowledge of learners and their characteristics*: this comprises a variety of issues – how learners develop with age (empirical or social knowledge); learners' cognitive development; child development; and knowledge of the needs of particular individuals or groups of learners.

6   *Knowledge of educational contexts*: political, curricular, sociological, cultural, geographical, historical and psychological factors may all be important here.

7   *Knowledge of educational ends (aims), purposes, values, and philosophical and historical influences*: both short- and long-term goals of education in general and of particular subjects.

Source: Adapted from Shulman (1986, 1987)

Subject content knowledge (SCK)

This is a declared body of knowledge about your subject; the concepts and skills pupils are expected to acquire. You amass this knowledge from a variety of sources: your education at home, at school and at university, as well as through personal study and reading. Together, these shape the quantity and quality of your SCK. Your explicit awareness of and engagement with these different sources of content knowledge will vary, but as you begin your career as a teacher, this is likely to be the area in which you are most confident. You should actively seek to extend the range of your SCK. This process supports your confidence for teaching and engages you with your subject on a personal level. A word of caution, however: you may see this body of knowledge as the key measure of your likely effectiveness as a teacher, but it is the way you transform that knowledge into effective teaching that is most important. Task 1.1.4 asks you to audit your SCK.

 Task 1.1.4 Auditing your subject content knowledge (SCK)

Analyse a copy of the curriculum for your subject, identifying areas where your SCK is good now, areas in which you require some additional knowledge, and areas in which totally new learning is required. Set yourself targets for developing your knowledge in the areas for development you identify. Discuss these areas for development with your tutor. Plan a course of action for this development. Keep a record of your progress in your PDP.

General pedagogic knowledge (GPK)

This body of knowledge and understanding relates to the effective transformation of your SCK into meaningful learning for pupils. This knowledge includes the broad principles and strategies that are designed to guide class instruction, organisation and management (for example, settling a class, managing the learning environment for effective learning, managing resources and other equipment, gaining and sustaining the attention and interest of the class, encouraging the disaffected, supporting the less able and extending the most able). By developing your general pedagogic knowledge, your classroom becomes a more varied and stimulating place both for yourself and your pupils.

Pedagogical content knowledge (PCK)

This is a combination of SCK and pedagogy that provides the specific knowledge you need for effective teaching and learning in your subject area(s). For example, the ways in which music teachers shape teaching and learning will be different in some ways to the shaping of teaching and learning in design and technology.

Teaching requires you to adapt your SCK to the classroom demands of teaching. It also requires you to consider the processes of your subject and how you can teach these to your pupils. What, for example, are the language and writing demands of your subject, and how are you going to teach them? What research skills and processes should pupils adopt? What forms does assessment (both formative and summative) take in your subject area(s), and how does this relate to content and process? PCK is effectively what pedagogy looks like in your subject area(s). Shulman (1986: 9) sums it up as follows:

> [PCK is] the most useful form of representation of . . . [the most regularly taught topics in one's subject area] . . . the most powerful analogies, illustrations, examples, explanations, and demonstrations – in a word, the ways of representing and formulating the subject that makes it comprehensible to others.

You should also think about the historical development of your subject, and think about how it came to be as it is. This dimension enhances your sense of what your subject is about and why it is studied. For further information, see the subject-specific textbooks in the Routledge *Learning to Teach* series.

Curriculum knowledge

This is your knowledge of the requirements and range of programmes for the teaching of your subject(s) across the age ranges you are preparing to teach. It also encompasses knowledge of the variety of instructional materials available to support those programmes. It includes knowledge of the curriculum required in your country and in your school(s), the public examinations they serve and the requirements of those examinations.

Knowledge of learners and their characteristics

Learners come with different kinds of knowledge. Shulman (1986, 1987) and Grossman (1990) define this as including empirical and social knowledge; that is, what children of a particular age range are like, how they behave in classrooms and school, their interests and preoccupations, their social nature, and how contextual factors such as weather or exciting events can affect their work and behaviour and the nature of the pupil-teacher relationship, as well as cognitive knowledge.

You will need to think about how children develop and what they know, which consists of two elements: knowledge of child development which informs practice; and knowledge of a particular group of learners, the kind of knowledge that grows from regular contact with these learners, of what they can and cannot know, do or understand.

Knowledge of educational contexts

Shulman (1986, 1987) and Grossman (1990) define an educational context as any setting where learning takes place. This includes formal settings (schools, nurseries, universities and colleges), informal settings (home, museums, concert halls, art galleries, and so on) and broader educational contexts (social, cultural and communal). The context often has a significant effect on teaching and learning and the work of teachers. It is important to think about issues such as:

■   the type and size of schools;
■   their catchment areas;
■   class size;
■   the extent and quality of support for teachers;
■   the amount of feedback teachers receive on their performance;
■   quality of relationships in schools;
■   expectations, philosophies and attitudes of the head teacher;
■   schools' policies, curriculum, assessment processes, monitoring and reporting, safety, school rules and expectations;
■   the 'hidden' and 'informal' curriculum, which includes the values demonstrated to pupils through the way the school is run (see also Unit 7.2).

The units in Chapter 7 in this book and on the companion website provide an overview of educational contexts in other countries (Finland, Northern Ireland, Scotland and Wales). In the multicultural classrooms of today, you can expect to be teaching pupils from a wide range of different educational and cultural systems where the expectations of teachers and pupils may be quite different to those you have personally experienced.

Knowledge of educational ends (aims), purposes, values, and philosophical and historical influences

This includes the values and priorities that shape the education pupils receive. Teaching is a purposeful activity, both in the short-term (goals for individual lessons or series of lessons) and the long-term (broader purposes, philosophies and functions of education). Views as to the purposes of education vary widely. Some would argue that its long-term goal is to produce efficient workers to serve the needs of society. Others see education as being of intrinsic worth in itself. Aims and purposes tend to be implicit rather than obvious and openly enacted.

Your personal subject construct

All of the above aspects of professional knowledge for teaching are brought together in your *personal subject construct* (Banks *et al.* 1999), which is the version of the subject that encapsulates your values and assumptions about your subject. This construct provides the basis of your work as a teacher – your understanding of the nature of your subject and how to teach it. Think, for example, about how your political, philosophical, theoretical and religious views shape the version of your subject you wish to teach. Within subject areas, specific questions may arise. What, for instance, is the role of sport in physical education? Should creationism be taught alongside evolution and the Big Bang in science lessons? And what about your wider role as a teacher, beyond your subject boundaries? What is your view of supporting language development or teaching mathematical skills as the need arises in your lessons? Such questions have a significant impact on the choices you make as a teacher. You should ensure that the personal beliefs and subject constructs you use in the classroom do not exclude colleagues and pupils with different views.

Some of the units in this book aim to develop your *general pedagogic knowledge* – your understanding of classroom management and organisation and what makes for effective teaching and deep learning; your *knowledge of learners and their characteristics*; and your *knowledge of educational contexts*. Subject-specific pedagogic issues are covered in the subject texts in the *Learning to Teach in the Secondary School* series. Task 1.1.5 asks you to consider PCK.

M

> **Task 1.1.5 Pedagogical content knowledge (PCK)**
>
> Look closely at the forms of PCK in Table 1.1.3. Consider carefully how you could apply your knowledge in each of the categories identified by Grossman (1990) to your work with pupils to make them more reflective learners and to personalise their learning experience. Record your notes in your PDP.

Managing the learning environment: a key part of your general pedagogic knowledge (GPK)

An important aspect of your job is managing the learning environment of your classrooms. *Learning to manage the classroom* is similar in many ways to learning to drive. At the outset, there seems so much to remember (using the clutch; braking; changing gear; watching other traffic; looking in the mirror; indicating; obeying the speed limit; and so on), but after a short time such skills become part of subconscious, internalised patterns of behaviour.

Much of what experienced teachers do to manage their classes has become part of their unconscious classroom behaviour. So much so that often teachers find it hard to articulate exactly what it is they are doing or why it is successful. This situation, of course, does not help you as a student teacher. It also gives weight to the spurious notion that teachers are born rather than made and that nobody can tell you how to teach.

Some teachers may well begin teaching with certain advantages such as a 'good' voice or organisational skills. Nevertheless, there are common skills and techniques to be learned that, when combined with an awareness of and sensitivity to the contexts within which you are teaching, will enable you to manage your classes effectively. Part of the pleasure of teaching is that *teaching is a continuously creative and problem-solving activity*. Learners and groups of learners each have their own characteristics and group dynamics that experienced teachers take into account in planning for teaching and learning. For example, if there has been recent controversy over environmental issues in the local area, teachers could adapt their teaching to incorporate this issue, thus allowing pupils to draw on their experience. Although lessons with different groups may have similar content, the same lesson is rarely delivered in the same way twice because of the variety in relationships between individuals, the whole class and the teacher.

Rogers (2002: 5) comments:

> Day-to-day school teaching normally takes place in a rather unusual setting: a small room (for what is asked of it), often inadequate furniture and space to move, a 50-minute time slot (or less) to cover set curriculum objectives, and 25 to 30 distinct and unique personalities, some of whom may not even want to be there. Why should there not be some natural stresses and strains associated with a teacher's day-to-day role?

One of your most important roles is to bring together the various personalities of your classroom (including your own) to create from these the best possible context for learning. This requires careful thought, planning and preparation. The key to success is to minimise the element of surprise. Of course, at some point, issues always arise to which you have to react. The majority of events and issues that arise in the classroom are, however, foreseeable, and can therefore be planned for. It is always better to be proactive rather than reactive.

When you plan, you should think not only of what you are going to teach and how you are going to teach it, but also of the implications of these choices. If, for example, you want your class to watch (part of) a DVD, have you checked that the equipment works and that you have located the relevant section of the DVD? If you want the class to move into groups halfway through the lesson, have you thought about the rationale for your groups, who is going to work with whom and how you are going to manage their movement? How are you going to manage the distribution of books or worksheets? Are all pupils working from books with the same page numbering? Such questions may seem small, but failure to think about such issues can cause significant interruption and disruption to learning. Effective teachers run efficient classrooms, and efficiency maximises the potential for learning and cooperation. Some of the important things for you to consider are:

- timing;
- seating plans;
- organisation of desks, materials, texts, and so on;
- how you plan to use teaching assistants (TAs) – meeting with them prior to the lesson is always advisable;
- pitch/differentiation/extension of work;
- range of activity;
- likely trouble spots (for example, using technology, writing on the board, distributing papers, setting homework, moving pupils into groups, and so on).

In Units 4.3, 5.1 and 5.3, we introduce you to theories underpinning educational practice and ideas that can provide a foundation for your development as an effective teacher whatever your subject. But what do we mean by effective teaching?

Effective teaching

Effective teaching occurs where the learning experience structured by the teacher matches the needs of each learner and when tasks effectively build on pupils' knowledge, skills and attitudes. A key feature of effective teaching is balancing pupils' chance of success against the level of difficulty required to challenge them. The units in Chapter 5 provide further information about pupil learning. Understanding the varied ways in which learning takes place and the ways in which pupils' learning styles and preferences can be used is essential.

Classroom rights and responsibilities

It is also important to think about rights and responsibilities in the classroom, including your own. Everyone should understand clearly that rights are counterbalanced by responsibility in terms of behaviour and participation, and that in the best interests of everybody, clear and appropriate sanctions will be applied to those who do not comply.

The following are useful areas to consider in relation to the rights and responsibilities of your classroom:

- *Respect*: all pupils and teachers deserve personal respect; everyone should employ respectful language; it is important to respect the views and beliefs of others.
- *Attention*: every pupil has the right to receive a fair share of teachers' attention; when invited to address the class, pupils have the right to be heard; everyone must pay full attention to the requirements of the lesson; when the teacher speaks, all must pay attention.
- *Learning/teaching*: all pupils have the right to learn; teachers have the right to teach; everyone has the responsibility of cooperating so that effective teaching and learning can take place.
- *Safety*: everyone should expect to be safe; everyone must ensure that safety is not compromised. Remember that teachers are responsible for the well-being and safeguarding of their pupils.

Think carefully about the activities that pupils engage with, consider their risks and take appropriate steps to ensure safe practice. Some subject areas, such as science, technology or physical education, carry more inherent risks, but all teachers need to take personal responsibility for ensuring safety and well-being in their lessons. Pupils should be made aware of the risks and take responsibility for acting safely.

■   *Safeguarding* of children is an increasingly high-profile issue. Some of the major areas that all teachers should consider are the following:
■   child protection issues;
■   physical abuse and neglect (including female genital mutilation);
■   mental abuse (including forced marriage);
■   sexual abuse and exploitation;
■   emotional well-being;
■   e-safety;
■   accident protection and prevention;
■   drug and alcohol misuse;
■   mental health.

National Institute for Health and Care Excellence (NICE) Pathways provide useful evidence-informed information (http://pathways.nice.org.uk) on many of these topics.

Teachers must be familiar with such issues, the common signs of problems, and procedures and channels for dealing with them. Each school is obliged to develop policies to support practice in these areas, and charities exist in some specialist areas.

There may well be other rights and responsibilities that you wish to establish for your classroom. Task 1.1.6 asks you to think now about what these might be and how you are going to establish and maintain them. See Unit 8.3 on your legal responsibilities.

 Task 1.1.6 Classroom rights and responsibilities

Working with fellow student teachers if possible, consider the rights and responsibilities operating in classrooms that you have observed. Draw up a list for your classes and store it in your PDP to refer to and develop as you progress through your ITE programme.

Your professional profile: what image do you want to project?

Lastly, in developing your professional code of conduct and ethical code, we suggest you consider what your digital footprint says about you. It is essential that you review your digital profile. Check how you are presented on social media and remove any references, images and connections that do not portray a professional image. You need to work to earn the respect of your pupils, parents and carers, your peers and employers, and adopting appropriate ways of representing yourself online is essential.

SUMMARY AND KEY POINTS

So let us return to the question that is the title of this unit. What do teachers do?

■ In some countries, teachers are free to choose what they teach and how they teach.

■ In others, the curriculum is set centrally and teachers' choices about how to teach may be more constrained.

■ Your own philosophy of teaching affects the way you approach your work and develops over time as you acquire further professional knowledge and judgement.

■ As a student teacher, you will test out and develop a repertoire of teaching styles and strategies. It may take you considerable time before you can apply the principles of effective teaching to your classroom practice, but you can monitor your development through regular evaluation of lessons. In this book, we aim to provide a basic introduction to what are complex areas, and it is up to you to develop systematically your professional knowledge and judgement by analysing and reflecting on your experience and wider reading.

■ As a teacher, you have responsibilities to your pupils, their parents and carers, your head of department, your school, your head teacher, and others.

■ Being an effective teacher does not mean simply knowing your subject. It also means:

  ■ knowing how to teach lessons that are intellectually robust, challenging and stimulating;

  ■ managing the classroom effectively and fairly; assessing and monitoring pupils' progress promptly and accurately;

  ■ modelling in your own behaviour and practice what you expect pupils to do; planning for inclusion and the needs of individual learners;

  ■ managing the rights and responsibilities of the classroom;

  ■ upholding school policies and procedures;

  ■ responding to the pastoral and personal needs of your pupils;

  ■ completing administrative duties;

  ■ contributing to the wider life of the school;

  ■ knowing your legal responsibilities.

As you progress through your ITE programme, you will develop knowledge, understanding and skills that enable you to fulfil your roles and responsibilities in all of these areas. Through your experiences in school, you should move from knowing about skills to a position where you can use them flexibly and appropriately in a range of situations. In other words, you will learn to do what teachers do - the school equivalent of plate-spinning - as you balance the many demands of the wonderful job that is teaching.

Check which requirements for your ITE programme you have addressed through this unit.

Further reading

Barton, G. (2010) *Grammar Survival: A Teacher's Toolkit*, London: Routledge.

Brindley, S. (ed.) (2015) *Masterclass* series of texts, London: Bloomsbury, available at: www.bloomsbury.com/uk/education/series/masterclass/
This series of texts provide subject-specific advice.

Eames, K. (2016) *Teaching Grammar in the English Language MESHGuide*, Bath Spa University, UK, available at: www.meshguides.org/meshguides-full-list./ (to be published in 2016).

Grossman, P.L., Wilson, S.M. and Shulman, L.S. (1989) 'Teachers of substance: subject matter knowledge for teaching', in M.C. Reynolds (ed) *Knowledge Base for the Beginning Teacher*, Oxford: Pergamon Press, pp. 23–36.
This chapter addresses a wide range of issues relevant to teachers at the beginning of their careers. It challenges you to think in detail about what precisely you need knowledge of if you are to be an effective teacher.

Harrison, C., Brookes, G. *et al.* (2014) *Spelling in English MESHGuide*, Universities of Nottingham and Sheffield, UK, available at: www.meshguides.org/meshguides-full-list./

Hayden, S. and Jordan, E. (2012) *Language for Learning in the Secondary School: A Practical Guide for Supporting Students with Speech, Language and Communication Needs*, London: Routledge.
This text provides a foundation in thinking about the functions of language for all secondary teacher. As language underpins work in every subject, this is strongly recommended.

Moore, A. (2004) *The Good Teacher: Dominant Discourses in Teaching and Teacher Education*, London: RoutledgeFalmer.
This book offers an insight into the background of a set of key educational issues and provides an overview of key debates.

Palmer, S. (2011) *Speaking Frames: How to Teach Talk for Writing*, London: Routledge.
This provides an introduction to teaching talk to support writing.

OECD TALIS (2015) *The Teaching and Learning International Survey*, Paris: OECD, available at: www.oecd.org/edu/school/talis.htm
This is an international study of practices in teaching and learning repeated periodically by the OECD.

Tokuhama-Espinosa, T. (2014) *Making Classrooms Better: 50 Practical Applications of Mind, Brain and Education Science*, New York: Norton.
Written by a teacher, this book links findings in psychology and neuroscience to education.

Vanes, R. (2012) *Tricks of the Writer's Trade and How to Teach Them to Children Aged 8–14*, London: Routledge.
You need to be able to teach the correct use of language, whatever your subject area, and to support learners in their language acquisition and use. These texts provide a strong foundation in teaching the effective use of language and grammar.

Volante, L. (2004) 'Teaching to the test: what every educator and policy-maker should know', *Canadian Journal of Educational Administration and Policy*, 35, available at: http://eric.ed.gov/?id=EJ848235

White, J. (ed.) (2004) *Rethinking the School Curriculum: Values, Aims and Purposes*, London: RoutledgeFalmer.
This text contains a series of essays discussing the place of each subject in the curriculum in England and giving an overview of curriculum developments within each subject.

Wragg, E.C. (ed.) (2004) *The RoutledgeFalmer Reader in Teaching and Learning*, London: RoutledgeFalmer.
This book offers an insight into the background of a set of key educational issues and provides an overview of key debates.

Other resources and websites

Association of American Educators (2015) *Code of Conduct for Educators*: www.aaeteachers.org/index.php/about-us/aae-code-of-ethics
   This site is for professional educators and has a range of resources, including an ethical code for educators.

Behaviour2Learn: http://behaviour2learn.co.uk/
   This site provides evidence-informed advice about behaviour.

GTCS (General Teaching Council for Scotland) (2015) *Code of Professionalism and Conduct*: www.gtcs.org.uk/standards/copac.aspx
   This site has a range of resources relevant to educators, as well as an ethical code for teachers and student teachers.

Mercer, N. (2015) *Thinking Together Project Materials*, University of Cambridge Faculty of Education: http://thinkingtogether.educ.cam.ac.uk/
   These materials support a dialogue-based approach to the development of pupils' thinking and learning, and include spoken language.

MESHGuides: www.meshguides.org

Subject associations (via the Council for Subject Associations) www.subjectassociation.org.uk/
   These provide evidence-informed advice about an increasing range of educational topics.

Teacher Support Network: www.teachersupport.info
   Teacher Support Network is a 24-hour confidential counselling, support and advice service. It also offers support lines in England (tel: 08000 562 561), Wales (tel: 08000 855 088) and Scotland (tel: 0800 564 2270).

Teacher Training Resource Bank: www.ttrb3.org.uk/
   These provide evidence-informed advice about a range of educational topics (this builds on an earlier version of the Teaching Training Resource Bank, funded by what was the Training and Development Agency for schools).

Appendix 2 on pages 591–595 provides examples of further websites you may find useful.

Capel, S., Leask, M. and Turner, T. (eds) (2010) *Readings for Learning to Teach in the Secondary School: A Companion to M Level Study*, London: Routledge.
   This book brings together essential readings to support you in your critical engagement with key issues raised in this textbook.

The subject-specific books in the *Learning to Teach* series are also very useful.

Any additional resources and an editable version of any relevant tasks/tables in this unit are available on the companion website: www.routledge.com.cw.capel

1.2 Student teachers' roles and responsibilities

Michael Allen and Rob Toplis

Introduction

Schools are busy places and teachers are often required to juggle many tasks at once. Unit 1.1 provides some insight into what it is to be a teacher. In this unit, we look at what it is to be a student teacher in a secondary school and consider the school experience itself. We look at your relationships with other people, both staff and pupils, that form part of the busy life of schools, discuss some specific expectations of student teachers in school and offer some guidance about your roles and responsibilities. We then link this to an examination of the concept of teacher professionalism. Finally, we discuss how your development as a professional is likely to pass through significant changes over your initial teacher education (ITE) programme.

OBJECTIVES

At the end of this unit, you should be able to:

- prepare for school experience;
- work with other staff and pupils on school experience;
- identify expectations, roles and responsibilities of student teachers in school;
- explain what it means to be a professional;
- chart aspects of your development as a teacher over your ITE programme and into your future learning and development.

Check the requirements of your ITE programme to see which relate to this unit.

Preparing for school experience

Before you start at any school, it is important to find out as much as you can about the school and its organisation, as well as the specific department you will be working with.

You can gather further information about schools from inspection reports (see other resources at the end of the unit for how to access inspection reports and other online information about schools for England, Scotland, Wales and Northern Ireland). Inspection reports provide you with a wealth of information about all aspects of the school as it was assessed at the time of the inspection; alternatively, the school may be able to lend you a copy of the school's last inspection report. This report provides you with questions to discuss with staff and areas to follow up as you learn more about the school.

Ideally, you will visit the school at least once before you start. On any visit, it is helpful to have a list of things you want to find out about the school, department and the activities in which you are going to be engaged. It is likely that your tutor will have given you a list of information to gather and questions to ask to help you with this. Task 1.2.1 is an orientation activity that will help you learn more about your placement school. Table 1.2.1 presents the key players in your ITE programme; nomenclature may differ from school to school, and the terms given in the first column of the table are those most used in this chapter.

 Task 1.2.1 Preparing for school experience

As you work through this unit, and as you read other relevant units in the book, make notes about what you need to do to prepare for school experience and what you might do to make the most of your school experience. Compare your notes with those of other student teachers. Store your notes in your professional development portfolio (PDP).

During your first visit(s), you may be introduced to the head teacher. However, you can expect to talk to the professional tutor and staff with specific areas of responsibility in the school. There are many policy and procedure documents in every school, covering a wide range of subjects; for example, school uniform; equal opportunities; behaviour management; marking policy; risk management; safeguarding and e-safety; and health and safety information such as the fire assembly points and how to record accidents. Often, these can be found in a staff handbook. You may be issued with a copy of this, or there may be a copy in the staffroom or school office. Your subject tutor may discuss the most relevant sections in the handbook, which you can then read in your own time after the visit. This discussion and reading of the handbook provides you with useful practical information about how the school operates and what you need to do to comply with its policies and procedures and routines. The staff handbook may also include a diagram showing the school's management structure and lines of accountability.

You can also expect to talk to the head of department or faculty, your subject tutor and others in your subject department about the curriculum, schemes of work and your teaching timetable. These discussions are likely to include specific aspects of teaching in the department; for example, safety issues, organisation of equipment and pupils, lesson plans, homework routines, and access to texts and resources, including informaton and communications technology (ICT). Some of the information may be in a departmental handbook.

On your visits (and later when you start in school), it is important to be aware of staffroom protocols. Some staffrooms are like lounges where teachers can relax and chat safely away from work and pupils during break and lunchtimes. Others have an additional function as a workroom

Table 1.2.1 The key players in your ITE programme

Key player	Alternative names	Role
Head teacher	Headmaster; headmistress; head	Carries overall responsibility for the care of pupils, the quality of teaching and learning, and many other aspects of school life.
Professional tutor	Professional coordinating tutor; professional coordinating mentor	Responsible for all student teachers in the school. Organises regular school-wide training sessions. Usually a senior member of staff.
Subject tutor	School-based mentor; class mentor; school tutor; mentor	Your first point of contact within the school. Organises your day-to-day training in the department, timetabling, weekly meetings, and so on.
Class teachers	Teachers; teaching staff	Members of staff whose classes you are given responsibility for during your time in school. Your school mentor may also be one of your class teachers.
Head of department	Head of subject; head of faculty; subject coordinator; subject lead	Responsible for running the subject department where you are placed.
University tutor	College tutor; higher education institution (HEI) tutor; link tutor; tutor	Responsible for your ITE programme both in school and the HEI. Delegates to school staff during the school experience.
Student teacher	Student; trainee teacher; trainee; beginning teacher	Yourself

(with or without allocated workspaces) where teachers can do marking and lesson preparation during their free periods. There are still some schools where the same staff have sat in the same chairs for 10, 20 or even 30 years! Colleagues may have brought in their own mugs for tea/coffee. There may or may not be a 'tea/coffee club'. Likewise, if you are planning to drive to school, check out the parking facilities and conventions; there may be reserved spots for some staff. If you check these things, you avoid upsetting the permanent members of staff.

Such visits also enable you to familiarise yourself with the geography of the building. This is particularly important if you are going to teach in a large school, perhaps with several different blocks or operating on more than one site. Secondary schools vary immensely not just in size, but also in physical features, ranging from the small rural or special school with under 100 pupils to the very large school with 1,000–2,000 pupils. Some schools are modern, or comparatively modern, while others are old, dating back to the 1880s, or even earlier. Each type of building has advantages and disadvantages. Whichever type of school you are in, it is important that you locate important facilities, such as the office, lavatories and the staffroom, before you start. The last thing you need to do on your first day is to get lost!

During school experience: work with other staff and pupils in school

Despite the fact that teaching involves spending large amounts of time away from colleagues and working autonomously or just with a teaching assistant, you still have to work with other staff and to be a team player. Taking on the role of a teacher as a student teacher means forging and managing professional relationships with adults (as well as pupils). During the initial days in school, you will introduce yourself to staff you did not meet on visits prior to school experience, including teaching and support staff in your department and key personnel outside the department such as the head teacher, deputies/assistant heads, heads of Key Stage, heads of year and the special educational needs coordinator (SENCO). In addition, you start to build a working relationship with school staff who are supporting you and observing your teaching. Try to make a good first impression on all these people. Figure 1.2.1 suggests some perceived attributes that help convey a positive image of a professional and well-prepared student teacher.

In this section, advice is presented with regard to developing and managing relationships with specific members of staff who play significant roles in your school experience. Relationships with pupils are also considered.

Relationship with the professional tutor

It is worth remembering that the professional tutor is a key element in your ITE programme, with oversight and management of all student teachers within the school and liaison with your HEI tutor, if appropriate. You may see the professional tutor in a formal context only once or twice a week, but they are normally senior members of school staff. They may organise sessions on general school issues. Likewise, you should be able to seek their advice on general school issues, if needed. They

Figure 1.2.1 Setting out to create a positive image

expect you to learn school routines, practices and procedures, including rewards/sanctions, and to follow these. They will also expect you to engage actively with the school-based programme they have put in place for student teachers.

Relationship with your subject tutor

In the early stages of learning to teach, your subject tutor is an important person. Your tutor supports your developing practice. As part of this, they observe you teaching and write reports on these observations. Your tutor is responsible for giving you a pass/fail or quantitative grade for your school experience, using these observations and the observations of other staff who have observed you teaching. There are a number of aspects of the relationship that you should consider.

There are likely to be agreed structures for your tutor to give you support, advice and guidance; for example, written feedback on one or more lessons each week and a weekly tutorial meeting. For other activities (for example, jointly preparing lessons or approval of lesson plans by your tutor, seeking advice on planning and preparation for lessons or on aspects of teaching with which you are less familiar, completing the required paperwork for your ITE programme, and keeping records of pupil attendance, classwork and homework), you should be clear about what your tutor expects of you and then do what is expected.

You should arrange regular meetings and clarify the purpose of those meetings, so that you are fully prepared for them. Your tutor is an experienced teacher from whom you can learn a lot. Do not think you know it all already and either do not seek advice or ignore your tutor's advice. Do not be afraid to ask for advice if you are not sure about anything, but check when is a convenient time – so that you know when to ask and when is inconvenient.

Also check with your tutor your status with support staff; for example, technical staff and office staff. In some schools, you approach them yourself; in others, you do so through your tutor. Likewise, discuss with your tutor your attendance at school and departmental staff meetings.

Your attendance and punctuality at school (and at lessons when in school) is important. Your school has an agreed procedure if you have an important reason (for example, an interview) to be off school or you are sick. Let your tutor know of any foreseen absences well in advance. If you find that one morning you are too ill to attend school, try to contact your tutor directly by phone/text message; otherwise, speak with the school office staff. If your ITE programme is in conjunction with an HEI, you are also required to contact them on the day of absence.

The tutor-student teacher relationship is vital to your success and it is worthwhile taking steps to ensure this remains cordial. However, from time to time, problems do occur, and can often be associated with the friction generated when the student teacher fails to seek or to act on the tutor's advice. If your relationship with your tutor breaks down, you need to contact your HEI tutor or senior staff member immediately and seek further advice. It is important to be aware that any breakdown in the relationship that ends in the student teacher leaving the placement may subsequently result in failure of the ITE programme.

Relationships with class teachers

You spend the bulk of your time in school in the company of the teachers whose classes you are teaching and so it is important also to establish good working relations with them. Remember that they are going to have to teach the class again after you leave, so discuss with them what they want you to do. Some teachers want you to follow their routines, practices and procedures; others allow you to experiment with what is best for you. Plan your lessons well in advance of when they are going to be taught to allow time for any planning meetings with, or checking by, the class teacher and any further planning or adjustment to take place. Collate resources well in advance, especially photocopying, and be flexible and be prepared to change lesson plans at short notice in the light of unexpected events. Avoid the situation where you are chasing the class teacher 10 minutes before the start of a lesson for an important resource or piece of information. Arrive early before a lesson. Keep teachers fully informed of any new approaches you are taking in your teaching and events that take place with their classes, particularly behavioural issues that need following up.

Relationships with pupils

Your main task as a student teacher is to ensure the pupils in your classes learn. This is most effective when you are able to treat each pupil as an individual. Learning pupils' names is a good first step, as is getting to know something about their interests (learning pupils' names is covered in Unit 2.3). It is important to greet pupils at the beginning of the lesson; this is most easily achieved by standing at the doorway as the pupils enter.

You also need to gain the respect of the pupils you are teaching. This is not usually automatic; it requires a proactive approach. A general guideline is that if you treat pupils with respect, the feeling is reciprocated (although some pupils may not necessarily respond in this way). For instance, you should be polite when dealing with pupils, and ensure they are polite back to you. At the same time, you should clearly define the boundaries of behaviour. Pupils are sensitive to actions they perceive as being unfair; for example, if one person has been talking, it is unfair to keep the whole class in for a detention.

Make sure you understand the material you are teaching and have planned and prepared your lesson and your resources. Do not be afraid to admit it if you are asked a question to which you do not know the answer, provided you follow it up in a later lesson.

Planning and preparation are essential for learning and to motivate pupils to learn (see planning in Unit 2.2 and motivation in Unit 3.2). Encouragement is one effective means of keeping pupils on task in your lesson. Motivation and encouragement work best when tailored to the needs of individuals. During the lesson, you need to keep pupils on task. To be effective, your approach needs to be tailored to each individual. However, this is difficult unless you have some knowledge of individual pupils.

Well-planned lessons support your approach to behaviour for learning (see Unit 3.3). Despite this, you may encounter some behavioural issues in the class; therefore, you should also be clear about how you are going to deal with any poor behaviour, in line with school behaviour policies. Here are some steps to take to deal with poor behaviour: never be drawn into a public confrontation with a pupil because you may lose your authority, which is difficult to recoup later. In any case, you do need to think of the effect on the rest of the class, and also on what the rest of the class are doing when a confrontation is going on. Simply saying 'I will see you later' allows you to choose the time and place to follow up. This enables you to maintain a working relationship with the particular pupil after the event.

Physical contact with pupils should be avoided unless there is an immediate health and safety concern, or is a requirement in a practical lesson such as physical education; for example, to support a pupil (see also Unit 8.3). It is unlikely that you will be called on to make decisions in contexts where physical restraint is necessary, because the supervising class teacher should be available on the very rare occasion when restraint is the pertinent action. Likewise, any contact with parents/carers in reaction to classroom events, both positive as well as negative, should be undertaken in conjunction with the class teacher. Further, more specific advice on encouraging behaviour to maximise learning is found in Unit 3.3.

A particularly important point to remember is to keep a professional distance in your relationships with pupils. It is easy with some classes to become over-friendly; this is especially the case during the first phase of development (see section on student teacher development below). To be the target of an adolescent 'crush' is not unusual for young student teachers, and if this is the case, maintaining an appropriate professional distance is imperative while nurturing mutual respect and good working relationships. In a similar vein, if you are alone in a room with any pupil (or parent), it is good practice to seek the presence of another member of staff or to leave the door wide open. Similarly, you should avoid texting or emailing pupils, or communicating with them via social networking websites. False allegations are uncommon but remain a threat. Task 1.2.2 presents some scenarios you might have to deal with.

 Task 1.2.2 Relationships with pupils

Consider your responses to the following events:

- There is a struggle between two pupils in the corridor.
- You observe a pupil going through another pupil's bag/locker.

Discuss your responses with your tutor or another student teacher and record your reflections in your PDP. Identify other scenarios to discuss – these may be real events that have taken place in school.

Expectations, roles and responsibilities of school experience

The main expectation of you as a student teacher is that you promote pupils' learning. To achieve this, there is a range of s*tructured teaching activities* that you are likely to engage in. These include:

- microteaching: a short teaching episode where you teach peers or small groups of pupils; it might be videotaped to enable analysis of different aspects of teaching;
- observation of experienced teachers: where you look at specific aspects of teaching in a lesson; for example, how teachers use questions to promote learning (see Unit 3.1);
- team-teaching: where you share the lesson with others; planning, teaching the lesson and evaluating together;
- whole-class teaching with the class teacher present;
- whole-class teaching on your own (as a student teacher, you should always have an experienced teacher nearby).

You should be given feedback on your planning and teaching in each of these situations to enhance your own learning. The amount of feedback you get from teachers watching your lessons varies. However, student teachers also have preferences. If you wish to have feedback on every lesson, ask if this can be done. Some student teachers prefer a small amount of very focused feedback; others can cope with more – a page or more of written comments. Written feedback is essential because it provides a record of your progress and ideas for your development. In practice, there are likely to be agreed conventions governing this aspect of your work. These take into account how you are to achieve the requirements to complete your ITE programme successfully.

Comments on your teaching divide into those relating to tangible technical issues that can be worked on relatively easily and those relating to less tangible issues relating to pupils' learning. Technical problems, such as the quality and clarity of your voice, how you position yourself in the classroom, managing transitions from one activity to another, your use of ICT and/or audiovisual aids, are easy to spot, so you may receive considerable advice on these issues. Problems with these aspects of your work are usually resolved early in your ITE programme, whereas less tangible issues that are directly related to the quality of pupil learning require ongoing reflection, attention and discussion; for example, your approach to the explanation of lesson content, your style of questioning and your evaluation of pupil learning. You may have access to videos of yourself teaching, in which case you are advised to spend some time in the detailed analysis of your performance in these different aspects of teaching. More detailed advice related to the teaching of your specific subject is given in the subject-specific texts in the Routledge *Learning to Teach in the Secondary School* series that accompany this generic text (see list on page ii).

Expectations relating to your social skills in developing relationships with staff and pupils and of your teaching are summarised in Table 1.2.2.

Thus, your main roles and responsibilities relate to teaching particular classes. Teachers have other roles and responsibilities such as planning the curriculum and liaising with outside agencies, but these are not usually undertaken by student teachers. You become involved in the wider roles and responsibilities of teachers after completing your ITE programme. This is part of your development as a professional (see also Unit 8.2).

The roles and responsibilities of teachers, including student teachers, are underpinned by the concept of *professionalism*. It is therefore appropriate to explore some ideas associated with the concept of professionalism and how these have changed over time, often as the result of policies and government initiatives.

Teachers as professionals

Research by Sammons *et al.* (2007) into teachers' lives, work and their effects on pupils identifies teachers' roles and responsibilities, educational policies and government initiatives as key influences on teacher professionalism.

Teachers' work changes constantly as a result of government initiatives and agendas about, for example, the curriculum, the care of children, the management of schools, teachers' professional standards and teachers' learning.

Views about other professions, such as medical doctors and lawyers, can be used as a lens with which to compare teachers' professionalism. The *main attributes of professionals* that distinguish them from other groups of workers are: their specialised knowledge (there is a substantial body of knowledge that a professional needs to acquire); that substantial training is required before an

Table 1.2.2 The school's expectations of student teachers

(i) Social skills

You are expected to:

■ Develop a good relationship with staff and pupils.
■ Be able to communicate with adults as well as pupils.
■ Work well in teams.
■ Learn to defuse difficult situations.
■ Keep a sense of humour.

(ii) Planning, teaching and evaluating lessons

You are expected to:

■ Be well organised.
■ Know your subject.
■ Plan and prepare thoroughly. Be conscientious in finding out what lesson content is appropriate to the class you are teaching. For some classes, you may be teaching material that is new to you or that you last thought about many years ago. You must know the subject matter you are teaching and you are expected to improve your own subject content knowledge. However, you are also expected to ask if you are unsure about the content for a particular lesson.
■ Share your plans with the class teacher, explaining why you want to do things the way you plan. Discuss any new/different teaching strategies or innovations in your teaching. Evaluate these carefully afterwards.
■ Check before the day on which you are teaching the lesson the availability of books and equipment; test out equipment new to you; talk to staff about the work and the pupils' progress; and clarify any safety issues.
■ Arrive in plenty of time for a lesson in order to arrange the classroom and lay out any equipment or books needed.
■ During the lesson, learn names of pupils, focus on and assess any learning that is taking place, and ensure that good behaviour is maintained during your teaching.
■ Evaluate the lesson.
■ Keep good records: keep your file of schemes and units of work, lesson plans, pupil attendance and homework up to date. Your evaluations of your lessons are best completed on the same day as the lesson, although sometimes you might want to add to this after you have marked pupils' work.

---

individual can be accepted into the profession; a commitment to meeting the needs of clients; a collective identity and a level of professional autonomy that controls their own practice; the profession is self-governing as well as publicly accountable (see, for example, Day 1999 and Unit 8.3). At this point, it is worth you thinking about teacher professionalism in these contexts by undertaking Task 1.2.3.

 Task 1.2.3 Compare professionals

Using the attributes of a profession, above, list some examples of the ways in which the practice of teachers is similar and the ways in which it is different to that of other professions such as medical doctors or solicitors. Discuss your findings with other student teachers and record in your PDP.

Becoming *a member of the teaching profession* means that you make the following commitments. That you will:

■ *Reach an acceptable level of competence and skill* in your teaching by the end of your ITE programme. This includes acquiring knowledge and skills that enable you to become an effective teacher and that enable you to understand the body of knowledge about how young people learn and how teachers can teach most effectively.

■ *Continuously develop your professional knowledge and professional judgement* through experience, further learning and reflection on your work.

■ *Be publicly accountable for your work.* Various members of the community have the right to inspect and/or question your work: the head teacher, governors, parents and inspectors. You have a professional duty to plan and keep records of your work and that of the pupils. This accountability includes implementation of school policies; for example, on behaviour and on equal opportunities.

■ *Set personal standards and conform to external standards* for monitoring and improving your work.

Table 1.2.3 summarises aspects of professionalism.

These aspects of professionalism are included in statements from the General Teaching Councils for Northern Ireland, Scotland and Wales, and in England are part of the Teachers' Standards for personal and professional conduct (Department of Education (DfE) 2012d). Similar statements are likely to be included in documents in other countries. The need to reflect, which is one of the important facets of professionalism, is discussed next (see also Unit 5.4).

Reflection can be defined in different ways. One definition includes reflection both *on* practice and *in* practice (Schön 1983). Reflection *on* your practice of teaching may involve the familiar lesson evaluations that follow planned, taught and assessed lessons. These reflections may be written and discussed with your tutor (this should be done sooner rather than later if all the important points are to be remembered accurately). An example may be a lesson where some aspect of pupil behaviour

Table 1.2.3 The school's expectations of your professionalism

Professionalism

You are expected to:

■ Dress appropriately (different schools have different dress codes).
■ Act in a professional manner; for example, be punctual and reliable; act with courtesy and tact; and respect confidentiality of information.
■ Take active steps to ensure that your pupils learn.
■ Discuss pupil progress with parents.
■ Become familiar with and work within school procedures and policies. These include record-keeping, rewards and sanctions, uniform, and relationships between teachers and pupils.
■ Be open to new learning: seek and act on advice.
■ Be flexible; for example, if there is a change in the timetable on a particular day.
■ Accept a leadership role. You may find imposing your will on pupils uncomfortable, but unless you establish your right to direct the work of the class, you are not able to teach effectively.
■ Recognise and understand the roles and relationships of staff responsible for your development.
■ Keep up to date with your subject.

affected learning. What was this? Who was involved? What was the real issue? Why did you respond in this way? Did it work? Can/should you respond differently in a similar situation in future? How can you organise your next lesson to reduce or help to eliminate this behaviour? This reflection involves careful analysis, evaluation and subsequent planning; it involves you being self-critical and open to advice from experienced teachers. It is an inherent part of learning to teach and should not be ignored or underestimated. Importantly, it is not necessarily a failure on your part. Reflection *in* practice involves your thoughts and the actions you take at the time of your actual teaching. Experienced teachers appear to do this automatically but it's worth remembering that they have built up a stock of intuitive responses to a number of situations over their years of practice. Your reflection *in* action will be limited but you may respond to some everyday examples as you build up your knowledge of pupils and situations. One example may be the timing of pupil activities, where you have allowed 10 minutes for the activity, only to find restless pupils after only four minutes; your reflection *in* action may lead you to move the lesson on to the next stage or to use another pupil activity (Unit 5.4 considers reflective practice).

It is important to consider the process you go through to become an experienced teacher. We do this next.

A model of student teacher development

The aim of your ITE programme is to facilitate your transformation from a student teacher to a competent professional. Plainly, this change is not instantaneous; instead, it proceeds by increments, with each little piece of experience contributing to your development. Your perception of yourself as a teacher alters as different aspects become the focus of concern at different points during your ITE programme. A major change for you might be assuming the role of the teacher after being a learner; for example, on a university course. You become one of them (teachers) instead of being one of us (learners). This role reversal requires significant behaviour modifications. Observing other teachers to see how they act in and out of the classroom helps you through these phases of development.

Various models of student teacher development have been identified. For example, Fuller and Brown (1975) described three phases of development: self concerns, tasks concerns and impact concerns. The three phases identified by Leask and Moorehouse (2005) are:

Self	Class	Pupil
Self-image and class management	Whole-class learning	Individual pupil's learning
How do I come across?	Are the pupils learning?	What are the different needs of my pupils?
Will they do what I want?	What are the learning outcomes?	How effective are my strategies for ensuring all pupils learn?
Can I plan enough material to last a lesson?	Am I achieving my objectives?	How can I find out?
	How do I know?	

The rest of this section summarises a model of student teacher progression first described by Furlong and Maynard in 1995, itself being based on a body of previous work. The model (see Table 1.2.4) does *not* assume that everyone passes through a predetermined, invariable linear process during their ITE programme, because individual and contextual aspects differ in many respects, such as the school environment. That said, research (for example, Fuller and Brown 1975; Calderhead and Shorrock 1997) has suggested that student teachers have common foci for their concerns at different times during their development. Remember, your primary role as expected by a prospective employer is to *teach the curriculum*, with the aspiration being that every pupil in the class achieves the learning outcomes for each of your lessons, over and above any informal pastoral role that you may envisage for yourself. Attainment of the final mature stage in Table 1.2.4 is the aim. With its emphasis on individual pupil learning and the successful achievement of learning outcomes by all pupils, you need to develop aspects of this third phase right at the start of your first school experience. However, in this model, your self-perceived role shifts from being the pupil's friend, to a crowd controller, then finally to teacher of subject content knowledge.

Other units in this book – for example, classroom management (Unit 1.4), planning (Unit 2.2) and differentiation (Unit 4.1) – cover specific issues described in the model in Table 1.2.4. Timing of the phases is difficult to predict because some student teachers progress more quickly than others during their ITE programme, and because of the individual and contextual differences described above. The three phases may span a single school experience or the whole ITE programme; in some cases, phase 1 occurs at the start of the first school experience, with phase 2 being experienced after a couple of weeks, and with some aspects of phase 3 appearing right at the end. At the start of the second school experience, there may then be a repeat of this process, only the first two phases are shorter. It is important to note that some student teachers who have had difficult and problematic school experiences emerge, after a number of years of qualified experience, as among the best teachers in their schools. Each of these phases is described below.

Phase 1: idealism and insecurity – focusing on self-development

You may begin your first school experience holding certain idealistic views about your role as teacher, partly based on your own memories of school when you were a pupil. Some student teachers

Table 1.2.4 A model of student or student teacher progression

Phase 1: idealism and insecurity	Phase 2: getting on top	Phase 3: stability and further progression
■ Desire to portray a caring image ■ Disorientation ■ Feelings of being unable to cope	■ Anxiety about failing ■ Realisation of personal areas for development ■ Drive to impress others brings steady improvements in performance	■ Limited success brings a period of stability and satisfaction ■ Desire to improve wanes ■ External intervention often required to develop further ■ Mature stage involves ensuring learning outcomes have been achieved by *all* pupils

first adopt an empathetic self-image, wanting to create a caring persona, being 'there' for the pupils and hence identifying with the pupils more than the class teacher did, and being popular. You may want to avoid becoming too strict or scary, not wanting pin-drop silence in your classroom, but instead a good-humoured, industrious buzz, so avoiding an atmosphere that negatively affects pupils' emotions. The most important factor determining success is your relationships with pupils, and you feel that if this can be arranged satisfactorily, then accomplishment in other areas will naturally follow without a great deal of further effort.

Once you begin your first school experience, these idealistic views may begin to evaporate in the face of immediate issues presented to you, and you switch to a more pragmatic stance based on survival, triggered particularly by an urgent need to establish classroom control. You have not yet constructed adequate concepts regarding the boundaries of important features of the modern classroom environment. For instance, when first left alone with a class, you are unclear about whether a particular pupil behaviour such as chatting during written work needs challenging. On top of this, because of the directly challenging nature of some pupils' behaviour, your self-image suffers a blow and there may be insecurity about whether, if you were to challenge behaviours, the pupils would merely ignore you and carry on. Both of these feelings conspire to make you feel reluctant to assert your authority, and student teachers sometimes attempt to justify a failure to challenge poor behaviour by saying they would rather not interrupt the flow of the lesson, or insisting they must keep rigorously to the lesson plan. Pupils actively test your knowledge of these boundaries, as well as your willingness to act on them, and you begin to realise that to be seen as a caring friend and equal by the pupils is not appropriate to a working relationship, and unworkable in practice. Planning issues can also be a cause of anxiety, such as do you have enough work to last the whole lesson, or what if they ask difficult questions?

Thus, the first couple of weeks of school are likely to be a time of insecurity with respect to self-image and readjustment of some prior idealistic notions, and you will at times feel out of your depth and run off your feet. You may have previously felt comfortable handling small groups or one-to-one situations, but whole-class teaching brings fresh and sometimes seemingly insurmountable problems; fortunately, for most student teachers, these feelings are transient.

Phase 2: getting on top – focusing on whole-class learning

An inability to appreciate the limits of certain classroom elements during the first couple of weeks starts to give way in light of your experiences to clearly delineated boundaries of what is judged 'acceptable'. You begin to realise exactly what constitutes, for example, a tolerable level of noise, pupil movement around the classroom and what level to pitch your lessons at. Having said that, realising the boundaries does not mean you can yet find strategies that successfully address every one of these issues. You feel pressure to put on a 'good show' for the significant players in your own assessment as a student teacher, your class teacher, school subject tutor and professional and HEI tutors, and work hard on your creative planning, delivery and especially your behaviour management, in order to foster these relationships. You are concerned about 'passing your ITE programme', and so do not wish to upset others by, for instance, having a teacher come into your class and complain about the noise. In order to appear to be a competent teacher, you may begin to mimic the behaviours of competent teachers around you or those who taught you in school (for example, their class management routines, personal mannerisms and stock phrases), sometimes unconsciously, although you may not necessarily fully understand the reasons behind those behaviours.

As a consequence of your hard work in addressing these issues, you begin to experience some successes. The pupils behave better (although perhaps not consistently so), which increases your confidence. Getting to grips with managing behaviour allows you to think more about whether the pupils are achieving learning outcomes, and you begin to adjust your lesson content in the light of this knowledge, although you may avoid differentiating work for individuals. For most student teachers, these successes are inconsistent and largely unpredictable, and some blame may be displaced onto factors beyond your control, such as room arrangement, a lack of resources or a need to fit in with the school's established procedures.

This phase is typified by steady improvements in classroom performance as a result of realising the nature of issues at hand, as well as determining successful strategies to address them. You start to think more about your autonomy as a teacher, about things you would like to do differently, although these desires are tempered by the need to fit in with the clear expectations of your school and tutors.

Phase 3: stability and further progression – focusing on individual pupils' learning

During the last weeks of your final school experience, there is usually a period of stability. Tried-and-tested methods have brought with them hard-won success for you, albeit not consistently, and so your feeling is why fix what isn't broken? Because of this, there may be a certain relaxation of attitude or 'cruising', with less time spent on planning and evaluations, and a feeling you have 'got there', and will comfortably pass your ITE programme. You are less anxious about managing behaviour, and let slide pupil misbehaviours that you previously might have challenged. Teaching remains largely at a shallow level; in fact, a common idea held by student teachers is that if pupils have enjoyed a lesson, then this shows it was successful; there is no real effort to ensure *all* pupils are achieving the learning outcomes, and there is little differentiation of work for individual pupils. These learning outcomes reflect an epistemology of the transmission of concrete knowledge, with an avoidance of the more abstract ideas, because you judge simple facts to be the material that pupils understand most easily and so can be taught without difficulty. You begin to feel more like a teacher, and believe you outwardly display attributes of a competent professional, although some of these behaviours are merely mimicry, with no real understanding of the professional knowledge that lies behind them.

In order to move on from this phase and progress towards becoming a more effective professional, concerted efforts are necessary, often requiring the intervention of others such as class teachers or tutors. First, student teachers at this phase of development may not be aware that further improvements are indeed necessary or even possible, so the first step would involve bringing to their attention the specific areas where competence could be further advanced. For some, the realisation that there is more to learn about teaching comes as a disappointment after gaining a modicum of proficiency. Critical self-analysis of your own teaching informs these areas for development, and it is vital that *you* recognise the need to make the effort to move on.

The greatest challenge lies in ensuring that each and every member of the class has accessed the learning outcomes; currently, in English state-maintained schools, the view is one of inclusion of all pupils in the learning process. The purpose of lessons needs to swing towards the needs of pupils, and away from you as a student teacher, with content focused on learning. The first step is determination of the extent to which pupils have learned during your lessons, which may be indicated by an effective plenary, end-of-topic test, or more formative types of assessment, all of which need to be referenced in your lesson evaluations.

You may in fact already realise that there are certain aspects of your teaching that could obviously be furthered, but the ability to progress is hampered by classroom management issues; for instance, you avoid practical activities, or you do not feel confident enough to experiment with innovative pedagogies. If this is the case, advice from other members of staff will prove invaluable in moving you on to higher levels of achievement. Task 1.2.4 is designed for you to reflect on the phases of development as a teacher.

 Task 1.2.4 Phases of student teacher development

Consider the three phases of student teacher development above: self, class and pupil. Reflect on your strengths and areas for development on each of these. Describe possible strategies for making progress in each of these three phases in the context of the following three areas:

■ classroom management and focusing on individuals;
■ assessment;
■ subject content knowledge.

Discuss your views with another student teacher. As you progress through your ITE programme, record in your PDP what strategies you have used and how they have worked.

Beyond your ITE programme

Teaching is an ever-changing process and learning to teach never stops. The comment 'I've been teaching this topic like this for the last 20 years' is simply unacceptable: continuing professional development (CPD) is not only a necessity in schools; it is a professional requirement for high-quality teaching and learning. CPD is covered in Unit 8.2. Now complete Task 1.2.5.

 Task 1.2.5 Your CPD

Fairly early on in your ITE programme, you should be aware of your developing CPD needs. Record in your PDP two examples of your CPD needs and reasons why you consider these to be important for your own learning.

SUMMARY AND KEY POINTS

This unit has touched on your multiple, changing roles and responsibilities as a student teacher. We hope that it has given you a better understanding of:

■ the preparation you need to do prior to school experience;
■ what you need to do during school experience, focusing particularly on developing positive working relationships with other staff, including your tutors and class teachers, and with pupils;
■ the expectations of you, your roles and responsibilities in school.

The unit has also looked at the concept of teacher professionalism and a model of student teacher development over your ITE programme and into your future learning and development. As a result, we hope that this has given you a better understanding both of what it is to be a professional and your development as a professional.

Check which requirements for your ITE programme you have addressed through this unit.

Further reading

Cohen, L., Manion, L., Morrison, K. and Wyse, D. (2010) *A Guide to Teaching Practice*, 5th edn, London: Routledge.
This text covers the important basic skills and issues that you need to consider during your school experience, such as planning, classroom organisation, behaviour management and assessment.

Furlong, J. and Maynard, T. (1995) *Mentoring Student Teachers: The Growth of Professional Knowledge*, London: Routledge.
This book provides valuable insights into the process of learning to become a teacher. It draws on extensive research to inform the stages of learning from starting to become a student teacher to the later stages of professional development.

Phillips, D.K. and Carr, K. (2010) *Becoming a Teacher through Action Research: Process, Context, and Self-Study*, 2nd edn, New York and London: Routledge.
This guide interweaves the stories of student teaching with the process of action research. The text focuses specifically on the needs of student teachers by providing assistance for all stages of the research experience, including guidance on how to select an area of focus, design a culturally proficient study, collect and interpret data, and communicate findings.

Zwozdiak-Myers, P. (2012) *The Teacher's Reflective Practice Handbook: Becoming an Extended Professional through Capturing Evidence-Informed Practice*, London: Routledge.
This book is an accessible guide that supports the facilitation of reflective practice through self and peer assessment, problem-based learning and personal development planning. The multidimensional framework enables you to build a meaningful, personally relevant portfolio of evidence-informed practice.

The subject-specific texts in this series provide detailed advice about teaching in your subject area – see page ii.

Other resources and websites

To keep up to date, we recommend you join your subject association. A list can be found on the website of the Council for Subject Associations: www.subjectassociation.org.uk/index.php?page=44.

In the UK, the main teachers' professional associations (unions) include:

Association of Teachers and Lecturers (ATL), England, Wales and Northern Ireland: www.atl.org.uk/

Irish National Teachers' Organisation, Northern Ireland: www.into.ie/NI/

National Association of Schoolmasters Union of Women Teachers (NASUWT), England, Wales, Scotland and Northern Ireland: www.nasuwt.org.uk/

National Union of Teachers (NUT), England and Wales: www.teachers.org.uk/

Scottish Secondary Teachers' Association, Scotland: www.ssta.org.uk

The Educational Institute of Scotland (EIS), Scotland: www.eis.org.uk/

Ulster Teachers Union, Northern Ireland: www.utu.edu/

Voice, previously the Professional Association of Teachers, England, Wales and Northern Ireland: www.voicetheunion.org.uk/
    In addition to offering direct advice and support to members on employment-related matters, the associations produce useful newsletters and publications on a range of topics and offer special concessions (for example, on car and travel insurance and training courses).

School inspection reports and further information about education can be obtained from:

England: Office for Standards in Education (Ofsted): www.ofsted.gov.uk; and Department for Education: www.education.gov.uk/

Scotland: Education Scotland: www.educationscotland.gov.uk/scottishschoolsonline/; and The Scottish Government: www.scotland.gov.uk/Topics/Statistics/Browse/School-Education

Wales: Estyn – the office of Her Majesty's Inspectorate for Education and Training in Wales: www. estyn.gov.uk/; and the Welsh Government: http://wales.gov.uk/topics/educationandskills/ ?lang=en

Northern Ireland: The Education and Training Inspectorate Northern Ireland: www.etini.gov.uk/index/ inspection-reports.htm; and the Department of Education Northern Ireland: www.deni.gov.uk/

Starting Out Guide for Newly Qualified and Trainee Teachers, available at: www.teachersupport.info/search/ node/starting%20out%20guide%20for%20newly%20qualified%20teachers
    This is published by the Teacher Support Network, which provides a 24-hour information, support and counselling service (www.teachersupport.info/). Tel: England 08000 562 561; Scotland 0800 564 2270; Wales 08000 855 088.

Teacher Training Resource Bank: http://webarchive.nationalarchives.gov.uk/20101021152907/www.ttrb. ac.uk/
    The archive contains some material from the Teacher Training Resource Bank.

Appendix 2 on page 591–595 provides further examples of websites you may find useful.

Capel, S., Leask, M. and Turner, T. (eds) (2010) *Readings for Learning to Teach in the Secondary School: A Companion to M Level Study*, London: Routledge.
    This book brings together essential readings to support you in your critical engagement with key issues raised in this textbook.

The subject-specific books in the *Learning to Teach* series are also very useful.

Any additional resources and an editable version of any relevant tasks/tables in this unit are available on the companion website: www.routledge.com/cw/capel

1.3 Managing your time, workload and stress, and building your resilience

Susan Capel

Introduction

Although teaching can be rewarding and exciting, it can also be demanding and stressful. The three main reasons given by teachers as factors that are demotivating and lower morale, and by teachers who leave the profession within the first few years, are related to time and stress; that is, too heavy a workload, work is too pressurised and stressful, and too much administration. These reasons are also causes of concern for student teachers.

You may be surprised by the amount of time and energy you use while on school experience (and later as a teacher), inside and outside the classroom and outside the school day. There is little time within a school day in which you can relax. In order to cope with your workload, and prevent your teaching commitment taking over your whole life, you need to plan to use your time and energy effectively over a week, a school experience and, later, a term and year. For example, you must not spend so much time preparing one lesson that you do not have time to prepare others well (there are, of course, times when you want to take extra time planning one particular lesson; for example, for a difficult class with whom the last lesson did not go well or if you are less familiar with the material). Do make sure that you are aware of all of the resources available; for example, existing lesson plans, homework instructions and resources on the school's intranet or virtual learning environment. Likewise, you should see yourself as part of a team of professionals and paraprofessionals and use teaching assistants (TAs) effectively in the classroom.

This unit looks first at how you manage your time, then at causes of, and coping with, stress, and finally at how you can build your resilience as a teacher.

OBJECTIVES

At the end of this unit, you should be able to:

- identify ways you can use your time effectively in the classroom;
- develop ways to manage your time and workload effectively;
- identify factors that may cause you stress;

■   develop methods of coping with stress;

■   develop some ways to increase your resilience as a teacher.

Check the requirements of your initial teacher education (ITE) programme to see which relate to this unit.

Managing your time and workload

As Amos (1998) emphasised, everyone has the same amount of time. It cannot be lost, increased, saved, delegated, reallocated nor reclaimed by turning the clock back. Time can easily be misused or wasted.

Pupils spend little time in school each year. Assuming 200 days per year and six hours contact per day, secondary school pupils spend less than 14 per cent of their time in lessons, while primary school pupils spend less than 12 per cent of their time in lessons (assuming five hours contact each day). Over 12 years of compulsory schooling, pupils spend about 92 weeks in total in lessons. Using this total amount of time in school, calculate how much (or little) time pupils spend in lessons in your subject over a year. It is therefore very important that you use this time effectively.

Managing your time in the classroom

To use classroom time effectively and economically, you need to plan to maximise the use of time in the lesson by ensuring you:

■   plan and prepare in advance, including setting up your classroom and identifying and setting out the resources you need before the lesson starts;

■   reduce the time it takes for pupils to get to lessons, to settle down and to pack up at the end and to manage pupils' behaviour in the lesson;

■   maintain a good balance in the use of time on teaching, supervisory and organisational activities;

■   allocate a high proportion of available time for academic work (sometimes called academic learning time);

■   spend a high proportion of time in 'substantive interaction' with pupils (that is, explaining, questioning, describing, illustrating);

■   devise simple, fast procedures for routine events and dealing with recurring problems;

■   eliminate unnecessary routines and activities from your own teaching;

■   delegate (to a TA or pupils) responsibilities and tasks that are within their capability;

■   regularly review the conduct of lessons in terms of effective use of your own and pupils' time.

This should enable pupils to:

■   spend a high proportion of their time engaged on learning tasks;

■   experience a high degree of success during this engaged time.

You can apply these time management principles in many ways in the classroom; for example, you can:

■ Spend time at the start of the first lesson with the pupils (and as a teacher at the start of the academic year) establishing rules and routines. This saves time on organisation and management as you proceed through the year, scheme or unit of work. Pay special attention here to safety issues. See Units 1.2 and 2.2 for further information about organisation, rules and routines in the classroom and Unit 3.3 for further information about behaviour for learning.

■ Use TAs or pupils to help give out and collect textbooks, pupils' books or equipment, to mark straightforward homework tests in class, make sure the classroom is left ready for the next class with the chairs tidy, floor clear, board clean and books tidied away.

■ Get pupils to do anything they can do to help you; for example, pupils can stick their own worksheets into their books rather than you spending time sticking them in or picking them up from the floor when they fall out.

■ Use peer- or self-marking; for example, for class tests or homework; it is both effective as pupils can be very perceptive when marking work and it saves time; once pupils are used to doing this, they will get on and do it. However, pupils need to be taught how to do this and provided with support.

■ Teach pupils to seek answers themselves rather than putting their hand up as soon as they get stuck.

■ Carry a marking pen with you as you move around the class checking work. This enables you to make brief notes on the work at that time. This not only provides formative feedback to pupils to promote learning; it saves you wasting time by having to go back to the work at a later stage.

■ Collect in books that are open at the page where you should start marking.

■ Ensure that work is dated and that homework is clearly identified so that it is easy for you to check what work has been done and what is missing. Ruling off each lesson's work helps you to check this.

■ Keep one page of your mark book for comments about progress (folding the page over ensures that comments are not seen inadvertently by pupils). As you see pupils' work in class or when you are marking, you can make brief notes that are then immediately at hand for discussions with parents, head of year, report writing, and so on.

If your school is using technology for some of these tasks or pupils are undertaking work electronically, or compiling an e-portfolio, as they are in some schools, the same principles apply, but should be adapted to the technology being used.

There are many other ways of managing time effectively in classrooms, which you develop as you gain experience. Task 1.3.1 is designed to help you look at how you spend your time in lessons.

Planning outside the classroom

Carefully plan the use of time in each lesson. This planning takes time; indeed, it takes more time when you start out than it does later in your teaching career. Use a timeline in your lesson plan, allocating time for each activity, as described in Unit 2.2. Allow time for pupils moving from one part of the school to another for the lesson (and, in physical education, time for changing), getting the class settled, particularly at the beginning of the day, after a break or lunch. You may find initially

---

 Task 1.3.1 How you spend your time in lessons

Observe how several experienced teachers use their time effectively in lessons. For example, look at how they divide their time between teaching, supervisory, organisational and management activities; time spent on explaining and questioning; time spent on routine events such as collecting homework or giving back books and procedures for doing this; what is delegated to TAs or pupils; time spent managing pupils' behaviour. Ask another student teacher or tutor to observe how you use your time in the classroom in one lesson or over a series of lessons. Discuss with the observer the findings and possible ways of using your or the pupils' lesson time more effectively and economically. Store your findings in your professional development portfolio (PDP) and try these ideas out systematically in your teaching.

---

that you under or overestimate the time needed for each activity, including organisation and management activities. In your reflection and evaluation at the end of each lesson, compare the time taken for each activity with that allocated. Although this helps you gradually to become realistic about how long different activities in a lesson take, early in your learning to teach you take longer to organise and manage your classes. It is therefore important that you do not base your long-term planning on the time it takes to organise and manage classes initially; rather, you should work hard to develop routine procedures to reduce time wasted as much as possible so that you maximise the learning time in the lesson.

Similarly, in planning a series of lessons, allocate time carefully. You have a certain amount of work to cover over a given period of time. If you do not plan carefully, you may find yourself taking too long over some of the content and not leaving yourself with enough time to cover all the content. Pupils' knowledge and understanding develop over a period of time; therefore, if they do not complete the content required, their learning may be incomplete. Unit 2.2 provides more information about lesson planning and schemes of work.

In order to use your time outside the classroom effectively, you need to plan your use of time and prioritise your work. Preparing as far in advance as you sensibly can and keeping everything up to date means that you do not have to chase around and try to complete paperwork at the last minute, just before it is needed (for example, before a tutor visits). Keeping records of activities can help with this; for example, keep a file of activities for the week, such as lessons to plan, marking to do, assignments for your ITE programme, and completing specific records of your work, including how you have met certain standards. Also plan time for reflection on your teaching overall and your development as a teacher: what have you learned and how are you going to develop further?

To help you plan how to use lesson time, complete Task 1.3.2.

Managing your own time effectively

However well you use time in the classroom, there are so many things for you to do as a teacher that your workload is high. Indeed, in a study by Kyriacou *et al.* (2003), less than 10 per cent of student teachers were absolutely certain that they would have enough time to do a good job. A high workload can result in not doing a good job, working very long hours to get the task done and not having enough time mentally and physically to relax for work the following day or week.

 Task 1.3.2 Planning how to use lesson time

When planning your lessons, deliberately think about how best you can use the time available. Determine what proportion of time to allocate to each activity and indicate, next to each activity, the amount of time to be allocated to it. When you evaluate the lesson and each activity in it, look specifically at how the time was used. Ask yourself how you can organise pupils and establish routines to make more time available for teaching and learning. Store these in your PDP and include them in future lesson plans.

Some of this may be alleviated by using the time you put into your work and your own time to best advantage. Some people always seem to work long hours but achieve little, whereas others achieve a great deal but still appear to have plenty of time to do things other than work.

One explanation for this could be that the first person wastes time, through, for example, being unsystematic in managing time, handling paperwork or responding to emails, putting off work rather than getting on and doing it, trying to do it all rather than delegating appropriately or not being able to say no to tasks, whereas the second person uses time well by, for example, having clear objectives for work to be done, prioritising work, completing urgent and important tasks first and writing lists of tasks to achieve during the day. Which of these descriptions fits you? To check this, you need to analyse the way you work and, if necessary, try to make changes. Task 1.3.3 is designed to help with this.

Using your time effectively on teaching-related activities helps you to be more efficient and more productive, better able to plan long-term, more satisfied with your work and your job, less stressed, and with more time for yourself and more opportunity to switch off out of work. There are many different techniques you can use to manage your time effectively. Figure 1.3.1 highlights some of these. Draw your own clock and insert your own techniques to avoid working around the clock and achieve a balance between work and leisure time (a work-life balance).

Some specific examples of ways of using your time effectively include:

- Making a list of activities you are going to complete each day. If there are activities left on the list at the end of the week or the day, ask why this is; for example, are you spending too much time on each activity? Are you unrealistic in how much you can achieve in a day? Spend five minutes at the end of a day identifying what you need for the next day to help save time.
- Utilising your free periods effectively (plan what you are going to do in these in advance).
- Planning your time for completing your work at time(s) best for you. For example, some people stay late at school then do not work at the weekend; other people set aside one day of the weekend and do all their work on that day. Whichever you decide best suits you – be strict with yourself, otherwise you will be working all the time. Set yourself things to look forward to; for example, attending a sports event at the weekend. This helps with time management as it prevents you from working through the weekend. These should also help you to reduce your stress.
- Organising your files and other work so you can easily locate them (it is as important to organise electronic files and delete those you do not need again as it is to organise paper files and throw away paper you do not need again).

Task 1.3.3 Planning your use of time outside the classroom

Record for one week the amount of time you spend on schoolwork outside the classroom, both at school and at home; for example, planning, preparation, marking, record-keeping, extracurricular activities, meetings. You might want to use a grid such as the one below.

Day	Work undertaken (along with time for each activity)	Total time
Monday		
Tuesday		
Wednesday		
Thursday		
Friday		
Saturday		
Sunday		
Total time for one week		

Then answer the following questions:

▪ Is the time spent outside the classroom and total hours worked during the week reasonable?
▪ Are you using this time effectively; that is, is the balance of time spent on the activities right (for example, are you spending more time on record-keeping than on planning and preparation)?
▪ Do you need to spend more time on some activities?
▪ Could you reduce time on some activities; for example, can some of the work be delegated to pupils, such as mounting and displaying work?

Compare the time you spent and how you spent it with other student teachers. If time spent is excessive, plan what action you are going to take to reduce the time spent on school-related work each week (according to the European Union working time directive, employers can't force adults to work more than 48 hours a week on average – normally *averaged over 17 weeks*). Store this in your PDP and recheck the use of time outside the classroom by repeating the log for one week to see whether this has worked and, in light of the results, what further action you need to, and can, take.

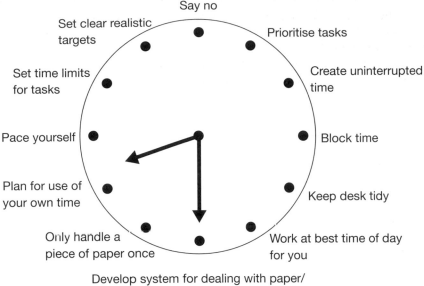

Figure 1.3.1 Working round the clock

 Do not do more than one job at a time or move from one thing to another, which can be disruptive, partly because you may not be concentrating fully on one task, which may result in inefficient use of time; hence, as one example, we suggest you manage your electronic communications effectively by, for example, switching off your phone so that you can focus on the task in hand and setting aside a time each day to respond to emails, rather than trying to respond as soon as they come into your mail box.

 Some teachers are now using iPads, Facebook and Twitter to keep up with colleagues, share resources and save time. However, you also need to be careful not to waste a lot of time using a variety of different technologies.

What other ways can you think of, appropriate to you?

Now complete Task 1.3.4 on balancing your work and leisure time.

✏ Task 1.3.4 Balancing your work and leisure time

In Task 1.3.3, you recorded the time spent outside the classroom over the course of a week on school-related work on school experience. Now do the same for the time spent on, and use of, leisure time. You may want to use a table similar to the one in Task 1.3.3. Looking at both tables, why is the balance between school-related work and leisure time as it is? Is this balance acceptable? If not, is it because of, for example, inefficiency, lack of experience or overload? How can you improve it? Discuss the balance of work and leisure with other student teachers and discuss with teachers how they achieve a work-life balance. Store the findings in your PDP and refer to it at intervals to check your work-life balance.

Preventing, managing and coping with stress

> Teacher stress may be defined as the experience by a teacher of unpleasant, negative emotions, such as anger, anxiety, tension, frustration or depression, resulting from some aspect of their work as a teacher.
>
> (Kyriacou 2001: 28)

Teaching has consistently been ranked as a high-stress occupation (see, for example, Johnson *et al.* 2005). According to the Health and Safety Executive (HSE 2013) Labour Force Survey, in 2013, work-related psychological/emotional ill-health, particularly stress, anxiety and depression that was caused or made worse by their job, was reported by more people working in the education sector, including teachers, than people working in other sectors. Compared to other social welfare professions, teachers experience high levels of stress (for example, Kyriacou 2000). Studies over time have consistently reported that between one-quarter and one-third of teachers frequently report being very or extremely stressed as a result of factors intrinsic to their work (for example, Gold and Roth 1993; Mills 1995), with Chaplain (2008) reporting 33–37 per cent of teachers. Reasons for teachers experiencing high levels of stress may be due to a range of factors, including teaching increasing numbers of pupils who are experiencing unhappy relationships at home that result in them being anxious and/or troubled, who have behavioural problems or who find it difficult to engage in learning. Such factors place ongoing demands on teachers on a daily basis, which may be very rewarding but are also emotionally draining and physically exhausting.

Research on teacher attrition has consistently indicated a high rate of new teacher attrition worldwide and over a period of time (see, for example, Darling-Hammond 1999; DeWert *et al.* 2003; Quartz 2003; Department of Education and Skills (DfES) 2005d; Changying 2007). Kyriacou and Kunc (2007) reported that about 40 per cent of those who start an ITE programme never become teachers, while 40 per cent of those who do become teachers are not teaching five years later. Smithers and Robinson (2011) reported a lower figure; about 17.4 per cent of those who completed an ITE programme were not recorded as being in teaching six months after completing. This does not mean that they do not ever become teachers; they may not have wanted to go into teaching (either at all or straight away) or not been able to get a job they wanted straight away, or they may have taken a gap year, for example. Likewise, in the United States, 30–50 per cent of new teachers have been reported to leave the field within their first five years (Quality Counts 2000; Ingersoll 2003); 14 per cent by the end of their first year, 33 per cent within three years and 50 per cent within five years (Alliance for Excellent Education 2004). At the other end of the teaching profession, Chaplain (2008), referring to Henry (2007) and Kyriacou and Coulthard (2000), reported the number of secondary teachers taking early retirement increased by 93 per cent in the period 2000–2007. One reason for this is the stress resulting from managing pupil behaviour and successive government initiatives. If student teachers work with teachers who are stressed, this may impact on their experiences in school.

Although it is preferable to prevent stress, this is not always possible; therefore, it is important that you identify causes of stress for you and develop strategies to be able to cope with it.

Causes of stress

Causes of stress may be different for different teachers or for the same teacher at different times. There may be a number of reasons for this; for example, whether a teacher has an internal or external locus of control. The most frequently reported factors contributing to teacher stress include discipline and dealing with pupils' disruptive behaviour, coping with a heavy workload, school ethos and lack of support from colleagues or managers (see, for example, Wilson 2002). However, many other causes of teacher stress have also been identified over a period of time (see, for example, Brown and Ralph 2002; Axup and Gersh 2008; Chaplain 2008; Akhlaq *et al.* 2010; Klaasen 2010; Klaasen and Chui 2010), including:

■ delivering material with which you are not very familiar;
■ motivating pupils and maintaining pupils' interest;
■ coping with the ability range of pupils within a class;
■ managing and controlling the class;
■ reprimanding a pupil;
■ conflict with pupils;
■ demanding work conditions.

It would also be unsurprising if the reasons were not similar for student teachers; indeed, studies have reported the same stress factors. However, in addition to factors that cause stress in all teachers, there may be additional causes of stress for student teachers; for example:

■ practical skills of teaching, techniques of lesson preparation and getting the teaching and/or planning right;
■ having unrealistic expectations of the profession;
■ having high expectations of own teaching performance;
■ not being regarded as a real teacher;
■ disagreement with the tutor;
■ observation, evaluation and assessment of teaching by the tutor, particularly receiving the tutor's or class teacher's opinion of classroom competence;
■ striking a balance between the school experience and personal commitments;
■ role ambiguity, role conflict and role overload.

Some of these points are addressed briefly below.

Stokking *et al.* (2003) identified shock and stress when starting to teach, which they suggested might be owing to student teachers having unrealistic expectations of the profession (which may be for a range of reasons) (see, for example, Hong 2010). This might be the result of lack of preparation or 'being thrown in at the deep end', and may be alleviated by gradually growing into more independent roles.

When you are being observed, evaluated and assessed, you are 'on show'. You are vulnerable because your developing skills are analysed and criticised constructively. This may be exacerbated where teachers are involved in assessing the teaching competence of student teachers because student teachers may feel unable to talk freely and openly to teachers about other concerns. Thus, the role of the teacher-tutor in assessment does not take account of student teachers' needs for friendship, counselling and tutoring. This may cause stress for student teachers.

Often, the role of a student teacher is ambiguous, so you are not quite sure how to perform in the role. Role conflict can result from doing a number of different activities within your job, each requiring different responsibilities, demands and skills; for example, teaching, form tutoring, talking to parents, administration (clerical work and committee duties), other tasks within the department, continuing professional development (inter-role conflict); or from trying to meet the different expectations of a number of people with whom you are working; for example, pupils, your tutor, other teachers, head of department, senior managers, parents (intra-role conflict). Likewise, role overload can be a factor (see workload above). Role ambiguity, conflict and overload may affect student teachers more than qualified teachers for a number of reasons. For example, as student teachers, you may, at any one time, be answering to and trying to please a number of people, who expect different things. You may also take longer to prepare each lesson than more experienced teachers. Further, you may be unsure of your role in a lesson, a department or the school as a whole.

In addition, student teachers are likely to have different concerns at different stages in learning to teach. Fuller and Brown (1975) classified changes in concerns over time in learning to teach as a three-way process; that is, concerns about self; concerns about tasks/situations; concerns about impact on pupils (this is covered in more detail in Unit 1.2). Thus, being concerned about specific aspects of your teaching or your development as a teacher at specific times is a natural part of learning to teach. As you go through your ITE programme, reflect on your own development as a teacher, particularly whether your concerns are the same or different at different times of the year.

It may also be that stressors outside work (for example, tensions of home and family or finances) are brought to, and add to stress at, work and make a person more vulnerable to stressors at work. Job stress may vary during the year according to the demands of a job, personal circumstances and/or other factors at any one time. A significant stressor at a particular time could account for differences in stress experienced by people at different times of a school year.

In Task 1.3.5, you are asked to look at causes of stress for you.

 Task 1.3.5 Causes of stress for student teachers

Write a list of factors that cause stress for you – both stressors as a student teacher and stressors outside your ITE programme. Compare these with causes of stress identified by another student teacher. Discuss similarities and differences. Store the list in your PDP and use this list for Task 1.3.6.

How can you cope with your stress?

Long-term stress may result in your teaching being less effective, more issues with pupils' behaviour, taking time off work or you becoming burned out (experiencing emotional exhaustion, depersonalisation and reduced personal accomplishment) (see, for example, Fernet *et al.* 2012). Different ways of coping with stress are appropriate for different people and for the same person at different times.

Ways of coping have been classified differently by different people. For example, Clunies-Ross *et al.* (2008) referred to proactive and reactive strategies. Arikewuyo (2004) classified strategies for coping with stress as:

■ active behavioural strategies (confronting the source of stress and attempting to change these sources by, for example, envisaging that you will get through in any situation whatever the circumstances, becoming more organised and devoting more time and energy to the job);

- inactive behavioural strategies (behaviours of escape, such as engaging in physical and recreational activities, and avoidance of the source of stress; for example, those individuals who might create stressful situations);
- active cognitive strategies (identifying the sources of stress and trying to tackle them by, for example, restructuring priorities, seeking more clarification, identifying strategies to manage and reduce stress);
- inactive cognitive strategies (conforming to, and trying to meet, expectations of, for example, tutors by, for example, meeting all duties and deadlines).

Murray-Harvey *et al.* (2000) identified personal and professional coping strategies. Five types of personal strategies were identified: cognitive; physical; behavioural; emotional; and rational/time organisation strategies. Three professional coping strategies were identified: knowledge of the curriculum and what a teacher is expected to teach and knowing the structure, organisation and culture of the school, which helped student teachers feel comfortable in that environment; use of self-management skills, such as preparation, planning and organisational skills; and professional qualities.

Some examples of specific coping strategies are identified below (these have been drawn from a number of sources; for example, Crothers *et al.* 2010; Leung *et al.* 2011; Titchmarsh 2012). This list is by no means exhaustive and you may find other strategies useful.

- *Prepare for stressful situations when you are not under pressure*; for example, prepare lessons before the day on which you are teaching them.
- *Have a good knowledge of what you are teaching*. There is nothing worse than being put on the spot if you do not have the knowledge. Read around a topic for which you do not have good knowledge prior to the lesson. If you are asked a question that you cannot answer, you can always say to pupils they should look it up and find the answer before the next lesson. You should then do the same.
- *Role-play a situation that is causing you anxiety and/or visualise what you can do to overcome the problem*. This helps you to focus on the problem and can be used to rehearse how you are going to cope.
- *Actively prepare for a situation*; for example, if you are anxious about a particular lesson, prepare it more thoroughly than normal. Plan thoroughly how you can reduce the likelihood of a problem occurring or deal with a particular problem. This strategy can help you to identify the reasons for a problem and to focus on possible ways of preventing or dealing with it.
- *Recognise and try to develop your strengths as well as your weaknesses* so that you can rely on your strengths as you work on improving any weaknesses.
- *Use any TA effectively*. TAs like to know what they are doing before they walk into the classroom; otherwise, you are putting them on the spot as well. It is important to communicate with them and keep them onside so that you work as a team in the classroom. Depending on the TA, and your relationship with them, they might be happy to team-teach, and so on.
- *Teach pupils to take responsibility for their own learning so that you are facilitating their learning*. Provide them with the resources they need to learn so you do not have to orchestrate everything. This takes the pressure off you.
- *Stamp out any behavioural issues as early as possible* because this creates stress and puts pressure on time (see also Unit 3.3).

- ■ *It is good to see pupils outside the classroom.* It can help to support their learning if you know something about what pupils do/are like outside the classroom.
- ■ *Develop effective self-management techniques;* for example, establish routines so that you can do things automatically, particularly when you are tired.
- ■ *Identify where you can get help.* You should get regular feedback on your teaching, but also identify other people who may be able to help.
- ■ *Develop social support systems that provide a network of people with whom you could talk through problems;* for example, other student teachers, your tutor, other teachers, a partner or friend. You may want to talk to different people for help with different problems. You may form a group with other student teachers to provide mutual support, talk about your anxieties/ concerns, develop a shared understanding of a problem and provide possible alternative solutions and practical help to address a problem; for example, a lesson being observed then discussed with another student teacher.
- ■ *Do not worry about incidents that have happened in school, and keep problems in proportion.* Try not to take problems home.
- ■ *Take account of the amount and variety of work you are doing to reduce both role overload and conflict.* This may mean, for example, that you need to try to take work home less often or take on fewer extracurricular activities. You may need to work on this over a period of time.

See also the strategies for managing your time and workload above.

However, it is important not only to focus on your concerns and fears, but also to pay attention to your aspirations and hopes as a teacher. Conway and Clark (2003: 470) suggested that focusing on resolving immediate concerns can result in 'an unduly pessimistic understanding of teachers and teaching'. You might find it difficult as a student teacher to focus on your development as a teacher, on the positive aspects of learning to teach and on your long-term goals and aspirations as a teacher. However, if you can do this, you are likely to have a more balanced view and be able to put things into perspective, and therefore reduce your stress (Unit 8.2 is designed to help you think about your continuing professional development). Task 1.3.6 is designed to help you to cope with your stress.

 Task 1.3.6 Coping with your stress

In Task 1.3.5, you listed factors that cause stress for you. Now identify ways that you can cope with this stress. Are the same or different methods appropriate for coping with stress, irrespective of the cause? Try out these coping methods as soon as you can and reflect on and evaluate whether these are effective. If they are not totally successful in all or some situations, what other methods are you going to try? Evaluate the effectiveness of these methods, store them in your PDP and adapt them or try new methods until you find those that work for you to cope with different stressful situations.

However, it is also important that you build up your resilience, as more resilient teachers are better able to manage the pressures of teaching and do not see periods when pressure builds up as times when they simply have to cope with stress. The next section looks at building your resilience.

Building your resilience

Resilience is what sustains and enables teachers to thrive rather than just survive in the profession (see, for example, Sumsion 2003; Kitching *et al.* 2009). It can be evidenced only in times of adversity and/or when there are challenges as it 'is activated and nurtured in times of stress' (Tait 2008: 58).

According to Beltman *et al.* (2011: 8), 'teacher resilience is a dynamic process or outcome that is the result of interaction over time between a person and the environment (for example, Bobek 2002; Sumsion 2003; Day 2008; Tait 2008)'; that is, the interaction of personal attributes with the contexts and the relationships in which teachers develop as professionals are important in building resilience. Some individual attributes enable teachers to do more than simply manage difficulties; rather, they sustain them when difficulties arise. They enable teachers to: adapt successfully despite obstacles; overcome challenging situations or recurring setbacks; bounce back quickly and efficiently; persevere and thrive (for example, Malloy and Allen 2007); and maintain their personal well-being (Howard and Johnson 2004). These individual attributes include altruistic motives, strong intrinsic motivation for teaching, high self-efficacy, feeling confident and competent, having coping strategies, and taking credit for and drawing sustenance from accomplishments. Gu and Day (2007: 1311) found that having an inner motivation to teach was associated with 'a strong sense of professional goals and purposes, persistence, professional aspirations, achievement and motivation'. On the other hand, personal risk factors include inability to ask for help (Flores 2006; Fantilli and McDougall 2009; Jenkins *et al.* 2009), a perceived conflict between personal beliefs and practices being used in school (Flores 2006; McCormack and Gore 2008) and personal challenges or difficulties such as negative self-beliefs or confidence (Fleet *et al.* 2007; Day 2008; McCormack and Gore 2008; Kitching *et al.* 2009).

According to Day *et al.* (2011), among others, some ways to build resilience both in your ITE programme on school experience and early in a teaching career include:

■ a formal mentoring programme and collegial support provided in the workplace;
■ establishing a mutually respectful, supportive relationship with your tutor, with open, honest, yet sensitive communication that challenges you;
■ understanding the role and responsibilities and establishing realistic expectations of your tutor;
■ working together with your tutor to improve teaching and learning;
■ devising challenging targets for development that also recognise success;
■ recognising the challenges in learning to teach and the reasons for these, and establishing a collaborative rather than individualistic approach to seeking solutions;
■ developing a reciprocal, mutually supportive, trusting network of peers and colleagues;
■ improving self-evaluation of your teaching; for example, through use of video analysis of teaching;
■ critiquing your own beliefs, values and practice;
■ developing social skills, assertiveness, self-regulation and empathy can help build resilience (Tait 2008);
■ valuing your own well-being.

Now complete Task 1.3.7.

🖉   **Task 1.3.7 Building your resilience**

Select two or three ways to build up your resilience from the list above. Reflect on: (i) your own current situation in relation to each; and (ii) how you might improve the situation in this area. For example, you might select identifying challenging targets for your development. What are your current targets for development? Are they challenging or are there aspects of your teaching that would be more challenging for you to develop?

Store your reflections in your PDP, work on them and review your progress in a month.

SUMMARY AND KEY POINTS

▪ We would be very surprised if, as a student teacher on school experience, you are not tired, do not feel as though you do not have enough time to do everything, are not anxious when someone comes in to watch your lessons, particularly if that person has a say in whether you become a qualified teacher, or if you are not worried about other aspects of your teaching and/or school experience.

▪ It may help to know that you are not going to be alone in this and many of the causes are the same for other student teachers.

▪ Where you are alone is in developing effective techniques that work for you to manage your time and cope with stress. There are no ready answers. Other people can help and support you with this, but nobody else can do it for you because what works for someone else may not work for you. You must work at managing your time and stress; there are no short-term, one-off solutions to these problems.

▪ It is also important that you build your resilience to enable you to thrive as a teacher. Collegial support in the workplace; a mutually respectful, supportive relationship with your tutor, with open, honest yet sensitive communication that challenges you; and a reciprocal, mutually supportive, trusting network of peers and colleagues are important in doing this. It helps also to focus on the positive aspects of teaching, your motivation to become a teacher, developing your self-efficacy, confidence and competence, which we hope this book will help you with.

Check which requirements for your ITE programme you have addressed through this unit.

 ## Further reading

Beltman, S., Mansfield, C. and Price, A. (2011) 'Thriving not just surviving: a review of research on teacher resilience', *Educational Research Review*, 6(3): 185–207.
This paper reviews recent empirical studies related to the resilience of early career teachers. These show resilience to be the outcome of a dynamic relationship between individual risk and protective factors and contextual challenges or risk factors and contextual supports or protective factors – an understanding of which can help to reduce risk factors and enhance protective factors and so enable new teachers to thrive, not just survive.

Bubb, S. and Earley, P. (2004) *Managing Teacher Workload: Work-Life Balance and Wellbeing*, London: Paul Chapman.
    This book provides guidance, along with a self-audit tool, on managing your workload, including, for example, how long you are working, what you are spending your time on and whether you are working efficiently.

Capel, S., Heilbronn, R., Leask, M. and Turner, T. (2004) *Starting to Teach in the Secondary School: A Companion for the Newly Qualified Teacher*, 2nd edn, London: RoutledgeFalmer.
    Although this book is written for newly qualified teachers, Chapter 2, 'Managing yourself and your workload', provides guidance on managing stress and time that is also appropriate for student teachers.

Child, D. (2007) *Psychology and the Teacher*, 8th edn, London: Continuum.
    Chapter 8, 'Human motivation', includes a section on stress in teachers and pupils.

Day, C., Edwards, A., Griffiths, A. and Gu, Q. (2011) *Beyond Survival: Teachers and Resilience*, Nottingham: University of Nottingham.
    This booklet reports on findings from a series of research seminars focused on addressing the question 'How does resilience in teaching arise and how is it sustained?' The findings reported should help you to understand better how to build your resilience as a teacher.

Galton, M. and MacBeath, J. (2008) *Teachers Under Pressure*, London: Sage with the National Union of Teachers (NUT).
    This book focuses on a five-year research project focusing on the government's remodelling agenda, including remodelling the workforce with a view to reducing teacher workloads. This sets factors relating to time and stress in schools into context.

Hayes, C. (2006) *Stress Relief for Teachers: The 'Coping Triangle'*, London: Routledge.
    This book looks at the nature of stress in the classroom in a clear, practical way. It focuses on how teachers can help themselves to cope. It focuses on a 'coping triangle'.

Holmes, E. (2009) *The Newly Qualified Teacher's Handbook*, 2nd edn, London: Routledge.
    This book covers all aspects of the first few months of teaching. The book is written in light of induction regulations introduced in 2008 for newly qualified teachers in England. Chapter 7 looks at work-life balance. Other chapters are likely to be of use in helping you with aspects of your work that may be stressful.

Kyriacou, C. (2000) *Stress-Busting for Teachers*, Cheltenham: Stanley Thornes.
    This book aims to help teachers to develop a range of strategies for coping with stress at work. It looks at what stress is, sources of stress, how to pre-empt stress, how to cope with stress, and what schools can do to minimise stress.

Other resources and websites

The Teacher Support Network: www.teachersupport.info
    These provide information, research evidence and a range of services, including conselling, to help.

Appendix 2 on page 591–595 provides further examples of websites you may find useful.

Capel, S., Leask, M. and Turner, T. (eds) (2010) *Readings for Learning to Teach in the Secondary School: A Companion to M Level Study*, London: Routledge.
    This book brings together essential readings to support you in your critical engagement with key issues raised in this textbook.

The subject-specific books in the *Learning to Teach* series are also very useful.

Any additional resources and an editable version of any tasks/tables in this unit are available on the companion website: www.routledge.com.cw.capel

1.4 Using information and communications technology/ digital technologies for professional purposes

Antony Stockford

Introduction

Teachers are expected to integrate various forms of information and communications technology (ICT)/digital technologies into their work in the classroom. The statutory framework of the 2014 national curriculum states: 'Pupils should be taught to develop their capability, creativity and knowledge in computer science, digital media and information technology' (Department of Education (DfE) 2013f: 64). The focus for this unit is the use of ICT to facilitate and enhance learning and the learning experience rather than the subject of information technology and computer science. This aspect is reinforced across a range of subjects. Good teachers in all subjects are already making highly successful use of ICT resources and are always looking out for new ways of using ICT to stimulate pupils and to extend their learning. ICT used innovatively to deliver your subject enhances learning for your pupils. These teachers understand that ICT is a tool to be applied selectively but is not the complete solution to meeting their pupils' needs. They are also able to learn from pupils. Talking with your ICT colleagues will also help you identify valuable learning experiences that help your pupils.

One concern for you if you are a non-ICT specialist may be that the pupils know more about computers and programs than you do. If this is a concern, or if you are uncertain about the use of ICT in your subject area or have not fully embedded it into your teaching, you are not alone, as was noted by the inspectorate in England in their ICT subject report 2008-11:

> Sometimes staff training in the use of basic ICT packages such as word processing or PowerPoint had brought staff capability up to the level of many of their students, but had not had any impact on teaching and learning or student achievement because staff had not yet embedded ICT use effectively into their teaching methodology.
>
> (Ofsted 2011a: 42)

The purpose of this unit is not to turn you into an ICT teacher, but to show how you can become a teacher who uses ICT creatively in your teaching to enhance pupil learning. One key objective is to raze some of your fears and present some clear signposts for you to using ICT to support your subject teaching. After all, in reality, 'The only thing we have to fear is fear itself' (Roosevelt 1933: 1).

OBJECTIVES

At the end of this unit, you should be able to:

■ understand the relevance of ICT for you and your pupils;
■ use frameworks for auditing your subject knowledge and understanding of ICT;
■ have ideas and examples for embedding ICT learning in your subject;
■ use some core techniques when teaching using ICT in your subject;
■ plan to teach using ICT resources to enhance the pupil learning experience.

Check the requirements of your initial teacher education (ITE) programme to see which relate to this unit.

The relevance of ICT for you and your pupils

You need to be clear about why you might use ICT in your subject lessons. Is it to amuse the pupils, is it to pique their curiosity for your subject, is it to help them learn? Hopefully it is the last two.

The following examples from the Ofsted Subject Report 2011 on English schools are excellent illustrations of this.

Examples of some of the particularly good practice observed by school inspectors for England (Ofsted):

An 11 to 16 secondary school provided two differing examples of how the use of ICT to support learning raised achievement. In the first example, two girls had produced a 17-minute film in French. They used the game Sims to modify 3D objects to create avatars of themselves in school uniform, avatars of their teachers and representations of their classroom and other areas of the school. The girls scripted a storyline, writing the dialogue in French, and the avatars were animated to perform the necessary actions. Finally they saved and compiled the animated scenes into a film and recorded the voiceovers in French to create the finished product. The use of ICT improved the girls' learning of French because the task really engaged them and they ended up spending longer on writing and speaking in the target language than would otherwise have been the case. In the process, they also developed their skills in 3D design.

In the second example, during a chemistry lesson the teacher's imaginative use of an animated photograph of a famous scientist 'talking' about his life's work was inspirational. Students were hugely engaged by this and the follow-up task, in which they were required to research and devise questions to ask of the scientist.

For a Key Stage 4 geography coastal study, from Burton Bradstock in Dorset to Porlock Bay in Somerset, a student used ICT to help with a sequence of investigations to plan and organise her work. This helped to demonstrate initiative and originality in her work. Her use of ICT deepened her analysis and understanding.

She looked at long shore drift from a western to an eastern coastline and learnt that the greater the wind speed the higher the wave frequency. The student used an anemometer to measure and compare wind speed and to see if there was any correlation between wind speed and how many waves broke in a minute. She used computerised charts and graphs to help her analyse her data and draw conclusions as well as to depict and illustrate her findings about the impact of waves on coastal erosion. This also led to a study of the impact on the shape of pebbles and their angularity. The student had downloaded maps from the Internet to show images of the two locations; she also used a digital camera to take photographs of them. The use of ICT helped to extend the student's learning.

(Ofsted 2011a: 34–5)

The key points these three examples of good practice illustrate are that:

■ The best use of ICT as a resource is context-driven.
■ If a pupil sees the benefit, they are more likely to use the same techniques again elsewhere.

What is common about the 'good practice' cited is that ICT was applied both in a contextual and in a practical applied manner. If you are going to develop your skills, resources and techniques to mirror this good practice, it is very important that you understand some of the theory behind these examples. The approach to using ICT in the examples above has theoretical support from the work of two educational theorists, Lev Vygotsky and Jerome Bruner. Both of these theorists took effectively a social constructivist approach to understanding the process of learning and how this might be applied to teaching. The underlying principle of social constructivist theory is that by a teacher modelling and scaffolding, learners are able to gain knowledge in a structured manner that they are able to retain and apply appropriately in the future; that is, they are learning (scaffolding is covered in Unit 4.1). Vygotsky (1978) developed a theory about helping pupils to develop problem-solving skills, which has been called the 'zone of proximal development' (ZPD). This is expressed as 'The distance between the actual development level as determined by independent problem solving and the level of potential problem solving as determined through problem solving under adult guidance or in collaboration with more capable peers' (Vygotsky 1978: 86). In a classroom context, this means that if you ask pupils to solve a problem type they have experience of successfully solving in the past, they are able to solve it when you ask them this time. If, on the other hand, you ask them to solve a problem type they do not have experience of doing, they require teacher input and, possibly, working together with others to successfully solve the problem.

Bruner (1976) extended aspects of the ZPD with his development of 'discovery learning'. This is an enquiry-based constructivist approach where the learner solves problems using their own knowledge and experience to develop new facts and relationships, which in turn form new knowledge.

As a teacher in a classroom context, you give the pupils 'clues' and choices, and then allow them to construct solutions using these and their prior knowledge and experience.

Learning theories are explored in greater depth in Unit 5.1 of this book, and how they are applied when using ICT to enhance learning is expanded on the companion website (www.routledge.com.cw. capel). In Task 1.4.1, you are asked to look at applying these theories.

In order to use ICT effectively to enhance pupils' learning, it is important that you are clear about your own level of knowledge, understanding and competence. The next section of the unit is designed to help you achieve this.

 Task 1.4.1 A framework to identify knowledge and understanding to solve new problems

Drawing on the pedagogical theories outlined above (in Unit 5.1 and on the companion website), develop a simple framework that you could use so that your pupils are able to suggest how knowledge and experiences they already have could be used to help solve new problems (transferrable skills). Discuss with another student teacher what skills you expect your pupils to demonstrate to problem-solve effectively, and use this to develop the framework. What will gaps in their completed frameworks tell you about their knowledge and the focus of your teaching?

Store your findings in your professional development portfolio (PDP) for later reference.

Frameworks for auditing your knowledge and understanding

In this section, you are going to undertake four tasks that, together, aim to take you through a self-audit of your ICT knowledge and skills. By working through these tasks, you plan how to develop your ICT knowledge and skills base. This forms a sizeable component of your PDP.

In Task 1.4.2, you are asked to identify forms of ICT, and in Task 1.4.3 (p. 65) to identify your current competences. In Task 1.4.4 (p. 65), you are asked to look at what your subject requires to be delivered with ICT, and in Task 1.4.5 (p. 66) to create an action plan to develop your skills.

 Task 1.4.2 What forms of ICT are you familiar with?

Using Table 1.4.1, answer three questions in relation to each form of ICT listed ('Forms of ICT' means knowing ways in which ICT is used or accessed):

■ Have you heard of this form of ICT?
■ Do you know the various uses for ICT?
■ Which are you able to use?

This is not an exhaustive list; however, it does aim to identify most common and current forms of ICT that you could use to enhance the learning experience (both yours and that of your pupils). Store the list in your PDP, revisit it and update your knowledge levels at regular intervals during your ITE programme.

Table 1.4.1 Forms of ICT

Form of ICT	Heard of		Know what it is/does		Know how to use	
	Yes	No	Yes	No	Yes	No
All-in-one PC						
Blog						
Bluetooth						
Camcorder						
Car computer						
CD player/recorder						
Cell phone						
Data logger						
Desktop PC						
Digital camera						
Digital radio						
DVD player/recorder						
e-Reader						
Home appliances						
(microwave/dishwasher)						
Interactive whiteboard (IWB)						
Laptop						
MP3/MP4 player						
Netbook						
PDA (Personal Digital Assistant)						
Satnav (GPS)						
Smartphone						
Tablet						
Television						
Twitter						
Visualiser						
Watch/clock						
Wi-Fi						

Task 1.4.3 Checking your basic ICT skills

In this task, you are auditing not just your knowledge about the ways ICT is used, but also how confident you feel about using ICT. You must be honest with yourself. It is better to be pleasantly surprised than claim what you cannot do.

Using Table 1.4.2 (p. 67), put a tick beside each skill indicating your level of competence/ confidence (0 = no confidence, 3 = very confident).

Store the table in your PDP, revisit it and update your knowledge levels at regular intervals during your ITE programme, as well as when undertaking Task 1.4.5.

 Task 1.4.4 How ICT is used in your subject

This task focuses you on your specialist subject. Look at one of the relevant examination specifications for your subject that you are going to teach and identify where ICT can be used to enhance both the learning and the assessment. (Unit 6.2 examines assessment in greater depth.) You can also complete this task using schemes and units of work (see Unit 2.2).

Examination specifications usually follow a common format. They are made up of units and each unit is made up of topics. Within each topic, there is specific subject content to be covered. Many specifications also identify wider skills that the examination programme addresses, one of which is usually ICT. Look at the topics in each unit and identify where you might use ICT opportunities to enhance teaching and learning within your subject. Remember, not all topics lend themselves to the use of ICT.

Using Table 1.4.3 (p. 70), map the units and the topics within the units. For each topic, identify where the use of ICT may enhance the pupils' understanding, interest and motivation for achieving their potential in your subject.

Some ideas for how you might use ICT for learning in your subject teaching are provided in Table 1.4.4 (p. 71), 'Elements of ICT in various subject areas'. Identify where you may need to enhance your skills and competences in using ICT to deliver and to enthuse your pupils to use appropriate ICT as an embedded part of their learning processes. Figure 1.4.1 provides guidance on completing Table 1.4.4, and Figure 1.4.2 demonstrates how the completed task might look.

This task requires honesty. You need to know where you are currently if you are going to make the most of your knowledge and skills and develop them. It is exactly what you do with your pupils in the classroom in assessing prior learning. Store the table in your PDP to use when undertaking Task 1.4.5.

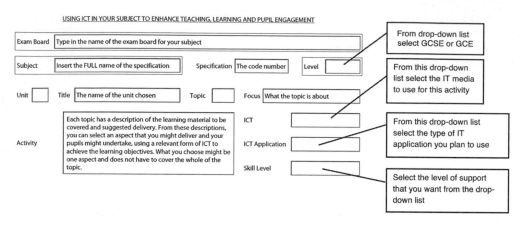

USING ICT IN YOUR SUBJECT TO ENHANCE TEACHING, LEARNING AND PUPIL ENGAGEMENT

Exam Board	Type in the name of the exam board for your subject		
Subject	Insert the FULL name of the specification	Specification: The code number	Level
Unit	Title: The name of the unit chosen	Topic	Focus: What the topic is about

From drop-down list select GCSE or GCE

From this drop-down list select the IT media to use for this activity

Activity: Each topic has a description of the learning material to be covered and suggested delivery. From these descriptions, you can select an aspect that you might deliver and your pupils might undertake, using a relevant form of ICT to achieve the learning objectives. What you choose might be one aspect and does not have to cover the whole of the topic.

ICT

ICT Application

Skill Level

From this drop-down list select the type of IT application you plan to use

Select the level of support that you want from the drop-down list

Figure 1.4.1 Guidance for completing Table 1.4.3

USING ICT IN YOUR SUBJECT TO ENHANCE TEACHING, LEARNING AND PUPIL ENGAGEMENT

Exam Board	Edexcel		
Subject	Geography	Specification: 9GE01	Level: GCE
Unit: 2	Title: Geographical investigations	Topic: 3	Focus: Increasing risks

Activity: Fieldwork and research to investigate how a small stream or part of a river catchment can suffer increased flood risks resulting from: growing urbanisation. Choose a local area and use local records to plot the changes over the past ten years. Use photographs to show how the areas have been developed.

ICT: Phone camera

ICT application: Photoshop

Skill level: Need guidance

Figure 1.4.2 Example of completed Table 1.4.3

✏️ **Task 1.4.5 ICT action planning**

This final task in this section is to enable you to develop your personal action plan. By looking at your responses in Tasks 1.4.2, 1.4.3 and 1.4.4, you are able to identify those areas you should develop to enhance your teaching and pupils' learning in your subject. Using the proforma in Table 1.4.5 (p. 75), identify the areas you want to develop and then the elements within those areas that you want to focus on. This encourages you to think about where you might be able to get support and the time frame for doing so. This enables you to prioritise your own development. Store the task in your PDP and refer back to it regularly during the year to record your progress and to identify the next aspects of developing your ICT competence.

Table 1.4.2 Basic ICT skills

General skills	0	1	2	3
Choosing appropriate software to help solve a problem				
Dragging and dropping				
Having more than one application open at a time				
Highlighting				
Making selections by clicking				
Moving information between software (for example, using the clipboard)				
Navigating around the desktop environment				
Opening items by double-clicking with the mouse				
Printing				
Using menus				
How to change the name of files				
Word-processing skills	0	1	2	3
Altering fonts: font, size, style (bold, italic, underline)				
Text justification: left, right, centre				
Using a spellchecker				
Moving text within a document with 'cut', 'copy' and 'paste'				
Adding or inserting pictures to a document				
Counting the number of words in a document				
Adding a page break to a document				
Altering page orientation (landscape, portrait)				
Using characters/symbols				
Using find and replace to edit a document				
Using styles to organise a document				
Using styles to alter the presentation of a document efficiently				
Adding page numbers to the footer of a document				
Adding the date to the header of a document				
Changing the margins of a document				
Email skills	0	1	2	3
Recognising an email address				
Sending an email to an individual				

Table 1.4.2 continued

Sending an email to more than one person				
Replying to an email				
Copying an email to another person				
Forwarding an incoming email to another person				
Adding an address to an electronic address book				
Filing incoming and outgoing emails				
Adding an attachment to an email				
Receiving and saving an attachment in an email				
Database skills (not now required but useful)	0	1	2	3
Searching a database for specific information				
Using Boolean operators (and/or/not) to narrow down searches				
Sorting database records in ascending or descending order				
Adding a record to a database				
Adding fields to a database				
Querying information in a database (for example, locating all values greater than 10)				
Filtering information in a database (for example, sorting on all values greater than 10)				
Categorising data into different types (numbers, text and yes/no Boolean types)				
Web browser skills	0	1	2	3
Recognising a Web address (for example, www. or .co.uk, and so on)				
Using hyperlinks on websites to connect to other websites				
Using the back button				
Using the forward button				
Using the history				
Understanding how to search websites				
Using Boolean operators (and/or/not) to narrow down searches				
Creating bookmarks				
Organising bookmarks into folders				
Downloading files from a website				

Table 1.4.2 continued

Spreadsheet skills	0	1	2	3
Identifying grid squares in a spreadsheet (for example, B5)				
Inserting columns into a spreadsheet				
Inserting rows into a spreadsheet				
Sorting spreadsheet or database columns in ascending or descending order				
Converting a spreadsheet into a chart				
Labelling a chart				
Adding simple formulae/functions to cells				
Applying formatting to different types of data, including numbers and dates				
Presentation skills	0	1	2	3
Inserting text and images on a slide				
Inserting a slide in a presentation				
Adding buttons to a presentation				
Using timers in a presentation				

Ideas and examples for embedding ICT learning in your subject

Think about the ICT you use yourself: your mobile phone; your television remote control; your microwave. You might have a wider range of ICT that you use, such as Twitter, Facebook, a tablet, a Kindle or e-book reader. Notice, we are not talking about your personal computer (PC) or laptop here as we are trying to use forms of ICT not normally associated with the classroom. In many cases, such forms of technology are not allowed in the classroom; however, with changes and development in digital media, the opportunities that are offered by much of the new technology cannot be ignored. The most important of these developments involves mobile media (see below).

If you use some of these devices and applications, or indeed others, consider ways in which using them could enhance, expand, illustrate and innovate in your subject teaching.

In English, for example, the use of e-book readers can, at times, be more effective than paper-based resources. Using a phone camera to take a photo and using the image as a stimulus for descriptive writing or poetry may be an effective way of engaging learners.

Thinking about home economics/food technology, there is a wide range of ICT/digital technology used both in the home and in the food industry that could be used in lessons.

Using mobile media devices to enhance pupil learning

As teaching and learning develops to meet the ever-changing global needs, teachers become aware of a greater range of media devices that their learners use. Industry has already recognised this and developed strategies where these can used to enhance employee efficiency and engagement.

Table 1.4.3 Using ICT in your subject

Exam Board				

Subject		Specification		Level

Unit	Title		Topic	Focus

Activity			ICT	
			ICT Application	
			Skill Level	

Unit	Title		Topic	Focus

Activity			ICT	
			ICT Application	
			Skill Level	

Activity			ICT	
			ICT Application	
			Skill Level	

Activity			ICT	
			ICT Application	
			Skill Level	

Activity			ICT	
			ICT Application	
			Skill Level	

Table 1.4.4 Elements of ICT in various subject areas

Art and design		Maths	
Finding things out	Surveys (for example, consumer preferences), Web galleries, online artist/movement profiles	Finding things out	Databases, surveys, statistics, graphing, calculators, graphical calculators, dynamic geometry, data logging/measurement (for example, timing), Web-based information (for example, statistics/ history of maths)
Developing ideas	Spreadsheets to model design specs	Developing ideas	Number patterns, modelling algebraic problems/probability
Making things happen	Embroidery, CAD (computer-aided design)/CAM (computer-aided manufacturing)	Making things happen	Programming (for example, LOGO turtle graphics)
Exchanging and sharing information	Digital imagery/CAD/ multimedia for students' design portfolios	Exchanging and sharing information	Formulae/symbols, presenting investigation findings, multimedia
Reviewing, modifying and evaluating	Real-world applications (for example, commercial art)	Reviewing, modifying and evaluating	Comparing solutions to those online, online modelling and information sources
Business and commercial studies		Technology	
Finding things out	Pay packages, databases, online profiling	Finding things out	Product surveys, consumer preferences, environmental data
Developing ideas	Business/financial modelling	Developing ideas	CAD, spreadsheet modelling
Making things happen	Business simulation	Making things happen	CAM, simulations (for example, environmental modelling), textiles, embroidery, control
Exchanging and sharing information	Business letters, Web authoring, multimedia CVs, email	Exchanging and sharing information	Advertising, product design and realisation, multimedia/Web presentation
Reviewing, modifying and evaluating	Commercial packages, dot-com, admin systems	Reviewing, modifying and evaluating	Industrial production, engineering/electronics

Table 1.4.4 continued

Performing arts		Physical education	
Finding things out	Online information sources, surveys	Finding things out	Recording/analysing performance, Internet sources (for example, records)
Developing ideas	Planning performance/ choreographing sequences	Developing ideas	Planning sequences/tactics
Making things happen	Lighting sequences, computer animation, MIDI, multimedia presentations	Making things happen	Modelling sequences/tactics, sporting simulations
Exchanging and sharing information	Video, audio, digital video, Web authoring, multimedia, animation, DTP (desktop publishing) posters/flyers/pro-grammes, email	Exchanging and sharing information	Reporting events, posters, flyers, Web/ multimedia authoring, video, digital video Reviewing, modifying and
evaluating	Ticket booking, lighting control, recording/TV studios, theatre/film industry	Reviewing, modifying and evaluating	Website evaluation, presentation of performance statistics, event diaries, performance portfolios
English		Modern foreign languages	
Finding things out	Surveys, efficient searching/keywords, information texts, online author profiles, readability analysis	Finding things out	Class surveys, topic databases, Web searching/browsing
Developing ideas	Authorship, desktop publishing (balancing text and images)	Developing ideas	Concordancing software, interactive video packages, DTP and word processing
Making things happen	Interactive texts/ multimedia/Web authoring	Making things happen	Online translation tools, interactive multimedia
Exchanging and sharing information	Exploring genres (for example, writing frames), authoring tools, text/ images, scripting, presenting, interviewing (audio/video)	Exchanging and sharing information	Word processing, DTP, Web/multimedia authoring, email projects, video/audio recording, digital video editing
Reviewing, modifying and evaluating	Website evaluation, online publishing, email projects	Reviewing, modifying and evaluating	Internet communication, website/CD-ROM language teaching evaluation, translation software

Table 1.4.4 continued

Humanities		Science	
Finding things out	Surveys, databases, Internet searching, monitoring environment (for example, weather), census data, and so on	Finding things out	Data recording and analysis, spreadsheets and graphing packages, Internet searching (for example, genetics info)
Developing ideas	Multimedia, DTP, modelling (spreadsheets/ simulations)	Developing ideas	Modelling experiments/ simulations
Making things happen	Simulations, interactive multimedia/Web authoring	Making things happen	Data logging, modelling experiments, simulations (what if . . .?)
Exchanging and sharing information	Web authoring, email projects	Exchanging and sharing information	Communicating investigation findings (DTP, Web/multimedia authoring, DV (digital video))
Reviewing, modifying and evaluating	Weather stations, satellite information, website/CD-ROM evaluation, archive information	Reviewing, modifying and evaluating	Accessing information (evaluating for bias on issues; for example, nuclear power)

Such an approach is called **B**ring **Y**our **O**wn **D**evice (BYOD) or **B**ring **Y**our **O**wn **T**echnology (BYOT) and utilises mobile devices and technology in the work environment.

This currently is the exact opposite of that in many schools, who prohibit the use of and even confiscate pupils' mobile phones on the principle that they will misuse them. However, adopting an industry approach to the use of pupils' mobile technology offers outstanding opportunities for enhancing pupils' learning.

The potential has been identified by the DfE (2013h) in the National Curriculum 2014, which clearly indicates across all Key Stages and subject areas that pupils must become digitally literate, being able to use, safely express themselves and develop their ideas for those subjects through information and communication technology, at a level suitable for the future workplace and as active participants in a digital world. Additionally, Ofsted requires that schools not only have e-safety policies, but also teach their pupils good and safe practice, which has been specifically updated by Ofsted (2014a).

Statutory guidance from the government and Ofsted requires teachers and schools to ensure that pupils know how to use digital media and the Internet effectively and safely. Again, because the National Curriculum requires this to happen across subjects, then it means that you, as a teacher, must be able to model good practice.

Of course, one of the best ways of doing this is to use the digital media, smartphones, tablets, laptops, and so forth that the pupils are familiar with and use them to enhance pupil learning.

If, as has been identified elsewhere in this unit, you as a teacher set an activity that requires pupils to take a series of themed photographs on their mobile phone and bring them in for a particular activity, then the engagement of the pupils is likely to be considerably higher than if you ask them to look something up, write about it and then bring that in.

As a teacher, the use of BYOD with your pupils also enables you to apply the 'flipped' classroom, where the pupils learn away from the classroom and then evaluate their learning back in the classroom (Shea and Stockford 2014). Using the Internet and mobile technology forms a core part of this, and in particular the opportunity for pupils to access their learning areas via, for example, the school intranet and downloading their field or homework from their own devices to their personal school learning area.

Developing such initiatives, which engage pupils, depends upon good practice. Underpinning this is an effective school and pupil BYOD policy. It is very possible that your school has not, as yet, developed such policies. However, Shea and Stockford (2014), using international exemplars, offer standardised policies that are freely adaptable for schools just for this purpose.

This should be starting to make you think, so let us extend the process to create a constructed learning activity. Try to be innovative and look at different ways in which you can deliver a lesson and enhance pupils' learning. The key to being innovative is to start with something familiar and in which you are interested. This should give you more confidence in being able to develop something new. We take the focus from Confucius (551–479 BC), 'I hear and I forget. I see and I remember. I do and I understand', and build on that theme via theories such as the ZPD (Vygotsky 1978) and Kolb's (1984a) theory of spiral exponential learning, where learning takes an active form (see also Unit 5.1).

Most of you, at some time, use or want to use the video feature on your mobile phone, digital camera or even your camcorder. You take the shots, but how many of you actually do anything with them? Task 1.4.6 (p. 76) is designed to show you how to use a mobile phone, as an example of everyday ICT, to enhance your teaching and pupils' learning.

Some core techniques when teaching using ICT in your subject

The fundamental thing to remember about using ICT is that it is applied and there are common techniques that underpin effective applied teaching; they are valuable as techniques in using ICT to support learning in the teaching of any subject.

Applied as a term means 'doing'. If the pupils are going to do an activity, it is important that they understand 'what they are doing', 'why they are doing it' and 'how they are doing it'. What is crucial is that you know that they understand these elements.

It is likely that when you use a form of ICT to enhance an aspect of your subject teaching, you bring the pupils together in an ICT suite/classroom where you have an environment, and sufficient computers, to draw their work together in a structured manner. So you need to know specific techniques needed for when you take your pupils into an ICT suite. There are options for how pupils enter the suite. Now complete Task 1.4.7 (p. 77).

The pupils have entered the suite and are seated. Now you need their attention, so to strategies two and three. There are two main types of teacher-pupil attention in an ICT suite: 'instruction' and 'briefing', which, wherever possible, require a particular technique.

■ Instruction covers taking the register and giving some additional guidance to the whole class, usually as a result of feedback from pupil activity.

The strategy to adopt here is to turn off all the computer monitors and/or turn each monitor so that it is not facing the pupil. The rationale for this is that if you just ask for their attention, pupils will continue with what they are doing or will be distracted and look at the screen, play with the mouse or keyboard rather than pay attention to you.

■ Briefing covers modelling, activity/task briefing, formative assessment.

A briefing is key as it is where you are engaging the pupils in the learning process by introducing the topic, task or activity and modelling as appropriate. At the same time, you are using the briefing to formatively assess prior knowledge, as well as the pupils' understanding of the context and the task activities.

Table 1.4.5 Information technology action plan

Areas for development	Methods of gaining knowledge	Target date and sign-off

The strategy to adopt here is to bring pupils away from the computers to the front of the suite or in front of the projector screen of the interactive whiteboard (IWB), if you are using one. The rationale for this is that you must not only have their full attention and concentration for briefing them, but you *must* establish that they know what they are doing, why they are doing it and how they are doing it. You are not able to assess progress and learning without this. Incidentally, you might notice the appearance of the virtuous three again: 'what', 'why' and 'how'.

Apart from the entry into an ICT suite, you do not just use these techniques once in a lesson. You may use each on a number of occasions. Most will be in your lesson plan, but some may be as a result of your formative assessment as you move round a class and you identify a common area of difficulty or the demonstration of an excellent piece of application or process that you would like to share with the rest of the class.

Task 1.4.6 Using everyday ICT

A key purpose of Task 1.4.4, 'How ICT is used in your subject', was for you to think about different ways in which you might use aspects of ICT to enhance your teaching and pupil learning in your subject. As an example of activities, Task 1.4.6 uses the video feature on a mobile phone in the classroom environment.

Take a video and then use that to create a subject-specific project that enhances pupils' learning, and engages and develops their learning skills. The processes are used to enhance teaching and learning within your subject and the topic provides the focus for the activity. Making a video as a task provides a hook for the topic as well as an activity that the pupils will not necessarily perceive as 'being taught', but an engaging way to learn with you and your subject.

 You haven't taken any videos? Not a problem; now is the time to do so. To help, there is practical guidance on the on the companion website (www.routledge.com.cw.capel), which 'walks' you through the task. A PowerPoint called 'Making a video', which can be used as a briefing tool for steps one to five, is also available for download at www.routledge.com.cw. capel. There are also some Internet links to give you access to more guidance should you need it.

By completing the task yourself (making a video), you are able to construct a lesson plan, brief the pupils and know how to answer the questions they are likely to ask, as you will have asked yourself exactly the same questions while you worked through the task. You can identify the points at which you have to stop and assess understanding before progressing to the next stage. This enables you to help your pupils understand elements of an activity and not disengage because you have not formatively assessed their understanding.

Remember that the purpose of this task is to provide you with both the experience of making a video and the resources to develop this as an activity for delivering a topic within your subject, so make notes for each step as you complete it so that you create your lesson activity as you go. Store these notes in your PDP.

As mentioned above, by doing Task 1.4.6, you can identify the 'difficult bits', which are where your pupils will ask questions. You will be able to either address these elements as you brief pupils on the task, or be able to answer questions that arise as the lesson activity progresses. You will have broken the task down into achievable elements that make up the parts of the lesson plan, which in turn indicate timing. You will also be able to assess your pupils formatively by understanding the topic and the activity as you move through the task. Your notes also act as a prompt while you are briefing or modelling the stages of the task.

Once you have completed this activity, in addition to the finished film, you will have the footage that you filmed on location. You will be able to use this as a resource for modelling the editing part of the task, an accompanying set of notes that you have written as you worked through the task. You can use these to develop two one-hour lessons, although the actual filming is best set as an 'out-of-school' assignment or homework task. With two lessons, pupils will want to do another topic in the same way. Longer than this and they are likely to stop finding it 'fun'.

By setting the context in terms of your subject, you are then using the making of a video as an innovative and practical strategy for teaching and learning. Using this task as a resource, you should be able to identify a suitable subject topic that lends itself to this type of task. The outcomes of Task 1.4.4, 'How ICT is used in your subject', should help you here to set focused learning outcomes for the lesson. The steps in making the video form the framework for the objectives. Both formative and summative assessment will have more relevance for the pupils as they will have ownership of the topic that they are using to address the subject context.

 Task 1.4.7 Entry strategies

Discuss with another student teacher why an orderly and structured entry to an ICT suite is important, and identify one strategy that you believe would be effective for you to implement and one strategy that you should never use. Write these down in your PDP. You may want to use Table 1.4.9, 'Entry to an ICT classroom: strategies', in the appendix to this unit (p. 85) for this task.

(Note: You can check your strategies against those in Table 1.4.9 (in the Appendix, p. 85), which provides a range of strategies for entry to an ICT suite.)

Planning to teach using ICT resources

When using ICT in subject teaching, planning has to reflect the many practical applications of ICT. Because pupils are interacting with varying forms of ICT, if they disengage, they tend to occupy themselves with other ICT-based activities, such as playing games or surfing the Internet, which makes it very difficult to re-engage and focus them; so the lesson plan must take this into account.

When using ICT to enhance your subject and your pupils' learning, your subject is the focus of the lesson. However, if ICT is to be a tool and not a barrier to learning, there are some things that must be addressed in any lesson plan involving the use of ICT.

Use the lesson plan your subject tutor has, by experience, developed as the most effective for your subject, and for the construction and delivery of the ICT element of your lesson, whether in an ICT suite, a subject classroom or even 'on location'. View the ICT element as a mini-lesson within a lesson, because it makes the components of the ICT activity more coherent. These are best viewed as a 'do and do not' table (see Table 1.4.6), which forms the reference resource for the lesson-planning task in this element of the unit.

There is a temptation to be prescriptive because it is easier, but it is important to separate instruction from innovation. The previous section showed what is meant by instruction. Innovation comes from the application of appropriate constructivist approaches such as 'discovery learning' (Bruner 1976), which is enquiry-based and takes place in problem-solving situations (see also Unit 5.1).

What may surprise you when you develop your lesson plan is how short each activity is. Practical experience of teaching ICT has shown that 12 minutes, including briefing and debriefing for each activity, results in the pupils being engaged in and understanding the purpose of what you are trying to achieve. What this means is that you are taking them through the stages of what you want them to be able to do, so that when you brief them on the full task, they have the tools and practice with which to tackle and complete it. It makes assessing what they have learned more effective and prevents pupils drifting and disengaging.

Having completed Task 1.4.6, 'Using everyday ICT', you have a good idea of what is involved, how long it took you to do each part, the difficulties you experienced and what kind of questions you asked yourself. These are going to inform your planning and delivery. The initial briefing is an opportunity to determine prior knowledge; who has it and the level of competency. Using questioning techniques based on 'what', 'why' and 'how' enables you to identify the level of prior knowledge your pupils have, which in turn means you are able to use pupils as a resource that can support you and other pupils (Units 1.2, 3.1 and 5.2 include more on questioning techniques). You must plan for this and what to do with prior knowledge.

Using an IWB, the virtual learning environment (VLE) and a visualiser can really benefit pupil confidence and learning when assessing knowledge and understanding at points in a lesson. The IWB allows you to both model the tasks and involve the pupils. The VLE, which is likely to be part of the school intranet, is where you can place the lesson and the resources for that lesson. The visualiser allows you to project hard copy resources and zoom in to be able to focus on particular parts of them. See if the school system allows the pupils to save their work to the school intranet as you can assess their progress outside of the lesson.

A task is made up of smaller elements, and it is particularly important that you break the task into the smaller elements. These elements may be covered by using a mix of resources and practical activity, according to your lesson outcomes and the type of task.

The key part (Task 1.4.8. p. 81) is writing the lesson plan for the task and activities within it using a framework that tells you where you want to get to, how you are going to do it, and how you are going to determine the effectiveness in achieving your aims, and hence intended learning outcomes for pupils' learning. The development of your planning and classroom must be based on feedback and your own critical reflection of the effectiveness of your practising the activity (see Unit 2.2 for more on lesson planning).

Some guidance for completing the proforma is given in Table 1.4.7 on page 80.

Table 1.4.6 Do and do not aide-memoire when planning an ICT media lesson or activity

Make sure that you do	Make sure that you do not
Use All, Most, Some in your planning. Not all pupils will achieve everything you have planned, but you *must* have core aims for the lesson.	Just write: ask questions – you must be specific about the formative assessment that you are doing; and they *must* link to your activity/lesson aims and outcomes.
Use what, why and how in your class, group and individual assessment. 'What' is knowledge recall; 'why' is understanding; and 'how' is application.	Ask rhetorical questions such as 'Everyone understand?' You *must* know that they know what they are meant to be doing. The pupils *must* know that you know as well. This is key to minimising disengagement.
Ten per cent teacher talk only in an ICT lesson. They will disengage. If you need to talk more than that, then what you are attempting is too complex. The term in ICT is 'decompose it', which means break it into small components.	'You know what to do, so everyone get on.' You do not know; you are making assumptions that they know what they are meant to be doing. You have to check before they start.
Tell them the aims and outcomes and how you propose that the pupils will achieve them.	Do not assume that despite the briefing and questioning, everyone will stay 'on task'. There are many distractions when using ICT media.
Check and get feedback as you brief and as the pupils undertake the task. It is too late to do it at the end, even if it is only a two-minute activity.	Do not allow friendship groups. They will talk rather than achieve. If you are using grouping or pairs, do it by ability. Ability in this term refers to ability to use the ICT media as well as 'educational ability'. They appreciate peer support.
Tell them how long the activity will take *and* count it down.	Do not assume that everyone will remember what they are doing, even though you have spent time specifically doing so (or thinking that you did so). You will need to have a one-to-one support strategy that is pupil-led.
Each activity has an 'entry', 'execute' and 'exit' to it. The entry is the briefing for that activity, and you must check using what, why and how before releasing them to that 'execute' part. 'Execute' is the pupil doing the activity, and 'exit' is the debriefing for that activity that they have just completed. The complete activity should be no more than 12 minutes, including briefing and debriefing. This minimises the opportunity for disengagement or incompletion.	Do not let the pupils just sit in front of the computer or ICT media all lesson. Making them get up, come to the front and then return to their seats refreshes their concentration and focus. It is much better for learning to be effective for eight minutes in each of three slots of 10 minutes than it is to be ineffective for a 30-minute unbroken tranche of time.

Table 1.4.7 Planning proforma guidelines

The learning aim	This is the task and the planned outcome. Pupil support will identify, based upon the SEN register and your experience of individuals, the type of resources and how those resources should be utilised to maximise learning. These are the intended learning outcomes that link to the task but address all learners by using All, Most, Some.
All	This identifies an aspect that everyone must be able to demonstrate by the end of the task. It could be pure knowledge or an outcome; for example: All – will be able to centre a title, change the font size and embolden it in a text document.
Most	This identifies an aspect that most of the pupils will be able to demonstrate by the end of the task. This is likely to show understanding by explanation; for example: Most – will be able to describe why it is important to be able to centre, change the font size and embolden a title in a text document.
Some	This is the discriminator element of the outcome process, and indicates those who will be able to demonstrate higher-order skills that may enhance the task outcome; for example: Some – will be able to selectively show how their outcome might be improved by the use of additional or different resources, such as media or software.
Assessment	At this point, you are only indicating the mix of assessment and whether it is formative or summative. So this might have markers such as: Peer to Peer Q&A, Presentation, Display.
Activity	This is the point at which you are breaking the task down into the individual activities that will equip the pupils to complete the task outlined in the aims. You will describe the activity, its purpose and duration.
Entry	Required – how you are going to model the activity that the pupils are going to do, the formative assessment to ensure understanding. Just putting 'Questioning' is *not* appropriate. You will need to be specific about 'what', 'why' and 'how'. You *must* know that they all understand what they are doing, why and how before they start the activity.
Execute	The activity that the pupils are going to do. Remember to allow transit time between the briefing and them starting. You may need to question the pupils to check they remember, as they may have forgotten. Give them the time duration, the start of the time and regular countdowns through the activity
Exit	The debriefing. Checking what they have learned, why it has relevance to the overall task, and how it could be used in another context.
Lesson resources	What you need to be able to deliver and assess the elements of the session; for example, digital camera, IWB, flip chart, sticky notes, and so forth.

Task 1.4.8 Planning to teach using ICT resources

Using the planning proforma in Table 1.4.8 as a framework and the outcome of Task 1.4.7, plan an activity using relevant methods of ICT for your subject that addresses each of the elements in the proforma.

   Discuss and critique your proposed plan with another student teacher. What amendments did you agree should be made? Why? Make notes on your proposed plan, as it is easier to amend the plan if you know where and why you have marked the areas for amendments. Record your discussions in your PDP.

Table 1.4.8 Planning proforma

The task/activity	
The learning aim	
Pupil support	
Learning outcomes	
Assessment	
The activity	
Entry	
Execute	
Exit	
Resources	

SUMMARY AND KEY POINTS

In this unit, we have taken you through:

- using ICT to enhance teaching and learning in your subject area;
- showing you that using ICT does not mean sitting in front of a computer all lesson just using a word-processing package;
- how ICT refers to many of the things that you see and use every day, without thinking about it, and ideas about how to use them;
- using ICT enables you to develop an enquiry-oriented lesson format to further enhance the learning experience for you and your pupils;
- your audits, which should encourage you, as they probably showed you knew more, not less, than you thought;
- a progressive series of knowledge and resource banks taken from your knowledge audit;
- a task that shows you how to use something you and the pupils use every day but enhances your subject teaching and pupils' learning;
- ways in which you are able to control the direction, pace and learning that will keep pupils engaged;
- how you can bring these elements together to produce the elements of a lesson plan for teaching using ICT as resources.

You may want to undertake the master's-level questions for reflection in Task 1.4.9.

Check which requirements for your ITE programme you have addressed through this unit.

M **Task 1.4.9 Master's-level questions for reflection**

Reading this unit and completing the tasks will help prepare you for using different types of ICT to enhance your teaching and your pupils' learning. The following is offered for you to be able to reflect on this unit and the use of ICT/digital technology in your subject, to critically analyse the potential benefits of doing so.

- Discuss the proposition that using ICT to encourage pupils to develop transferable skills is only effective if an application of ICT is used in different contexts and differing learning environments.
- Critically analyse the statement 'Understanding what you can do with ICT to enhance teaching and learning is more important than knowing how ICT works', and justify how you would support your conclusions.
- Using relevant sources to support your answer, evaluate how the use of different types of ICT can be used to enrich the learning experience for pupils with English as an additional language (EAL).
- Pupils who have been diagnosed with autistic disorders typically have limited social interaction, communication or interests, and can exhibit repetitive behaviour. Examine,

supported by relevant sources, a strategy using forms of ICT that you believe will benefit such a pupil's learning experience. Evaluate how you would determine the effectiveness of your strategy.

Store your findings in your PDP.

Further reading

The suggested sources for further reading have been selected to encourage you to think about opportunities for using all types of ICT in an innovative and effective manner to enhance teaching and learning. They also seek to demonstrate that inspiration can come from an unexpected range of sources, and so pose the question, 'That looks interesting; could I adopt that to enhance my subject?'

Beauchamp, G. and Kennewell, S. (2010) 'Interactivity in the classroom and its impact on learning', *Computers & Education*, 54(3): 759–66.
This paper explores the literature on interactivity in group and individual work with ICT, and characterises categories of interactivity for these types of work. A framework is presented for ways in which teachers and learners orchestrate the features of their classroom environment and interact with ICT to support action towards learning goals.

Burden, K. and Younie, S. (2014) *Using iPads Effectively to Enhance Learning in Schools MESHGuide*, University of Hull and De Montfort University, UK.
This MESHGuide gives a research-informed introduction to the use of iPads for learning.

Hennessy, S., Ruthven, K. and Brindley, S. (2005) 'Teacher perspectives on integrating ICT into subject teaching: commitment, constraints, caution and change', *Journal of Curriculum Studies*, 37(2): 155–92, available at: www.educ.cam.ac.uk/research/projects/istl/WP042.pdf (accessed 16 October 2015).
This paper examines how secondary teachers of the core subjects of English, mathematics and science are integrating ICT into mainstream classroom practice in English schools. The analysis culminates in a thematic model of professional thinking about how the integrated use of ICT can support subject teaching and learning.

Kennewell, S., Parkinson, S. and Tanner, H. (2002) *Learning to Teach ICT in the Secondary School: A Companion to School Experience*, London: Routledge.

Leask, M. and Pachler, N. (2014) *Learning to Teach Using ICT in the Classroom: A Companion to School Experience*, London: Routledge.
These texts provide an introduction to a wide range of ways of working with ICT/digital technologies in classrooms and for supporting your professional development.

Shea, J. and Stockford, A. (2014) *Inspiring the Secondary Curriculum with Technology: Let the Students Do the Work!* London: Routledge.
This book explores ways of using everyday technology to enhance pupil learning. The authors illustrate, with examples, a range of activities that pupils become involved in and those environments that might be used. The flipped classroom, interactive whiteboards, using mobile devices and social networking are explained in the context of using them in the learning environment to further enhance pupil learning experiences.

Younie, S. and Leask, M. (2013) *Teaching with Technologies: The Essential Guide*, Maidenhead: Open University Press.
This book brings together research findings to provide an evidence-based approach to using digital technologies in the classroom and highlights effective practice.

Younie, S., Leask, M. and Burden, K. (2015) *Learning to Teach Using ICT in the Primary School*, London: Routledge.
Although targeted at primary school, this book also covers areas highly relevant to secondary school, such as mobile learning, e-safety and games-based learning.

Other resources and websites

E-twinning: www.etwinning.net/en/pub/index.htm
This an EU initiative supporting collaboration between schools through projects across Europe.

European Schoolnet (EUN): www.eun.org
EUN is a network of 30 Ministries of Education in Europe and beyond. EUN was created 15 years ago to bring innovation in teaching and learning to its key stakeholders: Ministries of Education, schools, teachers and researchers. A number of projects relevant to particular subject areas are run through the EUN as set out on the home page. It also supports teachers and pupils working on collaborative projects across Europe (for the latter, also see the e-twinning site: www.etwinning.net/en/pub/index.htm).

NAACE: www.naace.co.uk/
This is the professional association for educators interested in school-based applications of ICT.

WebQuests UK: www.webquestuk.org.uk/
WebQuests were the original conception of Bernie Dodge from San Diego State University.

Appendix 2 on pages 591–595 provides further examples of websites you may find useful.

Capel, S., Leask, M. and Turner, T. (eds) (2010) *Readings for Learning to Teach in the Secondary School: A Companion to M Level Study*, London: Routledge.
This book brings together essential readings to support you in your critical engagement with key issues raised in this textbook.

The subject-specific books in the *Learning to Teach* series are also very useful.

Any additional resources and an editable version of any relevant tasks/tables in this unit are available on the companion website: www.routledge.com/cw/capel

Appendix

Table 1.4.9 Entry to an ICT classroom: strategies

Strategies to implement before entering an ICT classroom	*Rationale*
Settling the class	It is easier to quieten and direct a class before entering an ICT suite as it is a familiar practice.
Providing initial instruction	It is important with a classroom with electronic equipment that they enter in an orderly manner and know what the first requirements are; for example, that they take their coats off and put their bags under the computer desk.
Provide expectations	That they will take a chair and sit at the front of the classroom, or in front of the whiteboard/IWB/projector screen quietly.
Do not touch the computer	They do not switch computers on, and sit in front of them. You lose attention almost immediately. You must create a purposeful environment from the moment they enter the classroom.
Log on, and switch the monitor off	Provided that it is accompanied by ensuring that they sit at the front. The advantage is that they will be ready to start work after the briefing rather than waiting for a computer to start, which provides an opportunity for disengagement. This also means that any issues with logging on are localised to the particular pupil, and are hence addressed more easily.
Folders and so on to be handed out by a designated person and not taken; you may use the same strategy in reverse before you dismiss the class, as it allows for an orderly departure	Again, this ensures a purposeful environment, stops friendship groups chattering and scrimmages. With the pupils sat at the front of the class, there is an expectation for work.

2 Beginning to teach

The previous chapter was concerned with the role and responsibilities of the teacher and how you might manage those requirements. In this chapter, we look at how you might learn from observing experienced teachers and then move on to consider aspects of planning and preparing lessons.

For most student teachers, there is a period during which you observe other teachers working, take part in team-teaching and take part of a lesson before taking on a whole lesson. During this period, you use observation and critical reflection to build up your professional knowledge about teaching and learning and your professional judgement about managing learning. Unit 2.1 is therefore designed to focus your attention on how to observe the detail of what is happening in classrooms.

It is difficult for a student teacher to become fully aware of the planning that underpins each lesson, as planning schemes of work (long-term programmes of work) is usually done by a team of staff over a period of time. The scheme of work then usually stays in place for some time. The extent of the actual planning for each lesson may also be hidden – experienced teachers often internalise their planning so their notes for a lesson are brief in comparison with those that a student teacher needs. Unit 2.2 explains planning processes. Unit 2.3 combines this advice in an analysis of the issues you need to consider before taking responsibility for whole lessons.

The quality of lesson planning is crucial to the success of a student teacher in enabling the pupils to learn. Defining clear and specific learning objectives and learning outcomes for pupils' learning in a particular lesson is one aspect of planning that many student teachers initially find difficult. The following story (from Mager 2005: v) reinforces this need to have clear objectives and outcomes for lessons:

> Once upon a time a Sea Horse gathered up his seven pieces of eight and cantered out to find his fortune. Before he had travelled very far he met an Eel, who said, 'Psst. Hey, bud. Where 'ya goin'?'
>
> 'I'm going out to find my fortune,' replied the Sea Horse, proudly.
>
> 'You're in luck,' said the Eel. 'For four pieces of eight you can have this speedy flipper and then you'll be able to get there a lot faster.'
>
> 'Gee, that's swell,' said the Sea Horse and paid the money and put on the flipper and slithered off at twice the speed. Soon he came upon a Sponge, who said, 'Psst. Hey, bud. Where 'ya goin'?'

'I'm going out to find my fortune,' replied the Sea Horse.

'You're in luck,' said the Sponge. 'For a small fee, I will let you have this jet-propelled scooter so that you will be able to travel a lot faster.'

So the Sea Horse bought the scooter with his remaining money and went zooming thru the sea five times as fast. Soon he came upon a Shark, who said, 'Psst. Hey, bud. Where 'ya goin'?'

'I'm going to find my fortune,' replied the Sea Horse.

'You're in luck. If you take this short cut,' said the Shark, pointing to his open mouth, 'you'll save yourself a lot of time.'

'Gee, thanks,' said the Sea Horse and zoomed off into the interior of the Shark and was never heard from again.

The moral of this fable is that if you're not sure where you're going, you're liable to end up somewhere else. We hope that by the end of this chapter, you are able to plan lessons in which both you and the pupils know exactly what they are meant to be learning. Explicitly sharing your learning objectives with pupils provides them with clear goals and potentially a sense of satisfaction from your lesson as they achieve the goals set.

2.1 Reading classrooms

How to maximise learning from classroom observation

Ana Redondo

Introduction

How do you actively read a classroom rather than simply watch a teacher at work?

During your school placements, you can expect to observe experienced teachers as well as fellow student teachers. You should have the opportunity to observe lessons within and outside of your subject specialism.

What is important when observing in classrooms is to bear in mind that learners are not passive recipients or are not aware of who is in the classroom. They acknowledge the presence of all adults involved in a lesson, whatever their role, which means that they are in a certain way making a contribution to your learning through observation.

The more observations you carry out, the more comparative information you can gather between learners, classes, groups, teachers and pedagogical approaches. Asking questions about factors in the local context that have an impact on learning is an important part of the exercise. At the same time, you need to avoid being judgemental about what you observe while remaining a critical observer. As a professional, you are expected to behave ethically. As examples, the General Teaching Council for Scotland (2012) and the Teaching Council (in Ireland) (2012) ethical codes for teachers provide a framework for you to consider. (Web links are provided in the further reading at the end of this unit.)

It is important to develop a notion of learning as a transformative process and to identify key points in the lesson where learning happens in order to get the most out of the experience of lesson observation. Identifying what learning takes place, when and how by individuals and by the class as a whole is crucial to your understanding of what constitutes evidence of learning.

Teachers and pupils set up a working relationship in which both parties know the rules, the codes of behaviour and boundaries. In most classes, boundaries are kept and teachers work smoothly with the class, apparently without great effort. Beneath that order, there is a history of carefully nurtured practice by the teacher in establishing an appropriate atmosphere, usually in the first weeks of the new school year.

Sometimes, these boundaries are transgressed by pupils, and you may have observed ways in which the teacher restores a working atmosphere. Each teacher has his or her own way of dealing with this challenge. Watching the way other teachers deal with such issues helps you widen your own repertoire of skills.

OBJECTIVES

At the end of this unit, you should be able to:

- define the focus of your observations to achieve specific learning goals;
- use different strategies for recording your observations in forms that lend themselves to subsequent analysis;
- use observation to analyse teaching strategies and pupil learning behaviours to enhance your ability to plan and teach your own lessons;
- begin to understand the teaching and learning process and gain insights into how you wish to teach.

Check the requirements of your initial teacher education (ITE) programme to see which relate to this unit.

Preparing to observe: some general points

Qualified teachers expect to be observed in the context of continuing professional development (CPD), appraisal, inspections and preparation for inspections. Good practice includes peer observation between colleagues in order to support their learners more effectively. See Dudley's (2014) website on Lesson Study. You should look for opportunities to observe fellow student teachers and experienced teachers.

Teachers may be less used to being observed by people who are concerned about analysing what is happening in the lesson rather than measuring it against predetermined criteria such as teachers' standards. As an observer, it is advisable to engage in a dialogue with the teachers you observe at work, both prior to the lesson and afterwards. Before the lesson, you should agree areas for observation and what you plan to do with the data. After the lesson, you may wish to clarify aspects of the lesson you have observed, discussing the rationale for some of the actions taken that lead to a deeper understanding of the nature of learning. Equally, ascertaining their perception of the lesson, which you can then compare to yours, enables you to contextualise events and actions you observed, which at times are not necessarily obvious. *Remember that observation is fundamentally about enquiry: seeking to know what is happening, why it is happening and what its impact is likely to be.* It is not passive. It should focus on perception; that is, making sense of what you see, rather than judgement. Take an open, positive approach to observation but also be well prepared by reading and discussing key elements of a lesson with other student teachers and your tutor. Developing a kind of literacy by which to 'read' and recognise what takes place in a lesson is a skill you develop gradually, becoming more perceptive as you go along.

The form in which you record your observations varies according to the selected focus. Many schools use their own observation proformas or you may be given a different one by your tutors. When using either, you should adapt it to your own needs or alternatively create a new one, particularly for collecting and recording specific data in a targeted manner, which, in the flow of the lesson, you might otherwise forget. Lesson observation in pairs has great advantages for sharing an observation activity with another student teacher to compare notes and engage in a discussion about the significance of what you have both observed. Having a specific structure to collect information in turn can allow for a more focused dialogue, exchange and suggestions to feed into your own teaching. Among other sources, unions such as the National Union of Teachers (NUT), National Association of School Masters and Union of Women Teachers (NASUWT) provide guidance on lesson observation.

Who should you be observing and why?

Initially in observing lessons, you are naturally concerned with familiarising yourself with the dynamics of the classes with regard to how the pupils interact with each other and with the teacher, and how they respond to learning. These observations will be of particular value in preparing you for teaching these specific classes. However, you should not be observing the teacher with a view to imitating his or her teaching style, but with the idea of analysing what he or she is doing that is effective, and from that to make your own decisions as to what you wish to adopt in your own practice (see Unit 2.3 on taking responsibility for whole lessons). Building a rapport with pupils is something you will develop as time goes by and you gain more experience; also, as you spend more and more time with the same classes.

Through observation, you will find ways of developing your own professional practices with which you feel comfortable and which will enable you to be effective in what you teach, what methods and approaches you employ and which teaching strategies you prefer in order to impact positively on learners' experiences. It will also assist you in determining the best way of fostering attitudes in pupils and in creating a learning environment for pupils that are conducive to academic progress. See Unit 4.2 on adolescent well-being and Unit 5.1 on how pupils learn.

Having observed experienced teachers, and continuing to do so throughout your school placements, exposes you to a range of styles, a variety of strategies for teaching, learning and assessment from which to choose so that you can further develop your practice. See Unit 5.5 on personalising learning.

There are many aspects of a lesson that can form the focus for observation. Teachers modelling a respectful attitude towards pupils to enable them to achieve will be an important part of your observation of professional practice, as this is an important prerequisite for enjoying the respect of pupils. The learning environment and the ethos that the teacher wishes to create are central. Teachers establish rules and routines that then are often reinforced by just a single gesture or signal; for example, a raised eyebrow if a pupil speaks out of turn. As a student teacher, you should be observing the routines and teaching strategies of the teacher. This analysis enables you to select those aspects that you wish to adapt and adopt in developing your own teaching style. When you start teaching, existing classroom routines should be adhered to at the beginning until learners are able to adapt to your own routines.

Additionally, you should also observe what and how pupils learn. Use the guidance in Unit 4.1 on differentiation, Unit 5.2 on active learning and Unit 5.5 on personalising learning to construct observation schedules. You will have the opportunity to observe small groups of pupils working with support teachers who are specialist in working with pupils with learning difficulties outside the mainstream classroom or teaching assistants supporting individuals within the classroom. See Unit 4.6 on creating an inclusive classroom and Blamires (2014). Here, you have the opportunity to understand the learning needs of individual pupils in greater depth. Also, it is valuable to follow a class or pupil across the curriculum and observe teachers working in subject disciplines other than your own. All opportunities to observe teachers working with pupils are learning opportunities, and you may be able to note similar strategies across disciplines and teaching styles. Teachers in assembly, on duty at break or working with pupils in an extracurricular activity are all professionally engaged in their work, and how they work in these contexts directly relates to their work in the classroom. It is therefore a good idea to carry a small notepad with you at all times to record significant observations and any questions that occur to you at the time. These can be followed up later with the teacher or your tutor. Effective observation is a matter of intellectual curiosity, and to that end being alert, able to ask relevant questions and being supported by appropriate reading and discussion is a professionally rewarding experience as a student teacher.

Table 2.1.1 gives examples of questions to address through observation, perhaps prior to teaching a class. Add questions of your own.

What do classrooms look like?

As part of lesson observation, it is useful to 'read' the impact of the appearance and layout of the room on pupil and teacher learning and their experiences. The classroom or teaching space is more than a room with chairs, desks, boards and screens. It is a learning environment. It should both promote and support effective teaching and effective learning. See Unit 5.7 on critically appraising learning environments and Unit 5.8 on the language-rich classroom.

Classrooms often express the values and ethos of the school, and can reflect and promote specific subjects. You may find the planned approach in Task 2.1.1 useful.

How lessons begin and end

Lessons are structured into different parts carefully considering the time dedicated to each to maximise learning opportunities. As with all relationships and activities, how a lesson begins is significant to its success or otherwise. It is usual to begin with a starter task to engage learners from the very moment they enter into the classroom, taking them through activities that end with a plenary in which to summarise key points of the lesson and providing learners with a chance to rationalise for themselves what it is they have learned and how they have learned (see Unit 2.2 for further detail). This can be an opportunity for a teacher's skilful use of questioning in what is a very short period of time, between five and 10 minutes of a plenary, highlighting key points and enabling learners to understand the links between prior and future learning. Questioning (see also Unit 5.2) also provides the teacher with useful information about how learners have understood what they are asked to do and made sense of the work they are engaged in. Skilful teachers demonstrate good skills in managing learners and learning, have good subject knowledge and, at times, give the impression that it is all easy. When you first observe lessons, focusing on each of these parts of a lesson is a useful approach to analyse how timings for tasks, teaching materials and organisation of learning are managed. You might be asked to make an active contribution to one episode within a lesson as a way of beginning to teach the group that has been allocated to your teaching timetable.

Routines

Routines are important in ensuring smooth transition between tasks in lessons and to provide a backdrop of familiarity to learners (see Unit 5.2). They are particularly important when taking up

Table 2.1.1 Examples of research questions that can assist you in focusing your lesson observations

Briefing and preparing for observation

- Note the date, time and place of the lesson.
- Are you briefed on the topic being taught in the lesson and the composition of the class?
- With respect to professional ethics, have you agreed your role: a participant or non-participant?
- Have you agreed how and what you will observe?
- Have you agreed how you are going to feed back to the teacher and any future use you may make of your notes?

Teaching and learning questions

- What was the plan/structure/shape of the lesson?
- How was the lesson introduced? How did the pupils know the intended learning outcomes planned for the lesson?
- What were the different learning activities that the pupils undertook?
- Was there group or pair work?
- Did any pupils receive different work, degrees of help or resources?
- What were the different ways that pupils recorded or presented their learning?
- How did the teacher direct the pace of the lesson?
- What form of question-and-answer sessions did the teacher initiate?
- How were pupils encouraged to ask and answer questions?
- What resources were used to assist in learning and how were they used?
- How did the teacher provide a range of teaching strategies to ensure all learners can access what has been taught?
- Were digital technologies used during the lesson? How?
- Was the teacher handling the technology used?
- Did the pupils have a hands-on experience to complete tasks?
- What learning was supported through the use of technologies? (See Unit 5.3 on teaching strategies.)

Pupil and class management dimensions

- What were the teacher's expectations about pupils' responses to what has been taught?
- How did the teacher promote behaviour for learning?
- Were there established routines or codes of conduct? What were they?
- Were issues of health and safety referred to during the lesson? How? When?
- Did the teacher use any assertive behaviour management techniques? (Teaching College of New Jersey 2015) Sanctions? What was the intention and what were the outcomes?
- How did the teacher use seating plans? Why?
- How did the teacher use voice and gesture in the lesson to manage pupil responses?
- How did the teacher assess pupils' work during the lesson and how was this fed back to the pupils?

Other professional issues

- Was a teaching assistant or special educational needs teacher also in the room? What was their role and how did they work with the pupils and the teacher?
- Have you identified any gaps in your subject knowledge through observing this lesson? How are you going to address them?
- How has this observation made you consider your future professional practice as a teacher? What professional issues has it raised for you? Discuss these with other student teachers, tutors and peers in relation to the importance of becoming a reflective teacher.

Task 2.1.1 The learning environment

Consider a classroom or teaching space you are going to be teaching in at your placement school and how you can use this effectively. Is this space a specialist room or a general classroom? Is the space used mainly by one teacher and for one discipline?

■   Sketch the layout of the space and the seating arrangements. Identify the light source and how this affects visibility of the board, screen and other display boards that you will make use of to support your teaching; also, note other features, resources and the teacher's desk. Check how much space there is for you to move among pupils in order to evaluate what they are doing and support them when needed. Space will also be required by pupils when moving about. Obstacles that can cause concerns from a health and safety point of view (for example, tripping over chairs, bags, and so on) need to be avoided.

■   Note your perceptions of the advantages and limitations of the room layout to pupil and teacher learning and teaching. Does the layout support collaborative group working or not?

■   Describe any displays. Note the different proportions of pupil work and teacher/published material displayed. Are the displays colourful and well looked after? Do the displays prompt pupils to value their own work and the work of other pupils more highly?

■   What values does display material portray? What potential use can pupils make of them? Do displays portray positive images and information pupils can use to help with their work? Are they, in that sense, interactive and kept up to date? Are they relevant to the learning experiences of pupils?

■   Are any technological tools available in the room? If so, what are they? What can be said about their intended use?

■   Comment on whether you would like to be taught in this room and whether the environment promotes the subject and pupil learning. Give reasons for your response.

Unit 5.7 provides further guidance about critically appraising learning environments. Record your observations in your professional development portfolio (PDP).

new classes. Have a close look at how it is done. While you should follow existing school routines in the same way at the early stages of taking on a class, you can from then on develop your own ways of organising the lesson, following structures and policies set down by the school and subject departments. You can expect to introduce some of your own ideas as you become more confident and your tutors encourage you to become more assertive, independent and to begin to take some risks, albeit agreed beforehand with your tutor. Experienced teachers are very familiar with their learners, and vice versa, and that creates a specific dynamic that you cannot immediately reproduce. Be observant, discuss and ascertain the views of your tutors so as to develop confidence to adopt, to adapt and to align with your own style after a period of practice.

At the end of lessons, after summing up (sometimes called a plenary), it is important to allow enough time for pupils to be dismissed in an orderly manner, ensuring a well-organised exit. Therefore, observe techniques for dismissing pupils.

Timing

When planning lessons, careful attention needs to be paid to how long individual episodes should last. When observing lessons, you are advised to pay attention to the amount of time allocated to individual activities.

Task 2.1.2 is designed to help you to analyse the beginning, middle and end of a lesson.

 Task 2.1.2 Analysing the beginning, middle and end of a lesson

You may hear a lesson being described as being in three parts: starter, main body of the lesson and plenary. However, with experienced teachers, the lesson may appear to be a smooth flow of activities and the different features are noticeable in terms of content but not so much in format; for example, at times, some 'mini-plenaries' take place after a task to ensure understanding before moving on so that the end-of-lesson evaluative time becomes less formal.

There are three stages to the beginning of a lesson:

1   Starting: possibly lining up outside the classroom, particularly with younger pupils, to ensure an orderly entrance and settling them to a prompt start to learning. 'Starter tasks' (or 'hooks') (see Unit 5.2) are quick exercises that provide a good opportunity to link to previous learning (for example, revising work); also to get pupils to focus on work immediately rather than getting distracted with each other into chatter. Starters need only be between five and seven minutes.

2   The body of the lesson: presenting lesson outcomes, followed by presenting the work through chosen materials (either digital or print) and providing instructions to the work.

3   The plenary: invite learners to provide a summary, highlight key aspects of the lesson and link them to future learning, including homework tasks, where appropriate.

Useful prompt questions for observations are:

Outside the classroom

■   What procedures were used for pupils gathering outside the classroom? And their rationale?
  (a)   Were pupils free to enter as they arrived or did they have to line up?
  (b)   Did the teacher wait for the class at the classroom door – were they welcomed on arrival outside the classroom or did the teacher stay inside the classroom until the class was directed to enter?

Settling into place

■   Did the pupils sit where they pleased or did they have assigned places? Did they wait to greet the teacher standing before they were asked to sit down?
■   Was a register taken and in what manner?
■   What signals did the teacher use to indicate that the lesson had begun?

The beginning of the lesson

■ How did the teacher explain the intended learning outcomes (see Units 2.2 and 7.4) of the lesson?

■ How long was it before the lesson proper began?

■ What problems or issues did the teacher have to deal with before the lesson began? How did they do this?

■ In settling the class, what praise or conduct reminders did the teacher use and how did pupils respond?

The body of the lesson

■ How effective was the teacher in providing explanations and instructions to pupils to tell them what to do and how?

■ Were pupils encouraged to ask questions?

■ Were pupils expected to work independently from the teacher? Possibly sharing ideas with each other? Or to work quietly? In any other way?

■ Were pupils sufficiently challenged and engaged given their prior skills, knowledge and understanding?

■ Did pupils understand what they were being asked to do in every stage of the lesson?

■ Did pupils have opportunities and means to indicate their understanding (or lack) of the concepts being introduced?

■ Did pupils improve their understanding as a result of detailed and accurate feedback on their learning?

■ Were pupils who were having difficulty supported to help them understand?

■ How well was pupils' subject knowledge developed in terms of concepts, knowledge, skills and understanding?

■ Was the management of the pupils' behaviour effective to ensure that they make progress in a safe and secure environment?

The end of the lesson

■ Were pupils able to respond to questions satisfactorily during the plenary, demonstrating they: (a) could recall what they had learned; and (b) understood what they had learned?

■ How did the teacher find out what *most* pupils could recall and understand?

■ Were the intended learning outcomes achieved, and how did the teacher know that?

■ Were pupils dismissed quietly and as a class or in small groups?

If possible, discuss this list of questions with another student teacher and add to them. Then undertake the observation. In carrying out this task, you should arrive at least five minutes before the beginning of the lesson.

Using a similar checklist to that drafted below, record your observations.

Observer's name						
Date and time						
Class name and subject:					Number and composition of class: . . . male . . . female	
Real time	Place	Pupil actions	Teacher	Pupil talk	Teacher talk	Other notes

After the lesson, discuss with the teacher what you have noted to check for any misunderstandings and to discuss further the strategies you have observed. Record your observations in your PDP.

The structure of a lesson and transitions

The structure of a lesson is very important to its effectiveness (see Units 2.2 and 2.3). When an experienced teacher teaches a lesson, they work to a plan but equally they deviate from the plan when a new learning need becomes apparent. Good teaching is flexible and responsive. Experienced teachers use *transitions* in a lesson to summarise the learning at key points before moving on to the next learning activity. Figure 2.1.1 is a flow diagram of a lesson about communication where the transitions are highlighted in bold.

Teacher talk and oral feedback

It is useful to focus on teacher talk and feedback to pupils during a lesson to enable you to estimate its impact on learning and behaviour (see Units 3.1 and 5.8; and also Alexander 2015; Education Endowment Foundation 2015; University of Cambridge 2015b). There are various ways of doing this, including audio or video recordings of a lesson. However, on most occasions, written notes are sufficient. Task 2.1.3 is designed to help you analyse the way teachers talk to pupils. Unit 5.8 provides detail on the use of language in classrooms.

Task 2.1.4 asks you to focus specifically on questioning. Units 5.1, 5.2 and 5.8 provide more detailed background to the role of questioning in learning.

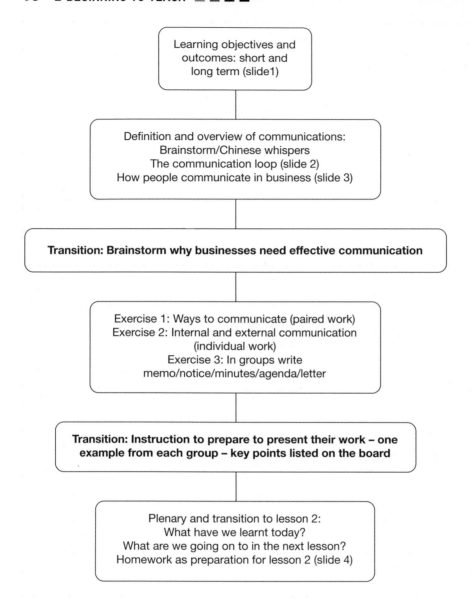

Figure 2.1.1 Flow diagram of a Year 10 business studies lesson, which is the first lesson of a
        double lesson on communication for business

Pupil talk and interaction

It is equally interesting and highly relevant to analyse pupil talk and interaction, which, if you follow
a class or group to lessons in different subjects or with different teachers, can change in significant
ways.

   You could simply use a class list and place a tick in red next to each pupil's name as they ask for
information and a tick in black against each pupil's name as they answer a question or offer information, to gauge pupil involvement in lessons.

M

 Task 2.1.3 Analysis of teacher talk

Complete the following checklist for a section of the lesson.

Oral feedback	Examples observed in the lesson	Learning impact on pupils
Giving information		
Correcting errors or misapprehensions		
Praising		
Questioning to check understanding		
Questioning to deepen understanding		
Asking pupils to focus on specific aspects		
Summarising learning		
Encouraging pupil reflection		
Coaching in skills		
Answering pupil questions		
Correcting poor behaviour		
Guiding pupils back on task		
Outlining next learning tasks		

Discuss your observations with the teacher after the lesson and record both the checklist and discussion in your PDP.

A more detailed observation with a small group of pupils, one pupil or the entire class can be undertaken using the checklist in Task 2.1.5 over a 20-minute period, recording minute by minute. A three-minute record is shown in the example.

Observing pupil management and encouraging pupil behaviours that maximise learning

Before beginning lesson observations, you should familiarise yourself with the school's and department's policies about managing learning and learners to maximise learning. These are used

Task 2.1.4 Teachers' questions and the development of questioning skills

Questions are often classified into 'closed' and 'open'. Closed questions are those about facts, with a single correct answer. Open questions may not a have a right answer or there may be several ways of responding. They require the pupil to speculate about events or anticipate new ideas or explanations (see Unit 3.1 for further information about questioning).

What types of question do teachers ask? Are they simple questions with one-word answers or are they more complex, involving explanation? Investigate the frequency of different types of questions. The following questions may help to focus your observation. Does the teacher:

- ask mainly closed questions?
- ask both open and closed questions according to purpose and circumstance? Are only right answers accepted?
- dismiss wrong answers?
- give enough time for pupils to give an answer?
- encourage pupils to frame a reply?
- provide scaffolding to encourage responses?

How does the teacher respond to right and wrong answers given by pupils?

Discuss your responses and your interpretation of them with the class teacher or your tutor.

Record your observations in your PDP.

to achieve a common approach to fostering appropriate behaviours for learning. It is essential that you work within these policies. (See also Unit 3.3. Task 3.3.4 asks you to record observations of unacceptable behaviours.) Discuss with teachers and tutors your own ideas about managing learners to maximise learning possibly drawn from literature or discussions at seminars so that you can implement and develop your own ways of interacting with pupils and manage learning effectively.

Focus upon pupil learning

Often, the instinct of student teachers in the classroom is to focus upon the teacher teaching rather than upon how and what the pupils are learning. This is not surprising. When we first 'go back to school', our memories are those of a pupil who watched and listened to the teacher (see Unit 5.7 for a framework for critically analysing the school environment). How individual pupils respond to the work set is something that needs to be closely observed and then related to their different abilities, interests and experiences in that subject. This information provides clues about their learning journey and how the teacher makes decisions about how to cater for the diverse needs of all pupils. Hence, you need to shift your focus and observe what and how the pupils are learning. Task 2.1.6 provides some examples of how to do this.

The teacher position is also critical in supporting learning. The position of the teacher in the room influences interactions, and you should make deliberate decisions about where you will stand and

Task 2.1.5 Analysis of pupil talk

Complete the following checklist to analyse individual, group or whole-class pupil talk over a 20-minute period.

Real time – minute intervals	Pupil(s) initiated questions of teacher	Pupil(s) answering teacher questions	Off-task(s) discussion with peers	On-task(s) discussion with peers	Other notes about the class activity or other events
9.10	Said B Safia Y				SB not paying attention Safia Y confused
9.11					
9.12		Seth S	Safia B		Good recall by Seth
9.13				Seth S Safia Y	

Discuss your observations with the teacher after the lesson and store both the checklist and the record of your discussion in your PDP.

how you move around during lessons. Task 2.1.7 asks you to consider this aspect of classroom management.

Observing assessment for learning

A common weakness identified in school inspections in England (Office for Standards in Education (Ofsted) 2008) is a lack of focus upon assessment for learning (see also Unit 6.1; Ofsted 2014b). Ensure that you know your school's assessment policies in relation to both teaching and learning, as well as national assessments and those of the subject department. Task 2.1.8 asks you to focus on assessment for learning (see Procter 2013 for an introduction).

How does the teacher use learning resources and aids during the lesson?

Teachers use resources and aids during lessons to help pupils learn most effectively by both employing a wide range of teaching strategies and to differentiate by matching the lesson activities to differing abilities, interests and school experience of pupils. All pupils learn best when exposed to a variety of activities at different levels and through many formats and approaches, be they

M

Task 2.1.6 Analysis of pupil learning

Before beginning your analysis, write down the intended learning outcomes for the lesson (see Units 2.3 and 7.4) and identify the task/activities on which you are going to focus.

If you are a participant observer, you are able to take notes of key information as the lesson unfolds, look over the work of pupils, and be actively engaged with coaching and guiding their learning activities. This enables you to begin to appreciate what strategies and resources are working effectively for their learning and why.

As a non-participant observer, your task becomes more subtle. If you are free to move around once pupils are involved in an activity, you can oversee their task completion. If it is appropriate, you can ask them brief questions but you must not disengage them from their task. Equally, do not be tempted to do the work for them. Always lead them to think through the task with your help.

In highly active lessons, there may be considerable chat and activity but there may equally be considerable learning taking place. Quiet lessons in which the pupils seem attentive to the teacher are not necessarily lessons where most learning occurs. Different teachers, depending on the subject and specific tasks pupils are engaged in, have different expectations of the degree of talk they allow pupils to have. Observe closely to what extent pupil talk is about the tasks in hand or not and how the teacher responds to that.

The most flexible way to record pupil learning is to make bullet points as you notice things; a proforma may not be appropriate because pupil learning is so complex. Once the lesson is over, ask the teacher if you may review the work the pupils have completed.

Discuss your observations with the teacher after the lesson and record both your analysis and discussion in your PDP.

practical, open-ended tasks that require exploring possible solutions or accessing and using audio-visual tools (see Keuchel and Beaudry on Visual Learning in the list of websites at the end of this unit). The important point here is that all pupils are learning. Providing a range of tasks and formats allows the teacher to be creative and embed variety and differentiation (see Units 4.1 and 5.5) in his or her approach to setting work for all pupils.

Task 2.1.9 provides an example of a proforma to use in analysing how learning resources help pupils learn.

Subject content focused observation

All teachers during the early stages of their career have to work hard to fill gaps in subject content knowledge and, as schemes of work and the curriculum change, experienced teachers also need to learn new content. You may want to focus an observation on the content of a lesson on a topic you are going to teach in which there is a gap in your own subject content knowledge (see also Unit 1.1).

Using video to support lesson observation

Lesson observation and the subsequent analysis is a very challenging activity. In five minutes of a lesson, so much can happen that is of significance and worthy of discussion. Recording part of a lesson

---

 Task 2.1.7 Where is the teacher during a lesson?

The movement of teachers in the classroom may say a lot about their relationship with pupils, about how they keep an eye on activity and behaviour, and about their interest in the pupils.

Draw an A4 map of the classroom in which you are observing. Mark on key points: teacher's desk, pupil desks, whiteboard, projector, and so on. Have several copies of the map available. At regular intervals throughout the lesson (for example, every minute or so), mark on your map where the teacher stands and where they have moved from, to build up a picture of position and movement. At the same time, record the time and what is going on in the lesson. This enables you to relate teacher movement to lesson activity. Analyse your map and discuss the following:

- Where is the teacher most often positioned during the lesson? What possible reasons are there for this: writing on the board; explaining with a projector; helping pupils with written work?
- Does the teacher keep an eye on all events in the room and, if so, how? Is it done by eye contact from the front or does the teacher move around the room?
- What does the teacher do to find out whether pupils were on task?
- Were some pupils given more attention than others? What evidence do you have for this? What explanations are there for this?
- Was teacher movement related to pupil behaviour in any way? Examine this idea and look for the evidence.
- Did the nature of the subject matter dictate teacher movement? How do movements change in different subject lessons? Give an example.
- Some teachers use their desk and board and equipment as a barrier between them and pupils; others move in among pupils and desks. Are there 'no-go areas' that the teacher does not visit? Are there similar spaces for teachers that the pupils do not visit?

Summarise your findings for your own records and reflect on what information your 'map' gives you about 'teacher territory' and 'pupil territory'. Share your information with other student teachers. Record your observations in your PDP.

---

for detailed analysis with the teacher is an ideal way of learning. By the same token, taking still images can be a very useful stimulus for post-lesson discussions about aspects of teaching and learning. However, this needs to be discussed and approved by the teacher you are observing and ethical issues need to be addressed.

Video recording your own lessons enables you to analyse your teaching and to identify ways to improve your practice. You may notice aspects of the lesson that otherwise you may have missed. This process is an effective way to reflect on your practice and set goals for improvement.

Established ethical procedures and guidelines about taking photographs or videos of children need to be adhered to and you need to gain formal consent from the school to video. Videos of pupils at school need to be kept confidential and within school premises. The use of photographs or video recordings of pupils normally requires parental consent. You need to familiarise yourself,

---

 Task 2.1.8 Assessment for learning

Undertake some research about assessment for learning choosing reputable sources. Make notes about this approach. Observe a class and, during the lesson, write detailed notes about any activities the teacher uses to assess pupils' understanding of the work. This may include:

1   How does the teacher find out:
    (a) whether the pupils know what they are supposed to be doing?
    (b) whether the pupils understand what they are doing?
    (c) whether the pupils know the possible learning outcomes?
2   Does the teacher:
    (a) talk to individual pupils as they work?
    (b) talk to small groups?
    (c) intervene with questions or suggestions when progress is slow or confused?
    (d) ask challenging questions to individuals or groups to move learning on?
    (e) address the whole class when a common problem emerges?
3   How does the teacher survey the whole class when working with small groups or individuals?

The teacher may use many strategies, but the most common include:

■   direct questions;
■   discussion;
■   asking pupils to present their work to their partner, the whole class or a group;
■   reviewing work on an iPad/tablet, computer, whiteboard or in exercise books;
■   role-play or display activities;
■   setting another task to test understanding;
■   posing a problem for pupils to solve in order to evaluate and deepen understanding.

Also note down what the teacher does to correct misconceptions and misunderstandings or to deal with a lack of understanding and to advance learning. How does the teacher reassure and motivate? (See Unit 3.2 on motivation.) How does the teacher consolidate learning? Discuss your observations with the teacher.

Record your observations in your PDP.

---

therefore, with school policy and ensure that parental consent has been sought by the school and allows for recordings to be made for the intended purpose. Many schools use video recording of lessons as part of their programme of CPD for all teachers, and in these circumstances pupils learn to ignore the cameras. Software can be used to annotate videos in real time so that key aspects of the lesson (for example, questions asked and explanations given) can be easily grouped for playback and analysis. IRIS Connect and Dart Fish are two commonly used platforms.

✏ Task 2.1.9 Learning resources and pupil learning

Identify the teaching/learning resources and aids used in activities in a lesson you observe and describe the benefits for pupil learning. Read Units 5.2, 5.3 and 5.5 for ways of observing learning.

The resource	Learning activity	Learning benefit
Printed texts		
Prepared study guide or worksheet		
Pictures, mind maps, graphics		
Internet and audiovisual material		
Computer programs, including games		
Experiments		
Games, puzzles, models and activity cards		
Digital tools; for example, interactive whiteboard, iPads/tablets		
Whiteboard		
Other types of equipment		

Discuss the lesson with the teacher and selected pupils. File the data in your PDP.

Collaborative teaching as a form of observation

Team-teaching or collaborative teaching is an interesting approach that can provide you with many interesting ideas about how the teacher and other adults in the classroom, be they another teacher or a classroom assistant, can approach lessons where they have planned them together. In that way, pupils can gain greater access to adults, thereby decreasing the pupil-teacher ratio. Individual pupils can be more effectively supported too. Collaborative or team-teaching is an ideal approach by which to organise learners in small groups to attempt practical work that otherwise is difficult to organise. For example, carousel tasks, discussions in small groups and engaging with work that involves finding solutions are activities that can be far more effectively conducted by more than one teacher.

You should seek every opportunity at your placement school to be involved in collaborative teaching because it is an active and powerful training experience where two-way observation and evaluative feedback can be very constructive; for example, by co-teaching with another student teacher. Mutual observation can facilitate joint planning, joint lesson evaluation and provide a reassurance that can be helpful when making decisions to inform new planning and teaching. You do need to agree success criteria for your lesson beforehand so as to help the observer focus on those aspects of your practice.

SUMMARY AND KEY POINTS

■ Lesson observation is something you can expect to take part in throughout your career. You may observe others in order to learn yourself or you may be observed as part of performance management in your school or the inspection process or when you are a supporting student and new teachers.

■ Observation is an important CPD activity for all teachers. It is also a key tool for reflective practice and practitioner research (see Unit 5.4).

■ Your observation skills will develop with practice and focused effort using some of the methods suggested here over your whole career.

■ The tasks in this unit were designed to help you develop your understanding and get the most out of observation; more importantly, they should enable you to inquire as you seek solutions to challenges arising in your own teaching.

Check which requirements for your ITE programme you have addressed through this unit.

Further reading

Altrichter, H., Feldman, A., Posch, P. and Somekh, B. (2008) *Teachers Investigate Their Work: An Introduction to Action Research across the Professions*, 2nd edn, London: Routledge.
This comprehensive text provides detailed advice about observations, as will most research methods textbooks.

Dudley, P. (2014) *Lesson Study: Professional Learning for Our Time*, London: Routledge; see also: http://lessonstudy.co.uk/about-us-pete-dudley/

General Teaching Council for Scotland (2012) *Code of Professionalism and Conduct*, available at: www.gtcs.org.uk/web/FILES/teacher-regulation/copac-0412.pdf
Lesson study is widely practised in schools as an improvement strategy.

Marsden, E. (2009) 'Observing in the classroom', in S. Younie, S. Capel and M. Leask (eds) *Supporting Teaching and Learning in Schools: A Handbook for Higher Level Teaching Assistants*, London: Routledge, pp. 133–46.
This resource provides further information about observation.

Ofsted (Office for Standards in Education) (2008) *Assessment for Learning: The Impact of National Strategy Support*, available at: http://dera.ioe.ac.uk/9309/1/Assessment%20for%20learning%20-%20the%20impact%20of%20National%20Strategy%20support.pdf
This resource provides an overview of assessment for learning from an Ofsted perspective.

Ofsted (Office for Standards in Education) (2014b) *Note for Inspectors: Use of Assessment Information during Inspections in 2014/15*, available at: www.gov.uk/government/uploads/system/uploads/attachment_data/file/379630/Note_20for_20inspectors_20-_20use_20of_20assessment_20information_20during_20inspections_20in_202014-15.doc
This site provides information about inspection and assessment.

O'Leary, M. (2014) *Classroom Observation: A Guide to the Effective Observation of Teaching and Learning*, London: Routledge.
This text has ideas and information that extend that in this unit.

Teaching College New Jersey (2015) *Anti-Violence Measures*, available at: http://oavi.tcnj.edu/tools-for-everyone/assertiveness/assertive-nonassertive-and-aggressive-behaviors/
This site provides examples of classroom issues from an American perspective.

The Teaching Council (for Ireland) (2012) *Code of Professional Conduct for Educators*, available at: www.teachingcouncil.ie/_fileupload/Professional%20Standards/code_of_conduct_2012_web%2019June 2012.pdf.
See the code of conduct and other resources available for teachers.

Other resources and websites

Keuchel, T. and Beaudry, J. (2015) *Visual Literacy MESHGuide*, Senior Mirandanet Fellow, NAACE Fellow, UK; University of Southern Maine, USA: www.meshguides.org/meshguides-full-list/
A MESHGuide outlining issues related to visual literacy.

Procter, R. (2013) *Assessment for Learning MESHGuide*: www.meshguides.org/meshguides-full-list/
A MESHGuide giving an introduction to assessment for learning.

The Education School Teachers' Qualifications, England, Regulations 2003: www.legislation.gov.uk/uksi/2003/1662/schedule/2/made
This sets out the requirements for teachers in England.

Appendix 2 on pages 591–595 provides further examples of websites you may find useful.

Capel, S., Leask, M. and Turner, T. (eds) (2010) *Readings for Learning to Teach in the Secondary School: A Companion to M Level Study*, London: Routledge.
This book brings together essential readings to support you in your critical engagement with key issues raised in this textbook.

The subject-specific books in the *Learning to Teach* series are also very useful.

Any additional resources and an editable version of any relevant tasks/tables in this unit are available on the companion website: www.routledge.com/cw/capel

2.2 Schemes of work, units of work and lesson planning

Sophy Bassett, Mark Bowler and Angela Newton

Introduction

Good-quality teaching depends on effectively planned lessons.

(Ofsted 2011b: 51)

In order to achieve an effectively planned lesson, a number of factors must be considered. These include pupil prior learning, the ways that pupils learn (see Unit 5.1), the requirements of the curriculum (Chapter 7), appropriate methods of teaching to suit the needs of all pupils and resources available (see Unit 4.1 on differentiation). In addition to these points, lesson evaluation informs the planning process (see Figure 2.2.1). This unit considers each of these factors in developing medium- and short-term plans.

Three levels of planning are particularly relevant to your work in the classroom – the *scheme of work*, which outlines lessons for a term or a year or so, the *unit of work*, which outlines a group of lessons around a particular topic, and the *lesson plan* for each individual lesson. You quickly gain experience of planning as you prepare lessons and units of work at your placement school. Evaluation is integrally linked to planning and teaching, and lesson evaluations form the basis of any changes or developments to your plans, both within and between lessons. For this reason, a flexible approach must be adopted.

OBJECTIVES

At the end of this unit, you should be able to:

- explain what is meant by the terms: 'aims', 'learning objectives', 'learning outcomes', 'progression' and 'differentiation';
- understand what is meant by a scheme of work, unit of work and lesson plan;
- construct units of work;
- construct effective lesson plans.

Check the requirements for your initial teacher education (ITE) programme to see which relate to this unit.

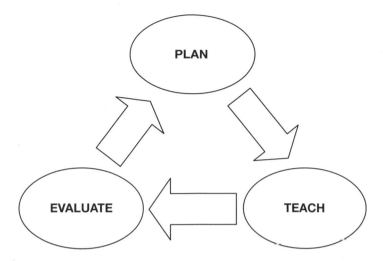

Figure 2.2.1 Plan-teach-evaluate cycle

Planning what to teach and how to teach it

The factors influencing *what* should be taught (content of lessons) are discussed in Unit 1.1 and Chapter 7, but how much you teach in each lesson and *how* you teach it (see Unit 5.3) are the teacher's own decisions.

Content of lessons

The knowledge, skills, understanding and attitudes appropriate for a young person entering the world of work in the twenty-first century are vastly different to those that were considered appropriate even 15 years ago. Ideas about what teachers should teach change regularly and the curriculum is under constant scrutiny by those responsible for education.

Before you plan individual lessons, you require an overall picture of what learning is planned for the pupils over a period of time. As a student teacher, you are usually given clear guidelines about what to teach and the goals for pupils' learning within your subject. These goals are often set out in nationally produced documents; for example, the Scottish Curriculum for Excellence, the English National Curriculum, the Welsh School Curriculum, the Northern Ireland Curriculum, school documents and specifications for accredited courses as issued by examination boards. You should become familiar with the curriculum requirements and the terminology relevant to your subject.

Teaching strategies

To repeat the earlier point, although the learning content may be prescribed, the decision about which teaching strategies to use is usually yours (see Unit 5.3). As you become more experienced as a teacher, you acquire your own personal teaching style. People learn in different ways and different teaching strategies are suitable for different learning objectives and different types of material. You should become familiar with a range of ways of structuring learning experiences in the classroom. For example, you might choose to use discussion, discovery learning or role play to achieve particular learning objectives. Unit 5.3 gives detailed advice on teaching styles and strategies that help you achieve different learning objectives. Task 2.2.1 asks you to reflect on your preferred approaches to learning.

 Task 2.2.1 How do you learn?

Spend a few minutes identifying the methods that help you learn and the teaching strategies used by teachers in situations where you felt you learned effectively (see Unit 5.1). Add notes identifying situations in which you did not learn. Compare these notes with those of other student teachers. People learn in different ways and different learning intentions require different strategies. You should take account of such differences in planning your lessons and demonstrate that you can use a range of teaching methods. This helps you to personalise learning (see Unit 2.1 on observations and Unit 4.1 on differentiation). Record your observations in your professional development portfolio (PDP).

Schemes of work, units of work and lesson plans

There are three main stages to planning for pupil learning:

1   a long-term plan – *the scheme of work*;
2   a medium-term plan – *the unit of work*;
3   a short-term plan – *the lesson plan*.

A number of formats for schemes of work, units of work and lesson plans are in use. We suggest you read the advice given for the teaching of your subject in the subject-specific texts in this *Learning to Teach* series and gather examples from the teachers and student teachers you are in contact with. However, while the level of detail may vary between different approaches, the purpose is the same – to identify learning objectives and learning outcomes in the long-term (scheme of work), in the medium-term (unit of work) or in the lesson (lesson plan) and the learning content to achieve these. Your initial teacher education provider may require you to use a specific proforma. However, it would be beneficial to try different approaches to planning in order to find those most appropriate to your situation. The best plans are ones that support you in your teaching so that your pupils learn what you intend them to learn. The illustrations in this unit are intended to provide examples with which you can work and later modify.

The scheme of work

This might also be called the 'programme of study' and is usually designed at department level. Different terms may be used in your school or in your subject, but the purpose is the same – to devise a long-term plan for the pupils' learning, usually across a term, a year or period of years. The purpose of a scheme of work is to ensure the continuity of pupil learning and build on the learning that has gone before. In some departments, schemes of work are very detailed and include a framework for teaching, learning and assessment, as well as safety issues.

Units of work

As with the scheme of work, different terms may be used for medium-term planning. A unit will normally provide a plan for pupils' learning from a few weeks to an entire term. Units of work are often informed by a department's scheme but will generally be written by an individual teacher.

Both schemes and units of work will plan for the development of pupils' knowledge, skills, capabilities, understanding and attitudes in order to ensure effective progression in learning. The term 'progression' means the planned development of knowledge, skills, understanding or attitudes over time.

Using a scheme of work to plan units of work

Often at your placement school you are given a scheme of work to inform your unit planning. The following questions should be considered when designing units of work:

1   What has been taught before?
2   What do you want the pupils to know, understand and be able to do?
3   How much time is available to do this work?
4   What resources are available?
5   How is the work to be assessed?
6   How does this work fit in with the work pupils are doing in other subjects?
7   What is to be taught later?

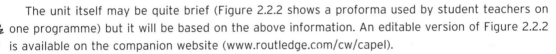

The unit itself may be quite brief (Figure 2.2.2 shows a proforma used by student teachers on one programme) but it will be based on the above information. An editable version of Figure 2.2.2 is available on the companion website (www.routledge.com/cw/capel).

Each question is now discussed in turn.

1   *What has been taught before?* This information should be available from school documentation (for example, the schemes of work) and from staff. In the case of pupils in their first year of secondary education, there is usually a member of staff responsible for liaising with primary schools who may have this information.

2   *What do you want pupils to know, understand and be able to do?* The aims of a unit of work are general statements about the learning that should take place over a period. *Learning objectives* are specific statements that set out what pupils are expected to learn across a unit. Learning outcomes are assessable learning objectives. They describe the action or behaviour of pupils that will provide evidence they have met the learning objectives. (Learning objectives are also prepared for each lesson, and further detail is provided later under lesson planning.) In devising each unit of work, a small aspect of the whole curriculum is selected and a route planned through it to provide the best opportunities for pupils to learn. Progression in pupil learning should be considered and built into units of work.

3   *How much time is available to do this work?* The number and length of lessons devoted to a topic are decided by the department or school in which you are working. Don't forget that homework has a valuable role to play in enhancing learning, and some time may be taken up by such things as assessments, revision, special events, bank holidays and school training days.

4   *What resources are available?* Resources include material resources as well as human resources, and what is available depends on the school where you are working. You need to find out the procedures for using resources in the school and what is available. You may find there are resources outside the school to draw upon; for example, parents, governors, charities and subject associations. Many organisations provide schools with speakers on current topics. There may be field study centres or sports facilities nearby. Before planning to use any resources, you should check whether there are any safety issues to consider.

5   *How is the work to be assessed?* Teaching, learning and assessment are interlinked. Most of the work you are doing with pupils is teacher-assessed, although some is externally assessed. A good deal of teacher assessment is formative, often referred to as assessment for learning – to check and guide pupils' progress; for example, in relation to learning objectives (see Procter's (2013) and Newton and Bowler's (2016) MESHGuides on Assessment for Learning and Bhatti (2015) on the alignment of curriculum, teaching and assessment). The key purpose of teacher assessment during a lesson is to check knowledge and understanding of the material and to guide the next steps of teaching.

Teacher assessment may also be summative – undertaken at the end of a piece of work to assess the progress achieved. In any case, you should keep good records of the pupils' progress (homework, class work, assessment results) in your own record book, as well as providing these in the form required by the school or department. Unit 6.1 focuses on assessment issues.

Task 2.2.2 asks you to consider how you might record the outcomes of your assessment of pupils.

 Task 2.2.2 Record-keeping and assessment

Ask staff in your department how they expect pupil assessment records to be kept and what forms of assessment you should use for the work you are doing. Make notes and compare practice in your school with other schools where your fellow student teachers are working. Record your observations in your PDP.

---

6   *How does this work fit in with the work pupils are doing in other subjects?* There are many areas of overlap where it is useful to discuss pupils' work with other departments. For instance, if pupils are having difficulty with measurement in technology, it is worth checking whether and when the mathematics department teaches these skills and how they teach them (see examples on De Geest's 2014 MESHGuide on aspects of learning of Mathematics; Eames (2016) on grammar and Harrison and Brookes *et al.* (2013) on spelling may also be of interest). Cross-curricular dimensions to the curriculum (see Unit 7.2) are usually considered by the school and responsibilities for different aspects shared out among departments. Ask staff in your department what responsibilities the department has in this area.

7   *What is to be taught later?* Progression in pupil learning has to be planned, and schemes and units of work are drawn up for this purpose. From these documents, you know what work is to come and the contribution to pupil learning that each lesson is to make.

Unit of work
Topic:
Related prior learning:

Class:	No in class:	Age:
No of lessons:	Duration:	Dates:

Unit aims: (from the NC or accredited course specification)

Unit objectives: (In relation to what pupils will know/understand/be able to do)

Cross curricular links:

Framework of lessons:	Ref. (NC/Spec.)

Resources:

Assessment strategies:

Other notes:

Figure 2.2.2 Unit of work proforma

Task 2.2.3 asks you to draw up a unit of work.

 Task 2.2.3 Drawing up a unit of work

In consultation with your tutor, draw up a unit of work to last about six to eight lessons. Focus on one particular class that you are teaching. Use the format provided for your ITE programme (or the one we provide in Figure 2.2.2). Ensure you consider questions 1–7 above in designing the unit of work. Record your planning in your PDP.

The lesson plan

The *lesson plan* provides an outline of one lesson within a unit of work. In planning a lesson, you are working out the detail required to teach one aspect of the unit of work. To plan the lesson, you use a framework, an example of which is provided in Figure 2.2.3.

The following questions should be considered when planning lessons:

1   What is the range of ability of the pupils?
2   What do the pupils know about the topic?
3   What are the aims, learning objectives and outcomes for this lesson?
4   What time is available for the lesson?
5   What resources are available?
6   What approaches to classroom management should I use?
7   What teaching strategies should I adopt?
8   How do I assess pupil learning?
9   What risks are associated with the work?

Each question is now discussed in turn.

1   *What is the range of ability of the pupils?* As you develop as a teacher, you are expected to incorporate *differentiation* into your planning. This refers to the need to consider pupils' individual abilities when work is planned so that all pupils, regardless of ability, are challenged and extended by the work. Differentiation can be achieved in different ways depending on the material to be taught. Differentiation may, for example, be achieved by *outcome* (that is, different types or qualities of work may be produced) or by *task* (that is, different tasks may be set for pupils of differing abilities) or by *teacher input* (Unit 4.1 provides further information). You provide continuity of learning for the pupils by taking account of and building on their existing knowledge, skills and understanding.

2   *What do the pupils know about the topic?* As your experience of the curriculum and of pupils' learning develops, it becomes easier to answer this question. You need to consider what has been taught before, as well as the experience outside school that pupils might have had. It may be appropriate to do some form of testing, or analysis of knowledge, skills, attitudes and understanding, or to have a discussion with pupils to discover their prior experience and attitudes to the work in question. As a student teacher, you should seek advice from the staff who normally teach your classes, as well as consulting national guidance materials.

3   *What are the aims, learning objectives and outcomes for this lesson?* Learning objectives and outcomes are informed by the aims of the unit. Learning objectives describe the learning intention for the lesson and are recorded in terms of what the pupils are expected to know, understand and be able to do. Objectives describe how pupils' behaviour is expected to change. Learning outcomes are assessable objectives. Drawing up effective objectives and specifying and planning for learning outcomes require considerable thought. Learning objectives are not the same for all pupils, and more often than not your objectives can be differentiated. One way of achieving this is to write objectives detailing what 'all', 'most' or 'some' pupils should be able to do.

An effective method of presenting learning objectives and outcomes is to begin each statement with 'By the end of this lesson, (all/most/some) pupils should . . .' When writing learning outcomes, you should include a verb (and in some subjects a quality) that ensures your outcome is measurable.

Verbs that help you be precise are those such as state, describe, list, identify, prioritise, solve, explain, create and demonstrate. These verbs force you to write outcomes that can be observed or measured. If you think your learning outcomes are vague, ask yourself whether they make it clear what the pupils have to do to demonstrate their learning. Task 2.2.4 supports your writing of measurable objectives.

To help pupils understand what is expected of them, you might use the acronym WALT (what am I learning today?) and WILF (what am I looking for?). These link with the use of objectives (WALT) and outcomes (WILF).

Task 2.2.5 challenges you to set learning objectives, specify learning outcomes and then analyse the learning that may result.

4   *What time is available for the lesson?* On the example lesson plan provided, a timeline is drawn down the left-hand side. You should plan for short learning episodes in order to maintain the engagement of the pupils. At the planning stage, think practically about how long it is likely to take to set up, complete and review each task. During the lesson, the timeline enables you to see easily if it is necessary to adapt the original plan to fit the time available.

5   *What resources are available for the lesson?* It is important to select and make available the most appropriate resources to achieve the learning objectives. Check how resources are reserved in your department and book them early because other staff may need them at the same time.

6   *What approaches to classroom management should I use?* You should plan for how you group pupils, integrate resources and manage transitions between activities and stages of the lesson (see Units 2.3 and 4.1).

7   *What teaching strategies should I adopt?* Teaching strategies should be selected as the best method to achieve your learning objectives (see Unit 5.3). Where possible, active learning strategies should be planned to engage all pupils (see Unit 5.2). Relevant questions should be planned for every lesson to assess pupils' knowledge and understanding during the lesson and to develop their higher-order thinking skills. Phrasing appropriate questions is a key skill for a teacher (see Unit 3.1).

8   *How do I assess pupil learning?* The assessment methods selected should enable the learning outcomes, and thus some learning objectives, to be accurately assessed. It is therefore important to choose reliable assessment methods, and you should seek advice from the teacher of the class. Ensure that you allocate sufficient time to carry out your chosen assessment methods effectively (see Unit 6.1).

Task 2.2.4 Writing measurable objectives

Using the Table 2.2.1 based on research into learning domains, collate a list of useful subject-specific verbs that will help to ensure your outcomes are measurable and progressive. Some generic verbs are provided to help you.

Table 2.2.1 Setting objectives based on learning domains to ensure measurable outcomes

Cognitive domain (based on Anderson and Krathwohl 2001)		
Progressive levels	*Example verbs*	*Subject-specific verbs*
Creating	Design, plan, invent	
Evaluating	Judge, assess, identify strengths/weaknesses	
Analysing	Analyse, compare, contrast	
Applying	Apply, use, select	
Understanding	Explain, discuss, identify	
Remembering	Define, list, label	

Affective domain (based on Krathwohl Bloom and Masia 1973)		
Progressive levels	*Example verbs*	*Subject-specific verbs*
Characterising by value	Influence, defend, support	
Organising	Modify, relate, integrate	
Valuing	Accept, initiate, endorse	
Responding	Agree to, reply, react	
Receiving	Listen, acknowledge, watch	

Psychomotor domain (based on Dave 1970)		
Progressive levels	*Example verbs*	*Subject-specific verbs*
Naturalisation	Manage, create, design	
Articulation	Adapt, reorganise, combine	
Precision	Master, refine, control	
Manipulation	Complete, improve, make	
Imitation	Copy, repeat, follow	

9   *What risks are associated with the work?* Safety is an important issue in schools. In some subjects, the assessment of risk to the pupils and incorporation of strategies to minimise this risk are a necessary part of the teacher's planning. Departmental and national guidelines are provided and should be followed to ensure the safety of pupils. As a student teacher, you should consult your head of department, class teacher or tutor for guidance on safety issues. Never undertake an activity until risk assessment has been considered. For examples of risk assessments, see HSE (2015), Eaton Vale Schools Activity Centre (2015) and CLEAPSS (2005). Your subject association will also be able to give you advice.

Task 2.2.5 Writing learning objectives and learning outcomes

Learning objectives link to the observable outcomes of the lesson; that is, to what pupils are expected to be able to do. Specifying the expected learning outcomes for the lesson will help you clarify your learning objectives. Discuss the writing of learning objectives with other student teachers in your subject area and your tutor. Choose a particular lesson and, as a group, devise appropriate learning objectives for all/most/some pupils that relate to changes in pupils' learning or behaviour. Pay particular attention to the quality and type of objectives you are setting – are they focused on the pupils' learning? Then identify the learning outcomes related to the learning objectives. How might learning be demonstrated by the pupil? Record your observations in your PDP.

Lessons have a structure and a rhythm to them. As you read this next section, think about the overall pattern to a lesson and the skills you use at each stage.

 An editable version of Figure 2.2.3 is available on the companion website (www.routledge.com/cw/capel).

Planning parts of a lesson

Planning is an important part of the teaching process. Figure 2.2.1 illustrates the planning, teaching and evaluation cycle that should occur for every lesson that you deliver.

Lessons can be divided into three parts. Each of these must be planned carefully in order that your lesson meets its learning objectives. These parts are called the starter, the main section and the plenary. Although there are three parts to a lesson, the main section usually includes several different activities, often referred to as episodes, that lead towards the achievement of the planned objectives. Starters and plenaries can also be referred to as episodes.

Starter

In order to actively engage pupils from the outset of the lesson, an interesting and relevant starter activity must be planned. Think of this as the 'hook' to draw pupils in to the lesson. This activity may draw upon and/or assess previous understanding or might present a challenge to pupils. Having such an activity displayed at the start of the lesson will give you time to organise your main activities as the class arrive.

Main section

Before you begin the main activities/episodes of the lesson, you need to clarify your learning objectives for the pupils. Sometimes you may elect to do this before the starter activity, whereas at other times you may complete the starter before explaining the learning objectives. It is considered good practice to display these objectives visually to your pupils. Pupils need to be aware of the purposes of the learning activities/episodes and how they will contribute to their learning journey within the lesson. Activities/episodes need to be 'chunked' as you must bear in mind that pupil concentration span is 10-15 minutes. You must also plan for the transitions between each activity/episode, and it may be necessary to conduct mini plenaries at the end of each episode to consolidate learning to ensure a smooth and well-paced lesson. Each episode should build upon the previous one.

Date:	Class:	Topic:
Lesson: (e.g. 2/8)	No. pupils:	Focus:
Duration:	Resources:	
Overall aim:		
Learning objectives: (all/most/some)		
Learning outcomes: (all/most/some)		
Learning support requirements:		
Assessment for learning strategies:		

Time		Teacher activity/strategy	Pupil activity (all/most/some)	Episode evaluation
	Starter			
	Main section			
	Plenary			

Lesson evaluation:

Were objectives/outcomes achieved by all/most/some? What evidence do you have to answer this question with certainty?

What went well? What didn't go well?

What needs to be addressed next time?

What are your priorities for pupil learning in the next lesson?

What are your priorities for improving planning, organisation and transitions?

What are your teacher performance targets?

Figure 2.2.3 Planning a lesson: one possible approach

Plenary

This is a very important part of the lesson, during which learning should be summarised. This involves referring back to the main learning objectives for the lesson. It is an important time for the teacher to check pupil learning, and this requires skilful questioning (see Unit 3.1). At this point, it may be appropriate to give a brief outline of the next lesson. Enough time should be set aside to record homework tasks and clear away any equipment.

General points to consider

Previous sections of this unit outline the key issues in effective planning. The following section highlights some general points that enhance the likelihood of overall success.

- *Resources*: Make sure your plan identifies the exact number of any resources that are required for the lesson. Ensure that you familiarise yourself with the equipment and know how to use it. If possible, set it up prior to the lesson.
- *Activities*: It is better to plan too many activities than too few. If one of your planned activities does not work or pupils complete the tasks more quickly than you anticipated, additional activities can be used.
- *Homework and forward planning*: Ensure you plan enough time to set homework and/or remind pupils of any materials they might require for the next lesson. This can then be recorded in their planner.
- *Group management*: Learn pupils' names as quickly as possible (see Buzan 2008; TeacherVision 2015). Consider whether there is a need to design a seating or workspace plan for your class. This can have both logistical and learning benefits.
- *Routines*: Classroom routines are important to ensure effective organisation of pupils and resources. These might include distribution and collection of resources, arrival and exit of pupils, and movement around the classroom. Ensure that you are at your teaching area before the lesson to greet the pupils on arrival. At the end of the lesson, pupils' departure should be supervised to ensure that they leave your teaching area in a safe and orderly manner. In subjects where there is a level of risk (for example, science or physical education), planning a safe routine is of paramount importance. Where effective routines are already in place, adhere to these: pupils will expect you to use the routines that their teacher will have worked hard to establish. When required, you may need to implement new routines after consultation with your tutor.

Evaluation and planning future lessons

As soon as you can after the lesson, evaluate its success. Were the learning outcomes, and therefore learning objectives, achieved by all/most/some? What went well? What didn't go well? What evidence do you have that allows you to answer these questions with some degree of certainty? Sometimes it is useful to wait until you have reviewed puplis' work before evaluating the lesson (see Unit 5.4). What are your priorities for pupil learning in the next lesson and how do they fit in with the unit of work? What are your priorities for improving planning for organisation and transitions? What are your priorities for your performance as a teacher? If you develop the practice of reflecting on your work as a matter of course, then modifying future practice on the basis of this reflection becomes second nature.

Task 2.2.6 challenges you to plan, teach and evaluate a series of lessons to support pupil progression.

✎ Task 2.2.6 Planning for pupil progression

Plan a unit of work to last between three and eight lessons. Plan, teach and evaluate lesson 1 in conjunction with your tutor. Identify the key points that should be considered when planning lesson 2. Repeat this plan, teach, evaluate cycle for the unit of work. Consider any adaptations you will need to make to your planned unit.

Review the quality of your planning and teaching using Brookfield's (1995) four critical reflection lenses of self-review, student review, peer review and theoretical literature. Identify your areas of strength and development in relation to promoting pupil progression through effective planning. Record this task in your PDP as an example of master's-level work.

SUMMARY AND KEY POINTS

You should now be able to:

■ explain the following terms: aims, learning objectives, learning outcomes, progression and differentiation;
■ construct units of work and lesson plans that are comprehensive and useful.

Check which requirements for your ITE programme you have addressed through this unit.

Further reading

Butt, G. (2006) *Lesson Planning*, 3rd edn, London: Continuum.
> This is a comprehensive book supporting student and qualified teachers to improve their planning in the short, medium and long term. Sections include planning for pupil differences and making plans work within the classroom.

Jerome, L. and Bhargava, M. (2015) *Effective Medium-Term Planning for Teachers*, London: Sage.
> This text provides advice and suggestions for effective medium-term planning. It includes examples of planning and justifications for the importance of medium-term plans, and explores links between pupil attainment and effective medium-term planning.

Kyriacou, C. (2014) *Essential Teaching Skills*, 4th edn, Cheltenham: Nelson Thornes.
> This provides an excellent and readable overview of the key skills that underpin effective teaching.

Mager, R. (2005) *Preparing Instructional Objectives*, 3rd edn, Atlanta, GA: Center for Effective Performance.
> Making the desired learning objectives and learning outcomes clear to *pupil*s helps ensure effective learning. This text provides useful information about objective setting.

Other resources and websites

Lesson plans are widely available on the Web but the quality will vary. See examples on the *Times Educational Supplement* (www.tes.co.uk/) or the *Guardian Teacher Network* (www.theguardian.com/teacher-network). Always check the strength of evidence of any advice you find.

MESHGuides (www.meshguides.org). The following have been cited in the text:

Bhatti, A.J. (2015) *Curriculum Alignment MESHGuide*, International Islamic University, Islamabad.

De Geest, E. (2013) *Mathematics: Reading and Writing Mathematics MESHGuide*, Open University, UK.

Eames, K. (2016) *Teaching Grammar in the English Language MESHGuide*, Bath Spa University, UK.

Harrison, C. and Brookes, G. *et al.* (2014) *Spelling in English MESHGuide*, Universities of Nottingham and Sheffield, UK.

Newton, A. and Bowler, M. (2016) *Assessment in Physical Education MESHGuide*, University of Bedfordshire, UK.

Procter, R. (2013) *Assessment for Learning MESHGuide*, University of Bedfordshire, UK.

Open University resources: The Open University's Open Learn website (www.open.edu/openlearn/education/educational-technology-and-practice/educational-practice) has a wide range of material that you may find helpful.

Remembering names: these websites will provide ideas

Buzan, T. (2008) *How to Remember Names and Faces*: www.open.edu/openlearn/body-mind/psychology/buzan-on-how-remember-names-and-faces.

TeacherVision (2015) *Learning Students' Names Quickly*: www.teachervision.com/teachingmethods/classroom-management/6708.html.

Risk assessments: see the CLEAPSS, Eaton Vale and HSE sites below

CLEAPSS (2005) *Managing Risk Assessment in Science Classrooms*: www.cleapss.org.uk/attachments/article/0/L196.pdf?Secondary/Science/Guides/.

Eaton Vale Schools Activity Centre (2015) *Risk Assessments*: www.eatonvale.co.uk/schools/riskassessments.aspx.

HSE (Health and Safety Executive) (2015) *Health and Safety Checklist for Classrooms*: www.hse.gov.uk/risk/classroom-checklist.htm.

Appendix 2 on pages 591–595 provides examples of further websites you may find useful.

Capel, S., Leask, M. and Turner, T. (eds) (2010) *Readings for Learning to Teach in the Secondary School: A Companion to M Level Study*, London: Routledge.
This book brings together essential readings to support you in your critical engagement with key issues raised in this textbook.

The subject-specific books in the Routledge *Learning to Teach* series are also very useful.

Any additional resources and an editable version of any relevant tasks/tables in this unit are available on the companion website: www.routledge.com/cw/capel

Acknowledgements

The authors are currently undertaking research into different models for lesson planning and their impact and rationale, and acknowledge with thanks the contributions to their research from teachers and student teachers.

2.3 Taking responsibility for the whole lesson

Michelle Lowe and Clyde Redfern

Introduction

This unit draws your attention to issues that have particular relevance to you when you are just starting to take responsibility for whole lessons. It focuses on particular aspects of planning and teaching to which you should pay particular attention. Recall the iceberg image of a teacher's work from Unit 1.1. The delivery of the lesson in the classroom represents the tip of the iceberg, while the bulk of the teacher's work for a lesson – routines, preparation, subject knowledge, professional knowledge and judgement, previous lesson evaluations – is hidden. Sometimes it can be helpful to remember the key elements of complex ideas using an acronym. We want to introduce you to the acronym of PROPS in the first part of this unit. The PROPs we ask you to think about are the following:

- P – personal attributes – being the teacher
- R – routines in the classroom
- O – outcomes
- P – planning
- S – subject.

In the first section of the unit we explore the importance of personal attributes and how you personify the role of 'the teacher'. We also look at how you can use verbal and non-verbal communication strategies to develop your confidence to deliver lessons. In the next section, we explore further the importance of understanding routines. We then move on to look at the importance of routines for pupils, other adults and for you as a teacher. A key element is to understand what you are trying to achieve in a lesson and the learning outcomes you intend for pupils. In this unit, we explore effective planning to ensure learning takes place and introduce you to the concept of the 'LOOP' for planning purposes. We also ask you to think about the importance of subject knowledge in relation to your planning. Finally, we explore the impact your first lesson might have on you personally.

OBJECTIVES

At the end of this unit, you should be able to:

■ have a greater awareness of your own persona as 'a teacher' and understand the impact this can have on others;

■ have an understanding of the power of routines to support the delivery of effective lessons;

■ recognise and apply the core principles in your future planning that ensure pupils can make progress;

■ have understood some of the barriers and enablers to your own confidence and identified strategies to use these to enhance your professional practice.

Check the requirements of your initial teacher education (ITE) programme to see which relate to this unit.

Persona: being the teacher

As a student teacher, you may find it hard to imagine yourself as a teacher. You may be asking yourself:

■ How do I dress?
■ How loudly do I have to talk?
■ Will the pupils listen to me?
■ Where should I stand?
■ How much should I talk?
■ What do I do with my hands?
■ Will they understand my accent?

This is very common and nothing to worry about. In the section below, we provide advice and ask you to explore your perceptions of what it is to be a 'teacher' and how this relates to your assessment of your own communication skills. You are asked to identify your strengths and areas for development. You will also understand how you can get the best out of your relationships with pupils and colleagues.

Personal attributes

First, complete Task 2.3.1.

When we talk about personal attributes, we are referring to the mannerisms, values and behaviours that all human beings have. Some people are generous, humorous, animated, smiley, kind, and so on. In your description of the 'teacher', you probably had lots of positive words such as these. It may be that some people who enter teaching have a set of personal attributes that predispose them to behaving in certain ways. For most people, the attributes needed for teaching

Task 2.3.1 What makes a great teacher?

You will already have observed teachers in the classroom. Reflect on this and imagine that you have to describe the key attributes of a great 'teacher' to someone from outer space. Think carefully about the attributes that impact upon pupils' learning.

Record the outcomes of your reflections and discussions in your professional development portfolio (PDP).

(for example, ability to explain, to give clear instructions, to appear even handed in settling disputes, your physical stance, your use of gesture) need to be developed or enhanced. This may take time and you shouldn't expect to have all of the desirable attributes perfected for your first lesson. You do, however, need a plan to enhance your existing personal attributes and to develop others. To do this, you first need to analyse your own personal starting point in a realistic and honest way. A tool used in management to assess personal attributes is the 360° self-evaluation. To complete your own self-evaluation, ask four trusted people to provide you with a list of your top five personal attributes as a teacher. Also ask them to identify three areas for development. Preferably, this would be colleagues in school, but you might also ask your friends or tutors. This will give you a balanced view of how others perceive you. Now complete Task 2.3.2.

 Task 2.3.2 Personal strengths and areas for development

Think back to the description of a great 'teacher' you developed for Task 2.3.1. Use the feedback from the 360° to assess how close you are to this. What do you need to do to close the gap and how will you do this? Store this information in your PDP.

Confidence

When you take responsibility for a class for the first time, this can feel daunting, as all eyes and expectations are upon you. You are no longer assisting someone else in the learning process, but are the person responsible for leading it. The most important of the personal attributes you need for this is confidence. To help you feel confident before you stand in front of the class, you need to feel that you understand the following:

- the routines and expectations of the classroom and the wider school – particularly the format and requirements of the lesson plan used in the school;
- the pupils' ability levels and any additional needs they may have;
- what has been covered in previous lessons and the focus for future lessons;
- what you will be teaching in terms of subject content;
- how both you and the pupils you teach will know that they have made progress;
- the resources needed and available to you.
- which other adults are available to support your lesson and how you will utilise them.

You will already have begun to collect information about your school and the pupils, which should help you with this (see forms of professional knowledge for teaching in Table 1.1.3). When you plan your first solo lesson, it will take a long time and you should be prepared for your tutor to offer advice and guidance. Although this may seem like criticism, remember they have a lot of experience that may be beneficial. This is an investment for the rest of your teaching career. This planning process will probably take longer than you anticipate, so allow plenty of quality time for discussion and modifications. Following this advice also means you develop and display other personal attributes that are valuable as a teacher. You will develop your patience, perseverance, resilience, ability to listen and take advice, and understand the value of reciprocity in professional life. Confidence is a state of mind that is fed by experience. It is not a fixed position and will be affected by how each individual lesson goes. A thorough plan is the key to confident delivery (see Unit 2.2 for the detail of lesson planning) and effective planning and evaluation of lessons can have an impact on your confidence. This is an area that you can develop and control.

Communication

Despite having a good lesson plan, you may still feel a little uncertain about your abilities as a teacher and it should be remembered that confidence can be affected by factors beyond the classroom. You need to be able to recognise if this happens and seek help and advice as appropriate. There are a number of other strategies you can employ to develop your confidence. Many of these are linked to verbal and non-verbal communication. In this section, we identify some simple ways in which you can project an image of confidence to your class. Recall the questions at the start of this unit.

How do I dress?

In most schools, you will need to conform to a dress code. Make sure you know what this is. Clothing should always be comfortable and practical. This is particularly important in relation to footwear. Similarly, you should also think about jewellery. Functional and in line with school norms is the most appropriate.

You may be a fashionista and tempted to wow pupils with your dress sense. You might argue that your clothing gives you confidence. However, this may not meet the school's dress code or be the best way to start a relationship with a group of pupils. You want them to remember you for the quality of your teaching, not the size of your heels or the pattern on your tie! If you really want to wear distinctive clothing that is in line with the school's dress code, leave this until you are able to deliver high-quality lessons on a regular basis.

Where should I stand?

Choosing where and how to stand in the classroom is important. Many student teachers position themselves almost exclusively at the front of the class as if attached to the teacher's desk. This is not helped in some modern classrooms where technology is controlled from a central location. Remember, you can control the computer from anywhere in the classroom using a relatively cheap remote pointer, which is a good investment. You may also be limited by the layout of the classroom. Although it may not be easy to change classroom layout immediately, this might be something you consider as you reflect on how the classroom layout impacts on learning. The most important thing is to position yourself where the pupils can see you and you can see them. You should also consider whether you need to move pupils to facilitate this; for example, bringing pupils closer to you at the start of a lesson and requiring their full attention on you. If you can plan to keep whole-class activities short and sharp, this will help pupils to maintain their focus on you.

Think of your classroom as a stage. You have the right to work in any part of it that you choose. Do not have the mindset that the teacher and pupil operate in separate zones. There are no teacher zones or pupil zones. Continuing with the analogy of a stage, if you were producing a play, you would control carefully as many elements as possible to ensure the audience get a rich experience. The same applies in a classroom. There are some basics. If the room is hot or stuffy, you should open a window. Think carefully about lighting – do not stand in front of a bright light or have bright lights shining at your pupils. Acoustics matter in the classroom (see Underwood *et al.*'s 2015 *Acoustic Accessibility MESHGuide*). Make sure your pupils can hear you and you can hear them. It is worth observing how good teachers use the space. Notice how they move and look for the key locations so that they can scan pupil activity on-task (Unit 2.1 gives guidance on observing classrooms).

How loudly do I have to talk?/Will the pupils listen to me?/Will they understand my accent?

Verbal communication is important (see also unit 3.1). Many student teachers focus on what they say and can spend a long time perfecting their teacher input, often learning a script like the lines of a play. Over time, you will move away from a script and towards a more natural performance. Through your communication style, you are aiming to be authoritative, not authoritarian. Teachers need to have clear speech. You need to develop an awareness and control of pace (how fast you talk), volume (how loudly) and tone (the ways in which your voice goes up and down). Some regional accents have particular tonal sounds. For example, some accents can be characterised with a rising inflection towards the end of sentences. This can leave the listener wondering if you have asked a question! You should be particularly aware of your own voice – try recording and listening to yourself and see how this is affected when you feel nervous or under pressure. Pay particular attention to vocalisations. Some people end every sentence with 'OK', 'erm', 'umm', and so on. We are not suggesting that you can change the way you speak overnight, but you need to be aware that you are moving from conversational language to presentational language. Just like an actor, you need to change into the character/persona of the teacher.

How much should I talk?

Remember that the aim of every lesson is to enable pupils to make progress in their learning. You have to make an assessment of whether they have done this and if you dominate the talk in the classroom it can be difficult to work out what a single pupil or groups of pupils have learned. A good lesson will have a balance of teacher talk and pupil talk and plenty of time for pupil activity. It is often the case in early lessons that the teacher will talk in the belief that this is a safe course of action. You may be scared to allow your pupils some freedoms and worry that they will not do what you ask them to do. A good lesson with engaging activities will keep pupils on-task. Unit 5.2 covers active learning. Over time, your role will change from the deliverer to the facilitator of learning.

What do I do with my hands?

Our voice is not the only way in which we communicate. Think about when you observe a play. The actions you see are as powerful as the words you hear. It is not just what you say but how you say it. Our hands are powerful communication tools. For example, if you cross your hands or arms in front of your body, this can be perceived as a sign that you are feeling vulnerable with the cross as a protection. Similarly pointing gestures can be perceived as aggressive and confrontational. You should also think about the eye contact you make with pupils. When you are nervous, you might not even look at the pupils, which may be perceived by them as you not being interested in them. Keep eye contact with pupils and link this to facial expression. It is very easy to appear pleased, disappointed, surprised or sad just by changing the position of your mouth or eyebrows. Your aim is not to make pupils your enemies or your best friends. Using a small nod of the head and a smile can be powerful tools in managing a classroom, which helps you to maintain your teacher persona. There are many books written about non-verbal communication and we signpost you to one of these in the Further reading. See also Unit 3.1 on communicating with pupils.

Interpersonal relationships

Student teachers often focus on their relationships with pupils, and this is very important to enable you to plan and deliver an effective lesson. You need to know what their abilities are, what personalities they have, what additional needs they may have, and so on, and you will be developing your communication strategies with pupils continually. However, during your first lessons, you may feel nervous about how to use other adults. You are now the leader of learning, which means you need to lead everyone. This can appear daunting. Now complete Task 2.3.3.

 Task 2.3.3 The role of the teaching assistant (TA)

Observe an experienced TA working with a teacher. What do they do? Why is this effective in supporting learning? How does the teacher include them in the lesson?
  Record the outcomes of your reflections and discussions in your PDP.

First of all, establish which adults are available to help you and what their role is. You may have a general teaching assistant (TA) or a TA to support pupils with additional needs. You may have a technician if you teach a science or an information technology (IT) related subject. These are highly skilled people who, like your tutor, will be willing to help you plan and deliver your lesson. When you make your lesson plan, you must plan for what they are going to be doing either before, during or after the lesson. Other adults in your classroom will be working with the same school routines and policies that you are, so you can expect them to support decisions that you make in relation to managing behaviour and learning in the classroom (see www.behaviour2learn.co.uk). Remember, if you plan for and carefully manage the pupils' learning, you will have a better chance of managing behaviour. A useful strategy in your early lessons is for you to ask your tutor to act as a TA. They can give you valuable feedback on how effectively you utilised them and included them in your lesson if they act in this role. It will also be helpful as they will be able to provide you with small interventions to keep your lesson on track; for example, they might spot the pupil who finishes the last page in their book and can intervene – you might not even know yet where to get new books! This strategy can also give your tutor a valuable and defined role in what is *their class*.

In this section, you have reflected upon your personal attributes and ways in which these can be developed or enhanced. You have also begun to think about how you can ensure that you have the confidence to deliver lessons as the lead teacher. In the next section, we explore further the importance of understanding routines.

Routines

Routines for class and lesson management provide a structure where the rules are understood by all so that learning can take place. In time, these routines become instinctive for you. Routines are not established in a vacuum. The pupils you teach have been in schools for at least seven years and they expect the teacher to establish 'norms' for classroom work, talk and movement. You are taking the lead for a class in a department and school that already has norms so it would not be appropriate for you to introduce completely new ways of working. School and department routines are normally non-negotiable and can be a support for you. The area in which you can focus and make your own impact over time is the teacher-controlled routines (see Unit 2.1 on observation of routines). There are routines for:

■ classroom management – the operational management of the physical space;
■ relationships in the classroom – the ways in which all people in the classroom interact and relate to each other;
■ expectations of and for learning

Classroom management

You need to think about how the classroom is managed. Completing Task 2.3.4 will help you to identify what current practice is in your school, and it can provide a helpful checklist for you to refer to when you take the lead as the teacher.

 Task 2.3.4 Classroom routines

Make a list of the routines in the classroom for the following:

■ entering the room/leaving the lesson;
■ getting the teacher's attention/the teacher getting attention;
■ pupils moving around the classroom;
■ getting equipment out and tidying away;
■ leaving the classroom (toilet/illness);
■ routine administration – taking registers/keeping records;
■ the use of time in the lesson.

Record the outcomes of your reflections and discussions in your PDP.

For your early lessons, one of your main goals is to get the pupils down to work promptly. To do this, you need to be confident in the operational routines of the classroom. Your concern is to establish yourself as an organised teacher, and earlier in the unit we discussed the idea of the classroom as a stage that you control. Your early lessons will go more easily if you fit in with established routines. You are 'borrowing' this classroom so always remember to leave it as you would expect to find it.

Relationships in the classroom

Other adults: There may be other adults in the room, and your job is to ensure that they are well utilised in supporting pupil learning. You will need to use or establish a routine for communicating the lesson plan in a timely and appropriate fashion and for gaining feedback from the other adults. Do not expect a TA to be able to do their own preparation if you only give them the lesson plan as the lesson starts!

Pupils: Pupils need to know what the routines are in your classroom. Adopting a *firm, fair, friendly* approach helps you develop good relationships with pupils. Pupils have certain expectations of you. You need to be explicit about your expectations of them and the routines you will use. Above all, they will expect continuity in their experiences at school. It is not helpful for pupils to be given conflicting routines as they move from class to class, subject to subject, teacher to teacher. You do need to know your class, and there will be influences on classroom relationships that come from the community. Information about the range of group 'norms' of behaviour for teenagers in the local area and background information about other social relationships (for example, which pupils are cousins, stepsisters or brothers) may help you understand more easily your pupils and their expectations.

Pupils may ask you inappropriate personal questions. Do not allow yourself to be distracted from the work in the lesson. You can choose whether or not to answer personal questions, but do set boundaries beyond which you will not go. Do not be personal, and do not take things personally. If you decide to share personal information with the pupils, then choose the time and place.

Routines for behaviour management: In terms of behaviour, pupils expect a teacher to be fair and consistent in applying the school rules. They expect those who comply to be rewarded and those who do not to be sanctioned (reprimanded). You need to think about how you will do this. Schools already have established routines to reward and sanction pupils. You should use this and ensure that you match the reward or sanction to the pupil action. One of your routines should be to reward rather than sanction to try to create a positive environment for learning in your classroom. Ask your tutor to observe your ratio of rewards to sanctions in your lessons. Behaviour management is cited as an area of concern by student teachers more often than any other area, and Units 3.2 and 3.3 provide more detailed guidance (see also www.behaviour2learn.co.uk/).

One of the more challenging areas is how to manage low-level disruptive behaviour. This is where a thorough understanding of the school policy on behaviour is vital. A key strategy is for you to be able to identify and defuse emerging situations. Confrontation in front of the whole class is generally to be avoided. You could use the following ladder of interventions:

■ First, try to use non-verbal gestures to remind a pupil to keep working.
■ Next, a quiet, individual conversation with the pupil. Use your voice sparingly to manage behaviour.

▪ If this doesn't work, try proximity praise, where you reward a pupil nearby who is on-task.

▪ At the next stage, try positioning yourself or another adult near a pupil who needs more encouragement to stay on-task.

▪ Before you use the school policy on sanctions, try a more detailed conversation where you highlight the issue and give a pupil clear options about how to correct the behaviour and what the consequences of continuing their behaviour will be.

Now complete Task 2.3.5.

 Task 2.3.5 Dealing with swearing

Discuss the following two scenarios with your tutor and identify an appropriate response:

▪ You overhear a pupil use swear words in conversation with another pupil.
▪ A pupil swears at you.

Record the outcomes of your reflections and discussions in your PDP.

You should always try to remain positive and try to hide any frustrations or anger that you might feel. This can be difficult; after all, you have planned a lesson in great detail and you want it to go right. You might be very worried about how a tutor perceives off-task behaviour. Remember, they will want to see that you have a routine for managing behaviour and that you are consistent. Now complete Task 2.3.6.

 Task 2.3.6 School policies: rewards and sanctions

Find out about the policies on rewards and sanctions at your placement school. Make notes of the key issues that affect your work. Check your understanding of the application of these policies with your tutor. Write down the approach you are going to take with respect to rewards and sanctions and discuss this with fellow student teachers and/or your tutor.

Record the outcomes of your reflections and discussions in your PDP.

Routines for gaining attention: Earlier in the unit, we discussed the non-verbal communication skills you can use to keep pupils' attention. Getting pupils' attention at the start of a lesson and getting the attention of the whole class at points during the lesson is a skill that experienced teachers do effortlessly. You must decide how you are going to get attention in both situations and then act confidently. You could try a verbal call for attention ('Stop what you're doing and just look here for a minute'). You might have a non-verbal signal (such as raising your hand in the air). You could use an auditory signal (a computer sound). A teacher may then follow this with a focus on an individual ('Guy, that means you too'), which acts as a reminder to all pupils that if they do not want to be the focus of the teacher's attention, they need to stop what they are doing. Think about what you want to call the class to attention for. You do not want to stop pupils when they are working well, but it can be helpful when, for example, pupils come to a difficult point or if you wish to draw their attention to a point on safety.

One of the fundamental rules of the classroom is that pupils should not speak when the teacher is speaking. Spending a few minutes in a lesson waiting for silence until you speak saves a lot of time later, as pupils know what you expect. Pupils may need reminding of your expectations and you probably need to reinforce the idea that this is one of your basic rules. You must be able to get the class's attention when you require it. When observing classes, the following questions may help you see some of the strategies used by teachers to establish this aspect of their authority:

- What verbal cues does the teacher use to establish quiet? Key phrases such as 'Right then' and 'Put your pens down now' establish that the teacher requires the class to listen. Some student teachers make the mistake of thinking the words 'quiet' or 'shush' repeated over and over will gain the required effect. Units 3.2 and 3.3 provide further advice.
- What non-verbal cues does the teacher use to gain attention? Look at the way teachers use gestures – eyes, face, arms, hands – to establish that they require the class to listen. They may stand still and just wait. Unit 3.1 contains more ideas.

There are also routines related to the way pupils gain the teacher's attention. The usual routine is that pupils put up their hands and do not call out. Again, we suggest you find out what the current practice is for the classes you are teaching and make sure you implement this consistently.

Expectations of and for learning

A good teacher has high expectations of and for learning. They plan for learning to take place. You need to establish a routine in your classroom whereby pupils are challenged through you clearly setting out the intended learning objectives for the lesson (see Table 2.2.1), sharing them with the pupils, planning activities that allow the pupils to engage with the learning objectives and assessing the extent to which the objectives have been met by individuals. Individual outcomes and tasks should all be directly related to the objectives and intended learning outcomes for the lesson. This should be reflected in your lesson planning (see Table 2.3.1). Part of the classroom routine is to help the pupils understand these steps for themselves. Checking and marking pupils' work during the lesson helps improve their work. It also helps if pupils are regularly involved in helping to assess their own work. It is a useful exercise, sometimes, to have pupils swap books so that they can check each other's work. Marking their work routinely helps you to set specific, well-matched and challenging targets for all. Your comments and discussions with them help pupils become aware of where and how to improve their work.

In this section, we have explored the importance of routines for pupils, other adults and you as a teacher. Do not underestimate the power of strong and clear routines, and strive to achieve these as soon as you can in your practice. You should expect some resistance from tutors and pupils to any change you wish to make as this can create unnecessary disruption.

Outcomes

Now you have begun to establish your identity as a teacher and have an understanding of the key routines that underpin your performance in the classroom, you can focus on the driver that underpins all lessons – pupil progress. It might seem an obvious statement that in your lessons pupils should make progress; however, achieving this requires a high level of skilful planning and delivery. Pupil progress is evidenced through the outcomes of a lesson. Put simply, outcomes are what pupils achieve in the lesson. There are obvious outcomes; for example, the amount of correct completed problems in a mathematics lesson. Outcomes can be planned for, and this is known as differentiation (see Unit 4.1). Sometimes there are unanticipated outcomes. When this happens, you need to understand why and adapt future lessons to accommodate this. We can keep the outcomes of a lesson in pupil record files. However, outcomes are often seen as the end product. This is not the case. We would want you to focus more on intended learning outcomes. If a pupil has learned in your lesson, if they have met the intended learning outcomes, they will be able to recall this at a later stage and use it in a variety of other contexts. In the next section, we explore the difference between actual outcomes and intended learning outcomes in more detail. You also need to think about outcomes for you. As a student teacher, you have to show how you have met the learning outcomes for your ITE programme. The outcomes of your ITE programme may become part of your evidence file against the professional standards. You are likely to feel that your outcomes are under constant scrutiny from many quarters, and this is right and proper to ensure that the best teachers enter the profession. Never lose sight of the fact that if you can establish an environment where pupil outcomes and the extent to which pupils achieve the learning objectives set for them are the main focus, you will be on the right lines to becoming a great teacher and most other things will fall into place.

Planning

Planning to ensure learning takes place means understanding this LOOP:

■ **L** – learning starting point – what pupils already know;
■ **O** – objectives – the new learning for the lesson;
■ **O** – outcomes – how you will see the learning happen;
■ **P** – progress – how you will know what learning has taken place.

The lesson plan is the obvious way in which your tutor can see what you intend to do and may be designed by you for two audiences – your tutor to check your planning and for you to deliver the lesson so that pupils learn (see also Unit 2.2 on lesson planning). It should contain enough information to satisfy both requirements and no more. It should not be a script, but the level of detail will vary with time and experience. The lesson plan is the culmination of the research and thinking that you undertake for the lesson and your evaluation of previous lessons. If a lesson is to be effective, you really need to be clear about what you are trying to do with your class and what you will be expecting of them. It is easy to fall into the trap of planning lessons that are relatively superficial but look busy with a series of activities that are not really having an impact on pupils' learning. You can use the checklist in Table 2.3.1 to support you in the planning process.

Now complete Task 2.3.7.

Table 2.3.1 Planning lessons

- Plan the lesson and ask for advice about your plan. Be clear about what you want to achieve. Have your plan to hand at all times. You need to work with the classroom teacher to understand what next steps pupils need in order to achieve.
- Think about your resource needs – are you using worksheets, pictures, cue cards, video, textbooks, PowerPoint, the interactive whiteboard? Some resources are easier and safer to use than others. You may find that equipment you had planned to use stops working or the specialist in your subject is not available to supervise you.
- Check that you have adequate extension and alternative work. Anticipate that additional work may be needed.
- Link tasks to earlier work (this is known as scaffolding) and set authentic tasks – ones that are relevant to the learners' lives and locality.
- Make the content challenging. Ensure the challenge is realistic and pupils are productive; do not make the work so difficult that the pupils give up.
- Know the class if possible through your observations and have a strategy for using and learning names. Try to learn names quickly – making notes beside the names in the register may help you remember. Drawing up a seating plan can help; pupils may always, or at least usually, sit in the same places. In any case, you can ask them to sit in the same seats until you know their names.
- Think about how you are going to assess pupils' work during the lesson. You will need to give them comments and feedback on what they are doing.
- Check which other adults will be in the room, and the need for any materials to help them with particular pupils. It might help, for example, to give them a copy of your lesson plan so that they are aware of what you are trying to do.
- Keep track (in your head, at least) of which activities 'worked' with the class and why.

 Task 2.3.7 Comparing lesson plans

Exchange a lesson plan with another student teacher. Discuss some of the questions below together. You can also use Table 2.3.1 to help structure the questions you ask for this task.

- Are the learning objectives and intended learning outcomes clearly specified and differentiated?
- Can you identify the types of outcomes expected?
- Are the pupils likely to be actively and appropriately engaged at every opportunity?
- Are the tasks 'authentic' tasks?
- Have you planned appropriate time sequences into your lesson?
- Is there scope for pupils to demonstrate to you what pupils have learned this lesson?

Record the outcomes of your reflections and discussions in your PDP.

Never start your planning just from an activity. You should always ask yourself if the activity that the pupils are doing or your actions as a teacher are directly related to the learning objectives and intended learning outcomes. If they are not, then you are diluting the impact your lesson will have. This is very common, and you may do this in the early stages of your planning. You may plan well-meaning activities that deflect pupils from focusing on the learning you want to take place in your classroom. If you can focus on planning for pupils' learning in your early lessons, you will have a focused impact on your pupils right from the beginning. This inevitably means you must spend a good deal of time thinking about the learning you want to take place and carefully crafting your learning objectives and intended learning outcomes. Unavoidable incidents occur to interrupt the flow of your carefully prepared lesson. We discuss below some of the more common incidents and possible solutions so that you are not taken by surprise.

Judging the timing during a lesson is one of the most difficult problems initially, and following a timeline on your lesson plan can help you see at a glance how the lesson is progressing in relation to the time allowed. Always keep an eye on the clock and keep your lesson plan to hand. If you spot that you are running ahead or lagging behind, you can intervene sooner to get your lesson back on track, but you need to consider also how the pupils are progressing. Monitoring the timing is useful for you and the pupils, and it may be that you use a displayed class timer for activities. It may be that you have too much or too little material. Pupils have to get to their next lesson on time and to have their break on time. So you must let them go on time! Five minutes or so before the end of a lesson (more if they have to change or put equipment away), draw the lesson together, reminding them of what's been achieved against the learning objectives and intended learning outcomes, what is expected in the way of homework and perhaps what they will be learning in the next lesson. Table 2.3.2 provides some examples of what you can do if pupils finish work early.

With experience, you acquire the skill of fitting work to the time available so the problem ceases to cause you anxiety.

Managing behaviour generally has been covered in an earlier section of this unit (it is also covered in Unit 3.3 in more detail). Inevitably, some pupils try to deflect you from your lesson goals. This needs to be addressed. Ignoring deliberately provocative remarks such as 'This is boring' can help you avoid confrontation. Try to motivate uninterested pupils by linking the work with their interests if possible and ensure the learning is relevant – if you cannot explain to pupils the relevance of the lesson to their current and future lives, then you cannot expect them to be motivated to learn. Ask your experienced colleagues for advice if particular pupils constantly cause you trouble. It is likely that they are also causing some other staff difficulties.

You may be worried that you will be asked a question and you do not know the answer. This is bound to happen. You can admit you do not know – 'What an interesting point, I've not thought of it that way Kate'; 'I just cannot remember at the moment'. It is possible to celebrate the moment:

Table 2.3.2 Backup plans in case pupils finish work quickly

> ■ Have questions prepared relating to the learning objectives/have a class test ready.
> ■ Let the pupils peer-assess each other's work and feed back against the learning objectives.
> ■ Go round and look at pupils' work, give a constructive comment and share this with the class if appropriate.
> ■ Use your lesson objectives and intended learning outcomes to devise questions about the work or get pupils to devise them. For example, devise a quiz related to the lesson; develop a spider diagram for summarising the key points in a topic; produce a mnemonic to aid the recall of key issues.
> ■ Homework (either past or just set) can be discussed in more detail. You may allow the pupils to discuss this together.
> ■ Pupils' existing knowledge on the next topics could be discussed through question and answer. (Learning is more certain where you, as the teacher, build on pupils' existing knowledge and experience.)

'Paul, that is a really good question. Where might we go for an answer to that?' Make arrangements for the answer to be found. The pupil can follow it up for homework, use the library to look for the answer or write to those who might know. You may also be able to find out from other teachers, student teachers or your subject association.

You will always have pupils who are not able to engage with the lesson because they do not have the appropriate equipment. You should aim to get most of the class working so that you can then direct your attention to those who require individual attention. Many schools have systems in place for dealing with pupils' lack of kit and equipment. You need to know what this is so that you follow the school system. It can be less disruptive to your lesson for you simply to supply the missing item for the lesson. But make sure you retrieve what you have loaned and indicate firmly that you expect pupils to provide their own.

You must check equipment in your teaching room beforehand and, in any case, have a backup planned if your lesson is dependent on equipment working, such as information and communications technology software. The more sophisticated your use of technology, the more likely you will encounter technical difficulties. Remember, your backup plan should still allow you to deliver the lesson's intended learning outcomes. Schools have different approaches to dealing with loss and breakage of equipment by pupils. The simple strategy of managing your lesson so that there is sufficient time at the end to check that equipment and books are returned saves you time in the long run. See also Unit 8.3 on health and safety.

Subject content knowledge and pedagogy

To use LOOP, you need to be aware of the importance of subject knowledge and specific pedagogic practices linked to your subject. This means that you must ensure your own personal knowledge of the subject is at a suitable level to teach the learning objectives and intended learning outcomes. You should audit your own subject knowledge and fill in any gaps you may have. It is also important for you to think about how you will remain at the forefront of current thinking in your discipline. You also need to be aware of the current pedagogic practices in your subject and endeavour to model best practice in your classroom.

Overview

In becoming a teacher, you are more vulnerable than when being educated for many other professions as you are exposed to a discerning audience (the class) early on. So much of your performance in the classroom depends on your own personal qualities and your ability to form good relationships with pupils from a wide range of backgrounds (see Unit 1.2). Your performance is analysed and commented on by those who observe your teaching. You are forced to face your own strengths and weaknesses as a result of this scrutiny. This can be stressful, particularly when you may be given apparently conflicting advice from different observers. As you become more experienced and you develop more analytical skills for use in appraising your performance, you should build your self-belief and confidence.

Despite following all of the advice given, it may be that you may have a poor lesson with a class. This does not mean that all lessons with that class will be like that. What it does mean, however, is that you must analyse the situation and put into place strategies for ensuring that the next lesson is better. Incidents will occur that leave you feeling deflated, unsure or angry. Try to adopt a problem-solving reflective approach to your work so that you maintain some objectivity and can learn from any difficult experiences you have. You will have seen from this unit that taking responsibility for the class is challenging and delivering your first lesson can call for all of your resilience. Time and stress management and developing resilience are important issues, and Unit 1.3 is devoted to them.

SUMMARY AND KEY POINTS

■ Your first encounters with the pupils are important in setting the tone for your relationships with them.

■ It is worth carefully considering the image you wish to project in these early lessons.

■ Aim to give an impression that you have created an organised learning environment.

■ Your professional persona as 'the teacher' is something you should create deliberately and not just allow to happen.

■ You should not underestimate the importance of planning your lessons to help reinforce this image.

■ Time invested in understanding and developing the LOOP will help you to develop as a skilled practitioner.

■ Most student teachers have to work on controlling their nerves and developing their self-confidence.

■ Covering the points in Table 2.3.3 in your preparation should prevent some of the difficulties you would otherwise encounter.

Table 2.3.3 Lesson preparations checklist

■ Set clear, simple and measurable learning objectives and intended learning outcomes for the lesson that are likely to be achieved.

■ Plan the lesson carefully and have extension work ready.

■ Obtain pupil lists and know pupils' names.

■ Check the room layout. Are things where you want them? What about safety issues?

■ Know the school, class and lesson routines.

■ Be on time.

■ Prepare resources beforehand.

■ Act as though you are in charge although you probably won't feel that you are.

■ Know the subject you are teaching.

■ Plan the lesson to give a balance between teacher talk and pupil activity.

■ Include a timeline in your lesson plan so that you can check during the lesson how the plan is working. Try not to talk too quickly.

■ Be prepared to manage behaviour and remember that learning should drive behaviour not behaviour drive learning.

■ Visualise yourself being successful.

■ Have a backup plan for the lesson (see Table 2.3.1).

One of the problems you may have will be believing you are indeed a teacher. This is a mental and emotional transition that you need to make. The pupils, parents and staff see you as a teacher, albeit a new one, and expect you to behave as such.

Check which requirements for your ITE programme you have addressed through this unit.

Further reading

Millar, R., Leach, J., Osborne, J. and Ratcliffe, M. (2006) *Improving Subject Teaching*, London: RoutledgeFalmer.
 This text is part of an *Improving Learning* series, and while this one is specifically around science teaching, more texts in the series have been published. They report findings from a major national research initiative into teaching and learning – the Economic and Social Research Council (ESRC)/TLRP programme.

Pease, A. and Pease, B. (2011) *Body Language in the Workplace*, London: Orion.
 This book will give you insights into verbal and non-verbal communication strategies. Further information is on their website and their YouTube videos, available at: www.peaseinternational.com/index.php?route=news/headlines (accessed 18 July 2015).

Westwood, P. (2007) *Commonsense Methods for Children with Special Educational Needs*, 5th edn, London: RoutledgeFalmer.
 Many of the approaches used with pupils with SEN work well with all pupils. This text outlines approaches to effective teaching and provides research to back up different strategies.

 Other resources and websites

Behaviour2Learn: www.behaviour2learn.org.uk
 Review information on this resource to support your work in establishing clear routine and boundaries.

Blamires, M. (ed.) (2014) *Special Educational Needs and Disability: Enabling Pupil Participation MESHGuide*, RIDDLE consultancy, previously Canterbury Christ Church University: www.meshguides.org/category/special-needs-2/enabling-pupil-participation-special-needs-2/
 Review information on this resource to support your work with pupils with different needs.

Burden, K. and Younie, S. (2014) *Using iPads Effectively to Enhance Learning in Schools MESHGuide*, University of Hull and De Montfort University, UK: www.meshguides.org/category/icttechnology/tabletsipad-pedagogy/

Queensland Government (2015) *Attributes of a Good Teacher*: http://education.qld.gov.au/hr/recruitment/teaching/qualities-good-teacher.html

Ofsted (Office for Standards in Education) (2014d) *Inspection Framework*: www.ofsted.gov.uk/resources/framework-for-school-inspection
 This will provide information about expectations in England.

Taylor, C. (2011) *Getting the Simple Things Right: Charlie Taylor's Behaviour Checklists*: www.gov.uk/government/uploads/system/uploads/attachment_data/file/283997/charlie_taylor_checklist.pdf

Underwood, A., Turner, R., Whyte, S. and Rosenberg, J. (2015) *Acoustic Accessibility MESHGuide*, BATOD Foundation, available at: www.meshguides.org/category/general-pedagogy/acoustics-listening-and-learning/

YouTube Teachers (www.youtube.com/user/teachers) and the Khan Academy (www.khanacademy.org/)
 Both have short videos explaining core concepts for many subjects.

Appendix 2 on pages 591–595 provides further examples of websites you may find useful.

Capel, S., Leask, M. and Turner, T. (eds) (2010) *Readings for Learning to Teach in the Secondary School: A Companion to M Level Study*, London: Routledge.
 This book brings together essential readings to support you in your critical engagement with key issues raised in this textbook.

The subject-specific books in the *Learning to Teach* series extend the information in this unit.

> Any additional resources and an editable version of any relevant tasks/tables in this unit are available on the companion website: www.routledge.com/cw/capel

3 Classroom interactions and managing pupils

Effective classroom interactions and management are essential to effective learning. Classroom interactions are those with (and between) pupils (and others) in the classroom to support learning. Classroom management refers to arrangements made by the teacher to establish and maintain an environment in which learning can occur; for example, effective organisation and presentation of lessons so that pupils are actively engaged in learning. Classroom management skills and techniques are addressed throughout this book in a number of different chapters and units. This chapter includes units about different aspects of classroom management related to interacting with pupils. Together, they give an insight into the complex relationships that are developed between teachers and pupils, and emphasise the need for well-developed skills and techniques that you can adapt appropriately to the demands of the situation. They reinforce the fact that although you must plan your lessons thoroughly, not everything you do in the classroom can be planned in advance, as you cannot predict how pupils will react in any situation on any given day.

One commonality of teachers from whom we have learned a lot is their ability to communicate effectively with pupils to enhance their knowledge, skills and understanding. Most of us tend to think we communicate well. However, communication is a complex process. Unit 3.1 is designed to help you communicate effectively in the classroom. The unit looks first at verbal communication, including gaining pupils' attention, using your voice and the language you use. It then considers types of communication, including explaining, questioning, discussion and active listening. Aspects of non-verbal communication are then considered, including showing enthusiasm, confidence and caring, and your appearance, gesture, posture, facial expression and mannerisms, particularly in relation to how you present yourself as a teacher.

Some pupils are motivated to learn and maintain that motivation; others are inherently motivated to learn but various factors result in them losing motivation; others may not be inherently motivated to learn but their motivation can be increased. A study of motivation therefore is crucial to give you some knowledge and insight into how you can create a motivational climate that helps to stimulate pupils to learn. Unit 3.2 looks at what motivation is, presents a number of theories of motivation and considers how these can inform your teaching and pupils' learning. It looks at the motivational learning environment in your classes and how this influences pupil motivation. It also looks at using performance profiling to enhance motivation. Finally, some specific factors that influence pupils' motivation to learn (for example, personal achievement (success), rewards, including the use of praise, punishment and feedback) are discussed.

We recognise student teachers' concerns about managing behaviour and misbehaviour. Unit 3.3 looks at adopting a positive approach to behaviour that focuses on positive relationships with pupils and a positive classroom climate in which all pupils can learn effectively. This approach is more consistent with an inclusive schooling approach. Thus, the focus of the unit is on preventing misbehaviour as far as possible rather than on a reactive approach that focuses on 'discipline' for misbehaviour. The unit starts by giving a brief overview of the policy context for promoting learning in the classroom. It then interrogates the term 'unacceptable' behaviour in order to help you understand the significance of its underlying causes. The unit then looks at factors that may cause unacceptable behaviour and then at the key principles of a behaviour for learning approach, which highlights the importance of getting the simple things right, building positive relationships in the classroom, structuring your lessons to promote positive behaviour, and rights, responsibilities, routines and rules in the classroom. It also highlights the importance of pupils knowing the consequences of sensible or inadvisable choices.

The final unit in this chapter, Unit 3.4, focuses on the transition between primary and secondary schools, recognising that this is only one of the many transitions pupils experience as they go through compulsory schooling. It considers conceptualisations of educational transitions and their impact on planning and preparation, focusing on a maturational and interactionist approach, whether this transition is a one-off event or ongoing event, and academic and life transitions. It highlights issues related to the primary-secondary transition, before considering theoretical perspectives that inform our understanding of transition, considering resilience, self-esteem and emotional intelligence theories. It then provides examples of planning and preparation for primary-secondary transition – focusing on administrative; social/user-friendly; curriculum; teaching and learning; and managing learning aspects of transition. Finally, it looks at what seems to work for pupils.

3.1 Communicating with pupils

Paula Zwozdiak-Myers and Susan Capel

Introduction

We can all think of people who really understand their subject but cannot communicate it to others. Effective teachers all have in common the ability to communicate effectively with pupils.

Communication is a complex two-way process involving the mutual exchange of information and ideas that can be written, verbal and non-verbal. Clear and effective communication includes not only delivering, but also receiving, information, which involves listening, observation and sensitivity. The quality of communication between pupil and pupil in lessons can enhance or hinder learning. Pupils can learn from communicating with each other; for example, through discussion or by talking about a task. Equally, such communication can be irrelevant to, and interfere with the progress of, the lesson, therefore detracting from pupils' learning. However, the focus of this unit is the quality of communication between a teacher and pupils, which is critical to effective learning.

Most of us tend to think we communicate well. However, when we study our communication skills systematically, most of us can find room for improvement. You cannot predict how pupils will react to an activity, a conversation or a question asked. Your verbal and non-verbal responses in any classroom situation will influence the immediate and, possibly, long-term relationship you establish with the class. In order to respond appropriately, you need well-developed communication skills combined with awareness and sensitivity to the diverse needs, experience and level of understanding of your pupils.

We first consider aspects of verbal communication, including using your voice (volume, projection, pitch, speed, tone, clarity and expressiveness), the language you use and the importance of active listening. We then consider aspects of non-verbal communication (for example, appearance, gesture, posture, facial expression and mannerisms), particularly in relation to how you present yourself as a teacher. Further aspects of communication are addressed in Unit 5.2.

OBJECTIVES

At the end of this unit, you should be able to:

■ appreciate the importance of effective verbal and non-verbal communication skills;
■ vary your voice consciously to enhance your teaching and pupils' learning;
■ appraise your use of language and use questioning more effectively as a teaching and learning tool;
■ understand the relationship between verbal and non-verbal communication;
■ gain awareness and control over your own self-presentation in order to present yourself effectively.

Check the requirements for your initial teacher education (ITE) programme to see which relate to this unit.

Verbal communication

Gaining attention

You need to establish procedures for gaining pupils' attention at the beginning of a lesson and also when you want the class to listen again after they have started an activity. This latter skill is especially important if there is a safety risk in the activity. Before you start talking to a class, make sure that all pupils can see and hear you, that you have silence and they are paying attention. To initiate and sustain group attention, it may help to stand at the front of the room: 'a centre-front position, facing the class group, standing relaxed and scanning the faces of the students while cueing for attention will normally (and positively) signal the teacher's readiness and expectation' (Rogers 2011: 58). Establish a means of getting silence (for example, say 'quiet please', raise your hand, blow a whistle in physical education or bang on a drum in music), and use this technique with the class each time to ensure consistency of approach. Wait for quiet and do not speak until there is silence. Once you are talking, do not move around. This distracts pupils, who may pay more attention to the movement than to what you are saying.

Using your voice

A teacher's voice is a crucial element in classroom communication. It is like a musical instrument, and if you play it well, then your pupils will be an appreciative and responsive audience. Some people have voices that naturally are easier to listen to than others. Certain qualities are fixed and give your voice its unique character. However, you can alter the volume, projection, pitch, speed, tone, clarity and expressiveness of your voice to use it more effectively and lend impact to what you say. These verbal dynamics are important elements of paralanguage, and your voice, if sensitively tuned, can become a powerful agent of expression and communication.

The most obvious way you can vary your voice is by altering the *volume*. It is useful to have the whole volume range available, from quiet to very loud, but it is rarely a good thing to be loud when it is not needed. Loud teachers have loud classes. If you shout too much, you may get into the habit of shouting all the time – sometimes people know somebody is a teacher because of their loud voice. Also, if you shout too much, you may lose your voice every September! Of course, you have to be heard, but this is done by projection more than by volume. (If you do have voice problems, see the advice at the end of the unit. Low-cost voice projection equipment is available.)

You *project* your voice by making sure it leaves your mouth confidently and precisely. This needs careful enunciation and breath control. If your voice is projected well, you are able to make a whisper audible at some distance. Equally, good projection brings considerable volume to your ordinary voice without resort to shouting or roaring.

Each group of words spoken has its own 'tune' that contributes to the meaning. A person may have a naturally high or low voice but everybody can vary the 'natural' *pitch* with no pain. Generally speaking, deep voices sound more serious and significant; high voices sound more exciting and lively. To add weight to what is being said, the pitch should be dropped; to lighten the tune, the pitch should be raised. A voice with a lower pitch can create a sense of importance as it comes across as more authoritative and confident than a high-pitched voice. It can also be raised more easily to command attention, whereas raising a naturally high-pitched voice may result in something similar to a squeak, which does not carry the same weight.

Speed variations give contrast to delivery. You can use pause to good effect. It shows confidence if you can hold a silence before making a point or answering a question. Having achieved silence, do not shout into it. Equally, have the patience to wait for a pupil to respond. Research (for example, Muijs and Reynolds 2011: 59) suggests that 'three seconds or slightly longer is the optimal wait-time' for a closed, lower-level factual recall question, whereas a longer wait-time (up to 15 seconds) is required for 'open-ended, higher-level questions'. Speaking quickly can be a valuable skill on occasion; however, this needs concentration and careful enunciation.

To use your voice effectively, these factors need to work together. For instance, you do not communicate effectively if the pitch of your voice is right, but you are not enunciating clearly or the volume is wrong; for example, you are shouting at a group, or pupils at the back cannot hear what you are saying. It is also important to put feeling into what you say to engage pupils so that your voice does not sound dull and monotonous. Often, pupils respond to *how* you say something rather than *what* you say. If you are praising a pupil, sound pleased, and if you are disciplining a pupil, sound firm. If you deliver all talk in the same way without varying the verbal dynamics, do not be surprised if pupil response is undifferentiated since the intended meaning behind the message may not be readily understood. Now complete Task 3.1.1.

 Task 3.1.1 The quality of your voice

Record your voice either reading from a book or a newspaper, or in a natural monologue or conversation. Listen to the recording with a friend or another student teacher. If you have not heard yourself before, the experience may be a little shocking! Your voice may sound different from the way you hear it, and a common response is to blame the recording equipment. This is probably not at fault. Remember that normally, you hear your voice coming back from the soft tissue and bone in your head. Most of your audience hear it coming forward. As you become used to listening to yourself, try to pick out the good points of your voice. Is it clear? Is it expressive? Is the basic pitch pleasant? When you have built up your confidence, consider areas for improvement. Do you normally speak too fast? Is the tone monotonous?

Repeat the task, but this time trying to vary your voice. For example, try reading at your normal speed, then faster, then as quickly as you can. Remember to start each word precisely and to concentrate on what you are saying. Then try varying the pitch of your voice. You will be surprised at how easy it is. Ask another student teacher to listen to the tape with you, comment on any differences and provide helpful advice for improving. Try these out in your teaching and store in your professional development portfolio (PDP) for future reference/ experimentation.

Language of the teacher

Teaching involves communicating with pupils from a variety of backgrounds and with different needs. To effectively support pupils with English as an additional language (EAL), for example, requires specialist knowledge and skill for teaching within the mainstream context in a way that promotes language learning alongside content learning. The learning of English for pupils with EAL takes place as much in the arts, humanities, mathematics and science as it does in the 'subject' of English, as well as the 'hidden curriculum', which implies that all teachers are teachers of language.

In order to develop pupils' language skills, a teacher's language must be accessible (see Unit 5.8 for detailed advice). There is no point in talking to pupils in language they do not understand. That does not mean subject-specific vocabulary cannot be introduced, but rather that you gradually introduce your class to the language of the subject. To do this, you must not assume that everybody knows the words or constructions that you do, including simple connecting phrases; for example, 'in order to', 'so that', 'tends to', 'keep in proportion', and so on. Start with a simple direct language that makes no assumptions.

It is easier for pupils to understand a new concept if you make comparisons or use examples, metaphors or references to which they can relate. Where appropriate, use a variety of words or explanations that ensure the meaning of what you intend to convey is understood by all pupils. As a teacher, your language must be concise. When you are speaking, you stress or repeat important words or phrases. Placing an accent on certain syllables of the words you use gives rise to rhythmic patterns that affect the meaning of your message. These are important techniques in teaching. If they help learning, repetition, accentuation and elaboration are valuable, but filling silence with teacher talk is generally unproductive. You take longer to deliver the same information and pupils' time may not be used most effectively. However, it is generally accepted that pupils understand something and learn it better if they hear it a number of times and if it is explained in different ways. A commonly used phrase to explain this is:

■ tell them what you are going to tell them;
■ tell them;
■ then tell them again what you have told them.

Task 3.1.2 focuses on the language of your subject.

Task 3.1.2 The language of your subject

Compile a list of specialist words and phrases used in your subject or in a particular topic that you may be teaching. How many of these might be in the normal vocabulary of an average pupil at your school? In your lesson planning, how might you introduce and explain these words and phrases? How might you allow pupils opportunities to practise their use of the words in the lesson? Tape a lesson that you are teaching, then replay the tape and consider your use of language, including words and phrases identified above. It can be particularly helpful to listen to this with a student teacher learning to teach another subject who does not have the same subject knowledge and language, and who therefore may be nearer to pupils' experience of the subject. How might you improve your use of language in future lessons? Record your responses in your PDP.

As well as conveying content, a teacher's language is also used to create and develop interpersonal relationships with individual pupils that make them more interested and motivated in learning. Using pupils' names, 'saying something positive to every pupil individually over a period of time and thanking pupils at the end of a good lesson' (DfES 2004c: 18), showing interest in their lives outside the classroom, valuing their experience, are all important in building mutual respect and creating a positive atmosphere for classroom learning (see also Unit 3.2).

Teachers also use language to impose discipline. Often, negative terms are used for this. This is not inevitable, and a positive approach may have more success (see also Unit 3.3). For example, can you suggest a constructive activity rather than condemning a destructive one? Could earlier praise or suggestion have made later criticism unnecessary? Hughes and Vass (2001) provide guidance on types of language that teachers can use to positively enhance pupils' motivation and learning, and Rogers (2011) unpacks the complex, dynamic relationship between language and behaviour management, particularly in relation to effective communication with challenging pupils and pupils with emotional and behavioural difficulties (see also Units 3.2, 3.3 and 5.8).

Types of communication

There are many different ways in which verbal communication is used in teaching. Explaining, modelling, demonstrating, questioning and discussion are core pedagogical tools for teachers and are briefly considered below.

Explaining, modelling and demonstrating

Teachers spend a lot of time explaining to pupils. In some teaching situations, it can be the main form of activity in the lesson, thus being able to explain something effectively is an important skill to acquire. Pupils learn better if they are actively engaged in the learning process and a good explanation actively engages pupils, and therefore is able to gain and maintain their attention. You must plan to involve pupils; for example, mix an explanation with tasks, activities or questions, rather than relying on long lectures, dictating notes or working something out on the board (see also Unit 5.2).

Explaining provides information about what, why and how. It describes new terms or concepts or clarifies their meaning. Pupils expect teachers to explain things clearly and become frustrated when they cannot understand an explanation. A good explanation is clear and well structured. It takes account of pupils' previous knowledge and understanding, uses language that pupils can understand, and relates new work to concepts, interests or work already familiar to the pupils. Use of analogy or metaphor can also help an explanation.

Table 3.1.1 identifies some key characteristic features of effective explanations. You might find this checklist and the sample questions useful when analysing and reviewing both your own and another student teacher's explanations.

Teachers often reinforce verbal explanations by providing pupils with a visual prompt, demonstration or model. Modelling is an effective learning strategy that allows pupils to ask

Table 3.1.1 Characteristic features of effective explanations

Characteristic feature	Sample question to ask yourself
Clear structure	Is the explanation structured in a logical way showing how each part links together?
Key features identified	What are the key points or essential elements that pupils should understand?
Dynamic opening	What is the 'tease' or 'hook' that is used at the start?
Clarity – using voice and body	Can the voice or body be used in any way to emphasise or embellish certain points?
Signposts	Are there clear linguistic signposts to help pupils follow the sequence and understand which are the key points?
Examples and non-examples	Are there sufficient examples and non-examples to aid pupils' understanding of a concept?
Models and analogies	What models might help pupils understand an abstract idea? Are there any analogies you could use? Will pupils understand the analogy? How might you help pupils identify the strengths and weaknesses of the analogy?
Props	What concrete and visual aids can be used to help pupils understand more?
Questions	Are there opportunities to check for pupils' understanding at various points, and to note and act on any misconceptions or misunderstandings? Are there opportunities for pupils to rehearse their understanding?
Connections to pupils' experience	Are there opportunities, particularly at the start, to check pupils' prior knowledge of the subject and to link to their everyday experiences?
Repetition	Are there a number of distinct moments in the explanation when the key points that should be learned are repeated and emphasised?
Humour	When and how might it be appropriate to use humour?

Source: DfES (2004d: 11)

questions about and hear explanations related to each stage of the process as it happens, since the teacher can:

■ 'think aloud', making apparent and explicit those skills, decisions, processes and procedures that would otherwise be hidden or unclear;
■ expose pupils to the possible pitfalls of the task in hand, showing how to avoid them;
■ demonstrate to pupils that they can make alterations and corrections as part of the process;
■ warn pupils about possible hazards involved in practical activities, how to avoid them or minimise the effects if they occur.

(DfES 2004e: 3)

Showing learners what to do while talking them through the activity and linking new learning to old through questions, resources, activities and language is sometimes referred to as scaffolding (see Unit 5.1). The idea is that:

[L]earners are supported in carrying out a task by the use of language to guide their action. The next stage in scaffolding is for the learner to talk themselves through the task. Then that talk can, in turn, become an internalised guide to the action and thought of the learner.

(Dillon and Maguire 2001: 145-6)

Combining verbal and visual explanations can be more effective than using verbal explanations exclusively, particularly with pupils whose dominant learning style is visual (see Units 5.1 and 5.3), who are learning EAL or have special educational needs and/or disabilities (see Unit 4.6).

Questioning

One technique in the scaffolding process for actively engaging pupils in their learning is questioning. Teachers use a lot of questions; indeed, 'every day teachers ask dozens, even hundreds of questions, thousands in a single year, over a million during a professional lifetime' (Wragg and Brown 2001: 1).

Asking questions effectively

Effective use of questioning is a valuable part of interactive teaching. However, if not handled effectively, pupils misunderstand and/or become confused. To use questioning effectively in your lessons requires planning (see Unit 2.2 on lesson planning), as you will need to consider:

■ what type of question(s) you are going to ask;
■ how you are going to ask the question(s);
■ when you are going to ask the question(s);
■ why you are asking the question(s);
■ of whom you are going to ask a question, how you expect the question answered, how you are going to respond if the pupil does not understand the question or gives an inappropriate answer, and how long you are going to wait for an answer.

However, you cannot plan your questioning too rigidly and follow a preset agenda, as this may result in pupils asking fewer questions themselves, producing undeveloped responses, rarely discussing ideas with their peers, presenting few thoughts of their own or demonstrating confusion. You must exercise flexibility and adapt your plan during the lesson to take account of the development of the lesson.

Asking questions is not a simple process. Questions are asked for many reasons; for example, to gain pupils' attention or check that they are paying attention, to check understanding of an instruction or explanation, to reinforce or revise a topic, to deepen understanding, to encourage thinking and problem-solving, or to develop a discussion. Wragg and Brown (2001: 16–17) classified the content of questions related to learning a particular subject, rather than procedural issues, as one of three types: *empirical questions* requiring answers based on facts or on experimental findings; *conceptual questions* concerned with eliciting ideas, definitions and reasoning in the subject being studied; and *value questions* investigating relative worth and merit, moral and environmental issues. These broad categories often overlap, and some questions may involve elements of all three types of question. Consider also the time that a teacher gives, after a question, for pupils to reply. Allowing thinking time is an important aspect of questioning.

Another classification that can be used to help you plan questions with specific purposes in mind is Bloom's (1956) taxonomy of cognitive objectives, through which questions can be arranged into six levels of complexity and abstraction. Lower-level questions usually demand factual, descriptive answers, whereas higher-level questions are more complex and require more sophisticated critical thinking from pupils. Research indicates that pupils' cognitive abilities and levels of achievement can be increased when they are challenged and have regular access to higher-order thinking (Black and Wiliam 2002; Fisher 2009; Muijs and Reynolds 2011). Table 3.1.2 links the hierarchical levels in Bloom's taxonomy with what pupils might be expected to do and the types of question that would help them to realise those tasks. Examples of possible question stems you could draw upon when planning questions to ask pupils in your lessons are provided for each cognitive objective.

There are a number of other ways in which questions can be categorised.

Closed and open questions

The most common reason for asking questions is to check that pupils have learned what they are supposed to have learned or memorised certain facts or pieces of information. These are questions such as: What is the capital of Borneo? What is Archimedes' Principle? How many furlongs are there in a mile? What does the Latin expression 'Veni, vidi, vici' mean, who first used it and when? How do you spell 'loquacious'? These are called *closed* questions. There is only one correct answer, which limits the scope of the response. The pupil either knows the answer or not; no real thought is required. Closed questions might be given to the whole class, with answers coming instantaneously. A short closed question-answer session might be used to reinforce learning, refresh pupils' memories or provide a link to new work.

Conversely, *open* questions broaden the scope for response since they have several possible answers and it may be impossible to know whether an answer is 'correct'. These questions are often used to stimulate thinking and learning and challenge pupils' capacity to frame ideas in words. Examples of open questions are: How could we reduce our carbon footprint? Should Western governments intervene in Middle Eastern politics? What words might you use to describe the Olympics? What do we know about the 'Big Bang' theory?

Table 3.1.2 Linking Bloom's (1956) taxonomy to what pupils need to do, thinking processes and possible question stems

Cognitive objective	What pupils need to do	Use of questioning to develop higher-order thinking skills	Links to thinking	Possible question stems
Knowledge	Define Recall Describe Label Identify Match	To help pupils link aspects of existing knowledge or relevant information to the task ahead.	Pupils are more likely to retain information if it is needed for a specific task and linked to other relevant information. Do your questions in this area allow pupils to link aspects of knowledge necessary for the task?	Describe what you see . . . What is the name for . . .? What is the best one . . .? Where in the book would you find . . .? What are the types of graph . . .? What are we looking for? Where is this set?
Compre-hension	Explain Translate Illustrate Summarise Extend	To help pupils to process their existing knowledge.	Comprehension questions require pupils to process the knowledge they already have in order to answer the question. They demand a higher level of thinking and information processing than do knowledge questions.	How do you think . . .? Why do you think . . .? What might this mean . . .? Explain what a spread-sheet does . . . What are the key features . . .? Explain your model . . . What is shown about . . .? What happens when . . .? What word represents . . .?
Application	Apply to a new context Demonstrate Predict Employ Solve Use	To help pupils use their knowledge to solve a new problem or apply it to a new situation.	Questions in this area require pupils to use their existing knowledge and understanding to solve a new problem or to make sense of a new context. They demand more complex thinking. Pupils are more likely to be able to apply knowledge to a new context if it is not too far removed from the context with which they are familiar.	What shape of graph are you expecting? What do you think will happen? . . . Why? Where else might this be useful? How can you use a spreadsheet to . . .? Can you apply what you now know to solve . . .? What does this suggest to you? How does the writer do this? What would the next line of my modelled answer be?

Table 3.1.2 continued

Cognitive objective	What pupils need to do	Use of questioning to develop higher-order thinking skills	Links to thinking	Possible question stems
Analysis	Analyse Infer Relate Support Break down Differentiate Explore	To help pupils use the process of enquiry to break down what they know and reassemble it.	Analysis questions require pupils to break down what they know and reassemble it to help them solve a problem. These questions are linked to more abstract, conceptual thought that is central to the process of enquiry.	Separate . . . (for example, fact from opinion) What is the function of . . .? What assumptions are being made . . .? What is the evidence . . .? State the point of view . . . Make a distinction . . . What is this really saying? What does this symbolise? So, what is the poet saying to us?
Synthesis	Design Create Compose Reorganise Combine	To help pupils combine and select from available knowledge in order to respond to unfamiliar situations.	Synthesis questions demand that pupils combine and select from available knowledge to respond to unfamiliar situations or solve new problems. There is likely to be a great diversity of responses.	Propose an alternative . . . What conclusion can you draw . . .? How else would you . . .? State a rule . . . How do the writers differ in their response to . . .? What happens at the beginning of the poem and how does it change?
Evaluation	Assess Evaluate Appraise Defend Justify	To help pupils compare and contrast knowledge gained from different perspectives as they construct and reflect upon their own viewpoints.	Evaluation questions expect pupils to use their knowledge to form judgements and defend the positions they take up. They demand complex thinking and reasoning.	Which is more important/ moral/logical . . .? What inconsistencies are there in . . .? What errors are there . . .? Why is . . . valid? How can you defend . . .? Why is the order important? Why does it change?

Source: Adapted from DfES (2004f: 13–14)

These questions are much more complex than closed questions. They are designed to extend pupils' understanding of a topic. To answer them, the respondent has to think and manipulate information by reasoning or applying information and using knowledge, logic, creativity and imagination. Open questions cannot usually be answered quickly as pupils need time to gather information, sift evidence, advance hypotheses, discuss ideas and plan their answers.

An example from a science lesson shows the difference in purpose between closed and open questions. 'What is the chemical formula of carbon dioxide?' is a closed question requiring factual knowledge, whereas 'How does carbon combine with oxygen during the respiration process?' requires understanding. Further, a question such as 'Do you think that reducing our carbon footprint can slow down global warming?' requires a deeper level of reflection and research by pupils.

You can ask closed or open questions or a combination of the two as *a series of questions*. The questions in the series can start with a few relatively easy closed questions and then move on to more complex open questions. A series of questions takes time to build up if they are to be an integral part of the learning process. They must therefore be planned as an integral part of the lesson, not as a time-filler at the end of a lesson where their effect is lost. Questions at the end of the lesson are much more likely to be closed-recall questions to help pupils remember what they have been taught in the lesson. There are implications for assessment of closed and open questions (see also Unit 6.1).

There are other aspects of questioning that are important to consider. Questions can be asked to the whole class, to groups, or to specific named individuals. Questions can be spoken, written on (an electronic) whiteboard, or given out on printed sheets. Answers can be given at once or produced after deliberation, either spoken or written. For example, you may set a series of questions for homework and either collect the answers in to mark or go through them verbally with the class at the start of the next lesson.

Effective questioning requires you to be able to ask clear, appropriate questions, use pauses to allow pupils to think about an answer before responding and use prompting to help pupils who are having problems in answering a question. Some key tactics identified by Wragg and Brown (2001: 28) for asking questions include: structuring; pitching and putting clearly; directing and distributing; pausing and pacing; prompting and pacing; listening and responding to replies; and sequencing. Muijs and Reynolds (2011: 58) identify three types of prompts to help pupils answer questions: *verbal prompts* (cues, reminders, instructions, tips, references to previous lessons or giving part of a sentence for pupils to complete); *gestural prompts* (pointing to an object or modelling a particular behaviour); and *physical prompts* (guiding pupils explicitly through motor skills).

Follow-up questions can be used to: probe further; encourage pupils to develop their answers; extend their thinking; change the direction of the questioning; and distribute questions to involve the whole class. Non-verbal aspects of communication such as eye contact, gesture, body language, tone of voice, humour, smiles and frowns are important in effective questioning because they go with the words that are used.

Common pitfalls or 'errors' in student teachers' use of questioning, as identified by Wragg and Brown (2001: 28), include:

■   asking too many questions at once;
■   asking a question and answering it yourself;
■   asking questions only of the brightest or most likeable pupils;
■   asking a difficult question too early in the sequence of events;
■   asking irrelevant questions;
■   always asking the same types of questions (for example, closed ones);
■   asking questions in a threatening way;
■   not indicating a change in the type of question;
■   not using probing questions;

- not giving pupils the time to think;
- not correcting wrong answers;
- ignoring pupils' answers;
- failing to see the implications of pupils' answers;
- failing to build on answers.

Errors of presentation (for example, not looking at pupils when asking a question, talking too fast, at the wrong volume or not being clear) are common errors and commonly detected (Wragg 1984). The second most common type of error is the way student teachers handle responses to questions; for example, they only accept the answer(s) to open-ended questions that they want or expect. Open questions are likely to prompt a range of responses that may be valid but not correspond to the answer expected: avoid the guessing game type of question-and-answer session where you have a fixed answer in mind as pupils then spend their time guessing what the teacher wants.

Other errors identified in this study were pupils not knowing why particular questions were being asked, pupils not being given enough background information to enable them to answer questions, teachers asking questions in a disjointed fashion rather than a logical sequence, jumping from one question to another without linking them together and focusing on a small group of pupils and ignoring the rest of the class. Student teachers tended to focus on those pupils sitting in a V-shaped wedge in the middle of the room.

Some aspects of questioning were not identified as common errors; for example, whether the vocabulary is appropriate for the pupils' level of understanding. Check that your questions are not too long, complex or ambiguous.

You can encourage pupils to actively participate in questioning by listening and responding appropriately to answers, praising good answers, being supportive and respecting answers and not making pupils feel they will be ridiculed if they answer a question incorrectly (see also Units 3.2, 5.2 and 5.5).

Discussion

Questioning may lead naturally into discussion to explore a topic further. Although pupils generally have more control over the material included in, and direction of, a discussion than in many teaching situations, the teacher is still in charge. Discussion should be planned. Seating arrangements and pupil grouping help develop a less structured atmosphere, which can encourage as many pupils as possible to contribute. Plan how you are going to stimulate the discussion and how you are going to respond if a discussion drifts off its main theme. By interjecting suggestions or key questions you can keep a discussion on the topic.

> For a fruitful discussion which allows pupils some significant say over what is discussed, while at the same time covering the ground that teachers judge to be important, it is best to think of questions that may be perplexing, intriguing or even puzzling to pupils. Skilfully chosen encouraging, broad questions are often effective in sparking off animated conversations. The process may begin with recall questions to extend and activate knowledge and then thought questions to lift the discussion.
>
> (Wragg and Brown 2001: 44)

To maximise pupils' learning through discussion you need to be able to chair a discussion effectively. Before you use discussion in your classes, it is wise to observe another teacher use this technique in their teaching. See also Unit 4.5 and the appendix to Unit 4.5, 'Handling discussion with classes'.

Active listening

Listening is not the same as hearing. For effective communication, *being able to actively listen and take account of the response* (for example, what pupils are communicating to you) is as important as being able to send the message effectively. Learn to recognise and be sensitive to whether or not a message has been received correctly by a pupil; for example, you get a bewildered look or an inappropriate answer to a question. Be able to react appropriately; for example, repeat the same question or rephrase it. However, also reflect on why the communication was not effective; for example, was the pupil not listening to you? If so, why? For example, had the pupil 'switched off' in a boring lesson or was the question worded inappropriately? Do not assume that pupils have your grasp of meaning and vocabulary (see 'Language of the teacher' above). It is all too easy to blame a pupil for not listening attentively, but it may be that you had a large part to play in the breakdown of the communication.

Wragg and Brown (2001: 34) identify four types of listening:

> *Skim listening* – little more than awareness that a pupil is talking (often when the answer seems irrelevant); *Survey listening* – trying to build a wider mental map of what the pupil is talking about; *Search listening* – actively searching for specific information in an answer; *Study listening* – a blend of survey and search listening to identify the underlying meaning and uncertainties of the words the pupil is using.

It is too easy to ask a question and then 'switch off' while an answer is being given, to think about the next question or next part of the lesson. This lack of interest conveys itself to the pupil. It is distracting to the pupil to know that the teacher is neither listening nor responding to what is being said. Also, you may convey boredom or indifference, which has a negative impact on the tone of the lesson. Effective listening is an active process, with a range of non-verbal and verbal responses that convey the message to the pupil speaking that you are listening to what is being said. Effective listening is associated with conveying enthusiasm and generating interest, by providing reinforcement and constructive feedback to pupils. These include looking alert, looking at the pupil who is talking to you, smiling, nodding and making verbal signals to show you have received and understood the message, or to encourage the pupil to continue, saying, for example, 'yes', 'I see what you mean', 'go on', 'oh dear', 'mmmm', 'uh-huh'.

Non-verbal communication

When we communicate, non-verbal cues can have as great an impact on the listener as the spoken word. Much teacher-pupil communication is non-verbal (for example, your appearance, gestures, posture, facial expression and mannerisms). Non-verbal communication supports or detracts from verbal communication, depending on whether or not verbal and non-verbal signals match each other;

for example, if you are praising someone and smiling and looking pleased or reprimanding them and looking stern and sounding firm, you are sending a consistent message and are perceived as sincere. On the other hand, if you are smiling when reprimanding someone or looking bored when praising someone, you are sending conflicting messages that cause confusion and misunderstanding. As Robertson (1996: 94) cautions, 'When non-verbal behaviour is not reinforcing meaning . . . it communicates instead the speaker's lack of involvement. Rather than being the message about the message, it becomes the message about the messenger.'

However, non-verbal communication can also have a considerable impact without any verbal communication; for example, looking at a pupil slightly longer than you would normally communicates your awareness that they are talking or misbehaving. This may be sufficient to gain the pupil's attention. You can indicate your enthusiasm for a topic by the way you use gestures. You can probably think of a teacher who stands at the front of the class leaning against the board with arms crossed waiting for silence, the teacher marching down between the desks to tell someone off or the teacher who sits and listens attentively to the problems of a particular pupil. The meaning of the communication is clear and there is no need to say anything, thus demonstrating that our actions can speak as loudly, if not more loudly, than our words. This illustrates that non-verbal signals are important for good communication, classroom management and control.

Effective communication therefore relies not only on appropriate content, but also on the way it is presented. Mehrabian (1972) found that 93 per cent of the meaning behind verbal messages was received through non-verbal channels: notably, 55 per cent through gesture; 38 per cent through tone of voice; and 7 per cent from the words actually used.

Presenting yourself effectively

There might seem to be some contradiction in discussing ways of presenting yourself as it could indicate that there is a correct way to present yourself as a teacher. However, the heading clearly refers to you as an individual, with your own unique set of characteristics. Herein lies one of the keys to effective teacher self-presentation: while there are some common constituents and expectations, it is also the case that every teacher is an individual and brings something of their own unique personality to the job.

Initial impressions are important, and the way you present yourself to a class on first meeting can influence their learning over a period of time. Having prepared the lesson appropriately, the pupils' impressions of the lesson, and also of you, are important. Part of the impression created relates to your appearance and pupils do 'value adults' in school who take pride in their appearance and who are well dressed (Sage 2000). Pupils expect all teachers to wear clothes that are clean, neat and tidy, and certain teachers to wear certain types of clothes; for example, it is acceptable for a physical education teacher to wear a tracksuit but not a history teacher. Thus, first impressions have as much to do with non-verbal as with verbal communication, although both are important considerations.

How teachers follow up the first impression is equally important; for example, whether you treat pupils as individuals, how you communicate with pupils, whether you have any mannerisms such as constantly flicking a piece of hair out of your eyes or saying 'er' or 'OK' – which reduce or prevent effective communication (pupils tend to focus on any mannerism rather than on what is being said and they may even count the number of times you do it!). It is generally agreed that effective teaching depends on and is enhanced by self-presentation that is *enthusiastic*, *confident* and *caring*. Why are these attributes important? How can you work towards making these attributes part of your self-presentation as a teacher?

Enthusiasm

Before many pupils will make an effort to get to grips with something new, the teacher needs to 'sell' it to them as something interesting and worthwhile. However, your enthusiasm should be sustained throughout a lesson, and in relation to each activity – not only when you are presenting material, but also when you are commenting on a pupil's work, particularly perhaps when a pupil has persevered or achieved a goal.

Your enthusiasm for your subject is infectious. However, there could be a danger of 'going over the top' when showing enthusiasm. If you are overexcited, it can give a sense of triviality, so the enthusiasm has to be measured.

There are perhaps three principal ways in which you can communicate enthusiasm both verbally and non-verbally. The first is via *facial expression*:

> An enthusiastic speaker will be producing a stream of facial expressions which convey his excitement, disbelief, surprise or amusement about his message. Some expressions are extremely brief, lasting about one fifth of a second and may highlight a particular word, whereas others last much longer, perhaps accompanying the verbal expression of an idea. The overall effect is to provide a running commentary for the listener on how the speaker feels about the ideas expressed. In contrast, a speaker who is not involved in his subject shows little variation in facial expression. The impression conveyed is that the ideas are brought out automatically and are failing even to capture the attention of the speaker.
>
> (Robertson 1996: 86)

The second way is via the *use of your voice*. The manner in which you speak as a teacher gives a clear indication of how you feel about the topic under debate and is readily picked up by pupils. Your voice needs to be varied and to indicate your feelings about what you are teaching. As you are engaged in something akin to a 'selling job', your voice has to show this in its production and delivery – it has to be persuasive and occasionally show a measure of excitement. A monotone voice is hardly likely to convey enthusiasm as 'Enthusiastic teachers are alive in the room; they show surprise, suspense, joy, and other feelings in their voices and they make material interesting by relating it to their experiences and showing that they themselves are interested in it' (Good and Brophy 2007: 385).

A third way to convey enthusiasm is via your *poise and movement*. An enthusiastic speaker has an alert, open posture and accompanies speech with appropriately expressive hand and arm gestures – sometimes to emphasise a point, at other times to reinforce something that is being described through indicating relevant shape or direction; for example, an arrangement of apparatus or a tactical move in hockey. If you are enthusiastic, you are committed and involved, and all aspects of your posture and movement should display this.

Think back to teachers you have worked with and identify some whose enthusiasm for their subject really influenced your learning. How did these teachers convey their enthusiasm? How do you convey your enthusiasm? To what extent does poise and movement reflect people's attitudes, emotions and intentions?

Confidence

It is very important that as a teacher, you present yourself with confidence. This is easier said than done because confidence relates both to a sense of knowledgeable mastery of the subject matter and to a sense of assurance of being in control, which takes time to develop and establish within the context of interpersonal relationships built by the teacher.

There is an irony in pupils' response to teacher confidence. Expression of authority is part of the role pupils expect of a teacher, and where exercised with confidence, pupils feel at ease and reassured. In fact, pupils prefer the security of a confident teacher. However, if they sense at any time that a teacher is unsure or apprehensive, it is in young people's nature to attempt to undermine authority (for further information, see Rogers 2011: 121–4).

Of course, in many cases, it is experience that brings confidence but regrettably pupils seldom allow that to influence their behaviour. Although the key to confident self-presentation is to be well planned, both in respect of material and in organisation, without the benefit of experience, all your excellent plans may not work and you may have no alternative 'up your sleeve'. Whatever happens, you need to cultivate a confident exterior, even if it is something of an act and you are feeling far from assured inside.

Confidence can be conveyed verbally in clear, purposeful instructions and explanations that are not disrupted by hesitation. Instructions given in a direct and business-like manner, such as 'Jane, please collect the scissors and put them in the red box', convey a sense of confidence. On the other hand, the same instruction put in the form of a question, such as 'Jane, will you collect the scissors and put them in the red box?' can convey a sense of your being less assured, not being confident that, in fact, Jane *will* cooperate. There is also the possibility of the pupil saying 'No'! Your voice needs to be used in a firm, measured manner. A slower, lower, well-articulated delivery is more authoritative and displays more confidence than a fast, high-pitched method of speaking. Use of voice is particularly important in giving key instructions, especially where safety factors are involved and in taking action to curtail inappropriate pupil behaviour. This is perhaps the time to be less enthusiastic and animated, and more serious and resolute in your manner.

Non-verbally, confidence is expressed via, for example, posture, movement and eye contact, both in their own right and as an appropriate accompaniment to verbal language. There is nothing agitated about the movement of confident people. They tend to stand still and use their arm gestures to a limited extent to reinforce the message being conveyed.

Eye contact is a crucial aspect of conveying confidence to pupils. A nervous person avoids eye contact, somehow being afraid to know what others are thinking, not wanting to develop a relationship that might ultimately reveal their inability or weakness. Clearly, it is your role as a teacher to be alert at all times to pupil reaction and be striving to develop a relationship with all pupils that encourages them to seek your help and advice. Steady, committed eye contact is usually helpful for both of these objectives. You must, however, also recognise that eye contact is perceived differently by people of different cultures: in certain parts of Africa, Asia and Latin America, avoiding eye contact is the way to show respect, whereas extended eye contact may be perceived as disrespectful or a challenge to authority. You should therefore take into account cultural sensitivities. This also applies to other aspects of non-verbal communication, such as dress, gesture, physical contact and spatial proximity to another person. For further information about cultural differences, take advice from your tutor, a staff member of that culture, staff at the local multicultural centre or the Commission for Equality and Human Rights (for additional guidance on cultural difference and diversity, see Knapp and Hall 2010, as well as the website www.naldic.org.uk).

Caring

It is perhaps not surprising that pupils feel emotional support and a caring approach are important in developing an effective relationship with teachers. Wentzel (1997) described caring teachers as those who demonstrate a commitment to their teaching, recognise each pupil's academic strengths and needs and have a democratic style of interaction. Wilson *et al.* (2007) found that an emotionally supportive environment in which the teacher also supplies plenty of evaluative feedback has a positive influence on pupils' social competencies. Wragg (1984: 82) reported that many more pupils preferred teachers who were 'understanding, friendly and firm' than teachers who were 'efficient, orderly and firm' or 'friendly, sympathetic and understanding'. It is interesting to note that firmness is also a preferred characteristic.

Notwithstanding pupils' preferences, interest in pupils as individuals and in their progress is surely the reason most teachers are in teaching. Your commitment to pupils' well-being and learning should be evident in all aspects of your manner and self-presentation. While this attitude goes without saying, it is not as straightforward as it sounds since it demands sensitivity and flexibility. In a sense, it is you as the teacher who has to modify your behaviour in response to the pupils, rather than it always being the pupil who has to fall into line with everything asked for by the teacher. There is a potential conflict, and balance to be struck, between firm confidence and flexible empathy. It is one of the challenges of teaching to find this balance and to be able to respond suitably at the appropriate time.

A caring approach is evident in a range of features of teaching, from efficient preparation through to sensitive interpersonal skills such as active listening. Those teachers who put pupils' interests above everything have taken the time and trouble to prepare work thoroughly in a form appropriate to the class. Similarly, the classroom environment shows thoughtful design and organisation. In the teaching situation, caring teachers are fully engaged in the task at hand, observing, supporting, praising, alert to the class climate and able to respond with an appropriate modification in the programme if necessary. Above all, however, caring teachers know pupils by name, remember their work, problems and progress from previous lessons and are prepared to take time to listen to them and talk about personal things as well as work. In other words, caring teachers show a real sensitivity to pupils' individual needs. They communicate clearly that each pupil's learning and success are valued.

Now complete Tasks 3.1.3 and 3.1.4.

 Task 3.1.3 Communicating effectively

Select in turn each aspect of verbal and non-verbal communication identified above; your use of voice, language, explaining/questioning/discussion, listening, presenting yourself effectively, enthusiasm, confidence, caring. Prepare an observation sheet for your tutors or another student teacher to use when observing you teach a class. Use this as a basis for evaluation and discussion about how you can further develop this aspect of your teaching. Store these in your PDP for future reference.

M

> ✏ **Task 3.1.4 Studying one aspect of communication in depth**
>
> Select one specific aspect of communication to study in greater depth. Review the literature on that aspect of communication. Design and conduct a piece of action research on that specific aspect of communication with one of your classes. Report critically on your research, identifying issues related to the assumptions underlying the methods of data collection and analysis. Critically analyse the outcomes of the study and reflect on your learning about improving your communication. Store in your PDP.

SUMMARY AND KEY POINTS

- Good communication is essential for developing sound interpersonal relationships with pupils, a positive classroom climate and effective teaching and learning.
- This unit has aimed to help you identify both the strengths and weaknesses in your verbal and non-verbal communication and in your self-presentation, to provide the basis for improving your ability to communicate.
- Developing your professional knowledge and judgement in this area should enable you to communicate sensitively and to best advantage.

Check which requirements for your ITE programme you have addressed through this unit.

 ## Further reading

Fisher, R. (2009) *Creative Dialogue: Talk for Thinking in the Classroom*, London: Routledge.
This book introduces a special form of dialogic teaching based upon an approach called 'Philosophy for Children' (P4C). It emphasises the development of critical and creative thinking through questioning and dialogue between pupils and teachers and between the pupils themselves. P4C helps to enhance communicative skills, as well as develop the habits of intelligent behaviour.

Knapp, M. and Hall, J. (2010) *Non-Verbal Communication in Human Interaction*, 7th edn, Boston, MA: Wadsworth/Cengage Learning.
Chapters embedded within Parts 2, 3 and 4 explore the non-verbal elements involved in any interaction: including the environment within which the interaction occurs; the physical features of the participants themselves; and their behaviour (for example, gestures, touching, territory and personal space, facial expressions, eye gazing and vocal sounds).

Muijs, D. and Reynolds, D. (2011) *Effective Teaching: Evidence and Practice*, 3rd edn, London: Sage.
Chapter 3 considers the important relationship between interactive teaching and pupils' learning. Elements of effective questioning techniques are identified and then reviewed in relation to class discussion. Chapter 11 introduces heuristic problem-solving strategies and guidance on how to promote higher-order thinking skills.

Ofsted (Office for Standards in Education) (2012a) *Questioning to Promote Learning*, available at: www.from goodtooutstanding.com/2012/05/ofsted-2012-questioning-to-promote-learning.
Advice and guidance is provided on how questions can promote learning along with a short three-minute video clip featuring Professor Dylan Wiliam speaking about how the IRE system (Initiation, Response, Evaluation) enables us to think more carefully about the way in which we ask questions and respond to pupils' answers.

Rogers, B. (2011) *Classroom Behaviour: A Practical Guide to Effective Teaching, Behaviour Management and Colleague Support*, 3rd edn, London: Sage.

> The author looks at the issues facing teachers working in today's classrooms. Describing real dilemmas and situations, he offers advice on dealing with the challenges of the job, and how building up a rapport with pupils and colleagues can support good practice. Examples of verbal and non-verbal communication skills are detailed within case studies that permeate throughout this highly accessible and informative book.

Walsh, J. (n.d.) *How Can Quality Questioning Transform Classrooms?*: www.sagepub.com/upmdata/6605_walsh_ch_1.pdf.

> This chapter is structured around three focus questions: (1) How can effective questioning help transform a traditional, teacher-centered classroom into a student-centered, inquiry-oriented community of learners? (2) What are the connections between quality questions and student achievement? (3) Why are there gaps between what we know about effective questioning and what we do in classrooms?

Other resources and websites

Teacher's non-verbal communication in the classroom.wmv: www.youtube.com/watch?v=vnbtxhZRcEs.

> This 11-minute film shows five teachers from secondary schools at Ras Al Khaimah addressing their classes at the beginning of a lesson – the soundtrack has been replaced with music so that the behaviour and body language are the main focus of the film.

National Association for Language Development in the Curriculum: www.naldic.org.uk.

> This website provides a professional forum for the teaching and learning of EAL, supporting bilingualism and raising the achievement of ethnic minority learners. The 'resources' link enables you to access important key documents and the 'ITTSEAL' link navigates you to the ITE section.

Voice Care Network: www.voicecare.org.uk.

> Their booklet 'More Care for your Voice' is intended to help people whose voice is needed for their work. This organisation is a registered charity with subscribing members. They provide advice and training. Relatively low-cost equipment is available to help with voice projection and to ensure that all pupils can hear the teacher.

Appendix 2 on pages 591–595 provides further examples of websites you may find useful.

Capel, S., Leask, M. and Turner, T. (eds) (2010) *Readings for Learning to Teach in the Secondary School: A Companion to M Level Study*, London: Routledge.

> This book brings together essential readings to support you in your critical engagement with key issues raised in this textbook.

The subject-specific books in the *Learning to Teach* series are also very useful.

Any additional resources and an editable version of any relevant tasks/tables in this unit are available on the companion website: www.routledge.com.cw.capel

3.2 Motivating pupils

Misia Gervis and Susan Capel

Introduction

Pupils' attitudes to school and motivation to learn are a result of a number of factors, including school ethos, class climate, past experiences, future expectations, peer group, teachers, gender, family background, culture, economic status and class. However, the link between motivation and educational performance and achievement is complex.

Some pupils have a more positive attitude to school and to learning; for example, it is valued at home or they see a link between education and a job. For example, if pupils see a relationship between success at school and economic success, they are more likely to work hard, behave in the classroom and be more successful. Many pupils want to learn but depend on teachers to get them interested in a subject. Even though some pupils may not be inherently motivated to learn, the school ethos, teachers' attitudes, behaviour, personal enthusiasm, teaching style and strategies in the classroom can increase their motivation to learn (see also, for example, Unit 5.3). On the other hand, pupils who do not feel valued at school are, in turn, unlikely to value school. Therefore, although some pupils may be inherently motivated to learn, they may become demotivated or have low motivation because of a learning environment that does not meet the needs of their learning style or does not stimulate them, or because a task is too difficult, or there is a negative impact of factors such as those identified above. Pupils for whom the motivational climate is not right are more likely to become disinterested and misbehave. If the teacher does not manage the class and their behaviour effectively, the learning of all pupils in the class can be negatively affected.

Thus, a central aim for you as a teacher is to create a motivational climate that helps stimulate pupils to learn. There is a range of techniques you can use to increase pupils' motivation to learn; for example:

- showing your enthusiasm for a topic, subject or teaching;
- treating each pupil as an individual;
- noticing and valuing effort in the classroom;
- providing quick feedback by marking work promptly;
- rewarding appropriate behaviour.

In order to use such techniques effectively, you need to understand why each technique is used. A study of motivation therefore is crucial to give you some knowledge and insight into ways of motivating pupils to learn. There is a wealth of material available on motivation. This unit tries to draw out some of the material we feel is of most benefit to you as a student teacher. However, the further reading list at the end of this unit, plus other reading in your library, will help you to develop your ability to motivate pupils further.

OBJECTIVES

At the end of this unit, you should be able to:

- understand the role and importance of motivation for effective teaching and learning and classroom management;
- appreciate some of the key elements of motivation for effective teaching;
- understand how to motivate pupils effectively;
- understand how to create a challenging classroom environment.

Check the requirements of your initial teacher education (IITE) programme to see which relate to this unit.

What is motivation?

Motivation 'consists of internal processes and external incentives which spur us on to satisfy some need' (Child 2007: 226). There are three key elements to motivational behaviour, which it is helpful for you to understand, as they can help you to interpret the behaviour of your pupils. These three elements are:

- direction (what activities people start);
- persistence (what activities people continue);
- intensity (what effort people put in).

These three key elements determine the activities that people start (direction) and continue (persistence) and the amount of effort they put into those activities at any particular time (intensity).

Motivation can be intrinsic (motivation from within the person; that is, engaging in an activity for its own sake for pleasure and/or satisfaction inherent in the activity; for example, a sense of achievement at having completed a difficult piece of work) or extrinsic (motivation from outside; that is, engaging in an activity for external reasons; for example, to receive a reward, such as praise from a teacher for good work, or to avoid punishment). Research has found that a person intrinsically motivated in an activity or task is more likely to persist and continue with that activity than a person extrinsically motivated. This can be illustrated by some (intrinsically motivated) pupils succeeding at school/in a subject despite the quality of the teaching, whereas other (extrinsically motivated) pupils succeed because of good teaching. Therefore, intrinsic motivation is to be encouraged in learning. A teacher's job would certainly be easier if all pupils were motivated intrinsically. However, pupils are asked to do many activities at school that are new to them, that are difficult, at which they may not be immediately successful or that they may perceive to be of little or no relevance to them. In order to become intrinsically motivated, pupils need encouragement along the way; for example, written or verbal praise for effort, making progress or success, feedback on how they are doing or an explanation of the relevance of the work. For example, the quality of the feedback that pupils receive can directly impact on their self-confidence. Teachers can deliberately plan extrinsic motivators (see below) into their lessons with a view to enhancing both self-confidence and intrinsic motivation (there is a cyclical relationship between self-confidence and intrinsic motivation, such that high self-confidence increases intrinsic motivation whereas low self-confidence decreases intrinsic motivation). Task 3.2.1 asks you to reflect on what motivates you as a learner.

 Task 3.2.1 What motivates you as a learner?

Reflect on your own experiences at school. What was it that motivated you in the subject that you are now learning to teach? Identify another subject in which you were less motivated and reflect on why this was the case. Discuss your reflections with another student teacher. Also identify anything you can learn from these experiences to build into your own teaching. Keep your notes in your professional development portfolio (PDP) for future reference.

Theories of motivation

There are a number of theories of motivation. In addition, we adopt our own, often unconscious, theories. Examples of theories of motivation, along with some of their implications for you as a teacher in determining learning activities, are given in Table 3.2.1 and in the text below.

What motivates people?

It is often difficult for a teacher to identify the exact reason for a particular pupil's behaviour at a particular time, and therefore what is motivating them. Likewise, it is often difficult for a pupil to identify exactly what is motivating them. As a teacher, you can often only infer whether or not pupils are motivated by observing their behaviour. Although there may be other reasons for a pupil not listening to what you are saying, talking, looking bored or staring out of the window, one reason may be that the motivational climate is not right and therefore the pupil is not motivated to learn.

Some of the factors that have been found to be motivating include: positive teacher-pupil relationships; supportive peer relationships; a sense of belonging; pupils' beliefs about their abilities; pupils' beliefs about the control they have over their own learning; pupils' interest in the subject; and the degree to which the subject or specific tasks are valued. Such factors have been categorised as:

■ achievement (for example, completing a piece of work that has taken a lot of effort);
■ pleasure (for example, getting a good mark or praise from a teacher for a piece of work);

■ preventing or stopping less pleasant activities/punishment (for example, avoiding getting a detention);

■ satisfaction (for example, feeling that you are making progress);

■ success (for example, doing well in a test).

The need for individuals to achieve can be encouraged by creating a learning environment in which 'the need for achievement in academic studies is raised' (Child 2007: 254). Each individual sets themselves a standard of achievement, according to their level of aspiration. It is therefore important to raise pupils' levels of aspiration. Pupils who are challenged are more likely to improve their performance than those who are not challenged. Research has shown that when people experience an activity as 'challenging' they have higher levels of self-confidence, feel more in control, experience more positive emotions and have reduced levels of the stress hormone cortisol. Conversely, when people experience an activity as 'threatening', their self-confidence is reduced, they perceive themselves to have limited control, experience more negative emotions and cortisol levels increase, which ultimately reduces their performance (Jones *et al.* 2009). Thus, setting tasks that are challenging but achievable for each individual pupil (that is, individualised tasks) can be used to raise aspirations. Tasks on which pupils expect to achieve approximately 50 per cent of the time are the most motivating. However, this means that pupils are likely to fail on the task approximately 50 per cent of the time, so it is important to plan to reduce loss of motivation when pupils fail (for example, by praising effort, giving feedback on performance, and so on).

Intrinsic motivation in pupils is related to interest in the activity and to effort (hard work), which leads to deep learning (Entwistle 1990; see also deep and surface learning in Units 5.2 and 5.3). Deep learning means that learners try to understand what they are doing, resulting in greater understanding of the subject matter. This is a prerequisite for high-quality learning outcomes (that is, achievement). According to achievement goal theory, Covington (2000) reported deep learning as being associated with task (or mastery) goals, whereas surface (superficial or rote) learning is associated with outcome (or performance) goals. In line with other studies, Lam *et al.* (2004) found that pupils with an outcome orientation were more likely to focus on better performance than on mastering a task.

Consideration of the types of goal that pupils use is important not only for their achievement, but also in determining the climate you create in the classroom. Research has shown that people's achievement is directly related to the types of goal they adopt (Elliot and McGregor 2001). Essentially, there are two key considerations when understanding the type of goal being used. First, is it a mastery or performance referenced goal? And second, is it an approach or avoid type of goal? These different components combine to create four possible types of goal: mastery-approach; mastery-avoid; performance-approach; and performance-avoid (see Figure 3.2.1). There seems to be a relationship between the types of goal adopted and whether pupils find an activity challenging or threatening. For example, work by Elliot and McGregor (2001) identified that pupils who set mastery approach goals perceived an examination situation to be challenging, whereas those who adopted performance-avoid goals perceived it as threatening. Individuals who set mastery-approach goals have the most control over their achievement, and consequently understand that their efforts determine their success. Consequently, it is important to work with your pupils to help them to adopt mastery-approach goals but also to be mindful of pupils who are only focusing on performance-avoid goals, as these are also associated with contributing to pupils experiencing higher levels of threat.

Table 3.2.1 Important theoretical perspectives and their implications for you as a teacher

Theory	Source	Main points	Implications for teachers
Theory *x* and theory *y*	McGregor (1960)	Theory *x* managers assume that the average worker is lazy, lacks ambition, is resistant to change, self-centred and not very bright. Theory *y* managers assume that the average worker is motivated, wants to take responsibility, has potential for development and works for the organisation. Any lack of ambition or resistance to change comes from experience.	Your treatment of pupils may be related to whether inherently you believe in theory *x* or theory *y*. A theory *x* teacher motivates pupils externally through a controlling environment; for example, by directing and controlling pupils actions, persuading, rewarding and punishing them to modify their behaviour. A theory *y* teacher encourages intrinsic motivation by allowing pupils to develop for themselves. This may be through an autonomy-support environment (see below).
Achievement motivation	Atkinson (1964) and McClelland (1961)	Motivation to perform an achievement-oriented task is related to the: (i) need to achieve on a particular task; (ii) expectation of success on the task; and (iii) strength of the incentive after the task has been completed successfully. This results in individuals setting themselves standards of achievement.	Create a learning environment that raises the need for achievement in academic studies by raising levels of aspiration. Plan tasks that are challenging but attainable with effort. Work should be differentiated according to individual needs.
Achievement goal theory	Ames (1992a, 1992b), Dweck (1986), Dweck and Leggett (1988) and Nicholls (1984, 1989)	A social-cognitive perspective that identifies determinants of achievement behaviour, variations of which result from different achievement goals pursued by individuals in achievement situations. In achievement settings, an individual's orientation towards one of two incompatible goals by which to judge success underpins how they strive to maximise their demonstration of ability. In a task- (or mastery-) oriented setting, the focus is on skill learning and exerting effort to succeed, and success is judged by self-improvement and mastery of a task. In an outcome- (ego- or performance-) oriented setting, individuals compare their performance and ability with others and judge success by beating others with little effort to enhance social status.	Pupils' goal orientation may be influenced by the motivational climate created by what teachers do and say. Therefore, plan a task-oriented learning environment that encourages pupils to improve their performance by trying hard, selecting demanding tasks and persisting when faced with difficulty, rather than an outcome-orientated learning environment that encourages pupils to select easy tasks that they can achieve with minimum effort and on which they are likely to give up when facing difficulties.
Attribution theory	Weiner (1972)	Success or failure is attributed to ability, effort, difficulty of task or luck, depending on: (i) previous experience of success or failure on the task; (ii) the amount of work put in; or (iii) a perceived relationship between what is done and success or failure on the task.	Reward effort as well as success, as pupils are more likely to try if they perceive success is owing to effort; for example, you can give two marks for work, one for the standard of the work, the other for effort. Use teaching and assessment that is individualised rather than competitive.

Theory	Reference	Description	Application
Expectancy theory	Rosenthal and Jacobson (1968)	A range of cues is used by one person to form expectations (high or low) of another. That person then behaves in a way that is consistent with their expectations. This influences motivation, performance and how the other person attributes success or failure. The other person performs according to the expectations, thus creating a self-fulfilling prophecy.	In order to avoid the self-fulfilling prophesy of pupils performing according to the way teachers expect them to perform (by forming expectations (high or low) based on a range of cues and conveying these expectations), do not prejudge pupils on their past performance. Rather, encourage pupils to work to the best of their ability all the time.
Hierarchy of needs theory	Maslow (1970)	Hierarchy (highest to lowest): (1) self-actualisation (need to fulfil own potential); (2) self-esteem (need to feel competent and gain recognition from others); (3) affiliation and affection (need for love and belonging); (4) need for physical and psychological safety; and (5) physiological needs (for example, food, warmth). Energy is spent meeting the lowest level of unmet need.	If a basic need (for example, sleep, food, warmth) is not met, a pupil concentrates on meeting that need first and is unlikely to benefit from attempts by teachers to meet higher-level needs. Try to create a classroom environment to fulfil basic needs first; for example, rules for using dangerous equipment provide a sense of physical safety, routines give a sense of psychological security, group work can give a sense of belonging/affiliation (Postlethwaite 1993).
Behavioural learning theories	Skinner (1953)	Activity or behaviour is learned and maintained because of interaction with the environment. An activity or behaviour reinforced by a pleasurable outcome is more likely to be repeated.	Positive reinforcement (reward, for example, praise) generally increases motivation to learn and behave. This has a greater impact if the reward is relevant to the pupils, they know how to get the reward and it is given fairly and consistently (there are, however, exceptions: see 'Praise' below).
Self-determination theory	Deci and Ryan (1985) and Ryan and Deci (2000a)	A broad framework that considers both social and environmental factors that contribute to either enhancing or diminishing intrinsic and extrinsic motivation. Key themes relating to intrinsic motivation are autonomy, competence and relatedness. Extrinsic motivation operates by engaging pupils in tasks so that they can willingly accept the value of the task even if the task itself may not hold any specific interest to them. This can lead to greater persistence and better engagement in the task. Key themes relating to extrinsic motivation are internalisation and integration.	In a teaching context, it is acknowledged that interpersonal interactions (for example, communication and feedback) between teachers and pupils are critical in facilitating or debilitating feelings of competency in pupils. As a consequence, intrinsic motivation can be elevated or diminished. Elevated intrinsic motivation does not occur unless also accompanied by a sense of autonomy. Research shows that autonomy-supportive teachers catalyse pupils' intrinsic motivation (Deci et al. 1981). Within a teaching context, highly intrinsically motivated pupils demonstrate high-quality learning and creativity.

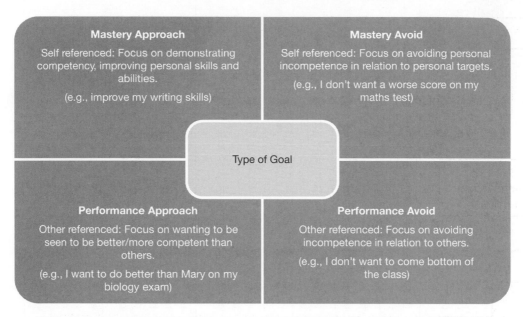

Figure 3.2.1 A representation of the different types of goals throughout the unit

Source: Adapted from Elliot and McGregor (2001)

Pupils' perceptions of the motivational context (that is, the goal orientation of the classroom and school) has been found to be important for their motivation and adjustment to school. Controlling environments (teachers attempt to guide pupils' thinking by providing specific guidelines for their academic and personal behaviours in class) have been found to have a negative effect on perceived competence and participation, which results in decreased intrinsic and self-motivation. On the other hand, pupils are motivated by teachers who know, support, challenge and encourage them to act independently from each other and from the teacher. An autonomy-support environment is one in which the teacher gives increasing responsibility to pupils (for example, for choices/options about what they want to do); encourages pupils' decision-making by spending less time talking, more time listening, making less directive comments, asking more questions and not giving pupils solutions; allows pupils to work in their own way; and offers more praise and verbal approval in class. Such an environment supports pupils' academic and social growth by increasing intrinsic and self-motivation to succeed at school, self-confidence, perceived competence and self-esteem. Research by Manouchehri (2004) has found a relationship between the motivational style adopted by teachers of mathematics and their commitment to implementing new teaching methods. Those adopting an autonomy-support style of motivation increase pupils' participation and engagement by, for example, creating more opportunities for pupils to examine and develop their understanding of mathematical ideas, to listen to the arguments and to ask questions of other pupils.

Figure 3.2.2 illustrates the link between teachers' actions in creating the motivational climate and pupils' responses, which influences their intrinsic motivation.

Further, pupils' goal orientations may be influenced by the motivational climate created by what teachers do and say. Research in physical education has found a relationship between pupils' perceptions of a lesson as being task-oriented and adaptive motivational responses, including increased

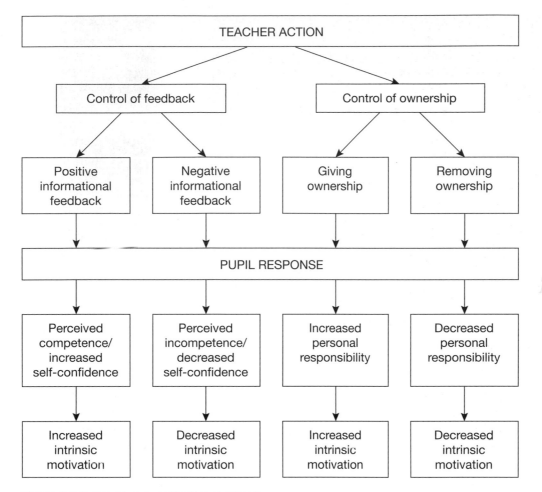

Figure 3.2.2 Creating a motivational climate

intrinsic motivation. In contrast, a relationship has been found between pupils' perceptions of a lesson as being outcome-oriented and maladaptive motivational responses. Such a lesson focuses on individual achievement and competition between individuals. This may foster extrinsic motivation, and discourage hard work and effort to achieve success by pupils who fail to achieve the outcome.

Although it changes with age, it is generally accepted that pupils are more likely to try harder if they can see a link between the amount of effort they make and success in the activity. Indeed, there is a link between achievement goal theory and attribution theory in that pupils with a high need to achieve attribute their success to internal causes (for example, aptitude and effort), while they attribute failure to lack of effort. On the other hand, pupils with a low need to achieve attribute their failure to external factors (for example, bad luck). Therefore, as a teacher, you should design activities that encourage pupils to attribute success or failure to effort. However, this is not always easy. Postlethwaite (1993) identified the difficulty of determining how much effort a pupil has made on a piece of work (especially that done at home) and hence the problems of marking the work. You can no doubt think of occasions where one person has made a lot of effort on a piece of homework, but missed the point and received a low mark, whereas another person has rushed through the homework and managed to achieve a good mark. In 'norm-referenced' marking, a certain percentage of the class are given a designated category of mark, no matter how good each individual piece of work. Thus, each pupil's mark for a piece of work is given solely for their performance compared to that of the rest of the group. This encourages success or failure to be attributed to ability or luck. In 'criterion-referenced' marking, all pupils who meet stated criteria for a particular category of mark are marked in that category. Thus, pupils are given a mark that reflects how closely the criteria for the assessment have been met, irrespective of the performance of other pupils. Although this overcomes some of the disadvantages of norm-referenced marking, it does not reflect how much effort the pupil has put into the work. Postlethwaite (1993) went on to say that effort can best be judged by comparing different pieces of the same pupil's work, as the standard of work is likely to reflect the amount of effort put in (that is, ipsative assessment). Giving two marks for the work, one for content and standard of the work and one for effort and presentation, can encourage effort. Thus, even if the content and standard are poor, it may be possible to praise the effort. This praise can motivate the pupil to try harder, especially if the pupil values the mark for effort. He suggested that another way of encouraging pupils to attribute success to effort is to ask them to write about the way they tackled the task (see also Units 6.1 and 6.2 on assessment).

According to expectancy theory, a teacher forms an impression of a pupil on which they base their expectations of that pupil; the teacher's verbal and non-verbal behaviour is based, consciously or unconsciously, on those expectations; the pupil recognises, consciously or unconsciously, the teacher's expectations of them from their behaviour and responds in a way that matches these expectations. Thus, there is a self-fulfilling prophecy. It is generally accepted that if a teacher expects high achievement and good behaviour, pupils perform to the best of their ability and behave well. Murdock (1999) found that where teachers held high expectations of pupils, they were engaged more academically. If, on the other hand, teachers have low expectations of pupils' achievement and behaviour, pupils achieve little and behave badly. In the same way, teachers can develop stereotypes of how different groups of pupils perform or behave; stereotypes can direct expectations (see also Unit 4.4 for further information).

One aspect of the organisation of a school that may particularly influence teachers' expectations of pupils is the way pupils are grouped. Pupils streamed by ability remain in the same group throughout the year, whatever their ability in different subjects. Whatever the labels attached to each stream, pupils are perceptive and judge their abilities by the stream they are in. This may be partly because teachers' verbal and non-verbal behaviour communicates clearly their expectations. Teachers expect pupils in the 'top' stream to do well; therefore, they behave accordingly; for example, actively encouraging pupils, setting challenging work. Teachers do not expect pupils in the 'bottom' stream to do as well; therefore, they behave accordingly; for example, constantly nagging pupils, setting easy work (or none at all). Both groups of pupils tend to fulfil the expectations of teachers. No doubt, many of you have heard of the notorious 'bottom' stream in a school. Setting (or banding) pupils for different subjects can overcome problems of streaming; that is, recognising pupils' ability in different subjects and changing the grouping of pupils according to their ability in a specific subject. The problem can also be overcome by grouping pupils in mixed-ability classes and providing differentiated work to enable pupils of different abilities to work alongside each other on tasks that are challenging but achievable for each pupil (see achievement motivation above). For further information about differentiation, see Unit 4.1.

Self-determination theory has had a significant contribution in the current understanding of motivation to learn in a classroom setting. As mentioned earlier, two distinct, yet interrelated, aspects of motivation need to be considered: intrinsic and extrinsic motivation. Unlike other one-dimensional theories, both are considered to be important in establishing an effective motivational climate in the classroom. There is an accepted view that intrinsic motivation refers to activities that an individual engages in because they find them inherently interesting and satisfying. We know that teachers can be instrumental in creating the 'right' conditions for intrinsic motivation to flourish. Furthermore, research has found that teachers have a significant contribution to make in either undermining or facilitating intrinsic motivation in their pupils (Ryan and Stiller 1991). When intrinsic motivation is elevated, pupils demonstrate high-quality learning and high levels of creativity, both of which are desirable and should be cultivated by teachers in the classroom. In order to understand why this happens, we need to look further into self-determination theory.

Ryan and Deci (2000b) highlight three important innate needs that underpin motivation; these are: competence, autonomy and relatedness. While each of these may appear to be separate and distinct, they interact with each other and mediate behavioural outcomes. Therefore, the motivation of an individual is a function of these factors. In order to enhance motivation in a pupil, the teacher needs to consider how they are working in relation to each of these. So, for example, effective positive feedback can enhance an individual's feeling of competence and, consequently, intrinsic motivation levels are elevated. However, this does not occur unless accompanied by an increased sense of autonomy. The role of a teacher can be instrumental in enhancing feelings of competence through their interpersonal interactions with pupils and frameworks such as reward systems that they put in place. There is substantive evidence to support the notion that teachers who adopt an autonomy-supportive approach are catalysts for their pupils' intrinsic motivation (Deci *et al.* 1981).

In self-determination theory, extrinsic motivation is also considered to be an important factor in regulating behaviour. The key factor is the degree to which an individual has 'internalised' the extrinsic factor as this directly impacts on autonomy. The greater the internalisation, the more

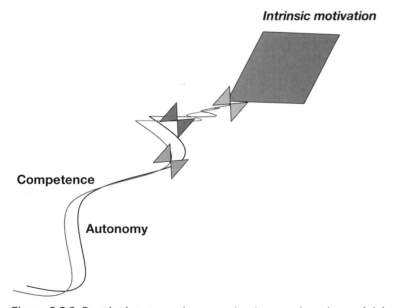

Figure 3.2.3 Developing competence and autonomy to enhance intrinsic motivation

autonomous the individual will feel, which in turn will enhance intrinsic motivation. Specifically, it is the relationship between 'internalisation' and 'integration' that is seen to be essential in contributing to how individuals perceive their own competence and self-determination. Figure 3.2.3 (p. 169) relates self-determination theory to flying a kite – it is important for a teacher to focus on developing both competence and autonomy at the same time (as it is important to pull both strings on a kite to keep it in the air).

Task 3.2.2 asks you to think about the hierarchy of needs theory. Task 3.2.3 asks you to think about the application of these theories to your teaching.

 Task 3.2.2 Hierarchy of needs

Consider some of the home conditions likely to leave pupils with unmet needs that prevent effective learning at school. Discuss with your tutor or another student teacher and record in your PDP what can be done in the school and what you can do in your lessons that may help pupils to meet these basic needs to provide a foundation for effective learning. Discuss when and to whom you should report if you suspect pupils' most basic needs are not being met, as this may require the skills of other professionals. Store the information in your PDP.

 M

 Task 3.2.3 Using theories of motivation in your teaching

Review a range of literature on theories of motivation. Write a reflective commentary on these.

Work in a group with other student teachers. Each select one theory of motivation. Use the information and the implications for teachers in Table 3.2.1 and in the text above as a basis for identifying practical implications of the theory for your lessons. Use this as the basis for planning for motivating pupils in one of your lessons based on this theory of motivation. Ask your tutor to observe the lesson and give you feedback on the effectiveness of your motivation. Record your own reflections. Meet with your group and discuss the theory, your lesson and reflection, then identify ways you can improve. Repeat the cycle of planning, teaching the lesson, reflecting and evaluating your effectiveness. Record the outcomes of your own and other student teachers' work in your PDP.

You might then like to try this using other theories of motivation.

Some specific factors that influence pupils' motivation to learn

One newly qualified teacher highlighted the following as factors that she has found important in motivating pupils to learn (Titchmarsh 2012):

■ If you are enthusiastic pupils are enthusiastic.
■ If you are in a bad mood, pupils pick up on it. You therefore need to cultivate a 'game face' for your teaching that does not show how you feel behind it.

- If pupils are bored, they are not going to be motivated. On the other hand, if they are doing an activity they enjoy, they are going to be motivated to learn.
- Give pupils ownership of tasks to enhance feelings of autonomy.
- Copying from a textbook is not advised as this is boring and does not encourage enquiry-based learning, which is generally more motivating.
- Many pupils find difficulty with independent learning as they have not learned how to do it or been encouraged. It takes time and effort to teach pupils how to be independent learners but it is worth it in the long run. If you do this from the start, they know what to expect. This then needs to be reinforced and they need to be encouraged to be independent.
- In subjects where it is applicable (for example, geography), taking pupils out of the classroom motivates them. However, once you get them out of the classroom, you need to have a good lesson plan for them.
- Pupils have to see the point in the activity, what they are going to have achieved and how they are going to have achieved it. There is no point in having an all-singing-and-dancing lesson if the pupils do not see the point. This has to be clear.
- Pupils will not be motivated or engaged if the work is too hard and they cannot access it, or it is too easy. Therefore, you need to differentiate the work.
- Some pupils are difficult. Sit and have a frank discussion with them about what interests them, what helps them learn, and so on so you can tailor your lessons for them.
- Give pupils (part of) a topic each to research and teach to others. This can be tailored to their ability. Tell them that what they teach will form the foundation for all pupils in the class. Normally, pupils do not want to let their peers down, so they work hard at this task.
- Using examples of good work gives a lift to those whose work is highlighted but also shows other pupils what is needed.
- Give verbal praise in the classroom.
- Give merits or credits, following the school's rewards and sanctions policy.
- Give stickers to younger pupils (for example, stars or smiley faces) for good work/answers.

Extrinsic motivation is sometimes used to encourage intrinsic motivation. However, it is important to recognise that motivating pupils extrinsically can have a detrimental effect when a pupil is already motivated intrinsically (see also Unit 5.6 on neuroscience).

Personal achievement (success)

Personal achievement (generally called success in an outcome-oriented learning environment) is generally motivating in itself. Some pupils struggle to succeed, whereas others succeed much more quickly. There are many ways to help pupils succeed; for example, using a technique often called whole-part-whole teaching. In this, pupils are shown the whole activity first so that they know what they are trying to achieve. The activity is then broken down into small, self-contained, achievable parts, which allows pupils to receive reinforcement for each small, successful step. The separate parts of the activity are gradually put together until the whole activity has been built up. Pupils are given appropriate feedback at each stage (see below for more information about giving feedback); therefore, when they attempt the whole, they are most likely to succeed. You may relate to this by thinking about when you learned (or tried to learn) front crawl in swimming. You probably practised

Task 3.2.4 Whole-part-whole teaching

As part of your normal lesson planning with a class, select one activity that you can break down into small, self-contained, achievable parts, which can be put together to build up gradually to the whole. Ask your tutor or another student teacher to observe you teaching this activity using whole-part-whole teaching. At the end of the lesson, discuss with some of the pupils how this went. Discuss with the observer how the pupils responded and how well they learned the task. Evaluate the lesson yourself, store in your PDP, and build on this experience in future lessons.

your arms, legs and breathing separately before you tried to put it all together (see Task 3.2.4). What other techniques can you use to help pupils succeed? (See also Unit 2.2 on lesson planning.)

The use of performance profiling techniques to enhance pupils' motivation by engaging them in self-assessment, but also in the process of goal setting, can be a valuable tool. This helps pupils identify their own personal successes but also areas for development. Performance profiling is based on Kelly's (1955) personal construct theory, which maintains that each individual holds unique cognitive constructs about the world and the self. It is through these that we all construct our own reality, and consequently we are the best experts on ourselves. As we develop, these constructs are changed and modified through our experiences and knowledge and understanding of the world. This theory suggests that in order to understand another, first we have to be able to see the world from their perspective. Thus, for the teacher to enhance motivation, it is helpful if they have an understanding of their pupils' perspectives. (Bourdieu's theory outlined in Unit 7.4 may give you a framework to identify factors influencing pupils' motivation.)

The process entails first asking pupils to identify key factors they think are essential to be successful learners; these could be subject-specific or more generic. This discussion should focus on identifying key factors perceived to be critical from the pupils' perspective. Through class discussion, you can agree on the final list. This can be as long or short as you want.

Once identified, these key factors can be added to the profile chart (see Figure 3.2.4). Each pupil can then complete their own profile by identifying their perceived strengths and weaknesses in relation to each of the key factors. The teacher can also complete their own chart for each pupil.

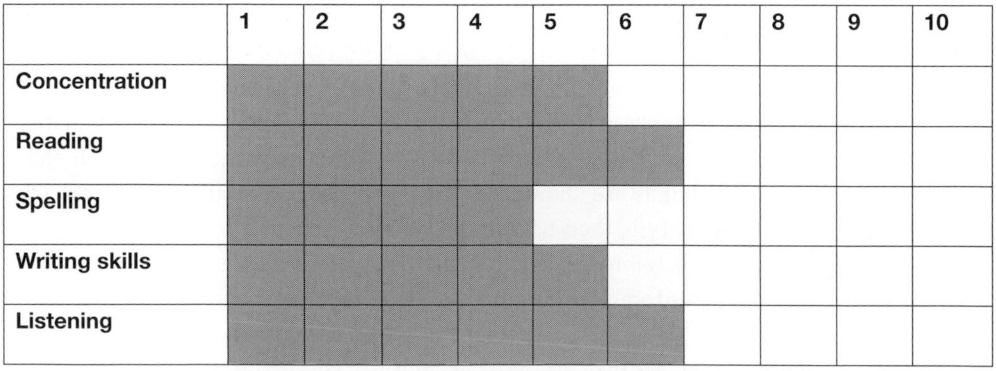
1
2
3
4
5
6
7
8
9
10
Concentration
Reading
Spelling
Writing skills
Listening

Figure 3.2.4 Example performance profile (1 = very poor, 10 = excellent)

Table 3.2.2 Identifying key areas of excellence and key areas of improvement

Key areas of excellence	Key areas for improvement
For example, *listening*	For example, *spelling*

This creates a means to compare the pupil perspective with that of the teacher and can be a starting point for discussion. Through discussion, pupil and teacher can gain better insight and understanding into how the pupil sees themself. So, for example, if a pupil has rated themself as a 4 on one factor and the teacher rated them as a 7, this provides a useful framework for mutual understanding. It also provides a clear visual representation of the pupil's strengths and weaknesses, which makes it tangible. Strengths and weaknesses can be recorded in a table such as Table 3.2.2.

Once the profile has been created, it can become an effective monitoring system and a focal point for goal setting. By agreeing the actions that need to be taken to address the profile and set goals, the pupil is able to take ownership of the process. In accordance with self-determination theory, we know that by increasing autonomy, intrinsic motivation is elevated. This process creates a platform from which this can develop. Furthermore, we know that changes in behaviour can only be initiated with the complete agreement of the individual, and this process ensures that the pupil is able to 'buy into' their own action plan to achieve success. Progress can be monitored through repeated profiles, which can provide a direct comparison to previous profiles, and serve to visibly map change, and achievement towards the agreed goals.

Rewards

Although personal achievement or success is motivating in itself, pupils may not be immediately successful on activities they undertake at school; therefore, they may need external rewards (positive reinforcements) to motivate them. Bull and Solity (1987) identified four types of rewards, listed below in the order in which they are used most often:

■ social rewards (social contact and pleasant interactions with other people, including praise, a smile to recognise an action or achievement or to say thank you, encouraging remarks or a gesture of approval);
■ token rewards (house points, grades, certificates);
■ activity rewards (opportunities for enjoyable activities);
■ material rewards (tangible, usable or edible items).

Task 3.2.5 focuses on these four types of reward.

Praise

Generally, pupils respond more positively to praise and positive comments about their work or behaviour than to criticism and negative comments. This, in turn, may produce a motivational

---

✎   Task 3.2.5 Using rewards

Develop an observation schedule with sections for the four types of reward listed above. Observe a class and mark in the appropriate category for any reward used by the teacher in the class. Discuss with the teacher the variety and frequency of use of the different possible methods of reward, as well as why a particular type of reward was used to achieve a particular purpose. Ask your tutor or another student teacher to undertake the same observation on one of your lessons. Discuss the differences in variety and frequency of reward used. As you plan your lessons, consider how you might use rewards. Ask the same person to observe a lesson a couple of months after the first one and see if you have changed your use of reward in your lessons. Relate this to what you know about behavioural learning theories. Record your notes in your PDP.

---

learning environment in which pupils work harder and behave better. If pupils misbehave in a classroom in which there is a positive motivational learning environment, Olweus (1993: 85) suggested that the use of praise makes pupils feel appreciated, which may make it easier for them to accept criticism of inappropriate behaviour and to attempt to change.

However, the Office for Standards in Education (Ofsted 1993) reported that teachers give relatively little praise and that their vocabulary is generally more negative than positive. Praise is given more often for academic than social behaviour, and social behaviour is more likely to be criticised than praised. One reason for this may be that teachers expect pupils to behave appropriately in the classroom.

Some teachers use very few different words to praise pupils; for example, 'good', 'well done', 'OK'. What other words can you use to praise someone or give feedback? Try to develop a list of such words because if you use the same word to praise pupils all the time, the word loses its effect. The range of words must be accompanied by appropriate non-verbal communication signals (see non-verbal communication in Unit 3.1 and Task 3.2.6).

Although it is generally accepted that praise aids learning, there are dangers in using praise. There are times when it may not be appropriate. For example, pupils who become lazy about their work as a result of complacency may respond by working harder if their work is gently criticised on occasion. If praise is given automatically, regardless of the work, effort or behaviour, pupils quickly see through it and it loses its effect. Praise should only be used to reward appropriate achievement, effort or behaviour.

Some pupils do not respond positively to praise; for example, they are embarrassed, especially if they are praised in front of their peers. Others perceive praise to be a form of punishment; for example, if they are teased or rejected by their peers for being 'teacher's pet' or for behaving themselves in class. Thus, conforming to the behaviours and values promoted in school results in negative social consequences. Therefore, although pupils know that they will be rewarded for achievement, effort or behaviour, they may also be aware of the norms of the peer group, which discourage them from achieving academically, making an effort or behaving well.

Other pupils do not know how to respond to praise because they have not received much praise in the past; for example, because they have continually received low marks for their work or because they have been in the bottom stream. They have therefore learned to fail. Some of these pupils may want to attribute failure to not caring or not trying to succeed. One way they may do this is by not making an effort with work; another is misbehaving in the classroom.

Thus, pupils respond differently to praise. In the same class, you may have some pupils working hard to receive praise from the teacher or a good mark on their homework, while others do not respond well to praise or are working hard at avoiding praise. You have to use your judgement when giving praise; for example, if you praise a pupil who is misbehaving to try to encourage better behaviour, you may be seen to be rewarding bad behaviour, thereby motivating the pupil to continue to misbehave in order to get attention. If you are not immediately successful in your use of praise, do not give up using it, but consider whether you are giving it in the right way; for example, would it be better to have a quiet word, rather than praise pupils out loud in front of their peers? As your professional knowledge and judgement develop, you become able to determine how best to use praise appropriately to motivate pupils in your classes.

Punishment

As well as using praise, teachers also use punishment to try to change behaviour. However, reward, most frequently in the form of praise, is generally considered to be more effective because it increases appropriate behaviour, whereas punishment decreases inappropriate behaviour. If pupils are punished, they know what behaviour results in punishment and therefore what not to do, but may not know what behaviour avoids punishment.

However, there are times when punishment is needed. At such times, make sure that you use punishment to best effect; for example, avoid punishing a whole class for the behaviour of one or a few pupil(s), always make it clear which pupil(s) are being punished for what behaviour, always give punishment fairly and consistently and in proportion to the offence. Also, make sure that the punishment does not include the behaviour that you want exhibited (for example, do not punish a pupil by requiring them to run round the football pitch if that is what you had wanted them to do). This sends mixed messages and is likely to put the pupil off that activity. Do not make idle threats to pupils by threatening them with punishment that you cannot carry out. In order to increase appropriate behaviour, identify to the offender any positive aspects of the behaviour being punished and explain the appropriate behaviour (see also Units 3.3 and 4.5).

Feedback

It may be that pupils who do not respond positively to praise are underperforming and have been doing so for a long time. You may be able to check whether they are underperforming by comparing assessment data over a period of time to measure current achievement with past achievement. The achievement of all pupils, including underperforming pupils, can be enhanced by receiving feedback on their work. Feedback is a formative process that gives pupils information about how they are doing and whether they are on the right track when learning something. This motivates them to make an effort and to continue.

A pupil is more likely to learn effectively or behave appropriately if feedback is used in conjunction with praise. A sequence in which feedback is sandwiched between praise (that is, praise-constructive feedback-praise) is designed to provide encouragement and motivation, along with information to help the pupil improve the activity or behaviour. Giving praise first is designed to make pupils more receptive to the information and, afterwards, to have a positive approach to try again. Try combining

---

✎ Task 3.2.6 The language of praise

Use the observation schedule below (or develop a similar one of your own with categories for praise and negative comments given to an individual, a group or the whole class, for both academic work and behaviour).

Tick each time praise or negative comment is given in each category					
Praise to individual for academic work					
Praise to group for academic work					
Praise to whole class for academic work					
Praise to individual for behaviour					
Praise to group for behaviour					
Praise to whole class for behaviour					
Negative comment to individual for academic work					
Negative comment to group for academic work					
Negative comment to whole class for academic work					
Negative comment to individual for behaviour					
Negative comment to group for behaviour					
Negative comment to whole class for behaviour					

Observe a class taught by an experienced teacher. Sit in a place where you can hear everything that is said. Record the number of times the teacher gives praise and makes negative comments to individuals, groups and the whole class in relation to academic work and behaviour. Observe the same experienced teacher in another lesson. This time, write down the different words, phrases and actions the teacher uses to give praise and negative comments in each of these categories and the number of times each is used.

Ask someone to conduct the same observations on your lessons. You might be surprised to find that you use a phrase such as 'good' or 'OK' very frequently in your teaching. Discuss the differences with your tutor and, if appropriate, develop strategies to help you improve the amount of praise you give and the range of words, phrases and actions you use to give praise. Record these strategies in your PDP and gradually try to incorporate them into your teaching.

---

feedback with praise in your teaching. Be careful how you use the word 'but' when giving feedback, especially when using the sandwich approach. The power of this small word has the effect of devaluing everything that comes before it. So, for example, if you said, 'Well done for your concentration in class today *but* your writing needs attention', the pupil will not acknowledge the praise; it is as if you have not said it. If, however, you replace 'but' with 'and', it changes the message and the emotional response to it. If you said, 'Well done for your concentration in class today *and* your writing needs attention', the praise element will still be acknowledged.

By observing pupils very carefully, you are able to spot small changes or improvements, which allows you to provide appropriate feedback (Unit 2.1 looks at observation techniques and Unit 6.1 focuses on assessment for learning). Feedback can be used effectively with the whole-part-whole teaching method (see above). If you give feedback about how a pupil has done on each part, this part can be improved before going on to the next part. If you give feedback immediately (that is, as an attempt is being finished or immediately after it has finished, but before another attempt is started), pupils can relate the feedback directly to the outcome of the activity. Thus, pupils are more likely to succeed if they take small steps and receive immediate feedback on each step. This success can, in turn, lead to increased motivation to continue the activity.

One problem with giving immediate feedback is how you can provide feedback to individual pupils in a class who are all doing the same activity at the same time. There are several methods that you can use to provide feedback to many pupils at the same time; for example, getting pupils to work through examples in a book that has the answers in the back, setting criteria and letting pupils evaluate themselves against the criteria or having pupils assess one another against set criteria (Unit 5.3 covers teaching strategies and styles, including the reciprocal teaching style of Mosston and Ashworth 2002). If they have been properly prepared for it, pupils are generally sensible and constructive when given responsibility for giving feedback. In Task 3.2.7, the focus is on pupils giving feedback to each other.

However, it is not always appropriate to give immediate feedback.

Not all feedback comes from another person (for example, the teacher or another pupil); feedback also comes from the activity itself. The feedback from an activity may be easier to identify for some activities than others; for example, a pupil gets feedback about their success if an answer to a mathematics problem matches that given in the book or the wicket is knocked down when bowling in cricket. In other activities, right or wrong, success or failure, is not as clear-cut; for example, there is often no right or wrong answer to an English essay. In the early stages of learning an activity, pupils find it hard to use the feedback from the activity; for example, they may notice that they were successful at the activity, but not be able to identify why. Normally, therefore, they need feedback from another person. This immediate, external feedback can be used to help pupils become more aware of what they are doing, how they are improving, why they were successful or not at the activity, and therefore to make use of feedback from the activity. Later in the learning (for example, when refining an activity), pupils should be able to benefit from feedback from the activity

---

 Task 3.2.7 Pupils giving feedback

As an integral part of your lesson planning, select one activity in which pupils can observe each other and provide feedback. Devise a handout with the main points/criteria to be observed. Plan how you are going to introduce this activity into the lesson. Discuss the lesson plan with your tutor. Ask your tutor to observe the lesson. Discuss the effectiveness of the strategy afterwards, determining how you can improve its use. Also try to observe teachers who plan for pupils to observe and give feedback to each other. Try the strategy at a later date in your school experience. Identify other ways in which you can get more feedback to more pupils when they are doing an activity and record in your PDP. Include these in your lesson plans, as appropriate (see also teaching styles in Unit 5.3).

itself, and therefore it is better to encourage this internal feedback by, for example, asking appropriate questions; for example, how did that feel? In this situation, the teacher should not give immediate feedback.

Finally, to be effective, feedback should be given about pupils' work or behaviour, not about the pupils themselves. It must convey to pupils that their work or behaviour is satisfactory or not, not that they are good (or bad) per se.

Motivating individuals and the class as a whole

As the discussion above has highlighted, there is no one correct way to motivate pupils to learn. Different motivation techniques are appropriate and effective in different situations; for example, pupils of different ages respond differently to different types of motivation, reward, punishment or feedback. Likewise, individual pupils respond differently. Further, any one pupil may respond to the same motivator differently at different times and in different situations.

Pupils need to feel that they are individuals, with their needs and interests taken into account, rather than just being a member of a group. Pupils need to be given opportunities to take ownership of the tasks in which they are engaged. If pupils are not motivated or bored, do not let them avoid doing an activity, but try to find ways of motivating them; for example, by relating it to something in which they are interested. You can motivate pupils most effectively by using motivation techniques appropriate for a particular pupil in a particular situation. Therefore, you need to get to know pupils as individuals.

Thus, you need to try to find out what motivates each pupil in your class. Learning pupils' names quickly gives you a start in being able to motivate pupils effectively (Unit 2.2 provides advice on learning pupils' names). You also need to get to know pupils as individuals. Observation of pupils, talking to them and discussing a pupil with the form tutor or other teachers all help. As you get to know pupils, you can identify what motivates them by finding out what activities they enjoy, what they choose to do and what they try to avoid, what types of reward they work for and to what they do not respond.

The sooner you can relate to pupils individually, the sooner you can manage a class of individuals effectively. However, this does not occur at an early phase of your development as a teacher (see phases of development in Unit 1.2). As a student teacher, you are at a disadvantage here because you can only know what motivates each pupil and what rewards they are likely to respond to if you know your pupils well and know something about their needs and interests. As a student teacher, you do not usually spend enough time in one school to get to know the pupils well, and therefore you can only try to motivate individual pupils by using your knowledge and understanding of pupils of that age.

However, there is one further element to motivation to consider briefly here. The same principles can also be applied to enhance the collective motivation of a class. By engaging pupils in discussions about 'what kind of a class' they want to be, you can encourage pupils to elicit the qualities that they think are necessary to enable all members of the class to succeed; for example, everyone to be on time and with the right materials, to respect others (and hence to listen quietly when someone else is talking), to work hard, to do their homework, and so on. Thus, in essence, they create a class profile (similar to that in Figure 3.2.4) that enables the collective perspective to be represented. Giving pupils ownership of the profile that they create contributes significantly towards collective motivation and behaviour modification in line with desired outcome. Consequently, if there is collective buy-in, pupils then monitor each other's behaviour and work to reinforce the key aspects identified on the profile. The benefit for you is that the pupils can help you with class management.

SUMMARY AND KEY POINTS

■ This unit has identified some theoretical underpinnings, general principles and techniques for achieving an appropriate motivational climate in your lessons, and therefore to increase pupils' motivation to learn. However, you need to be able to use these appropriately. For example, if you praise a group for working quietly while they are working, you may negatively affect their work. It is better in this situation to let the group finish their work and then praise them.

■ In addition, pupils are individuals and therefore respond differently to different forms of motivation, reward, punishment and feedback. Further, the same pupil responds differently at different times and in different situations.

■ To motivate each pupil effectively, therefore, requires that you know your pupils so you can anticipate how they will respond.

■ Motivation is supported by good formative assessment techniques (see Unit 6.1). Your developing professional knowledge and judgement enables you to combine theory with practice to motivate pupils effectively in your classes, which raises the standard of their work.

Check which requirements for your ITE programme you have addressed through this unit.

Further reading

Child, D. (2007) *Psychology and the Teacher*, 8th edn, London: Continuum.
> Chapter 8 provides in-depth consideration of motivation in education. It starts by considering three broad types of theories of motivation, then looks specifically at how some of the theories of motivation impact on you as a teacher and on your pupils.

Gilbert, I. (2002) *Essential Motivation in the Classroom*, London: RoutledgeFalmer.
> This book covers strategies, ideas and advice to help teachers understand how to motivate pupils and how pupils can motivate themselves.

Kyriacou, C. (2007) *Essential Teaching Skills*, 3rd edn, Cheltenham: Stanley Thornes.
> This book contains chapters on lesson management and classroom climate, both of which consider aspects of motivation; for example, whether lesson management helps to maintain pupils' motivation and whether the opportunities for learning are challenging and offer realistic opportunities for success.

Other resources and websites

Appendix 2 on pages 591–595 provides examples of websites you may find useful.

Capel, S., Leask, M. and Turner, T. (eds) (2010) *Readings for Learning to Teach in the Secondary School: A Companion to M Level Study*, London: Routledge.
> This book brings together essential readings to support you in your critical engagement with key issues raised in this textbook.

The subject-specific books in the *Learning to Teach* series are also very useful.

Any additional resources and an editable version of any relevant tasks/tables in this unit are available on the companion website: www.routledge.com.cw.capel

3.3 Managing classroom behaviour

Adopting a positive approach

Philip Garner

Introduction

This unit is designed to enable you to enhance your knowledge and skills in classroom management, and especially to support the development of positive approaches in dealing with pupil behaviour. It takes account of some of the most recent shifts in thinking and policy in this important dimension of your initial teacher education (ITE) programme. This includes advice that has emerged from a 'behaviour expert' nominated by the Department for Education (DfE), providing practical, hands-on information to teachers (DfE 2010a). More recently, this useful guidance has been reinforced (DfE 2014a: 6), with an emphasis that 'Teachers have statutory authority to discipline pupils whose behaviour is unacceptable, who break the school rules or who fail to follow a reasonable instruction'.

There has been a noticeable move away from reactive approaches to dealing with unwanted behaviour over the last 15 or more years. Such approaches were characterised by a preoccupation with 'discipline' being something that the teacher imposes on pupils (Robertson 1996). Instead, a greater awareness of 'behaviour for learning' has become apparent, which is consistent with the quest to develop inclusive schooling for all learners. Even so, it should be clearly understood that such an approach to pupil behaviour does not diminish the importance of clear and explicit classroom rules to govern pupil behaviour – and their consistent application. You need to ensure that pupils are under no illusions that, as class teacher, you are in control; it is, after all, what they expect of you!

A 'behaviour for learning' approach emphasises the teacher's role in creating an appropriate climate in which all pupils can learn effectively. It encourages you to link pupil behaviour with their learning via three interlinked relationships: how pupils think about themselves (their relationship with themselves); how they view their relationship with others (both teachers and fellow pupils); and how they perceive themselves as a learner, relative to the curriculum (their relationship with the learning they are undertaking). Recognition of the interplay between these three relationships is seen as the basis of a preventative approach. It also places importance on the role of the pupils themselves, in learning to manage their own behaviour.

Understanding this way of working remains an important facet of a teacher's role in managing pupil behaviour. The most recent advice has balanced this with a requirement that all teachers – and especially those newly qualified – understand some basic guidelines regarding the way in which the occurrence of unacceptable behaviour by pupils in a classroom can be minimised. Such behaviour has been a consistent cause of concern on the part of teachers themselves, educational professionals, parents and politicians for many decades; some aspects of these concerns are dealt with in the section dealing with 'policy context'.

Current approaches to 'behaviour' in ITE programmes reflect the shift in emphasis in the way that the issue is being tackled. The focus is on a middle ground between the earlier focus on 'control' and 'discipline' and a more recent holistic approach that focuses more upon linking behaviour with achievement.

This unit does not provide detailed accounts of individual behavioural needs or characteristics. There is now an extensive literature relating to the practical aspects of behaviour management, which is widely accessible elsewhere (see, for example, Dix 2007; Haydn 2008; www.behaviour2learn. co.uk). The unit concentrates on both the principles underpinning the links between pupil behaviour and the taught curriculum, as well as some of the important practical dimensions involved in effectively managing 'pupil discipline' in the classroom.

OBJECTIVES

At the end of this unit, you should be able to:

- recognise the policy context for promoting pupil learning in classrooms;
- interrogate a definition of the term 'unacceptable behaviour' and understand the significance of its underlying causes;
- recognise the importance of the links between pupil behaviour and their curriculum learning;
- understand the classroom implications of the current guidance to teachers regarding pupil behaviour;
- develop positive approaches to unacceptable behaviour that are based on relationships with pupils.

Check the requirements for your ITE programme to see which relate to this unit.

The current context: official advice and guidance

There has been an increasing emphasis upon the inclusion of a greater diversity of learners in mainstream schools in the last 20 or so years (DfEE 1999; DfES 2001a, 2003a). The underpinning ideology of educational inclusion is that the educational needs of all pupils in schools should be met, irrespective of their level of achievement or the nature of their behaviour (Evans and Lunt 2002). Thus, you will encounter a wide range of learner needs in your first encounters in the classroom. Pupils who exhibit what have been termed social, emotional and behavioural difficulties (SEBD) will almost certainly be present, even though recent changes in the Special educational needs (SEN) code of practice (DfE 2014k) have resulted in this category of pupils being removed from the remit of SEN provision. Such pupils have traditionally represented as many as 20 per cent of all pupils who have SEN (DfE 2014c). The challenging behaviour of these pupils is usually accompanied by underachievement or a specific educational need. In consequence, they will most likely be supported by the special educational needs coordinator (SENCO), teaching assistants and by other key workers in the school.

SEBD is a term that has previously referred to a continuum of behaviours, from relatively minor behaviour problems to serious mental illness (DfE 1994b). In this unit, the focus is principally on pupil behaviours that are viewed as low-level unacceptable behaviours – in other words, not those towards the more serious end of the continuum. However, you may sometimes encounter pupils who present more challenging behaviours in your classroom, including some who may abuse drugs and other substances; pupils with mental health needs and pupils who experience behaviour-related syndromes, such as attention deficit hyperactivity disorder (ADHD) or autistic spectrum disorders (ASD). Many of these behaviours, including those that are sometimes intense and very challenging to teachers, can be more effectively managed if you build proactive, positive strategies into your teaching. There are also existing school strategies and support (including a key teacher or tutor) who is directly involved in dealing with these more extreme behaviours. In addition, in instances where such pupils are present, such support will frequently be available from a teaching assistant who will work with the pupil in your classroom.

An important feature of a school's promotion of a 'positive climate', as well as its response to unacceptable behaviour, is the 'whole school behaviour policy' (DfE 2011d, 2014a). Its importance is stressed in straightforward terms: 'It is vital that the behaviour policy is clear, that it is well understood by staff, parents and pupils, and that it is consistently applied' (DfE 2014a: 5-6). As a matter of course, you should make sure that you familiarise yourself with its content. The government sets out clear guidelines regarding its content (below), although you should also recognise that individual schools vary according to the behaviour routines and rules they put in place:

1   a consistent approach to behaviour management;
2   strong school leadership;
3   classroom management;
4   rewards and sanctions;
5   behaviour strategies and the teaching of good behaviour;
6   staff development and support;
7   pupil support systems;
8   liaison with parents and other agencies;
9   managing pupil transition;
10 organisation and facilities.

A whole-school behaviour policy provides some of the basic building blocks that you use to help establish a positive classroom 'climate'; this term refers to the character or 'feel' of your classroom, as experienced by all those who experience it – teachers, pupils and any classroom visitors. A major influence on this is the class teacher's own repertoire of knowledge, skills and understanding about pupil behaviour and classroom management. To assist you in acquiring these attributes, you may be assisted by lead behaviour teachers, tutors and other suitably experienced professionals who provide practical support in positively managing behaviour (DCSF 2008c). In addition, further support can be provided by teachers from other educational settings; for example, pupil referral units (PRUs), special schools for pupils experiencing SEBD, teaching assistants and local authority (LA) personnel who have a specific brief for work in SEBD (Walker 2004).

Some of the key policy documents relating to pupil behaviour have already been referenced in this unit; a full listing is provided in the further reading at the end of the unit. These advice and guidance documents in England aim, among other things, to help teachers to promote positive behaviour and to support them in tackling issues of low-level unacceptable behaviour. They point to the importance of providing creative and positive learning environments for all pupils. They also provide a framework that you can use in order to develop a set of rules and routines based on the development of a positive relationship between yourself and the pupils. This is the first step in helping to insulate pupils from those factors (discussed later in this unit), which might cause them to behave inappropriately and, in consequence, fail to thrive as learners.

One related aspect of pupil behaviour that requires special mention is bullying. Like other unacceptable behaviours, bullying varies in its type and intensity. The current guidance on bullying in schools, which you should become familiar with, is provided in *Preventing and Tackling Bullying: Advice for Headteachers Staff and Governing Bodies* (DfE 2014h).

Finally, you are reminded that the Office for Standards in Education (Ofsted) framework includes 'behaviour and safety' as one of its key criteria for inspections (Ofsted 2012b). As well as being intrinsic to becoming a successful classroom teacher, there is a statutory emphasis that behaviour is a feature of teaching that will be under continuing close scrutiny in England, and no doubt in other countries, in the years ahead.

What is unacceptable behaviour?

Recent national advice and guidance on behaviour management in England emphasises the development of appropriate, positive behaviour. This has been identified as bringing significant benefits for all pupils (Redpath and Harker 1999). The guidance invites teachers to be clear about what behaviour they want pupils to engage in, and to model this as part of their teaching.

However, the term 'behaviour' has traditionally been taken to mean unacceptable behaviour. The Elton Report (DES 1989a) refers to misbehaviour as 'behaviour which causes concern to teachers'. The term is one that can variously be replaced by a range of other expressions that teachers use to describe unwanted, unacceptable behaviour by pupils. Thus, disruptive, challenging, antisocial, off-task, unwanted, emotional and behavioural difficulties (EBD) and SEBD are terms that are widely used, according to the personal orientation of the teacher concerned and to the type of problem behaviour being described.

The term 'unacceptable behaviour', as with its companion descriptors (see above), is often used as a catch-all expression for pupil behaviours that span a continuum (DfE 1994b). The so-called EBD continuum ranges from low-level unacceptable behaviour at one end (such as talking out of turn, distracting others, occasionally arriving late in class) to more serious, sometimes acting out behaviour, at the other (such as non-attendance, verbal or physical aggression, wilful disobedience and bullying). This confusion was recognised by DfE (1994b), which described EBD as all those behaviours that comprise a continuum from 'normal though unacceptable' to mental illness; confusion rather than clarity over definitions seemed to increase when the term EBD subsequently incorporated social difficulties into the spectrum to become SEBD (DCSF 2008c).

A previous version of the *SEN Code of Practice* (DfES 2001b: 93) defined 'children and young people who demonstrate features of emotional and behavioural difficulties' as those who are 'withdrawn and isolated, disruptive and disturbing, hyperactive and lacking concentration'.

DESIRABLE BEHAVIOUR	UNDESIRABLE BEHAVIOUR
L1. Attentive/interested in schoolwork	
• attentive to teacher, not easily distracted	• verbal off-task behaviours
• interest in most schoolwork/starts promptly on set tasks/motivated	• does not finish work/gives up easily
	• constantly needs reminders/low attention span
• seems to enjoy school	• negative approach to school
L2. Good learning organisation	
• competent in individual learning	• forgetful, copies or rushes work
• tidy work at reasonable pace	• inaccurate, messy and slow work
• can organise learning tasks	• fails to meet deadlines, not prepared
L3. Effective communicator	
• good communication skills (peers/adults)	• poor communication skills
• knows when it's appropriate to speak	• inappropriate timing of communication
• uses non-verbal signals and voice range	• constantly talks
• communicates in 1:1 or group settings	• lack of use of non-verbal skills
L4. Works efficiently in a group	
• works collaboratively	• refuses to share
• turn-takes in communication/listens	• does not take turns
• takes responsibility within a group	
L5. Seeks help where necessary	
• seeks attention from teacher when required	• constantly seeking assistance
• works independently or in groups when not requiring help	• makes excessive and inappropriate demands
	• does not ask 'finding out' questions
C6. Behaves respectfully towards staff	
• cooperative and compliant	• responds negatively to instruction
• responds positively to instruction	• talks back impertinently to teacher
• does not aim verbal aggression at teacher	• aims verbal aggression, swears at teacher
• interacts politely with teacher	• deliberately interrupts to annoy
• does not deliberately try to annoy or answer the teacher rudely	
C7. Shows respect to other pupils	
• uses appropriate language; does not swear	• verbal violence at other pupils
• treats others as equals	• scornful, use of social aggression (e.g. 'pushing in')
• does not dominate, bully or intimidate	• teases and bullies
	• inappropriate sexual behaviour
C8. Seeks attention appropriately	
• does not attract inappropriate attention	• hums, fidgets, disturbs others
• does not play the fool or show off	• throws things, climbs on things
• no attention-seeking behaviour	• calls out. eats, runs around the class
• does not verbally disrupt	• shouts and otherwise attention seeks
• does not physically disrupt	• does dangerous things without thought

Figure 3.3.1 Desirable and undesirable behaviour

Source: Adapted from QCA (2001b)

Key: L = learning behaviour; C = conduct/behaviour; E = emotional behaviour

DESIRABLE BEHAVIOUR	UNDESIRABLE BEHAVIOUR
C9. Physically peaceable • does not show physical aggression • does not pick on others • is not cruel or spiteful • avoids getting into fights with others • does not have temper tantrums	• fights, aims physical violence at others • loses temper, throws things • bullies and intimidates physically • cruel/spiteful
C10. Respects property • takes care of own and others' property • does not engage in vandalism • does not steal	• poor respect for property • destroys own or others' things • steals things
E11. Has empathy • is tolerant and considerate • tries to identify with feelings of others • tries to offer comfort • is not emotionally detached • does not laugh when others are upset	• intolerant • emotionally detached • selfish • no awareness of feelings of others
E12. Is socially aware • understands social interactions of self and peers • appropriate verbal/non-verbal contacts • not socially isolated • has peer-group friends; not a loner • doesn't frequently daydream • actively involved in classroom activity • not aloof, passive or withdrawn	• inactive, daydreams, stares into space • withdrawn or unresponsive • does not participate in class activity • few friends • not accepted or well-liked • shows bizarre behaviour • stares blankly, listless
E13. Is happy • smiles and laughs appropriately • should be able to have fun • generally cheerful; seldom upset • not discontented, sulky, morose	• depressed, unhappy or discontented • prone to emotional upset, tearful • infers suicide • serious, sad, self-harming
E14. Is confident • not anxious • unafraid to try new things • not self-conscious, doesn't feel inferior • willing to read aloud, answer questions in class • participates in group discussion	• anxious, tense, tearful • reticent, fears failure, feels inferior • lacks self-esteem, cautious, shy • does not take initiative
E15. Emotionally stable/self-controlled • no mood swings • good emotional resilience, recovers quickly from upset • manages own feelings • not easily flustered or frustrated • delays gratification	• inappropriate emotional reactions • does not recover quickly from upsets • does not express feelings • frequent mood changes; irritable • over-reacts; does not accept punishment or praise • does not delay gratification

Figure 3.3.1 continued

The definition also includes those who display 'immature social skills and those who present challenging behaviours arising from other complex special needs'.

One of the major difficulties in defining what inappropriate behaviour constitutes is that it varies according to the perception, tolerance threshold, experience and management approach of individual teachers. What might be an unacceptable behaviour in your own classroom may be viewed in another context, or by another (student) teacher, as quite normal. Alternatively, what you accept as normal may be seen as unacceptable in another context or by another (student) teacher. This leads to confusion in the mind of pupils, and to potential tension between individual teachers in a school or between a student teacher and tutor or other experienced teacher. So it is important to recognise that: (a) pupil behaviour is described explicitly in terms of observable actions; and (b) responses to it take full regard of a school's policy concerning behaviour and apply it with consistency. When you describe a pupil behaviour, you should always ensure that your definition is of the behaviour itself and not a description of the pupil as a whole. This avoids any likelihood of the pupil being labelled as a disruptive pupil or a problem pupil.

The Qualifications and Curriculum Authority (QCA 2001b) usefully identified 15 behaviours by which a pupil's emotional and behavioural development might be defined and assessed. These were divided into learning behaviours, conduct behaviours and emotional behaviours. Each group is subdivided into sets of criteria, depicting desirable and undesirable behaviours (see Figure 3.3.1). Now complete Task 3.3.1.

 Task 3.3.1 School policy on pupil behaviour

Familiarise yourself with your placement school's whole-school policy on behaviour and attendance. Discuss it with another student teacher who is placed in a different school. Consider both the similarities and differences in the two policies. What are the implications of the document for you as a student teacher, particularly in respect of classroom management?

Record your reflections in your professional development portfolio (PDP).

Identifying or defining unacceptable behaviour is important if you are going to develop strategies to deal with it in ways that promote learning. You need to describe exactly what any unwanted behaviour actually comprises in order to give a precise and objective description of what has occurred. Importantly, you need to describe the behaviour itself, not the pupil, otherwise there may be unwarranted negative labelling of the pupil. Task 3.3.2 helps you to develop a definition of unacceptable behaviour.

Scoping the causal factors

As Ayers and Prytys (2002: 38) noted, 'The way in which behaviour is conceptualised will determine the treatment of emotional and behavioural problems'. There are a number of causal factors that assist in explaining unwanted behaviour, disaffection and disengagement among some pupils; these are often multivariate and overlapping. The attribution of a cause can frequently result in the

Task 3.3.2 What is unacceptable behaviour?

It is important that you arrive at a personal definition of what comprises unacceptable behaviour. Divide a blank sheet of paper into three. Head the left-hand section 'Totally unacceptable' and the right-hand section 'Acceptable'. The middle section is reserved for 'Acceptable in certain circumstances'. Now examine your own classroom teaching, and complete each section. Remember, behaviour is as much about positive learning behaviour as it is those pupil actions that you regard as unacceptable or challenging. Reflect on your responses and discuss with your tutor and record in your PDP. Should the opportunity arise, you might wish to undertake this exercise with your pupils, in order to gather their thoughts. Comparing your list to theirs is likely to prove very revealing! You may also wish to discuss your responses with another student teacher.

acquisition of a negative label by the pupil. But, on the other hand, understanding and recognising the causes can give you clues as to what might be successful strategies. A brief outline of causal factors is given below. There is more exhaustive coverage in a variety of other sources (for example, Garner *et al.* 2014).

Factors that may cause unacceptable behaviour

You should recognise that for some pupils, their unacceptable behaviour is caused by several of the factors identified below:

Individual factors

- A pupil believes that the work is not within their grasp and as a result feels embarrassed and alienated and lacks self-esteem as a learner.
- A pupil may well experience learning difficulties.
- A pupil may have mental health, stress and possible drug misuse issues, all of which are important factors explaining underachievement and inappropriate behaviour in adolescence.

Cultural factors

- Adolescence can be a period of rebellion or resistance for many young people.
- Possible tension between societal expectation and the beliefs and opinions of the pupil.
- Group/peer pressure can result in various forms of alienation to school.
- Negative experience of schooling by parents, siblings or other family members.

Curriculum relevance factors (linked to both individual and cultural)

- The curriculum may be seen by a pupil to be inaccessible and irrelevant.
- The school may give academic excellence more value than vocational qualifications or curriculum options.

School ethos and relationships factors

■ Some schools can be 'deviance provocative' – their organisational structures and procedures are viewed by pupils as oppressive and negative.

■ Some schools are less inclusive, both academically and socially, to pupils who behave 'differently'.

External barriers to participation and learning factors

■ Family breakdown or illness usually impacts negatively on a pupil's mental health, and often on their sense of priority.

■ Poverty and hardship can mean that a pupil's physiological needs are not met – such pupils may be tired, hungry and consequently easily distracted (see also Maslow 1970 in Unit 3.2).

■ Sibling and caring responsibilities may mean that some pupils arrive late in your lesson – or not at all.

One aspect of causality that needs further consideration is that causal influences have been conceptualised as constituting three interlinked relationships first identified in what Bronfenbrenner (1979) called the *ecosystemic theory of relationships*. In the case of a pupil who is consistently behaving inappropriately, it is suggested that there has been a breakdown in one (or more) of these three relationships:

■ pupils' relationship with themselves (how pupils feel about themselves, their self-confidence as learners and their self-esteem);

■ pupils' relationship with others (how they interact socially and academically with all others in their class and school);

■ pupils' relationship with the learning they are undertaking (the curriculum) (how accessible they feel a lesson is and how best they think they learn).

The interrelationship between these is shown in Figure 3.3.2.

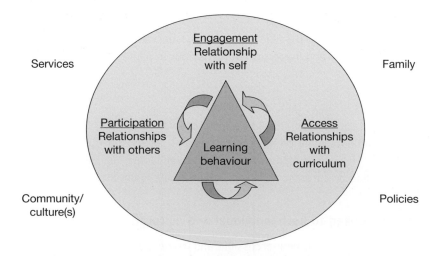

Figure 3.3.2 The behaviour for learning model

Source: After Tod and Powell (2004)

Subsequently, this theory was applied to pupil behaviour, in what was termed 'behaviour for learning' (Ellis and Tod 2009). This approach argues that all three 'relationships' need to be taken into account when planning your strategy to tackle unacceptable behaviour. The emphasis upon positive relationships is an integral component of the approach, with individual pupils as well as whole classes. This effort needs to begin from your first encounter with a group of pupils; over time, it will enable you to establish a classroom climate in which pupil learning can flourish.

Task 3.3.3 links causes to possible teaching strategies.

 Task 3.3.3 Linking causes to possible teaching strategies

Consider one pupil you are teaching who sometimes exhibits behaviour(s) unacceptable to you. Write a brief description of each of the behaviours, making sure that your language is clear and describes clearly observable pupil actions. Taking each behaviour in turn and referring to the causal factors identified above, assess which factors you feel might underlie that particular behaviour. Consider how amenable to change each of the causal factors you have identified is. Also identify any other teachers (for example, the SENCO) who might be able to provide you with advice and support. Finally, reflect on how your interpretation of cause might inform the way in which you choose to address the behaviour(s) shown.

Make notes in your PDP and discuss your responses with your tutor.

Key principles of a behaviour for learning approach

During the last six to seven years, there has been an increasing interest in the 'social and emotional aspect of learning' (SEAL). This recognises that an awareness of aspects of 'emotional intelligence' (Goleman 1995) can assist teachers in helping to create a positive climate for learning, in which good relationships between them and their pupils are paramount. It is based, in part, on the premise that 'generally a punitive approach tends to worsen or sometimes even create the very problems it is intended to eradicate . . . punishment alienates children from their teachers and does nothing to build up trust that is the bedrock of relationships' (Weare 2004: 63). Crucially, and linking SEAL to the notion of 'behaviour for learning', an understanding of 'self' is a cornerstone of learner motivation. As a result, pupils can:

- be effective and successful learners;
- make and sustain friendships;
- deal with and resolve conflict effectively and fairly;
- solve problems with others or by themselves;
- manage strong feelings such as frustration, anger and anxiety;
- recover from setbacks and persist in the face of difficulties;
- work and play cooperatively;
- compete fairly and win and lose with dignity and respect for competitors.

Although each of these represents a complex undertaking, your use of them as guidelines in developing your thinking about pupil behaviour will pay rich dividends as you progress in your teaching career. Discuss with your tutor how you might be able to do this.

A behaviour for learning approach accepts that most social and emotional aspects of learning (SEAL) are learned, and therefore can be taught or modelled by the teacher. Evidence strongly suggests that the most successful strategies for developing a positive learning environment are those that incorporate the promotion of positive relationships (Burnett 2002). As has been suggested, each of the three (interlinked) relationships is important in developing a positive learning environment in the classroom, and as a teacher you are at the very heart of orchestrating them. Although some pupils have relatively advanced 'social and emotional' skills when they arrive at school, others (often pupils who can sometimes behave unacceptably) might need support and the direct teaching of the specific skills they have not yet learned. So your task is to focus on helping to develop appropriate skills that enable each pupil to learn within a variety of learning contexts. This can be in whole-class or small-group situations in the classroom and elsewhere in the school. Some basic principles inform the way in which this can be done. These are as follows:

■ Behaviour for learning is a positive description. It tells pupils what you want them to do and why this helps them to learn, rather than focusing on behaviours that you do not want in your classroom.
■ It requires that you place value on (and praise appropriately) pupil behaviour that enables and maximises learning.
■ Effective behaviour for learning strategies can range from high-level listening and collaborative learning skills to remaining seated for two minutes. The emphasis is upon setting targets that are reachable by pupils.

Getting the simple things right!

So far in this unit, the focus has been placed upon the underlying principles of creating a positive learning environment. But your understanding of these must coincide with a parallel focus on the strategies that you can implement practically in order to establish yourself as a teacher who can manage pupil behaviour effectively.

In the words of the government's own Expert Adviser on Behaviour, 'managing a school or a class is a complex operation and because of this complexity it is easy to fail to get the simple, but essential, things right' (DfE 2011d). To assist you in avoiding some of the more obvious pitfalls, a helpful checklist has been devised (see Figure 3.3.3).

Each of the items in the checklist will most likely become 'second nature' to you; they are commonly understood by successful teachers as being crucial to organising effective learning in their classrooms. What you will notice is that each of the recommendations in the behaviour checklist (DfE 2011d) connects well with both Bronfenbrenner's ecosystem theory and the relationships that underpin a 'behaviour for learning' approach. Now complete Task 3.3.4.

Incorporating both a set of clear principles and some straightforward actions enables you to prevent the occurrence of unacceptable behaviour by pupils. It also assists you in giving a firm and consistent response to any instances of problem behaviour that might arise. What this also does is enable you to present yourself in a classroom leadership role. Most pupils will come to your classroom wanting to learn, although there will be times when some will either be unable or unwilling to learn on account of some of the factors described earlier in this unit. In dealing with this situation, it is important to develop certain classroom leadership skills that contribute to your being able to

Classroom

☐ Know the names and roles of any adults in class.
☐ Meet and greet pupils when they come into the classroom.
☐ Display rules in the class – and ensure that the pupils and staff know what they are.
☐ Display the tariff of sanctions in class.
☐ Have a system in place to follow through with all sanctions.
☐ Display the tariff of rewards in class.
☐ Have a system in place to follow through with all rewards.
☐ Have a visual timetable on the wall.
☐ Follow the school behaviour policy.

Pupils

☐ Know the names of pupils.
☐ Have a plan for pupils who are likely to misbehave.
☐ Ensure other adults in the class know the plan.
☐ Understand pupils' special needs.

Teaching

☐ Ensure that all resources are prepared in advance.
☐ Praise the behaviour you want to see more of.
☐ Praise pupils doing the right thing more than criticising those who are doing the wrong thing (parallel praise).
☐ Differentiate.
☐ Stay calm.
☐ Have clear routines for transitions and for stopping the class.
☐ Teach pupils the class routines.

Parents

☐ Give feedback to parents about their child's behaviour – let them know about the good days as well as the bad ones.

Figure 3.3.3 Behaviour checklist for teachers

Source: DfE (2011d)

 Task 3.3.4 Relationships and pupil behaviour

We have noted that promoting positive behaviour requires the teacher to understand three sets of relationships, with *self*, *others* and with the *curriculum*. But we have also noted that you need to take some practical steps in order to make these relationships happen. Examine the behaviour checklist (see Figure 3.3.3) and allocate each of the items in it to one or more of these relationship areas. Reflect on their distribution, compare and discuss your findings with another student teacher and store your findings in your PDP.

establish a well-organised environment for learning, forge positive relationships with all pupils, and establish a classroom ethos that allows pupils to demonstrate positive behaviour and optimum attainment.

A classroom leader needs to address three broad elements that help to define the ethos of the classroom. While these issues are important for all pupils, they are essential elements for promoting the engagement and positive behaviour of pupils who are at risk of misbehaviour. They are:

■ Motivation: you need to provide time at the start of each lesson to tell pupils what they are learning and why. Pupils need to be involved at every stage in assessing whether these learning intentions have been met (Unit 3.2 looks at motivation in more depth).
■ Emotional well-being: to help reduce pupil anxiety, you should share the lesson structure with pupils at the start, so they know what is going to happen during the lesson.
■ Expectations: you need to give time at the start of the lesson and before each new activity to make clear what behaviours are needed for this piece of learning to be successful.

These three underpinning elements are embedded in more specific teacher actions that allow you to demonstrate your role as the classroom leader to your pupils. These include:

■ good communication between yourself and your pupils (see Unit 3.1);
■ secure subject knowledge;
■ providing lively, well-paced lessons;
■ understanding and meeting the learning needs of all pupils in your class;
■ acting on your reflections and evaluations of previous lessons (feedback loop) (see also Unit 2.1);
■ demonstrating confidence and direction in managing pupils;
■ modelling desired behaviours yourself.

It is unlikely that, as a student teacher, everything clicks into place straight away; some of these will develop with experience. Nevertheless, it is worth noting that research has shown that student teachers who display confidence in managing their classes are less likely to encounter problem behaviour by pupils (Giallo and Little 2003).

Building positive relationships in classrooms

As has been discussed earlier in this unit, promoting positive behaviour places emphasis on the relationships you form with your pupils. Ineffective interventions are usually the product of unsatisfactory relationships with individual pupils. These interventions, even though they are ultimately unsuccessful, take up valuable teaching time and impact negatively on the learning of an individual pupil, the rest of the class, and also on your own confidence. Most interventions should take the form of positive actions that fit somewhere on a continuum from *positive reinforcement* through to *positive correction*. The actions you select should be those that enable learning to continue. They usually include eye contact, use of pupil name, description of the appropriate behaviour you would like the pupil to demonstrate, praise and affirmation (see also Units 3.1 and 3.2). For example:

■ modelling appropriate behaviour;

■ positive reinforcement and the appropriate use of targeted praise;

■ consistent and firm application of rules;

■ use of verbal and non-verbal communication;

■ listening to pupils and respecting their opinions;

■ remaining vigilant (pre-empting unacceptable behaviour);

■ dealing decisively with lateness and non-attendance.

By consistently using these approaches in your teaching, you are more likely to forge meaningful and positive relationships with your pupils. In sum, effective relationships mean that there is common ground between pupil and teacher. This is as vital in securing appropriate conditions for learning as it is for managing those behavioural issues that may be potentially problematic.

Structuring your lessons to promote positive behaviour

The design of effective lessons is fundamental to high-quality teaching and learning, and is vital to the job of promoting positive behaviour; the government's behaviour checklist provides a baseline set of headings that you need to take into account in doing this. As the commentary on the checklist states:

> Teachers who follow these guidelines find there is more consistency of approach to managing behaviour, both in the classroom and around the school. When children know that teachers will stick to the behaviour policy and class routines, they feel safer and happy, and behaviour improves.
>
> (DfE 2011d: 1)

As a result, pupil behaviour, as well as their learning, will improve. Effective lesson design takes into account behavioural differences between pupils as much as it does their levels of achievement or the subject or skill they are learning. Your teaching should be characterised by:

■ focus and structure so that pupils are clear about what is to be learned and how it fits with what they know already;

■ actively engaging pupils in their learning so that they make their own meaning from it;

■ developing pupils' learning skills systematically so that their learning becomes increasingly independent (see also Unit 5.2);

■ using assessment for learning to help pupils reflect on what they already know, reinforce the learning being developed and set targets for the future (Units 6.1 and 6.2 discuss assessment);

■ having high expectations of the effort that pupils should make and what they can achieve (see also Unit 3.2);

■ motivating pupils by well-paced lessons, using stimulating activities matched to a range of learning styles that encourage attendance;

■ creating an environment that promotes learning in a settled and purposeful atmosphere.

You can further promote a positive approach to behaviour by building individual teaching sequences within an overall lesson. The lesson (or a sequence of lessons) needs first of all to be firmly located, in the mind of the pupil, in the context of: (a) a scheme of work; (b) pupils' prior knowledge; and (c) their preferred learning styles. It is also important to identify clear learning outcomes. Structuring your lesson as a series of 'episodes' by separating pupil learning into distinct stages or steps, and then planning how each step should be taught, enables those pupils who are at risk of distraction or lack of concentration to regard the lesson as a series of 'bite-sized chunks'. Finally, you can secure overall coherence by providing: (a) a stimulating start to the lesson; (b) transition 'signposts' between each lesson episode, which reviews pupil learning so far and launches the next episode; and (c) a final plenary session that reviews learning (lesson planning is covered in Unit 2.2).

Rights, responsibilities, routines and rules

A framework for promoting positive classroom behaviour has been commonly constructed around the so-called 4Rs: rights, responsibilities, rules and routines (Hook and Vass 2000). You should recognise that such a focus operates best within the context of a fifth 'R', already encountered in this unit – 'relationships'. In applying aspects of the 4Rs, you need to be very sensitive, as a student teacher, to the existing arrangements in any class that you work in – these will have been established over a long period of time by the permanent class teacher. But you can begin by being conscious of how each of these 'Rs' can have a positive impact on your teaching.

Rights (R1) and responsibilities (R2)

Both rights and responsibilities are inextricably linked. They refer equally to teacher and pupils, and are the basis on which classroom relationships, teaching and learning are built.

- Teacher's responsibilities – you must seek to enable all pupils to learn, to seek out and celebrate improvements in learning, to treat pupils with respect and to create a positive classroom environment in which pupils feel safe and able to learn.
- Teacher's rights – you must be allowed to teach with a minimum of hindrance, to feel safe, to be supported by colleagues and to be listened to.
- Pupils' responsibilities – pupils must be willing to learn, to allow others to learn, to cooperate with teaching and other staff and peers, and to do their best at all times.
- Pupils' rights – pupils should be treated with respect, be safe, be able to learn and be listened to.

Rules (R3)

These are the mechanisms by which rights and responsibilities are translated into adult and pupil behaviours. They are best constructed collaboratively, so that the views of all pupils are taken into account.

Routines (R4)

These are the structures that underpin the rules and reinforce the smooth running of the classroom. The more habitual the routines become, the more likely they are to be used. Pupils who behave inappropriately often do so because they are unsure of what is happening in the classroom at a given time. Consistent application of your classroom rules will constitute a major step in establishing a routine in your class.

In using the 4Rs as a basis for promoting positive pupils, you should be encouraged to provide opportunities for your pupils to make choices about their behaviour, thus allowing them to take responsibility for their own actions. Choice is guided by their responsibilities and leads to positive or negative consequences according to the choice made by the pupil.

Consequences

Pupils need to know the consequences of sensible or inadvisable choices. Responsible choices lead to positive consequences; conversely, a choice to behave inappropriately leads to a known negative consequence.

Now complete Task 3.3.5, which is designed to help you to focus on the ways you use encouragement, positive feedback and praise in the classroom, and Task 3.3.6, which focuses on the impact of praise on your pupils.

In Task 3.3.7, you are asked to explore the links between behaviour and learning. Task 3.3.8 asks you to consider different definitions of unacceptable behaviour.

 Task 3.3.5 Monitoring your use of praise and encouragement in the classroom

A very useful starting point to promote the notion of positive approaches to behaviour is to examine the ways in which you provide encouragement, positive feedback and praise to your pupils. You can assess this by developing a log of praise and encouragement to use as a tool for measuring these positive interactions.

Add to the list of positive pupil behaviours identified below, which you can use to give praise. Underneath each one, note the words or actions you might use to convey to the pupil that your recognition carries value and meaning in that they are clearly directed towards a particular pupil and are linked to the positive behaviour that the pupil has demonstrated.

1   Queuing sensibly and quietly to enter the classroom.
2   Allowing another pupil to go first.
3   Lending an item of equipment to another pupil.
4   Putting waste paper in the bin.
5   Supporting another pupil's learning.
6   _____
7   _____
8   _____
9   _____
10 _____

During your observation of a lesson taught by a more experienced teacher in your placement school, record other ways in which that teacher acknowledges positive behaviour by pupils. Compare your notes on this topic with another student teacher working in a different setting. Store in your PDP for later reference.

Task 3.3.6 The impact of praise

Undertake a small-scale project designed to establish the impact of 'praise' on pupils in your class. In doing this, you should: (a) develop one or more research questions, so that your data collection has a focus; (b) identify a small, but recent and relevant, set of literature that contributes to a theoretical understanding of the issue; (c) define and provide a rationale for your methodology (including coverage of any ethical issues that might emerge in such a study); (d) gather and analyse data; and (e) consider the relevance of your findings to your practice. Store this in your PDP.

Among the possible research questions you might wish to consider are:

■ Do boys prefer different kinds of praise and encouragement than girls?
■ Does the nature and type of praise change according to age?
■ What types of praise do pupils prefer?
■ Is praise evenly distributed among your teaching group?
■ Is praise carefully targeted and in response to specific pupil actions?
■ Does personal praise link closely with a whole-school approach?

Task 3.3.7 Exploring further the links between behaviour and learning

To explore further the links between behaviour and learning, select one or more pupils who you currently teach in your placement school and who present you with a particular challenge on account of their unacceptable behaviour. You should explore the learning and behaviour interface by responding to the following key questions:

■ Does the educational achievement of this pupil vary from one curriculum subject to another?
■ What are the characteristics of those curriculum subjects in which the pupil appears to perform more effectively?
■ Has the pattern of educational achievement been inconsistent over time? Are there any logical explanations for this?
■ Do you know anything about the pupil's preferred learning style?
■ What are your own views about the capabilities of this pupil?
■ What do other subject teachers say about the educational achievements of this pupil?

Each of the above questions can form the basis of a small-scale classroom enquiry. For each, you could: (a) gather evidence from the school's pupil data; (b) obtain information from key personnel (for instance, the pupil's form tutor, or the SENCO); and (c) secure inputs from the pupil directly (subject to the appropriate permissions).

On the basis of what you discover, try to formulate a theoretical model for both the unacceptable behaviours displayed and their relationship with more positive aspects of this pupil's school performance. Store this in your PDP.

M

 Task 3.3.8 Interpretations of unacceptable behaviour

Interpretations of 'unacceptable behaviour', and the ways in which it has been defined, have changed over time. In spite of this, the educational literature is replete with material (research papers, books, official reports and guidance documents) looking at ways in which schools and teachers can manage behaviour more effectively. Two examples of this, separated by nearly 20 years, are the Elton Report (1989) and the Steer Report (2005). Using the links provided below, consider the similarities and differences in the recommendations of each report. What does the content of these documents tell you about official policy on pupil behaviour? Are there many commonalities regarding the practical advice that these reports offer to classroom teachers? Are you able to draw any inferences from the generic commentaries given concerning the nature and extent of pupil behaviour in schools?

Write up your analysis, discuss with your tutor or other student teachers and store in your PDP.

The Elton Report is available at: http://www.educationengland.org.uk/documents/elton/elton1989.html

The Steer Report is available at: www.educationengland.org.uk/documents/pdfs/2005-steer-report-learning-behaviour.pdf

SUMMARY AND KEY POINTS

■ Adopting a positive approach to managing pupil behaviour is crucially important.

■ Become familiar with your school's policies regarding behaviour management.

■ Take steps to understand what are the underlying causes of the problem behaviour in your class – this is the first step in taking positive action.

■ Try to establish a clear set of classroom rules and rewards and sanctions, and ensure that they are applied consistently and fairly.

■ Focus on your relationships with pupils – establishing an effective working relationship is crucial to a positive classroom 'ethos'.

■ Always try to lead by example – try to model the kinds of positive behaviours you want to see from your pupils.

■ Seek guidance and support from more experienced teachers in your school, and make use of all opportunities for professional development.

Check which requirements for your ITE programme you have addressed through this unit.

Further reading

Ellis, S. and Tod, J. (2014) *Promoting Behaviour for Learning in the Classroom*, London: Routledge.
This book provides a concise analysis of established behaviour management strategies that you can use in your own classroom. It recognises that no single approach will work for *all* pupils and that it is important to understand the individual needs, attributes and personalities of your pupils when deciding how best to intervene. The book covers a range of issues, including developing positive relationships in the classroom, understanding personal style and self-management, making use of effective feedback and rewards, individual differences and special educational needs, and dealing with challenging behaviour.

Haydn, T. (2012) *Managing Pupil Behaviour: Improving the Classroom Atmosphere*, 2nd edn, London: Routledge.
This book provides some very practical insights into how best you can manage behaviour effectively in your classroom. It will encourage you to think about the degree to which you are relaxed and in assured control of your class – so that you can really enjoy your teaching.
Managing Pupil Behaviour uses the views of over 140 teachers and 700 pupils to provide insights into the factors that enable teachers to manage learning effectively in their classrooms. It argues that this enables pupils to learn and achieve. Key issues explored include the factors that influence the working atmosphere in the classroom, the impact of that atmosphere on teaching and learning, and tensions around inclusive practice and situations where some pupils may be spoiling the learning of others.

Rogers, W. (2011) *Classroom Behaviour: A Practical Guide to Effective Teaching, Behaviour Management and Colleague Support*, London: Sage.
This book explores some of the issues that you will face when working in today's classrooms. It describes real situations and dilemmas and offers advice on dealing with the challenges of the job. Emphasis is placed on how to establish and enhance your relationships with pupils. The book also considers some more specialist aspects of teaching pupils who have additional needs, including sections looking at dealing with bullying, teaching students on the autistic spectrum in a mainstream classroom and working with very challenging students.

Roffey, S. (2010) *Changing Behaviour in Schools*, London: Sage.
This book will show you how to promote positive behaviour and well-being in your classroom. It provides examples of effective strategies for encouraging prosocial and collaborative behaviour in the classroom, the school and the wider community. It emphasises the importance of the social and emotional aspects of learning and introduces the idea that pupils should develop a sense of belonging in the classroom. Each chapter has case studies from primary and secondary schools, activities, checklists and suggestions for further reading.

Other resources and websites

Key policy documents relating to pupil behaviour

Improving behaviour and attendance in schools
www.gov.uk/government/policies/improving-behaviour-and-attendance-in-schools
Status: Departmental Policy, August 2014

Behaviour and discipline in schools: advice to headteachers and school staff
www.gov.uk/government/publications/behaviour-and-discipline-in-schools
Status: Departmental advice, September 2014

Getting the simple things right: Charlie Taylor's behaviour checklists: www.education.gov.uk/schools/pupilsupport/behaviour/a00199342/getting-the-simple-thingsright-charlie-taylors-behaviour-checklists
Status: Departmental advice, April 2012

Guidance for governing bodies on behaviour and discipline
www.gov.uk/government/publications/behaviour-and-discipline-in-schools-guidance-for-governing-bodies
Status: Statutory guidance, July 2013

Use of reasonable force
www.gov.uk/government/publications/use-of-reasonable-force-in-schools
Status: Departmental advice, July 2013

Screening, searching and confiscation
www.gov.uk/government/publications/searching-screening-and-confiscation
Status: Departmental advice (February 2014)

Preventing and tackling bullying
www.gov.uk/government/publications/preventing-and-tackling-bullying
Status: Departmental advice, November 2014

Appendix 2 on pages 591–595 provides further examples of websites you may find useful.

Capel, S., Leask, M. and Turner, T. (eds) (2010) *Readings for Learning to Teach in the Secondary School: A Companion to M Level Study*, London: Routledge.
This book brings together essential readings to support you in your critical engagement with key issues raised in this textbook.

The subject-specific books in the Routledge *Learning to Teach* series are also very useful.

Any additional resources and an editable version of any relevant tasks/tables in this unit are available on the companion website: www.routledge.com/cw/capel

3.4 Primary-secondary transitions

Divya Jindal-Snape

Introduction

Educational transition is an ongoing process that involves moving from one educational context and set of interpersonal relationships to another (Jindal-Snape 2010a). It includes moving from one educational setting to another but also moving from one class to another within the same school. Usually, educational transitions signal progression and 'moving up'. It may therefore be assumed that most pupils get positive messages and are very happy during these transitions. While most do find these transitions satisfying and fulfilling, with increases in opportunities and choices (Lucey and Reay 2000; Jindal-Snape and Foggie 2008), some pupils find them stressful and challenging, with dips in achievement, motivation and self-esteem (Jindal-Snape and Miller 2008). This period can also cause anxiety for parents/carers and family while they and their child adjust to a new system, 'unspoken rules' of schools and changing expectations of their role.

Similarly, teachers working with these pupils and families have to learn to implement new strategies according to their varying needs and ways of dealing with transition. Therefore, educational transitions are phases in which pupils, peer groups and teachers have to rebuild their learning environment.

This unit introduces you to the concept of transitions and their impact on planning and preparation for primary-secondary transitions. We discuss factors that have been found in research that pupils are excited by and look forward to, as well as what they worry about during this time. Resilience, self-esteem and emotional intelligence theories are used to explore the reasons behind any issues faced by pupils, as well as how you, as teachers, can support them.

OBJECTIVES

At the end of this unit, you should be able to:

■ explain the concept of educational transition and its impact on planning and preparation for primary-secondary transition;

■ be aware of what excites and worries pupils about moving to secondary school;

> ■ consider the best possible ways of supporting pupils during primary-secondary transition.
>
> Check the requirements for your initial teacher education (ITE) programme to see which relate to this unit.

Conceptualisation of educational transition and its impact on planning and preparation

There are some subtle changes that happen in our lives all the time, some more marked and visible than others. Within these life transitions, there is a distinct type of transition that most individuals go through; that is, educational transitions. To understand what is happening to the learner during transitions and what can be done to enhance that experience, it is important to reflect on how you might conceptualise primary-secondary transitions. You might be wondering what a successful transition might look like. Research suggests that this includes pupils having a sense of belongingness; no dips in educational attainment, self-esteem and motivation to learn; and a general sense of well-being (Peters 2010).

In an educational context, transition, also referred to as 'transfer' and 'moving on', has been conceptualised in various ways.

Maturational and interactionist approach

Some literature and practice tends to focus on pupils' skills and how they deal with any change in context and/or setting. This is particularly the case when looking at transition to formal schooling and considering the pupil's readiness to start school, but I believe this applies equally to primary-secondary transition. This approach to assessing a pupil's readiness to start school is called the maturational approach. It focuses on the learner's ability to perform at the norm expected at that level, being emotionally and socially ready, as well as the ability to look 'the right age'.

Another approach is an interactionist approach, which looks at the fit between the learner's readiness and the secondary school's readiness to adapt according to the learner's needs (Vernon-Feagans *et al.* 2008). This requires planning so that secondary schools are ready to receive pupils according to their specific and diverse needs. There are several aspects to this, which are addressed below.

One-off event or ongoing process?

Perhaps the biggest problem with planning and preparation comes from transition being seen by some teachers as a one-off event rather than an ongoing process in which pupils have to make sense of everyday changes and relationships (Jindal-Snape 2011). When conceptualised as a one-off event, practice focuses on activities such as meeting secondary school teachers prior to transition, school visits, induction days, residentials, and so on. As a result, the preparation *prior* to the move is the focus of attention. After the pupils have moved to secondary school, there might be a few days of getting to know each other and 'settling-in' activities, but little or nothing after that.

However, research clearly shows that there is no single pattern to how long pupils might take to adapt to the move. The results of one longitudinal study showed that some pupils who had reported transition to be difficult immediately after moving to secondary school reported they had no problems two months later (Jindal-Snape 2012). You might be thinking, 'yes, that is to be expected'. Interestingly, though, of those who had not found transition to be a problem immediately after the move, some reported problems by the end of the first term, and for one problems emerged at the end of the second term. How many schools would still be looking at any issues with adaptation at that stage?

Galton (2010) suggests that schools need to think longer term, and uses the example of Nicholson's (1987) work-role transition phases from the field of occupational psychology. These four phases are:

- ■ *Preparation.* This is similar to the pre-move programmes put in place by schools, such as induction weeks, open days, and so on.
- ■ *Encounters.* This includes a post-induction programme that, in the context of secondary schools, could include bridging activities. For example, an off-the-shelf computer game was used in some primary schools and their associated secondary schools as a contextual hub to facilitate transition from primary to secondary school. This project included ongoing work in secondary schools several months after the move.
- ■ *Adjustment.* At the adjustment phase, frequent and immediate feedback is provided on both success and failure. Pupils' reasoning is explored and strategies for identifying and correcting mistakes discussed.
- ■ *Stabilisation.* This involves future goal setting and appraisal of how the pupil might be developing, such as in the end-of-year reviews (these should be more than the typical end-of-year school reports). This should then look at those aspects of the pupil's adjustment (whether social, personal or academic) where improvement is required, as well as the setting of future goals for the following year.

Now complete Task 3.4.1.

 Task 3.4.1 Transition practices

Find out the primary-secondary transition planning and preparation practices of your placement school. Identify the purpose of each of the practices and make notes in your PDP. Reflect on where they would fit on Nicholson's (1987) work-role transition phases. Compare your findings with those from another student teacher in their placement school.

Academic and life transitions

During primary-secondary transitions, pupils and parents tend to focus more on the social aspects of transition, at least before the move or during the first few months of the move (Jindal-Snape and Foggie 2008; Galton 2010). Therefore, any academic transition has to be seen within the daily life experiences of a pupil. It is also important to remember that pupils moving to secondary school are experiencing several changes – that of moving to a new school, and the normative developmental

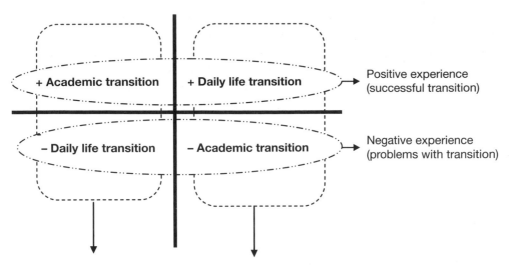

(++/−) Positive experience can reduce the impact of the negative experience
(−−/+) Negative experience can reduce the impact of the positive experience

Figure 3.4.1 Educational and life transitions (ELT) model depicting relationship between academic and daily life transitions

Source: Jindal-Snape and Ingram (2013)

and any associated physical and relationship changes. The education and life transitions (ELT) model in Figure 3.4.1, presented by Jindal-Snape and Ingram (2013), can be used to understand what might be happening for a pupil.

During the course of the day, even within the school, pupils adapt to their academic educational environment as well as daily life, such as making friends (see, for example, Pietarinen *et al.* 2010b). If one transition is going really well (that is, ++ positive experience), it could help the pupil to overcome any problems with other transitions (that is, - negative experience, a weaker negative experience) (Figure 3.4.1). For example, a pupil who might be finding it difficult to cope with studies (- negative) might still be happy if they have a strong support network of friends around them (++ positive). Obviously, this is by no means a static model and there are fluctuations all the time. However, as teachers, you could easily tap into and strengthen the positive experiences of transition to overcome any unavoidable negative experiences. For example, your positive interactions with the pupils might lessen their worries about getting lost in school and arriving late to your class or the homework being too difficult. Similarly, group work can be used in class to provide pupils with opportunities to develop friendship and learning networks.

Issues related to primary-secondary transitions

There is a significant change in identity for pupils when moving from being a primary to a secondary school pupil. This brings with it happiness but also some grief at losing the identity they had for the last six to seven years in primary school (which is more than half of their life at that time of moving to secondary school).

We suggest you undertake Task 3.4.2 to remind you of your own experience of transition.

Task 3.4.2 Remembering your own experience of transition

Answer the questions below in relation to transitions you have made; for example, when you first started school/secondary school/college/university.

1   How old were you?
2   What is your memory of the first day/first few days?
3   Draw/write how you looked and who was around you?
4   Can you remember any feelings/thoughts from that day?
5   What, if any, support was available to you?

Compare your answers with those of other student teachers to understand a variety of transition experiences. Keep your responses in your PDP.

Having refreshed your own memory of one of your experiences of education transition, we now consider what international research has found. Numerous studies have been conducted to understand what is happening during primary-secondary transition. It seems that despite the variation in educational systems, pupil's age or country, when they face primary-secondary transitions, the pedagogical, social and emotional challenges are quite similar (see, for example, Akos 2004; Adeyemo 2005; Jindal-Snape and Foggie 2008). There is clear evidence of a substantial decline in self-esteem, academic motivation and achievement (Eccles and Midgley 1989; Wigfield *et al*. 1991; Jindal-Snape and Miller 2008). However, as mentioned earlier, this is also a time that many pupils find to be satisfying and use it as a springboard to move on and up.

It is important to understand both what pupils are excited about and what they are worried about at this time. Interestingly, the same aspects of primary-secondary transitions can be exciting for some and stressful for others. In a study conducted by Jindal-Snape (2010d), 10 weeks before their move to secondary school, 139 primary school pupils were asked about their worries and things they were looking forward to about moving to secondary school (see Table 3.4.1).

As can be seen from Table 3.4.1, the same aspects were seen as exciting by some and challenging by others, with a particular focus on relationships with peers and teachers.

The issue of continuity in curriculum and pedagogical approach has been highlighted both in the educational literature (for example, Galton 2010) and government reports (for example, SEED 1999). Of course, these are not new issues as they were highlighted in government thinking in the UK as early as the 1960s (for example, Plowden Report 1967). Despite developments in practice, such as reciprocal visits of teachers, observations by peer teachers and use of bridging units, there are many challenges to be faced and further work is required to improve this aspect of transition practice. These challenges are, at times, tied to the unspoken values and cultural norms of primary and secondary schools. For example, there seems to be a big gap between primary and secondary schools' expectations of pupils in terms of independence, with some primary schools failing to make pupils independent and secondary schools expecting them to be independent. In a study conducted by Jindal-Snape and Foggie (2006), pupils, parents and professionals reported a difference in

Table 3.4.1 Aspects that pupils in final year of primary school were looking forward to or worrying about (*n* = 139)

	Looking forward to	Worried about
Making new friends	111	21
Losing old friends	N/A	88
More choices/opportunities	85	4
More independence	79	12
Several teachers	64	27
Different subjects	117	11
Travelling to school	34	1/
Bigger school	64	33
Bigger playground	60	7
Buying school dinners	53	16
Getting a locker	73	8
Variety of sports	2	0
Seeing old friends (already in secondary school)	3	0
Bullied	0	10
Getting lost/late for class	0	2
Too much homework	0	1

Note: Pupils could tick as many options as relevant.

discipline in primary and secondary schools: 'At Primary, if they are a bit late we comment but say that it's good that they've come, whereas at secondary, if they are late they get a punishment' (professional).

Research also suggests that a pupil might find transition to secondary school difficult if there is a big gap in their own expectations and reality. These can be both positive and negative. For example, Delamont (1991) found that pupils about to make the transition to secondary school had conceptualisations about secondary school that were greatly influenced by 'horror stories' communicated by their peers. When they reach the secondary school, they might find these concerns to be unfounded. However, the stress accompanying their prior perceptions might have already had a detrimental impact on the pupil. Now complete Task 3.4.3.

As you can probably see from Task 3.4.3, accurate and detailed information has to be provided to bridge the gap between expectations and reality. Therefore, schools invest a lot of time in giving pupils some knowledge of the new school and familiarisation through first-hand experience on induction days.

Task 3.4.3 Expectations versus reality

You can do this activity on your own or with other student teachers.

1   Note up to five expectations you had when starting your ITE programme or other transition; for example, going to a different country (expectations can be about everyday life, food, language, culture, and so on).
2   Against these expectations, identify what the reality was/is.
3   What are the differences/similarities?
4   For each expectation, add feelings/emotions that you experienced at that time.
5   Reflect on the impact of the gap/no gap between expectation and realities on your feelings.

Store your findings in your PDP.

Understanding transitions through theoretical perspectives

Researchers have identified different theories that help to understand what is happening during the transition period, as well as to understand how the experience can be improved. Three theories are discussed below: self-esteem, resilience and emotional intelligence.

Resilience

Resilience has been defined as a dynamic process encompassing positive adaptation within the context of significant adversity (Luthar 2006). Resilience literature looks at risk and protective factors that, at times, might be the same (for example, Newman and Blackburn (2002) identify that a family can be both a chaotic family, a risk factor, and a supportive family, a protective factor) (Jindal-Snape and Miller 2008). Research has been conducted to look at risk and resilience in the context of preschool-primary school (for example, Griebel and Niesel 2001) and primary-secondary transition (for example, Catterall 1998; Jindal-Snape and Hannah 2014). The findings emphasise the importance of internal protective factors (for example, self-esteem) and external protective factors (such as positive relationships at home and school) to help reduce multiple 'risks' or 'stressors' at the time of transition. Therefore, care needs to be taken to structure a supportive and safe environment for pupils at primary and secondary schools.

Self-esteem

Jindal-Snape and Miller (2008) have used Mruk's (1999) two-dimensional model of self-esteem. This proposes that self-esteem is dependent not only on feeling competent (self-competence), but also on messages that pupils might receive of their worth and value (self-worth). Primary-secondary transition involves several instances when a pupil's self-competence and self-worth might be shaken. For example, pupils can worry about their ability to do higher-level work despite there being gradual progression in the difficulty level (self-competence) and about being liked by teachers and peers, sustaining old friendships and making new friends (self-worth).

Further, those pupils with existing low self-esteem might respond more negatively to experiences of failure. On the other hand, those with higher self-esteem are more likely to persist in the face of difficulties (Tafarodi and Vu 1997). Thus, self-esteem might act as a protective factor but also the erosion of it might leave pupils vulnerable. The two-dimensional model of self-esteem seems to emphasise the role of significant others in the environment. Therefore, on the one hand, pupils' high self-esteem can be sustained by careful consideration of curricular progression and, on the other, by ensuring that pupils feel valued and welcome in your classroom.

Emotional intelligence

Goleman (1995) identified five 'domains' of emotional intelligence, namely: knowing your emotions; managing your emotions; motivating yourself; recognising and understanding other people's emotions; and managing relationships. Research has suggested that intervention in relation to emotional intelligence can enhance adjustment of learners (Adeyemo 2005, 2010). According to Adeyemo, this might be owing to the acquisition of emotional intelligence skills, which are the combination of intrapersonal and interpersonal factors that would help individuals cope with their own and others' emotions.

The boundaries are blurred between these three theoretical perspectives. There are overlaps, and sometimes cause-and-effect relationships seem obvious and sometimes they are very elusive. This might sit uncomfortably with some. However, it is important to generate and engage in this debate. Now complete Tasks 3.4.4 and 3.4.5.

 Task 3.4.4 Exploring these theories

Identify useful factors arising from the three theoretical models identified above. What factors can the school address and what are beyond its reach?

Compare your responses with those of another student teacher and record your responses in your PDP.

M **Task 3.4.5 Understanding the theories in the context of your and others' experience**

Undertake further reading related to these theories. You might want to start with those in the Further reading at the end of this unit. Reflect on where they would fit in with your own experiences of transition that you explored in the previous tasks. Discuss these theories and your view of them with other student teachers. Consider what you can learn from them to improve current transition practices. Store your notes in your PDP.

Examples of planning and preparation for primary-secondary transition

As mentioned earlier, schools are very aware of the issues pupils might face and try to provide support to enhance their experience of transition. Galton (2010) describes the *five bridges of transition*, namely: administrative; social/user-friendly; curriculum; teaching and learning; and managing learning. What these might involve is explored below.

Administrative

This involves good communication between schools through exchanging information about pupils, head teachers meeting, and guidance/special educational needs coordinator (SENCO) visiting the primary school. Our feeling is that the information exchanged is predominantly academic information, with less emphasis on social and emotional information about the pupil and no information exchanged about the pupil's other experiences of transition. This applies in an educational context when moving from nursery to primary school, within primary school or primary to secondary school, but also within life transitions such as a major bereavement in the family.

Social/user-friendly

At the very least, this involves familiarisation with the new school and staff, as well as with peers from other primary schools. This can take the form of an open day, induction events and residentials, usually in June/July for the move in August/September. Some schools have been known to organise treasure hunts around the school to help pupils navigate the physical environment and provide opportunities to work with other pupils they do not know. Pupils may be assigned buddies and, in the age of technology, this can also involve online links between pupils in primary and secondary schools.

Curriculum

Several countries around the world, including Scotland and Finland, have changed their national curriculum to enhance its continuity and progression. In England, for example, bridging units and summer schools have been introduced to assist with continuity.

Teaching and learning

This includes a clearer focus on pedagogical continuity, with teachers using similar strategies for teaching and learning in primary and secondary schools. There are examples of reciprocal visits with primary teachers going to secondary school to observe or teach, and vice versa. However, despite these practices, several differences in learning and teaching approaches are still noted within the school systems, including the use of space and layout of the class, use of group work, problem-solving, and so on. However, it must be recognised that there might be differences between subject teachers anyway.

Managing learning

The focus here is on preparing pupils for academic life after they start at secondary school. This might involve developing critical thinking and problem-solving skills. Examples of this might include activities such as critical analysis of a piece of literature or understanding the concept of globalisation where, as a group, they need to work on the learning intentions, sources of research, debating and unpacking their and others' understanding, and so on. The idea is to help pupils develop into 'professional learners' (Galton 2010).

In terms of planning and preparation for the move to secondary school, there are variations in when activities involving pupils start. There is an indication from parents that sometimes the preparation is left until too late. There is also strong evidence that these should start and carry on for at least six months before and six months after the move (Jindal-Snape and Foggie 2006), if not longer, as part of an ongoing process.

What seems to work for pupils?

A pupil's well-being can be dependent on feeling in control or having a voice (The Children's Society 2012). All pupils, especially in countries where education is compulsory, go through transition between primary and secondary school, irrespective of the educational system, terminology or age of this transition. For some, it might mean a move to a different school; others might carry on in the same school with some of the same teachers. It might be seen to be a normative transition with no choice in whether the pupil wants to make this move or not. So how can pupils be more in control of this transition?

Voice and opportunities to discuss concerns

Pupils can feel more in control if they are actively involved in decisions regarding the transition and associated planning and preparation. For example, teachers can involve pupils quite early on in the final year of primary school (or even earlier) in an exploration of what this change might mean to them, what they might be looking forward to or worrying about. Pupils can be given an opportunity to explore in a safe environment any concerns they might have or 'horror stories' they might have heard. They can share these with the aim of finding out whether others have similar concerns and how they might be able to resolve them. For example, Jindal-Snape (2010b) created a board game that includes key aspects that pupils have mentioned in the context of primary-secondary transitions (see Table 3.4.1 for some of these themes). Pupils can play this game at home or in school with an adult or a group of peers to explore and discuss transition-related aspects.

Familiarisation and knowledge of the new context

As mentioned earlier, schools are already doing a lot to facilitate familiarisation and knowledge of the new context. These attempts have been found to be most successful when familiarisation happens for a long period; for example, pupils starting to use the swimming pool in the secondary school a couple of years prior to transition.

There is also a clear indication from pupils that they want to move to the new school with pupils they know. However, it is important to remember that moving with friends cannot, alone, guarantee successful transition. Further, the link for some pupils is unclear, as some pupils who move with friends report difficulties and some who do not move with friends report no difficulties with transitions (Jindal-Snape 2010c).

Rehearsing in a safe environment

Jindal-Snape and colleagues emphasise the importance of rehearsing in a safe environment. This can be done, for example, through creative drama by constructing a possible real-life scenario in which the actors can depersonalise their actions and responses in the guise of 'playing the character' (Jindal-Snape *et al.* 2011: 2). This provides them with an opportunity to move from their concerns to 'Sam's concerns', a fictional character on whom everybody is comfortable projecting their own or another's concerns. Task 3.4.6 asks you to be involved in creative drama to experience how this might work.

We suggest, when ready, that you try this with pupils. You could also create similar scenarios in which you could use themes that might come from the pupils themselves; for example, making friends, bullying. This type of work can lead to a pupil being able to participate actively, as well as feeling in control by resolving any problems. It also gives pupils an armoury of strategies and responses they can use in similar real-life situations along with feeling more competent. However, it is important that you create a safe environment for pupils before doing this work.

 Task 3.4.6 Using creative drama to construct a real-life scenario

Try this task with other student teachers. You or another student teacher could play the role of the facilitator, as well as the other roles. Note down your learning and reflection in your PDP.

Scenario
It is the first day at secondary school. Robert and Mary are among the 80 pupils who are starting today. They were together at primary school. Mary has an older brother at secondary school and is feeling quite confident about starting school. Robert doesn't know anybody older than him in the school and is feeling concerned about the 'horror stories' he has heard from others.

In this scene, they are inside the school gates and have to be in classroom 1L10 to meet their mathematics teacher. They have been given a map but are having problems finding their way around school. They are overwhelmed by the size of the school and number of pupils around them. They had attended the induction event in the school before summer holidays but everything feels different. They ask Sheila for help but she mocks them and starts teasing them because . . .

Characters
- ■ Robert (11 years old) is nervous and under-confident but ends up coming across as overconfident and aggressive.
- ■ Mary (11 years old) is positive, cheerful, very sure of herself and tries to impress others by talking about her older brother in the same school, but this might lead to more teasing and name-calling.

■ Sheila (13 years old) enjoys teasing other children, and makes it difficult for Robert and Mary to find their way. *The character has to try to persistently block Robert and Mary in every way possible.*

Creative drama activity

Ask other student teachers to volunteer to play the part of each character. The audience are able to suggest change/come and replace the individual and take over that character. (*The facilitator asks the actors to freeze and then asks questions such as why do you think this is happening, what can be done, how do you think this person is feeling, and so on.*)

The ultimate purpose is to try to resolve the conflict through audience participation and for Robert and Mary to find their way to class.

Note in your PDP how this went and what you learned from it.

Active learning, learning agency, autonomy and choice

Learning agency, defined as 'a capacity for intentional and responsible management of new learning within and between school transitions' (Pietarinen *et al.* 2010b: 144) is crucial for well-being. Transitions are times when pupils can negotiate their learning within the school environment. Research suggests that choice and autonomy can have a positive impact on a pupil's sense of self and ability to manage their environment. Further, there is evidence that this is possible through active learning; for instance, through creative activities and a creative learning environment (Davies *et al.* 2013). In a project where pupils were actively involved in their preparation for transition and getting to know the school and peers through the use of a computer game, it was found that they benefitted from the opportunity to choose the game, as well as supporting their teachers in setting up the games consoles (Jindal-Snape 2012). Being involved in the game provided an opportunity for active learning and learning agency (Pietarinen *et al.* 2010a, 2010b). Now complete Task 3.4.7.

 Task 3.4.7 Your transition needs

Reflect on the following:

1   Having read this unit, and more widely around the area, how prepared do you feel about your own transition from student teacher to newly qualified teacher? Draw up a table, similar to Table 3.4.1, to identify your feelings about working as a newly qualified teacher (NQT) in a new school. Identify actions you might take to meet your concerns.
2   What professional development do you need to undertake to enable you to be prepared to support pupils in the context of primary-secondary transition?
3   How might you meet these professional development needs?

You might want to discuss these questions with other student teachers. It is also advisable to revisit these questions at different times on your journey as student teacher and teacher; hence, we suggest you store your thoughts and answers in your PDP.

SUMMARY AND KEY POINTS

■ This unit emphasises that transition is an ongoing process, with individual differences in when and how pupils adapt to their new school.

■ It is best to view transition in the context of the pupil's academic and daily life, with interactions between them.

■ Resilience, self-esteem and emotional intelligence theories provide an insight into the socio-emotional processes that a pupil might be going through, as well as providing a basis for effective transition practices.

■ Effective practices in primary and secondary schools should provide pupils with some opportunities to input into the transition process, giving them a voice, some control over the preparation and a degree of autonomy.

■ Pupils' involvement in the transition planning and preparation should help/allow them to voice their concerns in a safe environment, as well as promoting a successful transition.

Check which requirements for your ITE programme you have addressed through this unit.

 Further reading

Jindal-Snape, D. (ed.) (2010d) *Educational Transitions: Moving Stories from around the World*, London: Routledge.

This book provides further details on theoretical perspectives on transition (Chapters 2 and 3). Chapters 7, 8 and 9 cover transition research and practice in England, the United States and Finland. Chapter 13 pulls together international transition research and highlights examples of good practice from different countries.

Jindal-Snape, D., Douglas, W., Topping, K.J., Kerr, C. and Smith, E.F. (2006) 'Autistic spectrum disorders and primary-secondary transition', *International Journal of Special Education*, 21(2): 18–31.

This paper provides insight into the transition process for pupils with special educational needs (SEN) and emphasises the importance of early planning for transition.

Jindal-Snape, D. and Hannah, E.F.S. (2014) 'Promoting resilience for primary-secondary transitions: supporting children, parents and professionals', in A.B. Liegmann, I. Mammes and K. Racherbäumer (eds) *Facetten von übergängen im bildungssystem: nationale und internationale ergebnisse empirischer forschung*, Munster: Waxmann, pp. 265–77.

This chapter uses resilience theory to understand the transition needs and support systems. It is also an important chapter to understand about the multidimensional multiple transitions (MMT) model and how different individuals' transitions interact with each other.

Jindal-Snape, D., Roberts, G. and Venditozzi, D. (2012) 'Parental involvement, participation and home-school partnership: using the Scottish lens to explore parental participation in the context of transitions', in M. Soininen and T. Merisuo-Storm (eds) *Home-School Partnership in a Multicultural Society*, Turku, Finland: Turku University Faculty of Education B: 80, pp. 73–101.

In this unit, we did not have space to discuss the role of parents in primary-secondary transition. This chapter will give you an insight into parental participation and how it can be achieved.

Miller, D.J. and Moran, T.R. (2012) *Self Esteem: A Guide for Teachers*, London: Sage.

This book is based on the two-dimensional model of self-esteem. It looks at what this means for teachers, and provides advice on classroom techniques.

Other resources and websites

www.dundee.ac.uk/eswce/research/resources/
This website provides you with downloadable resources that you can use to facilitate transitions.

Appendix 2 on pages 591–595 provides further examples of websites you may find useful.

Capel, S., Leask, M. and Turner, T. (eds) (2010) *Readings for Learning to Teach in the Secondary School: A Companion to M Level Study,* London: Routledge.
This book brings together essential readings to support you in your critical engagement with key issues raised in this textbook.

The subject-specific books in the Routledge *Learning to Teach* series are also very useful.

Any additional resources and an editable version of any relevant tasks/tables in this unit are available on the companion website: www.routledge.com/cw/capel

4 Meeting individual differences

Every pupil in your class is unique. A class of same-age pupils is likely to contain individuals at different stages of development owing to the combined differences in physical development, cognitive development and background. Significant differences arise in the achievements of members of a class of pupils, including pupils in a class where setting is practised. The cultural, religious and economic backgrounds of your pupils can affect their response to schooling. Some pupils respond to academic challenge while others see no point in such demands. Others are gifted and need special attention, as do many pupils with learning or behavioural difficulties. Some pupils are at ease with adults while others find the experience less comfortable.

This chapter, comprising six units, invites you to consider several aspects of the background and development of your pupils. In practice, the features discussed interact, giving rise to the complex and varied behaviours that characterise human beings. For ease of discussion, some factors are discussed separately; we hope this approach helps you subsequently to integrate better your understandings of pupils and their learning and meet their individual needs.

Arguments for and against selection, the merits of banding, streaming or setting as opposed to mixed-ability classes, have been voiced ever since the 1944 Education Act, which advocated the separation of pupils by ability and sending them either to a grammar, technical or 'modern' school.

Unit 4.1 addresses pupil grouping for learning and goes on to discuss differentiation and progression, focusing on ways to improve the learning of all pupils in whatever type of grouping they are placed. Central to successful differentiation is the identification of pupil needs; thus, case studies invite you to enquire more deeply into the background and response of individual pupils and ways to plan differentiated work. You may want to return to this unit after dipping into other units.

Unit 4.2 focuses on the physical characteristics of pupils as they approach adolescence and young adulthood, and draws attention to the range of 'what is normal'. We address issues of diet and health of young people, and the ways in which schools contribute to healthy eating. We focus a section of this unit on obesity in pupils and the general population; we focus too on the ways in which schools can address this issue both through the academic curriculum and more widely.

Unit 4.3 addresses the issue of cognition and cognitive development. Logical reasoning is one important aspect of cognitive development, along with others such as problem-solving, developing skills and creative thinking. We note the importance placed on logical reasoning by Western societies through tests of ability. The notion of intelligence is introduced, including the 'nature-nurture' debate, and we touch on the theory of 'multiple intelligences'. Examples of teaching material from secondary school curricula are discussed in terms of their cognitive demand on pupils of different ages. Through set tasks, there are opportunities for you to work with pupils to see how they respond to different demands. We address, too, the importance of teaching pupils how to learn and to think about their own learning, and the central role of language in the development of cognitive skills is discussed.

In Unit 4.4, the background of pupils is considered, including class, gender and ethnicity. A significant factor related to class is poverty. These factors are discussed separately while recognising that for every pupil, these factors combine in different ways. We highlight some differences in performance of groups of pupils from various backgrounds, using research evidence, and discuss possible causes of those differences.

In Unit 4.5, moral education and values education are introduced and explained, and their development linked to the curriculum for schools in England, including citizenship and the importance of personal, social and health education (PSHE) courses. The emphasis is on the way schools contribute to moral education and values education through both the overt and hidden curriculum. While not stressing differences between pupils, the focus of the chapter does acknowledge the range of values and beliefs in our society and how schools not only have to respond to such differences, but also to contribute to the spiritual, moral and cultural development of pupils, as well as their cognitive and physical development. Opportunities for teachers to address moral and ethical issues are provided through tasks, and ways to introduce discussion between pupils are suggested.

Inclusion and special needs education is the focus of Unit 4.6 and it carefully considers the 2014 *Special educational needs and disability code of practice* (the first since 2001) for schools in England, which has established a new framework for the education of children and young people with special educational needs and disabilities (SEND). The unit draws attention to significant changes in recent years in the way in which pupils with SEND are supported, and emphasises the importance of the classroom teacher in the identification of need and response to need. There is a reference to sources of support and guidance, including the support of other professionals.

Pupil grouping, progression and differentiation

Alexandra Titchmarsh

Introduction

In your development as a student teacher, you are required to focus on a number of principles for planning and teaching. These include:

- setting suitable learning challenges;
- responding to pupils' diverse learning needs;
- overcoming potential barriers to learning.

You should also understand the principles of inclusion and work towards ensuring effective learning by all pupils through matching the teaching approaches used to the pupils being taught. As a student teacher, you also need:

- knowledge, understanding and ability to use/adapt a range of teaching, learning and behaviour management strategies to understand how children and young people develop (see Unit 3.3 on behaviour management, Unit 4.2 on growth and development and Unit 5.3 on teaching styles);
- to be able to plan for progression across the age and ability range, designing effective learning sequences within lessons and across series of lessons;
- to be able to manage the learning of individuals, groups and whole classes, adapting your teaching according to pupils' progress within the lesson; you must be flexible and versatile enough to recognise when a strategy is not working (see Unit 2.3 on taking responsibility for whole lessons);
- to know how to make effective personalised provision for those you teach and provide opportunities for all learners to achieve their potential (see Unit 5.5 on personalising learning);
- to assess the learning needs of those you teach in order to set challenging learning objectives (see Unit 2.2 on lesson planning).

There is an increasing acknowledgement of the need for a comprehensive and multifaceted approach to how to meet pupils' diverse learning needs (see Unit 4.4 on diversity and Unit 4.6 on special educational needs and disabilities (SEND). This is based on a more complex and inclusive view of ability, of how children learn, of the factors that affect learning and the effectiveness of particular teaching approaches. There has also been a major shift in expectations about what all pupils can and should achieve.

In this unit, we consider how different grouping arrangements have been and are currently used as a means of coping with differences in pupils' performance. There is evidence that pupil grouping may depend on the subject taught and the philosophy of the school (see the Education Endowment Foundation website on pupil grouping). We also consider how progression for all pupils can be achieved through teaching and learning approaches that ensure that account is taken of a range of learning needs. Strategies for developing differentiated units of work are provided, building on your subject specialist focus. See also Units 2.2 and 3.2, which address lesson planning and motivation, respectively.

OBJECTIVES

At the end of this unit, you should be able to:

■ understand the links between pupil grouping, progression and differentiation;
■ evaluate the implications of learning in a range of pupil grouping arrangements;
■ discuss definitions of progression and differentiation and their relationship to effective teaching;
■ discuss teaching methods that allow for differentiation;
■ begin to apply principles of differentiated approaches to learning in lesson planning.

Check the requirements for your initial teacher education (ITE) programme to see which relate to this unit.

Grouping pupils across the school

Schools have traditionally sought to cope with differences in pupil performance either through streaming, banding, setting or by setting work at appropriate levels for pupils in wide or mixed-ability classes. Streaming places the best performers in one class for all subjects, the least able performers in another class, with graded classes in between. Banding places pupils in broad performance groups for all subjects and tries to avoid producing classes comprising only pupils of low attainment or those unwilling to learn. Setting describes the allocation of pupils to classes by attainment in each subject; that is, streaming or banding for each subject. Broad streaming and banding support a notion of a general intelligence, whereas setting acknowledges that pupil aptitude and attainment may be different across subjects and contexts. The recent focus on the needs of more able or gifted and talented learners has led to renewed interest at a policy and school level in acceleration or fast-tracking; that is, moving a pupil or groups of pupils into a class with an older age group for some or all subjects. The effect of acceleration is one of the most researched aspects of educational intervention with 'gifted' pupils; for further reading, see Brody (2004).

In England, prior to the Education Reform Act (ERA) of 1988, many state schools grouped their pupils in mixed-ability classes for teaching purposes. The backgrounds, aptitudes and abilities of pupils, coupled with differences in interest and motivation, lead to differences in achievement between pupils that, by age 11, are substantial and widen even further as pupils grow older. Recognising these differences without prematurely labelling pupils as successes or failures was regarded as an essential prerequisite for organising the teaching of secondary pupils.

Following the move in many state comprehensive schools to mixed-ability teaching in the 1960s, strong arguments in favour of, and opposing, the practice arose. The effects of different pupil groupings became the subject of research, as reviewed by, for example, Hallam (2002) and Kutnick et al. (2005). One finding of these reviews is that all pupils gained socially from working in mixed-ability groups. Such groupings allowed pupils from a variety of backgrounds, as well as abilities, to work together, strengthening social cohesion. Another finding was support for some form of setting in mathematics and other subjects where learning is dependent on a more linear acquisition of skills and knowledge; for example, in modern languages and science (Harlen 1997; Ireson et al. 2002). An earlier comparative study of pupils in two comprehensive schools rigorously documented their differences in knowledge and understanding of mathematics and their motivation and attitude towards the subject (Boaler 1997). This study identified advantages and disadvantages to both setting and mixed-ability teaching and differences in approach to the teaching of mathematics by the subject staff. One conclusion from the study was that pupils in mixed-ability classes did as well as pupils taught in ability sets. However, the latter were taught in a more traditional way, through rule learning then application, whereas the former linked mathematics to the everyday life of pupils and used more open-ended project work as part of their teaching strategies. From this study, the evidence in favour of grouping pupils one way rather than another is not clear. More recent research paints a similar conflicting picture of the advantage of setting over mixed ability. For example, at Key Stage 3 (KS3), the advantage of a particular type of setting depended on the subject while at General Certificate of Secondary Education (GCSE) level setting appeared to offer little advantage over other forms of grouping. Since the introduction of the ERA (1988), mixed-ability grouping has been in retreat and successive governments in England have advocated a return to grouping by ability, together with increased whole-class teaching. See Gillard (2008) for a history of pupil grouping policies in England's schools up to 2008. A review of attainment and pupil grouping across schools does not support the contention that setting alone contributes to success or that setting improves the standards of those not achieving adequately (Kutnick et al. 2005: 6). For example, at KS3, the review identifies:

■ no significant difference between setting and mixed ability teaching in overall attainment outcomes;
■ ability grouping does not contribute much to the raising of standards of all pupils;
■ lower-achieving pupils show more progress in mixed-ability classes;
■ higher-achieving pupils show more progress in set classes.

(Kutnick et al. 2005: 5)

The advantages of grouping pupils one way rather than another is not clear-cut; the evidence suggests that in some circumstances, setting may promote the learning for some pupils in some subjects. The downside of setting may be some reduction in positive attitudes by pupils towards their peers, a heightened sense of anxiety of some pupils in higher sets, reduced motivation of those labelled 'not bright', and diminished cross-cultural mixing.

It is said to be less demanding on teachers to prepare lessons for setted groups. However, given that top sets are often large groups, top sets may contain not only very able pupils, who may be unchallenged by the work expected of the majority, but may also contain a wide spread of ability and motivation. Organising learning and teaching to maximise the potential of all pupils requires teachers to acknowledge that their classes, however grouped, are mixed ability.

So the best way to group pupils remains a vexed question. There is debate, for example, as to whether there should be less emphasis on how pupils are grouped and more on strategies that target individual achievement (for example, the use of data, assessment for learning (see Procter's (2013) and Newton and Bowler's (2016) MESHGuides), booster classes, differentiated challenge) and at the same time on approaches to learning that can maximise achievement for all pupils (emphasis on thinking processes, learning to learn, intervention via questioning, collaborative learning and literacy across the curriculum). There is also debate on 'personalised learning', which is intended to allow for greater tailoring of the curriculum to individual needs. Unit 5.5 looks at personalised learning. At the whole-school and class levels, groupings have a very direct link to how we differentiate to meet individual differences in learning and performance. A common theme in the conclusions to the best evidence studies of research into pupil grouping is that what goes on in the classroom, the pedagogic models and the teaching strategies used, is likely to have more impact on achievement than how pupils are grouped.

Finally, all the research reviews point to the long-lasting effects of grouping arrangements, not only on pupil self-esteem, but also on their future engagement in learning. Task 4.1.1 invites you to investigate pupil grouping in your school.

 Task 4.1.1 How are pupils grouped in your placement school?

Find out the ways in which pupils are grouped in your placement school, the reasoning behind the grouping and how it works in practice. Grouping arrangements often change after pupils have been in the school for a term, or a year. Different policies may apply often at the transition from KS3 to KS4, as well as between subjects.

Are primary school records (for example, their achievement levels) used to group pupils? Or are other tests used, such as the Year 11 Information System (Yellis) or the Cognitive Abilities Test (National Foundation for Educational Research (NFER) – Nelson) used to assess pupils and assign them to groups? See Chapter 6 for more about these tests.

Write a summary of your findings and discuss it with your tutor. Revise and file in your professional development portfolio (PDP).

Grouping within the class: jigsawing and rainbowing

Current thinking about effective teaching and learning sees the use of flexible groupings in class as an aid to learning and as a form of differentiation. The reviews on the effects of particular types of pupil grouping on pupils' achievement point to the positive effects of within-class groupings, which may include grouping by:

■ ability
■ mix of ability

- ■ gender
- ■ expertise
- ■ friendship and
- ■ age.

Learning activities that make use of flexible and different forms of grouping include paired tutoring, jigsawing and rainbowing. In jigsawing, the class is split into groups to study a topic. Jigsaw is a cooperative learning strategy that enables each pupil of a 'home' group to specialise in one aspect of a learning unit. Pupils meet with members from other groups who are assigned the same aspect, and, after mastering the material, return to the 'home' group and teach the material to their group members.

Rainbowing is similar to jigsawing. For example, pupils work in groups of four and discuss a problem or task. Each group member has a colour. Only four colours are used. After discussion, new groups are formed, getting together pupils with the same colour. This means that in a class of 28, new groups of seven members are formed, and the findings or ideas from each group of four can be shared. Pupils can then return to their original groups of four armed with new ideas. You could, of course, begin with four groups of seven, each with a colour of the rainbow, and then form seven groups of four in the same way.

Further information about these learning activities is available (see, for example, DfES 2004d).

Progression and differentiation

By far the greatest challenge to teachers is to ensure progression in the learning of all pupils in their class. Each pupil is different, whether in streamed, banded or wide-ability classes. Each pupil brings to school unique knowledge, skills and attitudes formed by interaction with parents, peers, the media and their everyday experience of their world. Pupils are not blank sheets on which new knowledge is to be written. Many pupils may have skills of which the school is not aware: some pupils care for animals successfully; others play and adapt computer games; yet others may work with parents in the family business. Some pupils may know more arithmetic than we dream of, as the following parody of stock market practice suggests:

Teacher: 'What is two plus two, Jane?'
Jane: 'Am I buying or selling, Sir?'

Your classroom is a reflection of your pupils' diversity of background and culture that interacts with their potential for learning. Each pupil responds to the curriculum in a different way. Some parents and their children may value a vocational, relevant education more highly because it is immediately applicable to earning a living, and may not subscribe to the values placed by the school on a broad, largely academic education.

The teacher must take account of personal interest, ability and motivation to design learning that challenges and interests pupils but, at the same time, ensures for each a large measure of success. Planning and teaching for progression in learning is the core business of teachers. It is important that you understand what progression means in your subject. In geography, for example, progression involves:

■ an increase in the breadth of studies;

■ an increasing depth of study to respond to pupils' growing capacity to deal with complexities and abstractions;

■ an increase in the spatial scale of what is studied;

■ a continuing development of skills to include specific techniques and more general strategies of enquiry, matched to pupils' developing cognitive abilities;

■ increasing opportunity for pupils to examine social, economic, political and environmental issues;

■ awareness and implications of interactions between people and their environments.

Now complete Task 4.1.2.

 Task 4.1.2 Progression in your own and other subjects

This task is in two parts.

In relation to the progression for geography above, consider how these characteristics might relate to teaching in your subject.

Access a copy of the relevant documents for progression in your subject and summarise how they describe progression, similar to the list for geography above.

With another student teacher, discuss: (i) similarities and differences between subjects; and (ii) what progression means for your teaching in your subject.

Keep your notes in your PDP for later reference.

Facilitating progression: approaches to differentiation and personalised learning

Planning learning for pupils, choosing learning objectives and learning outcomes based on knowledge of the pupils and of what constitutes progression in particular curriculum areas are critical in ensuring pupils' acquisition of the knowledge, skills and understanding underpinning progress (see also Unit 2.2). Progression and differentiation are therefore two sides of the same coin. The use and success of differentiated approaches depends on teachers knowing their pupils, being secure in their own subject content knowledge and having access to a range of teaching strategies. A straightforward way of thinking about planning for progression is the following:

1   What is it you want your pupils to know, understand and be able to do? This might be at the lesson level, the 'unit of work' level or by the end of year.

2   What is it that pupils know, understand and can do at the start of the topic?

3   What sequence of learning activities may help pupils progress from their present state to your objective(s)?

4   How do you know when pupils have reached where you want them to go?

(Levinson 2005a: 100)

To this, we would add:

5   Can pupils recognise that they have progressed either through the lesson or over a longer timescale?

In planning for progression, you need to start from where the pupils are, not where you would like them to be. Not all pupils are at the same level, so some degree of differentiation must be built into your day-to-day lessons, units of work and the wider scheme of work for most pupils if you expect to achieve points 1–4.

There is no one right way to differentiate for pupils. Effective differentiation is a demanding task and is about raising the standards of all pupils in a school, not just for those underachieving, with learning difficulties or the gifted. The purpose of a differentiated approach is to maximise the potential of each pupil and to improve learning by addressing each pupil's particular needs. But what exactly is meant by differentiation and how is it achieved?

Consider the following definitions. Differentiation is:

■   a planned process of intervention by the teacher in the pupil's learning;
■   the matching of work to the differing capabilities of individuals or groups in order to extend their learning;
■   about entitlement of access to a full curriculum;
■   'shaking up' what goes on in the classroom so that pupils have multiple options for taking in information, making sense of ideas, and expressing what they learn.

(Tomlinson 1999)

However differentiation is defined, the challenge begins with its implementation and practice, which in turn is affected by teachers' beliefs about the ability of their pupils, by expectations of particular groups of pupils and by an understanding of how we learn and of optimal learning environments. The nature of the subject itself and the kind of learning it involves may also affect differentiation.

Differentiation has sometimes had a bad press because at its worst it has implied an unrealistic and daunting demand on teachers to provide consistently different work and different approaches at the level of the individual pupil or has, unwittingly perhaps on the part of teachers, placed a ceiling on achievement for some pupils.

At its best, given what we know about effective approaches to learning, the influence of high expectations and the potential of all pupils, differentiation may be said to combine a variety of learning options that tap into different levels of readiness, interests, ability and learning profiles with more individualised support and challenge at appropriate times and in appropriate contexts. As we know relatively little about the potential of each pupil, differentiation should be used sensitively and judiciously.

A perspective on differentiation as liberating rather than constraining relies on a number of broader principles informing classroom learning and teaching:

■   a focus on key concepts and skills;
■   opportunities for problem-solving, critical and creative thinking;
■   ongoing assessment for learning;

- a balance between flexible groupings and whole-class teaching;
- identifying pupils as active learners with whom learning goals and expectations are shared;
- collaborative and cooperative learning;
- achievable but challenging targets;
- motivating and interesting learning activities;
- supportive and stimulating learning environments;
- effective use of learning support assistants (LSAs) within the classroom.

How would you describe/define differentiation? In Task 4.1.3, an aspect of the National Curriculum (NC) for England is interrogated for its implications for differentiation.

 Task 4.1.3 Differentiation in the English National Curriculum

In many curriculum documents, there are statements that identify actions teachers might take to promote inclusion, including a secure learning environment for all pupils, just one aspect of 'inclusion'. For example, in England, these statements include:

- Using teaching approaches appropriate to different learning styles.
- Using, where appropriate, a range of organisational approaches, such as setting, grouping or individual work, to ensure that learning needs are, for example, properly addressed. (This can be done within an individual classroom through seating plans or groups or differentiated learning outcomes that are shared with the class; however, this requires the class to know their current level.)
- Varying subject content and presentation so that this matches pupil's learning needs.
- Planning work that builds on pupils' interests and cultural experiences.
- Planning appropriately challenging work for those pupils whose ability and understanding are in advance of their language skills.
- Using materials that reflect social and cultural diversity and providing positive images of race, gender and disability.
- Planning and monitoring the pace of work so that all pupils have a chance to learn effectively and achieve success.
- Adapting your lessons to individual classes and being flexible and versatile to the needs of that class on that given day.

(Source: DfES/QCA, 2004, p. 32)

In a group with other subject student teachers, discuss which of these statements are statements of differentiation. To help you, use the definitions of differentiation mentioned earlier in this unit.

Write a working definition of differentiation and discuss it with your tutor. Keep a note of this in your PDP.

Managing differentiation

Differentiation starts with a clear view about what you want your pupils to achieve and what individual pupils may need as a particular learning goal, using and acting upon what you know about pupils' previous learning and achievement using assessment data from a range of sources. Pupils should know what they are aiming for both in the short and long term. Realistic targets need to be discussed and set through both knowledge of the individual and use of data. Then begins the consideration of appropriate differentiation strategies and how the process can be managed. It is unrealistic to expect one teacher to plan differentiated work separately for each pupil; it is perhaps better to identify groups of pupils who can work to a given set of learning outcomes using methods suitable to those pupils and the topic in question. However, you may find in some classes you do need to differentiate for individuals.

Differentiation always needs to be included as part of your day-to-day lesson planning. Your lesson planning proforma should include a reminder about differentiation (see also lesson planning in Unit 2.2).

It may be helpful to have a framework or steps in which to plan work:

■ *Step 1*: Your aims and short-term outcomes must be broad enough to apply to all pupils in your class. There are often a number of ways of achieving the same goal.
■ *Step 2*: Consider which activities to give pupils, linking them to what the pupil already knows and then identifying outcomes. Achievable outcomes are one way of ensuring motivation, but must set pupils a challenge; that is, not be too easy. By identifying achievable outcomes for different groups of pupils, the process of differentiation is begun.
■ *Step 3*: The selection of one or more activities. As well as factors in Step 2, check the availability of resources, the backup needed, for example, instructions are pupil-friendly, the language is suitable for your pupils, potentially provide samples or examples for pupils to work from, how any LSA is to be deployed.
■ *Step 4*: Planning must include assessment. This can be achieved in a number of ways; for example, by question-and-answer sessions, taking part in small group discussions, responding to queries in class, asking questions of pupils working on an activity, listening to pupils discussing their work, as well as marking books or short tests. The information gained helps you identify the next steps for the pupil. Assessment must reflect your objectives and be aligned with your learning outcomes.

Some lesson plans, units of work or schemes of work plan for differentiation by identifying different priorities for activities, such as:

■ must/should/could;
■ core/support/extension.

For example, an activity is selected that all pupils must attempt; it may contain the core idea of the lesson.

However, differentiation models should also recognise that pupils' learning needs may not be fixed or permanent and may relate to the learning context or topic at hand. Differentiation may therefore involve support or challenge being given to different pupils at different times; for example, sometimes to:

■ a whole group
■ a targeted group
■ those who work at speed.

Differentiation strategies: stimulus-task-outcome

The outcome of any particular task depends on the way it is presented to the pupil and how they respond. Teaching methods can be restricted by our own imagination; we are inclined to present a task in just one way with one particular learning outcome in mind, rather than to look for different ways to achieve the goals you have set for your pupils. One important, but limited, teaching goal is to ensure pupils remember things, which often involves rote learning (see Unit 5.5); for example, learning Mark Antony's speech on the death of Caesar. Very simply, this exercise is:

■ *Stimulus.* Play the role of Mark Antony in a class presentation of excerpts from *Julius Caesar*.
■ *Task.* Learn by heart the relevant text.
■ *Outcome.* Complete oral recall.

Much learning depends on recall methods: learning the names of element symbols in science; preparing vocabulary in a language lesson; recalling formulae or tables from mathematics; learning to spell. Recall is necessary, if unexciting, when compared with creative forms of learning.

If we wish to help pupils recall and use knowledge, then we move up a level, to consolidate and widen understanding. This situation opens opportunities to use a variety of contexts, including ones directly appropriate to pupils' needs; that is, differentiation by choice of stimulus. For example, to consolidate pupils' understanding of punctuation, you could:

1   ask pupils to punctuate a piece of text from which the punctuation has been removed;
2   as 1 above using a written report of an interview;
3   as 1 or 2 above but read it through first with the pupils;
4   engage in a taped discussion with pupils and ask pupils to write a short report of what was said, with verbatim examples;
5   ask pupils to interview other pupils, or staff, about a topic and write a report that includes a record of some interviews;
6   ask pupils to write a scene for a play.

Thus, for different stimuli, all pupils consolidate their understanding of punctuation, but the level of outcome is different according to the difficulty of the task and ability of the pupils; that is, differentiation and progression.

Now complete Task 4.1.4.

By contrast with Task 4.1.4, Task 4.1.5 invites you to discuss and identify ways in which one stimulus might be used for different outcomes.

Task 4.1.4 Lesson planning for differentiation: different tasks for a similar learning outcome

Choose a specific learning outcome for a topic you have taught or are about to teach. Identify two or three different tasks that allow pupils to achieve the identified learning outcome. In which ways are the tasks the same and different? Use the example above, of developing understanding of punctuation, to help you.

Discuss the tasks with your tutor. If possible, try out the tasks with your class and review the outcomes of the lesson. Keep a copy of the lesson plans and evaluation in your PDP.

 Task 4.1.5 Lesson planning for differentiation: one stimulus with different tasks and outcomes

You have a set of photographs showing the interiors of domestic kitchens covering the period 1850 to the present. Describe two or more ways in which you could use these photographs to teach your subject. Confine your discussion to a class you teach covering one to two lessons. For each example, identify:

■ how you use the photographs;
■ the activities you set your pupils;
■ the objectives and learning outcomes;
■ how you assess outcomes;
■ the ways in which the activities are differentiated.

Analyse your plan in terms of task and outcome for the differentiated approaches you develop.

If you do not like the choice of photographs, choose your own stimulus; for example, an astronaut working in a space lab, a Salvador Dali painting or an environmental activist at work.

Discuss your plan with your tutor. Identify how differentiation can be achieved for your pupils and why your choice of task, learning outcomes and assessment are appropriate. File your plan and a summary of discussion in your PDP.

Differentiation through teacher input and support

Differentiation also takes place at the point of contact with the group or individual. The level and nature of your response to pupils is itself an act of differentiation, and includes:

■ checking that pupils understand what they are supposed to do;
■ listening to a discussion and prompting or questioning when needed;
■ helping pupils to mind map or spider diagram an idea or problem (see also Unit 5.2);

- asking questions about procedure or techniques; suggesting further action when difficulties arise or motivation flags;
- giving pupils supporting worksheets or other written guidance appropriate to the problem in hand; the guidance might explain the topic in simpler terms or simpler language; you may, if appropriate, use word fills or add extra information;
- checking pupils' notebooks and noting progress;
- marking pupils' work;
- encouraging pupils by identifying success;
- setting achievable and realistic targets for improvement;
- increasing the demand of an existing task;
- noting unexpected events or achievements for a plenary session.

Now try Task 4.1.6.

 Task 4.1.6 Differentiation: class-teacher interaction

Discuss the above list of teacher support strategies with other student teachers and identify those strategies appropriate to the teaching of your subject. Add to the list of responses for your teaching. Store in your PDP for reference when appropriate.

Knowing how to set differentiated tasks depends on how well you know your pupils. The activity needs to be challenging yet achievable. Other ways in which activities can be differentiated include:

- the task's degree of open-endedness;
- the pupils' familiarity with the type of task (for example, pupils are often used to worksheet-based lessons where the information is given to them and they have to extract the information, and are not necessarily used to enquiry-based lessons);
- the pupils' degree of familiarity with the resources;
- whether the activity is a complete piece of work or a contributory part of a larger exercise;
- the amount of information you give pupils;
- the language level at which it is presented;
- whether the activity is set orally or by means of written guidance;
- degree of familiarity with the concepts needed to tackle the activity;
- the amount of guidance given to pupils; for example, in science lessons, the guidance given on making measurements, recording data or drawing a graph.

The activity suggested in Task 4.1.5 could be discussed in terms of these criteria. Task 4.1.7 invites you to appraise this list for your own subject teaching.

Task 4.1.7 Differentiation: how the task is presented and supported

Discuss the list above with other student teachers in your subject. In groups, say of two people, rewrite the list using strategies appropriate to your subject and the context of your teaching. Share your list with the group and go on to revise your own list. Store this in your PDP.

Differentiation by outcome and how the activity is assessed

Differences in outcome may be recognised by the amount of help given to pupils and how the activity was set and supported. This aspect of differentiation was referred to in Task 4.1.6. In addition, your expectations of what counts as a satisfactory response to the activity lies in your assessment criteria. Your assessment strategy reflects your criteria. These criteria might include:

- the extent to which all aspects of the problem have been considered;
- the adoption of a suitable method of approaching the activity;
- the use of more difficult concepts or procedures in planning;
- the recognition of all the factors involved in successful completion of the activity and limiting the choice appropriately;
- thoroughness and accuracy of recording data in a quantitative exercise;
- appropriateness and selection of ways to present information and the thoroughness and depth of analysis;
- use of appropriate ideas (or theory) to discuss the work;
- accuracy and understanding of conclusions drawn from an activity (for example, are statements made appropriate to the content and purpose of the activity?);
- distinction between statements supported by evidence from speculation or opinion;
- the way the activity is written about, such as the selection of appropriate style for the target audience;
- the ability of pupils to express themselves in an increasingly sophisticated language;
- the use of imagination or insight;
- the selection of appropriate diagrams, sketches or pictures;
- sensible use of information and communications technology (ICT) to support a task;
- recognition of the limitations of the approach to a problem and awareness of ways to improve it.

By choice of assessment criteria, you differentiate the work set. Statements such as those listed help you construct your assessment strategy.

Differentiation through curriculum design

Moving from differentiating your teaching in a lesson to one embracing the curriculum, one model of a differentiated curriculum suggests that the curriculum needs to be organised around the following core elements:

- learning environment or context (for example, changes to where learning takes place, open and accepting classroom climate);
- content (for example, greater levels of complexity, abstraction);
- process (for example, promotion of higher-level skills, greater autonomy, creative thinking);
- product (for example, encouraging the solving of real problems, the use of real audiences).

(Maker and Nielson 1995; DCSF 2008a)

You might refer back to the ideas in the list above, 'differentiation by outcome'.

Differentiation can therefore include different or enriched learning experiences that take place outside the classroom or beyond the school. The English NC exemplar schemes of work give examples of additional learning opportunities for each subject area (DfES 2005c). Government guidance on teaching gifted and talented pupils also gives guidance on enrichment and extension beyond the classroom, many examples of which are relevant for most pupils (DCSF 2008d).

Differentiation is good teaching and requires that you know your pupils. This knowledge enables you to judge the extent to which pupils have given an activity their best shot or settled for the easy option. Your role is to motivate your pupils and give support. Some pupils may present a greater challenge than others, and examples are given in case studies below. It is important to remember that you are unlikely to be successful with all pupils all the time. Read these case studies and then address Task 4.1.8. See Unit 4.6 on special educational needs (SEN) and Rose (2004) for further discussion of differentiation of pupils with SEN.

Case studies of pupils

Peter

Peter is a popular member of his group and has an appealing sense of humour. He can use this in a disruptive way to disquiet teachers while amusing his peers.

He appears very bright orally but when the work is of a traditional nature (that is, teacher-led), he often avoids the task in hand; it is at such times that he can become disruptive. His disruption is not always overt; he employs a range of elaborate avoidance tactics when asked to settle to work and often produces very little. His written language and numeracy attainments are significantly lower than those he demonstrates orally.

When given responsibility in groups, Peter can sometimes rise to the challenge. He can display sound leadership ability and, when he is motivated and interested in a group project, can encourage his peers to produce a good team effort. His verbal presentations of such work can be lively, creative, humorous and full of lateral thinking. At such times, Peter displays an extensive general knowledge.

Peter's tutor is concerned about Peter's progress. He fears that Peter will soon begin to truant from those subjects in which teaching is traditional in style. He is encouraging Peter's subject teachers to provide him with as much problem-solving work as possible.

Filimon

Filimon arrived a year ago from Ethiopia via the Sudan. He had not been at school for at least a year. He speaks Sunharic at home, as well as some Arabic, but knew no English on arrival. Eight months of the year he has spent at school here have been a 'silent period', during which time he was internalising what he was hearing. Now he is starting to speak with his peers and his teacher. He has a reading partner who reads to him every day and now Filimon is reading these same stories himself.

Joyce

Joyce is a very high achiever. She always seems to respond to as much extension activity as she can get. She puts in a lot of effort and produces very well presented work (for example, capably using ICT), and amply demonstrates her ability to understand, evaluate and synthesise. Joyce's achievements are maximised where she is able to work on her own or in a pair with one or a couple of other girls in the class. In other groups, she tends to keep herself to herself. Some teachers are concerned that she is not developing her social and leadership potential.

Joyce's parents put a lot of pressure on her and are keen for Joyce to follow an accelerated course wherever this is possible. Should she achieve her ambitions for higher education, Joyce will not be the first in her family to make it to Oxbridge.

These case studies were provided by Paul Greenhalgh, adapted by him from Greenhalgh (1994). You may find it instructive to select one of the pupils described above and consider how their presence in your class would modify your lesson planning.

Now address Task 4.1.8.

 Task 4.1.8 Writing your own case study

Prepare a short case study of two pupils in one of your classes. Identify two pupils for whom further information would be helpful to you in lesson planning and use the examples of case studies above to help you identify the information you need to collect. Do not use the pupil's real name in any report you make or discussion outside the school.

Collect information from the class subject teacher and the form teacher. The form teacher can give you background information about the pupils, as much as is relevant to your study.

After collecting the information and writing your report, ask the class teacher to read it and comment on it. Finally, use the information to amend Task 4.1.7 or plan a new lesson.

If there are other student teachers in your placement school, share your case studies with them. Use the case studies to identify some learning needs of these pupils and plan teaching strategies to take account of these needs. The study can contribute to your PDP.

Finally, we return to the topic of pupil grouping and the use of the teaching strategies of jigsawing and rainbowing (see the section 'Grouping within the class', above). Task 4.1.9 invites you to explore one of these strategies over a small number of lessons and evaluate the experience.

🖉 Task 4.1.9 In-class grouping and teaching strategies

Develop a plan to try out either jigsawing or rainbowing with a class you teach. Read the following two papers before embarking on the task:

1   *Grouping Pupils for Success* (DfES 2006b).
2   *Group Work Pedagogy and Practice: Teaching and Learning in Secondary Schools. Unit 10 Group Work* (DfES 2004b).

Suggested procedure:

■   Try out one of the strategies identified in 2 above with a class you teach (for example, one that would respond to a new grouping arrangement), or with a class with whom you are not making expected progress.
■   Select a topic suitable for subgroup working, draft a rough plan for a lesson, including a set of aims and objectives, and discuss the plan with your tutor or class teacher. Redraft and try out the plan on a small scale over one lesson to test out the groupings you can make, the instructions you give, how to move pupils around groups, and how to round off the lesson. Evaluate the lesson and decide whether to continue with this class or choose another.
■   Develop a set of lesson plans covering three lessons, including learning objectives and learning outcomes for each lesson:
    ■   Lesson 1: Identify the task, provide background for the pupils, including resources and perhaps homework. Brief your class for the second lesson.
    ■   Lesson 2: Introduce the activity, indicate how the groups will form and re-form and what pupils are expected to do in each group. Allow time for pupils to consolidate what they gained from the activity; for example, by a plenary session and introducing the final lesson.
    ■   Lesson 3: Consolidate the work done, leading to the final product.

Check your plans with your tutor/class teacher and teach the lessons.

You may find it helpful for your evaluation to keep a pocket notebook handy to jot down events that occur, the good things and bad things that happen, including pupil responses and comments. Flesh out these notes after each lesson.

Evaluate your teaching against your aims, including implicit aims such as enjoyment, enthusiasm, greater participation, improved behaviour pattern.

Identify the pupil gains from the strategy, including knowledge and skills both cognitively and affectively, the advantages and drawbacks of the strategies.

Discuss your evaluation report with your tutor and identify how you might develop this report into a piece of coursework. Retain the original report in your PDP.

SUMMARY AND KEY POINTS

■ This unit has discussed the ways in which pupils can be grouped for teaching, from streaming, setting and banding to mixed-ability classes. Relative merits of each strategy are mentioned in the light of research. The advantages of any one way of grouping pupils are not clear-cut and other factors strongly influence the achievement of pupils, such as the expectations of the teacher. The developments of in-class differentiation of work for pupils and personalised learning have moved the discussion away from grouping.

■ Progression and differentiation are addressed and several examples are provided. The ways in which tasks are selected, set, supported and assessed are each susceptible to modification to meet the needs of different pupils. Differentiation is addressed from a number of aspects, starting from a simple model of planning using stimulus, task and outcome. The importance of the role of the teacher in supporting and guiding their pupils is emphasised. Strategies for the management of differentiation are addressed, emphasising that in all classes there are pupils with different needs, irrespective of the way the pupils are grouped for teaching. Differentiating your teaching is a responsibility of all teachers, not just for those teachers addressing pupils with special educational needs.

■ We have suggested that tasks should be related to the experience of the learner whenever possible and, further, that the outcomes should be achievable. You may find the discussion about Vygotsky and Piaget in Unit 5.1 helpful in developing those ideas. For those wishing to go further, you can explore lesson planning in a different way, using a constructivist approach (see Unit 5.1).

■ The skills of teaching this way are acquired with experience and, importantly, better understanding of your pupils. While acknowledging that many student teachers move schools at least once in their ITE programme, it is important you begin to understand differentiated approaches to teaching and learning.

Check which requirements for your ITE programme you have addressed through this unit.

Further reading

DCSF (Department for Children, Schools and Families) (2008b) *Key Stage 3 National Strategy Materials*, available at: http://webarchive.nationalarchives.gov.uk/20110809091832/www.teachingandlearning resources.org.uk (accessed 7 December 2014).
   The archive of the National Strategies offers a range of supporting material for teachers and can be explored for materials on ability grouping and differentiation, as well as other teaching resources.

DfES (Department for Education and Skills) (2006b) *National Strategies: Grouping Pupils for Success*, London: DfES, available at: http://webarchive.nationalarchives.gov.uk/20130401151715/http://www.education. gov.uk/publications/eOrderingDownload/00844-2008DOM-EN.pdf.
   This document discusses the arguments for and against different ways of grouping pupils but moves on to explore more flexible ways of grouping, beyond rigid streaming and setting models and drawing upon evidence from research. It does not give subject-specific advice about grouping, but does identify contexts in which different ways of grouping pupils may be beneficial.

Imbeau, M.B. and Tomlinson, C.A. (2010) *Leading and Managing a Differentiated Classroom*, Alexandria, VA: Association for Supervision and Curriculum Development (ASCD).

> Differentiated instruction recognises that pupils are not the same and that access to equal education necessarily means that given a certain goal, each pupil should be provided resources, instruction and support to help them meet that objective. This text addresses these factors. See also similar texts on the ASCD website.

Kerry, T. (2002) *Learning Objectives, Task-Setting and Differentiation*, London: Nelson-Thornes.

> This book, part of a series addressing professional skills for teachers, clarifies each of these skills, explains their purpose and explores issues around, and the consequences of, the implementation of these skills. Practical application is discussed, supported by examples and activities. It also encourages readers to assess their own implementation and progress by analysing the tasks against standards.

Rose, R. (2004) 'Towards a better understanding of the needs of pupils who have difficulties accessing learning', in S. Capel, R. Heilbronn, M. Leask and T. Turner (eds) (2004) *Starting to Teach in the Secondary School: A Companion for the Newly Qualified Teacher*, 2nd edn, London: RoutledgeFalmer.

> This chapter addresses lesson planning for pupils who have difficulty learning. The author suggests an enquiry-based approach to teaching alongside cooperative teaching and learning.

Other resources and websites

See the Education Endowment Foundation on pupil grouping: https://educationendowmentfoundation.org.uk/toolkit/toolkit-a-z/ability-grouping/

Appendix 2 on pages 591–595 provides examples of websites you may find useful.

Capel, S., Leask, M. and Turner, T. (eds) (2010) *Readings for Learning to Teach in the Secondary School: A Companion to M Level Study*, London: Routledge.

> This book brings together essential readings to support you in your critical engagement with key issues raised in this textbook.

The subject-specific books in the Routledge *Learning to Teach* series are also very useful.

Any additional resources and an editable version of any relevant tasks/tables in this unit are available on the companion website: www.routledge.com/cw/capel

4.2 Adolescence, health and well-being

Ceri Magill and Barbara Walsh

Introduction

Adolescence is a transitional stage of growing up that changes a child into an emerging adult (teenager or young person) and involves biological, social and psychological changes, including dramatic changes to the body. The changing nature of family structure and social values play an important part in the adolescent phase of development. The expectation of different societies and/or families influences young people, especially in the school setting. Important factors that may affect adolescents' self-image and their schooling relate to the family, including the socio-economic status, employment history and family harmony. Negative features in any one of these may portend poor career prospects (Child 2007).

Adolescents begin to develop an independence from their parents, which on its own can cause many problems, especially because their parents' opinions become less important. This can be reflected in their behaviour in school, and this is sometimes seen as them being disrespectful and ignorant. It is important for you, as a student teacher, to understand these changes; how a pupil is feeling on the inside often affects how they cope and behave in the external environment.

One aspect of a good school is how successful it is in promoting the well-being of its young people. During personal, social and health education (PSHE), well-being is taught as a discreet focus during the adolescence phase. This includes sex and relationship education. A social and emotional aspects of learning (SEAL) course normally takes a whole-school overview of promoting well-being alongside behaviour, attendance, learning and employability.

The following statement, developed by the Whitehall Wellbeing Working Group in 2006, sums up this understanding:

> Wellbeing is a positive physical, social and mental state; it is not just the absence of pain, discomfort and incapacity. It arises not only from the action of individuals, but from a host of collective goods and relationships with other people. It requires that basic needs are met, that individuals have a sense of purpose, and that they feel able to achieve important personal goals and participate in society. It is enhanced by conditions that include supportive personal relationships, involvement in empowered communities, good health, financial security, rewarding employment, and a healthy and attractive environment.
>
> (Steuer and Marks 2008: 9)

OBJECTIVES

At the end of this unit, you should be able to:

■ describe aspects of the physical development of adolescents;
■ describe and understand some of the physical and cognitive differences between pupils during adolescence;
■ appreciate the effect of external pressures and influences on pupils' behaviour and identify some implications of these differences for teaching and learning;
■ discuss healthy eating and the role of the school in promoting this ideal.

Check the requirements for your initial teacher education (ITE) programme to see which relate to this unit.

About development and growth

Young people tend to have growth spurts, particularly after puberty, the point at which the sex glands become functional. Most girls mature physically earlier than most boys. There are differences in growth rates between boys and girls at the onset of puberty and, on average, girls show a growth spurt at an earlier age than boys. However, there is little difference, for example, in mean height of boys and girls up to the age of 13, but after the age of 16 boys are, on average, over 13 cm taller than girls. Height increases appear earlier than weight increases, and this has implications for physical activity. The differential rate of height and weight development is the origin of clumsiness and awkwardness of some adolescent pupils. As well as obvious gender differences between pupils in a co-educational context, the differences between individuals within a group of boys, or a group of girls, can be quite large and obvious. These differences in development can be worrying for the individual and may affect pupils' attitudes and performance to academic work. For example, it can happen that some pupils who have developed physically earlier than their peers may dominate activity in a class, causing a number of pupils to reduce their involvement for fear of being ridiculed by more 'grown-up' members of the class. On the other hand, those developing early may feel self-conscious in front of their later-developing peers.

Another feature of physical development is the onset of puberty. The age at which this occurs varies quite widely between both individuals and cultures, as does the period of puberty. Adolescence can begin at age 10 for some, for others much later and may finish around the age of 19. This means that a 12-year-old girl may be in a pre-pubertal, mid-pubertal or post-pubertal state. A 14-year-old boy may be similarly placed. Thus, it is not sensible to talk to a 14-year-old cohort of pupils as though they are a homogeneous group. The onset of puberty is affected too by environmental factors, including diet.

There is evidence that environmental factors affect growth (Sawyer *et al.* 2012).

In England, the uptake of free school meals may be used as a proxy measure of deprivation. Childhood poverty continues to have a significant impact on young people's well-being and education (Jackson *et al.* 2012; Sawyer *et al.* 2012).

Physical development and managing your classes

The variation in physical development of pupils shown, for example, in any particular class or any year cohort has implications for your management of classes. These differences are particularly apparent in Years 7–9 and may stand out in activities that prosper on physical maturity or physical control. Boys in early adolescence who develop late often cannot compete with their peers in games; and girls who mature earlier than their friends can also be advantaged in physical education and games but at the same time may feel embarrassed. Thus, competitive activities such as running or throwing or physical confrontation games such as football, hockey and rugby favour faster-developing pupils. Equally important is physical control, the ability to coordinate hand and eye, and to control tools and equipment properly and safely. In the past, some adolescents have been regarded as clumsy, which may be related to growth spurts. Activity in subjects such as physical education, art and design, technology, science and computing depend, in part, on good coordination and psychomotor skills.

Now try Task 4.2.1 to gain an understanding of the range of backgrounds, abilities and physical development in any one age group.

 Task 4.2.1 A profile of a class: background, abilities and physical development

Select a class you teach and find out as much as you can about the background of your pupils. Then shadow the class for a day and try to relate the ways pupils respond to teachers and different subjects. Link this with observation tasks from Unit 2.1 (see notes below for guidance on background).

Discuss your plan with your tutor, who can direct you to appropriate sources of information such as the form tutor. The school physical education staff may well be able to provide information on physical development. There may be special provisions for some pupils in your school that provide additional information; for example, homework club or other provision for pupils unable to work at home. See also the notes below in the section 'Pupil background: notes to help you with Task 4.2.1' for areas of focus for your data gathering.

When you visit classrooms, get permission from the teachers, tell them what you are doing, what is to happen to the information and what is expected to emerge. Be prepared to share your findings with them.

Write a short report for your tutor. Respect the confidentiality of information you acquire in any written or oral report. Reports should not quote names. The report may contribute to your professional development portfolio (PDP). Record in your PDP your personal response to this work and any implications it has for you.

Pupil background: notes to help with Task 4.2.1

Some of the information you might gather from the form tutor you are working with includes:

■ the names and the numbers of boys and girls;
■ the ethnicity of pupils; check the way the school reports ethnicity;

- the religious or cultural background of pupils;
- recent immigrants or children of families seeking asylum;
- patterns of absences and whether absences are supported by notes from parents or guardians;
- the regularity of completing homework and its quality (the class teacher should have such a record);
- the uptake of free school meals.

Gather data about:

- the height and weight of pupils; note any pupils deemed overweight or obese (see later in this unit);
- pupils who have statements of special need and the reason for this;
- the provision of a support teacher and why;
- pupils who do not have a support teacher but need one;
- pupils who have been identified as 'gifted and talented' in the school;
- pupils with specific learning difficulties; for example, dyslexia.

Some research suggests that pupils physically maturing faster score better on cognitive tests than pupils developing more slowly. On average, girls develop physically and cognitively faster than boys, and the results of standard assessment tasks (SATs) and General Certificate of Secondary Education (GCSE) results may be a reflection of this.

Large differences in performance in school subjects, taken together with differences in physical development, has raised the question of whether pupils should be grouped in classes by age, as they are now, or whether some other method should be used to group pupils for teaching purposes; for example, by achievement. Some other educational systems require pupils to reach a certain academic standard before proceeding to the next year, leading to mixed-age classes. Thus, underperforming pupils are kept back a year to provide them with an opportunity to improve their performance. Such practice has an impact on friendship, self-confidence and self-esteem. Equally, you may find schemes for extracurricular support of talented and able pupils.

When pupils feel good about themselves, they feel confident and ready to experience new things. By contrast, pupils who do not feel good about themselves may have their confidence damaged by every small setback. It is important for you to differentiate your teaching so every pupil achieves some success; personalised learning helps give pupils belief in their own abilities and the confidence to take on more challenging tasks (see Unit 3.2 on motivating pupils, Unit 5.5 on personalising learning and Unit 5.6 on neuroscience).

Everybody has feelings; it is impossible to be human and not have them, and during adolescence emotions are particularly strong. It is often easy for adolescents to feel helpless and overwhelmed by emotions. During this time, they may say things in anger or hit out only to regret it later. It is important for you to gauge the situation if, for example, they shout out, act out of character or tell you some personal details. Some pupils are happy to share their feelings while others hide them. If they are suppressing anger, sadness or bitterness, it might manifest itself in them blowing small situations totally out of proportion. The side effects of this could be headaches, lethargy and disaffection towards their work, and as a teacher it is important to be aware of these changes. See also Unit 3.3 on behaviour.

We have discussed the physical and cognitive development of pupils and drawn attention to the differences in development both within a gender group and between boys and girls. A large influence on physical development is diet, lifestyle and attitude to exercise and games. There is concern about the dietary habits of some young people, in part about risk of disease, in part about the level of fitness of many young people and issues of overweight and obesity. Yet others draw attention to the increased use of computers in entertainment and the accompanying sedentary habits this entails. Thus, we turn to consider diet, development and the curriculum. The advent of the concept of 'healthy schools' in England has required teachers to address 'health' issues, including health and well-being (including emotional health), healthy eating, physical activity and PSHE. This development has raised the profile of adolescent eating habits and recommendations for physical activity. This is the subject of the next section.

Diet, health and well-being

Background

In the past 100 years, the average height and weight of children and adults has increased and the age at which puberty arrives has decreased. Such average changes are owing, in part, to increased nutritional standards, better conditions of health and sanitation, and better economic circumstances for the majority. However, the increasingly sedentary lifestyle of young people and the rise in obesity has given rise to increased concern about their diet.

The current measure of body fatness is the body mass index (BMI). This is defined as a person's weight in kilogrammes divided by the square of their height in metres. Obesity in adults is defined as a BMI of 30 or more and overweight as between 25 and 29.9. BMI varies with age, and there are age- and gender-specific standards used by the medical profession. Table 4.2.1 shows recent data for children between the ages of 11 and 15 years.

Table 4.2.1 Children's overweight and obesity prevalence, by survey year, age group and sex (the body mass index (BMI) is defined as a person's weight (kg) divided by the square of their height (m))

BMI status	2003 %	2004 %	2005 %	2006 %	2007 %	2008 %	2009 %	2010 %
Boys 11-15								
Overweight	15.1	14.6	16.5	12.4	13.4	13.8	16.2	14.3
Obese	15.4	16.2	17.1	17.4	16.5	14.4	13.7	15.3
Obese and overweight	30.5	30.7	33.6	29.8	29.8	28.3	29.9	29.6
Girls 11-15								
Overweight	16.9	19.7	14.5	16.5	15.0	15.6	15.3	16.8
Obese	22.2	26.7	21.1	17.3	19.4	18.3	15.4	16.6
Obese and overweight	39.14	46.4	35.6	33.8	34.4	33.9	30.7	33.4

Source: NHS (2012)

Although the data for the period 2003–2010 show a fluctuating level of overweight and obesity in both girls and boys, the prevalence of obesity increased steadily in most years up to around 2006–2007 for both boys and girls aged 11–15, after which there are small but variable decreases in obesity. As a result, the trend in obesity in young people may be flattening out (NHS 2012).

Why is there an increase in overweight and obesity in childhood?

A simple answer is to do with energy balance. Physical activity (PA), sedentary behaviours and food intake are key variables implicated in childhood due to their influence on energy balance (Rowland 2004).

A national programme that measured children in Reception and in Year 6 for body mass and height showed that in 2010/11, 19 per cent of children were obese and 14.4 per cent overweight, meaning that over one-third of children were entering secondary school at an unhealthy weight (NOO 2011). In 2007, the Foresight Report stated that if current UK trends continue, in 2015, 36 per cent of males and 28 per cent of females will be obese, and, by 2025, the figures may rise to 47 per cent of men and 36 per cent of women (NHS 2012). This is a global phenomenon, with obesity rates in many Western countries increasing substantially over the last 10 years.

Many adolescents in the UK are not eating healthy diets or meeting the recommendations for exercise (DoH 2011a, 2011b). The National Diet and Nutrition Surveys carried out over the years by the Department of Health and Food Standards Agency have shown that adolescents eat more than the recommended level of sugar, salt and saturated fats and insufficient dietary fibre. The most frequently consumed foods were cereals and cereal products; that is, pasta, rice, white bread, savoury snacks, sugar and chocolate confectionery. Only 13 per cent of boys and 7 perc ent of girls ate the five-a-day fruit and vegetables recommended by government (DoH 2011a, 2011b).

Many intervention projects have been used to address the increase in child overweight and obesity levels through a combination of strategies to increase levels of PA, reduce time spent being sedentary and improve nutritional intake (Fairclough *et al.* 2013). It has been suggested that school-based interventions that combine PA and diet may prevent children becoming overweight in the future (Brown and Summerbell 2009). In addition, school-based interventions have proven to have more success when PA and dietary behaviours are reinforced at home thorough a family intervention (Brown and Summerbell 2009; Waters *et al.* 2011).

The immediate consequences of overweight and obesity in adolescence are social and psychological. Obese children are more likely to suffer from low self-esteem and behavioural problems. Those who are overweight are often seen as an easy target for bullying, with little peer pressure occurring to prevent it. Such marginalisation may contribute to the social and psychological effects of obesity. Obesity in adolescence and young adulthood has been found to have adverse effects on social and economic outcomes (for example, income and educational attainment) (NHS 2010).

The later health consequences are also serious. Increasing fatness is closely correlated with the development of Type 2 diabetes that used to be diagnosed in middle to later life but is now increasingly seen in young adults and children. Childhood obesity that continues into adult life increases the risk of various diseases, including cardiovascular disease, cancer and aggravation of rheumatic diseases and respiratory diseases, such as asthma, in later life (BNF 2011a).

The strategy of the government is to empower individuals through guidance, with information to enable people to make the best possible choices. In England the, NHS supports Change4Life, an

Internet campaign to encourage a healthy lifestyle that includes both healthy eating and exercise activities for children and their families (www.nhs.uk/change4life/pages/what-ischange-for-life.aspx). The NHS, through the Change4Life programme, also supports the 'Five-a-Day' campaign, which encourages the eating of fruit and vegetables. Guidelines for healthy eating, including the 'Eatwell Plate', can be found on the Food Standards Agency website (www.food.gov.uk).

Developing strategies to address obesity

The National Curriculum for physical education, which was revised in England from September 2014 (Key Stages 1-4), supports the delivery of a high-quality curriculum to inspire all pupils to succeed and excel in competitive sport and other physically demanding activities. In addition, some of the shared aims of the National Curriculum at Key Stages 1-4 include that all pupils:

- are physically active for sustained periods of time;
- lead healthy, active lives.

(DfE 2013l)

In support of the aims of the physical education curriculum, the National Institute for Health and Clinical Excellence (NICE) recommends participation in at least 60 minutes of moderate to vigorous intensity PA (MVPA) throughout the day for children and young people (5-18 years) (www.nice.org.uk). Yet, many young people fail to achieve this target. A study by Mersh and Fairclough (2010) assessed pupil activity levels, lesson context and teacher behaviours when delivering physical education and found that boys engaged in moderate to vigorous physical activity for 59.7 per cent of lesson time compared to 46.1 per cent for girls. While physical education lessons can provide some opportunity to take part in physical activity, much of the lesson is occupied by teacher explanation, disciplinary actions and equipment assortment. It is clear that an age-related reduction and gender differences exist in youth PA as a result of a complex interplay between biological, psychosocial, cultural and environmental factors (Malina *et al.* 2004; Van der Horst *et al.* 2007).

A simple answer to the problem of obesity is therefore that adolescents should eat less and exercise more. But this is a simplistic view. Adolescents today are not greedier; neither do they have less willpower than previous generations. There are many factors that contribute to what has become known as an 'obesogenic environment', a term used to describe environments that encourage and promote high energy intake and inactivity. The next section focuses on the factors relating to food and activity in the obesogenic environment of schools and how they affect adolescents.

Eating habits

The latest school food standards (England and Wales) were announced in June 2014. From January 2015, all local authority maintained schools, academies and free schools set up before 2010 and created from June 2014 onwards must meet these new standards for school food (Gov.uk 2014; www.gov.uk/school-meals-healthy-eating-standards). Many children (England and Wales) are eligible to apply for free school meals if families meet the local council assessment criteria.

The government has suggested that all food in schools must meet nutritional standards so that children have healthy, balanced diets.

This means that the following must be available on menus at schools:

■   high-quality meat, poultry or oily fish;
■   at least two portions of fruit and vegetables with every meal;
■   bread, other cereals and potatoes.

There can't be:

■   fizzy drinks, crisps, chocolate or sweets in school meals and vending machines;
■   more than two portions of deep-fried food a week.

To review the changes to school food standards, access the Children's Food Trust website (www.childrensfoodtrust.org.uk).

Ofsted (2010a) found that the majority of schools in England had a whole-school food policy and their school meals also met the nutritional standards set. Some schools provide voluntary breakfast clubs that are said to improve attendance, punctuality, concentration levels, problem-solving abilities and creativity (BNF 2011b). Breakfast clubs provide a range of healthy foods, and it is reported that this had been a successful first step in engaging pupils on healthy choices.

The school lunch may be the first meal of the day for some pupils. The School Food Trust (SFT) reports that there are 1.6 million children in the UK living in poverty. One consequence of this fact is that many of these children arrive at school hungry. This condition affects both their health and their education. Furthermore, these children only have a hot meal on school days (Dimbleby and Vincent 2013). Similarly, a small-scale research study by the SFT found that KS3 secondary school pupils were more on task (concentrating and engaged) and less off task (disengaged) in the classroom after lunch following a lunchtime intervention to improve the quality of the dining environment and the nutritional quality of the food (SFT 2009).

Further research carried out by the SFT (2011) in primary schools found that only 1 per cent of packed lunches met the standard nutritional standards for school lunches. The majority of packed lunches contained sandwiches, savoury snacks and sweetened drinks. Over half of the packed lunches included sweets, confectionery and savoury snacks, and they contained only half of the fruit and vegetables being provided by schools (SFT 2011). Ofsted (2010a) reported that the reasons why pupils did not take up school lunches were the price of school meals, peer pressure to bring packed lunches, lack of provision for those eating school lunches to sit with friends who had a packed lunch, parental preference and time spent queuing.

Most pupils have a good understanding of what constitutes healthy eating through food technology lessons and other subjects, particularly PSHE, physical eduction (PE) (Dimbleby and Vincent 2013) and science. In contrast, the 'Food in Schools' pilot project found that pupils' perceptions of the dining room were influential in the take-up of school meals. For example, 'students care as much about sitting with their friends as they do about what they actually eat. So the dining room is seen as a social environment' (DoH 2007). When queues are long and the dining room is crowded, the take-up of school meals is lower; this condition limits participation in extracurricular activities or the opportunity to sit with friends who bring packed lunches.

The environment outside school, in terms of influence on food habits, has changed in recent years. There has been, for example:

■   increased consumption of pre-prepared foods and carbonated drinks;
■   more 'eating out' in restaurants or 'eating in' through takeaways;
■   an increase in snacking, often high in saturated fats, sugar or salt;
■   increased pocket money for children; crisps and savoury snacks are the most popular after-school snack.

Shops near the school often provide an alternative to school lunches or after-school snacks. In London, foods chosen by secondary school pupils such as burgers, kebabs, pies, fried chicken and other fast food were analysed for their salt, fat and calorie content. The results showed that the local takeaway products exceeded not only the levels permitted in the average school lunch, but also similar food from national fast food chains (CASH 2010). There have been calls for local authorities to control the type of food outlets that can open up near schools.

Many advertising and promotional campaigns by the food industry to encourage the sale of their particular brands of food are mainly targeted at children. In 2007, the government introduced new regulations that restricted TV advertisements of foods high in fat, sugar or salt during programmes that are expected to be watched by children under 16. Research has shown that although almost all adverts shown during children's programmes did adhere to the restrictions, the amount of advertising for unhealthy foods that children are exposed to is the same as before the restrictions were introduced. This situation arises because children also watch programmes other than those for children, and there is an increase in exposure of all viewers to high fat, sugar and salt food advertising on television. The aim of the restrictions 'to reduce significantly the exposure of children under 16 to high fat, sugar or salt food advertising' has not been achieved; in fact, 'they appear to have had a perverse effect of increasing exposure of all viewers to high fat, sugar and salt food advertising' (Adams *et al.* 2012). Similarly, sponsorship of food products by companies for schools may raise money for books or sports equipment, but can give conflicting messages to pupils if the targeted food products are the 'less healthy' variety; for example, crisps, chocolates.

There is evidence to suggest a link between eating habits, social class and income (The Marmot Review 2010). While pupils from higher socio-economic groups tend to have a more varied diet, those from lower socio-economic groups have more restricted choice of food because parents purchased only food that is sure to be eaten. Many adolescents from low-income families eat less fruit and vegetables and more foods high in fat, sugar and salt. Social and economic differences in health status reflect, and are caused by, social and economic inequalities in society. It is what was termed in the Marmot Review 'the social gradient of health . . . put simply, the higher one's social position, the better one's health is likely to be' (The Marmot Review 2010).

The amount of alcohol consumed by young people in this country is one of the highest in Europe (NHS 2009). This problem alone causes physical, mental, emotional and social problems, which only exacerbate how adolescents may feel about themselves.

Physical activity

Inactivity starts with getting to school. In 2010, 36 per cent of secondary pupils walked to school, with 90 per cent of journeys being under a mile, and only 2 per cent cycled (DfT 2010). Safe storage for cycles is an issue for schools. Pupils who walk or cycle to school are likely to be fitter than those who journey by car, and are therefore more likely to enjoy and benefit from sport.

It has been mentioned earlier that one strategy for tackling obesity is exercise and that proposals have been made about the nature and extent needed for it to be beneficial. Physical education and school sport form less than 2 per cent of school life but are useful in fostering habits of activity that can last into adult life. In 2009/10, 87 per cent of pupils at KS3 had two hours of PE and sport, but this fell to 64 per cent at KS4 and 23 per cent for Years 12–13. There is some link between high levels of participation in at least three hours of PE and out-of-hours sport with the proportion of pupils eligible for free school meals. Free school meal entitlement and child poverty in England information is available at www.gov.uk/government/uploads/system/uploads/attachment_data/file/266587/free-school-meals-and-poverty.pdf (DWP 2013). There are also fewer opportunities available in terms of access to swimming pools and leisure centres for those in lower socio-economic groups than those in higher socio-economic groups.

Household income is also associated with sedentary behaviour, usually watching TV, for more than four hours a day. As the household income decreases, the average number of hours watching TV increases (NHS 2009). This increased sedentary behaviour contributes to obesity and overweight in pupils and affects the 'social gradient of health', as discussed earlier. By contrast, there is a parallel culture that values thinness. Images of men and women in the media, advertising and popular culture emphasise beauty, youth and thinness. Some adolescent boys, but in particular many girls, may compare themselves to extremely thin models working in the fashion industry and perceive themselves to be 'fat' in comparison, rather than healthy and attractive. This promotion of the 'ideal' thin body undermines self-confidence. Body image and self-esteem are closely connected. Self-esteem, especially in adolescents, is closely linked with self-confidence, and a lack of confidence may hinder progress both in school and outside school.

Moving forward

The National Curriculum in England addresses the issues of healthy living in a variety of ways. Nutrition is quite firmly based in the science curriculum in Key Stage 3 (KS3). In PE, pupils are to be taught knowledge and understanding of fitness and health. In PSHE, knowledge and understanding of a healthy, safer lifestyle is a part of the curriculum.

Now move on to Task 4.2.2.

Given all the teaching and learning opportunities provided within schools, there continues to be a problem with overweight and obese adolescents, in addition to the declining levels of PA. The effect of advertising on young people, especially through TV advertising, also contributes. Food marketing to children is a global phenomenon, and tends to be pluralistic and integrated, using

---

 Task 4.2.2 Food and health

Access the National Curriculum for England documents (online at www.gov.uk) or related documents in the country where you are learning to teach. Identify those areas of your subject area, and other curriculum areas, that address issues of healthy eating and healthy lifestyles, such as diet, nutrition and exercise. In England, address KS3 first.

Discuss with your tutor whether there is a coordinated approach in your placement school between the subjects and PSHE. Write a summary of your findings and file in your PDP.

multiple messages in multiple channels. The World Health Organization (WHO) stated that the primary concern was with products with high fat, sugar or salt (WHO 2010). Using the Internet, integrated media strategies advertise specific brands of food; through social media channels, companies can build a one-to-one relationship by communicating directly, and social sites can then extend the marketing messages when an adolescent opts to 'follow' a brand; 93 per cent of 12–15 year olds live in a household with Internet access and 75 per cent of them have a profile on an active social networking site. Over 75 per cent of the websites carrying high fat, sugar and salt products are linked to a corresponding product or brand page on a social networking site, with Facebook and Twitter being the most common. Such commercial messages are designed to persuade adolescents to consume unhealthy products. 'If the marketing didn't work, the food industry wouldn't devote multi-million pound budgets to developing slick campaigns to spread their messages' (BHF 2011).

There is a range of initiatives in schools in England to try to find a means of improving the health of pupils. The National Healthy Schools Strategy is an ongoing project where schools can work with pupils, teachers, families and the local community to actively promote the physical, social and mental well-being of all. It is an attempt by the government in England to bring together a multifaceted approach to the broad problem of improving the obesogenic environment of modern society. Now complete Task 4.2.3 to gain an understanding of the opportunities for exercise for pupils, as well as healthy food choices.

Now complete Task 4.2.4 to develop your understanding of health and well-being issues for pupils.

 Task 4.2.3 The school environment

The definition of an obesogenic environment is one that encourages and promotes high-energy intake and inactivity. Use the answers to the following questions and your observations to evaluate the environment of your placement school.

- How many of your pupils walk or cycle to school?
- Is there safe storage for cycles?
- What is the school food policy?
- Is there a breakfast club?
- How would you describe the environment of the dining room at lunchtime?
- What proportion of the school curriculum is given to PE and sports activities?

In addition, observe:

- the activities of pupils during break and lunchtime on two different weekdays;
- the food availability and food choices made at lunchtimes on one or two days;
- what proportion of pupils have packed lunches compared to school dinners.

Write a short account of this aspect of the school environment and discuss it with your school tutor. File the account in your PDP.

M **Task 4.2.4 Adolescence, health and well-being: a whole-school approach**

The task is in two parts.

Part 1

Write a literature review that focuses on a whole-school approach to adolescence, health and well-being. You could start by reading the research reports and literature referred to in this unit. Also, see the further reading at the end of this unit. You may need to focus on recent research over the last 10 years, for example, in order to manage the task. Your purpose is to convey the knowledge and ideas that have been established on these three areas and their strengths and weaknesses (not just a descriptive list of the material available, or a set of summaries).

Part 2

This can be followed by writing a proposal for a small-scale research study in your school. The proposed research should seek to explore the whole-school policy for 'health and well-being' for your pupils in your placement school and be evaluated in the light of evidence from your literature review.

We suggest that you discuss your review and the proposed research plan with your tutor as you proceed. The final document may be used as a basis for coursework and a copy placed in your PDP.

SUMMARY AND KEY POINTS

■ Adolescence involves physical, mental and emotional changes leading towards maturity and presents dramatic physical changes in young people. These changes may cause nervous introspection: 'Am I growing normally, am I too tall, too short, too fat? Am I physically attractive to others?'

■ Personal appearance assumes a growing importance and causes sensitivity. Girls mature physically earlier than boys, but the range of development of both boys and girls is wide. The range of physical differences between pupils means that, at the same age, pupils react quite differently to tasks and situations in school.

■ Young people are taller and heavier than previous generations, in part owing to improved diets. But the obesogenic environment of modern society, the more sedentary lifestyle and increased consumption of unhealthy foods can lead to overweight and obesity. There is growing concern about the rising numbers of overweight and obese pupils and adults and the physical, social and psychological effects this may have on the individual (DoH 2011a, 2011b).

■ The social and psychological effects on young people can be as damaging as the health risks. A number of issues affecting the health of adolescents have not been raised, including smoking, drinking and drug use, mental health and sexual health. These are discussed further in the report on *Adolescent Health* (BMA 2003).

- ■ Schools have a big role to play in helping pupils through adolescence with the minimum of disruption, to understand the changes in their bodies, to be comfortable with themselves as they are and how they look.

- ■ Schools play an important part in ensuring that pupils have access to a healthy diet and that they understand its importance to them now and in the future. This knowledge and understanding is achieved through a whole-school approach, including teaching and learning in PSHE and other areas of the National Curriculum. Involving pupils in understanding and learning about themselves through active participation encourages confidence and supports a positive self-image (see also Unit 5.2). The pupil who feels valued for their contribution is a pupil who is likely to have good self-esteem.

- ■ All teachers have the opportunity to contribute to the healthy development of their pupils and engender the self-confidence in young people to take control of this aspect of their lives. Self-confidence may help them to resist advertising pressures related to certain foods or, for example, to challenge what is said to be a fashionable appearance.

Check which requirements for your ITE programme you have addressed through this unit.

Further reading

Steuer, N. and Marks, N. (2008) *Local Wellbeing: Can We Measure It?* London: The Young Foundation, in collaboration with the New Economics Foundation (NEF).
    This is an excellent resource for those interested in statistics and how you can measure well-being quantitatively.

Other resources and websites

British Nutrition Foundation: www.nutrition.org.uk
    This site provides reliable information on diet and health. Particularly useful are the 'Teachers Centre' and 'Pupils Centre', which provide a wide range of resources for teachers, including activities for pupils that are downloadable free of charge. It also has research papers relating to diet and health and is an excellent resource for those teaching about diet and health.

Food Standards Agency: www.eatwell.gov.uk
    Government advice on food is given in this section of the Food Standards Agency site. This site has up-to-date, easy-to-read references with some resources for teachers. The Food Standards Agency main site is: www.food.gov.uk.

NICE (National Institute for Health and Care Excellence) guidance: www.nice.org.uk/guidance
    This site lists published guidance on and health and care relating to children and adolescents.

Appendix 2 on pages 591–595 provides examples of further websites you may find useful.

Capel, S., Leask, M. and Turner, T. (eds) (2010) *Readings for Learning to Teach in the Secondary School: A Companion to M Level Study*, London: Routledge.
    This book brings together essential readings to support you in your critical engagement with key issues raised in this textbook.

The subject-specific books in the Routledge *Learning to Teach* series are also very useful.

Any additional resources and an editable version of any relevant tasks/tables in this unit are available on the companion website: www.routledge.com/cw/capel

4.3 Cognitive development

Judy Ireson and Paul Davies

Introduction

During the secondary school years, pupils develop their knowledge and understanding of a wide range of subjects and also their ability to perceive, reason and solve problems. All of these skills are aspects of cognition (literally 'knowing'). A key feature of cognition is that it involves us as learners in making sense of the world around us. As such, it is unlike more basic forms of learning such as memorising a song or rote learning multiplication tables. It includes skills that involve understanding, such as map reading, following instructions to make something, analysing data and solving problems. Making sense, knowing, understanding, thinking and reasoning develop into adulthood and so cognitive development is an important feature of pupils' mental growth during the secondary school years.

Logical reasoning is one important aspect of cognitive development, along with others such as problem-solving, developing expertise in a particular field and creative thinking. Many school subjects require us to think and reason logically; for example, when handling evidence, making judgements, understanding when and how to apply rules, untangling moral dilemmas or applying theories. Most Western societies in their schooling of children privilege logical, mathematical and linguistic abilities over other ways of knowing about the world. The tests of ability used by some schools to select new entrants or to allocate pupils to teaching groups are often problem-solving exercises involving pattern seeking, pattern recognition and pattern using, and the capacity to think logically and quickly.

We consider some of the ways in which pupils' cognitive abilities develop and are identified, particularly logical reasoning, and discuss briefly some ideas about intelligence, including the possibility that there may be a number of discrete intelligences. We also illustrate some of the cognitive demands made by activities in some curriculum subjects. This unit is a continuation of Unit 4.2, which considered physical development and began to address cognitive development. Unit 5.1 addresses in more detail theories of how children learn and develop, and can be read in conjunction with this unit.

OBJECTIVES

At the end of this unit, you should be able to:

- ■ understand some features of cognitive development and the cognitive demands made by curriculum subjects;
- ■ explain and evaluate some ideas about the nature of intelligence;
- ■ identify types of thinking and relate them to learning activities;
- ■ begin to use tasks as a way of finding out about pupils' cognitive level;
- ■ evaluate the idea of 'matching' the curriculum to pupils' learning needs.

Check the requirements for your initial teacher education (ITE) programme to see which relate to this unit.

Differences between pupils

Differences between children are apparent from an early age. Even before they start school, some children pass developmental milestones such as walking and talking more quickly than others. Children may start reading and counting before they begin school, or become very confident in their physical skills. When pupils start primary school, some are better than others at school tasks and those who acquire good language and communication skills tend to be seen as more advanced and may be labelled as brighter than others, something that often leads to pupils being group by 'ability' in different subjects, especially mathematics and science.

In the secondary school, curriculum subjects call for the development and deployment of a range of cognitive skills. Each learning activity or task set by a teacher makes specific cognitive demands on the learner, who may be well equipped to meet them or may have gaps in certain areas. At a given point in time, several factors may contribute to the learner's capability, including their experience of similar tasks, their motivation to learn and cognitive abilities.

Motivational beliefs and learning

One of the reasons that children may be more advanced in certain areas is that they are interested in the kinds of learning valued in school. It can be argued that schoolwork is a game that children have not chosen to play, but that others, teachers and society, have chosen for them. If this assumption is correct, it is likely that some pupils are not highly motivated by the content and focus of lessons, and therefore these pupils may be less successful in school. An alternative view is that we all have an intrinsic motivation to acquire competence and a tendency to protect our sense of self-worth, so those pupils who fall behind in their learning and feel they are not competent become demotivated and act in ways to protect their self-image.

Unfortunately, this reaction often involves maladaptive activity such as procrastination, denying interest or playing the class joker. This is challenging for teachers, who often resort to extrinsic forms of motivation such as threats or praise. Such encouragement may be effective in the short term, but in the long run you are likely to find that it is more beneficial to develop learners' intrinsic motivation; that is, encourage pupils to see the point of their work and to emphasise their growing competence. It is well documented that learners work best at activities they themselves identify as worthwhile (see Unit 3.2).

Pupils who do well in school subjects are sometimes thought to be 'more intelligent' than others or, more accurately, display more intelligent behaviour. Some people are of the view that intelligence is a fixed capacity or 'entity' that sets a limit on what an individual can achieve. Neuroscientists (see Unit 5.6) have identified intelligence as 'incremental'; in other words, it can grow with learning. An incremental view of intelligence carries with it the potential for change through teaching, whereas an entity view suggests that the effect of teaching is much more limited. Dweck (1999, 2008) (see also Unit 5.5 on personalising learning) argues that entity beliefs place limits on learners' achievements, whereas young people and adults with incremental beliefs thrive by taking advantage of learning opportunities. These learners are willing to risk failure, as they believe that challenging tasks offer good opportunities for learning and that making mistakes is a natural part of the learning process.

As mentioned above, schools commonly group pupils by attainment (see Unit 4.1 on grouping), especially in some core curriculum subjects such as mathematics and science. Although common practice, grouping by ability has been shown to make very little difference to overall pupil attainment; Higgins *et al.* (2013) provide an accessible overview of evidence on this topic and also draw attention to the strength of evidence on which estimates are based. (Note their caution that care is needed when accessing information to ensure that sources of evidence for the ratings are evaluated carefully for relevance.) While ability grouping can make it more straightforward for the teacher to plan for a narrower range of learners who have similar attainment in the subject, it can be detrimental to pupil progress, particularly for pupils of similar attainment who are placed in low-ability groups (Ireson *et al.* 2005). Much research shows that grouping in this way can lead to the teacher not recognising the range within a group, and teaching as if the pupils are one supposedly homogenous group of individuals (Coe *et al.* 2014). This is a potential problem because, as discussed in Unit 4.1, pupils may require individualised support, and failing to recognise this impacts on their attainment.

Before reading on, complete Task 4.3.1.

 Task 4.3.1 Intelligent people

Think of two people who you would say are intelligent – they could be adults or children. In what ways are they similar and how do they differ? Share your ideas with other student teachers in your group and make a note of the characteristics in your PDP.

Thinking in different curriculum subjects

At this point, we turn briefly to some types of thinking and intelligent behaviour called for in different curriculum subjects. A closer look at a few subjects suggests that there are differences but also some overlapping demands. In general, linguistic and logical reasoning seems to be privileged in Western school systems.

It is generally thought that the demands of science and arts subjects are rather different. In a discussion about the teaching of art and design in secondary school, cognition is described in terms of the acquisition, assimilation and application of knowledge (Addison and Burgess 2007: 24). These cognitive processes are based on:

■ perception, observation based on experience; and
■ intuition and reason, both the unconscious and conscious making sense of experience.

These processes require the use of imagination, creativity and thinking skills, which are used to transform observations and experiences into material representations. The explicit inclusion of intuition and unconscious making sense of experience is emphasised in art and design in contrast with many other subjects; in the school curriculum, knowledge-based, analytical processes are valued in the appreciation and criticism of art and other creative activities (Addison and Burgess 2007: 24). By contrast, mathematics and science are usually thought to involve logical and mathematical thinking. Indeed, for some people, mathematics and art lie towards opposite ends of a spectrum or are 'different cultures', as described by Snow (1960). That the two cultures can coexist is demonstrated by 'Sciart', a 10-year programme of funding by the Wellcome Trust for scientists and artists to work together. Sciart aimed to stimulate interest and excitement in biomedical science and encourage interdisciplinary work. Fruitful symbiotic relationships were forged between scientists and artists, producing innovative outcomes that helped to demystify science and attracted widespread media and public interest (Glinkowski and Bamford 2009).

Recognising the creative nature of subjects such as mathematics and science is a key feature of good teaching. Not only has it been shown to support pupil learning, but it also helps them to understand how ideas and knowledge in particular subjects are constructed. TV programmes may be creative and imaginative, conveying the essence of important ideas and achievements in a way that is accessible and exciting for learners. The Internet also provides a wealth of ideas that teachers can use to support creativity in their classroom, but their use always requires careful consideration. Discoveries in science such as Archimedes' insight into floating and Watson and Crick's double helix model for the structure of DNA both required imaginative thinking. Nevertheless, teachers do tend to perceive their subjects in rather different ways, with teachers of mathematics being more inclined to view the subject as relatively linear, whereas teachers of English recognise that their subject may be accessed through a variety of routes. This may be linked to the extent to which work may be differentiated by outcome in the two subjects. When setting work for a class, an English teacher may set a single task for the whole class in the expectation that work will be differentiated by outcome, whereas a mathematics teacher is more likely to differentiate by task, setting work of differing levels of difficulty (see Unit 4.1 on differentiation, and Tasks 4.1.4 and 4.1.5 on lesson planning for differentiation).

Recognition of the overlap between the types of thinking used in different subjects is also beneficial for supporting cross-curricular learning opportunities. In primary school, project-based and holistic approaches to learning in non-core subjects are common, but this is seen much less in secondary schools. While teachers often identify the time pressures involved in teaching a busy curriculum as making collaborative work between different subject areas prohibitive, when done well, working in this way has been shown to support pupils not only in developing deep subject knowledge, but also flexibility, curiosity and confidence in their learning – attributes that are intrinsic to the curriculum. A good example of when this can work well is the Arts as a Tool for Learning Across the Curriculum (ATLAC) project, which brought together teachers from across the curriculum to work together in an interdisciplinary way, designing teaching approaches to promote creative learning (Das *et al.* 2011). Some curriculum subjects lend themselves more easily to this approach to teaching and learning (for example, design and technology) (see Task 4.3.2), but projects of this type have been shown to be beneficial in promoting good outcomes for pupils in all subject areas, and also help teachers to recognise the relationships between their and others' subject disciplines, as well as encourage them to take more risks and be more imaginative in their teaching.

A question of intelligence?

Intelligence is most often linked to a pupil's capacity to exercise linguistic and logical mathematical reasoning. This is what is measured by most tests of intelligence. There is considerable evidence to support classical theories of intelligence that suggest that there is a general factor underlying our performance in a wide range of activities in school and work. However, Gardner (1993a; and updated on his website) criticises these theories for being concerned with only a very narrow range of human ability, namely language and mathematics. He argues that they fail to take account of many other aspects that are important in the real world. In his 'theory of multiple intelligences', he proposes that there are a number of relatively autonomous intelligences. He describes intelligence as 'the ability to solve problems or fashion products that are of consequence in a particular culture, setting or community' (Gardner 1993b: 15). He has identified many intelligences, some added later as he developed his theory. They include:

- ■ *Linguistic*: use and understanding of language, including speech sounds, grammar, meaning and the use of language in various settings.
- ■ *Musical*: allows people to create, communicate and understand meanings made with sound.
- ■ *Logico-mathematical*: use and understanding of abstract relationships.
- ■ *Spatial*: perceive visual or spatial information, to be able to transform and modify this information, to recreate visual images even when the visual stimulus is absent.
- ■ *Bodily kinaesthetic*: use all or part of one's body to solve problems or fashion products.
- ■ *Intrapersonal*: knowledge of self and personal feelings. This knowledge enables personal decision-making.
- ■ *Interpersonal*: awareness of feelings, intentions and beliefs of others.
- ■ *Naturalistic*: the kind of skill at recognising flora and fauna that one associates with biologists such as Darwin.

(Gardner *et al.* 1996: 203)

- ■ *Existential intelligence*: concerned with 'big questions about one's place in the cosmos, the significance of life and death, the experience of personal love and of artistic experience'.

(Gardner, quoted in White 2005: 8)

Gardner proposes that these relatively autonomous intelligences can be exerted alone or combined in different contexts at different times. A number of intelligences may be needed in order to carry out some tasks; for example, in the case of art and design, both spatial intelligence and bodily kinaesthetic intelligence might contribute to learning.

Look back at the list of characteristics of intelligent people you identified in Task 4.3.1. How well do they map on to Gardner's set of intelligences?

Gardner's 'intrapersonal' and 'interpersonal' intelligences capture much of what has recently been called 'emotional intelligence' (Salovey and Mayer 1990). This is the ability to recognise, express and reflect on our own emotional states and those of other people, and also to manage these emotions. It is worth noting that for most people, learning is an emotional experience that may involve confusion, disappointment, apprehension, fascination, absorption, exhilaration and relief. These emotions can disrupt or facilitate learning, and it is easy to see that learners benefit from being able accurately to recognise and manage them effectively. For further reading on emotional factors and learning, see Goleman (1995) and Cherniss (2000), and within mathematics learning, see Goulding (2005: 56-8).

Some of the ideas behind the theory of multiple intelligences have received critical reviews (White 1998, 2005). It is not yet clear just how autonomous these intelligences are, and a common view is that a likely model of intelligence is one that operates through a general underlying intelligence backed up by a small number of special abilities. Thus:

> we are bound to look critically at evidence and the evidence of the existence for abilities in different intellectual areas, which are quite independent of each other, is not good . . . intelligence is not a monolithic unidimensional ability which allows us with one IQ number to define an individual fully. All measures of different aspects of intellectual ability correlate with one another.
>
> (Anderson 1992)

Any intellectual behaviour is then a product of a general processing ability and a number of special abilities (Adey and Serret 2010). The use of the word 'ability' above, rather than intelligence, may echo Gardner's early comments: 'nothing much turns on the particular use of this term [intelligences] and I would be satisfied to substitute such phrases as "intellectual competence", "thought processes", "cognitive capacities", "cognitive skills", "forms of knowledge"' (Gardner 1983: 284). In other words, it is not clear whether Gardner is describing an innate faculty, a learned process or a structure of knowledge. However, many teachers and advisers find Gardner's ideas helpful as they alert us to a variety of ways in which we might recognise and develop intelligent behaviour.

An opportunity to further explore multiple intelligence theory is provided in Task 4.3.2.

 Task 4.3.2 Multiple intelligences and design and technology (D and T)

Locate online the D and T curriculum for England (DfE 2013k). Select teaching D and T at KS3, download the Programme of Study and read the sections 'Aims', 'Attainment targets' and 'Subject content'.

Using these documents, identify the skills and intelligences demanded by D and T at KS3. These questions may help you.

1 In which ways do the demands of D and T link to the importance attached in school to linguistic and logico-mathematical aptitude?
2 Using Gardner's 'theory of multiple intelligences', discuss the teaching and learning of D and T as the utilisation and development of different intelligences.

> For discussion on the place of D and T in the school curriculum, see Owen-Jackson (2008: Chapter 1).
>
> Summarise your findings to discuss with your tutor or the D and T teachers in your school. File the final document in your professional development portfolio (PDP).

Logical thinking and reasoning

Logical thinking and reasoning skills enable pupils to draw inferences and make deductions, to give reasons for actions and opinions, to use precise language to explain what they think, and to make judgements and decisions informed by reasons or evidence. As such, they form an important part of thinking across the curriculum. Here, we elaborate on the nature of reasoning through examples of tasks that call on logical thinking for their solution.

The first pupil-related task we have selected (see Task 4.3.3) is adapted from a quiz book (Brandreth 1981: 118). The problems in these types of books are often abstract and lack a real context, but demand reasoning skills, perhaps not too far from the situation commonly found in school.

  Task 4.3.3 A logic problem

Try out the following problem on your own, then compare your answer with other student teachers and share how you set about solving the problem.

When Amy, Bill and Clare eat out, each orders *either* chicken or fish, according to these rules:

(a) If Amy orders chicken, Bill orders fish.
(b) Either Amy or Clare orders chicken, but not both.
(c) Bill and Clare do not both order fish.

Who could have ordered chicken yesterday and fish today? (For the solution, see Appendix 4.3.1).

The problem in Task 4.3.3 is essentially about handling information according to rules of the type 'If A, then B', commonly found in intelligence tests. In this example, the rules are arbitrary and, in this case, it is not a real-life problem because people don't behave in this way. The problem cannot be solved by resort to practical activity; it is a logico-mathematical task requiring abstract thinking. The puzzle can be done 'in the head', but many people need to devise a way of recording their thinking as they develop their answer and check solutions.

Another kind of reasoning task is a game used in *Thinking Through Geography* (Leat 1998). Pupils are given sets of words and asked to find the odd one out. See Task 4.3.4.

 Task 4.3.4 Odd one out

The following sets of words relate to traffic in urban areas. Which is the odd one out in each set? Try this yourself and then compare your answers with others in your group. What went through your mind as you thought about each set?

1	Park and ride	Shopping trips	Bus passes	Ring road
2	Wheel clamp	Tailbacks	Speed cameras	Sleeping policeman

We turn next to an exercise commonly given in science lessons to pupils aged between 12 and 15, the exact timing depending upon their level of development. Pupils are set a problem-solving task in which they are invited to identify the factors that affect the rate at which a pendulum swings (called a 'time period') (see Task 4.3.5). The task is practically based and has real-life connections, as pendulums are used to control timepieces, such as a longcase clock, which contains a rod (pendulum) with a heavy weight at one end. The length of the pendulum is adjusted to control the accuracy of the timepiece. The task comes from research into pupils' thinking about science concepts (see Whylam and Shayer 1978; Adey *et al.* 1989).

The activity concerns *understanding* and *how understanding is gained* rather than knowing and recall. The pupils' task involves planning an investigation, identifying patterns in data and making deductions; in other words, enquiry skills and thinking skills. The exercise illustrates, too, the ways in which pupils respond to data. The analysis of the data requires abstract thought and the ability to handle a complex situation in which several factors (variables) have to be considered.

 Task 4.3.5 Enquiry and understanding: which factors (variables) affect the swing of a pendulum?

Background information
A pendulum is essentially a rod pivoted vertically at one end and free to swing from side to side. A simple example of a pendulum is a piece of string suspended at one end with a weight at the other (see Figure 4.3.1). Pupils are sometimes expected to use experimental data to deduce factors that influence the rate of swing, or 'rules of the pendulum'. They may be given the data, or derive the data for themselves. The task is not to learn the rules, but to understand how the rules derive from observation. The exercise for you and for pupils is to work out what can, or cannot, be deduced from the set of data.

The pupils' task
Two pupils were given a task to find out which factors affected the time period, or rate at which a pendulum swings. They were not told exactly what to do but the teacher had suggested investigating the effect of length, weight and push on the time period. They decided to measure the number of swings made by a pendulum in half a minute. They changed variables of the pendulum each time, by varying:

- ■ the length of the pendulum; they had one short pendulum and one long pendulum (Figures 4.3.1a and 4.3.1b);
- ■ the size of the weight on the end of the pendulum, a heavy weight and a light weight (Figures 4.2.1b and 4.3.1c);
- ■ the height it was raised to set it going – the push; one 'push' was high up, the other 'push' low down (Figures 4.3.1c and 4.3.1d).

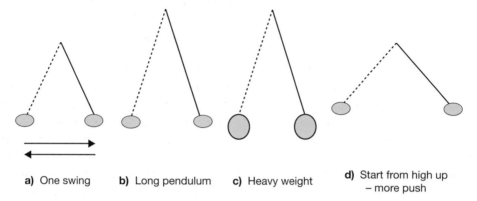

a) One swing   b) Long pendulum   c) Heavy weight   d) Start from high up – more push

Figure 4.3.1 The pendulum: three variables, length, weight and 'high up'

Your task

From the evidence *alone* in Table 4.3.1, what do you think the data tell you about the effect of *length*, of *weight* and of *position of release* on the number of swings per half-minute of the pendulum? See Appendix 4.3.2 for further information.

Table 4.3.1 Data on different pendulums obtained by pupils (for Task 4.3.5)

Experiment	Length of the pendulum	Size of weight on the end	Push at start	Number of swings in half-minute
1	long	heavy	high	17
2	short	heavy	high	21
3	long	light	low	17
4	short	light	high	21

Listening to pupils as they try to solve the problem can be very valuable as it provides clues about their thinking skills (cognitive processes).

There are some interesting features of this task. Intuitively, pupils expect the size of the weight and the 'push' to have an effect on the time period, or rate of swing. They tend to expect heavy weights to 'do more' than lighter weights. The results are contrary to common sense, and pupils often think they are wrong. This conflict with everyday conceptions is not an uncommon experience, even for adults. Evidence that the magnitude of the weight at the end of the pendulum has no effect on the time period is often rejected intuitively or put down to error. Common-sense notions can be in powerful opposition to evidence.

Some pupils also do not accept that if two variables are changed at the same time, then it is not possible on that evidence alone to make a deduction. In this situation, some pupils may then bring in evidence external to the investigation to support their argument, instead of using the data they have.

When pupils are faced with the need to get evidence for themselves, they frequently choose trial-and-error methods rather than logically constructed enquiries. Trial-and-error methods often lead to data that do not provide clear-cut answers to questions; this can lead pupils to make unwarranted inferences from the data in an attempt to get an answer.

As the data are not always clear-cut, your judgement may have to be withheld. This may cause mental conflict because there is a powerful expectation that experiments yield positive information. Saying 'this enquiry tells us nothing about the question' is often not an acceptable answer, especially if you have set up the enquiry. Such feelings mean that attitudes of persistence and honesty are critical for the generation of real understanding. For further information about the time period of a pendulum, see Appendix 4.3.2.

This investigation, and others like it, suggests that enquiries that involve handling together several variables (here, the weight, length and push) can be difficult for many pupils. Structured teaching is needed to improve achievement in these types of higher-level skills. One example of structured teaching is the five pillar model (Adey *et al.* 2001). The aim of this model is to encourage the pupil to move their thinking forward through a series of carefully planned activities so that the pupil not only solves the problem, but is able to articulate how it was solved (an example of metacognition) (see Unit 5.1). The higher-level thinking skills relate to Piaget's formal operational thinking, also discussed in Unit 5.1. For further discussion of this model, see the cognitive acceleration programme in this unit, on pages 263 and 264.

Common-sense beliefs and naive conceptions

Everyday beliefs and naive, or intuitive, conceptions are common in science, as shown in aspects of the pendulum task above, but they also surface in other subjects. Gardner (1991) gives many examples, including a classic case reported by I.A. Richards many years ago. Richards asked undergraduates at Cambridge University to read pairs of poems and then to offer their interpretations and evaluations. He found that the students were heavily influenced by the form of the poem; in other words, whether it rhymed, had a regular metre or rhythm, and avoided words that were too common or arcane. Many of them failed to understand the meaning of the poems.

Gardner (1991) suggests that many of our everyday understandings take the form of 'scripts' and 'stereotypes' that tend to simplify the world around us and make it more manageable. Unfortunately, pupils use these to interpret information presented in school subjects. For example, intuitive interpretations of historical events tend to be quite simplistic and stereotypical; there is often a good versus evil narrative, with evil leaders taking on great importance and the good usually winning in the end. Even when pupils have learned that events such as the Second World War have complex causes and that war is seldom due to the behaviour of a single evil leader, they may slip back into simplistic ways of thinking.

In art, children's intuitive conceptions of pictorial representation tend to start from an awareness of the relation between the picture and the world; in other words, what the picture represents.

As a result, all learners tend to focus on the picture-world relation and also tend to prefer realistic paintings and drawings. Interestingly, beauty appears to play a significant role in young people's thinking about art, and a beautiful painting is considered better than an ugly one. In secondary school, young people may move on to recognise and talk about relations between the picture and the artist, such as understanding that the mood of an artist may affect picture quality. Appreciating relations between the viewer and the picture is a later development (Freeman and Parsons 2001), and one that may not be realised by all.

It is worth getting to know about commonly held naive conceptions in your own subject as this can help you see why pupils have difficulty with some new ideas and ways of thinking. You may be able to plan activities to challenge specific conceptions. We return to this aspect of learning in Task 4.3.6.

Understanding percentages

The next task illustrates the demands made by problems involving percentages. Understanding percentage is an important part of everyday economic life, in retail, mortgages, investment and cost of living generally. It is an area of understanding where considerable confusion reigns for both pupils and adults (see Figure 4.3.2).

A supermarket offered olive oil for sale labelled '50% free'. The bottle contained 750 ml and was priced £2.99, the same price as a regular bottle of oil containing 500 ml. A group of adult customers were arguing that this offer was wrong because the price was not cheaper; that is, £1.50. Despite having the nature of the offer explained to them several times by another customer, most of the group refused to buy the item because it did not cost less than the regular item.

Figure 4.3.2 Percentages in the supermarket

Another example of a common confusion is financial inflation: many adults expect the cost of living to come down when the inflation rate is reduced from, say, 3 per cent to 2 per cent. Similarly, some adults have difficulty calculating real costs when sales advertising offers percentage discounts (see question c in Table 4.3.2). When pupils are faced with problems involving percentages, it appears that context is as important as the numbers themselves. In addition, the understanding of what constitutes a right answer is confused with 'what answer is good enough, given the context'. We might sympathise with this last point; for example, when preparing a dish for four people and faced with a recipe that requires half a litre of cream for six people, we might estimate rather than calculate exactly. The following example illustrates how context might influence pupils' responses to questions.

Pupils were given three questions on percentages, together with an introduction that explained the meaning of the symbol '%'. The questions (a, b and c) and the number of pupils getting the right answer (the success rate) for each of three year groups is shown in Table 4.3.2.

We suggest you read through the questions in Table 4.3.2 and check your own answers to the questions. Then consider possible reasons for the variation in the success rate shown by these pupils and the different contexts in which the mathematics is set. If ability is being judged by responses

Table 4.3.2 Pupils' performance on questions involving percentage

(a) Six per cent (6%) of pupils in school have free dinners. There are 250 pupils in the school. How many pupils have free dinners? The symbol '%' means per cent, or per 100, so 3% is 3 out of every 100.			
Age/years	13	14	15
Success rate %	36	45	57
(b) The newspaper says that 24 out of 800 Avenger cars have a faulty engine. What percentage of cars is this?			
Age/years	13	14	15
Success rate %	32	40	58
(c) The price of a coat is £20. In a sale, it is reduced by 5%. How much does it cost now?			
Age/years	13	14	15
Success rate %	20	27	35

Source: Hart (1981: 96). For further studies on the performance of pupils, see Keys *et al.* (1996).

to questions such as these, then clearly the context in which the mathematics is set matters. The author describes how pupils arrive at their different answers, the different strategies they use and implications for teaching (Hart 1981: 96-7).

Evidence from this investigation and others like it shows that most of us have several strategies we might use when attempting to solve problems such as these. Even young children may have three different strategies for simple addition problems. Pupils who are able to use more efficient strategies for the percentage problem above, such as multiplying by a fraction, are generally more successful but they might not always use the most advanced strategy. This might be because they are not very confident, or it takes time and effort, or the simpler strategy suffices.

Sometimes, it is getting the right answer that is the important factor, rather than the understanding of how a right answer can be obtained. Some of these difficulties for pupils may arise from differences in the use of mathematics in and out of school. In everyday life, approximations are often good enough, as in the cooking example above. For further discussion of the cognitive dimension of learning mathematics, see Goulding (2005: 58-63).

Understanding how pupils use mathematics in different contexts has important implications across the curriculum. A good example is how pupils think about and perceive ideas around risk and uncertainty. The science curriculum prescribes that pupils should be able to evaluate risks, both in terms of practical work but also, and possibly more importantly, wider societal contexts. Here again is a good example of overlap, but also differences, between curriculum areas and thinking skills. In a mathematics lesson, pupils would be taught about calculation of risks, often in a reductionist sense where risk is the product of likelihood and impact, while in the science classroom, the importance of how this knowledge might be used in decision-making would be the focus of discussion.

It is worth noting that adults are often quite happy to admit that they 'are not good at maths', whereas they are more reluctant to admit to literacy difficulties. The curriculum represents the drive by government to raise standards of literacy and numeracy, thereby demonstrating the importance of these skills.

Developing cognitive abilities

Nature and nurture

In general, pupils' cognitive abilities increase with age, as suggested by the percentage example in Table 4.3.2. Older pupils are more capable of abstract, symbolic thinking than younger pupils, who tend to use more concrete representations when solving problems (see the discussion of Piaget's theory of cognitive development in Unit 5.1). It is also clear that in any year group, there is considerable diversity, with some pupils able to cope with more demanding work, while others have great difficulty. Several different explanations have been suggested for this diversity and for the general pattern of development during the school years. In the remainder of this section, we briefly outline some of these.

So what might influence the development of cognitive abilities? Most answers to this question emphasise biological or environmental factors, or 'nature' and 'nurture'. 'Nature' refers to our inborn, genetic or inherited characteristics and how these unfold during maturation, while 'nurture' refers to the environment in which we grow and develop. Genetic factors undoubtedly affect development, but the extent of this influence is not entirely clear, as it is difficult to disentangle genetic and environmental processes. The most influential studies compare twins raised together with twins separated at an early age and raised in different families. These studies show that inherited characteristics do have a strong effect but they do not completely determine measured intelligence; the child's environment also makes an important contribution. Criticisms of the research include the view that the measures of intelligence used in these studies give a particular and quite restricted meaning to the notion of intelligence itself (Gardner *et al.* 1996).

A recent development in the nature-nurture debate is provided by the science of epigenetics. This explores the interactive process between nature and nurture, and argues development should be viewed as an interactive, dynamic process between the total environment of the genes and the genes themselves, instead of discussing the effects of genes and environment on development each as separate entities (see, for example, Day and Sweatt 2011).

Turning to the environment, a pupil's attainment on entry to secondary school is influenced by their experiences in the home and in primary school. Evidence has accumulated to suggest that a lack of stimulation in early childhood limits the capacity of children to benefit from school and other learning situations. A home life that forms a firm basis for later development is one in which children are well cared for and are encouraged to play, explore and talk, and later to enjoy books and learn about the world around them. Children from a good home learning environment have a head start when they enter primary school, as they have started to develop many of the cognitive, communicative and social skills needed in school. Later on, their parents may support them directly and indirectly; for example, taking them to the local library, explaining homework or enabling them to participate in a wide range of activities. While the majority of parents are able to provide a good home learning environment, some find this difficult, perhaps for economic, social or health reasons. Some parents find a good nursery and primary education for their children, while others find this a problem. The Child Care Act of 2006 was designed to provide free or affordable childcare for working parents, and, in addition, to provide an integrated education programme for this age group to address some of the inequalities described above.

A pupil's performance in attainment tests is thus a reflection of their innate abilities and the influence of the environment. Attainment tests tell you what a pupil knows, understands and can do at a particular point in time; however, they are not necessarily reliable predictors of future attainment. Pupils who have had less support for their learning in the past, or who do not speak English as their first language, may be more capable than suggested by these tests. For this reason, it is important to take care not to label pupils in a deterministic way as high, middle or low ability on the basis of attainment tests when they enter the school.

Knowledge base

Another important factor that is easily overlooked is the amount of knowledge an individual has acquired. It is sometimes assumed that the more advanced thinking of adults is owing to biological maturation, when in fact it may be owing to increased knowledge. Comparing children who are very knowledgeable about a subject with adults who are not (for example, children who are very good at chess and adults who are beginners) illustrates the power of knowledge nicely. When shown a chessboard with pieces laid out as they might be during a game, the expert children are better than the adult beginners at remembering the positions and, if the board is taken away, expert children are able to place more pieces than adults in the correct position on another, empty board. However, when the pieces are arranged randomly on the board, there is no difference between the adults and the children. This indicates that children who are good at chess build up knowledge of patterns and configurations as they play, and this knowledge helps them remember (see Bransford *et al.* 1999).

People who are experts are much better at recognising patterns in information and using principles to solve problems. This applies in domains as diverse as medicine, music, physics, computer programming and teaching. Experts build up a strong knowledge base and use it effectively to solve problems. Reading X-ray photographs is one such example (Abercrombie 1985). For pupils, the development of a strong knowledge base in school subjects is important for remembering and thinking. It also makes learning more enjoyable and satisfying. Good teaching and active learning (see Unit 5.2) should help pupils to build up a well-structured knowledge base, but this may be undermined by pressure to cover the curriculum, leaving insufficient time for understanding and consolidation.

Language and development

Language is the tool of cognitive development; without language, it would be difficult to construct ideas, convey ideas, challenge ideas and so effect change. When we think, we do so in symbols, both of language and image; thus, language is important for both community and personal development. This is why so much importance is placed on young children learning to talk, then to read and write. Whereas there may be arguments about when children should learn to read and write, no doubt exists that at some stage they should.

If language is crucial to development, then the first language or mother tongue is very important for pupils if they are to realise their full potential. For native English speakers, it is the full development of the linguistic abilities that becomes important. For pupils for whom English is a second language (E2L), another important issue arises. Whereas, for obvious reasons, it is important that such children learn English (the host language), at the same time, their first language is likely to be the one in which they think. The later a child comes to learning in a second language, the more likely it is that their thinking skills use the mother tongue. Thus, playing down or stopping the development of mother tongue learning not only diminishes its cultural significance, but crucially may inhibit their cognitive development and so reduce their opportunity to achieve (Lu 1998).

The first language skills they learn act also as a bridge to learning the second language, and children are able to use the visual, linguistic and cognitive strategies used in their mother tongue in learning to read and write English. Without this strong bridge, their chances of achieving academic success may be reduced and so limit their life chances (see Flynn's 2015 EAL MESHGuide).

Curriculum and development

Several ideas have now been introduced to explain pupils' performance in school. It has been suggested that performance is a product of inheritance and environment. Also that as they grow, develop and learn, pupils become more able to handle complex problems and situations and abstract (formal) thinking. You are not in a position to influence inheritance or the home learning environment, but you can influence classroom learning by providing activities that are aligned with pupils' current knowledge and understanding. To do this requires a careful analysis of the demands made by a piece of work and the current performance of the pupil or group of pupils with reference to relevant knowledge, skills and understanding needed to do the task.

Programmes of study for each of the National Curriculum subjects set out aims for all pupils, in terms of their thinking and learning, and even though each subject has different content knowledge and emphasis there are also some similarities in learning and thinking processes across subjects. You should turn to the programme of study for your subject and compare the aims with those for a different subject.

Each subject sets out requirements for pupils to acquire relevant knowledge and skills that form a foundation for that subject at a particular Key Stage. Each subject also specifies thinking and reasoning skills required to draw inferences and make deductions from foundational knowledge, as well as elements of problem-solving, reasoning and use of evidence to develop and justify arguments and give explanations. Some subjects place greater emphasis on pupil experience, imagination and creative thinking to generate and extend ideas.

For example, the programme of study for computing (DfE 2013f) states that it aims to ensure that all pupils:

■ can understand and apply the fundamental principles and concepts of computer science, including abstraction, logic, algorithms and data representation;
■ can analyse problems in computational terms, and have repeated practical experience of writing computer programs in order to solve such problems;
■ can evaluate and apply information technology, including new or unfamiliar technologies, analytically to solve problems;
■ are responsible, competent, confident and creative users of information and communication technology.

These aims clearly place emphasis on understanding, application and analysis, as well as practice of writing computer programs. Unusually, perhaps, the fourth aim also states personal qualities required for this subject.

Having identified the aims and subject content for your own subject, pick out statements that mention thinking skills. Which of these are likely to be the most and least challenging for pupils? Then turn to a specific piece of work or topic you are planning to teach and identify the cognitive and other demands for pupils. When you have clarified the task demands, a careful assessment of pupils' current performance may be carried out, through a process that represents an example of assessment for learning (AfL) (see Unit 6.1 and Procter (2013) and Newton and Bowler's (2016) MESHGuides on AfL). Thus, with evidence from assessment, future learning activities can then be planned so as better to guarantee some success while offering a comfortable level of challenge. Curriculum development then becomes a process of matching the curriculum to the needs of the pupils. This strategy depends on you being able to analyse the cognitive demands of the topic and associated learning activities and the relevant capabilities of pupils in order to achieve a match.

Some questions arise from proposing such an approach:

■ Does the cognitive demand made by the teaching material depend on the way the material is presented? Can most concepts be taught to most pupils if suitably packaged and presented?

■ If matching 'curriculum to pupil' is the goal of your teaching, how do you build in development, going beyond the current level of performance? How would pupils progress and is there a danger that reducing the chance of failure may remove challenge?

■ Records of pupil performance and development are needed in order to match material to pupil. How should you keep such records?

■ If each pupil has different prior knowledge and understanding, how can you cope with a whole class? See Unit 4.1 on grouping, progression and differentiation.

■ If pupils cannot cope with certain concepts because they are not yet ready for them, does this mean that some areas of the curriculum cannot be taught? Is rote learning an acceptable way to overcome this problem? See Unit 4.1 on differentiated learning, Unit 5.1 on theories of learning and Unit 5.2 on active learning.

You may wish to add your own ideas to this list.

An alternative to this approach is to think in terms of 'constructive alignment' (Biggs 2003). A basic assumption here is that the learner constructs meaning through relevant learning activities, hence 'constructive'. The 'alignment' part refers to what you do, which is to set up a learning environment that supports the activities appropriate to achieving the desired learning outcomes. The key is that teaching methods and assessment tasks are aligned to the learning activities. Less emphasis is placed on obtaining detailed information about each learner. Such an approach perhaps acknowledges that it is very difficult for you to match work on an individual basis, given the number of pupils in a class and the variety of differences between pupils. The key point is that during a course of teaching (for example, a unit of work), you should provide a variety of learning activities carefully designed to enable pupils to achieve the desired outcomes.

The cognitive acceleration programme offers a somewhat different approach (Shayer and Adey 2002) that incorporates several key components. This has been referred to above – the five pillar model (page 257). The emphasis is on helping pupils to understand the context, to 'learn how to learn' and begin to construct meaning for themselves. The first component is 'concrete preparation', which involves you setting activities to ensure that pupils are familiar with the context of a problem and any technical vocabulary. You then give pupils problems to discuss in small groups, designed in such a way that all pupils are able to contribute to the discussion (see jigsawing and rainbowing in Unit 4.1). An important feature of the programme is that pupils are encouraged to think about their own thinking (metacognition). Both you and your pupils are encouraged to think about links between their thinking in other aspects of the curriculum. Results suggest that pupils can be taught to think in generic ways that help them to learn better across a range of subjects and context (Adey and Serret 2010). Cognitive acceleration started in science but is now being developed in a variety of curriculum subjects (Shayer and Adey 2002).

Clearly, learning activities that are carefully designed can be very effective in helping pupils to learn and to become aware of their own learning strategies. Both these aspects of learning can also contribute to a pupil's sense of competence, which may be seen as a fundamental human need. Competence is an important aspect of motivation and one that may help to raise pupils' aspirations.

Creative problem-solving

In this unit, we have taken cognition to encompass acquisition, assimilation and application of knowledge, and also problem-solving and thinking. Earlier in the unit, we used an example from design and technology as fostering capability to integrate thought and skills into a holistic exercise, rather than a piecemeal exercise of isolated skills.

A different example of this type of problem-solving is shown in a collection of children's responses to problems set by adults. The collection shows the spontaneous work by pupils (upper primary, lower secondary) in response to problems related to everyday events (de Bono 1972). The tasks include:

■ How would you stop a cat and a dog fighting?
■ Design a machine to weigh an elephant.
■ Invent a sleep machine.
■ How would you build a house quickly?
■ How would you improve the human body?
■ Design a bicycle for postmen.

(de Bono 1972)

In this work, pupils need knowledge of the context from which the problem is drawn and also to use knowledge and skills from both inside and outside the classroom. The work of pupils is occasionally unusual and the solutions sometimes impractical. The responses show much imagination and insight into their everyday world. The book is out of print but used copies are available cheaply on the Web.

Measuring cognitive development and intelligence tests

Much work has been carried out to help us understand pupils' (and adults') responses to problem situations. For example, Piaget devised many tasks that have been used extensively and adapted by others (see Donaldson 1992; Child 2007: Chapter 4; Adey and Serret 2010). These tasks provide a window on the type and sequence of thought process adopted by learners and reveal much about how pupils' thinking develops. Hopefully, if you have tried some of the tasks in this unit, you are starting to see how you might use problems to help you learn more about your pupils' cognitive processes.

The main purpose of many tests and examinations is to assess, rank, select and make predictions about progress (see Unit 6.1). IQ tests were first developed by Binet to identify pupils who may be in need of special education (Gould 1981: 148). Later, tests of intelligence were designed to assist educational and occupational selection on a fair, meritocratic basis. Most people are familiar with the notion of 'intelligence quotient' (IQ), which is reported as a single number. This is derived from test scores and shows the extent to which the pupil is below or above an average score based on a large sample of pupils. The test is norm-referenced and the average score is given an arbitrary value of 100. As indicated above, intelligence tests generally tap a range of cognitive abilities involving language, numerical and non-verbal thinking and reasoning.

Intelligence testing assumed great importance in the UK after the Second World War owing to the 1944 Education Act. Pupils were selected for grammar, technical or 'modern' schools by means of the 11+ examination, a type of intelligence test. Despite being developed into a reliable sophisticated tool, the examination failed to take account of late developers or the effects of pupils' social background. The tests also favoured pupils with good linguistic skills, those who had a good vocabulary and were familiar with middle-class culture, and girls. Girls, on average, mature faster than boys, and the 11+ entry had to be modified to ensure equal access to grammar school for boys and girls. It was shown, too, that performance on the tests could be improved by training, which suggested that, in part at least, learned skills were being tested rather than purely innate intelligence. Confidence in the whole issue of selection was undermined by research from Ireson and Hallam (2001), showing that it had negative impacts on pupils from less advantaged backgrounds. In due course, many local authorities abolished grammar schools and moved to a fully comprehensive secondary system on grounds of equity, although some retain selection; for example, Kent and Buckinghamshire (Ireson and Hallam 2001). Concerns about the impact of home background on pupils' achievement in national examinations have led to a call for the use of cognitive abilities tests in selecting young people for gifted and talented programmes and entrance to university.

Standardised testing is a skilled process and many commercially available tests must only be used by approved persons. IQ testing is sometimes used by educational psychologists to assess pupils who, in various ways, find school difficult. This procedure may be necessary for the identification of special educational needs such as dyslexia (see Unit 4.6). Other reasons for standardised assessment may be for research purposes as part of monitoring a population (see Unit 6.1 for further information on assessment).

We have described some challenges that arise in teaching aspects of a few subjects and drawn attention to the role of cognition in teaching art and design. Task 4.3.6 asks you to assess the cognitive challenge in your teaching subject.

 Task 4.3.6 Cognitive challenge in your teaching subject

This leads to master's-level Task 4.3.7.

Select a coherent piece of work, say a topic in a unit you teach, and identify the concepts pupils usually get wrong, stumble over or misunderstand, or you find hardest to teach. As well as your day-to-day classroom experience, use the results of end-of-unit tests or GCSE examination. What is it that makes the concept(s) difficult? Here are some reasons:

- The subject matter is too abstract.
- Pupils do not have the necessary vocabulary.
- The subject matter lacks relevance to everyday life.
- Pupils cannot access sufficient background knowledge.
- Pupils are asked to apply existing knowledge to new situations.

- ■ Pupils are expected to make connections between different areas of knowledge.
- ■ Pupils need to consider multiple factors in a situation.
- ■ The task requires pupils to look for patterns in information.
- ■ Pupils are expected to abstract generalisations from a situation.
- ■ The task asks pupils to make judgements or criticisms about propositions or generalisations.

As part of your classroom experience, select a topic covered or a task you set and ask pupils to talk about how they completed it and to identify any aspects of the work they found easy and those they found difficult. How pupils experience difficulties varies in different subjects. For example, in mathematics, pupils find modelling, proportionality, estimating and probabilistic reasoning challenging. In learning languages, vocabulary and following grammatical irregularities can be a problem. Pupils' intuitive explanations of phenomena in science result in what are commonly termed 'naive conceptions'. Two examples that explore the difficulties that pupils may have in different subjects are explained below.

As we have already discussed in the pendulum task, there are phemomena in science – sugar 'disappears' when it is added to water, heavy objects sink and light objects float, light coming out of our eyes helps us to see – that have counter-intuitive explanations. One of the most difficult explanations for pupils (and indeed most people) to understand is that plants' food does not come from the soil. Plants are watered, given plant 'food', compost and fertilisers are sometimes mixed into the soil, so how can there be any other explanation? That the main component of plant growth is carbon, which comes entirely from the air, can seem extraordinary given that air appears 'empty' to many young children and that the wood of tree trunks can weigh many tons. For pupils to be able to make sense of such an explanation, they need a set of concepts in place on which they can draw. To understand photosynthesis, they need to be able to use concepts:

- ■ Air is a gas.
- ■ Gases are material substances.
- ■ It can be demonstrated that air is material (for example, feeling wind, trying to squeeze an inflated balloon).
- ■ Leaves deprived of light do not make starch.
- ■ The presence of starch in leaves can be demonstrated.
- ■ Plants can be deprived of carbon dioxide.
- ■ The presence of carbon dioxide in the air can be demonstrated.
- ■ Plants deprived of carbon dioxide die.

Hence, when approaching the teaching of photosynthesis, you need to ensure that pupils are familiar with some of these concepts prior to learning and that they are able to make use of all of them at the end of the lesson.

Another example comes from geography, where pupils often have difficulty in understanding the structure of the Earth and geological processes such as continental drift. The Earth's crust appears to be very stable and solid, and, for most of us, our everyday life experiences confirm this to be the case. It is only when earthquakes and volcanic eruptions occur that we are able to observe the dynamic nature of the thin crust on which we live. To properly understand the changing structure of the Earth, pupils would need to be able to use these concepts:

■ The Earth's crust only forms a small fraction of the total mass of the Earth.
■ Most of the Earth is composed of liquid, molten rock.
■ The solid crust floats on the molten rock beneath it.
■ Very high temperatures and enormous pressure causes rock to melt and move.
■ The Earth is around 4.6 billion years old.
■ Most geological processes take hundreds of thousands of years before they can be observed.

As with the science example above, when teaching about topics such as continental drift, you would have to ensure pupils were familiar with many of these concepts at the start of the lesson, and make sure they are able to make use of them by the end of the lesson.

M

Task 4.3.7 Helping pupils to understand difficult ideas

Make a plan for a short teaching episode that may make a difficult idea more accessible to pupils. (This plan does not have to be set out formally, more a sketch of your ideas.) This might be an aspect of photosynthesis in science, a challenging section of a poem in English, interpretation of complex evidence in history, and so on. In devising your plan, address some of the points we have made in this chapter.

1   Establishing what required knowledge pupils already have (you might, for example ask pupils in a previous lesson to put forward their own ideas or explanations of what you are about to teach and make notes of what they say or do; ask more experienced teachers what pupils might be expected to know and do).
2   Making the learning purpose worthwhile (think about contexts that help pupils make sense of new content).
3   Using a range of strategies (think about two or more strategies you might use to support learning; discuss with peers and colleagues).
4   Incorporating required thinking (for example, inference-making, deduction, problem-solving).

Write about 500 words justifying your plan. In so doing, you should draw on what you have learned in this chapter, as well as two other academic texts (these might be referenced in this chapter or texts drawn from your particular subject area). Such a justification would be in the form of an explanation backed up by literature that makes a convincing argument for your approach.

SUMMARY AND KEY POINTS

Cognitive development is described as a process through which pupils develop their knowledge, understanding, reasoning, problem-solving and creative thinking. All these aspects of thinking develop into adulthood, and so cognitive development is an important feature of pupils' mental growth through the secondary school years.

In thinking about cognitive development across various secondary school subjects, this unit brings together the following key ideas:

■ Research reveals that there are differences between pupils in terms of the cognitive processes they use in, and the cognitive demands made by, different curriculum subjects.

■ Carrying out the practical tasks in this unit encourages you to analyse the cognitive abilities involved in completing them, as well as provide you with opportunities for finding out more about your pupils' capabilities.

■ Key to this is listening to your pupils and finding out about their perspective on learning activities; through this, you learn more about their understanding and thinking. This process helps you to design activities to assist their development.

We refer you to Units 3.2, 5.1 and 5.2 for further discussion of related topics.
Check which requirements for your ITE programme you have addressed through this unit.

 ## Further reading

Adey, P. and Serret, N. (2010) 'Science teaching and cognitive acceleration', in J. Osborne and J. Dillon (eds) *Good Practice in Science Teaching: What Research Has to Say*, Buckingham: Open University Press.
Although written in the context of teaching science, the authors discuss what it might mean to be intelligent and theories about its origin and function, and then go on to discuss the implications for learning science in secondary school. The evidence provided is based on extensive research into pupils' understanding of science and of interventions to improve understanding and promote cognitive acceleration. The conclusions not only have implications for the teaching of other subjects, but also provide some evidence for enhanced learning in other subjects as a result of interventions in science lessons.

Child, D. (2007) *Psychology and the Teacher*, 8th edn, London: Continuum.
This edition is an updated and expanded version of a classic text that provides a useful review of cognitive development, theories of learning and intelligence. It includes research into classrooms, practice, management and special needs, and is a useful source of references.

Donaldson, M. (1992) *Human Minds: An Exploration*, London: Allen Lane.
The author expands on ideas expressed in *Children's Minds* (1978), a classic text on developmental psychology and Piaget's work on cognitive growth, and presents a study of the development of the mind from birth to maturity.

Gardner, H. (2006a) *Multiple Intelligences: New Horizons*, New York: Basic Books.
Gardner provides a summary of the original theory first propounded in *Frames of Mind* (Gardner 1983). He argues that the concept of intelligence should be broadened, but not so much that it includes every human faculty and value. He also describes how multiple intelligence (MI) theory has evolved over the course of 25 years and includes a section on educational experiments based on MI theory.

Other resources and websites

TED Talks

www.ted.com/talks/sir_ken_robinson_bring_on_the_revolution?language=en
    A Ted Talk where Ken Robinson gives a useful overview of learning theory and discusses ideas about creativity and intelligence in the classroom and school curriculum.

www.ted.com/talks/sarah_jayne_blakemore_the_mysterious_workings_of_the_adolescent_brain?language=en
    A Ted Talk where Sarah-Jayne Blakemore discusses the developing adolescent brain and its link to learning in school.

DfE Qualified Teacher Status (QTS) Skills Test: http://sta.education.gov.uk

DfE Families in the Foundation Years: www.gov.uk/schools-colleges-childrens-services/early-years

Appendix 2 on pages 591–595 provides examples of further websites you may find useful.

Capel, S., Leask, M. and Turner, T. (eds) (2010) *Readings for Learning to Teach in the Secondary School: A Companion to M Level Study*, London: Routledge.
    This book brings together essential readings to support you in your critical engagement with key issues raised in this textbook.

The subject-specific books in the Routledge *Learning to Teach* series are also very useful.

Any additional resources and an editable version of any relevant tasks/tables in this unit are available on the companion website: www.routledge.com/cw/capel

Appendix 4.3.1: Answers to Task 4.3.3

From rules a and b, if Amy orders chicken, Bill orders fish and Clare orders fish. This contradicts rule c. So Amy orders only fish. Then from rule b, Clare can order fish or chicken. Clare orders chicken, then Bill orders fish or chicken. If Clare orders fish, then Bill can order only chicken. So Clare could have chicken yesterday and fish today.

Appendix 4.3.2: Commentary on Task 4.3.5

The time period of a pendulum depends on the length of the pendulum; neither the magnitude of the weight nor the position from which the pendulum starts swinging (high or low) affects the time period.

From the pupil readings shown in Table 4.3.2, it follows that investigations 1 and 2 tell you the length has an effect on the time period, since only length was changed, weight and position of release being held the same.

Investigations 2 and 4 tell you that weight has no effect on the time period, since length and position of release are held the same.

Finally, from investigations 1 and 3, *if weight has no effect*, then since the length is constant in both experiments, the position of release has no effect on the number of swings per half-minute.

Responding to diversity

Stefanie Sullivan

Introduction

Teaching is a complex process, made interesting by the vast range of educational, social and political contexts and purposes that shape it. Your classroom is likely to be a mix of boys and girls, contain pupils from several ethnic origins, and have pupils from family backgrounds with differing views on the value and purpose of education, as well as pupils who have disabilities. In addition, there may be differences in the financial status of your pupils' families and, for some families, unemployment. Some pupils may split their time living in two different homes owing to divorce, and other pupils may not be living with their parents but are looked after in other ways. This unit helps you to understand better the complex make-up of modern UK society, particularly how social diversity, educational opportunity and attainment are interrelated. As well as considering a big-picture perspective, you are expected to take account of such diversity in your classroom practice and encouraged to examine critically the ways in which you respond to diversity in your teaching.

The standards that student teachers are expected to meet include the ability to adapt their teaching to the needs of all pupils so that all pupils are challenged and supported. This is easy to write but much more difficult to implement. It is important to recognise that your own experiences of education and your perspectives on the educational, social and political contexts of the day have a significant influence on the way in which you respond to diversity. In this unit, we focus on issues around gender, ethnicity and social class, which, although they are examined separately herein, clearly overlap and intertwine.

OBJECTIVES

At the end of this unit, you should be able to:

■ access evidence about the relative academic performance of pupils in relation to gender, ethnicity and class;
■ discuss issues of discrimination and bias in relation to gender, ethnicity and class;

A history of diversity in the UK

The presence of people originating from other cultures, faiths and backgrounds has been a feature of British society for many centuries. The notion of 'other' suggests that British society is easily described but 'Britishness' is neither a clearly defined nor a fixed concept. Immigration into the UK continues since joining the European Union. A few examples draw attention to the changing ethnic mix that contributes to present-day society. The Roman conquest of England at the dawn of the Christian era lasted some six centuries, at the end of which came invasion by Germanic peoples. About two centuries later, the Viking invasion brought Danes and Norwegians to the mix of peoples. In 1066, the Normans took over much of England, and many French people stayed and were assimilated. In the sixteenth century, many people fled mainland European countries to escape, for example, religious persecution.

The ethnic mix was added to by Jewish immigration following their persecution at the end of the nineteenth century. Two world wars saw a further migration of people in mainland Europe away from conflict. As many former colonial countries have gained independence, immigration from Africa and Asia altered the ethnic mix in the UK. The important difference associated with this latter wave of immigration was the visibility of newcomers. The 1950s in the UK saw the active recruitment of black and Asian families to fill the gaps in the workforce (Briggs 1983: 310–12).

Throughout the last century, the population of England and Wales grew steadily, from 35.5 million in 1901 to nearly 49 million in 1991. The 2013 mid-year population estimate suggested that the population of England and Wales was 57 million. According to the Office for National Statistics (ONS, 2012a: 10), the minority ethnic population reached 14 per cent of the population in 2011, and some studies suggest this may reach around 30 per cent by 2050. The freedom of movement of EU citizens and the widening of EU membership has added further to the cultural mix. For example, between 2008 and 2013, the estimated number of people resident in the UK born in the EU8 (Czech Republic, Estonia, Poland, Hungary, Latvia, Lithuania, Slovakia and Slovenia) rose from 689,000 to 1,077,000.

Up to the early 1950s, immigration was largely white. Many immigrants prior to that date were assimilated into the host culture, although a few immigrant groups maintained their distinctive lifestyle; for example, the Jewish community. At first, the host community adopted the same attitude towards the black and Asian immigrants and expected them to adopt the values and lifestyle of the host nation. Black people, however, were not accepted in the same way as white immigrants of the past. This attitude towards immigrants and asylum seekers remains today among a minority of people.

The increased diversity of our society does not just come from the range of ethnic and cultural backgrounds it represents. Advancements in health and social care mean more children are surviving with complex needs and the number of people with disabilities in the UK is increasing. Though the number of divorces has remained stable over recent years, the number of marriage separations has increased dramatically over the last 50 years (ONS 2014), resulting in a changing notion of 'family'. The Joseph Rowntree Foundation monitors poverty and social exclusion on an annual basis, and highlights that British society is becoming increasingly polarised. Their 2011 report showed that in 2009/10, 29 per cent of children lived in poverty (Aldridge et al. 2011). Although their 2014 report shows an improvement, it highlights that the poverty threshold is lower and 'almost all of the major cities in the UK, and a large number of London's boroughs, have more than 30 per cent of children in poverty' (MacInnes et al. 2014: 34).

Equal opportunities and educational equity

By equal opportunities, we refer to the lack of discrimination between pupils on the grounds of gender, ethnicity, class and disability. This notion links to the idea of equity in education by which we refer to the achievement of fairness in education; for example, that all pupils should have equal access to state-maintained schools. For many people, it is self-evident that the implementation of equal opportunities policies is a reflection of basic human rights, but how does the notion of equality of opportunity relate to a teacher's response to diversity? Should the same curriculum, teaching styles, and so on, be used consistently, or does such 'equality' in fact perpetuate inequality? Sociologists of education have argued for many years that if you assume that all pupils come to school equally prepared, and treat them accordingly, then in reality you advantage those who have been better prepared in their social milieu to succeed at school (Bourdieu 1974: 32–56; Bernstein 1977; Willis 1977). Although society has changed in the 35 years since these observations were made, there remain substantial differences between pupils in their educational experiences; that is, readiness for secondary school (see also Units 4.2 and 4.3, which discussed examples of difference in 'cognitive development' and 'health and well-being'). The notion of the dilemma of difference (Norwich 1993; Dyson 2001) is at the heart of this educational debate:

> the dilemma lies in the choice between identifying children's differences in order to secure appropriate provision, with the risk of labeling and discriminating, and accentuating learners' 'sameness' and offering common provision, with the risk of not paying due attention to their needs.
>
> (Terzi 2008: 245)

Concerns about educational achievement have shifted between different groups of pupils over the years. In the 1980s and earlier, there was concern about the underachievement of West Indian pupils (Short 1986). Now there is growing concern about the low performance of many white working-class pupils, with only 36 per cent of white British children from low-income backgrounds achieving five or more GCSEs at A*–C, including English and mathematics, in 2012 (Ofsted 2013). Although much progress has been made in the last three decades as regards equal opportunities for men and women in the workplace and boys and girls at school, the mean gender pay gap for women and men working full time in 2012 was 24.5 per cent for annual earnings, with men still predominating in many of the highest-paid occupations (EHRC 2013).

These issues around gender, ethnicity and class comprise the foci of the remainder of the unit.

In many cases, explanations of pupil underachievement have focused on the shortcomings of the pupil or their families. More recently, the focus has shifted to addressing the educational system as one of the factors contributing to underachievement. This focus is not only at the level of government and school policy, but also in the classroom where such policies are interpreted and implemented by teachers (see the Joseph Rowntree Foundation website for reviews of the relationships between underachievement and gender, ethnicity and class).

Gender

The EHRC has regularly produced overviews of social differences in our society (see www.equality humanrights.com). These overviews are available online and include performance in national examinations, take-up and achievement post-16 and in further and higher education, as well as employment patterns and rates of pay in England. There remains considerable difference in the ways in which boys and girls/men and women exist and move through our society. Focusing on secondary schooling, both boys and girls have been steadily improving their performance in school examinations over the past 20 years, but there is a clear gender gap. Table 4.4.1 compares the performance of boys and girls at General Certificate of Secondary Education (GCSE) gaining five or more grade A*-C, including mathematics and English, over the five-year period from 2008 to 2013. Noticeable from this table is that over the last two years, girls have continued to improve but boys' performance has stayed virtually static, resulting in an increased gap between the genders.

Given the different performance at GCSE level in England, Figure 4.4.1 shows examination entries for General Certificate of Education (GCE) A-level courses (IOP 2013). There is clear gender delineation in some areas between what might be considered masculine and feminine subjects (for example, physics, English, psychology).

Table 4.4.1 Percentage of pupils achieving five or more A*-C grades, including mathematics and English

	2008/09	*2009/10*	*2010/11*	*2011/12*	*2012/13*
Boys	47.1	51.5	54.6	54.2	55.6
Girls	54.4	58.9	61.9	63.7	65.7

Source: DfE (2014m)

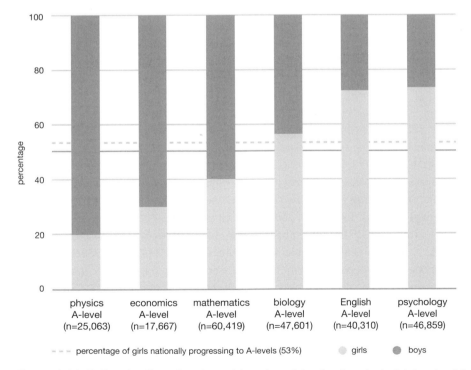

Figure 4.4.1 National ratios of male and female entries to six selected A-level subjects averaged over 2010 to 2012 in England

Source: IOP (2013: 8)

Pupils often have very stereotyped ideas about the roles of men and women. Hartley and Sutton (2010) found that by the age of 8, children of both genders believe that boys are less focused, able and successful than girls. There is the potential for such beliefs to lead to a self-fulfilling prophecy, with boys accepting this myth as fact and resigning themselves to being unsuccessful (Hartley and Sutton 2013). Boys' and girls' responses to school are shaped by society's views of how each gender behaves or should behave. In this sense, each identity is socially constructed rather than one reflecting the views of individual boys and girls. There is much research on the different ways in which boys and girls are positioned by, and respond to, learning and the curriculum (Paechter 2000; Smith 2005), classroom interactions (Myhill 2002), teachers (Younger *et al.* 1999; Myhill and Jones 2006), and moving to a new school (Jackson and Warin 2000; Noyes 2003). Rudduck (2004) explores the challenges of developing, and possibilities for, gender policies in secondary schools in some detail.

So far in this section, we have been looking at the relationship between performance and biological differences between pupils; however, the notion of gender is more nuanced, including different masculinities and femininities. Traditional stereotypes are being broken down and at the same time are more fragmented. Such differences are increasingly celebrated, and this includes pupils' sexuality. The Office for National Statistics Household Survey in 2011 found that 1.5 per cent of adults identified themselves as gay, lesbian or bisexual (with 95 per cent valid responses provided) (ONS, 2012b: 1). Stonewall (the national lesbian, gay and bisexual charity) feels that 5–7 per cent of the population being gay, lesbian, bisexual or transgender is a reasonable estimate (Chalabi, 2013). However, there are no hard data on the number of lesbians, gay men and bisexuals in the UK as no national census has ever asked people to define their sexuality.

As we said at the outset, teachers' responses to this level of diversity are influenced by their personal views and experiences. Whatever your views, many issues in this area require a thoughtful, professional approach; for example, towards homophobic bullying (both the Intercom Trust and Stonewall have good websites with useful guidance and resources concerning homophobic behaviour).

Ethnicity

The report *How Fair is Britain?* (EHRC 2010) showed that considerable progress has been made by groups of minority ethnic pupils over recent years, and ethnic differences at GCSE are narrowing. In 2011, only people from the white Gypsy or Irish Traveller, Pakistani, Bangladeshi and black Caribbean groups were less likely than white British people to have degree qualifications or equivalent (Lymperopoulou and Parameshwaran 2014). Two reports at the turn of the century identified the serious underachievement of black Caribbean pupils (Fitzgerald *et al.* 2000; Gillborn and Mirza 2000). Though this is a group that is still lagging behind, they have shown the largest improvement in recent years; in 2012/13, the percentage of black pupils achieving five or more GCSEs at grade A*–C or equivalent, including English and mathematics GCSEs or iGCSEs, was 2.5 percentage points below the national average. This gap has narrowed by 1.7 percentage points since 2011/12, but over the longer term has narrowed by 3.7 percentage points since 2008/09 (DfE 2014m).

The issues of underachievement of particular groups of pupils is an ongoing concern for government at both a local and central level. There have been various government initiatives over the years designed to address the issues of underachievement of particular groups of pupils; however, there is still a wide gap between the high and low achievers. The underperformance of many white working-class boys serves to emphasise the importance of taking into account how class and gender effects are embedded within the data showing attainments of ethnic groups (see Gillborn and Mirza 2000; Strand 2008).

Girls in all ethnic groups continue to score higher than boys in GCSE examinations, although both groups of pupils have improved year on year (DfE 2014m). Black Caribbean pupils improved their performance in GCSE; about one-third of pupils gained five or more grade A*-Cs at GCSE, including mathematics and English, in 2007, rising to over one-half in 2013. However, the proportion of people with no qualifications in the black African group was roughly equivalent in 2001 and 2011 (Lymperopoulou and Parameshwaran 2014).

The evidence accumulated by the Swann Enquiry 30 years ago suggested that many minority ethnic pupils were underachieving (DES 1985). The data above, and more recent research (for example, Gillborn and Gipps 1996; Smith 2005; Archer and Francis 2007) shows that although achievement has been raised for most pupils, underachievement still persists and is often linked to particular ethnic groups.

Table 4.4.3 shows the attainment gaps over the last five years between pupils whose first language is English and those who have a different first language. When gaining grades A*-C in mathematics and English is included as an indicator, the data show that pupils whose first language is English are consistently achieving better than their counterparts. Interestingly, however, a higher proportion of pupils whose first language was not English achieved the expected levels of progress in English and mathematics than those whose first language was English. For English, the gap was 7.6 percentage points in 2012/13, and for mathematics 8.7 percentage points (DfE 2014m).

For teachers working with pupils from a range of ethnic backgrounds, the issue of supporting those for whom English is an additional language is important. See Flynn's (2015) MESHGuide on English as an additional language. The issue of language goes far wider than classroom oracy. Many classroom resources are heavily text-based and their use of language requires not only a level of literacy, but also cultural awareness. Teachers need to ensure they are adequately challenging pupils whose first language is not English and they should consider carefully the language requirements that are made by textbooks, classroom talk and homework tasks to identify whether these are creating barriers to learning. There is evidence that giving pupils opportunities and time to use their mother tongue to think about ideas and, where possible, to discuss concepts, allows them to operate at a higher cognitive level (see the section on language and development in Unit 4.3).

Despite levels of educational attainment improving across ethnic groups, this has not translated to the labour market (Tackey *et al.* 2011). The 2011 census showed large differences across ethnic groups in rates of employment (Nazroo and Kapadia 2013). In the year to September 2013, the

Table 4.4.2 First language attainment gaps 2008/09 to 2012/13 (English as a first language minus first language other than English expressed as difference between the two percentage scores)

	2008/09	2009/10	2010/11	2011/12	2012/13
5 or more A*-C grades at GCSE and equivalent	1.2	0.2	-0.4	0.4	-0.4
5 or more A*-C grades at GCSE and equivalent, including English and mathematics GCSEs	3.4	3.1	2.7	2.9	2.6

Source: DfE (2014m)

unemployment rate for the black and the Pakistani/Bangladeshi communities was 12 per cent, and 6 per cent for white jobseekers (DWP 2014). Relatively high levels of unemployment have an impact upon the future economic status of groups, and therefore, in a complex way, the chances of their children in school. This is not to say that such inequality of attainment cannot be addressed, or is somehow cyclical, but rather to highlight the limitations of schools' ability to affect social change. Archer (2008: 102) argues that the dominant educational discourse in Britain contributes to excluding minority ethnic pupils from 'the identity of the "ideal pupil"', and, as a student teacher, it is important to unpack your own notion of success and ensure it does not favour a particular group of pupils. Recent government initiatives in England have attempted to raise attainment and improve the employment and access to higher education of different pupil groups (explore 'DfE *Raising Attainment*' in the useful websites at the end of this unit).

Class

Class, or social class, is a contested categorisation of people but is usually related to social standing and economic role. The economic role is linked to the person's type of employment, ranging from professional to unskilled. A frequent broad classification is working class, middle class and upper class; for further discussion of class, see Savage *et al.*'s (2013) analysis of the BBC's 2011 Great British Class Survey.

The effect that pupils' economic circumstances have upon their education is very real. Connolly (2006) makes a convincing argument from statistical analyses of performance data that pupils' social class and ethnicity have a far greater effect on GCSE performance than gender.

Understanding social class goes beyond simply looking at economic capital (for example, measures such as free school meals) but relates to other 'capitals' that pupils' families possess. This might be social capital or the cultural capital that includes having well-educated parents and ready access to books and media, and pupils may be exposed to a wider range of learning and cultural experiences than pupils of less well-educated parents. Although the use of computers and mobile phones is widespread, not all families can afford advanced technological equipment.

There is much evidence to signal the relationship between culturally rich homes and pupil attainment (see Bourdieu 1986 for an explanation of cultural capital and its potential effects on academic success) (see also Unit 7.4). When exploring the data referred to in this unit, it is clear that gender, ethnicity and class effects are overlapping and intertwined. In that sense, data that show the performance of different ethnic groups might have as much to do with class as with gender. Using the rather crude measure of free school meals (FSM) to show how socio-economic status relates to GCSE performance, in 2012/13, 38.7 per cent of pupils eligible for FSM achieved an A*–C grade in English and mathematics GCSEs, compared with 65.3 per cent of those pupils not eligible for FSM (DfE 2014m).

In the same way that our response to gender issues needs to become more nuanced, so here we should include the increasing number of looked-after children and the needs of refugee and asylum seekers' children.

The challenge for teachers is, of course, that we cannot necessarily see who these pupils are, but they might well require different kinds of support. Class works in many subtle ways to disadvantage those already disadvantaged. Through language, manners, cultural awareness, and so on, the middle classes have a better sense of the 'rules of the game' and so can capitalise better on their educational opportunities.

Another aspect of this class discussion is poverty, the effect of which has been described graphically by Davies (2000: 3–22) and can be seen in the GCSE attainment data in Table 4.4.3. For some time, there has been evidence of the growing gap between rich and poor (Woodward 2003: 8; Reardon 2011), and the Organisation for Economic Co-operation and Development (OECD) found that inequality in income has risen faster in Britain than in any other country since 1975 (OECD 2011). An Oxfam report in 2012 further highlighted the impact of the recession on those living in poverty and the rise of inequality (Oxfam 2012).

Typically, more well-educated, middle-class parents have a better understanding of the school system (Power *et al.* 2003), where to get information from (Hatcher 1998) and how to best support their children's schooling, and so generally stand a better chance of maximising the opportunities afforded by the new educational markets (Ball 2003). Class and ethnicity remain the main factors in educational disadvantage, and yet class is possibly the most difficult factor to define, identify and respond to in a way that can precipitate meaningful and long-term change.

The Joseph Roundtree Foundation monitors what is happening to poverty and social exclusion in the UK. The foundation's website would be a good starting point to explore data on the impact of socio-economic status on educational achievement and life chances.

A key policy development in England in relation to raising the attainment of disadvantaged pupils is the introduction of pupil premium funding in April 2011. In an attempt to close the gap between disadvantaged pupils and their peers, additional funding is given to schools for each of their pupils eligible for free school meals or who are classed as a looked-after child. At this point in time, it is difficult to judge the effects of this still relatively new funding, and there is disagreement as to whether there are signs of impact, particularly at secondary level. Higgins (2015) gives a good analysis of available data to date and where pupil premium may be seen to have impacted on attainment.

The above discussion reminds us that the performance of pupils is related to many factors, including gender, ethnicity and class. The variables used here, gender, ethnicity and class, are not causes; variables hide causative factors, some of which are identified above, that contribute to underachievement.

Table 4.4.3 Attainment gap between pupils resident in the most deprived and least deprived areas (least deprived minus most deprived)

	2010/11	2011/12	2012/13
5 or more A*-C grades at GCSE or equivalent, including English and mathematics GCSEs	33.7	30.6	29.5
A*-C grade in English and mathematics GCSE	33.7	20.5	29.4

Source: DfE (2014m)

School policy and classroom practice

In this section, we begin to examine both school policies and your classroom practice, in the light of the earlier discussion. If schools play a role in the ongoing structuring of inequality in society, albeit not deliberately, then teachers need to reflect critically upon their practice. This involves examining how your own position and action in a diverse society both help and hinder you in challenging unequal treatment in the classroom. See Task 4.4.1.

 Task 4.4.1 Policies towards equal opportunities (EO)

1   Obtain a copy of the equal opportunities (EO) policy in your school. Read it and try to identify:
- Who was involved in developing and writing the policy.
- How old it is.
- Whether there are any later documents; for example, working party reports.
- What areas of school life it covers. Are any areas of school life omitted from its brief?
- The focus of the policy. Are issues around gender, ethnicity, social class or disabilities part of the policy or are they addressed separately?

2   Who knows about the policy? Devise a way of sampling knowledge, understanding and opinion of pupils and staff about the policy. For example:
- Are copies of the policy displayed in the school?
- How many staff know about it/have read it? How many pupils know about it/have read it?
- Who is responsible for EO in the school? Can you arrange to talk to them about their role?

3   Is the policy treated seriously in the school? For example:
- Has any in-service course been devoted to EO issues?
- Does the school EO policy influence departmental policy or classroom practice?
- Can you identify examples of the policy in action? Within the classroom environment? During the school day?

Summarise your findings to discuss with your tutor then file in your professional development portfolio (PDP).

No matter how concerned the school is to promote equity through good policies, implementing them in the classroom is not an easy matter. It is instructive to use lesson observation time to look at specific aspects of teaching and then to report back to your tutor or tutor group. Some ideas are listed in Tasks 4.4.2 and 4.4.3 (see Unit 2.1 for details on observation techniques).

When you first start teaching, your concern is to promote learning through well-ordered lessons. When you feel more confident, ask a colleague to observe one of your lessons, focusing on the questions in Tasks 4.4.2 and 4.4.3. As you develop as a teacher, you can consider wider issues of inclusion and diversity. These issues might be regarding language or the textual materials used by pupils who, like us, are influenced by words and pictures, particularly moving pictures. Access to the World Wide Web has opened up all sorts of material to pupils, and not all of this is helpful for their academic or social development. Task 4.4.4 asks you to review teaching materials for their implicit messages.

Now complete task 4.4.5.

Task 4.4.2 Responses to gender: classroom observation

Ask a class teacher if you can observe their lesson. Explain the purpose of your enquiry, which is to find out which pupils participate in the lesson more than others, and which pupils the teacher invites to answer questions or volunteer information. Be prepared to share your findings with the teacher.

Keep a tally of the frequency of attention to, and the time given to, boys and girls. Devise a recording sheet to collect information to explore one or two of the following:

■ Who puts their hand up to answer a question?
■ Who does the teacher select?
■ In class activities, how much time is spent by the teacher with boys/with girls?
■ How does the teacher respond to a pupil? With praise, criticism or further questioning?
■ When pupils are reprimanded, is there any difference in what is tolerated, or not, by the teacher? The action taken by the teacher?

Consider whether different messages are conveyed to boys, or girls, by the teacher's response to classroom interactions.

See if you can interview a focus group of pupils to ask them whether they feel their gender makes a difference to their experiences in school.

Draft notes for discussion with other student teachers in your placement school. Afterwards, identify and record the implications for your teaching and file in your PDP.

 Task 4.4.3 Responses to ethnicity: classroom observation

Redesign the record sheet you used in Task 4.4.2 to collect data about teachers' response to pupils of different ethnicity. For some pupils, their ethnic background may mean that the mother tongue is not English. Use similar questions as listed under Task 4.4.2 and observe the same protocols about observing classrooms. You may wish to add to the list of questions:

■ How does the teacher support pupils whose first language is not English?
■ How does the teacher adapt resources for these pupils?
■ How does the teacher adapt their own language for these pupils?

See if you can interview a focus group of pupils to ask them whether they feel their ethnicity makes a difference to their experiences in school. Talk to pupils whose first language is not English and ask them to explain what support they find most helpful to enable them to be successful in school.

Draft notes for discussion with other student teachers in your placement school. Modify the notes after discussion, as needed, and then file in your PDP.

Task 4.4.4 Bias and stereotyping in teaching resources

Select a resource in general use in your school (for example, a book or DVD) and interrogate it for bias and stereotyping. Some questions you could use to address this issue include:

- Are women and girls shown in nontraditional roles?
- Are men shown in caring roles?
- Who is shown in a position of authority? Who is the employer, the decision-maker, the technologist?
- Are people and jobs stereotyped; for example, black athletes, male scientists, female social workers, male cricketers?
- What assumptions, if any, are made concerning minority ethnic citizens in the UK? How accurate are the images shown of people and of places?
- How are people in the developing world depicted? Is it to illustrate malnutrition, or their living conditions, or the technology employed? Are the images positive or negative?
- What assumptions, if any, are made concerning underdevelopment in the developing world?

Identify some issues for discussion with your tutor and file your notes in your PDP.

 Task 4.4.5 Who is recruited to post-16 courses?

If your school has a sixth form, compare the number of pupils in the first year academic and vocational courses by gender and ethnicity and then compare those numbers with the numbers in the previous year's Year 11 cohort. Identify the subject preferences.

How many pupils left school to carry on education in another institution and what are their gender and ethnic characteristics?

Identify questions arising from the exercise for discussion with your tutor. File your notes in your PDP.

Responding to diversity in the classroom

Your immediate concerns are focused on the classroom, but much of what goes on in the classroom has its origins outside the classroom. These origins include the cultural background of pupils, which includes their class and ethnicity. Yet, other pupils may have special educational needs (see Unit 4.6). Other factors to consider when trying to make sense of what goes on in the classroom are the teachers' expectations of pupils, the effect of an externally imposed curriculum and the school's ethos realised through its policies and practices.

Expectations of academic performance are often built upon both evidence of what a pupil has done in the past and their social position: male/female; white/black; working/middle class; stable/unstable family background. A perceived social position is sometimes, if unconsciously, used by teachers to anticipate pupils' progress and their capacity to overcome difficulties (Noyes 2003). You might have found yourself thinking things, or even making assumptions about pupils from the time you first saw their names on the class register. It is crucial you take time to explore your own beliefs and values in relation to gender, ethnicity and class, and explore what prejudices you may be subconsciously harbouring. It is through honest self-reflection that you are able to develop into a teacher committed to inclusive practice.

The interaction of the teacher with pupils in the classroom is often revealing. Some teachers may subconsciously favour asking boys, rather than girls, to answer questions. Once established, the reasons for this behaviour can be explored. Similar questions can arise about the way teachers respond to pupils' answers. Whereas one pupil might make a modest and partly correct response to a question to which the teacher's response is praise and support, to another pupil offering the same level of response, a more critical attitude may be adopted by the teacher.

Are these different responses justified? Is the pupil who received praise gaining support and encouragement from praise, or is the pupil being sent a message that low-level performance is good enough? It is teacher expectations that direct and control such responses. If, as has been documented in the past about the performance of girls, the praise is implicitly saying 'You have done as well as can be expected because you are a girl' and the critical response is implying 'Come on now, you're a boy, you can do better than this', then there is cause for concern.

Such interpretations depend very much on the context. A comparison of teacher behaviours in different lessons might reveal the influences on teaching and learning of the subject and the gender, age, and social and cultural background of teachers and pupils (Pearce 2005). Tasks 4.4.2 and 4.4.3 addressed this suggestion.

Now complete Task 4.4.6.

 Task 4.4.6 Diversity and learning

Some schools have much more diverse populations than others; however, the issues of diversity are relevant for all schools and pupils. What has been the impact of legislation and initiatives on the achievement of pupils in your placement school?

Find out from staff, school documents and inspection reports information about the following features of your placement school:

- the mix of the pupil population in terms of gender, ethnicity and socio-economic status;
- the different languages spoken by pupils;
- the number of pupils needing and receiving support because English is not their first language;
- the cultural background of pupils, which includes their ethnicity, class and family religion;
- the academic performance of different groups of pupils; for example, in school progress tests, GCSE and GCE A level.

How does the school analyse and use data about their pupils?

Find out to what extent your subject department policy and practice relates to the whole school equal opportunities policies. Focus particularly on the curriculum; for example:

■ Identify whether there is a commitment to multiculturalism at subject level? If so, identify how this policy influences teaching and learning.
■ Examine teaching and learning resources to see whether they reflect the school policies.
■ Explore whether there are different strategies for supporting pupils from different backgrounds.

Is there evidence of positive approaches to diversity in the broader life of the school; for example, in display material, in assemblies, in the recognition of different cultural and religious practices at different times of the year, in extracurricular activities? You may find other examples.

Summarise your findings and analyse the information. Draw out some key issues for discussion with your peers and tutor as a draft document. You could develop this enquiry into a piece of coursework, researching recent equal opportunities legislation (for example, the 2010 Equality Act) or government policy (for example, the introduction of pupil premium funding) to provide background for your coursework. Keep a copy in your PDP.

SUMMARY AND KEY POINTS

■ In order to promote equity in educational contexts, teachers need to 'have a secure understanding of how a range of factors can inhibit pupils' ability to learn, and how best to overcome these' (DfE 2011i).
■ Beyond 'understanding' needs to come action, and this involves noticing, critiquing and changing your own practices if necessary, in order to create learning environments in which all pupils can thrive and succeed, and where prejudice is rooted out.
■ Teachers might develop their practice by changing resources, adopting different approaches to grouping procedures and developing other teaching styles. Through such actions, teachers can begin to challenge some of the inequalities in our society. Alternatively, teachers can simply maintain the status quo and although their discourses might welcome diversity, their practices might be maintaining inequity.
■ Sometimes you hear a teacher say 'I didn't notice their colour, I treat them all the same'. Learning opportunities are enhanced by not being 'gender-blind' or 'colour-blind' or 'class-blind'. I suggest that not recognising pupil differences is just as inadequate a response to teaching demands as is the stereotyping of pupils. Teachers need to recognise those differences without placing limits on what can be achieved.
■ Teachers need to reflect on their expectations, preconceptions and even prejudices (however unintended). If you expect most Asian girls to be quiet and passive and good at written work, then that is not only what they do, but also perhaps all they do. Individuals respond in different ways to teachers; you should try to treat each person as an individual and respond to what they do and say, making positive use of your knowledge of the pupils' culture and background.

Check which requirements for your ITE programme you have addressed through this unit.

Further reading

DfE (Department for Education) (2014b) *Child Poverty Strategy 2014-17*, London: HMSO.

Flynn, N. (2015) *Teaching English as an Additional Language MESHGuide*, University of Winchester/University of Reading, UK.
This interactive evidence-based resource has been developed by university, school and local authority staff to help student teachers and new teachers teach children with EAL effectively.

Kingdon, G. and Cassen, C. (2007) *Understanding Low Achievement in English Schools*, London: Centre for the Economics of Education, LSE.

Ofsted (Office for Standards in Education) (2013) *Unseen Children: Access and Achievement 20 Years On*, London: Ofsted.

Smith, E. (2005) *Analysing Underachievement in Schools*, London: Continuum.

Other resources and websites

Department for Education - Raising Attainment: www.gov.uk/search?q=raising+attainment
This section of the Department for Education's site includes reports and advice on how schools may raise achievement, addressing a variety of different circumstances in which schools are placed and the particular factors affecting achievement in their geographical area. It also includes information on how the pupil premium might be used.

Department for Education - Statistical Data: www.gov.uk/search?q=gcse+and+equivalent+attainment
The GCSE and equivalent attainment section of the DfE website contains extensive information that helps you to consider the performance and characteristics of pupils from different backgrounds. The GCSE and Equivalent Attainment by Pupil Characteristics reports on the number and percentages of pupils achieving various outcomes at the end of KS4.

Equal and Human Rights Commission (EHRC): www.equalityhumanrights.com
This site provides a wealth of information and includes many easily downloadable statistical summaries of social life in Britain. *How Fair is Britain?* is a triennial review that monitors the progress that society makes towards becoming one that is more equal.

Joseph Rowntree Foundation: www.jrf.org.uk
The Joseph Rowntree Foundation aims to identify the root causes of poverty and injustice. The website provides a wealth of information and research on the barriers to educational achievement and the impact of gender, ethnicity, social class and poverty.

Stonewall: www.stonewall.org.uk
Stonewall's mission is to ensure all lesbian, gay, bi and trans people are able to participate fully in society. The website provides a wide range of information and resources that support you to develop your understanding of the issues involved and consider how you can make a difference for LGBT pupils.

Appendix 2 on pages 591-595 provides further examples of you may find useful.

Capel, S., Leask, M. and Turner, T. (eds) (2010) *Readings for Learning to Teach in the Secondary School: A Companion to M Level Study*, London: Routledge.
This book brings together essential readings to support you in your critical engagement with key issues raised in this textbook.

The subject-specific books in the Routledge *Learning to Teach* series are also very useful.

Any additional resources and an editable version of any relevant tasks/tables in this unit are available on the companion website: www.routledge.com/cw/capel

4.5 Values education
Discussion and deliberation

Ruth Heilbronn

Introduction

In discussing the area of values education, the unit focuses first on you as a practitioner; second, on your pupils and their development; and lastly, on how discussions of issues relating to values and to ethics might be supported in the classroom. First, in common with other professional practitioners, teachers are obliged to behave with integrity and to uphold the values of the profession (see your notes from Task 1.1.1 on your code of conduct as a teaching professional). These values may be encapsulated in a particular code of conduct or embedded in competency statements, such as those in the Teacher Standards that apply in England (DfE 2011i), where the preamble states that 'Teachers make the education of their pupils their first concern, and are accountable for achieving the highest possible standards in work and conduct. Teachers act with honesty and integrity.'

The second focus on teachers as educators draws on the fact that teachers are not only responsible for their own behaviour, but to a great extent for that of their pupils, and must intervene if necessary to arbitrate and guide the way pupils behave. Values underpin the choices we make as teachers, and our behaviour and attitude to others. For example, teachers are expected to develop a positive relationship with pupils by being fair, respectful and supportive to them and to their achievements. Teachers need to demonstrate the same qualities that they expect of their pupils. Teaching can be considered a practice in which the good teacher exemplifies both the skills and the values of the practice (Dunne 2003: 353-71): we expect teachers to be exemplary figures in the course of their work (McLaughlin 2004: 339-53). When teachers stop a class because they have overheard a racist remark, which they tackle sensitively, knowledgeably and successfully, while upholding the value of tolerance, we would say they dealt competently with the situation, drawing on their own values and their experience, in a 'deliberate exercise of principled judgement in the light of rational knowledge and understanding' (Carr 1993: 253-71).

> Morality is the area of values which affects how we treat each other and hence the area of values which in an important sense are not optional. It is about what we owe to each other, what we may blame others for not living up to.
>
> (Haydon and Hayward 2004: 165)

OBJECTIVES

At the end of this unit, you should be able to:

■ understand the place of values education and ethical deliberation in a subject and school context;
■ understand the various legal responsibilities of schools in the area of moral, social and cultural development, including civic responsibility;
■ identify core common values for yourself and those of the school in which you are teaching;
■ identify opportunities to promote understanding and practice of these core common values in the school context;
■ try out some methods of teaching, leading discussion and promoting ethical deliberation in the classroom.

Check the requirements of your initial teacher education (ITE) programme to see which relate to this unit.

Values education

First, a look at the terms 'values education' and 'moral education'. These are often used interchangeably, but they do not have the same meaning. 'Morality' involves wider notions of 'goodness' and particular views on the nature of right and wrong, which the term 'values' does not. Any adult in a relationship with a child is, in some sense, teaching about values, and such teaching takes place in various situations, such as in one-to-one conversations, classroom teaching, and parent or carer interactions. The unit picks this up later when discussing particular schools' ethos, such as that of a faith school. 'Values' might be defined as:

> the principles and fundamental convictions which act as general guides to behaviour, the standards by which particular actions are judged to be good or desirable. Examples of values are love, equality, freedom, justice, happiness, security, peace of mind and truth.
>
> (Halstead and Taylor 2000: 169)

It follows that:

> 'values education' is a broad term and may carry a particular emphasis on education in civic and wider moral values, or 'character education' and be closely related to other terms in current use, including spiritual, moral, social and cultural development, for example in some of the formulations of the English National Curriculum.
>
> (DfE 2014o)

Our values determine how we choose a course of action or a belief in situations where different views are held; this is important because sometimes our values might be in conflict with other values in situations in which we find ourselves. Value judgements on controversial issues differ from judgements of fact, for which evidence can provide a foundation. The third focus of the unit is on ethical deliberation, the kind of moral reasoning that goes on when making ethical judgements, and the focus is particularly on how we might help pupils to develop this kind of judgement. The kinds of situations involved are those when a course of action is not clear, when teacher or pupil is unable to decide what to do and when more facts about a situation cannot help, because the particular dilemma is an ethical one. At the end of the unit, some support is provided on a way of developing this form of discursive reasoning, which can be adopted in a classroom, for pupils dealing with difficult issues or choices, or in a community of practitioners similarly searching for guidance on a difficult choice of action.

In many countries, some form of civic education is a vehicle through which values can be promoted and pupils can be encouraged to develop their ability to deliberate on moral matters. Schools as well as individual teachers uphold values and express these in their policies and practices, which often makes for considerable differences in ethos between different schools, as evidenced in the behaviour, attitudes and priorities of the pupils and staff. Research shows that these differences are important to the individual teachers' ability to thrive and develop in school (Heilbronn *et al.* 2002: 371-89) and to the pupils' expressions of respect for one another and their socially responsible behaviour in the classroom (Hansen, 1995: 59-74). The ethos of the school is created largely through the school leadership and the way in which it develops and manages a vision of the kind of school it wishes to maintain. Some tangible expressions of a school's ethos might be found in the way parents are welcomed into the school; the relationships between adults and young people outside as well as inside the classroom; staff sensitivity to cultural and faith differences in the school; or how the school celebrates the success of its pupils. The ethos of a school contributes as much to values education as does the prescribed curriculum.

Values underlie all aspects of school life. In some schools, there is a common understanding about where many of the values come from, as they are based on definable moral codes. So in a faith school, there is a clear understanding about what is 'right' and 'wrong', based on tradition and 'scripture'. In a secular school, the basis for this understanding is not so clearly defined. Nevertheless, even in a faith school, there are many areas where value judgements are made, which are not clearly indicated by the underlying faith ethic, such as judgements about what is 'fair' in a particular situation, which may involve judgement in choosing one claim above another. Teachers frequently have to make such judgements in particular situations. School policies may provide guidelines; for example, when dealing with racist or bullying incidents. In these policies, 'respect' is usually a core value and many of the school rules and procedures may derive from this stated value. However, what cannot be prescribed in advance of any situation is what any individual person *ought* to say and to do in response to any particular situation. As a teacher, it is a matter of judgement how to mediate the policy. So in acting and being in the classroom, a teacher stands as a moral example. An example of such a situation might be that a teacher might punish a pupil who steals from another pupil without much discussion; alternatively, the teacher might decide to talk to the pupil, to get them to understand that what they had done was wrong. Choosing how and when to have this discussion is also a matter of judgement (see Heilbronn 2008).

Talking with pupils about the rights and wrongs of an aspect of their behaviour is important, as it acknowledges and respects the pupils' ability to develop an understanding of the consequences of their actions and behaviour. Such talk encourages a sense of responsibility and agency, and so helps pupils to develop moral understanding. The policies of the school are, in some sense, a formal interface between the individual pupil and teacher. So the teacher in the example could relate the discussion about why stealing is wrong to the school's formal statement or rule relating to respect. In fact, 'everyday classroom life is saturated with moral meaning. Even the most routine aspects of teaching convey moral messages to students' (Hansen 1995: paragraph 2).

Pupils judge their teachers on the way they develop good relations with them, and believe that without good relationships they do not learn effectively (ESRC 1997; Wiedmaier *et al.* 2007; Liu and Meng 2009; Wang and Holcombe 2010). It is significant that pupils tend to have good relationships with teachers who are good at engaging in reasoned discussion and who are able to articulate the values that underlie the rules about what is acceptable and non-acceptable behaviour. These teachers are more likely to develop trusting and respectful relationships than those who merely dictate what the rules demand (Lickona 1983). Although written over 30 years ago, the nature of Lickona's enquiry means that the research is still as relevant today, as is Nucci's corroboration that:

> students rated highest those teachers who responded to moral transgressions with statements focusing on the effects of acts ('Joe, that really hurt Mike'). Rated lower were teachers who responded with statements of school rules or normative expectations ('That's not the way for a Hawthorne student to act'). Rated lowest were teachers who used simple commands ('Stop it!' or 'Don't hit').
>
> (Nucci 1987: 91)

It may not be possible to take all the time necessary to deal in depth with particular issues as they arise, but this too can be acknowledged with the pupils. What is important is to reflect back to pupils the example of the kind of behaviour that is acceptable and the reasons behind the values expressed, rather than ignoring or suppressing what is not acceptable. It is important to attend to issues of values in any particular classroom situation since pupils experience lessons as individual young people and not as disembodied 'learners' of a particular curriculum area. As participants in the classroom, their experiences need to be attended to. Van Manen (1991) has written of 'the tact of teaching' and how good, trustful relationships rely on 'pedagogical thoughtfulness' on the part of the teacher. This is not always easy to achieve, of course, and teachers have testified that they sometimes find judgement over the right thing to do can be difficult; for example, being fair to all while also taking individual needs into account.

Cultural diversity and common values

Quite young children can distinguish moral judgements related to justice and fairness from judgements about social conventions, such as how to address people properly or follow dress codes (Nucci 1987). It is important in a pluralistic society to be able to distinguish a number of fundamental common values that do not rely on any specific cultural or religious foundations. For example, work carried out some 20 years ago, but still relevant today, was led by a group called the National Forum for Values in Education and the Community. It had representatives from all the faith groups and non-faith members. This forum developed guidance for teachers in the form of a 'statement of values' that set out to identify common and enduring values in society about which most people would agree, irrespective of culture or belief, and this was then incorporated into the National Curriculum (NC) for England. The published statement is shown in Figure 4.5.1. The National Forum moved from the broad general statement of values to the translation of those values into practice. For example, under the heading of 'the Self' the National Forum team listed the following goals for pupils:

■   develop an understanding of our own characters, strengths and weaknesses;
■   develop self-respect and self-discipline;
■   clarify the meaning and purpose in our lives and decide, on the basis of this, how our lives should be lived;
■   make responsible use of our talents, rights and opportunities;
■   strive, throughout life, for knowledge, wisdom and understanding;
■   take responsibility, within our capabilities, for our own lives.

(DfEE/QCA 1999a: 219–221)

Figure 4.5.2 shows the values underlying the English National Curriculum (2011)

In England, subsequent revisions of the NC contained clearly stated underlying aims, to promote 'the spiritual, moral, cultural, mental and physical development of learners at the school and within society' (DfEE/QCA 1999a: 148). However much this curriculum may change in the coming years, it is hard to escape the idea that schools have a responsibility to promote values education in some form. Currently, in England, the government has required schools to promote 'fundamental British values', a term that 'is taken from the definition of extremism as articulated in the new Prevent Strategy, which was launched in June 2011. It includes "democracy, the rule of law, individual liberty and mutual respect and tolerance of different faiths and beliefs"' (HMG 2011: 9).

Successive Education Acts since 1988 have required the Office for Standards in Education (Ofsted) to inspect the contributions that English schools make to pupils' spiritual, moral, social and cultural education and how well pupils' attitudes, values and other personal qualities are developed. Ofsted

---

1 The self
We value ourselves as unique human beings capable of spiritual, moral, intellectual and physical growth and development.

2 Relationships
We value others for themselves, not only for what they have or what they can do for us. We value relationships as fundamental to the development and fulfilment of ourselves and others, and to the good of the community.

3 Society
We value truth, freedom, justice, human rights, the rule of law and collective effort for the common good. In particular, we value families as sources of love and support for all their members, and as the basis of a society in which people care for others.

4 The environment
We value the environment, both natural and shaped by humanity, as the basis of life and a source of wonder and inspiration.

Figure 4.5.1 A set of values

Source: QCA (2005: 220)

> The curriculum should reflect values in our society that promote personal development,equality of opportunity, economic wellbeing, a healthy and just democracy, and a sustainable future.
>
> These values should relate to:
>
> - ourselves, as individuals capable of spiritual, moral, social, intellectual and physical growth and development
> - our relationships, as fundamental to the development and fulfilment of happy and healthy lives, and to the good of the community
> - our society, which is shaped by the contributions of a diverse range of people, cultures and heritages
> - our environment, as the basis of life and a source of wonder and inspiration that needs to be protected.

Figure 4.5.2 Values underlying the English National Curriculum

Source: DfE (2011i)

published guidance entitled *Promoting and Evaluating Pupils' Spiritual, Moral, Social and Cultural Development* (2004), subsequently updated in school inspection guidance (Ofsted 2015). However, there is considerable debate about how the term 'spiritual' is to be defined and whether it is the job of schools to promote spirituality, and more than any other area of the curriculum it is difficult to see how the development of spirituality could be measured, assuming an acceptable definition of what it is could be agreed (Hand 2003). So it seems sensible to concentrate on schools as ethical places, and teachers as ethical people, with responsibilities to develop pupils' sense of values and their ability to act ethically. See Unit 4.3 on Gardner's (2006a) multiple intelligence theory, Gardner considers that spirituality is part of 'existential intelligence'.

Settings and opportunities for values education

How does the ability to reason in situations of dilemmas and conflicting choices develop? How does a child develop a sense of moral judgement? This question is a source of continuing interest and research. Building on Piaget's foundational work (Piaget 1932), Kohlberg developed his own detailed theory of the development of moral reasoning. Both writers stressed maturation factors, linking the development of moral judgement with cognitive capability and arguing that mature moral judgement is dependent on a capacity to reason logically: it develops as children's reasoning ability develops (Kohlberg 1985). In discussing the development of children's ability to use increasingly nuanced moral reasoning, the term 'moral development' is frequently used, particularly in policy and curriculum documents (see Units 4.3 and 5.1 on maturation of reasoning and cognitive development).

The structured nature of both Piaget's stage theory and the Kohlberg framework is a contested matter (see Donaldson 1978; Stern 1985; Weiten 1992), and for further study, the following articles provide an introduction to their work: Huitt and Hummel (2003), Nucci (2007) and Atherton (2011). The Further reading and Other resources and websites sections give Web links and further suggestions for reading.

Arguably, pupils' understanding of the school's values, and more widely of right and wrong, is 'caught', rather than 'taught'. Many argue that the only way for values and moral reasoning to develop is through experience, in particular experiences that arise from a real situation and subsequent discussion of that experience with others, such as peers or adults. Research has shown that there are common features of schools that seem to have a positive impact on the development of pupil values, such as participation in the communal life of the school and the classroom, encouragement to behave responsibly, provision of an orderly school environment, and clear rules that are fairly enforced (Battisch *et al.* 1998). A school's explicitness about its values and the extent to which teachers actually practise shared values also has an important influence on the pupils' own development of moral understanding and responsibility. The home influence in values' formation is, of course, far more significant than that of the school, given the early nurture period and the time spent in the family. This reinforces the importance of a partnership approach between schools and their local communities (Nucci 1987).

The curriculum is one vehicle through which 'moral development' can be channelled, for example in individual subjects, such as religious education (RE) and some kind of civic education as in the citizenship curriculum in England. Citizenship education, because of its subject matter, is inherently related to values. Political and social issues concern the question of how we should collectively live, which is at root an extension of the basic moral question 'How should I live my life?' (Haydon and Hayward 2004). Although many areas of public life can be an occasion for teaching and discussing in a fairly descriptive manner, they remain value-laden in nature and may often call for sensitive handling (see later tasks).

The curriculum can also outline courses of study for matters relating to pupils' personal lives, such as health education and careers education more generally, under the auspices of a personal, social and health education course (PSHE). An example of aims and objectives for a PSHE course is the English NC from early in its inception (DfEE/QCA 1999b: 136–42). This curriculum outlined a strong, though not statutory, programme of PSHE, aiming to foster moral development and values education. There are also curriculum initiatives to foster the development of moral reasoning through specific learning activities, such as various courses of 'character education'. In England, the Jubilee Centre for Character and Virtues is involved in this work (see www.jubileecentre.ac.uk). Resource books such as Freakley *et al.* (2008) have also been developed with teaching material.

In examining these curriculum possibilities, there remains the underlying question as to whether values can be *taught* or only *caught*. Kohlberg did comment on the artificiality of creating a specific curriculum area purely to foster moral development. In an evaluation of one of his own early projects in school, he stated, 'While the intervention operation was a success, the patient died. When we went back a year later, we found not a single teacher had continued to engage in moral discussion after the commitment to the research had ended' (Kohlberg 1985: 80). This underlines the importance of personal experience and continued commitment to engaging with discussion about values. When we talk to a pupil about something we have both experienced, we engage in a process of talking about values in a direct and practical way.

Ethical deliberation through discussion

A common technique for raising moral and ethical issues is through discussion. Discussion activities have great potential to develop this kind of reasoning, sometimes called ethical deliberation. Young people can be taught some rules and practices of these kinds of discussion, in which they grapple with ethical dilemmas and consider moral choices they may find difficult. Accordingly, their discussions may not end in clear decision or agreement, and one of the key factors in such discussions is the ability to live with ambiguity and uncertainty. This ability generally develops as young people become adults, but the drive to embrace certainty is a powerful one. The ability to make moral judgements wisely depends on weighing up fine balances of possible actions, within an understanding of context, and we expect this ability to develop as children mature. In their discussions, the pupils may not reach agreement, but the discussions can lead to a deeper understanding of the issues and the positions of others. Evidently, from what was said earlier, underlying all these discussions are the values that the participants hold, although they may not be able to articulate them fully. Taking part in well-managed and well-conceived deliberation on ethical matters enhances pupils' social interaction, because they need to listen to each other and respect each others' opinions. See Hand and Levinson (2011) for a consideration of discussing controversial issues in the classroom, as well as Appendix 4.5.1.

> The use of discussion acknowledges that social growth is not simply a process of learning society's rules and values, but a gradual process in which students actively transform their understanding of morality and social convention through reflection and construction. That is, students' growth is a function of meaning-making rather than mere compliance with externally imposed values.
>
> (Nucci 1987: 89)

The new understandings that are 'constructed' in peer exchange can be powerful in developing pupils' moral understandings (Berkowitz *et al.* 1980). It is clear that engaging in ethical deliberation through discussion involves respect for the opinions of others, sincerity in seeking to clarify what is said by others and skill in relating what is said to one's own situation and choices. Managing such discussions or explorations requires skill, to avoid them becoming merely ritualistic or worse, a confirmation of prejudices and an opportunity for the strongest characters to dominate. Discussions need to be appropriately related to the pupils' own experience or imaginative capacities (see Appendix 4.5.1 for advice on handling discussions in the classroom). At any given time, there are likely to be 'hot topics' that concern young people in their lives outside the classroom. Often, these can be based on personal choices that pupils might raise anonymously, or that teachers can narrate as a story. Opportunities or possibilities for work on values may arise through attending to the pupils' interests; for example, social networking through Internet linking could raise questions about relationships, trust and privacy that draw on the ethics of a responsible online community. In the public domain, the debates and dilemmas are usually, although not always, age-related and may involve concerns for the environment, endangered species, fair trade, equality of opportunity – or legal decisions, such as the medical case regarding the separation of conjoined twins, where the operation to separate them would lead to the survival of only one of the babies. At the time, the case made English legal history when the unresolved conflict of views about what to do became a case in the Court of Appeal (Wasserman 2001). The debate about conflicts on moral issues continues to be relevant as medicine's technical possibilities grow.

> As medicine drives us past the limits of our settled moral deliberations, it becomes increasingly important to take stock of the rules and principles by which our lives, and those of others, are ordered. We should be painstaking in our attempts to resolve moral and legal dilemmas that threaten the most basic rights of individuals, such as the separation of conjoined twins.
>
> (Clucas and O'Donnell 2002)

Some worked-through discussion of examples of controversial issues can be found in Levinson (2005b: 258-68). Also, Appendix 4.5.1 provides some suggestions for developing the capacity for ethical deliberation through discussion, giving some rules and procedures that may be helpful in managing such discussions.

In addition to discussion as a pedagogic technique, there are also educational games that foster moral development, which includes digital computer games, some of which have been specifically designed to increase values awareness, such as the RealLives simulation that enablers players to learn more about different cultures and develop intercultural competence (Struppert 2010). In a critical consideration of digital games-based learning, Younie and Leask (2013) argue gaming can help engender values and resilience in young people through learning to manage emotions (from frustration of losing to elation at winning) by following rules and in team-based games, through cooperation to achieve shared goals. Citing Piaget (1932), they outline how games can help pupils' emerging social and cognitive capabilities, especially for boys (Hromek and Roffey 2009), and particularly aid working with rules and the development of self discipline, which underpins society and social order. Similarly, Mead (1934) outlined how role-playing fosters empathy in children, which is essential for developing a sense of morality. So playing games, whether it is online, or classroom-based simulations, or in the playground, can be understood to aid the socio-emotional, moral and cognitive development of pupils. For further information on the psychosocial benefits of computer gaming in relation to developing values, see Younie and Leask (2013: Chapter 4).

The following section of the unit identifies some relevant areas for reflection about values. These are generic areas and not the kinds of issues that might arise in a particular subject such as citizenship or religious education, where there are many opportunities for discussions about values. Our approach is to make suggestions for tasks from which you select those appropriate to your school and your needs. It is not intended that all tasks be undertaken.

Reflecting on teacher values

Task 4.5.1 focuses on the expression of values in the Teachers' Standards in England and asks you to reflect on these or the values relevant to your ITE programme and the country in which you wish to teach, with regard to the way in which the standards express a view of the personal and professional conduct expected of teachers, as in Figure 4.5.3.

Aims of schools

Task 4.5.2 focuses on the aims of a school and how these are interpreted.

Subject teaching

Task 4.5.3 relates to subject teaching.

Class management

Task 4.5.4 relates to class management.

Task 4.5.1 Reflecting on teachers' values

The following task draws on the Teachers' Standards in England (DfE 2011i), which is available on the Internet. To understand the full context of the task, you particularly need to look at the section entitled 'Preamble'. It is available at: www.education.gov.uk/publications/eOrdering Download/teachers%20standards.pdf.

Refer to Figure 4.5.3 and read the statement of values defined there, which teachers should uphold.

■ Do you believe that these should be your core values as a teacher? Are there any you do not agree with?
■ Are there any aspects that may be more difficult to apply than others?
■ Are there any issues that you think you might experience in putting these values into place?
■ Are there any aspects of the values relating to teaching that you think are missing here?

Summarise your views, identifying the values you currently hold. Keep the summary in your professional development portfolio (PDP). Return to this task at a later date and review your opinions.

Part Two: Personal And Professional Conduct

A teacher is expected to demonstrate consistently high standards of personal and professional conduct. The following statements define the behaviour and attitudes which set the required standard for conduct throughout a teacher's career.

- Teachers uphold public trust in the profession and maintain high standards of ethics and behaviour, within and outside school, by:

  - treating pupils with dignity, building relationships rooted in mutual respect, and at all times observing proper boundaries appropriate to a teacher's professional position
  - having regard for the need to safeguard pupils' well-being, in accordance with statutory provisions
  - showing tolerance of and respect for the rights of others
  - not undermining fundamental British values, including democracy, the rule of law, individual liberty and mutual respect, and tolerance of those with different faiths and beliefs
  - ensuring that personal beliefs are not expressed in ways which exploit pupils' vulnerability or might lead them to break the law.

- Teachers must have proper and professional regard for the ethos, policies and practices of the school in which they teach, and maintain high standards in their own attendance and punctuality.

- Teachers must have an understanding of, and always act within, the statutory frameworks which set out their professional duties and responsibilities.

Figure 4.5.3 Teachers' Standards in England part 2

Source: DfE (2011i)

🖊 Task 4.5.2 Aims of the school and how they are interpreted

This task contains several sub-tasks that focus on the aims of the school. Carry out one or more sub-tasks, either alone or in pairs, and discuss your findings with other student teachers or your tutors.

1   Collect together the aims of your placement school and, if possible, that of another school. Compare and contrast the aims of each school.
   ■ Does the school in its aims express a responsibility for the moral development of pupils?
   ■ How are these aims expressed and in what ways do the school statements differ?
2   Many school curricular statements are prefaced with some broad aims, relating to fostering pupils' self-esteem, valuing their contribution and helping them to develop independently, while also enabling them to work with peers. How might these aims of this school curriculum be translated into opportunities for the pupil to achieve them?
3   In what ways does the PSHE course contribute to the education of your pupils in the area of values? Select a topic; for example:
   ■ identifying bias and stereotyping and developing strategies to deal with it;
   ■ care of the environment;
   ■ practices and attitudes towards adult relationships.
4   How might a school assembly contribute to the moral and values education of pupils? Some opportunities for reflection on this might arise by:
   ■ Attending assembly – keep a record of its purpose, what was said and the way ideas were presented. Interview some pupils afterwards and compare your perception of the assembly with theirs. Did they understand the underlying point of any 'message'? If so, did they agree with it? Is the message relevant to their life and their family, and if so, how?
   ■ Helping to plan an assembly with a teacher and with the support of other student teachers. Some questions that may be helpful are:
      ■ Does the school have a programme for assemblies? How is the content and approach agreed within your school?
      ■ How does the content and messages of assemblies relate to the cultural mix of your school?
      ■ Does assembly develop a sense of community or is it merely authority enhancing? How is success celebrated and whose success is mostly recognised?
      ■ What is the school's programme of in-service education and training (INSET)? Is there any provision relating to moral, ethical and values education? How is such work focused and by whom? (Your school tutor can direct you to the staff responsible for INSET.)

Write a short report on one of the four exercises above to discuss with your tutor. Review the report after meeting with your tutor and file the final statement in your PDP.

Task 4.5.3 The place of subject work in promoting moral development and values education

Identify a social, ethical or moral issue that forms part of teaching your subject.

Review the issue as a teaching task in preparation for discussing it with other student teachers. Your review could include:

■ a statement of the subject matter and its place in the curriculum;
■ the ethical focus for pupils;
■ a sample of teaching material;
■ an outline teaching strategy (for example, a draft lesson plan);
■ any problems that you anticipate teaching the issue;
■ any questions that other student teachers might help you resolve;
■ resources to support the ethical focus.

Keep notes on the teaching task in your PDP for later use.

 Task 4.5.4 Classroom management

Class detention

Consider the following scenario:

A class is reading from a set text and from time to time stopping to discuss points. Some pupils get bored and start to flick pellets at other pupils sitting near the front. The teacher knows it is happening but cannot identify the main culprits. One or two pupils take offence at being hit by pellets and start to complain. The teacher tries unsuccessfully to stop the disruption. The noise level rises and the whole class gets involved. The teacher says that the person who started throwing the pellets will be given a detention and needs to own up. No one owns up and the class is given time to sort it out among themselves if they can. No one owns up and the whole class is kept in after school for 15 minutes. This causes resentment among the pupils and some walk out and refuse to stay.

How might the teacher have dealt differently in each case with the following:

■ the whole incident;
■ those left in detention;
■ those who walked out;
■ complaints about unfair practice/injustice?

What larger themes does this incident raise (for example, the justice of collective punishment)? Keep notes of your responses, identifying the implications for classroom management. File in your PDP.

Critical incidents

Many incidents with which teachers deal in school have an ethical dimension. How we respond to them is, to a large extent, a function of our own ethical beliefs, and what we do also models our underlying values. Whether we act judiciously, for example, or react inappropriately in haste, may determine whether we are just and fair or not, and pupils quickly pick up which is the case. Two examples of such incidents are presented in Task 4.5.5. Consideration of the incidents is designed to show the kinds of judgements that may need to be made. In the first incident, an individual pupil

---

 Task 4.5.5 Critical incidents

Read through the following extracts and discuss the two cases with another student teacher, or in a group. There are prompt questions to support your reflections.

1   Wayne is in school during break in order to keep an appointment with a teacher. On the way to this appointment, walking past his form room, he sees a pupil from his form going through the drawers of the teachers' desk. The pupil is not facing Wayne but it seems obvious to him that the pupil is taking things out of the desk and putting them in his pocket. Wayne walks away unseen by the other pupil. Wayne decides to tell his class teacher.

2   This incident concerns a 13-year-old girl who attends a local girls' school. Her parents do not approve of her mixing with other pupils outside school hours and expect her to return home promptly after school. But she often goes home with other girls and part of the way with boys from the nearby boys' school. One day, she makes an arrangement to meet one of the boys after school and she gets another girl in her class, Serena, to give her an alibi. On the day of the meeting, Serena decides that she does not want to provide the alibi and to lie to her friend's parents. During the afternoon, the two girls argue in class to the extent that the teacher keeps them back after school. The teacher then learns the cause of the argument and so finds out about the arrangements.

Some questions to support discussion:

■   What would you do in each of these cases if you were the teacher?
■   What advice would you give to the pupils?
■   Can you imagine any difficult decisions you might have to take? If so, explain the considerations.
■   If you didn't know what to do, do you know where to get the advice and support you need to help you manage challenging situations?
■   How do the situations relate to the particular formulation of the ethical responsibilities of teachers as stated in your ITE programme requirements or accreditation standards?

Summarise your response to each incident and share it with your tutor. File this and any further comments in your PDP.

has to decide what to do – a question of conscience – and a teacher has to act accordingly. In the second example, the teacher is faced by a situation in which there is a conflict of responsibilities towards the parents, on one hand, and the pupils, on the other, and is required to take a stand.

Now complete Task 4.5.6.

M

 Task 4.5.6 Teaching right and wrong

Consider the following questions and draft a response to them before reading the extracts from Smith and Standish (1997). In the light of your reading, review your responses.

1   In your opinion, can values be explicitly 'taught' or only 'caught' by example and through experience? Draft a response to this question before reading the text. See Smith and Standish (1997: 75–91).
2   'If we are supposed to instil values in the young, whose values are these?' Where do values come from?
3   What do you think about the statement of values of the National Forum as a basis for education in schools? See Figure 4.5.1 in this unit and Smith and Standish (1997: 1–14).
4   Investigate the Kohlberg stages of moral development; for example, through the paper by Nucci (2007). What is your view of these stages? Do they tally with your views on how a moral sense develops? Do people pass through various stages of moral development as they grow up? See Smith and Standish (1997: 93–104).

Respond to these three issues around the requirement of schools and teachers to provide a set of moral values through which to help the growth and development of their pupils. Summarise your thoughts and discuss them with other student teachers before finalising your response. Finally, this topic could be written up as an essay (5,000 words) with a title such as 'Teaching right from wrong'. Keep a copy in your PDP.

SUMMARY AND KEY POINTS

■   Moral judgement and moral behaviour derive from personal, social, cultural, religious and political viewpoints and conventions.
■   Societies with diverse groups have a potential for enrichment or friction. In this respect, the National Forum on Values in Education is helpful in developing a consensus about values that may support social cohesion.
■   Young people develop an ability to reason about values and to make ethical choices. They are helped towards maturity in this respect by parents and carers, teachers and peers. This mature stage of development may lead to questioning the values they have grown up with.

■ Some moral and ethical matters can arise naturally in dealing with children but subject work may afford opportunities for approaching them (see Task 4.5.3). While some subjects lend themselves more easily than others to these matters – such as English, religious education, citizenship and civic education – all subjects can provide an opportunity. The use of discussion and simulations are good ways of introducing moral and ethical matters (see advice on both in Appendices 4.5.1 and 4.5.2, respectively, at the end of this unit).

■ Teachers have a particular responsibility to promote pupils' development as ethically responsible people. In some countries, there is a legal responsibility, such as England, where teachers have to promote 'the spiritual, moral, cultural, mental and physical development of pupils at the school', as outlined in the National Curriculum (DfE 2011i).

■ Ethical dilemmas continually arise in practice and you need to exercise good judgement when faced with them. It is important that you know the school policy about the issue that confronts you and the expected response in your school.

■ When you find it difficult to respond by yourself, you should refer to experienced and qualified staff for help. These dilemmas are part of being a teacher with responsibility for others.

Check which requirements for your ITE programme you have addressed through this unit.

Further reading

Dewey, J. (1909) *The Moral Principles in Education: The Middle Works of John Dewey, 1899–1924. Volume 4: 1907–1909, Essays*, Carbondale and Edwardsville, IL: Southern Illinois University Press.
> While over 100 years old, this book is easy to read and as valid today as then. It is open source and freely downloadable at: www.gutenberg.org/ebooks/25172.

Haydon, G. (2006a) *Values in Education*, London: Continuum.
> This book addresses the questions: what are the fundamental aims and values underlying education and how can education promote values in a world of value pluralism? The text also discusses morality and if schools should teach it. In a secular society, how should schools treat the links between morality and religion? This is an updated version of an earlier text, *Teaching About Values* (1997).

Haydon, G. (2006b) *Education, Philosophy and the Ethical Environment*, London: Faber & Faber.
> This book offers a critical analysis of some of the fundamental questions about the nature and purpose of education, using the concept of 'ethical environment'. It addresses many ideas about values education, including the contrasting ideas of relativism and universal values, indoctrination, the relationship between values and sense of identity, and the demands of pluralism.

Langford, P. (1995) *Approaches to the Development of Moral Reasoning*, Hove: Erlbaum.
> A survey of approaches to the development of moral reasoning, including the contributions of Freud, Kohlberg and Piaget. The text provides a critical review of stage theory of moral development, and alternative approaches are described.

Smith, R. and Standish, P. (eds) (1997) *Teaching Right and Wrong: Moral Education in the Balance*, Stoke-on-Trent: Trentham.
> This discusses the work of the National Forum on Values Education and also argues for alternative approaches to values education.

Other resources and websites

There are many resources for developing a values education course in schools, or for finding ideas and materials for work with pupils, where values education appears in a specific curriculum area, such as PSHE, RE or citizenship. The following websites are helpful:

British Humanist Association: www.humanism.org.uk/education/education-policy

Citizenship Foundation: www.citizenshipfoundation.org.uk

CitizED subject resource bank: www.citized.info

Jubilee Centre for Character and Virtues: www.jubileecentre.ac.uk

Appendix 2 on pages 591–595 provides examples of further websites you may find useful.

Capel, S., Leask, M. and Turner, T. (eds) (2010) *Readings for Learning to Teach in the Secondary School: A Companion to M Level Study*, London: Routledge.
This book brings together essential readings to support you in your critical engagement with key issues raised in this textbook.

The subject-specific books in the Routledge *Learning to Teach* series are also very useful.

Any additional resources and an editable version of any relevant tasks/tables in this unit are available on the companion website: www.routledge.com/cw/capel

Appendix 4.5.1: Managing discussion

The following notes may help you develop your strategies for conducting discussion. They adopt the neutral chairperson approach.

A useful model for discussion is to engage with the following four principles:

1   There should be rules and procedures for discussion that all understand.
2   Speakers should provide evidence and information to back up their comments.
3   A neutral chairperson should have overview of the discussion.
4   The expected outcomes should be understood and communicated to everyone.

1 Rules and procedures

You need to consider:

■   choice of subject and length of discussion (young pupils without experience may not sustain lengthy discussion);
■   physical seating; room size; arrangement of furniture so that most pupils have eye contact;
■   protocols for discourse; taking turns; length of contribution; abusive language;
■   procedures for violation of protocols (for example, racist or sexist behaviour);
■   how to protect the sensitivity of individuals; pupils may reveal unexpected personal information in the course of a discussion;
■   stance of the chairperson.

2 Provision of evidence

In order to stimulate discussion and provide a clear basis for argument, you need to:

■ know the age, ability and mix of abilities of the pupils;
■ know what information is needed;
■ know sources of information;
■ decide at what point the information is introduced (before, during).

3 Neutral chairperson

A neutral stance may be essential because:

■ the authority of the opinions of the chair should not influence the outcome;
■ the opinions of pupils are to be exposed, not those of the teachers;
■ the chairperson can be free to influence the quality of understanding, the rigour of debate and appropriate exploration of the issues;
■ pupils will understand the teacher's stance if it is made clear at the start.

4 Possible outcomes

The strategy is discussion, not instruction. Pupils should:

■ learn by sharing and understand the opinion of others;
■ be exposed to the nature and role of evidence;
■ realise that objective evidence is often an inadequate basis for decision-making;
■ come to know that decisions often rely on subjective value judgements;
■ realise that many decisions are compromises.

Action

Try out these rules by setting up a discussion with other student teachers on the topic of: 'Equal opportunities for girls enable them to join the power structure rather than challenge it.'

Appendix 4.5.2: Simulations and role play

General and specific subject advice may be found in some of our companion subject books in the series; for example:

Art and design:
Addison and Burgess (2007)

Geography:
Lambert and Balderstone (2009: 114-46)

History:
Haydn (2008 *et al.*: 18-20, 50-1)

Science:
Levinson (2005b: 258-68)
A fuller description of simulations is given in Turner (1995).
Frost (2010)

See Unit 5.4.

4.6

An introduction to inclusion, special educational needs and disability

Nick Peacey

Introduction

In England, the 2014 Children and Families Act[1] (UK government 2014) and the 2014 *Special educational needs and disability Code of Practise*[2] (the first since 2001) have established a new framework for the education of children and young people with special educational needs and disabilities (SEND).

The new framework:

■ covers provision for children and young people between 0 and 25 years of age;
■ makes collaboration between services and all types of educational institution mandatory;
■ provides for local authorities (LAs) to publish a 'local offer' explaining exactly what is available in their area and 'to make provision more responsive to local needs and aspirations' (the 2014 code para 4.2);
■ introduces an 'Education, Health and Care Plan (EHCP)' to replace the 'statement of special educational needs' and 'learning difficulties assessment';[3]
■ seeks to emphasise schools' duty to optimise 'ordinary differentiation' before intervention, partly by reducing what were two school levels of intervention to one, known as 'special education needs support';
■ strengthens the rights of pupils with SEND and their parents/carers.

Article 24 of the UN Convention on the Rights of Persons with Disabilities (UNCRPD) guarantees all disabled learners a right to participate in all forms of mainstream education with appropriate support. The UK ratified this Convention in 2009 with specific restrictions on its obligations. Understanding approaches to the diverse needs of all their pupils is essential to all teachers' professional development (see also Unit 4.4).

Definitions

The abbreviation SEN is used throughout the unit to refer to special educational needs as set down in the law governing the 2014 Code of Practise. The abbreviation SEND is used to refer to special educational needs and/or disability. Pupils learning English as an additional language (EAL) and 'gifted and talented' pupils are not per se regarded in law as having special educational needs, though of course they may be so identified if they are also assessed as having an impairment or learning difficulty.

The publication *Index for Inclusion*, which was sent with government support to every school in England, describes inclusion in these terms:

The authors of *Index for Inclusion* noted that schools cannot remove all barriers to inclusion. There are limits; for example, to how much schools can do about the barriers created by poverty.

The Centre for Studies on Inclusive Education (CSIE) definition of inclusion is comprehensive. Documents often use the term in what we might call a 'placement' sense to mean the process by which pupils with SEND are placed in mainstream institutions as opposed to specialist provision such as special schools or units.

Defining SEN and disability

The 2014 Act and 2014 code are conservative on terminology: they have retained this definition dating back to the 1996 Education Act: 'A child or young person has SEN if they have a learning difficulty or disability which calls for special educational provision to be made for them.'

The definition of disability is rather different: the Disability Discrimination Act (DDA) (DfEE 1995), now subsumed into the Equality Act 2010, describes a disabled person as having 'a physical or mental disability which has an effect on their ability to carry out normal day-to-day activities'. That effect must be substantial (that is, more than minor or trivial), adverse and long term (has lasted or is likely to last at least a year or for the rest of the life of the person affected).

The Equality Act disability discrimination legislation applies to a wider group of pupils than those defined as having SEN. For example, it covers those with medical or physical impairments for whom there are no educational barriers to learning. It applies across the United Kingdom and to all educational establishments, public or private, whereas the 2014 code applies only to publicly funded schools in England.

Some authors feel we should have outgrown the notion of SEN. They feel it places too much emphasis on locating difficulty within the individual, the 'medical model', and that the model discourages consideration of removing barriers to the learning of minorities, such as those with SEND, by changing the school culture, policies and practice, particularly that in the classroom, for all individuals.

In contrast, the Scottish Parliament has adopted the concept of additional support needs (ASN), rather than SEN. '1. *A child or young person has additional support needs for the purposes of this Act where, for whatever reason, the child or young person is, or is likely to be, unable without the provision of additional support to benefit from school education provided or to be provided for the child or young person*' (Scottish Government 2009).

The breadth of this definition ensures that those benefiting from the Act's powers include, for example, looked-after children.

But much English, Northern Irish and Welsh government statute and regulation (including that related to funding) is still set in an SEN model. In this unit, we use the terminology of the 2014 Code of Practise, which, while not claiming that there are hard and fast categories of SEN, groups SEN under four main categories, which it calls 'broad areas of need and support':

■ communication and interaction;
■ cognition and learning;

- social, emotional and mental health;
- sensory and/or physical needs.

The code suggests that:

> These four broad areas give an overview of the range of needs that should be planned for. The purpose of identification is to work out what action the school needs to take, not to fit the pupil into a category.
>
> (DfE/DoH 2015: para. 6.27)

We return to these categories later in the unit and consider some of the classroom approaches involved. By the end of your initial teacher education (ITE) programme, you are expected to meet certain standards with respect to your understanding of SEND issues.

Inclusive pedagogy

The literature on learning and teaching in relation to pupils with SEND has moved decisively over the last few years to the adoption of inclusive teaching approaches, usually known as 'inclusive pedagogy'. This is based on developing understanding that:

- advice on teaching pupils with particular SEND frequently involves methods that could support individuals in all sorts of diagnostic categories;
- many 'SEND methods' are not qualitatively different from those used in ordinary teaching, but simply extensions or emphases of standard approaches;
- we should therefore prioritise development of ordinary teaching methods before assuming anything different will be needed for some individuals.

> Our conceptualisation of inclusive pedagogy focuses on how to extend what is ordinarily available in the community of the classroom as a way of reducing the need to mark some learners as different. This is underpinned by a shift in pedagogical thinking from an approach that works for *most* learners existing alongside something 'additional' or 'different' for those (*some*) who experience difficulties, towards one that involves providing rich learning opportunities that are sufficiently made available for *everyone*, so that all learners are able to participate in classroom life.
>
> (Florian and Black-Hawkins 2011, original emphasis)

So the good news is that you do not need to craft an infinite number of pedagogies for different 'needs', but can develop a more limited repertoire, to extend or diversify your teaching for particular individuals or groups.

Disability-specific insights and knowledge are valuable and have their place in your planning. For example, when teaching English literature to pupils on the autistic spectrum, you should know that careful approaches to metaphor and simile will often be important (they will support many other pupils as well). But you should prioritise developing your inclusive pedagogy as the foundation of your teaching of SEND.

What does 'inclusive pedagogy' consist of?

The Institutes of Education at London and Exeter disseminated one research-based model of 'ordinary teaching' in a well-evaluated programme of SEND training for new teachers (Lindsay *et al.* 2011) commissioned by the now closed Training and Development Agency for Schools (TDA).

It offered a three-part planning model:

1 approaches that help all and can be modified to remove barriers for those with SEND (the 'pillars of inclusion');
2 approaches drawn from specialist studies of subject/curriculum area learning;
3 insights from disability-specific knowledge.

Planning to help everyone learn and participate: 'the pillars of inclusion'

The TDA documentation characterised eight aspects of planning as 'the pillars of inclusion':

- ■ inclusive learning environments;
- ■ multisensory approaches including the use of information technology;
- ■ working with additional adults;
- ■ managing peer relationships;
- ■ adult-pupil communication;
- ■ formative assessment/assessment for learning;
- ■ motivation;
- ■ memory/consolidation of learning.

The TDA advised that all eight pillars should be considered. The model is not the only way of demarcating the significant areas: the point is that if teachers are not to create barriers to access before they walk into the classroom, they need some such holistic model or checklist of differentiation in their minds.

Now complete Task 4.6.1.

 Task 4.6.1 The pillars of inclusion applied to the teaching of English

TDA extension materials explored the possibilities and potential barriers of all subjects within the model of pedagogy outlined above. You will also find, on the same site, booklets relating to most other secondary subjects. Download the English booklet and also the booklet for your own subject in the TDA series of curriculum booklets developed to show how the pillars of inclusion apply to subject teaching. http://webarchive.nationalarchives.gov.uk/20111218081 624/http://tda.gov.uk/teacher/developing-career/sen-and-disability/sen-training-resources/ one-year-itt-programmes/~/media/resources/teacher/sen/secondary/english.pdf (accessed 29 March 2015).

Use the tables relating to the pillars of inclusion in the English booklet, or that for your own subject, to find ideas to discuss with your tutor or colleagues and record in your professional development portfolio (PDP).

The National Curriculum (NC) for England 2014

Teachers have long been able to design their lessons in ways that they feel meet the needs of pupils with SEND, whatever the current national curriculum may say. The statutory principles involved have become known as the 'general inclusion statement'. Nothing in the 2014 NC or the revised SEND framework has affected the position.

The current inclusion statement is based on:

1   The need to set suitable learning challenges. This principle encourages high expectations for all within a teaching and learning model, which matches the approach used to the pupils.
2   Responding to pupils' diverse learning needs. Lessons should be planned to ensure there are no barriers to *every* pupil achieving.

This will include, for example:

■   the way adults structure communication with pupils;
■   the layout of the classroom space;
■   making sure that all pupils can hear.

Some background: the developing legislative framework

1971   Legislation in England and Wales brings those considered 'ineducable' into education.
1981   The 1981 Education Act included specific duties of local education authorities (LEAs) and school governors to make provision for SEN, defining responsibilities and procedures for SEN and the establishment of parents' participation in special educational assessments, along with a right of appeal.
1988   The 1988 Education Act introduced the National Curriculum and reinforced the duty to consider SEN, though many felt that proper attention was not given to the area.
1994   *The Code of Practice on the Identification and Assessment of Special Educational Needs* (DfE 1994a) came into effect on 1 September.
2000   The revised National Curriculum for England (containing the 'inclusion statement') became law. It remains the law at the time of writing.
2001   The Disability Discrimination Act 1995 was revised by the addition of a Part 4. This, for the first time, placed duties on schools and other educational institutions not to treat disabled pupils less favourably and to make 'reasonable adjustments' to ensure that disabled pupils are not put at a substantial disadvantage. Disabled school staff have rights under Part 2 of the Act.
2001   A revised SEN Code of Practise re-emphasised the importance of whole-school approaches. 'The effective school will identify common strategies and responses across the secondary curriculum for all pupils designed to raise pupils' learning outcomes, expectations and experiences.' The curriculum available for all pupils will directly affect the need to intervene at an individual level (DfEE 2001b).
2004   *Removing Barriers to Achievement: The Government's SEN Strategy* (DfES 2004h). This document gives a detailed outline of the government's planning for SEN over the next 10 years and provides a useful summary of many areas of development.

2005 The Disability Discrimination Act 2005 put a duty on public bodies to 'promote disability equality'. This brought disability equality the same legislative status as gender equality and race equality.

2009 *The Lamb Inquiry: Special Educational Needs and Parental Confidence* (DCSF 2009a). This inquiry concluded that while relatively small-scale changes to legislation were necessary, the most important systemic aim was the proper implementation of legislation and regulation currently in force. At the same time, the then government set in place the highly significant *Achievement for All* programme (see Knowles' *Achievement for All MESHGuide*, 2016). This stressed three elements for development across schools: 'Key features of the programme included:

■   rigorous tracking of children's progress in English and mathematics with intervention when pupils fall behind;

■   a termly structured conversation on educational outcomes between the teacher that knows the pupil best and the parent;

■   a common-sense approach to addressing what is getting in the way of learning, such as bullying, persistent absence or poor social skills.

These approaches were led and championed at senior leadership and headteacher level' (DfE, 2011b)

Evaluation concluded that the parental engagement element had been particularly successful: schools were said to have been 'really listening' to parent views and translating what they heard into changes that made a real difference to the social and academic progress of pupils. This programme also represented a response to concerns about classroom teaching for SEN and disability identified by Blatchford *et al.* (2009) (see Task 4.6.2).

2010 The Office for Standards in Education (Ofsted) published its *Special Education Needs and Disabilities (SEND) Review* (Ofsted, 2010b). While the press focused on the review finding that there was overidentification of SEN in many schools, the inspection team's greatest concern was the low quality of education on offer to many of those who had been identified.

2010 A revised Ofsted framework for inspection included specific provisions for the inspection of SEN in schools. The current framework can be consulted on the Ofsted website (www.ofsted. gov.uk) (Ofsted, 2015). It includes as a key element of an inspection: 'the extent to which the education provided by the school meets the needs of the range of pupils at the school, and in particular the needs of disabled pupils and those who have special educational needs.'

2010 The Equality Act pulled together legislation on equality, including that concerning: disability; race; gender, pregnancy and maternity; sexuality; age; and religion and belief.

These are 'protected characteristics'; that is, they can be brought into discrimination claims.

2011 The coalition government published a Green (consultative) Paper on SEND, *Support and Aspiration: A New Approach to Special Educational Needs and Disability* (DfE, 2011f). This set out detailed proposals and questions for consultation on five areas: early identification and support; giving parents more control; learning and achieving; preparing for adulthood; and services working together for families.

2014 The 2014 Act and 2014 Code of Practice are approved by Parliament. The Code of Practice (approved by both Houses of Parliament) cannot be ignored by any institution or service to which it applies. They must 'have regard' to its provisions: they can implement them with some flexibility, but must be able to justify any departure from them if challenged.

The Act and Code:

- ■   replace the Statement of SEN and the Learning Difficulties Assessment by a single ECHP running from 0–25 years of age (the Statement only covered 3–18 years of age);
- ■   mandate all parties across education, health and social care, and all types of government-funded schools, including academies and free schools, to work together to provide services for SEND. This includes the duty to provide health services in EHCPs (section 42);
- ■   make clear that the duty applies to helping the child or person achieve the best possible 'educational and other outcomes' (section 19).

Section 19 of the 2014 Act makes clear that LAs 'must have regard to' the views, wishes and feelings of the child or young person and the children's parents and support them through joint decision-making processes and in the facilitation of the individual's development. Within this, it gives parents the right to express a preference for any state-funded school, including academies and free schools, and encourages the extension of the scope of personalised funding, developing a voucher system within special education.

The SEND Code of Practice 2014: a little more detail

The SEND code 2014:

- ■   is jointly published by the Department for Education and the Department for Health;
- ■   covers the full age range (0–25 years) of provision and all services;
- ■   gives only 19 pages of its 282 to the SEND provision that should ordinarily be in place in mainstream schools;
- ■   says that schools should:
  - ■   ensure that children and young people with SEN engage in the activities of the school alongside pupils who do not have SEN;
  - ■   designate a teacher to be responsible for coordinating SEN provision – the SEN coordinator, or SENCO (this does not apply to 16–19 academies);
  - ■   inform parents when they are making special educational provision for a child;
  - ■   prepare an SEN information report and report on arrangements for the inclusion of disabled children;
  - ■   appoint a governor with SEND responsibilities;
  - ■   regularly review how expertise and resources used to address SEN can be used to build the quality of whole-school provision.

The two-stage approach to meeting needs

The Ofsted thematic review of SEND practice in schools (Ofsted 2010b) raised two major concerns:

- ■   Pupils are too often identified as having SEN when what they need is really good quality ordinary teaching.
- ■   Pupils identified as having SEN too often do not receive the support required to allow them to catch up with their peers.

Task 4.6.2 Special educational needs and disability code of practice: 0-25 Years

- ■ Read the school policy on SEND provision in your placement school and the extracts from the 2014 code of practice above.
- ■ Discuss the implementation of the 2014 code of practice and school policy with your tutor and the SENCO in your placement school. Useful questions include: How does your school ensure that the requirements of the SEND code are met? How are all the teachers in school involved in implementing the code of practice?
- ■ Discuss your findings with those of another student teacher who has undertaken the same exercise in another school.

Make a summary of the similarities that arise and try to account for the differences. Store these in your PDP.

The press furore about the first finding ('too many identified as having SEN') rather drowned out the second message. Ofsted did, however, review its inspection frameworks and now has in place schedules that concentrate on ordinary learning and teaching and SEND, rather than more specialist arrangements.

The 2014 code offers a response to 'overidentification'. It cuts the three stages of school action in the 2001 code to two, which is certainly likely to reduce the numbers identified.

The two stages are:

- ■ SEN support: intervention planned and delivered by the school within its own resources, sometimes using external specialist help. If SEN support does not result in appropriate progress, moves may be made towards assessment for an EHCP.
- ■ An EHCP: a multi-professional agreement, overseen by the LA, with statutory force on what intervention and resources are appropriate for the pupil to make appropriate academic and social progress. In many cases, schools are expected to have the funding in their budgets to make the provision specified, but it is possible for them to seek help from the LA where interventions are likely to be very expensive.

SEN support

The 2014 code stresses the importance of high-quality teaching for all: 'making higher quality teaching normally available to the whole class is likely to mean that fewer pupils will require such [SEN] support' (DfE/DoH 2015: para. 6.15).

The phrase 'knowledge of the SEN most frequently encountered' refers to the expectation that schools should help all teachers to develop their learning about such conditions as speech, language and communication needs, autism, dyslexia, moderate learning difficulties and mental health issues, the areas that schools most frequently identify as SEN in the DfE annual census every January.

If things are not going well for a pupil, the school is expected to consider and plan an intervention as 'SEN support'. This is to be done after appropriate consultation of all records and discussion with parents/carers and the pupil themselves.

In the past, such plans would often have been set out as an individual education plan (IEP). You may find that schools still use this device, intended as a way to communicate details of the intervention to all staff, though IEPs have often been felt to be more bureaucratic than effective. A school may have a learning passport system, where the pupils themselves take intervention ideas and objectives, as well as their own preferences in ways to learn, to their various classes; it may be that the planning and review of SEN support is incorporated into the school's ordinary planning and review systems for all pupils.

Whatever the details of communication of the SEN support plans, the 2014 code expects the processes to be carried out within the overall model: 'Assess, Plan, Do, Review.' This formula is to drive a cycle within schools, whereby the assessment, planning and review are carried out by the SENCO and appropriate others from inside or outside the school, in full consultation with the parents and pupil, particularly in the setting of intended outcomes and review dates. Subject teachers are to remain responsible for day-to-day implementation, perhaps with the support of a teaching assistant (TA) for all or some lessons (see below).

The review process is emphasised:

> The effectiveness of the support and interventions and their impact on the pupil's progress should be reviewed in line with the agreed date.
>
> The impact and quality of the support and interventions should be evaluated, along with the views of the pupil and their parents. This should feed back into the analysis of the pupil's needs. The class or subject teacher, working with the SENCO, should revise the support in light of the pupil's progress and development, deciding on any changes to the support and outcomes in consultation with the parent and pupil.
>
> Parents should have clear information about the impact of the support and interventions provided, enabling them to be involved in planning next steps.
>
> (DfE/DoH 2015: paras 6.53–6.55)

It may be that as the result of a review, school or parent(s) may decide to seek an LA assessment to decide if an EHCP should be prepared. But it is the clear intention of the code that schools should use 'Assess, Plan, Do, Review' to try different approaches to intervention themselves, before moving to that step.

Additional staff in the classroom

Where other adults are supporting pupils in your classroom, you are in charge. You need to liaise closely with them to ensure the pupil gains maximum benefit from this support. The support staff should have the lesson plans well in advance. You can check with them that the materials you are providing are appropriate for a particular pupil (see Task 4.6.3).

Teaching staff should be clear that the learning of all pupils in lessons is their responsibility. There are concerns that in some schools, pupils with SEN and/or disabilities are substantially taught by TAs.

Task 4.6.3 Working with support staff in the classroom

For a pupil with SEND to be fully supported in the classroom, the classroom teacher and support staff must develop an effective working relationship. Ask some support staff for advice about how you can best work together. Observe support staff working in classrooms and consider what has to be done to ensure the pupils make maximum progress.

Identify the implications for lesson planning for your classes and file your notes in your PDP.

Extensive research, including audio recordings of classroom interactions, reported by Blatchford *et al.* (2009: 34) found that many support staff working with pupils with SEN in schools were inappropriately deployed and that this was affecting pupil outcomes. The statement in their report that caused the most comment was this:

> The more support pupils received, the less progress they made, even after controlling for other factors that might be expected to explain the relationship such as pupils' prior attainment, SEN status and income deprivation.

The team argued that the least expert/trained professionals, TAs, were often taking the major responsibility for the education of the pupils who needed the most sophisticated and expert teaching. Blatchford and his colleagues were clear that the situation was not the fault of the TAs, but of the teaching staff who managed them.

Nationally, there is a budgetary aspect to this: it was easily demonstrable that the bulk of the money spent annually on SEN was going on the salaries of TAs, so misdeployment on the scale identified represented a significant waste of resources across the country.

Finally, the belief that a TA would 'look after' the needs of the pupil with SEN effectively deskilled many teachers, who felt they did not have the expertise to help such pupils learn.

The Education Endowment Foundation has published useful guidance on making the best use of TAs (Sharples *et al.* 2015). Now complete Task 4.6.4.

Records from transfer between schools

When working with pupils with SEND, you can consult the records created at transfer from primary to secondary school. These records can include:

- detailed background information collated by the primary school SENCO;
- copies of any plans prepared for primary school SEND intervention.

You can contact the SENCO or the pupil's form tutor if you feel such information would help your planning. Task 4.6.5 allows you to find out more about the assessment of pupils with SEN.

Task 4.6.4 Measuring outcomes for pupils with SEND

The 2010 Ofsted review and studies of classroom practice with pupils with SEND (such as Blatchford's) have emphasised the need for all schools to have appropriate methods in place to measure the outcomes of those with SEND and those less likely to make progress. Undertake the exercise below to find how your school tackles this.

Plan a meeting with the SENCO or inclusion manager and briefly record an account of your school's systems for:

1   tracking the attainment of all pupils and, within that, monitoring the progress of pupils with SEN and/or disabilities (academic progress and social inclusion);
2   monitoring the outcomes of planning and interventions to support pupils with SEN and/or disabilities across the school (for example, provision mapping and management, data on the results of specific intervention programmes, views of pupils and parents/carers, input from external professionals, results of reviews of pupils' progress, attendance data).

This activity is likely to take around an hour to complete, and you will probably need to spend half an hour of that time speaking to the school's SENCO or inclusion manager.

The record you make of your discussion should help to enhance your knowledge of your school's systems for meeting the needs of pupils with SEN and/or disabilities. Store these in your PDP.

 Task 4.6.5 Pupil assessment on entry to school

Ask what, if any, assessments are carried out on pupils on entry to the school and if you can see examples of them. You should also ask what use is made of the information collected by these assessments. Select the assessments made on one, or two, pupils with SEND and describe how the information is used to plan their learning. File the information in your PDP.

The EHCP: the second stage of the Code of Practise for SEND

If SEN support is not succeeding, schools and parents or carers may consider a multidisciplinary assessment to examine the possibility of a pupil's having an EHCP. Because the process is expensive – assessment alone can cost several thousand pounds – LAs have a duty to consider carefully whether to embark on it. Many LAs have, in recent years, reduced the number of statements, the predecessors of EHCPs, they issue. Funds are released directly to schools for SEND provision.

The statement was popular with parents and schools because it guaranteed the resources written into its clauses. There is every sign that the EHCP will have similar status. But while welcoming the mandatory involvement of health services in the EHCP, the voluntary bodies that support parents and carers of pupils with SEND suggest that full checks and balances are not yet in place to ensure the whole EHCP has to be honoured. Any form of 'failure to provide' within the area covered by a statement could be challenged in the tribunal for SEN and disabilities (SENDIST) and, if necessary, in the courts. But the SENDIST does not have equivalent powers in relation to the new health element of the EHCP.

Assessing for an EHCP and (if it results) an EHCP's implementation and review are 'high stakes' operations. So, unlike SEN support, where schools have very substantial freedom in how they implement the code, everything to do with the statement is embedded in a network of statutory rules. Teachers need to know about pupils with EHCPs in their class. You should discuss with your head of department or faculty how you can plan for pupils in your classes who have one. Find out more about pupils with an EHCP in your placement school through Task 4.6.6.

 Task 4.6.6 How does an EHCP come about in your school?

Arrange a convenient time with the SENCO to discuss the procedure by which an EHCP is drawn up for a pupil and how it is reviewed. Has the LA's/school's practice been changed recently? Summarise your findings and arrange to have it checked by your tutor or the SENCO. Store these in your PDP.

The response of schools

English as an additional language (EAL) and SEN

The 2014 code says:

> Identifying and assessing SEN for children or young people whose first language is not English requires particular care. Schools should look carefully at all aspects of a child or young person's performance in different areas of learning and development or subjects to establish whether lack of progress is due to limitations in their command of English or if it arises from SEN or a disability. Difficulties related solely to limitations in English as an additional language are not SEN.
>
> (DfE/DoH 2015: para. 6.24)

For advice on EAL, see Flynn's (2015) EAL MESHGuide.
The main points to be aware of are:

- Pupils learning English go through well-researched stages: they may, for instance, say little or nothing for some time after arriving in a new country, but are learning nonetheless.
- Pupils learning English benefit from high-quality learning environments: they do not as a rule need individual programmes; see, for example, Unit 3.2, which discusses motivation.
- If the English learning stages are not proceeding as they should, the possibility of a learning difficulty may be considered. This is the time for teachers to consult specialist help, such as the school SENCO.

Those wishing to take this area further should explore the ideas discussed in Hall (1996).

Special schools, units and resource bases

The proportion of pupils with statements educated outside the mainstream has remained almost the same between 1999 and 2014, though the number of LA special schools has gone down. Mainstream schools often have special units or resource bases attached to them:

> Inspection reports identify increased interest in resourced mainstream provision by rating it highly compared to that in other primary, secondary and special schools. Overall, pupils were as likely to make good progress with their academic, personal and social development in primary, secondary or special schools. But pupils had the best chance of making good progress in all three areas in resourced mainstream schools. A greater proportion of this provision was outstanding and it was seldom inadequate. High-quality specialist teachers and a commitment by leaders to create opportunities to include all pupils were the keys to success.
>
> (Ofsted 2006b: para. 280.3)

Access arrangements for examinations and assessments

All awarding bodies for public examinations, such as General Certificate of Secondary Education (GCSE) and General Certificate of Education (GCE) Advanced (A) level make access arrangements for pupils with EAL or learning difficulties. Access arrangements are also available for other pupils with SEND. If you feel that a pupil you are teaching needs such arrangements for an examination or national test and such arrangements are not in place, you should contact the SENCO or the school's examination coordinator to find out what can be done. It is important that the arrangements are in place well before the assessment: their use benefits from practice, like so many other things.

Concerns about a pupil not recognised by the school as having SEND

You may feel a concern about a pupil's progress and wonder if they have unrecognised SEND. It is always worth comparing notes with another teacher to see how the pupil responds in their class. While sensory impairments of hearing or vision are sometimes not picked up until secondary age, some of the most frequently unrecognised SEND relate to 'receptive' impairment in language or communication that is, an impairment in comprehension; see 'communication and interaction' below.

Concerns raised by pupils

Children and young people may raise concerns about their own progress. Their views should, of course, always be treated seriously.

Looking back to your time in secondary school, you may reflect that bringing worries to a member of staff will frequently require some courage from the pupil. The issues brought to you can be the tip of the iceberg. Once again, discussion with a colleague can help to get the perspective clear.

You should be particularly alert to signs of eating disorders, particularly anorexia, whether they emerge through observation, written work or conversation; such concerns should always be reported for urgent consideration.

More legalistically, failure to take appropriate steps when a disabling condition is brought to staff attention may well be an offence of disability discrimination under the Equality Act 2010.

Helping pupils with SEND to learn

This section provides some guidance on working with pupils with SEND in mainstream classrooms. Overall, you need to remember that the evidence from research supporting the effectiveness of differentiated pedagogies (teaching strategies; see Unit 5.3) for different groups of SEN is slender.

Part of your planning should involve (at a tactful moment) asking pupils with SEND how they like to be taught. A good example of how to do this is provided by the British Stammering Association, which has produced excellent materials on consulting youngsters worried about speaking up in class (www.stammeringineducation.net/england/secondary/).

We suggest that you develop your teaching approaches; that is, concentrate on good normal pedagogy. Seek advice from your tutor. You should:

■ concentrate on developing your overall teaching style and the best possible learning environments in classrooms you use;
■ use the education plan, the knowledge of others in the school and books and websites to build your awareness of the issues in learning for a pupil; do not assume that you need to teach that pupil differently or separately;
■ remember that motivation is a key part of learning, whatever the SEN: special treatment can 'turn off' adolescents (see Unit 3.2);
■ remember that the timing and intensity of interventions often makes the difference rather than the pedagogy;
■ have high expectations of homework and classwork; clarity in setting homework and care in checking it has been recorded properly helps those likely to find the work difficult.

Using information and communications technology (ICT) is an important way of helping some pupils with SEN (see Unit 5.5). If you would like to check that you are covering all aspects of preparation for SEND in planning lessons, have a look at the TDA pillars of inclusion (above) and the associated subject booklets.

Specific educational needs

We turn now to discuss briefly the particular groups of pupils with specific educational needs. The headings are derived from the 2014 Code of Practise (DfE/DoH 2015).

The 2014 code separates SEN into four broad areas.

It explains:

These four broad areas give an overview of the range of needs that should be planned for. The purpose of identification is to work out what action the school needs to take, not to fit a pupil into a category. In practice, individual children or young people often have needs that cut across all these areas and their needs may change over time. For instance speech, language and communication needs can also be a feature of a number of other areas of SEN, and children and young people with an Autistic Spectrum Disorder (ASD) may have needs across all areas, including particular sensory requirements. A detailed assessment of need should ensure that the full range of an individual's needs is identified, not simply the primary need. The support provided to an individual should always be based on a full understanding of their particular strengths and needs and seek to address them all using well-evidenced interventions targeted at their areas of difficulty and where necessary specialist equipment or software.

(DfE/DoH 2015: para. 6.27)

The four areas 1: communication and interaction

This area covers pupils with speech and language delay, impairments or disorders, specific learning difficulties, such as dyslexia and dyspraxia, hearing impairment and those who demonstrate features within the autistic spectrum. These difficulties may apply also to some pupils with moderate, severe or profound learning difficulties.

Pupils with language impairment

Pupils in this group may have receptive (that is, limitations in comprehending what is said to them) or expressive (that is, they find it hard to put their thoughts into words) language impairments. Obviously, the first impairment is the harder to identify. You need to be aware that:

■ emotional and relationship difficulties often go with language and less often with hearing impairments;
■ language impairments need specialist attention, normally from a speech and language therapist.

   When teaching these pupils, you should be sure:

■ to check understanding;
■ to use visual aids and cues to the topics being discussed;
■ that the pupil is appropriately placed to hear and see;
■ that you explain something several different ways if you have not been understood the first time;
■ like a good chairperson, you repeat what pupils say in discussion or question and answer sessions (in any case, others in the class may not have heard);
■ that you allow time for pupils to respond in question and answer sessions and, if necessary, ensure they are pre-prepared for responding, perhaps by a TA (see the section on questioning in Unit 6.1).

   For further information, see the websites of the charities the Communication Trust and ICAN.

Pupils with autism spectrum conditions, sometimes known as autism spectrum disorders (ASD)

Those with autism spectrum conditions typically lack 'mentalisation'; that is, the ability to picture what another person is thinking. Any social context can create barriers for them.

   Autistic pupils' absorbing interests (such as train timetables) and lack of social focus mean that coordinated planning is essential. You need to be aware that:

■ many researchers feel autistic pupils' behaviour is a form of stress management for their hypersensitivity to many different stimuli, including touch and sound;

■ pupils with conditions on the autistic spectrum can learn 'intellectually' how to act socially (for example, in the matter of eye contact);

■ suggestions on approaches to autism vary widely; you need to be absolutely clear what agreed strategies are being used at school and home and work within them.

Further help may be obtained from the National Autistic Society and the Autism Education Trust (see the useful websites listed at the end of this unit).

The four areas 2: cognition and learning

Support for learning difficulties may be required when children and young people learn at a slower pace than their peers, even with appropriate differentiation. Learning difficulties cover a wide range of needs, including moderate learning difficulties (MLD), severe learning difficulties (SLD), where children are likely to need support in all areas of the curriculum and associated difficulties with mobility and communication, through to profound and multiple learning difficulties (PMLD), where children are likely to have severe and complex learning difficulties as well as a physical disability or sensory impairment (DfE/DoH 2015).

Learning difficulties

Pupils identified in this group are likely to be attaining well below others of their age in a range of areas. Fletcher-Campbell (2004a) argues that such pupils do not need different teaching approaches from those used with typically developing pupils, but benefit from planning that sets appropriate objectives at appropriate levels. Pupils with severe learning difficulties are described as 'unlikely to reach level 2 of the National Curriculum by the age of 15 (DfEE/QCA 2001). The term 'learning difficulties' thus covers a wide range of need so you need to check exactly what any individual learning plan advises and seek specialist advice.

Working memory

There is increasing concern that this group and many others, such as pupils with dyslexia, are not receiving the help they should have in relation to working memory. Working memory is the memory system that allows us, for example, to do mental arithmetic or transfer information accurately from a whiteboard to a writing book.

Gathercole (2008) has suggested Table 4.6.1 key themes in a classroom teacher's support in this area (see Table 4.6.1).

All of this is the strongest possible argument:

■ against setting homework or another independent study task right at the end of a lesson;

■ for ensuring that those who are not clear what the task is (or their parents/carers if they are involved) have a simple way of checking exactly what is required!

Table 4.6.1 Working memory

Principle	Watch out for
Recognise working memory failures	Warning signs include incomplete recall, failure to follow instructions, place-keeping errors, abandoning tasks or guessing at answers.
Monitor pupils	Look out for the warning signs and ask pupils to let you or a buddy know if something is going too fast for them.
Evaluate working memory loads	Think about the loads on working memory caused by lengthy sequences, unfamiliar and meaningless content and demanding mental processing activities.
Reduce working memory loads	Reduce the amount of material to be remembered, use shorter sentences, make the material more meaningful and familiar, simplify the mental processing required and restructure your explanation of complex tasks.
Structure activities so that the pupil can use available resources, such as word banks	Check that any new learning fits into the framework of what the pupil already knows.
Repeat important information	Repetition can be supplied by teachers, TAs or fellow pupils nominated as 'memory guides'.
Encourage the pupil to use memory aids	These can include wallcharts and posters, useful spellings, personalised dictionaries, cubes, counters, abacus, Unifix blocks, number lines, multiplication grids, calculators, memory cards, audio recorders and computer software.
Support memory through motivating approaches	Use visual or concrete ('real') materials, or activities involving movement, to reinforce learning through a range of sensory channels. Plan so that the new knowledge can be tried out in a range of enjoyable applications; for example, by using computer software or simulations.
Develop the pupil's own strategies	Strategies can include setting up an agreed approach for the pupil to own strategies, ask for help, rehearsal, note-taking, use of long-term memory, and strategies for place-keeping and organisation.

Dyslexia

You should be aware that:

■ the term dyslexia covers a wide range of needs;
■ the current emphasis is now on examining the individual's skills, such as phonological awareness, and working on them as a way forward.

Phonological awareness is the conscious sensitivity to the sound structure of language. It includes the ability to auditorily distinguish units of speech, such as a word's syllables and a syllable's individual phonemes (the smallest functional unit of sound such as 'c' in *cat* or 'th' in *that*).

Most schools and LAs have staff with specialist knowledge in this area. Help can also be sought from the major voluntary organisations. These include the British Dyslexia Association, Dyslexia Action, the Dyslexia Forum and the Professional Association of Teachers of Students with Specific learning difficulties (PATOSS) (see website addresses at the end of this unit).

Dyspraxia

Dyspraxia often shows as clumsiness and/or a lack of coordination. It may be defined as difficulty in planning and carrying out skilled, non-habitual motor acts in the correct sequence. Pupils with dyspraxia can need the support of whole-school systems, particularly in terms of ensuring that they are taking enough exercise. If you are concerned about a pupil with dyspraxia, it may help to talk to the physical education staff as well as to the SENCO. Engagement and building on strengths are as important for improving coordination as they are in any other learning, and physical education (PE) specialists are often expert at developing such approaches.

Difficulties with handwriting are a specific coordination issue. The publications and conferences of the National Handwriting Association and Dyspraxia Foundation are helpful (see the useful websites at the end of this unit).

The four areas 3: social, emotional and mental health difficulties

'Social, emotional and mental health difficulties' has replaced the 2001 Code of Practise category 'behavioural, emotional social difficulties'. That category had been much criticised, not least because it suggested that behaviour was a specific condition. It is now accepted that behaviour concerns may be associated with every form of learning difficulty or disability.

The 2014 code says:

> Children and young people may experience a wide range of social and emotional difficulties which manifest themselves in many ways. These may include becoming withdrawn or isolated, as well as displaying challenging, disruptive or disturbing behaviour. These behaviours may reflect underlying mental health difficulties such as anxiety or depression, self-harming, substance misuse, eating disorders or physical symptoms that are medically unexplained. Other children and young people may have disorders such as attention deficit disorder, attention deficit hyperactive disorder or attachment disorder.
>
> Schools and colleges should have clear processes to support children and young people, including how they will manage the effect of any disruptive behaviour so it does not adversely affect other pupils.
>
> (DfE/DoH 2015: paras 6.32–6.33)

Behavioural concerns

Behavioural problems are discussed in Units 3.1, 3.2, 3.3 and 4.1, and tasks are set there to develop your skills in this area. The differentiation case studies in Unit 4.1 are relevant here.

As the code suggests, a pupil presenting consistent problems of behaviour may well have special needs, such as a language impairment or an autistic spectrum disorder or have mental health needs:

they may be depressed, for instance. The code does not discuss the possibility that the behaviour is a response to something in the school environment that the pupil finds hard to tolerate, such as bullying in the playground or an irrelevant curriculum.

While you should always be alert for the issues in the school environment that trigger concerns, pupils who consistently act out or display withdrawn behaviour not related to the situation will benefit from the coordinated approach encouraged by the code.

Traditionally, secondary schools have three management approaches to such concerns: (1) the pastoral teams (form tutor, year/house head, and so on); (2) SEND teams; and (3) subject department or faculty.

The interrelationship of these management teams is critical to a school staff's success with emotional, social and mental health difficulties. Important points to bear in mind in your response to pupils who cause concern by their behaviour include understanding that:

- learning, not counselling, is the teacher's contribution to resolving behaviour concerns: many heads of schools talk of the 'therapy of achievement';
- recognising that many pupils whose behaviour is a concern have speech, language and communication needs and benefit from teaching that addresses those needs;
- being aware that 'scaffolding' success for such pupils can be demanding and you should expect support with your planning (and lessons learnt) from experienced colleagues (scaffolding is discussed in Unit 5.1).

Your lesson planning should address:

- knowing the strengths and interests of any pupils whose behaviour is worrying;
- knowing the levels of language and literacy of those pupils;
- considering alternatives within lesson plans if one learning activity is not succeeding.

Attention deficit hyperactivity disorder (ADHD)

ADHD is a medical diagnosis. The diagnosis in itself tells you nothing about teaching pupils with ADHD. While medication by means of a stimulant (such as Ritalin) is widely known as a treatment for this condition, the National Institute for Health and Care Excellence (NICE) guidance is clear that children and young people with mild or moderate forms of ADHD should first be offered referral to a psychological group treatment programme and their parents offered referral to a parent training programme (www.nice.org.uk/guidance/qs39/chapter/list-of-quality-statements). Further help and guidance may be found in the websites at the end of this unit.

The four areas 4: sensory and/or physical needs

The 2014 code advises that:

Some children and young people require special educational provision because they have a disability which prevents or hinders them from making use of the educational facilities generally provided. These difficulties can be age related and may fluctuate over time. Many children and young people with vision impairment (VI), hearing impairment (HI) or a multi-sensory impairment

(MSI) will require specialist support and/or equipment to access their learning, or habilitation support. Children and young people with an MSI have a combination of vision and hearing difficulties. Information on how to provide services for deafblind children and young people is available through the Social Care for Deafblind Children and Adults guidance published by the Department of Health.

Some children and young people with a physical disability (PD) require additional ongoing support and equipment to access all the opportunities available to their peers (DfE/DoH 2015: paras 6.34-6.35).

Deafness and hearing impairment

If you have a deaf pupil in your class, you should be aware that:

■ specialist advice is usually not difficult to come by; you should ask the SENCO for direction in the first instance;
■ many of the teaching checkpoints set out under language impairment apply;
■ pupils have individual communication needs; you need to know what they are.

Further advice can be obtained from Action on Hearing Loss (formerly the Royal National Institute for the Deaf (RNID)) and the National Deaf Children's Society (see the list of useful websites at the end of this unit). Action on Hearing Loss produces useful booklets on teaching deaf and hearing-impaired pupils.

Visual impairment

If you have a pupil with visual impairment in your class, specialist advice is again not difficult to come by. The SENCO in your school and the individual plan for the pupil concerned can help in the first instance. There is substantial online support to teachers from the Royal National Institute for the Blind (RNIB) (see the list of useful websites at the end of this unit). The RNIB argues strongly for commitment to the development of independence in blind learners.

Less obvious visual problems may affect pupils' reading. Specialist optometrists sometimes prescribe overlays or tinted spectacles to help with this problem.

Further information may be found on the RNIB website. We suggest you investigate in depth some pupils with SEN in your classes (see Task 4.6.7).

Physical disability

Specific guidance on any barriers to learning that a pupil's physical disability may present should normally be sought from school records, from the pupil and their parents and from any staff, such as TAs, who have worked with them. The core message should be the same as that for dyspraxia above: engagement and building on strengths will be central to any learning plans.

Medical conditions

Medical conditions are not addressed in the code's four categories, but you should be aware of its guidance on the statutory position and the possible interrelationship with SEN:

The Children and Families Act 2014 places a duty on maintained schools and academies to make arrangements to support pupils with medical conditions. Individual healthcare plans will normally specify the type and level of support required to meet the medical needs of such pupils.

Where children and young people also have SEN, their provision should be planned and delivered in a co-ordinated way with the healthcare plan. Schools are required to have regard to statutory guidance 'Supporting pupils at school with medical conditions.'

(DfE/DoH 2015: para. 6.11)

A medical condition can affect a child's learning and behaviour. The effect may also be indirect: time in education can be disrupted, there may be unwanted effects of treatment, and through the psychological effects that serious or chronic illness or disability can have on a child and their family. Schools and the pupil's carers and the medical services should collaborate so that pupils are not unnecessarily excluded from any part of the curriculum or school activity because of anxiety about their care and treatment.

 Task 4.6.7 Thinking about individual pupils

Identify, with the help of your tutor, pupils with whom you have contact who have SEND of different types. Draw up a table similar to the one below in your diary and complete it, drawing on the expertise of different staff as necessary. Use fictional names to preserve confidentiality and compare practice in your school with student teachers from different schools.

Description of pupil's SEND	Paul has severe hearing loss. He can lip-read reasonably well and his speech is fairly clear.
Pupil's strengths and interests	
Interaction with classroom work and environment in my subject	
General interaction with school environment	
The role of the school/SENCO	
The role of outside agencies (LA services, educational psychologists, educational welfare officers)	

For one or more of your pupils, identify:

■ the implications of your findings for lesson planning;
■ how you can work with the support teacher/TA.

Share your ideas with your tutor and/or the SENCO. Store these in your PDP.

SUMMARY AND KEY POINTS

This unit has introduced you to a range of issues relating to pupils with special needs and/or disabilities and set those issues and possible responses in the context of the *Special educational needs and disability code of practice: 0-25 Years* (DfE/DoH 2015).

■ In your work as a student teacher, we expect you to develop your understanding of the teacher's responsibilities for pupils' SEND so that, when you are in your first post, you are sufficiently aware of your responsibilities, including those set out in the code of practice, and that you ensure that your pupils' SEND are met.

■ You cannot expect to solve all pupils' learning problems on your own. You must seek advice from experienced staff. And never forget to listen to the pupils on what works for them.

■ Every child is special. Every child has individual educational needs. A major problem experienced by pupils with SEN is the attitudes of others to them. For example, pupils who have obvious physical disabilities such as cerebral palsy often find they are treated as though their mental abilities match their physical abilities when this is not the case. How will pupils with SEN find you as their teacher?

■ Teachers need to ensure that all their pupils learn to the best of their abilities and that pupils with SEN are not further disabled by the lack of appropriate resources to support their learning, including software (Leask and Pachler 2013).

Check which requirements for your ITE programme have been addressed through this unit.

Further reading

Alloway, T.P. and Alloway, R.G. (2015) *Understanding Working Memory*, 2nd edn, London: Sage.

Blatchford, P., Bassett, P., Brown, P., Koutsoubou, M., Martin, P., Russell, A. and Webster, R. with Rubie-Davies, C. (2009) *Deployment and Impact of Support Staff in Schools: The Impact of Support Staff in Schools. Results from Strand 2, Wave 2*, DCSF Research Report DCSF RR148, available at: www.ioe.ac.uk/DISS_Strand_2_Wave_2_Report.pdf

Centre for Studies on Inclusive Education (2011) *Index for Inclusion: Developing Learning and Participation in Schools*, available at: www.csie.org.uk/resources/inclusion-index-explained.shtml

DfE/DoH (2015) *Special educational needs and disability code of practice 0-25 Years*, available at: www.gov.uk/government/uploads/system/uploads/attachment_data/file/398815/SEND_Code_of_Practice_January_2015.pdf

Farrell, M. (2009) *The Special Education Handbook: An A-Z Guide for Students and Professionals*, 4th edn, London: Routledge.

Flynn, N. (2015) *Teaching English as an Additional Language MESHGuide*, University of Winchester/University of Reading, UK.

Knowles, C. (in press) *Achievement for All 3As MESHGuide*, London: Achievement for All.

Lindsay, G., Cullen, M.A., Cullen, S., Dockrell, J., Strand, S., Arweck, E., Hegarty, S. and Goodlad, S. (2011) *Evaluation of Impact of DfE Investment in Initiatives Designed to Improve Teacher Workforce Skills in Relation to SEN and Disabilities*, London: DfE RR115.

Sharples, J., Webster, R. and Blatchford, P. (2015) *Making Best Use of Teaching Assistants*, London: Education Endowment Foundation.

Other resources and websites

See also Unit 1.4 relevant websites for more Web addresses.

Action on Hearing Loss (formerly Royal National Institute for the Deaf (RNID)): www.actiononhearing
    loss.org.uk

ADDISS Attention Deficit Disorder (ADD) Information Service: www.addiss.co.uk

Autism Education Trust: www.autismeducationtrust.org.uk

British Dyslexia Association: www.bdadyslexia.org.uk/

The Communication Trust: www.thecommunicationtrust.org.uk

Dyspraxia Foundation: www.dyspraxiafoundation.org.uk/

ICAN: www.ican.org.uk.
    This charity supports speech, language and communication development in schools and elsewhere.

MESHGuides (Mapping Educational Specialist knowHow): www.meshguides.org
    This website hosts a growing number of research informed guides for teachers, including specific guides
    on SEND, including 'EAL' and 'Reluctant Writers'.

NASEN (National Association for Special Educational Needs): www.nasen.org.uk/
    The NASEN site hosts a number of valuable resources produced by the Department for Education: www.
    nasen.org.uk/onlinesendcpd/

National Autistic Society: www.nas.org.uk

National Curriculum 2014: www.gov.uk/government/uploads/system/uploads/attachment_data/file/210969/
    NC_framework_document_-_FINAL.pdf

National Deaf Children's Society: www.ndcs.org.uk

National Handwriting Association: www.nha-handwriting.org.uk

Professional Association of Teachers of Students with Specific Learning Difficulties (PATOSS): www.patoss-
    dyslexia.org

Royal National Institute for the Blind: www.rnib.org.uk

Appendix 2 on pages 591–595 provides further examples of websites you may find useful.

Capel, S., Leask, M. and Turner, T. (eds) (2010) *Readings for Learning to Teach in the Secondary School: A
    Companion to M Level Study*, London: Routledge.
    This book brings together essential readings to support you in your critical engagement with key issues
    raised in this textbook.

The subject-specific books in the Routledge *Learning to Teach* series are also very useful.

Any additional resources and an editable version of any relevant tasks/tables in this unit are available
on the companion website: www.routledge.com/cw/capel

Notes

1   'The 2014 Act' in this unit.
2   'The 2014 code' in this unit.
3   Learning difficulties assessment has been the term used in post-16 education.

5 Helping pupils learn

This chapter is about teaching and learning. As you work through these units, we hope that your knowledge about teaching and learning increases and that you feel confident to try out and evaluate different approaches.

Unit 5.1 introduces you to a number of theories of learning. Theories about teaching and learning provide frameworks for the analysis of learning situations and a language to describe the learning taking place. As you become more experienced, you develop your own theories of how the pupils you teach learn and you can place theories in the wider context.

In Unit 5.2, teaching methods that promote learning are examined. How you use these methods reveals something of your personal theory of how pupils learn. At this point in your development, we suggest that you gain experience with a range of teaching methods so that you are easily able to select the method most appropriate to the material being taught.

Unit 5.3 provides you with details about teaching styles. Again, we suggest that as you gain confidence with basic classroom management skills, you try out different styles so that you develop a repertoire of teaching styles from which you can select as appropriate.

We have talked at various points in this book about the characteristics of effective teaching.

Unit 5.4 is designed to provide you with information about methods for finding out about the quality of your own teaching and that of others through the use of reflection using action research techniques and drawing on the evidence base underpinning educational practice. During your initial teacher education programme, you are using action research skills in a simple way when you observe classes. In this unit, we explain the key aspects of action research and reflective and evidence-informed practice.

Unit 5.5 focuses on the concept of personalising learning. Digital technologies or information and communications technologies (ICTs) have made it possible to monitor pupils' actual attainment in tests against their expected grades across all subjects, and this means that teachers can be sent alerts automatically where pupils are not achieving what is expected. This allows for teachers to intervene more quickly to help pupils falling behind and provide a more 'personalised' learning experience. The concept of 'personalised learning' has many other features and these are discussed in this unit.

Unit 5.6 introduces you to research in neuroscience, which is yielding knowledge about brain function and how teachers can maximise pupil learning. This area of work is possible because activity of the brain can be monitored more easily than before using the latest MRI scanners and other techniques.

Unit 5.7 builds on the focus on personalising learning, which was new to the last edition. It invites you to develop your own critical thinking skills and those of the pupils.

Unit 5.8 focuses on the use of language in the classroom so as to improve the learning of pupils.

5.1 Ways pupils learn

Diana Burton

Introduction

Given that teaching is a means to an end, not an end in itself, good teachers do not simply concentrate on subject content; instead, they ensure that pupils learn *how*, *what*, *whether*, and so on in relation to their subject of study. However, the interaction between the activities of teaching and the outcomes of learning is critical. In order to develop presentation and communication techniques that facilitate effective learning, a teacher must have some understanding of how pupils learn. Programme lectures and school placements add to and refine the ideas you already have about learning and reveal differences in how individuals learn. Psychological research is concerned with this individuality of *cognition*: knowing, understanding, remembering and problem-solving. Research reveals information about human behaviour, motivation, achievement, personality and self-esteem, all of which impact on the activity of learning.

Several theoretical perspectives contribute to our understanding of how learning happens; for example:

■ behaviourism, which emphasises external stimuli for learning;
■ gestalt theory, which expounds principles of perception predicated on the brain's search for 'wholeness';
■ personality theories that are located in psycho-analytic, psycho-metric and humanist research traditions.

Discussion of such work can be accessed quite easily in libraries and journals (see Child 2007 or Long *et al.* 2011 for very good overviews), so this unit is organised around theories that have been particularly influential on pedagogic strategy. These theories include:

■ Piaget's cognitive-developmental theory of maturation;
■ metacognition, the way in which learners understand and control their learning strategies;
■ social constructivist theories that emphasise social interaction and scaffolded support for learning;
■ constructivist theories about the strength of pupils' existing conceptions;

- information processing explanations of concept development and retrieval;
- learning style theories, which question qualitative distinctions between ways of learning, stressing instead the matching of learning tasks to a preferred processing style.

In Unit 4.3, you met multiple intelligence theory, which suggests a multidimensional rather than a singular intelligence (Gardner 1983, 1993a, 1993b, 1995, 2011). Many educators consider this to have application when considering how individuals learn. Similarly, emotional intelligence theory, addressed in Unit 4.3 and emphasising the potency of the learner's emotional state, is also of interest to teachers (Salovey and Mayer 1990; Goleman 1995, 2006, 2011; Mayer and Salovey 1997; Mayer *et al.* 2004; Petrides 2009; Petrides *et al.* 2011).

OBJECTIVES

At the end of this unit, you should be able to:

- appreciate the interaction between ideas about learning and pedagogic strategies;
- begin to explain and differentiate between some psychological perspectives on learning;
- appreciate more about your own approach to learning.

Check the requirements of your initial teacher education (ITE) programme to see which relate to this unit.

How ideas about teaching and learning interact

Decisions you make about how to approach a particular lesson with a particular pupil or group of pupils depend on the interplay between your subject knowledge and pedagogic knowledge, your knowledge of the pupils and your understanding about how learning happens. Let us imagine that you have spent 10 minutes carefully introducing a new concept to your class but a few pupils unexpectedly fail to grasp it.

You test the reasons for their lack of understanding against what you know about the pupils' and their:

- prior knowledge of the topic;
- levels of attention;
- interest and motivation;
- physical and emotional state of readiness to learn, and so on.

You consider also factors relating to the topic and the way you explained it; for example:

- the relevance of the new material to the pupils;
- how well the new concept fits into the structure of the topic;

- the level of difficulty of the concept;
- your clarity of speech and explanation;
- the accessibility of any new terminology;
- the questioning and summaries you gave at intervals during your explanation.

Finally, you draw on explanations from educational psychology that have informed your understanding of how pupils learn and provided you with questions such as:

- Does the mode of presentation suit these pupils' learning styles?
- Has sufficient time been allowed for pupils to process the new information?
- Does the structure of the explanation reflect the inherent conceptual structure of the topic?
- Do these pupils need to talk to each other to help them understand the new concept?

A teacher's ideas about learning usually derive from a number of theories rather than from one specific theory. This is fine because it allows for a continual revision of your ideas as you gain more experience. This process is known as 'reflecting on theory in practice'. Some of the theories from which your ideas may be drawn are reviewed in this unit. In order to contextualise that review, it may be helpful to think about the types of learning activities in which you engage your pupils.

Gagné (1977) identified five factors that contribute to effective learning (see Task 5.1.1). Each of these factors is used in teaching all subjects in the curriculum, interacting in complex ways. It is helpful to consider them separately so that a particular pupil's learning progress and needs can be monitored and so that you can plan lessons that foster all types of learning (see also Unit 2.2) and employ different pedagogical strategies depending on the type of learning planned (see also Unit 5.5). Task 5.1.1 invites you to analyse the demands on pupils in a lesson using the factors identified by Gagné.

M

 Task 5.1.1 Analysing learning activities for demands on pupils

Select a learning activity from a lesson you have taught or observed. Describe the types of learning involved using the table below for each of the five factors. An example from science has been provided to guide you.

Activity	Intellectual skills	Verbal skills	Cognitive	Attitudes strategy	Motor skills
Science: a group activity using particle theory of matter	Discussing how to set up the activity to test an hypothesis	Defining solids, liquids and gases	Recalling previous knowledge about particles	Listening to and sharing ideas	Manipulating equipment

Share your findings with other student teachers, your tutor or class teacher. Identify the implications for planning future lessons and record these in your professional development portfolio (PDP).

The theory of multiple intelligences provides a different, and possibly more attractive, framework than Gagné's typology for categorising the different ways pupils learn (Gardner 1983, 1995, 2015). Gardner proposes that there are a number of relatively autonomous intelligences, such as 'linguistic intelligence' and 'musical intelligence', and includes nine or more different 'intelligences'. These intelligences may act alone or be combined in different ways in different contexts (for further information, see Unit 5.6). It is arguable whether it is actually possible to identify separate intelligences in this way – they could equally be described as different forms of processing with the strength of each varying from individual to individual. Gardner was not concerned about the use of the word 'intelligence' as such, so the words 'gift' or 'skill' would be equally appropriate. This theory is discussed more fully in Unit 4.3. Noble argues that it helps teachers make sense of their observations that pupils have different strengths and learn in different ways (Noble 2004: 194). Since each intelligence has a different developmental trajectory, pupils may engage in higher-order thinking in areas of intellectual strength and engage in lower-order, less abstract thinking in areas of weaker 'intelligence'. Noble relates this to Bloom's (1956) revised taxonomy of educational objectives, which orders cognitive processes from simple remembering to higher-order creative and critical thinking. From this viewpoint, Noble developed a matrix with multiple intelligence (MI) dimensions on the horizontal axis and the revised Bloom taxonomy of educational objectives (RBT) on the vertical axis (Noble n.d.) (for Bloom's taxonomy, see Stanford University 2015). Teachers used this matrix to design learning outcomes and activities so that pupils could demonstrate what they had learned at different levels of complexity across intellectual domains.

This approach has clear application in terms of differentiation in the classroom (see Unit 4.1 for more about differentiation). For instance, in a science project about the processes involved in the formation of volcanoes, pupils were given the opportunity to explain the process in a number of ways, such as drawing a flow chart (spatial intelligence) or setting the words to the tune of a well-known song (musical intelligence). Thus, a pupil understands better how volcanoes are formed by using, for example, a flow chart rather than by writing a paragraph. In this way, the types of learning pupils engaged in were broadened so that each pupil had greater access to the curriculum and could tackle a task at the relevant level of complexity depending on the strength of a particular intelligence.

Psychological perspectives on learning

A determining factor in lesson preparation is the knowledge that learners already possess. Unfortunately, identifying this knowledge is not as simple as recalling what you taught the pupils last time, for knowledge is, by definition, individualised. Each pupil's experiences of, attitudes towards and methods of processing prior knowledge are distinct. Psychologists are interested in how learners actively construct this individualised knowledge or 'meaning', and different theories offer different notions about what constitutes knowledge. *Cognitive developmental theory* depicts knowledge as being generated through the learners' active exploration of their world (Piaget 1932, 1954). More complex ways of thinking about things are developed as the individual matures. *Social constructivism* explains knowledge acquisition by suggesting that learners actively construct their individual meanings (or knowledge) as their experiences and interactions with others help develop the theories they hold (Rogoff 1990; Brown 1994). The constructivist approach draws attention to pupils' prior knowledge, which interacts with new knowledge offered through the curriculum. The interaction may support or conflict with the teacher's objectives. *Information processing theories* view knowledge as pieces of information that the learner's brain processes systematically and that are stored as abstractions of experiences (Anderson *et al.* 1996). Interestingly, the theory of *situated cognition* does not recognise knowledge as existing outside of situations, but rather as 'collective knowledge'; that is, the shared, ongoing, evolving interaction between people (Lave and Wenger 1991; Davis and Sumara 1997). See Hara (2009) for a full account of communities of practice and peer learning.

The first three of these theories have been particularly influential in shaping pedagogy, while situated cognition has helped us to theorise the impact of 'collective knowledge' on learning. They are outlined briefly below.

Cognitive developmental theory

Piaget

Jean Piaget was a Swiss psychologist who applied Gessell's (1925) concept of maturation (genetically programmed sequential pattern of changing physical characteristics) to cognitive growth. He saw intellectual and moral development as sequential, with the child moving through stages of thinking driven by an internal need to understand the world. His theory implied an investigative, experiential approach to learning.

According to Piaget, the stages through which the child's thinking moves and develops is linked to age. Piaget thus provides a criterion-referenced rather than norm-referenced explanation of cognitive development (Shayer 2008). From birth to about 2 years, children understand the world through feeling, seeing, tasting, and so on. Piaget called this the *sensory-motor* stage. As children grow older and mature, from about 2 to 6 years, they begin to understand that others have a viewpoint. They are increasingly able to classify objects into groups and to use symbols. Piaget termed this the *preoperational* stage.

The third stage, from 6 to about 12 years, identified by Piaget is the *concrete operational* stage. Children are still tied to specific experience but can do mental manipulations as well as physical ones. Powerful new internal mental operations become available, such as addition, subtraction and class inclusion. Logical thinking develops.

The final stage of development sees children manipulating ideas in their heads and able to consider events that haven't yet happened or think about things never seen. Children can now organise ideas and events systematically and can examine all possibilities. Deductive thinking becomes possible. Piaget suggested that this final stage, called the *formal operational* stage, begins at about 12 years of age.

The learner's stage of thinking interacts with experience of the world in a process called *adaptation*. The term *operations* is used to describe the strategies, skills and mental activities that children use in interacting with new experience. Thus, adding 2 and 2 together, whether mentally or on paper, is an operation. It is thought that discoveries are made sequentially, so, for example, adding and subtracting cannot be learned until objects are seen to be constant. Progress through the sequence of discoveries occurs slowly and at any one age children have a particular general view of the world, a logic or structure that dominates the way they explore the world. The logic changes as events are encountered that do not fit with their *schemata* (sets of ideas about objects or events). When major shifts in the structure of children's thinking occur, a new stage is reached. Central to Piaget's theory are the concepts of *assimilation*, taking in and adapting experience or objects to existing strategies or concepts, and *accommodation*, modifying and adjusting strategies or concepts as a result of new experiences or information (see Bee and Boyd 2013 for a full description of Piaget's theory).

The influence of stage theory

Piaget's work influenced the way in which some other psychologists developed their views. Kohlberg (1976) saw links between children's cognitive development and their moral reasoning, proposing a stage model of moral development (see also Unit 4.5). Selman (1980) was interested in the way children make relationships, describing a set of stages or levels they go through in forming friendships. Stage models of development were also posited in relation to personality growth, quite independently of Piaget's work. Influenced by Freud's (1901) psychoanalytic approach, Erikson's (1980) stages of psychosocial development explain the way in which an individual's self-concept develops, providing important insights into adolescent identity issues, such as role confusion. You may be aware of the fragility of an adolescent's self-concept, of the fundamental but often volatile nature of adolescent friendships and of the increased interest adolescents show in ethical issues. It is essential to consider these factors when planning for learning since they impact so heavily on pupils' motivation for, and capacity to engage with, lesson content. Research has identified the significance of teacher-pupil relationships for pupils' feelings of self-worth in relation to learning competence (see Bartlett and Burton 2016 for discussion of this), and an eight-year study by Davies and Brember (1999) showed significant correlations between self-esteem and attainment scores.

Jerome Bruner, a prolific American cognitive psychologist, also developed a stage model of the way people think about the world. He described three stages in learning: the enactive, iconic and symbolic. Unlike Piaget's stages, learners do not pass through and beyond Bruner's different stages of thinking. Instead, the stage or type of representation used depends on the type of thinking required of the situation. It is expected, however, that as pupils grow up, they make progressively greater use of symbolic representation (Bruner 1966).

The stress on the idea of 'stages' in Piaget's theory was far-reaching, especially the implication that pupils need to be at a particular developmental level in order to cope with certain learning tasks. However, research studies have substantially refuted such limitations on a pupil's thinking (Donaldson 1978). Thus, the construct of a staged model of cognitive maturation probably has less currency than the features of development described within the various stages. Flavell (1982), a former student of Piaget, argued that while stage notions of development are unhelpful, Piaget's ideas about the sequences learners go through are still valid. They can help teachers to examine the level of difficulty of topics and curriculum material as a way of deciding how appropriate they are for particular age groups and ability levels (see, for example, Unit 4.3, which discusses with examples aspects of cognitive development). The key task for teachers is to examine the progress of individuals in order to determine when to increase the intellectual demand on them. Bruner (1966) argued that difficult ideas should be seen as a challenge that, if properly presented, can be learned by most pupils.

Metacognitive awareness

Work by Adey and colleagues has revealed that learning potential is increased if pupils are metacognitively aware; that is, if they understand and can control their own learning strategies. These strategies include techniques for remembering, ways of presenting information when thinking, approaches to problems, and so on. Shayer and Adey developed a system of cognitive acceleration in science education (CASE; see Unit 4.3), which challenges pupils to examine the processes they use to solve problems (Adey 1992, 2008; Shayer and Adey 2002). In doing so, it is argued that pupils are enhancing their thinking processes. It was Flavell who first proposed the notion of metacognition, arguing that becoming 'aware of one's own "cognitive machinery" is a vital component of intelligence' (Flavell 1979: 907). It has become fashionable to refer to metacognition as 'learning to learn', and whole systems explaining to teachers how to achieve it are available (see, for example, Guy Claxton's long-established 'learning power' approach in Claxton 2002, 2015; Claxton *et al.* 2011; or a scheme for secondary schools by Best and O'Donnell 2011). Hall *et al.* (2006) suggest that this concept has potential for moving learning away from a curriculum and assessment dominated education system, and Hattie (2009) claims it enables learners to attain better outcomes.

It is argued that if pupils are helped by their teachers to become more reflective and aware of processes they are deploying, they are more able to take control of their learning and to achieve better outcomes. See, for example, Namrouti and Alshannag's (2004) study with Jordanian 7th graders, or Black *et al.*'s (2002) study in London, in which mathematics and science teachers' use of structured questioning and encouragement of pupils to discuss their understanding of concepts led to pupils of all abilities scoring higher in their national assessment tests or General Certificates of Secondary Education (GCSE) exams than pupils in ordinary lessons. Being metacognitively aware can be likened to having a commentator in the learner's mind who analyses and comments upon the methods they are using to learn a new concept or skill while the learning is happening. The transfer of learning between tasks can also be enhanced where the teacher cues learners into the specific skill being learned and encourages them to reflect on its potential for transfer (Anderson *et al.* 1996). Spada *et al.* (2006) found that taking a metacognitive approach with social science undergraduates reduced the tendency for their test anxiety to lead to a surface approach to their learning. See Goswami (2008) and the publications of her Centre for Neuroscience in Education for early research on metacognition and its relationship with reasoning, memory and cognitive development.

It seems, then, that the higher-order cognitive skills of Piaget's stage of formal operations can be promoted and encouraged through a focus on metacognition. Learners need, above all, to learn to learn, and teachers' endeavours would be more profitable if they concentrated on teaching pupils how to learn (Claxton 2002, 2015). Task 5.1.2 asks you to plan a lesson in which metacognitive strategies are introduced. The project 'Learning How to Learn', part of the 'Teaching and Learning Research Programme' (TLRP/ESRC 2006), confirms that emphasis should be placed on practices that have potential to promote autonomy in learning (Black *et al.* 2006). The ready availability of instant information via the Internet requires pupils to have the confidence and skills to sift through it and judge its utility and relevance to their work. See Wegerif *et al.*'s (2015) handbook for a number of chapters on metacognition and teaching creative thinking.

 Task 5.1.2 Analysing learning activities: learning how to learn

Consider how you can give pupils at least one opportunity during each lesson to think about the strategies they are using in their learning. Ask them, for instance, how they reached a particular conclusion, how they tackled the drawing of a 3D shape or how they would undertake a journey from point A to point B. Summarise your findings and file in your PDP.

Social constructivist theory

The ideas of Russian psychologist Lev Vygotsky and of Jerome Bruner in the USA have increasingly influenced educators in recent years. Vygotsky's work dates from between the 1920s and 1930s (he died in 1934). His most influential work, *Thought and Language*, was not available in English until 1962 (Vygotsky 1962).

Vygotsky

Juxtaposing Piaget's and Vygotsky's theories shows their 'common denominators as a child centred approach, an emphasis on action in the formation of thought, and a systematic understanding of psychological functioning', and their biggest difference as their understanding of psychological activity (Kozulin 1998: 34). For Vygotsky (1978), psychological activity has sociocultural characteristics from the very beginning of development. Conceptual understanding can be generated from a range of different stimuli, implying a problem-solving approach for pupils and a facilitator role for the teacher. Whereas Piaget considered language a tool of thought in the child's developing mind, for Vygotsky language was generated from the need to communicate and was central to the development of thinking. He emphasised the functional value of egocentric speech to verbal reasoning and self-regulation, and the importance of sociocultural factors in its development. His work has spawned much interest in sociocultural theory (Mercer and Littleton 2007), wherein thinking and learning are shaped by culture, and human development is understood by reference to its social and communicative form. In communicative talk, the development is not just in the language contrived to formulate the sentence, but also through the process of combining the words to shape the sentence because this shapes the thought itself (see resources on the University of Cambridge and Neil Mercer's *Thinking Together* website referenced at the end of this unit).

Thus, Vygotsky's work highlights the importance of talk as a learning tool and a number of important reports in the UK reinforced the status of talk in the classroom, highlighting its centrality to learning (Bullock Report 1975; Norman 1992). Vygotsky believed that such communicative instruction could reduce pupils' 'zone of proximal development' (ZPD); that is, the gap between their current level of learning and the level they could be functioning at with adult or peer support: 'What a child can do today in cooperation, tomorrow he will be able to do on his own' (Vygotsky 1962: 67). Social constructivism thus stresses the necessity for group interaction and adult intervention in consolidating learning and extending thinking. Many teachers are familiar with these key ideas, but Kutnick *et al.* (2002) cautioned that they may not think strategically about the size and composition of groups in relation to the tasks assigned, calling for educationalists once again to pay attention to the social pedagogy of pupil grouping (see Unit 4.1; DfE 2006). This issue was compounded in the UK by the requirement for whole-class teaching within the national literacy and numeracy strategies. Whole-class teaching tends to place the emphasis for talking with the teacher through whom all interactions are routed. Myhill (2006) (see also Unit 5.8) investigated the nature and quality of classroom discourse, how teachers use questions, how they capitalise on pupils' prior knowledge and how they help pupils become independent learners. She found that teacher discourse can variously support or impede pupil learning and that cognitive or conceptual connections in pupils' learning are often ignored. Task 5.1.3 invites you to investigate pupil talk in your lessons.

Unit 5.2 provides discussion and examples of active learning strategies that often involve pupil-teacher and pupil-pupil dialogue, both examples of strategies illustrating a Vygotskian approach to learning.

Task 5.1.3 Analysing learning activities: pupil talk

Review the advice for teachers on the University of Cambridge *Thinking Together* website and Professor Robin Alexander's *Dialogic Teaching* website. Consider how often you make opportunities for your pupils to talk in lessons, to each other, to you, to a digital or video recorder or via a DVD. Listen to how the talk develops the thinking of each member of a small group of pupils. Notice how well-timed and focused intervention from you moves the thinking on. Write up examples of showing the advantages of promoting pupil talk with your pupils; file the report in your PDP.

Bruner

Bruner also placed an emphasis on structured intervention within communicative learning models. He formulated a theory of instruction, central to which is the notion of systematic, structured pupil experience via a spiral curriculum where the learner returns to address increasingly complex components of a topic. Current and past knowledge is deployed as the pupil constructs new ideas or concepts. Thus, the problem of fractions in Year 5 will be tackled via many more concrete examples than when it is returned to in Year 7. Learning involves the active restructuring of knowledge through experience; the pupil selects and transforms information, constructs hypotheses and makes decisions, relying on a developing cognitive structure to do so.

Teachers should try to encourage pupils to discover principles by themselves through active dialogue with the teacher. Thus, for Bruner, the teacher's job is to guide this discovery through structured support (for example, by asking focused questions or providing appropriate materials); he called this process 'scaffolding' (Bruner 1983; Verenikina n.d.). The ideas of pupils emerging through their talk are scaffolded or framed by the teacher putting in 'steps' or questions at appropriate junctures. When hearing an idea emerge, the teacher can intervene by asking a question that requires the pupils to address that idea explicitly, which may help them find the solution.

Bruner argued that the scaffolding provided by the teacher should decrease in direct correspondence to the progress of the learner.

Wood (1988) developed Bruner's ideas, describing five levels of support that become increasingly specific and supportive in relation to the help needed by the pupil (see Table 5.1.1).

Having established the task the pupils are to complete, a teacher might give general verbal encouragement to the whole class and follow this up with specific verbal instruction to groups who need it, perhaps targeting individuals with guidance on strategies for approaching the task. Some

Table 5.1.1 Scaffolding: Bruner's levels of support

Five levels of support a teacher may use in scaffolding learning:

- general verbal encouragement;
- specific verbal instruction;
- assistance with pupil's choice of material or strategies;
- preparation of material for pupil assembly;
- demonstration of task.

pupils need physical help in performing the task and yet others need to be shown exactly what to do, probably in small stages. Thus, the different ways in which teachers support pupils is a further example of differentiation (see Unit 4.1). Scaffolding is also discussed in Unit 3.1.

The five levels of support above can help you think systematically about the nature of the support you should prepare for particular pupils, and to keep a check on whether the level is becoming more or less supportive. This has obvious relevance for differentiation in your classroom, workshop or gym. Task 5.1.4 addresses scaffolding and differentiation.

✎ Task 5.1.4 Analysing learning activities: scaffolding learning

Try scaffolding a pupil activity during a school placement.

- ■ How easy or difficult was it to work out when to intervene?
- ■ How far did the influence of an idea reflect the strength of the pupil's personality or the validity of the idea?
- ■ How did you, as the teacher, handle this without demotivating the pupil/pupils?

File your comments in your PDP.

Studies have warned of the dangers of casually incorporating 'scaffolding' into the professional lexicon as a proxy for generalised help or support rather than, as was originally intended, a very precise means of helping pupils master a specific task (Mercer and Littleton 2007). Furthermore, Russian neo-Vygotskians have argued that there has been considerable misunderstanding in educational circles of what Vygotsky said about ZPDs and about meaning being socially constructed (Goswami 2008). Teachers therefore need to heed Burton's (2007) warning that advances in communication technologies have led to the global popularisation of some psycho-pedagogical ideas that may not have been fully researched, and beware over-interpreting their impact within their classrooms. Now complete Task 5.1.5.

✎ Task 5.1.5 Analysing learning activities: differentiation

For a topic you are planning to teach, use Bruner's levels (Table 5.1.1) to prepare the type of support you think might be needed during the first lesson. Once you start teaching the topic, choose two particular pupils who need different levels of support. Plan the support for each one, lesson by lesson, noting whether they are requiring less or more support as the topic progresses. What does this tell you about the way you are teaching and the way the pupils are learning?

Choose an example of scaffolding you have used and write a report to discuss with other student teachers, your class teacher or tutor. File the report and comments in your PDP.

Constructivism

Another theory of learning, called 'constructivism', is that described by Driver and Bell (1986). While sharing a Brunerian and Vygotskyan emphasis on the social construction of meaning, constructivism places much more importance on learners' individual conceptions and gives them responsibility for directing their own learning experiences. Thus, pupils construct meaning for themselves from their experiences and do not learn ready-made knowledge; they already have explanations for events and phenomena in the world from their own experience. These explanations may conflict with accepted views, thus raising the importance of knowing about your pupil's prior knowledge. The pupil's prior understanding has to accommodate new experiences, such as that provided by the school curriculum. The pupil then has to accommodate the new experiences. Development of knowledge and understanding thus becomes a dynamic process constantly changing in response to new experiences. This process creates a demand on the pupil's willingness to accommodate new knowledge, thus motivation becomes a challenge. One useful teaching strategy is 'cognitive conflict', moving the pupil from a comfortable state of understanding to an uncertain state by providing experiences that challenge that current understanding. Constructivism implies that understanding is the goal, not just recall of knowledge, which, unless placed in an explanatory framework, may soon be forgotten. It is this framework that the pupil has to construct and develop. It is in the science subject area that constructivist ideas have been most influential (Levinson 2005a: 95–100). Naylor and Keogh (1999), for instance, devised concept cartoons that strike at the very heart of learners' misconceptions about scientific ideas in an effort to help them rethink the problem. (For examples of concept cartoons, see the UK National STEM Centre (2015) (now STEM learning)).

In the constructivist approach, little emphasis is placed on the role of instruction; rather, the teacher must create situations that facilitate individuals constructing their own knowledge. According to Liang and Gabel (2005), the teacher is expected to support, guide and facilitate rather than perform the functions of teaching, information providing and information transferring. Pupils synthesise new information according to their former knowledge, experiences, belief and attitudes, and then shape the information and find their own meanings within it rather than simply receiving the information (Seker 2008). If pupils harbour misconceptions, they must be helped to take them apart at the root since long-held conceptions are very difficult to shake off and are resistant to change even when teachers and others explain the error. Constructivism emphasises the need to give learners responsibility for directing their own learning experiences (Seker 2008).

Information processing theory (IP theory), including rote learning

This approach to learning originated within explanations of perception and memory processes and was influenced by the growth of computer technology. The basic idea is that the brain attends to sensory information as it is experienced, analyses it within the short-term memory (STM) and stores it with other related concepts in the long-term memory (LTM).

Psychologists saw the functioning of computers as replicating the behaviour of the brain in relation to the processing of information. Information is analysed in the STM and stored with existing related information in the LTM. This process is more efficient if material can be stored as abstractions of experience rather than as verbatim events. If I ask you to tell me the six times table, you recite 'one six is six, two sixes are twelve', and so on. You do not explain to me the mathematical principle of multiplication by a factor of six. On the other hand, if I ask you the meaning of the term 'economic enterprise', it is unlikely that you will recite a verbatim answer. Instead, your STM searches your LTM for your 'schema' or idea of enterprise. You then articulate your abstracted understanding of the term, which may well be different from that of the person next to you. In terms of intellectual challenge, articulating the second answer requires greater mental effort, although knowing one's multiplication tables is a very useful tool. Thus, teachers need to be absolutely clear that there is a good reason for requiring pupils to learn something by rote, because rote learning is not inherently meaningful so cannot be stored in LTM with other related information. Rather, it must be stored in its full form, taking up a lot of 'disk' space in the memory. Information stored in this way is analysed only superficially in STM; the pupil does not have to think hard to make connections with other pieces of information. For further information about information processing theory, see Unit 5.3.

It can often be difficult in secondary schools for teachers to determine precisely the prior knowledge of their pupils. You observe that good teachers cue learners in to their prior knowledge by asking questions about what was learned the lesson before or giving a brief resume of the point reached in a topic. Such strategies are very important because if previous learning has been effective, information is stored by pupils in their LTMs and needs to be retrieved. Seminal psychological work established that learning is more effective (that is, more likely to be understood and retained) if material is introduced to pupils according to the inherent conceptual structure of the topic (Ausubel 1968; Gagné 1977). By this is meant identifying the basic concepts that need to be taught first, then broadening the concepts to widen their application, thus introducing new concepts. To understand, for example, momentum, you need to understand mass and velocity (which in turn requires an understanding of speed and direction), and so on. Concept maps can reflect the conceptual structure of a topic. Information that is stored using a logical structure is easier to recall because the brain can process it more easily in the first instance, linking the new ideas to ones that already exist in the memory. As a teacher, this requires you to have thought through the structure in advance, and to know how the concepts fit together, hence the importance of spending time on schemes of work even where these are already produced for you. See Task 5.1.6 and concept maps in Unit 5.2. Contrast this point of view and practice with the textbook/workbook approach used in Finland (see Unit 7.4).

This emphasis on structure and sequence can be found perhaps most readily in the teaching of modern foreign languages (MFL) and mathematics. In MFL, for instance, teachers encourage recognition and acquisition of vocabulary first, followed by the construction of spoken and written sentences. This approach might be described as moving from the general to the specific. Thus, in mathematics, we start with number recognition, moving to the general concepts of addition, subtraction and multiplication, and on to more specific computations such as calculating area, solving equations or estimating probabilities.

Concept development

It is helpful to consider briefly how information processing relates to concept development. The material held in the LTM is stored as sets of ideas known as 'schemata' ('schema' is the singular). A schema is a mental structure abstracted from experience. It consists of a set of expectations with which to categorise and understand new stimuli. For example, our schema of 'school' consists of expectations of pupils, teachers, classrooms, and so on. As teachers, our school schema has been refined and developed as more and more information has been added and categorised. Thus, it

Task 5.1.6 Structuring a topic for effective learning

Choose a topic from your subject area, one covering some four to six lessons and one you are expecting to teach. For a couple of minutes, think freely about some of the ideas contained within it, jotting them down haphazardly on paper. Now think about how those ideas fit together and whether, in teaching the topic, you would start with the general overarching ideas and then move to the specific ones, or vice versa.

You can organise your topic by drawing up a conceptual hierarchy of it like the one started below for a personal, social and health education (PSHE) topic. This hierarchy moves from the general to the specific.

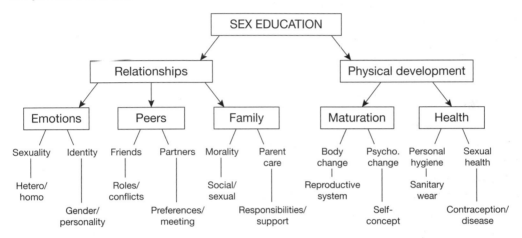

Give your completed structure to other student teachers in your subject for comment. Use their responses to finalise your hierarchy, adding notes for clarification as needed.

From the school's scheme of work (SoW), identify the topic and the lessons that are related to it. Sketch out the sequence of ideas in the SoW and identify how the teaching is organised, from general to specific, or vice versa. Compare the sequencing of ideas in your framework and that in the SoW.

Try to account for the differences and discuss them with your subject tutor. How are the differences explained? Are they to do with an understanding of the topic, or related to the ways pupils respond to the topic, or a practical issue to do with resources?

Write an account of the study, including implications for the way you approach teaching this topic. File in your PDP.

includes expectations about hierarchies, pupil culture, staffroom behaviour, and so on. It is probable that our school schema is different from, and more complex than, the school schema held by a parent, simply because of our involvement in schools.

When children are young, their schemata do not allow them to differentiate between pieces of information in the way that those of older pupils do. A one year old's schema of dog might include expectations about cats too because they have insufficient experience of the two animals to know them apart. As they experience cats as furry, dogs as hairy, cats meowing, dogs barking, and so on, greater differentiation is possible. Since the object of school learning is to promote pupils' concept differentiation in a range of different subjects, teachers should encourage comparison between objects or ideas and introduce new ideas by reference to concrete examples. Even as adults, while we can think abstractly, we find new ideas easier to grasp if we can be given concrete examples of them. Teaching in the context of IP theories stresses the application of knowledge and skills to new situations. The teacher's role is to help pupils find new ways of recalling previous knowledge, solving problems, formulating hypotheses, and so on. Critical thinking tasks in which learners have to wrestle with new ideas and issues are important in encouraging connections to be made between areas of subject knowledge or experience. Rote learning, copying information from a book or taking dictated notes from the teacher are very unsuitable for promoting concept development.

We have discussed cognitive development theories, social constructivist theories and information processing theories. In each of these theories about how learning occurs, there has been an emphasis on the individual and the differences between them. Looking at what is known about how learners' styles and strategies differ equips us further to understand individual differences.

Learning styles, strategies and approaches

You may encounter teachers who try to identify whether learners are predominantly visual, auditory or kinaesthetic learners (VAK) (Dryden and Vos 2001). However, there are a number of such classifications based on different constructs and using a range of measurement tools. Some of these ideas, such as the VAK construct and preferred environmental conditions or stimuli for learning, have been incorporated along with a range of other ideas, such as neurolinguistic programming, into accelerated learning programmes such as that of Alastair Smith (Smith and Call 2002). Such approaches were readily embraced at first but have since been heavily critiqued (see, for example, Burton 2007). See also Unit 5.6 for a perspective from neuroscientists.

It can be attractive to feel that we can categorise pupils into fixed learning approaches or styles and then teach to a formula that such a categorisation suggests. However, we know that learning is complex and context-dependent, with pupils employing different approaches in different settings. It is important that you take an eclectic approach to learning style classification and measurement lest you too readily pigeonhole pupils and fail to provide a range of approaches to learning, including choice of activities and resources to maximise access for all to the curriculum. In this section, you are introduced to categorisations that have been researched over a considerable number of years, but for a full overview of the range of research in this area, consult Riding and Rayner (1998), and for a systematic review of 71 different constructs, see Coffield *et al.* (2004a, 2004b). As Coffield (2008) has complained:

> the learning styles movement has muddied the waters by producing endless dichotomies such as 'pragmatists' v 'theorists', 'field independent' v 'field dependent' learners, and 'left' v 'right brainers'. Most of these terms have no scientific justification whatsoever; nevertheless too many tutors succumb to the intuitive appeal of these pseudo-scientific concepts.
>
> (Coffield 2008: 33)

There is often confusion about what constitutes learning style as distinct from learning strategy. The *cognitive* or *learning style* may be a fairly fixed characteristic of an individual, is static and a relatively in-built feature of them (Riding and Cheema 1991). In contrast, *learning strategies* are the ways learners cope with situations and tasks. Strategies may vary from time to time and may be learned and developed (see also Unit 5.3 on teaching styles).

Learning style

Understanding how in-built features of learners affect the way they process information is important for you as a student teacher. Riding and Cheema (1991) studied a huge number of cognitive and learning style constructs developed by a range of established psychological researchers. They proposed that learning styles may be grouped into two principal cognitive styles. The first, the *wholist-analytic style*, identifies whether an individual tends to process information in wholes (wholist) or in parts (analytics). The second, known as the *verbal-imagery style*, describes whether an individual is inclined to represent information during thinking verbally (verbalist) or in mental pictures (imagers) (Riding and Rayner 1998).

The two styles operate as dimensions, so a person may be at either end of the dimension or somewhere along it. Think about what your own learning style might be. Do you:

- Approach essay writing incrementally, step by step, piecing together the various parts, or do you like to have a broad idea of the whole essay before you start writing?
- Experience lots of imagery when you are thinking about something, or do you find yourself thinking in words?

Discuss your style with other student teachers. In doing so, you are developing your metacognitive knowledge about your own way of learning.

These styles are involuntary, so it is important to be aware that your classes contain pupils whose habitual learning styles vary. You need to ensure that you provide a variety of ways in which pupils can work and be assessed. It would not be sensible to present information only in written form; if illustrations are added, this allows both 'verbalisers' and 'imagers' easier access to it. Similarly, 'wholist' pupils are assisted by having an overview of the topic before starting while 'analytics' benefit from summaries after they have been working on information.

This is not to suggest that you must determine the style of each pupil, but that there must be opportunities for all pupils to work in the way that is most profitable for them. Unlike the way in which intelligence quotient (IQ) is used, the higher the IQ score, the better the performance is expected, the determination of learning style does not imply that one way of processing is better than another. The key to success is in allowing learners to use their natural processing style. It is important for you to be aware of your own style because teachers have been found to promote the use of approaches that fit most easily with their own styles.

Learning strategy

Learning strategy describes the ways in which learners cope with tasks or situations. These strategies develop and change as the pupil becomes more experienced. Kolb's work describing two dimensions of learning strategy is the most widely known in the area of strategy theory (Kolb 1976, 1985). Kolb envisaged a cyclical sequence through four 'stages' of learning (concrete experience, reflective observation, abstract conceptualisation, active experimentation) arising from the interaction of two dimensions (see Figure 5.1.1). The east-west dimension represents 'processing' (how we approach

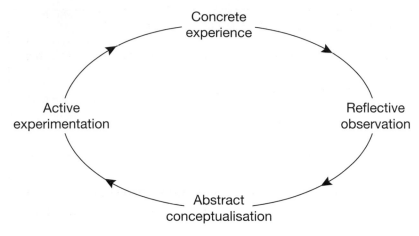

Figure 5.1.1 Kolb's experiential learning cycle

Source: Adapted from Kolb (1985: 21)

a task) and the north-south dimension 'perceiving' (our emotional response, or how we think or feel about it). Kolb argued that these two dimensions interact, and that although learners use preferred strategies, they could be trained to develop aspects of other strategies through experiential learning. Thus, Kolb suggests that learners need, at the concrete experience stage, to immerse themselves in new experiences. Learners reflect on these experiences from as many perspectives as possible at what Kolb calls the reflective observation stage. This reflection enables the learner to create concepts that integrate their observations into logically sound theories at the abstract conceptualisation stage, which are then used to make decisions and solve problems at the active experimentation stage (Fielding 1996). Learners have a predilection for one of the stages, so it can be argued that when you are planning a sequence of lessons around a topic, learners should be provided with experiences that ensure that they use each of the stages in the cycle at some time, in addition to their preferred one.

Indeed, without involving pupils in each of the stages, deep learning (higher-order learning) may not emerge (cf. Bloom's taxonomy of educational objectives, in Anderson and Krathwohl 2001). Kolb's work continues to be influential, and a study by Kayes (2005) confirmed the reliability and validity of his assessment instrument, the Learning Style Inventory (for an example of an assessment instrument, see http://clinteach.com.au/assets/LEARNING-STYLES-Kolb-QUESTIONNAIRE.pdf).

Try Task 5.1.7.

Learning approaches

Other researchers are interested in the motivations and attitudes pupils and students bring to their learning, described as 'approaches to learning'. Researchers have investigated learners' approaches to study and how learning approaches interact with learning strategies (Biggs 1978, 1987, 1993, 2001; Entwistle 1981, 1993; Entwistle *et al.* 2001).

Entwistle described different orientations to learning, such as being oriented towards discovering the meaning of a topic or being oriented simply to scratch the surface. Combinations of these orientations with extrinsic factors, such as the need to pass examinations or the love of a subject,

Task 5.1.7 What is your preferred strategy for learning?

Try to work out which stage of Kolb's cycle describes the way you learn yourself most of the time (see Figure 5.1.1).

Think about how you process information; for example:

■ Are you more comfortable reflecting on ideas where you have had lots of concrete experience?
■ Do you prefer to draw from abstract theory and experiment with it to solve problems?

Do you think Kolb's ideas could help you to process information differently? Would it be helpful to 'practise' different ways? What are the implications for your work with pupils? Record your ideas in your PDP.

were thought to lead to learning strategies that characterised certain approaches to study, from 'deep' to 'surface' levels of thinking.

A pupil's approach is a function of both motive and strategy and motives influence learning strategies (Biggs 1993). Thus, a pupil with an instrumental (surface) motive is likely to adopt reproducing or rote learning (surface) strategies. Deep motive results from an intrinsic desire to learn and can inspire the use of deep strategies, emphasising understanding and meaning. An achieving motive might be an egotistical need to pass examinations; from this perspective, the learner can derive achieving strategies that stress time management, well-ordered resources and efficiency.

Pupils whose motives and strategies are compatible with the demands made by learning tasks are likely to perform well. Pupils are likely to be less successful where motives and strategy are incompatible with task demand. For example, a pupil with a deep approach to learning is constrained by superficial task design such as a requirement for short answers, whereas a pupil with an achieving motive may be deterred if set very long-term objectives or vague objectives. Task 5.1.8 invites you to investigate your own approaches to learning.

Successful learning, if defined in terms of understanding and permanence, is linked with deep approaches that achieve higher-order thinking, which can be taught. A number of researchers have stressed the impact of social and cultural environment on learning approaches; Phan and Deo (2007) further confirmed this finding in two large-scale studies in the South Pacific region.

  Task 5.1.8 Your own approaches to learning

Refer to the paragraphs above on learning approaches. Do you recognise any of these learning approaches in relation to your own learning? Do your motives and associated learning strategies stay the same over time or do they depend on the task and the reason you are completing it? In your PDP, record some notes on your own ways of learning for discussion with your tutor.

The achievement-driven context within which secondary school pupils in England currently learn, for instance, could militate against the possibility of teaching deep approaches because of time constraints. Greater use of individualised learning, facilitated by technology, may encourage the use of deep approaches to learning if pupils have the time and autonomy to pursue a topic in depth. Currently, there are worries that the use of the Internet develops a surface approach, with learners simply cutting and pasting from unregulated information sites.

What the vast array of research into styles, strategies and approaches tells us is *not* that you need to identify every learner's distinctive profile, but that you should endeavour to maintain variety in the learning experiences you design for pupils, in the ways you present information, in the resources pupils use and the tasks they undertake, and in the ways you assess their progress.

SUMMARY AND KEY POINTS

- The importance of developing your own models of learning and refining these as you gain more experience of pupils and learning contexts has been established.
- You continually draw on your knowledge of the pupils, of the subject and of how learning happens in the teaching process.
- The symbiosis between theoretical positions and pedagogic practices has been emphasised. For instance, concept development is enhanced where pupils are introduced to new ideas via concrete examples and retention is aided if topics are taught according to their inherent conceptual structure.

The key features of cognitive development, social constructivism and information processing theories, as they apply to pupil learning, have been outlined and your attention has been drawn to the implications of learning style and strategy for teaching techniques. The benefits of adopting a facilitative, interventionist approach and of aiming for a variety of approaches in presentation, resource, task and assessment can be extrapolated from all the theories that have been discussed. Learning is likely to be most effective where pupils are actively involved with the material through critical thinking, discussion with others and metacognitive awareness of their own learning strategies.

Check which requirements for your ITE programme you have addressed through this unit.

 ## Further reading

Bartlett, S.J. and Burton, D.M. (2016) *Introduction to Education Studies*, 4th edn, London: Sage.
  Chapters 8 and 9 provide a full outline of major psychological theories and contemporary psychological research into how pupils learn.

Bee, H. and Boyd, D. (2013) *The Developing Child*, 13th edn, Boston, MA: Pearson Education.
  This excellent text covers all aspects of human development. The latest edition of this classic brings the research right up to date.

DfE (Department for Education) (2006) *Grouping Pupils for Success: National Literacy and Numeracy Strategies*, available at: http://webarchive.nationalarchives.gov.uk/20110809101133/http://wsassets.s3.amazonaws.com/ws/nso/pdf/bbd59a99cf4ad4a66ac8a25069a72063.pdf

Long, M., Wood, C., Littleton, K., Passenger, T. and Sheehy, K. (2010) *Psychology of Education*, London: Routledge.
   Written in an accessible and engaging style, key concepts from psychology that relate to education are addressed together with practical suggestions to improve learning outcomes and opportunities to apply your theoretical knowledge to real-world contexts.

Riding, R. (2002) *School Learning and Cognitive Styles*, London: David Fulton.
   Incorporating psychological developments on individual learning differences with practical classroom applications, Riding shows how processing capacity, cognitive style and understanding the structure of knowledge are central to our understanding of pupil differences and how pupils can be helped to learn, why pupils find some aspects of their schoolwork difficult, and why pupils behave as they do.

Verenikina, n. (n.d.) *Understanding Scaffolding and the ZPD in Educational Research*, University of Wollongong, NSW, Australia, available at: http://ro.uow.edu.au/cgi/viewcontent.cgi?article=1695andcontext=edupaper

Wegerif, R., Li, L. and Kaufman, J.C. (eds) (2015) *The Routledge International Handbook of Research on Teaching Thinking*, London and New York: Routledge.
   A comprehensive guide to research on teaching thinking in a range of contexts. Key topics include: approaches for teaching thinking; developing creative thinking; metacognition; and neuroeducational research on teaching thinking.

Other resources and websites

The titles of these websites give a clear indication of the information they cover that relates to the discussion in the text:

Alexander, R. (2015) *Dialogic Teaching*: www.robinalexander.org.uk/dialogic-teaching/

Claxton, G. (2015) *Building Learning Power*: www.buildinglearningpower.co.uk/

Centre for Neuroscience in Education led by Professor Usha Goswami: www.cne.psychol.cam.ac.uk/people/ ucg10@cam.ac.uk

Gardner, H. (2015) *Multiple Intelligences*: http://howardgardner.com/multiple-intelligences/

National STEM Centre (2015) *Concept Cartoons*: www.nationalstemcentre.org.uk/ellbrary/resource/1482/ concept-cartoons

Noble, T. (n.d.) *Integrating the Revised Bloom's Taxonomy with Multiple Intelligences: A Planning Tool for Curriculum Differentiation*, National Australian Catholic University: www.bounceback.com.au/sites/ default/files/Integrating%20the%20Revised%20Bloom%E2%80%99s%20Taxonomy%20With%20Mul tiple%20Intelligences_0.pdf

Stanford University (2015) *Teaching Commons: Bloom's Taxonomy of Educational Objectives*: https:// teachingcommons.stanford.edu/resources/course-preparation-resources/course-design-aids/bloom %E2%80%99s-taxonomy-educational-objectives

TLRP (Teaching and Learning Research Programme) (2006) *Learning How to Learn – in Classrooms, Schools and Networks*: www.tlrp.org/pub/documents/no17_james.pdf

University of Cambridge/Professor Neil Mercer (2015) *Thinking Together*: http://thinkingtogether.educ.cam. ac.uk/resources/

Appendix 2 on pages 591–595 provides further examples of websites you may find useful.

Capel, S., Leask, M. and Turner, T. (eds) (2010) *Readings for Learning to Teach in the Secondary School: A Companion to M Level Study*, London: Routledge.
   This book brings together essential readings to support you in your critical engagement with key issues raised in this textbook.

The subject-specific books in the Routledge *Learning to Teach* series are also very useful.

Any additional resources and an editable version of any relevant tasks/tables in this unit are available on the companion website: www.routledge.com/cw/capel

5.2 Active learning

Michelle Lowe

Introduction

As a teacher, one of your most important tasks is to encourage the development of pupils' understandings of key curriculum 'concepts'. Vygotsky (1986) provided a definition of a concept that can help us understand the role teachers must play in the process:

> a concept is more than the sum of certain associative bonds formed by memory, more than a mere mental habit; it is a complex and genuine act of thought that cannot be taught by drilling but can be accomplished only when the child's mental development itself has reached the requisite level.
>
> Practical experience also shows that direct teaching of concepts is impossible and fruitless. A teacher who tries to do this usually accomplishes nothing but empty verbalisation, a parrot like repetition of words by the child, simulating knowledge of the corresponding concepts but actually covering up a vacuum.
>
> (Vygotsky 1986: 149-50)

The quotation suggests that a teacher cannot do the learning for the pupil, and that in order for understanding to occur, the pupil has to be active in the learning process.

This unit addresses ways in which you can help pupils to become active learners through providing active learning in your classroom. Some writers argue that active learning underpins 'deep learning', as opposed to 'surface learning', which is learning with little understanding. They argue that 'deep learning' is the only meaningful learning (see Unit 5.1 for detailed references). Active learning underpins meaningful learning because it enables learners to develop knowledge of the subject taught and skills for learning, including the ability to reflect on the processes involved in that learning.

In this unit, learning is defined in the first section, then active learning, and then there is a discussion of different forms of learning that can be related to active learning: lifelong learning, deep learning, learning to learn, discovery learning, rote learning and aids to recall. The unit concludes with a section on directed activities relating to texts (DART).

> **OBJECTIVES**
>
> At the end of this unit, you should be able to:
>
> ■ explain the term 'active learning' and discuss the advantages of active learning to the teacher and the learner;
> ■ be aware of ways of embedding active learning in the classroom;
> ■ consider the use of resources to support active learning in your lessons.
>
> Check the requirements for your initial teacher education (ITE) programme to see which relate to this unit.

What do we mean by 'learning'?

Before we can begin to understand what active learning might be and why we should want to encourage it we need to think about what 'learning' is.

Säljö (1979) carried out an interview study in which he asked a group of adults what learning meant to them. Analyses of the transcripts produced five qualitatively different conceptions. Learning was seen as:

1 a quantitative increase in knowledge
2 memorising
3 acquisition of facts, methods, etc. that can be retained and used
4 the abstraction of meaning
5 an interpretative process aimed at understanding reality.

In general terms, the first two types of learning can be described as *surface* learning or *atomistic* learning in which learning focuses on specifics, on details, and on memorising facts without necessarily understanding the whole message or concept. This type of learning is essentially passive, and is often associated with learning environments where the learners see the aim of learning as fulfilling requirements of the course; in order to pass the exam; or in order to please the teacher (see Unit 5.1).

The last two types of learning can broadly be described as *deep* or *holistic* learning that is characterised by a search for meaning that demands an active engagement with the learning and leads to a broader understanding of the whole topic (see Unit 5.1 for detail). It involves the learner in realising that the study deals with some aspect of the real world that the learner is trying to understand more fully.

A number of writers have since added a sixth level of learning (for example, Mezirow 1997): changing as a person, which reflects the fact that learning at its deepest level changes the pupil's perception of reality, and therefore changes them as a person.

Case studies: two pupils learning mathematics

Manjeet and Robert are two pupils in Year 9. They are taught the same syllabus at the same school and complete the same activities and assignments but with different teachers. They had similar scores on entry from primary school. Here's what they have to say about one of the subjects they take.

Robert: I enjoy maths because I can think, which is not something I always do in other subjects. I try to see the maths that is being taught in other areas as well. For example, I use it at home to help my younger brother and when I go to town with my friends. I'm the one who always manages to save money and get deals! I like watching TV programmes too, there are quite a few now about maths . . . it's really interesting to find out where our maths comes from. All the time I like to think about how it links to what we've been doing in class. It's funny because I never liked maths in my primary school, but I do now. I even do the homework, and ask the teacher for some additional work. I also try to make up sums and problems of my own. The way I work is to try to understand the information first, then try it out. If I don't understand, I will ask the teacher, or a friend, or my mum, she's good with maths! I think that someone who is not so good at maths would struggle a bit. You know, to get interested in it. To find different ways to understand it. In our class, we do a lot of group discussions and pair work and the teacher really makes us think by asking some very difficult questions. She also lets us work on our own by getting us to do investigations and surveys and looking on the Internet. It must work because I passed the latest tests and I'm predicted to get a good grade in General Certificate of Secondary Education (GCSE).

Manjeet: The way I do it is to keep trying the same activity until I get it right, you know, trying different techniques to solve the same problem. I know I have to get the maths right because my parents say it will be useful for me in the future to get a good job. I usually try to write down formulas and learn them by heart. I always do the classwork and homework the teacher has given me so I can get a good enough mark but I only spend a short time on it as I like to go out with my friends. The lessons are usually the same. The teacher explains something to us, then shows us some examples on the board. Then we usually have to do some exercises from a textbook or worksheet. We usually work on our own. Sometimes we do past test papers as practices, but I didn't do well on the last one!

Task 5.2.1 helps you to reflect further on the different perceptions of learning that Robert and Manjeet have.

 Task 5.2.1 Two pupils' experiences of mathematics

Discuss with other student teachers the observations made by these pupils from the standpoint of: (1) their response to the tasks set and possible reasons for these responses; and (2) the way the tasks may have been set by their teachers.

Record your findings in your professional development portfolio (PDP).

The responses of Robert and Manjeet suggest two important things. The first of these is that they experience mathematics differently. They appear to approach their learning in two qualitatively different ways. Robert appears to take a deep approach to his work, while Manjeet appears to adopt a shallow (surface) approach. Nevertheless, Manjeet's willingness to try different ways of solving problems is a positive feature of his attitude to work. Those who take a deep approach tend to have an intrinsic interest in the topic and the tasks, and aim to understand and seek meaning. They adopt strategies that help them to satisfy their curiosity and to look for patterns and connections in other areas. They think about the task. Those who adopt a surface approach see tasks as work given to them by others. They are pragmatically motivated and seek to meet the demands of the task with the minimum of effort (Entwistle 1990; Prosser and Trigwell 1999).

We suggest that Robert is engaged mainly in active learning and Manjeet is engaged more in passive learning. This may mean that Robert is able to think abstractly and is actively involved in the process of learning. This may involve, for example, learning through doing, trying things out, getting it wrong and knowing why. It is not just the learner's attitude, but the way the task is set. Active learning has to be encouraged. Perhaps the way Manjeet engages with the subject is as much to do with the way the lessons are taught and the learning structured as it is with Manjeet's own approach to learning.

What is active learning?

Active learning draws from the theories of learning that were outlined in Unit 5.1, perhaps taking the best from each!

Active learning occurs when a learner takes some responsibility for the development of the activity, emphasising that a sense of ownership and personal involvement is the key to successful learning.

Unless the work that learners do is seen to be important to them and to have purpose and unless their ideas, contributions and findings are valued, little of benefit is learned.

Active learning can also be defined as purposeful interaction with ideas, concepts and phenomena, and can involve reading, writing, listening, talking or working with tools, equipment and materials, such as paint, wood, chemicals, and so on. In a simple sense, it is learning by doing, by contrast with being told.

Active learning may be linked to experiential learning. Experiential learning is also learning by doing but with the additional feature of reflection upon both action and the results of action; only where pupils are 'engaged actively and purposively in their own learning is the term experiential appropriate' (Addison and Burgess 2007: 35-6). Both active and experiential learning contribute to meaningful learning.

Active learning strategies benefit both teachers and pupils. As a teacher, they enable you to spend more time with groups or individuals, which allows better-quality formative assessment and feedback to take place (both of these are key features of 'assessment for learning'; see Unit 6.1; Procter 2013). Active learning can also enhance your support for learners with special educational needs (see Unit 4.6 on special educational needs; Blamires 2014). Activity methods encourage autonomous learning and problem-solving skills, important to both academic and vocationally based work. There is, of course, an extra demand on you in the planning and preparation of lessons. The advantages of active learning to pupils include greater personal satisfaction, more interaction with peers, promotion of shared activity and team work, greater opportunities to work with a range of pupils, and opportunities for all members of the class to contribute and respond. It can encourage mutual respect and appreciation of the viewpoint of others (see also Unit 5.5 on personalising learning).

It is important to realise that learning by doing, by itself, is not enough to ensure learning. The proverb 'Tell me, I will forget. Show me, I may remember. Involve me, and I will understand' at the beginning of Unit 1.1 was reformulated by a prominent educationalist as 'I do and I am even more confused' (Driver 1983: 9). The essential step to learning and understanding is reflection through discussion with others, especially the teacher; such discussions involve 'thinking' as well as recalling; that is, experiential learning.

Matt, a newly qualified teacher, articulates his experience of trying to embed active learning in his classroom:

A NEWLY QUALIFIED TEACHER'S VIEW ON IMPLEMENTING ACTIVE LEARNING

It was difficult to understand this aspect when I began teaching. Of course you want to plan lessons that engage pupils but the English National Curriculum almost implies that as a teacher you have to 'put on a show' in order to have exciting and stimulating lessons. What I realised very soon was that entertainment isn't the focus. If you take that approach, you cannot do it for every lesson you teach. Using the principals of active learning made a real difference. When I started to think about how I structure activities to maximise each pupil's engagement and activity in the learning, I noticed that their attainment and achievement also improved. It takes time to become familiar with all of the different active learning strategies, and I think you need to introduce them carefully and build them up over time in the classroom. Now I have a range of strategies I can use and nothing beats the buzz of seeing pupils actively engaged in their own learning.

Lifelong learning

Some writers believe that building the individual's capacity to learn should be the main focus of education in our schools. Guy Claxton (2002, 2015) argues that in order for this to happen, the following principles should be taken into account:

- The focus for learning should move from predominance on content to predominance on the learning process itself.
- Learners should be given the skills needed to learn under any conditions.
- Learners should be equipped with a range of learning methods, some rational and precise, some experimental or even unconscious.
- Learners must be made aware of their own learning process (TLRP 2006).

In his work, Claxton has described four characteristics of expert, lifelong learners, commonly referred to as the four Rs.

Claxton's four Rs are resilience, resourcefulness, reflectiveness, reciprocity:

- *Resilience* describes the learners' enjoyment of learning and their ability to resist distraction and persevere with their learning, despite setbacks.
- *Resourcefulness* refers to the learners' ability to look more deeply into issues and question taken-for-granted assumptions.

■ *Reflectiveness* is about the learners' ability to consider and adjust approaches and concepts in the light of changing understandings and information.

■ *Reciprocity* encompasses the learners' ability to contribute to and learn from others' understandings and approaches.

Task 5.2.2 asks you to apply these ideas.

 Task 5.2.2 The four Rs

Think of a lesson you have taught recently and answer the following questions on it:

1   What opportunities were there in the lesson for the pupils to display or develop skills in the four Rs?
2   How could you adapt the lesson, or series of lessons, to enable pupils to develop or improve one or two of these characteristics as appropriate?

Record your notes in your PDP.

Active learning encourages the development of the four Rs in learners. A similar approach has been taken by Hargreaves (2005), who has argued that the best schools personalise learning to ensure that 'deep learning' happens. Most schools recognise that enabling pupils to perform well in exams is only a part of their wider educational purpose (see Unit 7.1 on aims of education). Schools are increasingly seeking to support the development of their pupils as learners equipped for the twenty-first-century world in which being a lifelong learner is paramount. 'Deep learning' is best developed through encouraging pupil voice, assessment for learning (Procter 2013) and learning to learn (TLRP 2006). See also Unit 5.1. In addition, Hargreaves identified the importance of 'deep experience', arguing that pupil engagement was the key to better relationships between staff and pupils, and was a prerequisite for the development of good learners who possess independence, responsibility, confidence and maturity.

Learning how to learn (see also metacognition in Units 4.3, 5.1, 5.5 and 6.1)

Learning how to learn is a feature of active learning (TLRP 2006). By promoting activities that engage pupils and require them to participate in the task from the outset, teachers encourage an approach to learning that is both skills-based and attitude-based. Active learning methods promote habits of learning that it is hoped are valuable in the workplace, the home and generally enhance pupils' capacity to cope with everyday life. School can be a place where pupils learn to do things well and in certain ways, thereby developing skills that are used throughout life. For example, pupils learn to consult a dictionary or a thesaurus in book form, as part of a word processing program or online in order to find meanings or to check their spelling and grammar. These skills become habits, capable of reinforcement and development. Reinforcement leads to improved performance. However, unless teachers can engage pupils with their need to know, learning is done under sufferance, leading to problems. Such problems may include poor recall of anything learned or rejection of learning tasks, which in turn may lead to behaviour problems.

Active learning, discovery learning and rote learning

Discovery learning

Discovery learning at its simplest occurs when pupils are left to discover things for themselves. This is a common approach taken with younger learners but in the secondary school a more structured framework is often used to facilitate learning. This is called 'guided discovery'.

But is the intention of guided discovery that pupils come to some predetermined conclusion or is it that learning should take place but the outcomes vary from pupil to pupil? You need to be clear about your reason for adopting guided discovery methods. If the intention in discovery learning is to move pupils to a specific end point, then as discovery it could be challenged. This approach might preclude, for example, considering other knowledge that surfaced in the enquiry. If discovery learning focuses on how the knowledge was gained, then the activity is concerned with processes; that is, how to discover and how to learn. The question is one of means and ends. Are discovery methods then concerned with discovery as 'process', learning how to learn? Or discovery as 'motivation', a better way to learn predetermined knowledge and skills and to support personalised learning with pupil and teacher working together to set the direction of open-ended work? Or is it discovery as 'change in self', learning something about yourself as a teacher and using this knowledge to deal with pupils' learning differently? This is also called reflection and is a key component of professional learning (Schön 1983).

Rote learning

It is a fallacy, we suggest, to assume that pupils can learn everything for themselves by discovery methods. Teachers are specialists in their fields of study; they usually know more than pupils, and one, but not all, of their functions is to tell pupils things they otherwise might not know but need to know. You need to consider what you want to achieve and match the teaching style with the purpose (see Unit 5.3 on teaching styles). Pupils need to be told when they are right; their work needs supporting. On occasions, you need to tell pupils when they are wrong and how to correct their error. How this is done is important but teachers should not shirk telling pupils when they underperform or make mistakes. See Unit 3.2 on motivating pupils, which includes a section on giving feedback. The Education Endowment Foundation (2015) reports research on the importance of feedback as well as on many other issues affecting pupil attainment (See the list of websites at the end of this unit).

Rote learning may occur when pupils are required to listen to the teacher. There are occasions when you need to talk directly to pupils; for example, to give facts about language, of spelling or grammar; about formulae in science; or health matters such as facts about drug abuse or safe practice in the gymnasium. Other facts necessary for successful learning in school include recalling multiplication tables, or remembering vocabulary, or learning the reactivity series of metals, or recalling a piece of prose or poetry. Some facts need to be learned by heart, by rote methods. There is nothing wrong with you requiring pupils to do this from time to time, provided that all their learning is not like that. Such facts are necessary for advanced work; they contribute to the sub-routines that allow us to function at a higher level. Habits of spelling, of adding up, of recalling the alphabet are vital to our ability to function in all areas of the curriculum and in daily life.

Sometimes, pupils need to use a routine as part of a more important task that they may not fully understand. You may decide that the end justifies the means and that through the experience of using the routine in different contexts, understanding of that routine develops. Many of us learn that way.

Learning facts by heart usually involves a coding process. For example, recalling a telephone number is easier if it is broken into blocks such as 0271 612 6780, and not as 02716126780. Another strategy is the use of a mnemonic to aid recall, such as recalling the musical notes E G B D F by the phrase 'Every Good Boy Deserves Fun'. Do you know any other mnemonics? What other ways are there of helping pupils to learn by rote?

Use Task 5.2.3 as a starting point to evaluate the different types of learning your teaching provides.

 Task 5.2.3 Identifying types of learning

Review a selection of lessons that you have taught and identify where you have used active learning, guided discovery and rote learning. Critically reflect on the reasons for your choices and whether these were appropriate. If you have not given the pupils opportunities to learn in these ways, try to work out some lesson plans where you build them in. Record your reflections in your PDP.

Active learning in the classroom: aids to recall and understanding

Sometimes information cannot easily be committed to memory unless a structure is developed around it to help recall. That structure may involve other information that allows you to build a picture. In other words, recall is constructed. Structures may include other words, but often tables, diagrams, flow charts or other visual models are used. Another way of helping learners to remember ideas or facts is to construct summaries in various forms. Both the act of compiling the summary and the product contribute to remembering and learning. Figure 5.2.1 shows a model of learning based on the idea that personal development proceeds best by reflection on your own actions. Reflection in the model is incorporated in the terms 'review' and 'learn'. This model is presented as a cyclic flow diagram that enables you to keep in mind the essential steps.

This model can be applied to pupils' learning as well as your own. See also Figure 6.1.1, 'The planning/teaching/assessment/planning loop' (Unit 6.1), where the model is applied to lesson planning. However, you might also want to develop a more sophisticated model of active learning in relation to your own practice. We recommend you consider carrying out research in your own classroom (see Unit 5.4).

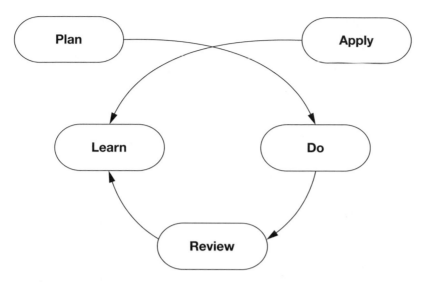

Figure 5.2.1 An active learning model: plan, do, review, learn, apply

Source: Watkins *et al.* (2007: 77)

Mapping tools: spider diagrams and mind maps

It is often helpful to pupils and teachers to 'brainstorm' as a way of exploring their understanding of an idea. One way to record that event is by a spider diagram (or Burr diagram) or mind map in which the 'legs' identify the ideas related to the topic. Figure 5.2.2 shows a spider diagram constructed by a pupil of some ideas associated with 'fruit'.

Concept maps, more commonly called 'mind maps', are developments from spider diagrams and are used to display important ideas or concepts that are involved in a topic or unit of work and, by annotation, show the links between them. An example is shown in Figure 5.2.3. Concept maps can be made by pupils as a way of summarising their knowledge of a unit of work. The individual map reveals some of the pupil's understanding and misunderstandings of the topic. Making a concept map at the start of a unit helps to probe pupils' prior knowledge of the subject. In either case, you may need to provide a list of ideas with which pupils can work and to which they can add their own ideas, as illustrated in Figures 5.2.2 and 5.2.3.

Concept mapping is useful as part of your lesson preparation, particularly when beginning a new unit of work. See also Task 5.1.5 in Unit 5.1. Concept maps have their origin in the learning movement called constructivism. In particular, constructivists hold that prior knowledge is used as a framework to learn new knowledge. In essence, how we think influences how and what we learn. Concept maps identify the way we think, and more importantly the way we see relationships between knowledge. Concept mapping enables you to gain an overview of the unit, to consolidate links between several ideas, and may reveal weaknesses or gaps in your own understanding. Concept mapping is a useful way of linking topics in the curriculum so as to promote continuity and breadth of understanding in your teaching (see, for instance, concept maps in science in Frost and Turner 2005: Chapter 5.2). Concept maps are difficult to construct but the process of drafting one is a valuable exercise. Task 5.2.4 asks you to prepare a concept map.

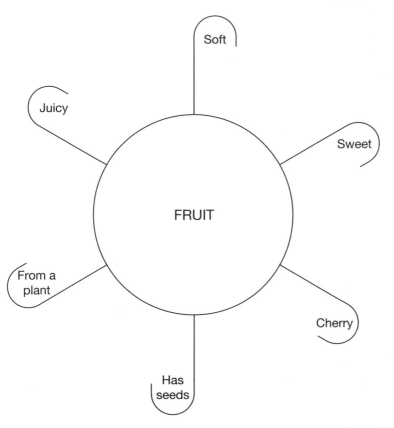

Figure 5.2.2 A pupil's meaning of fruit or a pupil's understanding of the concept of fruit

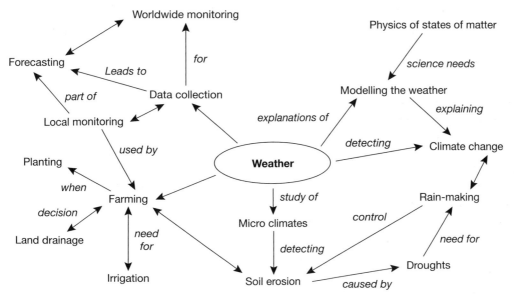

Figure 5.2.3 Concept map: weather

Task 5.2.4 Using concept mapping

Prepare a concept map for a unit of work that you are going to teach. Discuss this map with other student teachers or your tutor and reflect on its value to enhance active learning in the lesson. Record in your PDP ideas for the use of concept maps in your lessons.

Directed activities related to text (DART)

DART (directed activities related to text) are ways of engaging pupils in active reading, writing and listening in order to foster their understanding of a text and their ability to reflect. These are long-standing classroom teaching strategies (see, for instance, Davies and Greene 1984; Gilham 1986: 164), which continue to be widely used (for example, Davison and Dowson 2003: 69, 79, 254). DART can involve the use of textbooks, but take in ways of using a variety of written and other visual materials, including resources downloaded from the Web. DART are devised to ensure that pupils interact with a text. Interaction includes, for example, underlining certain types of word, listing important words, drawing diagrams or reformulating a labelled diagram into continuous prose. The level of demand (that is, differentiation) is adjusted by you to meet the needs of the pupils. A listening activity may be designed to help pupils understand instructions given by the teacher. DART and related types of learning activity emphasise the importance of language in learning and in assessing learning. For further discussion on the role of language in learning, see, for instance, Burgess (2004). Some examples of DART in the classroom are discussed below (see also Unit 5.5).

DART: giving instructions

This includes activities as diverse as making bread, carrying out a traffic survey or gathering information on the effects of the Black Death. A common complaint by teachers is that pupils do not read instructions or, if they do, are unable to comprehend them. Sometimes, the language level is too high, or pupils may understand each step but not the whole, or just lack confidence to act. Sometimes, it is because pupils do not have any investment in the project; it is not theirs. Ways of alleviating such problems depend on the ability and attentiveness of your pupils, but can include:

- Co-writing the instructions for an activity. Pupils then use their own checklist as they complete each stage of the task.
- Writing instructions on numbered cards. A set of cards can be given to a group who are instructed to put the cards into a working order. Discrepancies are discussed and the order checked against the purpose in order to agree the acceptable sequence, which can then be written or pasted in pupils' books.
- Matching instructions to sketches of events: ask pupils to read instructions and select the matching sketch and so build a sequence.
- Discussing the task first and then asking pupils to draft their own set of instructions. After checking by the teacher, the pupils can begin.

The same approach can be applied to how to do something or explain a process; for example, helping pupils explain how ice erodes rock or how to interrogate a database.

DART: listening to the teacher

Sometimes, you want pupils to listen and enjoy what is being said to them. There are other occasions when you want pupils to listen and interact with the material and keep some sort of record. It may be to:

- explain a phenomenon (for example, a riot);
- describe an event (for example, a bore in a river);
- describe a process (for example, making pastry);
- demonstrate a process (for example, distillation);
- design an artefact (for exmple, a desk lamp); or
- give an account (for example, of work experience or a visit to a gallery).

There are a number of ways you can help pupils in their work. For example:

- Identifying key words and ideas as you proceed, signalling to pupils when you expect them to record them.
- Identifying, or getting pupils to identify, key words and ideas in advance on a worksheet and asking pupils to note them, tick, underline or highlight as they are discussed. These words can be written on the board.
- Using a diagram that pupils annotate as the lesson proceeds. This diagram might be used to: label parts; describe functions; and identify where things happen. Pupils could keep their own notes and then be asked to make a summary and presentation to the class. Some pupils may need a word list to help them.

A possible way to support pupils in preparing a summary could be to give them a depleted summary and ask them to complete it. The degree of help is a matter of judgement. For example:

- Give the summary with some key words missing and ask pupils to add the missing words.
- Give the depleted summary with an additional list of words. Pupils select words and put them in the appropriate place. The selection could include surplus words.
- Vary the focus of the omitted words. It could be on key words, or concepts, or focused on meanings of non-technical words; for example, on connecting words or verbs, and so on (Sutton 1981: 119; Frost and Turner 2005: 181-4).

Another possibility could be to provide pupils with a writing frame. A writing frame consists of 'visual guidance on the construction of each paragraph or section of a piece of writing, which includes all or part of a topic sentence and bullet points identifying items which pupils should include' (see Moss in Davison and Dowson 2003: 151). So, in the example given above of writing an account of a visit to a gallery, a possible frame might look like this:

- give details of the journey to the gallery (for example, times of departure and arrival, mode of transport, route);
- describe the gallery (for example, size, age of the building);
- list three artists whose work is exhibited there and give some information about what you have learned about them;
- say whether you would recommend this gallery to friends and give at least two reasons.

DART: characterising events

You may wish to help pupils associate certain ideas, events or properties with a phenomenon; for example, what were the features of the colonisation of the West Indies, or what are the characteristics of a Mediterranean-type climate? As well as reading and making notes:

■ List ideas on separate cards, some of which are relevant to the topic and others not relevant. Ask pupils to sort the cards into two piles, those events relevant to the phenomenon and those not directly related. Pupils compare sorting and justify their choice to each other.

■ Mix up cards describing criteria related to two phenomena. Ask pupils to select those criteria appropriate to each event. A more complex task would be to compare; for example, the characteristics of the Industrial Revolutions of the eighteenth and twentieth centuries.

DART: interrogating texts or reading for meaning

Learners often feel that if they read a text (a book or an online source), they are learning, and don't always appreciate that they have to work to gain understanding. Learners need to do something with the material in order to understand it. There are a number of ways of interrogating the material in order to assist with learning and understanding. There are some general points to be considered. It is important that pupils:

■ are asked to read selectively – the length of the reading should be appropriate;
■ understand why they are reading and what they are expected to get out of it;
■ know what they are supposed to be doing while they read, what to focus on, what to write down or record;
■ know what they are going to do with the results of their reading; for example, write, draw, summarise, reformulate, précis, tell others, tell the teacher, carry out an investigation.

To help pupils read for meaning, you could try the following activities.

DART: getting an overview

Using photocopies of written material is helpful; pupils annotate or mark the text to aid understanding. Pupils read the entire text quickly, to get an overview and to identify any words they cannot understand and to get help from an adult or a dictionary. Ask pupils to read it again, this time with a purpose, such as to list or underline, or group key words or ideas.

DART: reformulating ideas

To develop understanding further, pupils need to do something with what they have read. They could:

■ make a list of key words or ideas;
■ collect similar ideas together, creating patterns of broader concepts;
■ summarise the text to a given length;
■ turn prose into a diagram, sketch or chart;

- make a spider diagram;
- design a flow chart, identifying sequence of events, ideas, and so on;
- construct a diagram (for example, of a process or of equipment with labels);
- turn a diagram into prose, by telling a story or interpreting meanings;
- summarise using tables, such as relating structure to function (for example, organs of the body), historical figures' contribution to society (for example, emancipation of women) and form to origin (for example, landscapes and erosion).

Where appropriate, pupils could be given a skeleton flow chart, spider diagram, and so on, with the starting idea provided and asked to come up with further ideas.

DART: reporting back

A productive way of gaining interest and involvement is to ask pupils to report their findings, summaries or interpretation of the text to the class. The summary could take one of the forms mentioned above. In addition, of course, a pupil could use the board, overhead projector, poster or a computer-assisted presentation such as PowerPoint. Pupils need to be prepared for this task and need to be given sufficient time. Public reporting is demanding on pupils and it is helpful if a group of pupils draft the presentation and support the reporter. The presentation could be narrative, a poem, a simulation, diagram, play, and so on. A suggested sequence of events is shown in the feedback loop, from 'Class discussion' to 'Task', in Figure 5.2.4, which can be introduced depending on the time available and the interest and ability of the class.

Lesson planning for active learning

It is important to distinguish between 'activities' and 'active learning'. It is relatively easy to fill a lesson with a series of activities that keep pupils busy and apparently enjoying it, yet these may provide an insufficient learning challenge. Such work may be well within the pupils' grasp and so they do not have to think much about what they are doing or why. Many pupils take seriously copying from the board, book or worksheet but such activities are often superficial and should be used very sparingly, even though they can keep a noisy class quiet.

Some lesson planning in the early stages of learning to teach may be to ensure that all your learning outcomes are addressed, or that your discipline is effective; this requirement may lead to a lesson that is teacher-dominated. For example, you may have explained orally the lesson and its purpose and have asked some bridging questions; you may have then used a video and asked the pupils to complete a worksheet in response to watching the video; finally, you may have given out homework based on the class work. You, as the teacher, have been very active in the lesson and may well feel exhausted at the end of it! From the pupils' point of view, however, the lesson may have been quite passive because they were told what to do at every step, with little or no input into what they were to do and learn. In these circumstances, many pupils may not fully engage in learning except in a superficial sense.

Task 5.2.5 provides a springboard to explore these issues.

This short lesson sequence illustrates how to scaffold the learning at the initial stage (see references to scaffolding in Units 3.1 and 5.1). It provides ample opportunities for pupils to take part, but the cognitive demands remain mostly at word or phrasal level and the activities are tightly

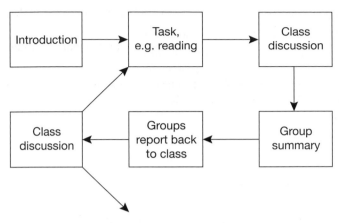

Figure 5.2.4 Reporting back

    Task 5.2.5 Active classroom or active learning?

You may find this task best discussed in a tutor group.

A structured sequence for the learning of new vocabulary in a modern foreign language lesson is presented in Table 5.2.1.

The pupils seem to be busy, but to what extent do you think the pupils are actively engaged in learning?

Identify any changes you would make to the lesson and explain why.

Record your notes in your PDP. After you have carried out this task, compare your response to that of an experienced teacher.

---

controlled by the teacher. For pupils to progress further, they would need to be led gradually towards the challenge of identifying patterns, generating sentences of their own, integrating this vocabulary into new structures and contexts. Furthermore, the memorisation techniques illustrated here may well be helpful in the short term but are unlikely to be sufficient to secure deep learning by way of retaining the newly acquired words in the longer term.

To begin to use active learning, you need to have a clear idea about what you want to achieve. Monk and Silman (2011) suggest that the way to begin is to visualise the learning atmosphere you are aiming to achieve by the end of the term and then to plan the steps that get you there. You need to consider your knowledge of the pupils, the curriculum, the learning space available (your classroom or perhaps somewhere else in the school) and then begin to plan activities that signal to the pupils that your classroom is an active not passive one, where their views, interest and opinions are central to their learning experience. These issues suggest some key questions to keep in mind when planning for active learning:

■   What will the pupils actually do that enhances their learning?
■   How will I ensure that as I am talking the pupils are processing what I am saying?
■   Does the majority of the class have the life experiences to understand what I am trying to teach?

■ Am I planning my teaching to cover the curriculum or am I planning the teaching of the curriculum to ensure the pupils are actively learning?

(Monk and Silman 2011: 189)

Some teachers might use the word *hook* to describe an activity planned at the start of a sequence of lessons that engages pupils in their learning. 'Hooks' can involve:

■ challenges
■ problems to solve
■ role play to bring an experience to life
■ visits and visitors, in addition to visual and auditory stimuli.

A multisensory classroom experience can contribute towards active learning. Visual aids can generate interest, bring 'reality' into the classroom and enable an interactive approach to be adopted. Visual aids may take the form of a simple prompt; for example, a picture, a poster, an object, an overhead projector transparency, a PowerPoint presentation or an interactive whiteboard.

Visual aids are a powerful tool for focusing attention, stimulating memorisation and conveying meaning, all of which contribute to active learning. They enable the teacher not only to present information, but also to clarify concepts and meanings and build ideas, models, diagrams and sequences with the class. For example, you can hide definitions that the pupils then complete. Pupils can hypothesise from partly revealed screens, share their ideas and complete some creative writing

Table 5.2.1 An example of a structured sequence for the oral introduction of new vocabulary for beginners in a modern foreign languages lesson

Activity	Pupils' physical involvement	Pupils' mental involvement
Teacher presents new vocabulary items with visuals (for example, downloaded pictures, flash cards, and so on)	Pupils repeat each word at a time, in chorus and individually at random	Pupils try to work out the meaning of the word. The repetition helps them to start to commit the new vocabulary to their short-term memory.
Teacher numbers visuals on the board, then calls out the words at random (or this could be done with the use of a list on tape)	Pupils write the number that corresponds to the word they have heard	Pupils draw upon their short-term memory to identify the correct item.
Teacher asks question: 'What is this' in the target language	Pupils put their hands up, selected individuals speak	Pupils draw upon their short-term memory to produce the words.
Teacher asks pupils to work in pairs and ask each other what the new words are; teacher encourages the class to answer in short sentences; for example, 'this is a . . .'	All pupils involved in speaking	Pupils recall the words as well as the question. They begin to formulate a simple sentence.

from these ideas as a class activity. Equally importantly, the pupils can use these aids to display their own understanding.

Increasingly, pupils have access to iPads or tablets (Burden and Younie 2014) and the teacher often has an interactive whiteboard (a touch-sensitive projection screen that is connected to a computer and a projector that allows you or your pupils, using a pen or finger, to highlight or move what is displayed on the board). Text can be written on the whiteboard (for instance, a whole-class correction of an exercise) and then saved for further use at a later date. You and your class can also interface with downloaded interactive materials from the Internet, or simply use downloaded images, graphs, texts, and so on. These added advantages make the interactive whiteboard and tablets/iPads or other digital devices powerful tools for engaging pupils in learning. Although this way of working requires a fair amount of preparation time, it helps to make smooth transitions between activities, and there is an increasing range of time-saving resources being developed for use in the classroom.

Task 5.2.6 invites you to consider the use of 'hooks' in one of your units of work.

Whatever visual aids you choose to use, it is worth bearing in mind that they require management. There are practical implications for maximising the impact of visual aids, including their clarity, lack of ambiguity and appropriateness of the language level to your class. Another practical implication is to make sure all pupils can see and, if appropriate, read your visual prompts. It is useful, for example, when using visual aids to practise where to stand so as not to obstruct pupils' vision. You do need to be careful that your 'hook' doesn't become the main focus for your planning. Planning for learning requires you to focus on what the pupil is doing as well as what you are doing. To encourage pupils to participate fully in the lesson and hence promote meaningful learning, there are some important features to bear in mind when planning your lesson. As well as planning strategies that include an input from pupils into the development of the lesson, you should:

- share the learning outcomes with your pupils and give an example of what your pupils' finished work should look like (that is, what counts as a successful piece of work);
- focus some learning outcomes on process rather than content (that is, on pupil action and contribution to their own learning);
- illustrate your criteria for assessment;
- link the lesson to the pupils' prior knowledge and include your strategies for eliciting it;
- prepare contingency plans for differentiating for both faster and slower pupils;
- think about ways to help pupils in difficulties (that is, give support) (see Units 4.1 and 5.1).

Task 5.2.7 helps you to consider strategies to activate pupils' prior knowledge.

  Task 5.2.6 Using hooks

In one of your units of work, plan how you can involve pupils through the use of a 'hook' (see examples in the list earlier in this unit) to promote active learning. Teach the lessons incorporating this 'hook' and then evaluate the effectiveness of this approach and how you might improve their use in future lessons. Record the outcomes in your PDP, focusing on analysing the learning outcomes using guidance in Units 5.1, 5.3 and 5.5).

M

✏️ **Task 5.2.7 Activating pupils' prior knowledge**

(See also short-term and long-term memory in Unit 5.1 and Unit 5.3.)

Select a strategy for probing pupils' prior knowledge of a topic and use it in a lesson in which you are being observed. Evaluate the effectiveness of the activity yourself and also ask your tutor or class teacher to give you feedback on its effectiveness. Strategies you could use include a question and answer session, brainstorming in small groups (that is, eliciting spontaneous recall of relevant information or randomly listing ideas/suggestions in relation to a particular topic or question), followed by a plenary session, asking pupils to prepare a spider diagram summarising what they know. You then use these to plan the next lesson. File feedback in your PDP.

Active learning goes hand in hand with an approach to teaching that encourages pupils to develop and progress as individuals and not merely to receive information from the teacher. Active learning, therefore, is a process that is:

■ structured and organised – a purposeful activity through which pupils can achieve the intended learning outcome as you have planned it;
■ transformational – enables pupils to consider alternatives, to think differently and develop attitudes and values;
■ communicative – involves engagement with others within and beyond the classroom and develops higher-order skills such as analysis, communication, investigation and listening;
■ generative – pupils are engaged in the process of their own learning; the task generates deeper understanding by challenging pupils' understanding;
■ supportive of meaningful learning.

If this description is correct, then a lesson must invite pupils to participate in the work, contribute to its development and, consequently, begin to shape their own learning. The demands on the pupil in such a situation move learning to higher-order skills, to which we now turn.

Developing pupils' higher-order thinking skills

It is now generally acknowledged that the explicit development of thinking skills needs to take place alongside teaching of factual content and that the emphasis in learning is not just on the outcomes, but also on the processes. Teaching, therefore, needs to be designed to enable pupils to:

■ develop logical reasoning in order to apply it to new contexts (formal thinking approach);
■ deconstruct problems in order to find solutions to them (heuristic approach);
■ reflect on and evaluate their own learning (metacognitive approach) (Muijs and Reynolds 2005).

These three approaches are at the heart of active learning because they promote the learners' engagement with the task and encourage pupils to make sense of their learning (see also Unit 5.1). Bloom identified six levels of thinking of gradually increasing complexity, which make increasing demands on the cognitive processes of learners (Bloom 1956; see also Units 3.1 and 5.1). These six levels are listed in the first column of Table 3.1.2 in Unit 3.1. While there is the potential for active learning at every level, the last three levels can be linked to the higher-order thinking skills mentioned above.

Providing suitable challenges is fundamental to active learning. One strategy used extensively by teachers is questioning (see also Unit 3.1). The importance of questioning as a teaching and learning strategy is long established and well documented in educational research (for example, Wragg and Brown 2001; Kerry 2004). Many studies show how questions can take various forms and how they can be adapted to serve a variety of purposes to promote active learning such as:

■   capturing pupils' attention and interest;
■   recalling and checking on prior knowledge;
■   focusing pupils' attention on a specific issue or concept;
■   checking and probing pupils' understanding;
■   developing pupils' thinking and reasoning;
■   differentiating learning;
■   extending pupils' power of analysis and evaluation;
■   helping pupils to reflect on how they learn.

To the student teacher, questions asked by experienced teachers may appear intuitive and instinctive, whereas in reality good questioning develops by reflection on experience. Questions should not just be 'off the cuff', but prepared in advance and related to the learning outcomes, so that pupils' learning is structured. A useful observation schedule identifying good principles for effective questioning is available (Good and Brophy 2000: 412). Morgan and Saxton (1991) identify six different types of questions that stimulate thinking:

1   questions that draw upon knowledge (remembering);
2   questions that test comprehension (understanding);
3   questions that require application (solving);
4   questions that encourage analysis (reasoning);
5   questions that invite synthesis (creating);
6   questions that promote evaluation (judging).

Experienced teachers have the skill of asking questions beyond those planned in response to pupils' replies. Experience here depends largely on knowing your subject and how to use this knowledge (that is, how to put across your knowledge of the subject to the pupils in a way that enables them to learn), and on knowing your pupils and how they respond to your subject and your teaching. You also need to know the ideas/concepts that pupils find difficult, and therefore need to probe their understanding/misunderstandings.

Effective questioning is central to the teaching and learning process. How Bloom's taxonomy relates to the use of questions by the teacher is shown in Table 3.1.2 in Unit 3.1. This table identifies the purposes of questioning at the various levels and gives examples of the sort of question that may be asked.

Finally, complete Tasks 5.2.8 and 5.2.9.

Task 5.2.8 Developing higher-order thinking skills through the use of questioning

Observe a lesson and script the questions used by the teacher to promote learning. Try to classify them against Bloom's (1956) taxonomy of educational objectives. How does the type and frequency of question used impact upon active learning? Discuss your observations with the teacher or your tutor and record them in your PDP folder.

 Task 5.2.9 Reflecting on your use of active learning

Read the article: Powell, E. (2005) 'Conceptualising and facilitating active learning: teachers' video-stimulated reflective dialogues', *Reflective Practice*, 6(3): 407-18.

Make notes in your PDP. Arrange to videotape a lesson, or a part of a lesson, that aims to promote active learning. If possible, discuss the video extract with other student teachers or your tutor, using Moyle's reflective framework (see Appendix 1(b) of Powell's article). Alternatively, analyse your questioning technique using the information in the text boxes and other research literature on questioning that you have selected. Write a critical analysis of your teaching, drawing upon the research literature that you have read, and store this in your PDP.

SUMMARY AND KEY POINTS

■ Teaching is an enabling process; teachers can guide pupils' learning but cannot do the learning for them.

■ Pupils need to engage mentally with a task if learning is to take place; thus, you need to enthuse and motivate pupils, give purpose to their learning tasks, and provide active learning experiences. Some of these activities (for example, DART) introduced study skills, and are important for pupils preparing for public examinations.

■ This unit has used examples of reading, writing, listening and talking activities designed to improve learning and learning skills.

■ There is hands-on activity in practically based subjects, such as art and design, science and technology. Working with your hands does not guarantee that learning takes place; both hand and brain need to be involved.

■ Pupils need to have a say in the design, execution and evaluation of practical work in the same way as we have stressed the need for their active involvement in reading and listening.

The advantages claimed for the active learning include, too, an emphasis on cooperative learning, which can provide opportunities for pupils to take some responsibility for their own learning by, for example, active participation in the development of the task. This approach requires pupil self-discipline and may contribute to that wider goal of education. For the teacher, it opens up a wider range of teaching methods to develop personalised learning, allows the growth of resource-based learning and provides space for monitoring pupil progress and giving formative feedback. Aims can be widened; as well as encouraging acquisition of knowledge and understanding, active learning can be used to promote process skills and higher-order skills.

The key to good teaching is preparation. This is particularly important if you select active learning strategies. These strategies are a major part of your teaching repertoire, and as such contribute significantly to the professional standards required of a newly qualified teacher (NQT). Further advice and guidance on active learning is available in the further reading section.

Check which requirements for your ITE programme you have addressed through this unit.

Further reading

A wide range of literature is available on developing memory and thinking skills; for example, Edward de Bono's work. The texts below provide specialist information relating to this unit.

Muijs, D. and Reynolds, D. (2005) *Effective Teaching: Evidence and Practice*, 2nd edn, London: Paul Chapman. This book provides a comprehensive introduction to what are considered to be key elements of effective teaching, as evidenced by recent research on practice. The chapters on interactive teaching, collaborative small group work, constructivism and problem-solving and higher-order thinking skills are particularly useful for deepening your understanding of what active learning involves and how you can bring it about in your own teaching.

Watkins, C., Carnell, E. and Lodge, C. (2007) *Effective Learning in Classrooms*, London: Paul Chapman. This book focuses on learning, what makes it effective and how to promote it in classrooms. The authors identify active learning as a core process for promoting effective learning in classrooms. Drawing upon international research as well as case studies involving practising teachers, they provide you with useful ideas and frameworks for developing your own conception of active learning.

Other resources and websites

The websites below give access to a host of materials relevant to this unit.

Blamires, M. (ed.) (2014) *Special Educational Needs and Disability: Enabling Pupil Participation MESHGuide*, RIDDLE consultancy, previously Canterbury Christ Church University: www.meshguides.org/category/special-needs-2/enabling-pupil-participation-special-needs-2/

Burden, K. and Younie, S. (2014) *Using iPads Effectively to Enhance Learning in Schools MESHGuide*, University of Hull and De Montfort University, UK: www.meshguides.org/category/icttechnology/tabletsipad-pedagogy/

Claxton, G. (2015) *Building Learning Power*: www.buildinglearningpower.co.uk/

The Education Endowment Foundation (2015) *Feedback*: https://educationendowmentfoundation.org.uk/toolkit/toolkit-a-z/feedback/

Education-line (www.leeds.ac.uk/bei/COLN/COLN_default.html) holds a repository of papers presented at the British Education Research Association conferences (BERA): www.bera.ac.uk.

These provide a useful starting point to find out about recent research projects on active learning and thinking skills.

Education Scotland (2015) *Skills in Practice: Thinking Skills*: www.educationscotland.gov.uk/resources/s/skillsinpracticethinkingskills/knowing.asp

Google Scholar also provides open access to a wide variety of research papers: http://scholar.google.co.uk/.

University libraries subscribe to online journals so that members of libraries can gain access to the worldwide body of research literature. In the UK, local neighbourhood libraries are usually able to borrow copies of the wide range of literature held by the British Library.

Kagan: www.kagan-uk.co.uk/
Kagan UK trains teachers to use Kagan Structures, a set of research-based instructional strategies that have been created to teach pupils cooperation and learning strategies to enhance achievement.

Keuchel, T. and Beaudry, J. (2015) *Visual Literacy MESHGuide*, Senior Mirandanet Fellow, NAACE Fellow, UK; University of Southern Maine, USA: www.meshguides.org/meshguides-full-list/

Lee, C. (2013) *Mathematics: Assessment for Learning: The Four Operations MESHGuide*, Open University, UK: www.meshguides.org/assessment-for-learning-the-four-operations/

Noble, T. (n.d.) *Integrating the Revised Bloom' Taxonomy With Multiple Intelligences: A Planning Tool for Curriculum Differentiation*, National Australian Catholic University: www.bounceback.com.au/sites/default/files/Integrating%20the%20Revised%20Bloom%E2%80%99s%20Taxonomy%20With%20Multiple%20Intelligences_0.pdf

Online Education Research Journal (OERJ) is an open access online journal giving access to recently published research papers: www.oerj.org.

Procter, R. (2013) *Assessment for Learning MESHGuide*, University of Bedfordshire, UK.

Stanford University (2015) *Teaching Commons: Bloom's Taxonomy of Educational Objectives*: https://teachingcommons.stanford.edu/resources/course-preparation-resources/course-design-aids/bloom%E2%80%99s-taxonomy-educational-objectives

TLRP (Teaching and Learning Research Programme) (2006) *Learning How to Learn – in Classrooms, Schools and Networks*: www.tlrp.org/pub/documents/no17_james.pdf

University of Cambridge/Professor Neil Mercer (2015) *Thinking Together*: http://thinkingtogether.educ.cam.ac.uk/resources/

Appendix 2 on pages 591–595 provides examples of further websites you may find useful.

Capel, S., Leask, M. and Turner, T. (eds) (2010) *Readings for Learning to Teach in the Secondary School: A Companion to M Level Study*, London: Routledge.
This book brings together essential readings to support you in your critical engagement with key issues raised in this textbook.

The subject-specific books in the Routledge *Learning to Teach* series are also very useful.

Any additional resources and an editable version of any relevant tasks/tables in this unit are available on the companion website: www.routledge.com/cw/capel

Acknowledgements

The author would like to thank Matthew Lowe for his willingness to try the strategies advocated in this unit.

Teaching styles

Chris Carpenter and Hazel Bryan

Introduction

This unit is concerned principally with *individual teaching styles*. In the same way that assessment, curriculum and pedagogy are closely interrelated, we suggest that while teaching style is a topic highly worthy of close study in its own right, it is informed by other aspects of teaching. Therefore, while teaching style will be at the heart of the unit, we will draw on aspects such as learning theory, pedagogy and the activities that teachers employ in helping pupils to learn to shed light on teaching styles. In this way, you will be supported in building knowledge about teaching styles and in considering how the styles that teachers use are related to other aspects of teacher knowledge that you will be developing as a part of your initial teacher education (ITE) programme. The section

OBJECTIVES

By the end of this unit you should:

■ understand the possibilities for a repertoire of teaching styles that you can draw upon to enable pupils to learn in various situations;

■ have thought about the relationship between the teaching styles that you employ in the classroom and what you intend pupils to learn;

■ have developed an understanding that the focus of your teaching is enabling learning (that is, helping *particular* pupils to learn *something specific* and therefore teaching styles need to be specific to what is learned, the learners and teacher who is carrying out the teaching);

■ be able to apply knowledge that you have about how pupils learn to underpin the teaching styles that you employ;

■ map your developing style to the requirements of your ITE programme and use your mapping to set targets for your further professional development.

Check the requirements of your ITE programme to see which relate to this unit.

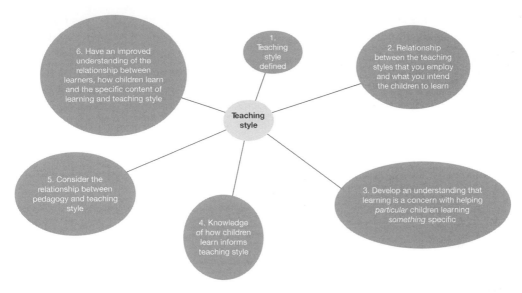

Figure 5.3.1 Developing a repertoire of teaching styles

Source: 'Forms of professional knowledge', pp. 18–21, Unit 1: a response to Task 1.1.5)

'Classroom approaches: teaching/pedagogical strategies' in Unit 5.5 provides a list of strategies to consider together with the styles outlined in this unit.

Figure 5.3.1 looks at developing a repertoire of teaching styles. Anyone who has been to school will be familiar with the kinds of things that teachers do. Indeed, the modes of teaching that teachers employ are often a feature of film, television series and novels that use schools as a place to situate a drama. You might reflect for a moment on memorable scenes from film or book: in what way would you describe the teaching style of that teacher? There is a vast array of approaches that teachers use in classrooms, ranging from telling, describing, setting tasks, assessing learning and modelling various learning activities. The problem can be that if we do not understand the underpinning principles of teacher activities and develop a growing appreciation of why teachers do what they do, we can be guilty of 'impersonating a teacher', or focusing merely on 'procedural display' aspects. In other words, that, as a student teacher, you might carry out certain tasks but are not necessarily clear as to why you might be doing them, other than because we know that those are the kinds of things that teachers do. This unit introduces ideas about teaching styles and provides opportunities for you to use theories encountered in other units in this book to widen your range of teaching styles and their associated strategies so that your actions as a teacher are informed.

The teaching styles we introduce in this unit include the following:

■   closed, framed and negotiated strategies (see Table 5.3.1); and
■   command, practice/task, reciprocal, self-check, inclusion, guided discovery, convergent discovery, divergent discovery, learner initiated and self-teaching strategies (see Table 5.3.5).

In developing this idea of teaching styles, we draw upon a model developed by Barnes (1987) that can be used to identify the basic elements of different teaching styles. This model works on a continuum of 'closed' to 'negotiated' styles.

In the 'closed' teaching style, the teacher assumes a high degree of control in relation to all decisions. This is a most authoritative teaching style: in this mode, the role of the pupil is to learn from the teacher and from the activities the teacher provides. This is a highly interventionist style of teaching where the teacher may even demonstrate what is to be achieved. In the more 'negotiated' teaching style, the teacher foregrounds the learners more explicitly in the process; that is, a context where learners are actively involved in planning and evaluating. Between these two poles is the 'framed' approach, where the teacher still controls the overall topic but pupils are invited to play an active role:

In order to illustrate the ideas behind the teaching styles suggested by Barnes (1987), we have used the example of a secondary mathematics lesson, where the teacher is teaching algebra (see Table 5.3.2, p. 371).

Now complete Task 5.3.1.

Table 5.3.1 Teaching styles

	Closed	*Framed*	*Negotiated*
Content	Tightly controlled by the teacher; not negotiable	Teacher controls the topic, frames of reference and tasks; criteria made explicit	Discussed at each point; joint decisions
Focus	Authoritative knowledge and skills; simplified monolithic	Stress on empirical testing processes chosen by teacher; some legitimation of pupils' ideas	Search for justifications and principles; strong legitimation of pupils' ideas
Pupils' role	Acceptance; routine performance; little access to principles	Join in teachers' thinking; make hypothesis; set up tests	Discuss goals and methods critically; share responsibility for frame and criteria
Key concepts	'Authority'; the proper procedures and the right answers	'Access' to skills; processes criteria	'Relevance'; critical discussion of pupils' priorities
Methods	Exposition; worksheets (closed); note giving; individual exercises; routine practical work; teacher evaluates	Exposition; with discussions eliciting suggestions; individual/group problem-solving; lists of tasks given; discussion of outcomes; teacher adjudicates	Group and class discussion and decision making about goals and criteria; pupils plan and carry out work; make presentations; evaluate success

Source: Adapted from Barnes (1987: 25)

Table 5.3.2 Examples of teaching styles in the teaching of algebra

Closed	Framed	Negotiated
■ pupils learning to solve equations in a mathematics lesson ■ teacher models the process ■ teacher gives pupils the sums to complete ■ teacher insists on the pupils using the method they have demonstrated ■ teacher marks the sums	■ teacher sets the tasks ■ pupils are shown a method, or a range of methods, depending on the school approach ■ pupils are encouraged to try the method or range of methods and reflect upon the efficacy for them; if, in the course of this activity, new methods are discovered, this will align with a 'framed' approach; this approach merges into the 'negotiated' style and demonstrates how there is natural overlap between styles	■ teacher presents the 'unknown' as a problem to be solved ■ pupils suggest ways this might be solved; they must test their methods on other pupils ■ pupils are encouraged to try their methods and then reflect on what happened ■ new methods proposed ■ teacher models 'correct' solution ■ when pupils are 'stuck', they ask

Source: Adapted from Barnes (1987)

 Task 5.3.1 Closed, framed and negotiated teaching styles

Consider a lesson that you have either taught or have observed. Map the key components of the lesson from a closed teaching style:

■ How would the topic be introduced?
■ What resources will you need?
■ How will the pupils work?
■ What will your role be?
■ How will the work be assessed?

 Now repeat this task from a framed and then negotiated teaching style perspective and reflect upon the following questions:

■ What was the learning experience like for pupils in each mode?
■ How effective were the assessment methods in each mode?
■ What implications are there for resources in each mode?

 Record your reflections in your professional development portfolio (PDP).

Task 5.3.1 asked you to work through one lesson, but taught using three different teaching styles. You will notice that we have invited you to reflect upon this activity from the point of view of the pupil in terms of their overall experiences in each of the modes. The reason for this is because the 'processes' that pupils go through necessarily shape what it is they learn about the task. This is because we know that cognitive processes are not separate from emotional ones. Therefore, the more control over the processes the learner has, the more likely they are to feel empowered and the more likely they are to have positive feelings about the task. It then follows that if they have positive feelings, they are more likely to persist and, even more importantly, the more likely they are to care about getting to a point of some level of mastery. There is a relationship, then, between the teaching style that is adopted and the learning experiences of the pupils (Kyriakou 2009). Meaningful learning happens best where active social interaction is encouraged (Kintsch 2009) and where there is a cooperative and supportive ethos. Teaching styles therefore need to take account of the need for negotiation both between pupils and following constructivist ideas (see Unit 5.1) between pupils and teacher. Your teaching style should make allowances for the learning process and should not only promote discussion, but encourage pupils to challenge their own and others' ideas and to go back and forth in a non-linear way. To do this, you may need to move from *closed* strategies (Barnes 1987), where the teacher tightly controls the content of the lesson, the learning environment and the outcomes of the lesson, through *framed* strategies, where the teacher controls the topics and has clear expectations of outcomes but allows the pupils to propose and test alternatives, to *negotiated* strategies, where the pupils have much more freedom in determining the area of investigation and the way in which work is reported, with possibly variable outcomes. In a meta-analysis relating to achievement, Hattie (2009: 246) argues that teachers need to be 'adaptive learning experts' who have high levels of flexibility that can be employed to guide their pupils in their learning goals. This, Hattie proposes, includes ensuring a positive learning climate. Table 5.3.1 describes the main differences between these strategies.

As you progress through your school placements, you should refine your practice to develop teaching styles that suit different circumstances and achieve diverse learning outcomes. *Usually, you need to adopt a range of styles within a single lesson in order to ensure all of the pupils are deepening their understandings about the topic being considered.* However, teachers may not always develop or use the most suitable teaching style for their pupils. Research (DfES 2003b) suggests that mismatch between pupils' preferences and teachers' styles arises for a number of reasons, including a belief on the part of individual teachers that what helps them to learn also helps pupils. Of course, there may be an element of habituation here. That is to say, pupils may become used to being taught in a particular way and to some extent become 'conditioned' to expect that, so even if a teacher uses a different style and they then get something potentially richer, they may find it initially unsettling. It is worth bearing in mind that teachers may well prefer to adopt styles of teaching that are actually best suited to themselves and not necessarily to their pupils. The position may be even worse for student teachers. Calderhead and Shorrock (1997) suggest teachers, especially student teachers, are initially more comfortable with structures and styles they experienced as pupils than with new ideas, and Evans (2004) reports 41 per cent of a sample of student teachers felt they taught in the way they had been taught, even though many of them had not enjoyed that way. Therefore, it is important that when you critically reflect on your own teaching, you take active steps to incorporate effective practice, including ideas gained from discussion, observation of other teachers and reading, to become comfortable and confident with a wide repertoire of strategies (Bolton 2005; McGregor and Cartwright 2011; Sellers 2014). This can be related to Lortie's (1975) contention that student teachers have experienced an 'apprenticeship of observation'. By this, he means that student teachers will have a close knowledge of classrooms as pupils and will be very aware of the kinds of things that their teachers did. This can be linked to the idea of 'procedural display' that was referred to above.

At this point, we would wish to draw a clear distinction between the *style* of teaching and the *activities* that teachers may employ. We feel that they are clearly related but not the same. We would argue that there are a multitude of activities that teachers may use in the classroom, such as those shown below (in Table 5.3.3).

Table 5.3.3 Examples of activities that teachers might use in the classroom

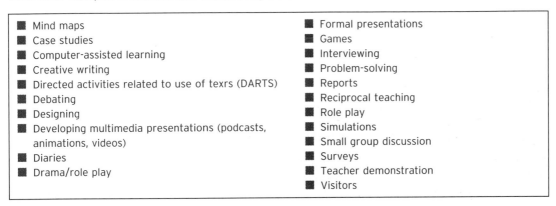

- Mind maps
- Case studies
- Computer-assisted learning
- Creative writing
- Directed activities related to use of texrs (DARTS)
- Debating
- Designing
- Developing multimedia presentations (podcasts, animations, videos)
- Diaries
- Drama/role play
- Formal presentations
- Games
- Interviewing
- Problem-solving
- Reports
- Reciprocal teaching
- Role play
- Simulations
- Small group discussion
- Surveys
- Teacher demonstration
- Visitors

We argue that the *activities* that teachers employ are a *part* of teaching style but not the same thing. For example, a secondary geography teacher might employ a directed activity related to texts (DARTS) (see Unit 5.2), however they might do this using different teaching styles. The teacher might give pupils a 'Water Aid Report' on developing irrigation projects in Ghana (www.wateraid.org/uk/where-we-work/page/ghana) but might approach this using different teaching styles. The decision the teacher makes in determining which teaching style to adopt is influenced by a range of complex factors, as Hattie (2009) discusses. It might be that a particular teaching style is used because that is what is expected in that department – it is a predominant culture of the department and 'how we do things round here'. On the other hand, it might be shaped by what the teacher wants their pupils to learn through the process of addressing the task. That is, not simply the facts of the Water Aid project, but the experience of working together, developing an inquisitive mindset and some research skills. It may be that the teacher's own values about the purpose of the activity, and indeed the teacher's views on the purpose of schooling itself, influences the teaching style adopted, as shown in Table 5.3.4.

The relationship between learning activities and teaching styles can be thought of like the cover version of a song. To give an example, in 2011, Amy Winehouse covered 'The Girl from Ipanema' (www.youtube.com/watch?v=Sn7UrA-2vt4), a song originally released in 1964 by Joao Gilberto and Stan Getz (www.youtube.com/watch?v=UJkxFhFRFDA), featuring Astrud Gilberto.

As you would expect, Winehouse's version was a very different interpretation from the 1964 version. In our analogy, the song represents the activity and the style is the artist's interpretation of the song.

Table 5.3.4 Water Aid project Ghana

Water Aid project in Ghana (www.wateraid.org/uk/where-we-work/page/ghana)	Closed style	Read the piece together. Pupils answer the questions set by the teacher (for example, on the work of a cocoa plantation).
	Framed style	Read the piece together. Take one aspect of the project (for example, the work on a cocoa plantation). Teacher explains what is to be learned and sets activities for pupils to undertake.
	Negotiated style	Read the piece together. Ask the pupils what they might do next if they are to learn more about the issues of running a cocoa plantation. What do they know? What do they want to know? Where might this information be held? How will the information be collected?

Mosston and Ashworth's continuum of teaching styles

A helpful way to frame the styles that teachers employ is to look at it from the point of view of how much 'say' the learner has and how much 'say' the teacher has in terms of the decisions being made in the learning context. In a physical education setting, Mosston and Ashworth (2002) describe this as a continuum that is illustrated graphically in Figure 5.3.2.

In reflecting on the Mosston and Ashworth continuum, it can be seen that in the left-hand side (closed style), the teacher makes all the decisions about what is to be learned, how it will be learned and also exactly how this will be achieved. In this sense, the teaching style is formal and authoritative. An example of this is an aerobics class where the teacher models what is to be done and then the class members copy precisely what the instructor does there and then. Towards the right-hand side (negotiated style), the learner has increasing amounts of control to the point where, at the extreme right-hand side, they might decide what they will learn and how they will go about it: this learner-initiated approach affords pupils a greater amount of intellectual freedom, creativity and enquiry. This negotiated style is commonly found in early-years settings where a belief in the importance of pupils constructing their own understandings of the world frame the style the teacher adopts.

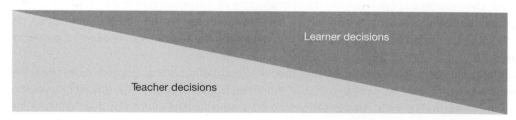

Closed teaching style   More negotiated teaching style

Figure 5.3.2 Mosston and Ashworth teaching styles

Source: Adapted from Mosston and Ashworth (2002)

Linking the 'closed' teaching style of the aerobics teacher and the highly negotiated teaching style is a *continuum* of teaching styles: we feel that thinking about teaching styles on a continuum is helpful as it allows you to understand that having a range of teaching styles – a repertoire – at your fingertips will enable you to employ the most appropriate style for any given context. In the famous scene of the football lesson in the film *Kes*, Mr Sugden the PE teacher adopts a predominantly closed style (www.youtube.com/watch?v=v3cayRMnVb8).

By contrast, the most skilful and creative teachers are able to tap into their repertoire of teaching styles according to the given context.

At this point, it is helpful to acknowledge the ways in which different teaching styles shape the balance of pupil talk to teacher talk (Mercer 2015; University of Cambridge 2015b). This is not simply a matter of balance, but of understanding the demand that particular teaching styles make of the learner. Research has shown that where the teacher's focus is oriented towards *learning* rather than performance, there tend to be fewer reports of disruptive behaviour (Watkins *et al.* 2007).

Mosston and Ashworth's continuum of teaching styles offers a nuanced means by which teaching styles can be understood (see Table 5.3.5 and the text below).

Now complete Task 5.3.2.

 Task 5.3.2 Teaching style observation (see also Unit 2.1)

Observe a lesson in your school placement.

- ■ How might you describe the teaching styles that the teacher employs?
- ■ How involved were the pupils in making decisions?
- ■ What were they able to make decisions about?
- ■ Why did the teacher employ that style?
- ■ What were the issues that emerged?

Record your observations in your PDP.

Teaching style as an element of 'constructive alignment'

So far, we have suggested that teaching styles might best be considered on a continuum, and that the most skilful teachers have a repertoire of teaching styles that they use for differing learning contexts. We have considered also the relationship between the teaching style, what is to be learned, activities that teachers might use in learning contexts and the learning experiences of the pupils. In this section, we will locate teaching style in the slightly wider context of learning intentions and the assessment of learning (Moore 2012). This leads into what Biggs (1996) refers to as 'constructive alignment'. In other words, what the teacher intends the learners to learn, the activities that enable the learners to build deeper understanding and the way that this is assessed should all 'line up' or be coherent and mutually supporting. That is, constructively aligned. There are implications for teaching styles here: the teacher will need to adopt a teaching style that enables the pupils to have plenty of opportunities to be able to practise the thing to be learned. The teacher needs to have

Table 5.3.5 Mosston's 'continuum of teaching styles' (2002 version)

Below, we present Mosston and Ashworth's spectrum of teaching styles. You will see that they have structured these in a particular order, ranging from the command style to the learner-designed individual programme.

The command style

This style is often described as autocratic or teacher-centred. It is appropriate in certain contexts; for example, teaching safe use of equipment, learning particular routines in dance.

The practice style

While similar to the command style, there is a shift in decision-making to pupils and there is more scope with this style for the teacher to work with individuals while the group is occupied with practice tasks such as writing for a purpose in English or practising skills in mathematics.

The reciprocal style

The pupils learn by working in pairs. Each partner is actively involved – one as the 'doer' and one as the 'teacher partner'. The class teacher works with the 'teacher partner' to not only improve mastery of the topic under consideration, but also to help develop their capacity to evaluate and provide feedback. This style provides rich possibilities for interaction and communication among pupils. Pupils can also learn to judge performance against criteria.

The self-check style

This style is designed to develop the learner's ability to evaluate their own performance. The teacher sets the task and the pupils evaluate their own performance against set criteria and agree goals in collaboration with the teacher.

The inclusion style

In this style, differentiated tasks are presented to ensure that all pupils gain some feeling of success and so develop positive self-concepts; for example, if an angled bar is provided for high jump practice, all pupils can succeed as they choose the height over which to jump. They decide at what level to start.

Guided discovery style

Mosston sees this as one of the most difficult styles. The teacher plans the pupils' learning programme on the basis of the learners' competence. The teacher then guides the pupils to find the solution – reframing the question and task if necessary but always controlling the teaching agenda. Pupils with special educational needs are often taught in small groups, and this approach might be used by the teacher to develop an individualised learning programme for each pupil.

Convergent discovery style

In this style, there is a single desired outcome to the learning episode but the learners have autonomy over processes and presentation. The teacher provides feedback and clues (if necessary) to help them reach the correct outcome.

Divergent discovery style

Learners are encouraged to find alternative solutions to a question; for example, in approaching a design problem in art. Multiple solutions are possible and the learners assess their validity, with support from the teacher if necessary.

The learner-designed individual programme

A pupil designs and carries out a programme of work within a framework agreed and monitored by the teacher. Pupils carrying out open-ended investigations to answer a particular question in science provide an example of this style. The knowledge and skills needed to participate in this method of learning depend on the building up of skills and self-knowledge in earlier learning experiences.

Learner-initiated style

At this point on the continuum, the stimulus for learning comes primarily from the pupil, who provides the question to investigate as well as the method of investigation. Thus, the pupil actively initiates the learning experience and the teacher provides support. Giving homework that allows pupils freedom to work on their own areas of interest in their own way might fall into this category. However, Mosston and Ashworth make the point that this kind of learning arises 'only when an individual approaches the teacher (authority figure) and initiates a request to design his/her own learning experiences' and 'when teachers ask learners to *do a project* it cannot be construed to be an example of this style' (Mosston and Ashworth 2002: 284–5).

Self-teaching style

This style describes independent learning without external support. For example, it is the type of learning that adults undergo as they learn from their own experiences.

Source: Adapted from Mosston and Ashworth (2002)

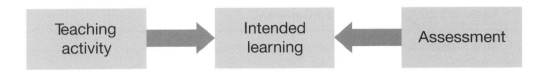

Figure 5.3.3 Biggs' (1996) model of constructive alignment

Source: Developed from Biggs (2003)

the opportunity to make judgements about how well the learner is mastering the thing under consideration as they progress and to be able to make helpful suggestions about the next steps, as in Figure 5.3.3.

For example, if a history teacher wants the pupils in their class to learn to make interpretations about historical events, they might show the pupils a picture of a Victorian street scene and then ask questions such as:

- What do you notice?
- What can we say about the times from this?
- What do you think it might have been like to live in those times and why?

Pupils might then discuss their ideas in pairs, engage in some further joint reading – either online or from texts provided by the teacher – and carry out a brief piece of joint writing. Pupils might then present their writing to the rest of the class.

In order to help you make the connections between the learning the teacher wishes the pupils to achieve, the teaching style adopted, pedagogical activities and assessment, we have placed this example within Biggs' model of constructive alignment (see Table 5.3.6).

Now complete Task 5.3.3.

Table 5.3.6 Example of constructive alignment

Learning intention	Teaching style	Assessment
To understand what it was like to live in Victorian times	Framed style: ■ teacher provides the picture ■ teacher generates initial questions engaging in whole-class discussion ■ teacher sets up the sequence of activities	■ Using criteria made clear to the learners, the teacher listens to pupil discussions in relation to the learning intentions. We call this 'intentional listening'. For a recent research project on teacher feedback, see the Education Endowment Fund website (https://educationendowmentfoundation. org.uk/projects/anglican-schools-partnership/). ■ teacher listens to pupil's discussions ■ teacher reads the written work ■ teacher monitors the presentations

---

✎ Task 5.3.3 Constructive alignment

Learning intention	Teaching style	Assessment

Think about your own subject. Work through some examples of 'constructive' alignment. Discuss with a fellow student teacher.

By undertaking the constructive alignment task, you will begin to make rich connections between what is to be learned, the style of teaching adopted, and activities that enable pupils to engage in deep learning and assessment.

The relationship between skills, attitudes, concepts and knowledge (SACK) and teaching styles

The skills, attitudes, concepts and knowledge that you are intending particular groups of pupils to learn will determine the teaching styles that you employ. You may be familiar with the acronym SACK, which is intended to remind you to check whether the balance of your lesson outcomees between skills, attitudes, concepts and knowledge is appropriate (see also Unit 2.2). Developing process skills by, for example, training pupils to perform a simple action might best be achieved through the use of *closed* strategies, whereas developing an attitude or coming to understand a concept that does require meaningful learning to take place might best be achieved through the use of *negotiated* strategies. When one of the intended learning outcomes for the lesson concerns the development of knowledge, it can be more difficult to decide on the best strategies to use and you might need to refer to other theories, such as information processing models, to help you.

Information processing models and teaching style

As well as constructivist models of learning (see Unit 5.1), there are models that represent learners as information processing systems. These can run parallel to constructivist models and do not necessarily contradict them; pupils with poor information processing capabilities, who need a lot of help and progress slowly, would be those who had small zones of proximal development (Vygotsky 1986)[1] (see also Unit 5.1).

Information processing models can illustrate why your teaching style may need to change depending on whether your lesson's intended learning outcomes relate to skills, knowledge or attitudes or concepts.

Learners can only take in a certain amount of information in a set time. There is limitation of capacity, and bottlenecks can occur when a lot of information is transmitted. When bottlenecks occur, not all of the transmitted information is received in the memory. Therefore, your teaching style must not deliver too much information too quickly or introduce digressions. Reflect on whether using closed or framed strategies will enable you to get your key points across with most effect. At the start of the lesson, when learning outcomes and activities are outlined or, for example, when demonstrating a technique or ensuring safety, a very focused, closed, instructional style might be required.

After information is received, short- and long-term memory work together dynamically. Information is processed in short-term memory, where fresh information and retrieved existing knowledge are used together to make meaning of new situations. This meaningful learning can then be stored in long-term memory. A teaching style that incorporates a range of teaching strategies to present information in different ways and provides a variety of perspectives matches a range of preferred learning styles. More pupils are able both to take in the information and to link it to existing knowledge, increasing the probability that it is processed rather than disregarded.

Once you have considered the teaching styles most likely to support the achievement of your lesson's intended learning outcomes, consider your strategies. Because pupils learn in different ways, you might use talk in conjunction with, for example, a visual presentation of key themes. You might also think about your strategy for grouping. Kutnick *et al.* (2006) have carried out an extensive literature review and suggest no one form of grouping benefits all pupils. Grouping by ability can benefit the most able but demotivate the less able; friendship groups can sometimes provide a non-threatening environment that promotes learning, but at other times they can reinforce peer group norms/cultural stereotypes that prevent progress. Be prepared, therefore, to seek advice about the organisational strategies you employ within the classroom and how best to exploit the different opportunities they present (see Figure 5.3.4).

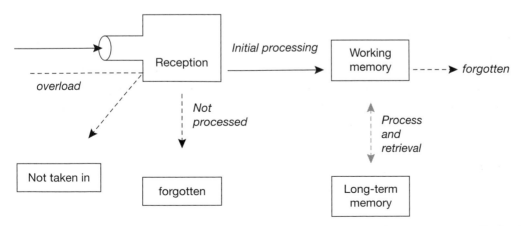

Figure 5.3.4 A flow chart for an information processing model; the flow chart shows the typical pattern of information flow and processing suggested by a multi-store model of memory proposed by Atkinson and Shiffrin (1968)

Personalised learning and independent learners

Personalised learning requires that you 'shape teaching and learning around the different ways children learn' (after Barnes and Harris 2006: 1). In some circumstances, such as using resistant materials workshops, science labs or working with javelins, your choice of actions is quite constrained. Nevertheless, it is unlikely that you adopt a complete command style during your school placement and allow pupils no discretion over their work. It is even less likely that you have the confidence or desire to adopt a discovery style, and hand over the majority of the decisions to the pupils. However, it is important that you do encourage learners' independence in order to further the personalisation of their learning. Mosston and Ashworth (2002) argue that there is a 'discovery threshold' and independent learning is not possible if teachers do not use discovery styles or styles that afford the learner greater autonomy. Therefore, your repertoire should incorporate at least the discovery style and associated strategies and provide pupils with challenging opportunities for independent work both within and outside the classroom. Rudduck *et al.* (2006) have advice to offer here. Their project used discussions with pupils to investigate personalised learning. Two of the key strategies identified by the pupils as important were oral praise and feedback, which provide immediate support and help clarify misunderstandings, and the use of negotiated and realistic targets. Combining these contributes to a style that encourages all pupils to develop the skills of independent learning. Task 5.3.4 asks you to consider how you might develop independent learners.

Unit 5.5 provides further advice on personalising learning.

Pedagogy and teaching styles

Student teachers sometimes talk about 'teaching styles' and 'pedagogy' as if they are the same thing. We would suggest that 'pedagogy' needs to be understood as something far wider than merely the acts of teaching and the styles that teachers employ. We feel that teaching is an act that is deeply embedded in cultural norms, and as such is saturated with the values and customs of particular communities:

> Pedagogy is the act of teaching together with its attendant discourse. It is what one needs to know, and the skills one needs to command, in order to make and justify the many kinds of decisions of which teaching is constituted.

> (Alexander 2004: 11)

In this way, we would argue that teaching is never 'innocent'. By that, we mean that when a teacher is teaching a class, the pupils will be 'making sense' not only of the explicit content of the lesson but also the teacher themselves and the teaching styles that they use. In her book *Psychology in the Classroom*, Phillida Salmon (1995) describes how pupils will inevitably get an impression of their teacher not only from what they do, but the *way* that they do it. Now complete Task 5.3.5.

There will no doubt be times when you feel pressures to inhabit a teacher identity that you feel uncomfortable with and also to employ teaching styles that may not feel right to you. However, by developing a deep understanding of the potential of different teaching styles, the uses and limitations of such teaching styles and the constructive alignment needed between learning, teaching style and assessment, you will develop as a skilful, responsive teacher.

Task 5.3.4 Developing independent learners

Teaching styles create the environment within which learning can take place. Independent learning is a mode of learning that has been advanced in recent years. Consider the following extract:

> Recent years have seen a drive by teachers to promote independent learning in a variety of guises, whether in the form of Building Learning Power (Claxton 2007) or as 'self-regulated' learning (Zimmerman 1989; Boekaerts 1999; Pintrich 2004). For some teachers, this movement has been interpreted mistakenly as undermining their role. In reality, the move to student-centred learning raises different challenges for teachers and infers new agendas for their professional development.
>
> (Stoten 2014: 452)

Now consider the following questions:

- When you set and clarify learning outcomes, expectations and boundaries, how do you share these with pupils? Do you instruct or allow pupils to construct their own understanding?
- How do you help pupils to acquire knowledge, skills and understanding? Do you tell them or do you ask them open-ended questions? Do you accept different answers as being of equal value?
- How structured are the opportunities you provide for pupils to demonstrate, practise and apply what they have learned? Who decides the format for demonstrating learning?
- How do you support learners in becoming independent? Is it by helping them to reflect and build on their existing learning through open-ended questions or allowing trial and error? Alternatively, do you have a 'this is how to do it' approach?

The questions above are open-ended. They do not all have hard and fast answers. If your answers are of the 'usually I would but sometimes' or 'when I started I would but now I', you are beginning to adjust your style in response to your experience and to develop as a teacher.

You are beginning to widen your repertoire and developing *mobility ability* in order to develop independent learners. Record your observations in your PDP.

The 'hidden' curriculum

In Unit 5.1, you were introduced to the idea that we can use theory to explain how children learn. If we adopt a constructivist theory of how children learn, it can be seen that no matter what teaching styles the teacher uses, the pupils will make sense of classrooms and the activities they undertake in their own way. In other words, that they will 'construct' their own understandings. It is also suggested here that the way in which the teacher carries out the teaching style will convey messages about other aspects, such as their enthusiasm for the subject, how much they are enjoying being with the pupils and how confident they are in their subject. It follows, then, that there can often be

Task 5.3.5 Memorable teachers

Ask anyone about their most significant experiences in learning and they will almost certainly start talking about the people who taught them. That awkward, memorable, young man whose own ardent passion for mathematics created from a dry-as-dust subject a distinctive, fascinating world.

Salmon (1988)

When you think about memorable teachers that taught you:

■   Who do you remember?
■   What do you remember?
■   What activities did they employ with you?
■   How would you describe their style?

unexpected learning that is not visible to the teacher or the pupils. This is sometimes referred to as the 'hidden curriculum' (see Unit 7.2). There are a number of ways that this can be conceptualised. For example, Jackson (1968) describes it in terms of 'unofficial expectations of the school conveyed by implicit messages'. Martin (1976) talks in terms of 'consists of some of the outcomes or by-products of learning . . . particularly those states which are learned but are not openly intended'. In this way, it is important for student teachers and teachers to bear in mind that the lack of 'innocence' can result in 'hidden' learning (see Task 5.3.6).

 Task 5.3.6 Hidden curriculum

A Year 8 class are asked to write a creative poem about a memorable experience. Josh gets very excited about this and writes a long descriptive piece about the time he went to the park and helped a child retrieve their football from a tree.

The teacher sees this and their first comments are to point out transcriptional features of text rather than authorial features.

What might be the explicit and 'hidden' messages about what the teacher values being transmitted?

Record your observations in your PDP.

It is important therefore to remember that although you may have thought carefully about what you will teach and how you will go about it, there is always likely to be 'unexpected' or 'hidden' learning.

SUMMARY AND KEY POINTS

Although any teaching style is individual, it tends to be identifiable within a continuum of styles and associated strategies. In this unit, we have explored:

- the nature of pedagogy and how it relates to teaching style;
- Mosston and Ashworth's spectrum of teaching styles (in order to empower you to make informed choices in relation to teaching styles);
- the way in which both the topic under consideration and the learners should influence the teaching styles to be adopted;
- the fact that, inevitably, there will be 'noise' in the communication between the teacher and the learners; this 'unintended' learning is called the 'hidden curriculum';
- the notion that if independent learning is to take place, teaching styles that provide learners with optimum conditions should be employed.

Check which requirements for your ITE programme you have addressed through this unit.

Further reading

Alexander, R. (2008) *Essays on Pedagogy*, London: Routledge.
   This provides a useful introduction to issues around pedagogy.

Biggs, J. (1996) 'Enhancing teaching through constructive alignment', *Higher Education*, 347–64.
   This text introduces constructive alignment.

Gipps, C. and Stobart, G. (1997) *Assessment: A Teacher's Guide to the Issues*, London: Hodder & Stoughton.
   Chapter 2 provides a useful discussion of deep and shallow learning.

Jensen, E. (2009) *Super Teaching*, 4th edn, San Diego, CA: The Brain Store.
   This is an easy-to-read book that contains many ideas that help the development of teaching strategies and styles.

Joyce, B., Weil, M. and Cahoun, E. (2009) *Models of Teaching*, 8th edn, Boston, MA: Allyn & Bacon.
   The authors identify models of teaching and group them into four 'families' that represent different philosophies about how humans learn. This is a comprehensive text designed for those who wish to deepen their knowledge of teaching and learning issues.

Mercer, N. (2000) *Words and Minds: How We Use Language to Think Together*, London: Routledge.

Mosston, M. and Ashworth, S. (2002) *Teaching Physical Education*, New York: Maxwell Macmillan International.

Salmon, P. (1988) *Psychology for Teachers: An Alternative Approach*, London: Hutchinson.

Street, P. (2004) 'Those who can teach deconstructing the teacher's personal presence and impact in the classroom', *Triangle Journals*.
   This paper on the impact of personal attributes on teaching was presented as a paper at a Vocational Education conference in 2004.

Wegerif, R. and Dawes, L. (2004) *Thinking and Learning with ICT: Raising Achievement in Primary Classrooms*, London: Routledge.

Other resources and websites

British Council/British Broadcasting Corporation Learning Styles and Teaching: www.teachingenglish.org.uk/
articles/learning-styles-teaching
   This site has a useful summary of teaching and learning styles. Do note that some of these conflict with
   the advice in Unit 5.6, which reports research from neuroscientists.

Geoff Barton's website: www.geoffbarton.co.uk
   Geoff Barton has been an English teacher for years. His website is well worth a visit.

Appendix 2 on pages 591–595 provides further examples of websites you may find useful.

Capel, S., Leask, M. and Turner, T. (eds) (2010) *Readings for Learning to Teach in the Secondary School:
A Companion to M Level Study*, London: Routledge.
   This book brings together essential readings to support you in your critical engagement with key issues
   raised in this textbook.

The subject-specific books in the Routledge *Learning to Teach* series are also very useful.

Any additional resources and an editable version of any relevant tasks/tables in this unit are available
on the companion website: www.routledge.com/cw/capel

Note
1   'The discrepancy between a child's actual mental age and the level he reaches in solving problems with
   assistance indicates the zone of his proximal development' (Vygotsky 1986: 187).

5.4

Improving your teaching

An introduction to practitioner research, reflective practice and evidence-informed practice

Marilyn Leask and Tony Liversidge

Introduction

As a student teacher, you might ask yourself why such an emphasis is placed on reflective practice and the use of evidence to underpin your professional judgement in your initial teacher education (ITE) programme (see Unit 1.1 on professional judgement and forms of professional knowledge). The analysis of your practice is one of many activities that you are asked to do, such as lesson evaluations, lesson debriefs with tutors, critical reflection on aspects of school-based experience and taking part in lecture and seminar discussions.

Developing your professional judgement through analysing what you are doing, why you are doing it and how to do it effectively, as well as systematically evaluating what you have done, particularly in terms of improving pupils' learning experiences, is a central part of your practice. This reflective practice is undertaken to ensure your teaching produces new learning. Using data from the sources above helps provide evidence for your answer to the question 'How do you know that your lesson went well?' Observing that pupils are quiet, busy, happy or good and look as if they are working industriously is no guarantee that the learning you have intended is taking place. Detailed advice about evaluation of your lessons is provided in Units 2.1 and 2.2.

OBJECTIVES

At the end of this unit, you should be able to:

- demonstrate an understanding of the terms practitioner research, action research, reflective practice and evidence-informed practice;
- identify different forms of evidence on which you can draw to enable you to make an informed decision concerning an aspect of practice;
- apply research strategies to evaluate and improve aspects of your teaching;
- develop your ability to reflect on practice based on evidence from research to acquire higher levels of professional knowledge and judgement.

Check the requirements for your ITE programme to see which relate to this unit.

Reflective practice and evidence-informed practice

Wright (2008) argues that developing the habit of reflecting on your work is perhaps the most significant driver of your learning to teach, and your tutors will push you on this aspect from the very start so that you will develop these good habits. However, they will recognise that you will need constructive guidance on reflective practice and they will give feedback on your teaching, suggest new strategies to try out, and encourage you to spend time and energy thinking about how to develop your teaching.

Casting a critical eye over what you do, including carrying out the tasks throughout this book, and sharing and discussing your 'findings' with fellow professionals, will bring new insights and new levels of understanding and enable you to refine your teaching methods, discover new approaches and compare how others have tackled similar situations. Rather than relying on your own opinions or superficial anecdotal observations, this reflective practice will allow you to gather evidence that can be examined critically. In this way, your evaluation of practice becomes more rigorous and can be regarded as bringing practical research into teaching with a view to enhancing the quality of learning and teaching at the same time. You become what Handscomb (2013) calls a 'teacher enquirer'.

In this unit, we introduce you to simple techniques that may help you find more systematic answers to questions about your teaching and other school activities, and provide a brief introduction to practitioner research more generally. This type of research is undertaken in many schools to support school improvement and the approach stems from long-standing research into how professionals can work to improve practice (Stenhouse 1975). We also suggest that once you gain qualified teacher status, you extend your knowledge and understanding of the tools of practitioner research. Here, as Biggam (2015) notes, the incorporation of information skills (or i-skills) plays a crucial role: you need to establish what information you need; where to get that information; how to access, retrieve and organise it; assess its relevance and worth; and exploit it and communicate it to your advantage. In addition, you should aim to develop techniques for reflective thinking and reviewing evidence of effective practice as part of your continuing professional development (CPD).

Increasingly, teachers are able to access research and evidence to inform their decisions. This approach gives rise to the phrase 'evidence-informed' practice. Oversby (2012) (in quoting from Morris 2004) offers that such practice involves the 'conscientious, explicit and judicious use of current best evidence in making decisions about the learning and learning experience offered to students'. It is no coincidence that recent governmental responses to reports such as the *Carter Review of Initial Teacher Training* (ITT) (DfE 2015f) and the *Teacher Workload Challenge* (DfE 2051g) and its championing of evidence-based teaching through the Education Endowment Foundation (EEF), have recognised that the Teachers' Standards should be amended to be more explicit about the importance of teachers taking an evidence-informed approach, and that there needs to be a strong evidence base to build arguments about effective practice. We use the term evidence-informed rather than evidence-based as educational contexts and learners backgrounds vary so we define *evidence-informed practice as the exercise of your professional judgement in the light of evidence from a range of sources.*

You may at some point find that you have the opportunity to join teacher-researcher networks that have the goal of building the evidence base for practice. Schools may be part of networks, and you may be part of a subject specialist network. There are networks on LinkedIn, groups on Facebook and one such set of professional networks is developing through MESH – Mapping Educational

Specialist KnowHow Initiative and an educational charity, which aims to provide a sustainable system using resources already in the education system to generate, quality assure and update evidence-based summaries written for educators (MESH Guides). (See the link to the MESH and Education Communities Web 2.0 environment at the end of this unit.)

Processes of reflective practice and practitioner research

Schön (1983) used the phrase 'reflective practitioners' to explain how enlightened professionals work in modern society. Dewey (1933) introduced the notion of 'reflective thinking'. These concepts signify how professionals, such as teachers, are able to analyse the effectiveness of their actions and to develop different ways of working as a result. Thus, professionals are constantly learning about what they do and so improving their practice. Drawing upon the concepts advanced by Schön and Dewey, in addition to those proposed by Stenhouse (1975, 1983) of the 'teacher as researcher' and Hoyle and John's (1995) distinctions between 'extended and restricted' professionals, Zwozdiak-Myers (2009) identifies nine dimensions of reflective practice. You may find it helpful to keep these in mind as you work through this unit and consider how you might collect data on your own practice to provide a foundation for improvement. Figure 5.4.1 sets out these dimensions.

However, merely thinking about what you do is not the same as researching it. A teacher researcher, while also being a reflective practitioner, adds to this by using research techniques to enhance and systematise that reflection to justify their actions and thus to improve their practice and continue to develop professionally. Such investigation into their own practice by professionals themselves has come to be known as 'action research', 'practitioner research' or 'teacher enquiry'.

In practitioner and action research, the aim is to look at some aspect of your own or the school's practice, which is giving rise to some concern, identify the precise nature of the problem, collect

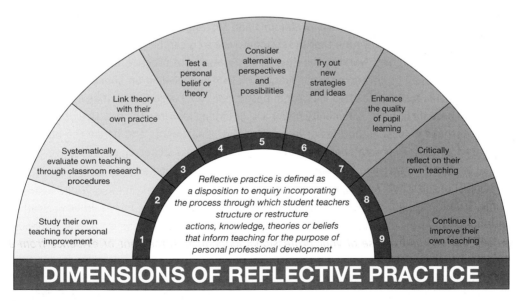

Figure 5.4.1 Dimensions of reflective practice

Source: Zwozdiak-Myers (2009)

some data concerning the problem and then devise a solution. In this respect, McNiff and Whitehead note that:

> Action research involves learning in and through action and reflection . . . Because action research is always to do with learning and learning is to do with education and growth, many people regard it as a form of educational research.
>
> (McNiff and Whitehead 2002: 15)

However, Sharp (2009) notes that although action research might also be considered synonymous with practitioner research, particularly in terms of 'hands-on', small-scale projects, practitioner research is perhaps less attached to some of the more defining characteristics of what is referred to as the action research cycle. For the beginning practitioner researcher, a more 'manageable' type of action research might be that termed by Cain *et al.* (2007) as 'literature-informed, one-turn action research', where 'literature-informed' indicates the guiding role played by relevant literature and where 'one-turn' indicates one turn of the planning, acting, observing and reflecting cycle is sufficient to effect significant improvement in practice.

The additional aspects of true action research are that the devised solution is then implemented and evaluated, which may then lead a series of cycles of research and to further reflection on the problem, additional data collection and another solution being devised, implemented and evaluated. It is the link between action and research that Hopkins (2008) suggests has a powerful appeal for teachers and in this 'living theory' action research methodology (McNiff and Whitehead 2009), which is something of an ongoing, formative, proactive and evolutionary process, the teacher can be 'at the heart of the action and at the heart of the research' (McDonagh *et al.* 2012: 112).

In theory, an action research cycle may be repeated a number of times before suitable solutions are found. Thus, evaluation, reflective teaching and practitioner (action) research are closely bound together, sharing a similar concept of cyclical or spiral development, often going through several iterations (see the action research models of Kemmis and McTaggart, 1988: 14; Elliott, 1991: 71).

In addition, Menter *et al.* (2011) note that practitioner research can be collaborative and involve a group of teacher researchers working together, investigating the practice of others as well as their own across a school or college or other educational setting, scaling up small-scale research. They also add that this research is often classroom-based, but could include activities in staffrooms, or enquiries with parents or other community members, or indeed look into the practice of education policymaking, perhaps in local authorities or in government departments and hence the outcomes might be shared with other practitioners beyond the individual researcher or collaborative group. For example, teachers researching into an issue they have noticed, such as pupil achievement in a particular subject or the school monitoring process, may have identified areas such as pupil behaviour at lunchtime, truancy or pupil preparation for assessment at Key Stage 3 (KS3) as being in need of investigation.

Table 5.4.1 outlines points to consider in planning a practitioner research project. Schools have access to benchmarking data and pupil data, which can provide a useful foundation for researching the impact of different forms of teaching on different types of pupils; for example, from the Centre for Evaluation and Management (Durham University) pupil tests (ALIS and YELLIS, MidYS, SOSCA, as described on www.cemcentre.org/) tests or the GL Assessment Cognitive Abilities Tests (previously called National Foundation for Educational Research (NFER) CATS tests).

Table 5.4.1 Planning a practitioner research project

Research focus
You need to be clear about the focus of the research. It is a useful exercise to write a paragraph at the outset explaining what is going to be investigated and why this is worth doing. When the focus is decided, a number of research questions need to be devised in order to identify precisely what it is you wish to find out. These are the central questions of the research and are important as they provide you with a clear trail to follow. Patterson's (2016a, 2016b, 2016c) research methods MESHGuides are designed to support teacher research.
Data sources
It is important to consider current research findings and what has already been written about your focus (many schools have links with universities and so can access university libraries, and increasingly there are open online resources – see the websites at the end of this unit as well as the further reading). This will add to your professional knowledge and inform your research. You then need to decide what data you need to collect and where those data might be held. The most likely sources of data for teacher researchers include pupils, teachers from the same or different schools, parents, other adults working with children, documents such as pupil reports, school records and written policies, inspection reports, government or similar publications.
Research methods
After identifying the sources, you can now decide upon appropriate methods of data collection. Designing the 'tools' to gather information may at first seem daunting but this should not be the case. In your teaching, you are continually using data collection skills through questioning pupils, scanning your classroom, marking pupils' work and analysing curriculum documents. Carrying out practitioner research enables you to use and further develop these skills. Basic tools for collecting data are through interviews, questionnaires, observation and analysis of documents.
Timeline
Now that you have a clear research focus and research questions, the sources of data have been identified and the methods have been decided upon, you can develop a timeline for the collection and analysis of data. A clear plan helps ensure that nothing important has been missed out and gives you more control over the process by fitting the research into your existing work commitments. It is particularly important to have a clear timeline when evaluating initiatives where data has to be collected at specific points. For instance, the evaluation of a curriculum initiative on the teaching of a history module, using drama techniques, to a Year 7 class would have to be carefully planned beforehand as data could only be collected during the teaching and immediately after.

Very often when new initiatives are introduced into schools, such as the development of person-alised and flexible approaches to learning, they are evaluated through the techniques of practitioner research and enquiry.

Before embarking on practitioner research, you, along with other colleagues involved, need to have thought through and discussed the purpose of the enquiry. This enables you to construct a plan that identifies what is going to be investigated, what questions you want to try to answer, how the research will be carried out and what will be the expected outcomes in terms of data and analysis. These factors can then be put in a time frame that offers targets to work towards. While it is important to have a clear plan, as a researcher you must be prepared to adapt and change according to altering circumstances. In this way, planning and conducting classroom research mirrors the teaching process itself. The research encompasses some of the methods you have already been using, such as observation, keeping a diary, obtaining the perspective of different interested parties (pupils, staff, parents) by the use of interview and questionnaire, and examining documents (Patterson 2016b). Table 5.4.1 provides you with guidance for planning a practitioner research project. Evaluating evidence from practice and research is a professional skill. Task 5.4.1 is designed to give you practice in this.

More detailed advice, including undertaking a literature review and reporting your research, are provided in Patterson's MESHGuides (Patterson 2016a, 2016b, 2016c).

 Task 5.4.1 Evaluating research and evidence

You need to understand data collection methods not just so that you can conduct research yourself, but also to evaluate evidence from other larger-scale research projects that may be used to make informed judgements on your own practice. In this way, teaching becomes an evidence-based profession.

Choose a research article from an education research journal, the Online Educational Resources Journal or the Education Resource Information Center (ERIC) or a systematic review from the Evidence for Policy and Practice Information Centre (EPPI) Centre on an area of teaching that particularly interests you. How were the data in the article collected? What are the key findings and do they add to your knowledge or understanding in any way?

Record your reflections in your PDP.

Research techniques for use in the classroom

As mentioned previously, the usual methods of collecting data are interviews (group or one-to-one), questionnaires, observations, diaries and analysis of documents (the texts in the further reading provide more detail). When used, these methods need to be carefully designed to ensure the information you want is obtained while also considering the feelings of those from whom it is being collected.

Ethical issues

An ethical approach is a key aspect of any educational research. Teachers and other professionals working in classrooms have a duty of care for their pupils. Within this professional way of working, there is a need to respect others and share information as appropriate, yet also maintain trust and individual confidentiality. There are ethical considerations to be taken into account when you are collecting data from pupils and teachers. You must be open about the purposes of your research and obtain agreement from those who are in a position to give it; your tutor may advise you to get the permission of the head teacher and others involved. You should consider the role of the pupils in your research and how much to involve them. Pupils are invariably as interested as teachers in educational improvements and the positive developments in school life that can result from such research. You need to take your responsibility in the area of ethics seriously. It is worth consulting

Table 5.4.2 An ethical approach to practitioner research

You must take responsibility for the ethical use of any data collected and for maintaining confidentiality. Before starting, check the ethical requirements at your higher education institution. We suggest that you should, as a matter of course:

1   Ask a senior member of staff as well as teachers directly involved with your classes for permission to carry out your project. Get ethics approval from you ITE provider. They will have a formal process for this.

2   Before you start, provide staff involved with a copy of the outline of your project, which should include:

   (a) the area you are investigating;
   (b) how you are going to collect any evidence;
   (c) who you are going to collect evidence from;
   (d) what you intend to do with the data collected (for example, whether it is confidential and whether it will be written up anonymously or not);
   (e) who the audience for your report will be;
   (f) any other factors relevant to the particular situation.

3   Consider if you need to ask for pupil and/or parental consent.

4   Think about how you want the pupils to be involved in the research.

5   Check whether staff expect to be given a copy of your work.

6   If you store data electronically, then you should check that you conform to the requirements of the Data Protection Act. For example, you should not store personal data on computers without the explicit authorisation of the individual.

the British Educational Research Association ethical guidelines (www.bera.ac.uk) for a more detailed consideration of ethical issues. Table 5.4.2 outlines the key areas to consider.

Interviewing

Interviews can take many forms depending upon whom you are interviewing, where the interview is being held and what the focus is. Interviews can be very formal, as is the case when a candidate is interviewed for a teaching post, or they can be very informal and part of an everyday conversation, as when a teacher asks a pupil from their tutor group how they are getting on with their General Certificate of Secondary Education (GCSE) coursework. Different types of interview are a normal part of a school day, and teachers can become very skilled at gathering information from pupils by such methods. Consider, for instance, how you might 'interview' a pupil about an incident on the corridor between lessons, or a pupil who is finding work in a particular subject difficult. These are both instances where you employ your professional judgement and skills to find out what has been going on and what the issues are. You are then in a position to act appropriately. Teachers are also used to 'interviewing' or talking with parents when working together to aid the progress of their children. It is also helpful to ask small groups of pupils about particular issues in what can be termed 'focus group interviews'.

When conducting interviews as part of practitioner research, it is important to consider beforehand what questions need to be asked, how they will be asked and how the data will be recorded. You may wish to tape-record them, though it is often easier to make brief notes under key headings during or immediately after the interviews.

Questionnaires

A questionnaire is useful for surveying pupil or parental views. They can enable the collection of information from a large number of people comparatively quickly and anonymously if appropriate. Here, you might want to consider the use of an online survey tool such as Survey Monkey or Bristol Online Surveys (BOS), which can also do some analysis of the data for you. In a questionnaire, the wording and layout of the questions is very significant. They need to be framed so that those being asked, Year 7 pupils, for instance, can understand and answer appropriately. How the completed questionnaires are collected in also needs to be considered. If they are given to whole groups of pupils, it is possible to explain the purpose of the questionnaire, read out the questions and then collect them all in at the end of a lesson. Always test out the questions with a small group to check the questions are understood and that the answers are likely to be relevant to the topics being researched.

Observation schedules

An observation schedule provides a structured framework for recording classroom behaviours. Observations should be carefully planned so as to cause the least disruption to the lesson. Unit 2.1 provides information about observation schedules, as does Unit 5.3. You should by now have used forms of observation schedules to observe classroom routines. It is not possible to record everything that happens in a classroom so you need to focus on, for example, a particular group or pupil or aspect of the teacher's work and record behaviour over time. It is important that you devise your own observation schedules to suit your particular purpose. Video recordings provide an additional way of recording data about classroom activities.

Paired observation

This is a streamlined procedure that enables you to obtain feedback on aspects of your work that are difficult for you to monitor. The example in Unit 5.3, of two student teachers working together with one providing feedback on the topic chosen by the other, is an example of paired observation in practice. Paired observation works in the following way: two colleagues pair up with the purpose of observing one lesson each and then giving feedback about particular aspects of the lesson or the teaching of the person observed. The person giving the lesson decides the focus of the observation. The three stages of a paired observation are:

■ Step 1: You both agree the focus of the observation and what notes, if any, are to be made.
■ Step 2: You each observe one lesson given by the other. Your observations and notes are restricted to the area requested.
■ Step 3: You give each other feedback on the issue under consideration.

The cycle can be repeated as often as you wish.

Research diaries and other documents

Diaries can provide valuable data and useful records over a period of time. The researcher and also those involved in the research, such as pupils or teaching colleagues, could keep them. They can be designed in different ways; for instance, a decision may be made to write under specific headings giving short relevant pieces of information such as the subjects that give homework each night, the particular tasks set and the length of time spent on each. Alternatively, the diarists could be allowed to express themselves more freely; for example, explaining how they feel each day's lessons have gone and the reasons why they think this. The structure chosen depends upon the nature of the research project and is a decision to be made by the researcher, often in conjunction with the participants. All sorts of documents can provide useful information to the practitioner researcher; for example, government, local authority (LA) and school policies, pupil work and curriculum documents. In addition, analysis of pupil work, asking pupils to write about or draw images of a topic/issue being researched and biographical accounts written by participants all provide useful insights into life in school and the learning that is taking place.

You need to be aware that there are in fact many ways of collecting information, and it is important to be creative as well as adaptable in considering data collection. For instance, the use of social media, such as Facebook, Twitter, LinkedIn, blogs, crowdsourcing and open community research sites, can be a source of data or information and enable you to network with other researchers (Bell and Waters 2014). In addition, YouTube has a huge number of videos about aspects of research that are accessible and informative for teacher researchers. Note that some of the texts and Web resources in the recommended reading give more detailed advice on how to design and use the methods mentioned above.

Task 5.4.2 is designed to give you practice in planning the kind of research project that student teachers are likely to undertake.

 Task 5.4.2 Planning your research project

Your ITE programme will normally include a small research project as an assignment. Check your programme requirements with your tutor. The process is as follows:

- Identify an issue or problem associated with your teaching for further investigation (for example, challenging the more able pupils or the development of active learning techniques).
- Outline the focus of the research and explain why this is an important area for you to investigate.
- Write a number of key research questions (about three) that identify what you need to find out.
- Undertake a literature review to check what has been done before (use the websites at the end of this unit). List the likely sources of data.
- Identify methods to collect the data.
- If they are available, have a look at some of the projects that have been done previously by people on your programme.

We suggest you discuss your findings with your tutor and other student teachers. Store your findings in your PDP.

Analysing evidence about teaching and learning

As a practitioner-researcher, you need to develop a strategy for data collection that is most appropriate for the chosen research focus. This strategy often involves the use of both quantitative and qualitative data. Decisions that you make have implications for the type of data analysis that will be appropriate for you to use. However, whatever types you use, the onus will be on you to present your analysis in a way that can be understood, so that, for instance, patterns can be more easily identified. The evidence available for drawing conclusions about teaching and learning can take different forms. This evidence includes:

■ quantitative data in numerical form that can be collected from a range of sources; for example, statistical returns, questionnaires and school management information systems. League tables of school performance are a good example of how quantitative data can be presented and used. These types of data are useful for measurement and comparison on a large scale but often lack explanation for individual differences and can feel very impersonal;

■ qualitative data, which are more descriptive and often include detailed personal explanations. These data are 'richer' and give a feel for particular cases but are sometimes harder to analyse and do not lend themselves easily to measurement. Such data are collected through observation, interview, analysis of documents, diaries, video, photographs, discussions and focus group brainstorming.

For instance, if you were investigating a problem of pupil truancy at your school, you would be likely to require quantitative data showing the extent of truancy and any relationship this has to factors such as age, gender, pupil performance, the time of day or particular lessons. You may also want qualitative data that gives a more in-depth and personal explanation of truancy from the perspectives of truants, their teachers and parents. Using both types of data helps to give a fuller understanding of the issues.

Task 5.4.3 is designed to give you an overview of the performance data available in your school.

As part of any previous school experience, you may have been set assignments that involved the collection of a range of information to support your analysis. These tasks will have started with a clear focus or a question to answer, such as 'What routines does the teacher use in managing the work of the class?' You may have collected evidence from various literature sources to help you to answer that question initially. In addition, you may have observed and made notes about what

---

 Task 5.4.3 Reviewing performance data at your school

Schools have information systems that provide data showing how pupils are performing. Subject departments collect such data as part of the annual reviewing process and to inform future development plans. Find out about the different types of evidence and the process used in your school to evaluate the effectiveness of teaching, pupils' learning and the monitoring of individual pupil progress. Consider how these data inform the setting of future targets for pupils, teachers, subject departments and the school. Store your findings in your PDP.

the pupils and the teacher actually did during a variety of lessons; you may have looked at the pupils' work and the teacher's lesson plans; you may have cross-checked your perceptions with those of the teacher as a way of eliminating bias, improving accuracy and identifying alternative explanations. In doing such assignments, you have been involved in basic classroom research. In such research, data are gathered from different sources, checked for alternative perceptions/explanations, as exemplified in the fifth dimension of Zwozdiak-Myers' (2009) model of reflective practice, and conclusions are drawn from this information so as to develop teaching in the future. This process, whereby you approach the topic of the research from as many different angles and perspectives as possible, gathering a wide range of data in order to gain a greater understanding, is called triangulation. Miles and Huberman (1994) have suggested that the constant checking and double-checking involved means that triangulation becomes a way of life in such research. Burton *et al.* (2008) provide a more detailed discussion of how to improve the validity of your research project in this way.

SUMMARY AND KEY POINTS

In this unit, we have provided simply a brief introduction into an important area of professional practice and accountability.

- Evidence-informed practice = professional judgement + evidence. Critical reflection aided by practitioner research, by individuals or by teams, provides the means by which the quality of teaching and learning in the classroom can be evaluated as a prelude to improvement.
- Developing your teaching skills is one important aspect of your professional development. But other important attributes of the effective teacher that we stress in this book are developing the quality and extent of your professional knowledge and judgement through reflective practice.
- Building your professional knowledge and judgement are longer-term goals, which are developed through re ection and further professional development.
- In this unit, we have opened a door on information and strategies that you can use to reflect on the quality of your teaching.
- We suggest that you come back to this work during the year and again later in your career, because increasingly as a professional you can expect to be asked to provide evidence to underpin your approach to education. The application of practitioner research to your work at that later stage opens your eyes to factors influencing your teaching and learning that you may not have known existed.
- You should now have ideas about practitioner research and how to evaluate the quality of your teaching through using a continuous cycle of critical reflection so that you can plan improvement based on evidence. If you intend to develop your research skills, then we suggest that you join relevant communities of practice on the Web and read several of the texts and review the materials on the websites referenced below and on page 591–595, and consult with experienced colleagues.

Check which requirements for your ITE programme have been addressed through this unit.

Further reading

Bell, J. and Waters, S. (2014) *Doing Your Research Project: A Guide for First Time Researchers*, 6th edn, Berkshire: McGraw-Hill.
This is an excellent text that gives step-by-step advice on completing a research project, including how to prepare for research and draft and finalise a methodologically sound and well-written report. It also warns you of potential pitfalls to prevent you wasting time on false trails.

Burton, D. and Bartlett, S. (2004) *Practitioner Research for Teachers*, London: Paul Chapman.
This text discusses the nature of practitioner research and its importance for your professional development as a teacher. It also provides useful practical guidance on the designing of research projects and data collection.

Burton, N., Brundrett, M. and Jones, M. (2008) *Doing Your Education Research Project*, London: Sage.
The authors take you through the process of designing and conducting a research project. It is a useful text for studying research methods as part of an academic qualification or if you are seeking to conduct research in your professional situation.

Costello, P.J.M. (2011) *Effective Action Research: Developing Reflective Thinking and Practice*, London: Continuum.
This title provides clear and accessible advice to the research novice on the key issues in action research.

Hopkins, D. (2008) *A Teacher's Guide to Classroom Research*, 4th edn, Milton Keynes: Open University Press.
This book is concerned with the development of teachers as researchers as a means to improving classroom practice. It gives clear advice on all aspects of the research process.

Koshy, V. (2005) *Action Research for Improving Practice: A Practical Guide*, London: Paul Chapman.
This provides practical advice on action research in the classroom.

Patterson, E.W. (2016a) *Research Methods 1: Doing a Literature Review: How to Find and Make Sense of Published Research*, MESHGuide, University of Winchester www.meshguides.org.

Patterson, E.W. (2016b) *Research Methods 2: Developing Your Research Design*, MESHGuide, University of Winchester www.meshguides.org.

Patterson, E.W. (2016c) *Research Methods 3: Considering Ethics in Your Research*, MESHGuide, University of Winchester www.meshguides.org.
These MESHGuides are written specifically for teachers interested in research.

Thomas, G. (2009) *How to Do Your Research Project: A Guide for Students in Education and Applied Social Sciences*, London: Sage.
This book takes you through what should happen at each phase in a research project's schedule and provides down-to-earth advice on how to weave the various elements of a project together into a coherent whole.

Wilson, E. (2009) *School-Based Research: A Guide for Education Students*, London: Sage.
The book is focused clearly on the needs of the new classroom researcher and offers a guide to the research process. It offers ideas on how to research issues that teachers are likely to be concerned with, such as ability grouping, pupil voice, pupil behaviour, teaching approaches and pupil motivation.

Other resources and websites

British Educational Research Association: www.bera.ac.uk
This is one professional association where educational researchers (teachers or academics) will present their work.

ERIC – the Education Resources Information Center: www.eric.ed.gov/ERICWebPortal/resources/html/about/about_eric.html
This is the US-based online digital library of education research and information. ERIC is sponsored by the Institute of Education Sciences (IES) of the US Department of Education.

Evidence for Policy and Practice Information Centre: www.eppi.ioe.ac.uk
This has a list of systematic reviews of practice in education.

MESHGuides: www.MESHGuides.org
> This site gives you access to research summaries and researching networks.

Online education communities: https://knowledgehub.local.gov.uk/
> This provides access through a people and 'community' finder to others with similar interests and includes teacher researcher/academic and teacher/academic research review networks. Other professional networks are subject association networks, via Twitter and LinkedIn. Some people do use Facebook as a professional community, but this is also a social networking site and it is wise to keep professional activities separate from social activities.

Online Educational Research Journal: www.oerj.org
> This is an open access educational journal provided by Durham University.

Teaching and Learning Research Programme: www.tlrp.org/
> This archive provides access to resources developed under a major national programme.

Teacher Training Resource Bank Archive: http://webarchive.nationalarchives.gov.uk/20101021152907/ http://www.ttrb.ac.uk/
> This was a major source of evidence to inform practice until it was archived by the coalition government elected in the UK in 2010. Some links still work.

Appendix 2 on pages 591–595 provides examples of further websites you may find useful.

Capel, S., Leask, M. and Turner, T. (eds) (2010) *Readings for Learning to Teach in the Secondary School: A Companion to M Level Study*, **London: Routledge.**
> This book brings together essential readings to support you in your critical engagement with key issues raised in this textbook.

The subject-specific books in the Routledge *Learning to Teach* series are also very useful.

> **Any additional resources and an editable version of any relevant tasks/tables in this unit are available on the companion website: www.routledge.com/cw/capel**

Acknowledgements

Research underpinning the advice in this unit stems from a number of research and development projects funded by the Local Government Association, Becta, the European Union, the Manpower Services Commission, the Department for Education/Department for Education and Skills (DfE/DfES), and what was the Training and Development Agency for Schools (TDA) over a 25-year period. Further information on these initiatives is provided in the following:

Leask, M. (1988) Teachers as evaluators: a grounded approach to project evaluation, MPhil thesis, University of Cambridge library, available at: http://library.beds.ac.uk/record=b1468955~S20.
> This work researched reliability and validity of the Teacher Evaluator approach, building on Lawrence Stenhouse's seminal work.

Leask, M. (2004) 'Accumulating the evidence base for educational practice: our respective responsibilities', Paper presented at the British Educational Research Association Annual conference, 16–18 September 2004.

Leask, M. (2011) 'Improving the professional knowledge base for education: using knowledge management and Web 2.0 tools', *Policy Futures in Education*, **9(5).**

Leask, M. and Younie, S. (2014) 'National models for CPD: the challenges of twenty-first century knowledge management', Special Edition, *Journal for Professional Development in Education (PDiE)*.

5.5 Closing the achievement gap
Personalising learning

Carrie Winstanley

Introduction

Successive English governments have been concerned with closing the achievement gap through different approaches to school improvement, general education policy and social initiatives. Early secondary school education has been identified as a key stage for the introduction of 'intensive catch-up programmes' to address problems persisting from early years and primary school contexts (Wellings and Wood 2012: 7:D.2). Units considering the issues around social initiatives and education policy can be found in Chapter 7. This unit is concerned more with pedagogic practices that can help in the struggle to raise achievement through matching learning tasks to pupils' strengths and supporting them effectively where necessary. Primarily, the unit focuses on personalising tasks and feedback, and on helping pupils to improve how they understand their own learning through self-regulation.

Personalised learning occurs when learning is tailored to individual needs, interests and aptitudes. The aim is to ensure that each pupil achieves the highest standards possible for their abilities, regardless of their background and circumstances. A further emphasis is on equipping pupils for more autonomy in their learning, which is considered vital to cope in the rapidly changing world of work. Closely related to this is the notion of self-regulated learning; pupils can be helped to learn about how they learn and to control and improve their learning.

This unit explains, first, the concepts of personalising learning. It then places these ideas in a classroom context. The next section discusses self-regulation, with a focus on helping pupils become independent learners. All of the concepts in this unit are linked to aspects of good practice in learning and teaching, such as the importance of knowing pupils' interests, motivations, strengths and problems. The role of the teacher in ensuring consistent best practice, meeting pupils' needs and facilitating acceptable levels of achievement is therefore very important.

OBJECTIVES

At the end of this unit, you should be able to:

■ show awareness of the issues surrounding the aim of closing the achievement gap;
■ understand what is meant by personalising learning and by self-regulated learning;
■ recognise instances of good practice in personalising learning and self-regulation;
■ be better equipped to embed personalising learning in your own teaching and to support pupils developing self-regulation.

Check the requirements of your initial teacher education (ITE) programme to see which relate to this unit.

Closing the achievement gap

Raising achievement is a vital part of education and so the means required to close the gap extend beyond the teacher in the classroom. Through effective systems and organisation, school structures need to help with the development of a supportive ethos. A positive school culture promotes teachers and school leaders with high aspirations for all pupils and facilitates significant levels of engagement. This in turn helps to maximise achievement for all.

Schools do not operate in a vacuum. It is incumbent on local authorities (LAs) and government agencies to provide a supportive and flexible environment to help schools achieve their learning aims. Similarly, pupils' parents and carers should be encouraged to develop active partnerships with schools in order to help them understand, value and contribute to their children's education. By involving families and communities with their children's education, the high aspirations and support are not restricted to the hours in a day when the child is in school. This is helpful in developing self-regulation and fostering positive attitudes to learning, as you will see as this unit unfolds (Dweck 2012). Since the first priority for you as you learn to teach is how to manage general classroom learning, however, the rest of this unit focuses on personalising learning in practice and on self-regulation. A range of teaching and learning techniques and strategies are included that will help close the achievement gap if harnessed effectively, including many that are part of personalised learning and self-regulation such as metacognitive strategies and subject-specific tactics. The English Department for Education (DfE) suggests some 'generic strategies which are beneficial for low attainers', and many of these overlap with the ideas in this unit:

> Early intervention; monitoring of pupils' progress; tailoring teaching to the appropriate needs of individual pupils; coaching teachers/teaching assistants in specific teaching strategies such as cooperative learning; cognitive approaches, based on mental processes; one-to-one tuition; peer-to-peer support; aspects of the home-school relationship; and study support.
>
> (DfE 2012f: 6)

Task 5.5.1 asks you to reflect on issues around closing the achievement gap for your pupils.

Task 5.5.1 Considering the achievement gap

Thinking about your current school experience and previous experiences with learners, identify pupils who you feel did not always perform as well as you anticipated. What evidence did you have that their actual performance was less good than their potential performance? Was this underachievement consistent across different curriculum subjects? What did you learn about the pupils outside of the curriculum requirements?

   Record your responses in your professional development portfolio (PDP) and discuss with other student teachers.

Task 5.5.2 asks you to compare resources you have put together to support personalising learning in your classroom with those of other student teachers. Collegial support and collaborative working are important features of teaching where the goal is for every pupil to succeed.

 Task 5.5.2 Resources to support closing the achievement gap

If you are a student teacher in Wales, Scotland or Northern Ireland, there are considerable resources available online to support the curriculum and teaching in each country. We suggest you become familiar with the specific resources developed by the department for education in your country. The links below provide a starting point.

Education Scotland: www.educationscotland.gov.uk/

Learning Wales: Raising Standards Together: http://learning.gov.wales/?skip=1&lang=en

Department for Education Northern Ireland Raising Standards and School Improvement: www.deni.gov.uk/index/curriculum-and-learningt-new/standards-and-school-improvements.htm

The Education Endowment Foundation (https://educationendowmentfoundation.org.uk/) has been funded by the UK government specifically to support closing the gap in attainment. Research-informed toolkits for many areas of education are available.

   Also ensure that you are familiar with the pupil progress tracking tools used in your placement school. Compare what you have found with other student teachers.

   Record your findings and responses in your PDP.

Raising achievement through self-regulation and personalised learning

When researching theory and ideas about how to support pupils' achievement, it is worth searching for the terms 'underachievement' and 'underachiever'. These are less often used in current literature; the shift in focus is helpful as it focuses on the positive, but much relevant research is published under the auspices of 'underachievement'.

   The concept of 'achievement' is less straightforward than it might first appear. Of course, we can measure it through examination and test results, but taken out of context these results do not give us the whole picture of a child's development and learning. Remember that achievement and ability can be easily confused; see Dweck's work for a contemporary take on how we think about ability (for example, Dweck 1999, 2008). Different types of underachievement can be identified; for some interesting work on various typologies of underachieving pupils, see Wallace *et al.* (2009). It is worth considering the characteristics of high and low achievers when thinking about how to improve performance in all pupils (see Table 5.5.1).

Table 5.5.1 Characteristics of low and high achievers

Characteristics of low-achieving pupils	Characteristics of high-achieving pupils
Rarely monitor their performance	Continually self-monitor
Stick to the same strategies	Adapt their strategies to contexts and tasks
Vague learning goals	Set specific learning goals
Tend to have static learning goals	Willing to adapt their learning goals
Have a narrow range of learning strategies	Use a wide range of learning strategies
Focus on performance goals (comparing with others)	Mastery goals (focusing on self-improvement)
Give up readily in the face of failure	Demonstrate persistence in the face of failure

What is meant by personalising learning?

There are no widely agreed definitions of personalised learning, and so there can be some confusion about what is meant by the term, in particular as it relates closely to individualised learning. You might find slightly different interpretations in official documents and in general education publications and even see diverse definitions in policy documents in different schools. Generally, however, both terms refer to matching learning tasks to pupils' needs wherever possible.

Individualising learning usually suggests pupils working alone, following solo agendas, essentially working in isolation. There may be several pupils working individually, yet all aiming to achieve the same intended learning outcomes, perhaps working through a planned programme at their own individual pace, but essentially completing the same tasks. This is usually led or constructed by the teacher.

Personalising learning differs as it generally incorporates whole-class work and, in particular, interactive group work with interventions for pupils who need additional support. Personalising learning means shaping teaching and learning around the different ways pupils learn. The onus is on schools and teachers to ensure that what they provide in terms of the teaching, curriculum and school organisation is designed to reach as many pupils as possible by providing a wide range of learning experiences for diverse pupil needs across a unit of work. Thus, every pupil's learning is maximised in the context of the current curriculum; it does not mean that each pupil has a personalised curriculum.

One other type of learning should be mentioned when discussing learning being matched to individual needs: *tailored learning*, *personal curricula* or *learning*, or *individual education plans* (usually referred to as IEPs). This type of learning is generally for pupils with specific learning needs who may have been assessed by a psychologist or other specialist. In these instances, pupils can be provided with a very detailed modified curriculum for each and every subject that goes way beyond the more straightforward personalising and individualising learning discussed here. For more details on this type of work, see Unit 4.6 on inclusion and special educational needs.

As the personalisation of learning is such a broad concept, many of these approaches are already discussed in other units; you should therefore also refer to these other units (see, for example, Units 2.3, 3.1, 4.1, 4.3, 5.3 and 6.1).

The principles and practices of personalising learning

The principles of personalising learning in the classroom are a reflection of existing good practice. Pupils' individual needs must be assessed and the curriculum and work being set should be responsive to these needs, creating an inclusive approach to teaching. Useful assessment supports learning and is linked to personal targets, making use of effective feedback primarily from teachers, but also including peer and self-assessment. Peer support should be harnessed, including the use of mentoring for learning matters, as well as social and emotional concerns. Learning strategies should be directly taught, and this links directly to self-regulation.

So, what should personalised learning be like in the classroom? Effective ways to personalise learning include:

■ focusing assessment on its value for learning rather than merely for measuring; making use of assessments and the associated data in order to plan pupils' targets;

■ preventing pupils falling behind through earlier interventions; pupils taught in smaller groups to meet their needs better (accomplished by using teaching assistants and by extending the school day);

■ focusing on developing learning strategies and independent learning skills; dynamic approaches to grouping pupils; matching tasks to ability and providing appropriate challenge; negotiated and realistic targets;

■ information and communications technology (ICT) used more often and with a creative approach; making better use of a virtual learning environment that is pupil-friendly and accessible off-site;

■ providing additional support for pupils when needed to facilitate achievement; a focus on safe school environments where hindrances to learning and teaching (for example, bullying, poor behaviour) are tackled promptly and decisively; ensuring that all pupils have increased opportunities to study safely, particularly pupils from disadvantaged backgrounds (achieved through opening libraries in the evening, running supervised homework sessions, and so on);

■ teachers and managers celebrating achievement and keeping expectations of pupil performance high; relaxing the timetable to increase choice and opportunities; oral praise and prompt feedback to clarify misunderstandings;

■ augmenting or replacing parents' evenings with 'pupil review days' that allow personal meetings for pupils to discuss targets and progress with teachers; shifting the way that parents and carers are involved in their child's education so they have a more active role rather than merely receiving reports of progress or problems; reorganising school staffing to create different approaches to leadership and teaching.

The benefits for pupils

Some of the main potential advantages for pupils in terms of the skills developed through more personalised and individual learning are listed below (assembled from a range of teaching and government Web resources). Note the repeated emphasis on increasing independence and the account taken of pupils' emotional development. Pupils should:

- become more independent workers, requiring less supervision as they build project management techniques;
- develop team work skills through varied small group work;
- learn about the importance of being a reliable, consistent team member;
- become increasingly confident in their approach to problems, building resilience and demonstrating persistence in resolving difficulties through expanded opportunities to control their own work;
- improve their written and oral communication skills owing to increased small group work and more contact with teachers in deeper-level conversations (rather than short answers in a class context);
- increase the responsibility for their own actions by planning their own work, not just responding to short in-class tasks and homework;
- respond to resources with an evaluative and critical mindset, questioning new ideas effectively;
- become more motivated, engaged and excited by their work, encouraging creative responses and deeper learning.

As a student teacher, your major concern is what this means you might do in the classroom. We now turn to some commonly recommended approaches closely associated with personalising learning that you can adopt in your classroom, with short explanations and some suggestions for further developments.

Classroom approaches: teaching/pedagogical strategies

Various factors in approaches to teaching and learning will impact on the personalisation of learning, and in this unit those that link to self-regulation are considered in detail. Other concerns are noted here below; each one is covered in more depth in other units in this volume.

Grouping pupils and group work (see also Units 2.3 and 4.1)

Collaborative group work is central to personalising learning and differs from individual learning in this respect, so it is well worth spending some time considering different options for grouping pupils. Flexibility is the key to ensuring pupils have a range of experiences, and you must be willing to move groups around for different tasks and sometimes even just for a refreshing change.

The importance of questioning techniques (see also Unit 3.1)

The quality of questions both to pupils and from pupils is important, and the 1956 work of Bloom is a still much-used (often adapted) way of thinking about higher-order questioning. Numerous different versions of Bloom's taxonomy exist (Stanford University 2015), but a useful rule of thumb is to ensure that the higher-level aspects or types of thinking – analysis, evaluation and synthesis – are incorporated into all lessons.

Task setting, problem-solving and investigations (see also Units 5.2 and 5.3)

Real-life problems, interesting investigations and meaty projects in which pupils can be involved in depth are preferable to isolated, disconnected tasks and activities. One useful technique for helping pupils plan and execute projects is 'Thinking Actively in a Social Context' (TASC) (Wallace 2000), a model that can be used by pupils to plan long-term project work or short-term activities. It is a flexible tool for thinking and discussing ideas and tasks. The elements are below. There is no prescribed order; the model is usually presented in a circle with no specified start or end point and there are verbs to explain what is being done with a linked trigger question.

- *Gather/organise* – What do I know about this?
- *Identify* – What is the task?
- *Generate* – How many ideas can I think of?
- *Decide* – Which is the best idea?
- *Implement* – Let's do it!
- *Evaluate* – How well did I do?
- *Communicate* – Let's tell someone!
- *Learn from experience* – What have I learned?

The model works well for a variety of ages, and there is plenty of guidance on its use on the National Association for Able Children in Education website (www.nace.co.uk/).

Cognitive issues: accelerated learning, learning styles and metacognition (see also Units 4.3 and 5.1)

Many contemporary ideas about how children's cognitive processes should be harnessed have been controversial. There is little empirical evidence to support the notion of 'accelerated learning', and there is some suggestion that relying on 'learning styles' can even be detrimental (Bjork *et al.* 2013). The idea of metacognition is to focus on how we learn and how we can improve our learning. Useful metacognitive techniques aim to help pupils analyse their own strengths and weaknesses and develop their self-understanding in relation to their work (see Units 4.3 and 5.1 for more on multiple intelligences and metacognition).

Emotional intelligence and motivation

Together with understanding your pupils' metacognition and learning styles, knowledge of their emotional intelligence allows insights to their responses to tasks and assists you with pupil groupings (see Units 4.1 and 4.3). Personalising learning should make it easier to keep pupils motivated as they have been involved in choosing much of their learning (see Unit 3.2).

Differentiation (see also Unit 4.1)

Central to personalising learning is differentiation in order to meet pupils' individual needs. There are many varied ways to differentiate, and you need to choose what is most appropriate in relation to the required learning outcomes. Options include differentiating by adjusting, for example, the content, pace, outcome, level of support or resources.

Self-regulated learning

Self-regulated learning (often referred to as 'self-regulation') refers to the use of strategies and techniques that help learners to reflect actively on their attitudes and to adapt behaviours to improve the achievement of suitable goals to improve learning. Pupils need to be taught techniques and strategies for self-regulation that work for them; it is an individualised process. It requires careful consideration of activities and behaviours, in which pupils evaluate what they have done and how well they achieved their goals. Through repeatedly asking themselves if the strategy they have used really works well for them, they can try to reduce negative behaviours and increase the use of positive behaviours. Through this active process of reflection, pupils learn to take more responsibility for their own learning and focus on improving and developing their own performance and learning.

Zimmerman (2002) describes self-regulation as a self-directive process. Learning becomes a proactive pursuit that pupils do for themselves. Zimmerman and Schunk (1989) identify three aspects of learning that pupils can be taught to self-regulate in order to improve performance:

■ Behaviour – actively controlling resources for study (such as time, place of study and use of staff and peer support).
■ Motivation and affect – controlling feelings about work (such as reducing anxiety) and setting reasonable goals.
■ Cognitive strategies – aiming for deep learning by using effective processing strategies.

More recently, Bjork *et al.* have reviewed the value of self-regulation and concluded that it has become increasingly important, but that 'research on learning, memory, and metacognitive processes has provided evidence that people often have a faulty mental model of how they learn and remember' (Bjork *et al.* 2013: 417). In addition to not carefully scrutinising how they learn, pupils are prone to lapse into making assumptions that can be counterproductive, such as 'over-attributing differences in performance to innate ability' and 'assuming that learning should be easy' (Bjork *et al.* 2013: 436). Self-regulation requires a flexible, growth mindset (Dweck 2012) in which pupils believe that their effort can reap rewards, and that success is achievable as a result of hard work.

Now complete Task 5.5.3, which serves as your own self-regulation activity as well as one you can use with pupils.

Goal setting and self-regulation of tasks (see also Units 3.2 and 6.1)

Goal setting is a vital aspect of self-regulation that pupils can be actively taught to develop. Teachers should support pupils to develop strategies for reviewing their own performance. Once these have been cultivated, pupils can be more involved in setting their own realistic and negotiated learning goals in collaboration with their teachers. This provides vital clarity and transparency, and making the next steps explicit helps keep pupils and teachers on target. Where pupils are progressing

Task 5.5.3 Self-regulating how you study and approach homework

- Study time: How long do you study for each day? Does this depend on the tasks you have been set, or do you have a fixed amount of time for working each day? How often do you take breaks and what do you do when you have a break?
- Study space: Have you access to a dedicated study space? Is it always the same space? Shared? Personal? How is it laid out? Do you enjoy studying there? What would make it even more comfortable?
- Personal timetables: Do you study best in the morning or evening? What other activities do you do during the week and are there days when it is better or worse for you to study? What about the weekends?
- Keeping on track: What distracts you when you are supposed to be studying? How do you manage the distractions? How do you record what you have done and what is left to do? Have you made a study plan or timetable? Do you stick to it?
- Planning: Are you able to accurately plan how long tasks will take? Have you tried timing yourself? How do you manage your deadlines? Do you ever find yourself working right up to a deadline? How does this make you feel? How good are you at prioritising and ordering your work?

You should complete this task individually and then come together with other student teachers to discuss your responses to the questions, as well as thinking about your emotional response to the task. You may find you were making excuses to yourself or being harsh and chastising yourself for poor work habits. Consider how this task might work with pupils and adjust the questions to meet your group's needs and interests.

Try some of the questions with a group of pupils in your teaching and evaluate their effectiveness. Present the findings to the rest of the group. Record the outcomes in your PDP.

particularly well, there is potential to compact curricula, allowing pupils to skip tasks that do not provide them with challenge.

Self-regulation can be approached in different ways, but these ways commonly include: self-evaluation; goal-setting; completing the activity; and monitoring and evaluation. All of these steps are best undertaken with the help of the teacher until the pupil is able to take responsibility for their own learning. So, pupils can be helped to evaluate where they are at the start of a task by thinking about how much they already know about a topic and through linking new experiences to their existing understanding. They then analyse the set task and break it down into manageable learning goals, thinking about the sequence of tasks, timing and the pace of work. The next step is to choose appropriate strategies from a wide range of strategies that have been used in previous tasks. Some teachers help by providing a list of ways to engage in active study such as:

Recording my ideas/understanding; explaining the information to another person; transfering key ideas to electronic or paper index cards; creating quiz questions for a friend to answer; translating the information into a diagram; and so on.

These tactics are no different from effective study skills strategies, but self-regulation requires careful and thorough self-monitoring of pupils' own performance once they have attempted the task and received feedback. Pupils should note what could be improved.

Feedback

Pupils learn to develop their self-regulation through the feedback they receive. When assessing pupils' work, you should emphasise progress and achievement, rather than failure, and avoid making unhelpful comparisons between pupils. Feedback must be constructive and should nurture learners' strategies to help them manage their work. The aim is to involve both teachers and learners in reflection and dialogue, enabling all to have learning opportunities and ensuring that pupils are recognised for their efforts. The feedback should be about the task rather than the pupil and should be linked to attainable standards expressed clearly.

Actively helping pupils learn how to self-regulate can be done by teachers modelling reflection, through thinking aloud and encouraging pupils to practise the same processes together with the teacher and with peers. This can be done in groups, as collaborative learning. Feedback can also be used to help deepen pupils' learning, and, as well as correcting the mechanics of presentation, writing and accuracy of information, teachers can help learners make links between concepts. They can be directed to relevant information and helped to focus their attention on relevant ideas and shown how to develop an analytical approach.

Teaching for self-regulation

As you will have noted, there are implications for the teacher's role in supporting pupils to develop effective self-regulation. In order to help with goal setting, teachers can help to tease apart the components of tasks so they can be tackled effectively. This can be done very clearly at first and then phased out as the pupils see how to break down the tasks themselves. The intention is to shift the responsibility for learning from the teacher to the pupils. Teachers should also encourage a wide range of learning strategies through allowing different responses to tasks where appropriate so that pupils can provide audio and visual answers and not be confined to writing.

The key point to remember is that pupils require direct and explicit teaching if they are to develop effective self-regulation, and that these strategies have been shown to improve learning (Bjork *et al.* 2013).

SUMMARY AND KEY POINTS

Personalising learning involves shaping teaching and learning around the different ways that pupils learn. This has implications for teaching methods, curricular structure and school organisation. Self-regulating learning has been shown to be an effective way to improve motivation and achievement.

You are likely to find that many of the elements of these aspects of learning are already part of what you plan to do in the classroom as they emphasise ideas widely recognised as best practice. These include really getting to know your pupils, varying pedagogies in the classroom, encouraging learners to understand their own learning strategies in order to raise their achievement and using assessment to help with learning.

Check which requirements for your ITE programme you have addressed through this unit.

Further reading

Dweck, C.S. (2012) *Mindset: How You Can Fulfill Your Potential*, London: Constable & Robinson.

> This book addresses what is one of the principal barriers to learning pupils experience – the belief their abilities are fixed. It raised the importance of pupils being helped to adopt a 'growth mindset'. Further references to Dweck's work can be found through her Wikipedia entry or the Mindset website (www.mindsetonline.com/).

Wallace, B., Leyden, S., Montgomery, D., Winstanley, C., Pomerantz, M. and Fitton, S. (2009) *Raising the Achievement of All Pupils within an Inclusive Setting: Practical Strategies for Developing Best Practice*, London: Routledge.

> For some really practical examples of proven effective classroom and whole-school practices, this book is extremely useful. Based on case studies of schools, each chapter combines theory with illustrative examples and covers areas including multiple exceptionalities and social and emotional issues, as well as leadership and inclusion.

West-Burnham, J. and Coates, M. (2007) *Personalising Learning: Transforming Learning for Every Child*, London: Network Educational Press.

> This book is written with a teacher audience in mind and presents a useful combination of theory and practice, taking in ideas such as multiple intelligences and the restructuring of the curriculum. It focuses on the importance of personalised learning for equity, inclusion and effectiveness, and includes some case studies of successful schools that have taken the agenda on board.

Winstanley, C. (2010) *The Ingredients of Challenge*, Staffs: Trentham Books.

> This book is an exploration of the provision of an appropriate challenge for pupils and provides practical suggestions, as well as a theoretical grounding. Understanding pupils as learners is central to the book, and many aspects relate closely to individual and personal learning.

Other resources and websites

BBC *Assessment for Learning*: www.bbc.co.uk/northernireland/forteachers/curriculum_in_action/assessment_for_learning.shtml

Lee, C. (2013) *Mathematics: Assessment for Learning: The Four Operations*, MESHGuide, Open University, UK: www.meshguides.org/category/general-pedagogy/assessment/

National Association for Able Children in Education: www.nace.co.uk/

National College of School Leadership: *Personalising Learning*: www.nationalcollege.org.uk/transfer/open/adsbm-phase-3-module-1-enabling-learning/adsbm-p3m1s2/adsbm-p3m1s2t4.html

> This website is the National College of School Leadership and has links to some of the archived documents from the PL strategy, containing practical ideas.

Open University, *Open Learn: Self Regulated Learning*: www.open.edu/openlearnworks/course/view.php?id=1490%3F

> This is an open access Open University supported course focusing on self-regulated learning and on creating personalised technology-enhanced learning environments.

Procter, R. (2013) *Assessment for Learning*, MESHGuide, University of Bedfordshire, UK: www.meshguides.org/category/general-pedagogy/assessment/

Stanford University (2015) *Teaching Commons: Bloom's Taxonomy of Educational Objectives*: https://teachingcommons.stanford.edu/resources/course-preparation-resources/course-design-aids/bloom%E2%80%99s-taxonomy-educational-objectives

Appendix 2 on pages 591–595 provides further examples of websites you may find useful.

Capel, S., Leask, M. and Turner, T. (eds) (2010) *Readings for Learning to Teach in the Secondary School: A Companion to M Level Study*, London: Routledge.

> This book brings together essential readings to support you in your critical engagement with key issues raised in this textbook.

The subject-specific books in the Routledge *Learning to Teach* series are also very useful.

> Any additional resources and an editable version of any relevant tasks/tables in this unit are available on the companion website: www.routledge.com/cw/capel

5.6 Neuroeducation
The emergence of the brain in education

Paul Howard-Jones

Introduction

> Education is about enhancing learning, and neuroscience is about understanding the mental processes involved in learning. This common ground suggests a future in which educational practice can be transformed by science, just as medical practice was transformed by science about a century ago.
>
> (Royal Society 2011: 1)

In recent years, there has been a step change in efforts to bring neuroscience and education together in dialogue. This is largely owing to the insights that are emerging from neuroscience that have relevance for many areas of education. These insights involve literacy, mathematical development, creativity, adolescent brain development and cognitive enhancing drugs, as well as the understanding, early identification and treatment of development disorders such as dyslexia and attention deficit hyperactivity disorder (ADHD).

A new, exciting and rapidly developing area of research is springing up that focuses explicitly on neuroscience in education: neuroeducation (also called brain, mind and education or educational neuroscience). It is not possible here to provide a comprehensive review of this new area. Instead, this unit is something of a taster. It introduces some initial concepts that can be applied immediately in your practice, highlights some pitfalls worth avoiding, and identifies sources of further information for finding out more. Websites and further reading at the end of the unit provide starting points for exploring this area in more depth.

OBJECTIVES

At the end of this unit, you should be able to:

■ understand why neuroscience is increasingly relevant to educational practice;
■ avoid some popular neuromyths;

- understand brain development and educational achievement are an interaction of genes and experience (such as education), and so educational achievement is not biologically determined;
- understand how an awareness of brain plasticity can benefit learners;
- consider new ways in which you can use reward in the classroom.

Check the requirements of your initial teacher education (ITE) programme to see which relate to this unit.

Neuromyths to avoid

Most teachers think knowledge of the brain is important when developing their practice and, given the central role of the brain in the learning process, this belief appears justified. However, a lack of valid information about neuroscience and training for teachers has helped a parallel world of pseudo-neuroscience to develop within schools. Many concepts that claim a brain-basis are unscientific and educationally unhelpful, so let's first identify some of the most popular but unscientific beliefs about the brain (also called 'neuromyths'). These often originate from authentic science that has then become misinterpreted or over-interpreted. That makes it difficult, but also important, to understand which part is fact and which is fiction. Task 5.6.1 introduces some neuromyths.

Surveys of teachers in countries as diverse as the United Kingdom (UK), Turkey and China show over 90 per cent of teachers believe teaching to pupils' learning styles can improve outcomes (Howard-Jones 2014). Learning preferences do exist, in the sense that different individuals may

---

 Task 5.6.1 Neuromyths: true or false?

Carry out this quick true/false survey on some teachers, learners and friends. You may be surprised how common neuromyths are. The answers are in brackets.

1   We mostly only use 10 per cent of our brains (*false* – we use all our brains all the time).
2   Exercise can improve mental function (*true* – see main text).
3   Coordination exercises can improve integration of left and right hemispheric brain function (*false* – see main text).
4   Pupils are more attentive after sugary drinks and snacks (*true* – although not healthy in other ways, sugary snacks actually increase attention; Busch *et al.* 2002).
5   Regular drinking of caffeinated drinks reduces alertness (*true* – regular caffeine (for example, two cans of caffeinated soft drink a day) reduces children's cognitive function by initiating counter-regulatory changes in the brain; Heatherley *et al.* 2006).
6   Individuals learn better when they receive information in their preferred learning style (*false* – see main text).
    Record the outcomes in your professional development portfolio (PDP).

prefer to receive information in different ways. For example, it is possible to categorise learners' preferences in terms of visual, kinaesthetic or auditory (VAK). However, there seems little educational value in doing so. The functionality of different brain regions is sometimes used to support learning style theory. For example, different regions of the brain are more involved than others in processing visual, auditory and somatosensory (touch) information. But performance in most everyday tasks, including learning of information provided in just one modality (for example, visual), prompts many regions in both hemispheres to work together in a sophisticated parallel fashion.

In reality, the brain is so massively interconnected that sensory experience is always cross-modal in nature so that, for example, visual experience activates auditory brain activity. As Kayser (2007: 24) puts it, 'the brain sees with its ears and touch, and hears with its eyes'. (This interconnectedness of the brain also means that neuroscience cannot be used to support multiple intelligences theories since the distributed nature of neural function suggests we should not characterise individual differences in terms of some limited number of capabilities.) Scientific evidence from laboratory experiments shows that providing information in a learner's preferred VAK style is 'wasted effort' (Kratzig and Arbuthnott 2006).

At the end of their extensive educational review, Coffield *et al.* (2004a) concluded there were no clear implications for pedagogy arising from any existing models of learning styles. However, the effectiveness of multimodal teaching is supported by both educational and scientific research. That is, using a wide variety of modalities (visual, auditory, touch, taste, smell, and so on) to teach every child really can support their learning.

Educational kinesiology (or Edu-K, also often sold under the brand name of Brain Gym®) draws on ideas about perceptual-motor training; that is, that learning problems arise from inefficient integration of visual, auditory and motor skills. This idea spawned several training programmes to remediate learning difficulties through exercises but these were shown to be ineffective by numerous studies in the 1970s and 1980s (Cohen 1969; Sullivan 1972; Hammill *et al.* 1974; Bochner 1978; Arter and Jenkins 1979; Kavale and Forness 1987). A major review of the theoretical foundations of Brain Gym® and the associated peer-reviewed research studies failed to support the contentions of its promoters (Hyatt 2007). Despite this, many teachers remain enthusiastic about Brain Gym® and convinced that it supports learning, with reports of increased reaction times following Brain Gym® exercises suggestive of some positive effect on cognition (Sifft and Khalsa 1991). If Brain Gym® can contribute to learning, it may be for entirely different reasons than those used to promote it.

There is an emerging body of multidisciplinary research showing the beneficial effect of aerobic exercise on selective aspects of brain function, and some of these aspects happen to be particularly important for education (Hillman *et al.* 2008). For example, a study of adults revealed increased levels of brain-derived neurotrophic factor (BDNF) after two three-minute sprints (Winter *et al.* 2007). When compared to sedentary or moderate exercise conditions, participants showed a 20 per cent increase in the speed of recall for words they learned immediately following their intense exercise. BDNF plays an important role in synaptic plasticity, the making of connections between neurons, which is thought to underlie our ability to learn. Neuroscience is shedding light on how exercise and fitness can promote learning. But it seems that aerobic exercise is what's needed, rather than the rehearsal of motor-perception skills.

Drinking water is often promoted as a way to improve learning, and it is true that even mild dehydration can reduce our ability to think (Cian *et al.* 2000). However, a recent adult study has shown that drinking water when not thirsty can also diminish cognitive ability (Rogers *et al.* 2001). Luckily, forgetting to drink water is not usually a problem, because our brains have evolved a sophisticated system that makes us thirsty when our bodies (and brains) need more fluid. So, encouraging and enabling children to drink water when they feel thirsty may be a more sensible approach than constantly monitoring the amount of water they consume. Exercise and unusually hot weather are the exception to this rule, when there is evidence that the body's own monitoring system becomes less reliable, suggesting children might then need encouragement to drink in order to avoid dehydration (Bar-Or *et al.* 1980; Bar-David *et al.* 2005). Apart from these special circumstances, there is no evidence to suggest that normally functioning children are generally prone to voluntary dehydration. Indeed, the only study showing voluntary dehydration in the classroom comes from the Dead Sea region – the lowest point on the planet and notoriously hot (Bar-David *et al.* 2005). Our survey also revealed 20 per cent of student teachers thought their brain would shrink if they failed to drink six to eight glasses of water a day. Very serious dehydration can do this, as graphically illustrated when a man in Japan tried to commit suicide by overdosing on soy sauce (Machino and Yoshizawa 2006). Three weeks later, after appropriate treatment, the man's brain was shown to have returned (mostly) to its original dimensions. However, this was a rare case, and one caused by vast amounts of soy sauce, not by forgetting to drink water.

Brain development and brain plasticity

Brain development results from our genes interacting with our experience. That means that our genes have a major influence on outcomes such as our educational achievement, but these outcomes are not biologically programmed by our DNA. It is important for teachers to understand this, because teachers who develop strong beliefs in the role of genetics are more likely to believe their pupils are limited by their biology (Howard-Jones *et al.* 2009). So, there is a relationship between how teachers think about brain development and their attitude towards learners in the classroom.

However, whatever your age and stage of development, the brain always remains plastic. That means that the way our brain functions, the way its neurons connect with each other and even the shape and size of its various parts can change as a result of experience, and that includes educational experience. Of course, the brain is more plastic during childhood, but even the adult brain remains plastic and able to learn, as in the example shown in Figure 5.6.1.

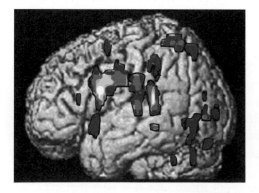 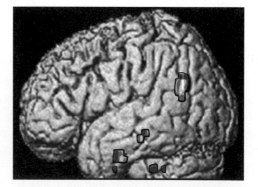

Figure 5.6.1 Changes in brain activity following training (scan 1: activity decrease; scan 2: activity increase)

Source: Delazer *et al.* (2003: 82-3)

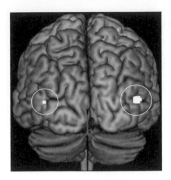

Figure 5.6.2 Increase in brain activity associated with training

After adults undertook mathematics training, the images show how their brain activity when doing mathematical problems shifted from the front of the brain to the back of the brain. This left image (scan 1) shows where activity reduced after training, and the image on the right (scan 2) shows where activity increased. This shift is owing to a decrease in working memory load (that is, a reduced amount of information to hold in one's immediate attention such as the steps that must be followed) and more automatic processing (that is, doing some parts of the mathematical processes without thinking about it).

When we learn, even the structure of the brain can change. In a study of learning to juggle (Draganski *et al.* 2004), researchers demonstrate learning-induced transient volume increases of the brain areas activated by daily training. After three months of training, visual regions associated with motion processing (shown in white in the rear-view image of the brain in Figure 5.6.2, supplied by the authors of the study with grateful thanks) increased their size by approximately 3 per cent. After another three months without practice, these regions partially shrunk back again nearly to their original size.

It is important that teachers and their pupils understand about brain plasticity, because many learners feel their brains limit their potential and prevent them from learning. However, when we decide we want to learn, we are choosing to change our brains in terms of their function, connectivity and structure. Research has shown that simply knowing about brain plasticity can improve the self-concept and academic potential of learners. So tell your pupils: their brain isn't something they're stuck with – they can change their brains! Task 5.6.2 asks you to put some of these ideas into practice.

Brains, games and learning: pupil engagement

Teachers have always offered rewards (whether they are prizes, points or praise) for achievement. Usually, teachers strive to ensure reward consistency; for example, that every pupil with a correct answer should receive a point. Yet, researchers have struggled to find any relationship between the rewards offered and learning achieved. In contrast, there seems a strong relationship between how the brain responds to reward and the likelihood of learning (Howard-Jones *et al.* 2011).

So, if we know how the brain responds to reward, we can use this to promote learning more effectively. For example, 'uncertain' reward generates a greater brain response than predictable reward, which is probably why we love games. It is important, however, that the uncertainty is owing to chance rather than a lack of academic confidence. Learning games in which pupils' learning earns them the *chance* to win points can make learning more fun and more memorable. This can involve

---

🖉 Task 5.6.2 Implement your own brain plasticity intervention

Understanding about brain plasticity has been shown to influence pupils' theories about intelligence, which in turn can influence the effort they make in their studies. Assess the extent to which your pupils think their intelligence is a fixed entity, by asking them to record their agreement with the following statements:

1   You have a certain amount of intelligence and you can't really do much to change it.
2   No matter who you are, you can change your intelligence.
3   You can learn new things, but you can't really change your basic intelligence.

   Use a Likert-style scale from 1 (*disagree strongly*) to 6 (*agree strongly*). For each pupil, add up the score for questions 1 and 3 and take away the score for question 2.
   Then discuss with your pupils about brain plasticity, perhaps using the illustrations in this book. A week later, assess their ideas about intelligence again, in exactly the same way as before. Do pupil scores suggest they have improved their theory of intelligence? Record the outcomes in your PDP.

---

alternating delivery of learning content with gaming rounds. In a typical gaming round, every team answers a multiple-choice question testing them on the content they've just encountered. Before the correct answer is revealed, pupils must also decide whether they would like to 'game' their points. Then, the correct answer is revealed and non-gamers with the correct answer receive their points immediately. Gamers who have the correct answer, on the other hand, then wait for the outcome of a random 'game' event (similar to the toss of a coin) to find out whether they've doubled or lost their points. Pupils make the decision to game or not at the start of each round and no one, whether gaming or not, can win points unless they answer the question correctly. As the stakes are gradually raised by the teacher with each round, the lesson can become an emotional roller coaster in which the winner remains impossible to predict. Classroom research has demonstrated how entire topics stretching over several lessons can be delivered entirely through this approach, with good learning gains and very positive pupil feedback (Howard-Jones *et al.* 2014). Related brain imaging research has shown that, in competitive games, our reward system is also responding to our competitors' fortunes, so we can expect pupils' neural reward systems to be stimulated even when it is their competitor's turn (Howard-Jones *et al.* 2010). A free app (Zondle Team Play) for whole-class games based on this research can be found at www.zondle.com. Now complete Task 5.6.3.

🖉 Task 5.6.3 Explore different ways of using reward

Develop a learning game that involves uncertain rewards. You can use freely available resources such as those on www.zondle.com, or you can simply toss a coin or spin a wheel to determine the points awarded when pupils give a correct answer. Other ways of using uncertain reward include offering raffle tickets rather than prizes for good work. Try this systematically with pupils and discuss whether they find these approaches are more fun than consistent reward. Record the outcomes in your PDP.

SUMMARY AND KEY POINTS

■ Teachers' views about brain development can affect their work with learners.

■ There is a lack of evidence for many supposedly brain-based ideas meant to improve learning; for example, teaching to learning styles, through rehearsing perceptual-motor exercises or by increasing water intake.

■ In contrast, a better understanding of authentic neuroscience; for example, brain plasticity can have a positive influence on teacher and learner attitudes.

■ Authentic neuroscience is also providing insights into a number of educational issues, including the use of reward as a means to support learning.

Check which requirements for your ITE programme you have addressed through this unit.

Further reading

Blakemore, S. and Frith, U. (2005) *The Learning Brain: Lessons for Education*, Oxford: Blackwell.
One of the first readers on the relevance of neuroscience to education, written by two prominent neuro-scientists.

Geake, J.G. (2009) *The Brain at School*, Milton Keynes: Open University Press.
A guide for teachers, written by an expert in education, who want to know whether and how neuroscience can be applied in the classroom.

Howard-Jones, P. A. (2010) *Introducing Neuroeducational Research*, London: Routledge.
An in-depth text on the issues, opportunities and methods by neuroscience may be used to inform educational practice.

Howard-Jones, P. (2013) *Neuroscience and Education: A Review of Educational Interventions and Approaches Informed by Neuroscience*, London: Educational Endowment Foundation, available at: http://education endowmentfoundation.org.uk

Royal Society (2011) *Brain Waves Module 2: Neuroscience: Implications for Education and Lifelong Learning*, available at: http://royalsociety.org/policy/projects/brain-waves/education-lifelong-learning/.
A free and forward-looking review of how neuroscience may inform education in the future.

Other resources and websites

Neuroscience for Kids: http://faculty.washington.edu/chudler/neurok.html
There are very few sites that translate neuroscience into something understandable. Don't be put off by the title; it's a useful site for grown-up neuroscientists too!

The Brain from Top to Bottom: http://thebrain.mcgill.ca
Delivers neuroscience facts and diagrams differentiated by three levels of complexity. (Work your way up!)

The International Mind, Brain and Education Society: www.imbes.org
You can also find out here about the journal associated with this society.

Royal Society: http://royalsociety.org/policy/projects/brain-waves/education-lifelong-learning
The full report and further details about the recent work by the Royal Society on the implications of neuroscience for education are available on this site.

Appendix 2 on pages 591–595 provides further examples of websites you may find useful.

Capel, S., Leask, M. and Turner, T. (eds) (2010) *Readings for Learning to Teach in the Secondary School: A Companion to M Level Study*, London: Routledge.
This book brings together essential readings to support you in your critical engagement with key issues raised in this textbook.

The subject-specific books in the Routledge *Learning to Teach* series are also very useful.

Any additional resources and an editable version of any relevant tasks/tables in this unit are available on the companion website: www.routledge.com/cw/capel

5.7 Developing critical thinking

Hazel Bryan

Introduction

When you first go into school, you may be dazzled by the sheer volume of activity that you encounter. Secondary schools are large, complex organisations that take time to understand, as there are multiple systems operating at any given time. The core business of teaching pupils is at the heart of the organisation. As a professional, you bring with you your graduate subject knowledge and your developing pedagogical skills. You have an increasing amount of 'professional capital' (Hargreaves and Fullan 2012: 2). However, as an 'extended professional' (Hoyle 1974), you also need to develop critical thinking skills that enable you to adopt an objective, questioning perspective. Critical thinking skills enable you to take a step back from any immediate situation (Barnett 1994; Education Scotland 2015) and 'read' it from an objective position, whether this is in relation to teaching, learning or the introduction of, for example, a new syllabus. The development of a critical perspective provides you with the skills to read any given text (for example, a government policy document or a more localised school policy) from an informed position. Such a perspective also supports you in the development of problem-solving skills (King and Kitchener 1994). Well-honed critical thinking skills empower you to ask questions of any given context and text and, by having this model of enquiry at the core of your professional self, you develop as an inquisitive practitioner, seeking to enhance your practice by understanding better any given context. However, 'critical thinking' should not be reduced simply to a set of skills. Rather, it should be regarded as an 'attitude, underpinned by curiosity . . . the motivation to understand at deeper levels' (Bryan *et al.* 2010: 62). Indeed, Brookfield (1993) uses the rather beautiful analogy of a conversation about learning to describe critical thinking. You adopt this approach in evaluating your lessons (see Unit 2.2 on planning and evaluating) and in undertaking reflective practice and action research (see Unit 5.4 on action research).

Poulson and Wallace (2004) suggest the following as indicators of a critical perspective:

- adopting an attitude of scepticism;
- habitually questioning the quality of your and other's claims to knowledge;
- scrutinising claims to see how convincing they are;
- respecting others as people;
- being open-minded to other perspectives;
- being constructive by using your scepticism to find better ways or interpretations.

Similarly, Scott (2000) offers the following four indicators:

■ identifying and challenging assumptions;
■ challenging the importance of context;
■ imagining and exploring alternatives;
■ developing reflective scepticism.

The model outlined in this unit, the linden tree, supports your pedagogy in two ways. First, it provides you with a simple, elegant tool to develop your critical thinking capacity from the first time you enter a school. It supports you in understanding the school as an organisation, the learning spaces within school and learning as a concept. Throughout the process, the models offered above by Poulson and Wallace (2004) and Scott (2000) are drawn upon to illuminate critical issues. Second, this unit supports you in developing critical thinking, as a critical disposition in your pupils.

OBJECTIVES

At the end of this unit, you should be able to:

■ read the physical environment of your school (the architecture and icons) with a critical eye;
■ understand the learning spaces you construct from a critical perspective;
■ approach the interactions and pedagogical encounters you have with your pupils from a critical perspective;
■ develop critical thinking in your pupils.

Check the requirements of your initial teacher education (ITE) programme to see which relate to this unit.

The linden tree

As a starting point, consider a cross-section of the tree, and the concentric layers revealed in this cross section (Figure 5.7.1).

Each concentric circle represents that which is visible as you approach, enter and spend time in school. Within each concentric circle, you are introduced to theory and practice from a national and international perspective and offered tasks that develop your critical thinking.

Architecture

The outer layer, the bark, is what you see as you walk up to the tree. If you apply this model to the school, the outer layer is that which is visible from the outside. What is there to see as you approach the building? The design of the school represents the intentions of the architects, and those who commissioned the building of the school. It is common practice today for architectural design teams to work with stakeholders (community representatives, governors, parents, teachers and pupils) in

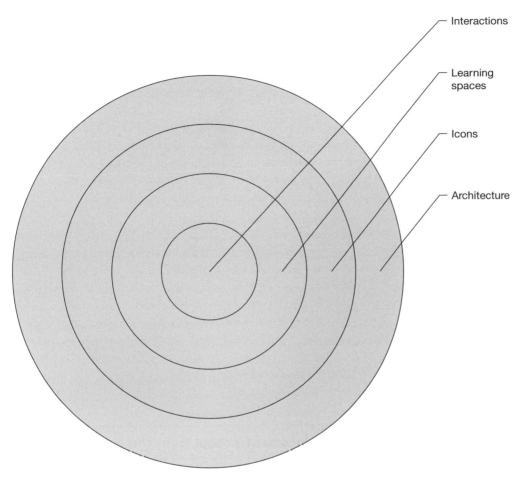

Interactions

Learning
spaces

Icons

Architecture

Figure 5.7.1 Critically evaluating the learning environment

discussions around school design, but of course this was not always the case. The school architect Mark Dudek discusses his work in terms of the psychological and spatial requirements needed in school design to accommodate and respond to theories of learning and cognitive development that inform pedagogy today: 'More esoteric factors such as the effects on behaviour of colour, light, surface texture and imagery are considered in addition to the more practical aspects of designing for comfort and health' (Dudek 2000, dustcover). So, as you might expect, a boys' grammar school built in the 1930s has a different provenance from, for example, an academy commissioned and built in 2016. And yet, embodied within the obviously visible, the design of the school represents a range of values in relation to beliefs about learning, teaching and the place of the school in any given community.

At the award-winning Rumi Jiya School in Hyderabad, India, the architects sought to design a school that would challenge assumptions about traditional models of rote learning. The design principles include:

■ building a learning community;
■ treating stakeholders as partners;

■   making nothing rote;
■   extending the spirit of entrepreneurship;
■   celebrating constraints.

(http://architecture.about.com/od/schooldesign/ig/
Winning-School-Designs/Rumi-School-of-Excellence.htm)

Similarly, in the Building Tomorrow Academy, Kiboga, Uganda, the design principles included the importance of community use, as the community had invested so much in the building. The design principles also included a requirement for the teacher to be able to see all the pupils in her classroom at any one time, as, in Uganda, teachers are scarce and numbers of pupils in each classroom are relatively high (http://architecture.about.com/od/schooldesign/ig/Winning-School-Designs/Rumi-School-of-Excellence.htm).

There are, of course, other design features in each of these schools that focus upon green initiatives and safety requirements, but the design principles outlined above relate to the ways in which the buildings have been conceived in relation to learning and teaching.

In Reggio Emilia in Northern Italy, the Reggio schools are designed in partnership with the famous Domus Academy, Milan. The resident Reggio architect, Professor Andrea Branzi, refers to the concept of 'liquid modernity' when articulating his vision for the school buildings (Branzi 2004). That is, buildings within which everything is moveable, including walls and floors, in order to respond to the changing needs of pupils. Task 5.7.1 invites you to critically evaluate the external features of your placement school.

✏ Task 5.7.1 Consider your placement school from the outside

Questions	Critical thinking indicators
What, in your opinion, were the design principles upon which the school was constructed?	Being open-minded to other perspectives (Poulson and Wallace 2004)
In what way is this a community school?	Challenging the importance of context (Scott 2000)
How well does this design work for the purpose of educating young people today?	Imagining and exploring alternatives (Scott 2000)

In this task and the following tasks in this unit, record your notes in your professional development portfolio (PDP) and reconsider your observations when you know the school better. Then make notes about what you would like to see in the school in which you are working when qualified and consider these points when you are being shown around the school prior to interview.

Icons

The second concentric circle of the cross section of the tree relates to the things that are visible as you enter the school. These are referred to here as icons. Icons were traditionally Christian images represented in art form, but today are used widely in marketing and fashion to depict values through well-known symbols.

It is likely that you enter the school on your teaching placement via the school reception, in order that you can sign in. Reception in secondary schools in the UK today is likely to be used by visitors and parents, rather than the main entrance for pupils. By learning to read the messages relayed by these icons, you are developing a critical perspective on what the school is saying to visitors. As such, the reception area is a space where values about the school are expressed, and a critical reading of the icons in this area provides you with a sense of how the school wishes to be understood by visitors.

If your school is a faith school, there may be religious artefacts in the reception area, if this is appropriate to the faith. What can you see? Are these artefacts what you would also see in, for example, a church? If so, what does this say about the relationship between the school and the church?

Secondary schools welcome visitors every day, including prospective parents and Office for Standards in Educatin (Ofsted) inspectors. There is likely to be a mission statement in the reception area. Similarly, there are likely to be badges of school success or school validation by external bodies such as Healthy Schools or Investors in People. Schools increasingly provide visitors with a file containing newspaper clippings of events and pupils' success, promoting the positive image of the school. There might be a noticeboard for parents and school prospectuses. Finally, there might be work by the pupils on display in the reception area. Task 5.7.2 invites you to critically evaluate the reception area of your placement school.

🖉 Task 5.7.2 Consider the reception area

Questions	Critical thinking indicators
What artefacts are in the reception area? What is the relationship between these and the mission statement?	Being open-minded to other perspectives (Poulson and Wallace 2004)
What are the badges of school success or sponsorship? What does this suggest to you in terms of the way the school values external validation?	Identify and challenge assumptions (Scott 2000). Adopting an attitude of scepticism (Poulson and Wallace 2004)
Is pupil work on display in reception? If yes, is it written work or only art work? How long has the work been on display?	Adopting an attitude of scepticism (Poulson and Wallace 2004)
What would you expect to see in this school's reception area?	Being constructive by using your scepticism to find better ways or interpretations (Poulson and Wallace 2004)

As suggested in Task 5.7.1, record your notes in your PDP and reconsider your observations when you know the school better.

The learning space

As you leave the reception area and walk to your classroom, pause. On entry into your classroom, take a moment to consider the learning space. If you are in a traditional classroom, start by looking at the layout of the classroom furniture. How have the desks and chairs been arranged? In what ways has the furniture been organised to accommodate or reflect what you know about effective learning? Is there flexibility for the teacher to rearrange the furniture to create specific learning environments for specific purposes?

From a behaviourist perspective (see Unit 5.1 on how pupils learn and Unit 5.3 on teaching styles), the teacher is placed at the centre of the learning process. The role of the teacher in a predominantly behaviourist-influenced classroom would be as director, instructor and transmitter. The role of the pupil in such a classroom would be as passive recipient of a predetermined, tightly structured, linear curriculum. Knowledge in such an environment is conceived as residing with the teacher or within selected texts, and pupils are rewarded for correct answers or behaviours. Task 5.7.3 invites you to critically evaluate learning spaces from a behaviourist perspective.

✏️ Task 5.7.3 Consider the learning space – from a behaviourist perspective

Questions	Critical thinking indicators
Does the layout of the furniture suggest a behaviourist approach to learning? If yes, why do you think the classroom is laid out in this way? What has been the guiding principle for the teacher whose layout this is?	Being open-minded to other perspectives (Poulson and Wallace 2004). Imagining and exploring alternatives (Scott 2000)
Does the layout suggest the teacher plays a dominant role in addressing the class?	Identifying and challenging assumptions (Scott 2000)
Does the furniture dictate a passive role for the pupils?	Imagining and exploring alternatives (Scott 2000)

Discuss your responses with another student teacher and store your findings in your PDP.

Within a classroom organised upon constructivist principles of learning (see Unit 5.1, 'Ways pupils learn', and Unit 5.2, 'Active learning'), the pupil is regarded as an active agent in their own cognitive development. They are viewed as meaning makers, motivated to construct their own understandings of the world, rather than passive recipient sponges, if you like, of knowledge. Of course, meaning making is a complex concept, 'whether learning is meaningful can only be judged by the learner because meaningfulness is an expression of the relationship between the material of learning and the learner's existing understandings' (Moon 2005: 106).

Within the constructivist classroom, the role of the teacher is to scaffold the individual pupil's learning, to provide appropriate learning experiences and opportunities so that the pupil can actively make sense of their world, and create understanding themselves. As such, the place of knowledge shifts from residing with the teacher or text, to the pupil, who, given the right conditions, naturally moves through stages of learning. Vygotsky built upon Piaget's constructivist theory by making the case for language within learning. Vygotsky's model of social constructivist learning emphasised the centrality of language in cognitive development (see Unit 5.1). Other modes of learning (imitation and learning from observation) come to the fore within this approach (Bandura 1969). Task 5.7.4 invites you to critically evaluate learning spaces from a constructivist perspective.

✎ Task 5.7.4 Consider the learning space – from a constructivist perspective

Questions	Critical thinking indicators
Does the layout of the furniture facilitate group learning? If yes, why do you think the classroom is laid out in this way? What has been the guiding theory of learning or pedagogical principle for the teacher whose layout this is?	Being open-minded to other perspectives (Poulson and Wallace 2004). Imagining and exploring alternatives (Scott 2000)
Does the layout of the furniture facilitate an active role for the pupil?	Developing reflective scepticism (Scott 2000)
Does the furniture suggest a scaffolding role for the teacher?	Identifying and challenging assumptions (Scott 2000)

Discuss your responses with another student teacher and store your findings in your PDP.

Within a classroom organised around a belief in experiential learning (see Unit 5.1), experience is the starting point for learning (Miller and Boud 1996). Kolb's four-point model of experiential learning suggests that concrete experiences, followed by reflection, enable the learner to theorise what they have learned in order to use it in future (Kolb 1984b). As learning is viewed in this model as subjective, when it does happen it is transformative as it occurs through a process of reflection. Task 5.7.5 invites you to critically evaluate learning spaces from an experiential learning perspective.

✎ Task 5.7.5 Consider the learning space – from an experiential learning perspective

Questions	Critical thinking indicators
How might first-hand experiences occur in this classroom?	Developing reflective scepticism (Scott 2000)
In what ways are pupils supported in reflecting on their experiences in this classroom?	Being open-minded (Poulson and Wallace 2004)
What would it take to enable pupils to reflect upon their learning?	Imagining and exploring alternatives (Scott 2000)

Discuss your responses with another student teacher and store your findings in your PDP.

Interactions

Teachers create the conditions within which learning opportunities occur. In addition to the concrete structures of classroom organisation considered above, teachers also construct opportunities for pupils to interact with each other and with texts, with the teacher themself or other adults. For example, within the behaviourist classroom considered above, the pupil interacts mainly with the teacher and selected texts. On the other hand, the principles that underpin a constructivist classroom would give rise to interactions between the pupil, teacher and first-hand resources. The social constructivist classroom brings into play interactions between pupils, resources, texts and the teacher or knowledgeable other, and within the experiential classroom, pupils are interacting with first-hand resources including texts, other pupils, the teacher and other adults.

It is possible, then, to map visible interactions against learning theories. Interactions, though, can be understood differently, as pedagogical actions within consciously created contexts. The term pedagogy is used to describe the 'artistry' of teaching (Moon 2005), collaborative practices (Pickering *et al.* 2007) and the 'science of teaching' (Bryan *et al.* 2010). Pedagogy, though, is far more than practices undertaken by teachers to bring about specific learning outcomes. Pedagogical practices have the potential to oppress or liberate the learner, and as such can be understood to be political actions (see Giroux's notion of 'critical pedagogy'; Giroux 2011). Critical pedagogy locates learning within the wider context of society, and as such positions the teacher as a significant agent in this endeavour. This is in line with Freire's belief that pedagogies create social justice or injustice, thereby creating or denying the 'humanising' potential of education (Freire 1992). Task 5.7.6 invites you to critically evaluate interactions within your placement school.

🖉 **Task 5.7.6 Consider the interactions**

Questions	*Critical thinking indicators*
In what way do you construct your role in relation to your pupils and talk about your role to other student teachers in relation to pupils?	Scrutinising claims to see how convincing they are (Poulson and Wallace 2004)
What are your expectations of pupil relationships?	Scrutinising claims to see how convincing they are (Poulson and Wallace 2004)
Do the learning opportunities draw from a range of disciplines?	Imagining and exploring alternatives (Scott 2000). Habitually questioning the quality of others' specific claims (Poulson and Wallace 2004)
What would you do differently?	Being constructive by using your scepticism to find better ways or interpretations (Poulson and Wallace 2004)

Discuss your responses with another student teacher and store your findings in your PDP.

By now, you have begun to develop an inquisitive, consciously questioning state of mind in relation to the school. That is, the start of a disposition of criticality. By working through the concentric circles of the tree, you have looked at that which is visible from the initial impressions given by the architecture, and then applied the linden tree model to take you step by step through the school into the heart of classroom practice. The activities you have undertaken using the concentric circles lead you towards a 'critical stance . . . [which] has the connotation of sharpness and precision' (Moon 2005). That is, a disposition that enables you to analyse, question, interrogate to engage in different 'ways of seeing' (Berger 1972). This approach emerges in some methodological approaches. Clough and Nutbrown (2007) refer to 'radical looking' and 'radical listening' when introducing pupils to data analysis. That is, they encourage pupils to actively seek information. Similarly, Holliday (2007) encourages pupils when considering research in familiar settings or with colleagues, to make the 'known strange'. That is, to step back, remain objective, look for details and resist complacency. The section that follows supports you in developing a critical disposition in your pupils in school.

Fruits of the tree: creating a critical disposition in your pupils

The development of critical thinking in your pupils requires you to focus first upon the word 'thinking'. Guy Claxton, in his very accessible book *Wise Up* (Claxton 2001; see also Claxton 2015) draws upon the work of Diane Halpern (1998) in promoting a fourfold model of critical thinking that you might develop in your pupils. Halpern's model is as follows.

Part 1: develop the right disposition

Halpern argues that pupils should expect thinking to sometimes be hard, and that they should not be dispirited in this possibility. Developing the right disposition involves your pupils in persisting with complex tasks. In a sense, this is about developing 'learning resilience' and 'thinking resilience' (Johnston-Wilder and Lee 2010). A task for you in relation to developing the right disposition in your pupils is to reflect upon the opportunities you provide for your pupils: do you include complex thinking tasks as part of your pedagogical menu? When do your pupils have good opportunities to discuss, rationalise and problematise in their work?

Part 2: skills training

Halpern suggests that in order for critical thinking to be able to be engaged in successfully, certain skills need to be developed in young people. For example, Halpern advances the case for a focus upon the use of language in learning. Ask yourself, when do your pupils have opportunity to think about developing a precise language; a sound, persuasive argument; a questioning mind that interrogates arguments and claims? In addressing these areas, your pupils are engaging with issues of validity and reliability.

Part 3: recognising when to activate critical thinking

Halpern argues that the teaching of thinking skills involves you in supporting your pupils in finding out for themselves how to approach complex problems, and having opportunities to reflect with others upon the success or otherwise of the approach.

Part 4: metacognition

Developing in your pupils an awareness of the process of critical thinking brings about a state of self-awareness, and this, Halpern suggests, is crucial to the teaching of thinking. In this way, your pupils develop an ability to use critical thinking with 'conscious intent in a variety of settings' (Claxton 2001: 130).

Halpern's fourfold model is a useful starting point for focussing the mind on developing critical thinking in pupils in school.

Thinking

Your pupils need time to think. Moon (2008) suggests that you introduce your pupils to the concept of 'think time' or 'quick think'. This has the potential to be valuable to your pupils, but there are implications for you to consider to ensure your practice is appropriate. The following approach set out in Tables 5.7.1–5.7.4 is based upon Moon's (2008) 'pedagogy of critical thinking'.

The suggestions in Tables 5.7.1–5.7.4 provide you with approaches to the development of critical thinking in class. They offer the opportunity for pupils to work collectively in the development of critical reading, the development of a critical perspective and the start of critical writing.

Table 5.7.1 Introducing 'think time' and 'quick think'

Concept	Pupil activity	Implications for your practice
Pupils are invited to 'stop and think' or take part in 'think time' at appropriate times in the lesson.	Pupils might reflect upon the task independently or discuss with other pupils.	You should ensure that pupils have adequate time to engage in deep thinking and discussion.
Pupils are invited to 'quick think'.	Pupils write down notes based upon their deep thinking and discussions with fellow pupils.	Moon (2008) reminds us of Tobin's (1987) concept of 'wait time'. Thinking takes time: do not be tempted to fill the pauses with teacher talk.

Table 5.7.2 Developing critical thinking through real-life scenarios

Activity	Pupil activity	Implications for your practice
Provide pupils with extracts from current newspapers of issues that are controversial (for example, global warming, legal rulings).	Pupils should work in small groups to discuss the issues and: ■ list the further questions they have; ■ offer a range of possible solutions in bullet point format; ■ consider the consequences of each solution, possibly written in a short paragraph.	You need to find current events that are well written in newspapers. Pupils need plenty of time to engage in this activity.
Provide pupils with the same current story, but presented in a range of newspapers	Pupils should read the same story in each newspaper and consider the ways in which each newspaper has presented the same event. What are the features of text in each paper that are effective? What is the overall impression of the event from each newspaper? Thoughts can be presented as a concept map or bullet points.	As above, but you need a range of newspapers offering the same event/storyline.

Table 5.7.3 Developing critical thinking through personal critical incidents

Activity	Pupil activity	Implications for your practice
Invite pupils to consider a personal critical incident at a time when they were faced with a dilemma that they are happy to discuss and explore.	Pupils work in small groups to first describe the dilemma. Pupils then move on to explain how the actions they took/the dilemma made them feel. Finally, other pupils ask *questions* to encourage the pupil to explore other ways in which they might have acted. This activity lends itself best to discussion rather than writing.	This activity must be set up in a sensitive manner, and only involve pupils who wish to discuss a critical incident. You should ensure that the 'rules' are followed in terms of the supportive nature of this activity.

Table 5.7.4 Developing critical thinking through creative scenarios

Activity	Pupil activity	Implications for your practice
Watch an extract from a film that provides opportunity for robust debate and differing perspectives; for example, *Titanic*, *Jumaji*, Baz Luhrman's *Romeo and Juliet* . . .	Explore options from various characters' perspectives – what could have been done differently? Invite pupils to consider a different storyline/different ending based on characters acting differently.	You need to find films that lend themselves to robust debate.
Watch an extract from, for example, *Dr Who*, *Star Wars* or *Men in Black* that provides complex ethical dilemmas for the characters.	Invite your pupils to consider all the options open to the characters, setting out the pros and cons, and seeking a resolution.	Pupils need time to watch the extracts, and maybe rewatch them. Pupils need to have been introduced to the notion of pros and cons in action.
Offer pupils dilemmas from literature; for example, Goldilocks' hunger and exhaustion. Present it as a critical incident. Pupils in the secondary school will appreciate the irony in this activity and enjoy the playful nature of the activity. Of course, any character (with imaginary related relatives/friends) can be hot-seated, such as the key characters from poetry (for example, 'The Charge of the Light Brigade') or literature (Anne Fine's *Tulip Touch*).	Hot-seat the following characters: Goldilocks; Goldilocks' parents; the three bears. Invite the hot-seated pupils to work collaboratively to create their storylines. The rest of the pupils should work together to construct questions for the hot-seated characters.	Pupils need time to construct their storylines and time to engage in the hot-seating activity.

SUMMARY AND KEY POINTS

This unit has introduced you to the concept of critical thinking as an empowering, creative disposition.

■ You have been offered a thinking tool in the shape of the linden tree to develop your skills of interrogation and analysis.
■ You have begun to understand the benefits of stepping back from any immediate situation, asking questions and looking for details. In developing a critical mindset in relation to education, you are enhancing your ability to engage in a 'critical confrontation with your problems' (Smyth 1989).
■ Developing such a critical disposition in relation to education is in line with Habermas' notion that 'empowerment and political emancipation' result from critical and evaluative engagement (Moon 2008: 15).

■ You may have begun to notice throughout this unit that critical thinking and reflective practice are closely linked (Smyth 1989). In essence, reflective thinking, developed by Dewey in 1933, seeks to *understand* phenomena, whereas critical thinking results in a 'critical being' (Barnett 1997), who is both creative and *empowered* in practice (Habermas 1971).

■ This unit has also introduced you to the possibility of developing a *critical disposition* in the minds of your pupils and this is demonstrated in the classroom activities suggested above, where pupils are encouraged to arrive at solutions, rather than simply debate issues.

■ And why the linden tree? Known as a sacred tree in Slavic tradition, the linden tree is also known as the Holy Lime in Poland. Pre-Christian Germanic tradition held that the linden tree had such properties that it would reveal truths; judicial meetings were held beneath the linden tree as it was believed the tree would help to restore justice. The linden tree is associated with cultural and spiritual significance in Greek and Roman mythology – in both, it is regarded as a tree symbolising the virtues. The linden or lime tree can live for centuries, and is revered for its medicinal lime blossom and practical versatility. In all these societies, the linden tree has symbolised justice, the virtues and practical applicability. As such, the linden tree has provided a fitting metaphor upon which a model to develop critical thinking in teachers and pupils has been constructed.

Check which requirements for your ITE programme you have addressed through this unit.

Further reading

Moon, J. (2008) *Critical Thinking: An Exploration of Theory and Practice*, London: Routledge.
This comprehensive text introduces the reader to theory underpinning critical thinking. The book sets out for the reader the conceptual issues surrounding the notion of critical thinking. It introduces the individual as a critical thinker, exploring emotions, language and curiosity in thinking. The text engages well with the concept of knowledge, setting complex ideas out with a lightness of touch. Finally, Moon offers practical suggestions for the development of critical thinking in educational settings.

Bryan, H., Carpenter, C. and Hoult, S. (2010) *Learning and Teaching at M Level: A Guide for Student Teachers*, London: Sage.
This text is designed for all student teachers. It promotes the importance of enquiry in professional practice, and as such makes explicit links between theory and practice. Starting with a belief in the importance of teachers having a deep understanding of learning, the book immerses the reader in issues relating to pupil learning. There is a chapter dedicated to the development of critical thinking, reading and writing.

Johnston-Wilder, S. and Lee, C. (2010) 'Developing mathematical resilience', BERA Annual Conference 2010, 1–4 September 2010, University of Warwick: http://oro.open.ac.uk/24261/2/3C23606C.pdf

Other resources and websites

Claxton, G. (2015) *Building Learning Power*: www.buildinglearningpower.co.uk/

Education Scotland (2015) *Skills in Practice: Thinking Skills*: www.educationscotland.gov.uk/resources/s/skillsinpracticethinkingskills/knowing.asp

Appendix 2 on pages 591–595 provides further examples of websites you may find useful.

Capel, S., Leask, M. and Turner, T. (eds) (2010) *Readings for Learning to Teach in the Secondary School: A Companion to M Level Study*, London: Routledge.
This book brings together essential readings to support you in your critical engagement with key issues raised in this textbook.

The subject-specific books in the Routledge *Learning to Teach* series are also very useful.

Any additional resources and an editable version of any relevant tasks/tables in this unit are available on the companion website: www.routledge.com/cw/capel

5.8 Creating a language-rich classroom

Annabel Watson and Debra Myhill

Introduction

Language is fundamental to learning and fundamental to being human: it is language that distinguishes us from animals. Although animals can communicate, only humans can use language to reflect on the past, to communicate complex abstract ideas or emotions, and to shape or imagine new futures. And language shapes how we see and interpret the world; as Wittgenstein famously proposed: 'The limits of my language are the limits of my world. All I know is what I have words for' (Wittgenstein 1961: 5-6).

What we can articulate and express is influenced by the language we have to express it, and language itself influences how we think. Think, for example, of the common metaphor of the sun setting over the horizon, creating a conceptual image of the sun moving rather than the correct scientific understanding that it is the earth rotating that causes the sun to disappear. Or consider the fact that in English we can discriminate between a foreigner and a stranger, whereas in French there is only one word (*étranger*) to cover both these ideas. When new learning or discoveries occur, we have to create new words to express them. Language is the most powerful tool we have as learning beings.

The relationship between thinking and language has been explored most comprehensively by Vygotsky, who highlights the symbiotic relationship between the two: thoughts are not mentally 'translated' into words; rather, thought and language interact together to generate new knowledge and understanding. It is a dynamic, constructive process:

> The relation of thought to word is not a thing but a process, a continual movement back and forth from thought to word and from word to thought. In that process the relation of thought to word undergoes changes which themselves may be regarded as development in the functional sense. Thought is not merely expressed in words; it comes into existence through them.
>
> (Vygotsky 1986: 218)

Although this might seem an abstract philosophical idea, it is one we all experience many times in our own social interactions with others. Most of us have had the experience of beginning a sentence and being surprised at where we end up, or of trying to articulate a half-formed idea and getting tangled up in our own words as we struggle to bring thoughts and words together. In the classroom, then, it is important that we see opportunities to use language to talk, read and write not as reductivist representations of thought, but as the very processes that facilitate thinking and learning. This unit sets out to encourage you to think how you can capture the affordances of language to make learning in your classroom a meaningful, dynamic and vibrant process.

OBJECTIVES

At the end of this unit, you should be able to:

- ■ begin to establish participatory and interactive classrooms;
- ■ begin to set up effective exploratory, dialogic talk;
- ■ begin to create tasks and activities that generate active reading;
- ■ support the development of writing in your subject.

Check the requirements of your initial teacher education (ITE) programme to see which relate to this unit.

Creating an interactive classroom

Talk is the dominant mode of communication between any teacher and their pupils. Teachers typically use talk to explain, give instructions, assess learning and control behaviour. However, talk can also be a powerful tool for learning. It allows us to formulate and express ideas, to reformulate or clarify thinking, to communicate ideas and receive feedback from others, and to reflect on learning (Howe 1992). Language is thus not only an *intra*personal 'psychological tool' that allows us to crystallise and represent thought to ourselves, but also an *inter*personal 'cultural tool' that provides 'a means for people to think and learn together' (Mercer 1995: 4). The implication of this is that an effective classroom is not one in which you, as a teacher, dominate conversation, using talk to channel information from expert to novice, but rather one where you help pupils to use talk to formulate, test and evaluate their own ideas, developing their thinking through conversations with you, the teacher, and each other.

Research over the past 30 years indicates that teachers dominate whole-class talk (Edwards and Westgate 1994; Galton *et al.* 1999b), and more recent research suggests that the patterns of basic classroom interaction have changed very little (Myhill 2006; Mercer and Littleton 2007). The pattern of turn taking in discussion tends to follow what is often called an IRF or IRE structure: initiation response feedback/evaluation. Typically, the teacher initiates with a question to which a pupil responds, and the teacher then offers some form of feedback. The consequence of this is that the teacher's voice is consistently dominant, and pupils' involvement in discussion is limited and subordinate. Other factors exacerbate the situation: teachers ask many questions but pupils ask few; questions tend to invite factual recall only; pupil answers tend to be brief; and feedback from teachers tends to praise, but not explore, pupil answers (Alexander 2001). Furthermore, the fact that teachers often echo or repeat pupil answers reinforces the implicit message that the teacher's voice is the only one to which pupils need to listen. The level of control exerted by teachers is highlighted by Edwards and Westgate (1994: 46):

> The teacher takes turns at will, allocates turns to others, determines topics, interrupts and reallocates turns judged to be irrelevant to those topics, and provides a running commentary on what is being said and meant which is the main source of cohesion within and between the various sequences of the lesson.

Of course, you need to control the pace and focus of whole-class discussion in order to meet the demands of your curriculum. However, you should consider how far you can make use of these episodes to really extend pupil learning, how to genuinely involve your pupils, and how to provide opportunities 'for the children to develop their individual understanding or ideas' and 'to articulate their thoughts and comments' (Myhill and Warren 2005: 67).

You need to plan carefully for whole-class discussion in order to do this. You should consider the balance of closed, factual questions to more open, speculative ones in advance, and check that open questions genuinely invite open responses. It is important to plan sequences of questions that invite pupils to use higher-order thinking skills of analysis, synthesis and evaluation, and to ask 'process' questions that invite them to explain their thinking. You should also actively prompt pupils to ask their own questions about what they are learning. Think about the 'wait time' you allow pupils before they answer – do they have enough time to formulate their ideas? Could they talk through their thoughts with a partner before sharing them with the whole class? Also, consider alternatives to questions. Some research suggests that questions can actually 'inhibit students' intellectual creativity' (Mercer 1995: 28), and that teachers can use other kinds of conversational strategies, such as offering your own observations and speculations in order to prompt pupils to do the same. Most importantly, try to give your full attention to your pupils' responses, explore their thinking and use mistakes as opportunities to collaboratively explore misunderstandings or miscommunication. Task 5.8.1 is designed to help you with this.

It is equally important to consider the role of language in effective group work. Research suggests that pupils want to be trusted to learn and collaborate with their peers (McIntyre *et al.* 2005), but also that they need to be taught how to do this effectively. A dialogic approach, discussed in the next section, is one way to promote effective group discussion.

M **Task 5.8.1 Observing and analysing whole-class discussion**

Observe a 5–10-minute episode of whole-class discussion.
  Make a note of:

■ how many conversational 'turns' the teacher takes;
■ how many turns pupils take.

  Reflect and evaluate:

■ How far does the pattern of interaction fit the 'IRF' pattern described above?

■   What does the teacher do to try to encourage pupil participation in the discussion?
■   How successful are they in doing this?

Discuss your reflections with a peer. Record the outcomes of your reflections and discussions in your professional development portfolio (PDP). Now pair up with a colleague and undertake the same exercise in one of the lessons you are teaching. Were the results what you had planned for? If not, why not?

Again, reflect on and record the outcomes.

Exploratory talk for learning

You learn a lot more if you can talk and communicate and discuss things with people rather than a teacher standing and drumming information into you: and I don't think teachers realise that.

(15-year-old pupil; Des Fountain 1994: 55)

Introducing exploratory talk into your classroom can be a powerful and exciting way to actively involve your pupils in their learning. The aim is to enable pupils to use talk to independently explore and make sense of what they are learning, rather than simply absorbing (or ignoring) teacher summaries. It is characterised by 'thinking aloud', where teachers and pupils talk together to speculate, develop, test and evaluate ideas. The talk should be informed by a spirit of enquiry in which disagreement and differences of opinion are seen as an opportunity to extend learning, moving together towards a greater understanding of a concept or issue. By explaining their ideas to others, pupils have the opportunity 'to reorganize and clarify material, to recognize misconceptions, to fill in gaps in [their] own understanding, to internalize and acquire new strategies and knowledge, and to develop new perspectives and understanding' (Webb *et al.* 2009: 49–50). Most importantly, exploratory talk is a form of scaffolding (Wood *et al.* 1976) (see Unit 5.1) in which the knowledge or understanding reached is greater than that which could have been achieved by a pupil working alone.

One particular theorisation of exploratory talk is the concept of 'dialogic talk' that has been developed by Robin Alexander. Dialogic talk moves away from the routine pattern of IRF exchanges, 'aiming to be more consistently searching and more genuinely reciprocal and cumulative' (Alexander 2004: 1; see also Robin Alexander's website referenced at the end of the unit). While a monologic teacher is characterised by a desire to transmit knowledge, convey information and maintain control of talk, a dialogic teacher is focused on creating authentic conversational exchanges, creating opportunities for pupils to learn through exploration and collaborative talk.

Dialogic talk is founded on five principles: collectivity, reciprocity, support, cumulation and purposefulness (Alexander 2004: 27). Teachers and pupils *collectively* address learning tasks together, in groups or as a whole class. They *reciprocate* by sharing ideas, listening to each other and considering alternative views. They are *supportive* in allowing all members of the group to freely express their ideas without fear of embarrassment, and they support each other to reach common understandings. The discussion is *cumulative* in that teachers and pupils respond to each other's ideas, building them into a coherent line of enquiry. The talk is also *purposeful* in that it is planned and steered by the teacher in order to reach a specific educational goal (Alexander 2004). Skidmore

Table 5.8.1 The features of typical pedagogic (monologic) dialogue versus a dialogic pedagogy

Pedagogic dialogue	*Dialogic pedagogy*
Teacher-controlled	Teacher-managed
Closed interactions	Open interactions
Limited participation	High participation
'Right' answers valued	All answers valued
Teacher owns truth	Shared quest for truth
Teacher talks most	Extended pupil contributions
Closed structure	Open structure

Source: Drawing on Skidmore (2000)

(2000) contrasts this purposeful dialogic pedagogy with the more monologic dialogue, which he calls pedagogic dialogue, in many classrooms (see Table 5.8.1).

In a truly dialogic discussion, there is a common goal or purpose shared by the members of the group: a problem to be solved, a topic to be understood, or an issue to be considered, resolved or decided upon. Pupils need to try to express their own point as clearly as possible, and to be prepared to give arguments or explanations to support their ideas. They also need to be comfortable in expressing uncertainty or tentativeness, and to be prepared to explore differences of opinion regardless of the strength of their own convictions. They should allow each other to speak, ask questions in order to understand better, and paraphrase or reflect back each other's words to show their own understanding and offer others the chance to correct misunderstandings. To enable your pupils to succeed in this, you need to explicitly teach a range of skills. They need guidance in how to work together, how to include others, and how to monitor their own contributions (forexample, to check that they're not dominating the discussion). They also need to learn about how to express disagreement politely and constructively, how to listen effectively and how to be sensitive to other people's reactions. Such skills are essential for effective group work in all areas of the curriculum, and you should make opportunities to model good (and bad!) practice. Now complete Task 5.8.2.

Creating active readers

Active reading involves readers in engaging with interpreting, questioning, and meaning-making from the texts they read, rather than simply decoding the words on the page (Gough and Tunmer 1986; Stuart *et al.* 2008). In order to understand how to develop active readers, you need to understand a little about the nature of reading and reader behaviour. Constructing meaning from texts involves a complex interaction between the reader, the text being read, and the context in which we are reading. As we read, we bring to the act all our previous reading experiences, our own life experiences and our cultural knowledge and values: there are 'as many different possible readings of text as there are readers' (Fleming and Stevens 1998: 64). What we already know influences how we interpret the text: reading a historical account of the reign of Queen Elizabeth I could be influenced by having seen Miranda Richardson's portrayal of her in *Blackadder*; an explanation of volcanic

Task 5.8.2 Analysing pupil discussions

Read this extract from a whole-class episode in which Year 8 pupils discuss the smoking ban. At the end of each pupil's contribution, they nominate another pupil to continue. Pupil names have been changed.

- ▪ What features of dialogic talk are evident?
- ▪ What would be a suitable topic of enquiry within your own subject area?
- ▪ How would you prepare your pupils to take part in an activity such as this?

Record your ideas in your PDP.

Claire: I also think that smoking should be banned because people think it's sexy and cool but really it's just a health hazard. Sarah?

Sarah: But smoking is part of some people's personality, and if you had to say about somebody who smokes, if you had to describe them, you'd probably, one of the first things you'd say is that they smoked, and I feel that if they banned it in public places, then it wouldn't be the right of freedom. Jack?

Jack: I also feel that the ban could have been the wrong decision because people may like feel loss of freedom, like they're being told what to do. John?

John: Yeah, but it also means less people killed, less people dying because of it, and children are healthier. Ella?

Ella: I agree with John when he says that other people might not want the smoke near them. It's not really the choice of people that do smoke, it's the decision of the government to protect the people that don't smoke against becoming ill. Sophie?

Sophie: I agree with Sarah and Jack. It's not nice if you don't smoke, but like Sarah said it's their personality and their own right of freedom. And you'd kind of feel like you're being bossed around. It's not really free. Jess?

Jess: But I think they should ban it because it's doing everyone a favour, by making people cut down. Even if they do feel bossed around, it's better for them. Chris?

Chris: It depends what you think is more important. The right of freedom for smokers, or protecting people who don't smoke, like Ella said.

Record the outcomes in your PDP.

craters could be influenced by a holiday trip to Vesuvius; and it is impossible for post-Holocaust readers to read *The Merchant of Venice*, with its cutting anti-Semitism, in the same way as Shakespeare's audience. Cultural influences are significant too, and we read very much from our own cultural perspective. A description of a loyal dog has many cultural resonances in England, with our view of a dog as 'man's best friend', but many readers from other countries would have very different views of dogs, perhaps as scavenging pests to be deterred. And words and phrases carry many cultural overtones: think about 'afternoon tea', for example, or 'blood sports'. Readers who have English as an additional language or come from different cultural backgrounds may draw different meanings from texts. (See Flynn's *English as an Additional Language* MESHGuide referenced at the end of the unit.)

Confident readers know instinctively that we don't read every text in the same way: it would be foolish to read a telephone directory from the beginning, just as it rarely makes sense to begin a novel in the middle of the book. As we read, we predict and anticipate what comes next, drawing both on our life knowledge and our knowledge of similar texts, and we constantly strive towards making sense of the text. This is why, when we are revising our own writing, it is hard to find mistakes in expression, as we read what we intended it to say, rather than what we have actually written. Good readers are also constantly self-monitoring their understanding of the text, being alert for misunderstandings or misreading. This is comprehension monitoring (Pressley 2000; Yuill and Oakhill 2010) and is an important skill for all readers, including for supporting pupils with special educational needs (Berkeley *et al.* 2010). When you are devising an activity involving reading, you might use Table 5.8.2 to help you plan for the development of reading skills.

DART: directed activities related to text

Another way to approach developing active readers is to use a DART strategy (directed activities related to text). These were originally developed by Lunzer and Gardner (1979) and are particularly relevant to non-fiction texts. DART are not intended to be reading exercises or comprehension keep-fit! Try to choose a DART strategy that fits the work you are doing with your class and try to select a DART strategy that naturally accompanies the kind of text you are using or the particular skill or learning you are hoping to develop. For yourself, always be clear about what the learning point of any given strategy is, otherwise the learning pupils may derive from the activity is fortuitous rather than planned. Through a successful DART activity, 'the processes of comprehension, of gaining meaning and drawing inferences from text, are brought out into the open, and it is from this that one reader can learn from another how to become a better or more thoughtful creator of meaning' (Harrison 2004: 100). These activities all encourage close reading: always encourage readers to explain and articulate how they made their decisions so they become explicitly aware themselves of the reading strategies they are using. The list below groups the DART strategies into clusters and explains what reading skills each strategy might develop.

DART strategies (see also Unit 5.2) include the following:

Text marking

Text marking includes underlining, annotating or numbering the text to show sequence. Skills include:

■ skimming or scanning to find specific information;
■ differentiating between different categories of information;

Table 5.8.2 Devising activities to develop reading skills

Reading skill	Typical activity
Developing vocabulary through encounters with new words	Introducing new vocabulary relevant to the text before beginning reading
Strengthening decoding skills when encountering complex subject-specific vocabulary	How would you say *pteridophyte*; *hebdomadarian*?
Developing morphological awareness of how words are built	What might *homograph* mean? *Photosynthesis*?
Developing strategies for using context cues	Prediction; drawing analogies between text and other texts; using life experience
Developing self-monitoring strategies	Reading back over the text to check if something does not make sense
Developing text questioning strategies	Questioning the content of the text – 'Why did Mr Bennet prefer Elizabeth?' Questioning the author's intentions – 'Is the perspective provided in the text a biased one?'

- deciding what is relevant information;
- finding the main ideas;
- questioning the information presented in the text.

Graphic reorganisation

Text restructuring involves reading and remodelling the information in another format, such as flow charts, diagrams, grids, lists, maps, charts or concept maps. These diagrammatic representations of texts are sometimes called graphic organisers. Skills include:

- identifying what is key and relevant in a text;
- applying what is known in a new context;
- summary and prioritisation;
- synthesising information and ideas.

Sequencing

Sequencing activities involve reconstructing a text that has been cut into chunks. Skills include:

- reading and rereading;
- paying close attention to the structure of the text;
- paying close attention to link words;
- hunting for the logic or organising principle of the text (for example, chronological order);
- using previous experience and earlier reading.

Cloze

Cloze procedures are gap-filling tasks that involve the reader in actively constructing meaning. Skills include:

- paying close attention to the meaning of the sentence;
- choosing a word that fits grammatically;
- using one's existing knowledge of the topic;
- working out what is likely from the rest of the text;
- working out what fits with the style of the text;
- attending to the sense of the whole by reading and rereading, backwards and forwards.

Prediction

Prediction activities invite intelligent, informed speculation about what happens next, either immediately or eventually. Skills include:

- looking for clues in the text to inform prediction;
- drawing on reader knowledge of other similar texts;
- justifying decisions with textual evidence.

Text reformulation

Text reformulation involves re-presenting the information or ideas in a text in a different format. Skills include:

- selecting key information for reformulation;
- sifting the relevant from the irrelevant;
- awareness of the characteristics of different genres;
- writing as well as reading skills.

(adapted from DfES 2002: 31)

Now complete Task 5.8.3.

 Task 5.8.3 Incorporating DART strategies into lessons

Take a text for your subject that you might use in a lesson and create a lesson activity that uses one of the DART strategies above.

Write a short paragraph explaining what reading skill you are hoping to develop and the rationale for the task you have developed.

Include this in your PDP.

Supporting writing

As a teacher, you are most likely to use talk as a tool for communicating with pupils and fostering learning; however, it remains the case that the dominant mode of assessment is writing. In terms of mental effort, writing is one of the most sophisticated and complex activities we engage in: Kellogg (2008) argues that writing makes as much demand on our cognitive abilities as playing chess. The reason it is such a challenging task is because all writers are, in effect, having to multitask. We have to think about who the writing is for and what we want it to achieve; we have to think about how to organise and structure it; we have to make decisions about word choices, images, tone and formality; we have to think about punctuation and spelling; and we have to physically produce the text, either on paper or digitally. Writers have to learn that writing 'is not simply the language of speech written down' (Perera 1987: 17) and have to manage shaping written text to match the writing task set. Sometimes writers do not have the linguistic repertoire that they need and this has to be more explicitly taught: Perera (1987: 22) noted that 'teachers need to be aware of some of the linguistic difficulties that pupils encounter as they attempt to master a formal written style', and Myhill (2009) has shown that writers of differing levels of competence have mastered different linguistic constructions. While some writers learn an enormous amount implicitly from their reading and talking, this is not the case for all learners, and it is important to be explicit in your teaching of writing. (See Gardner's (2013) *Reluctant Writers* MESHGuide referenced at the end of the unit.)

One way to be explicit is to consider what the written genres for your subject are. Genres in writing are 'how things get done, when language is used to accomplish them' (Martin 1985: 250); they are a collectively and implicitly agreed set of conventions for writing and 'preferred ways of creating and communicating knowledge within particular communities' (Swales, 1990: 4). Ask yourself what kinds of writing you ask pupils to complete in your subject: it might be evaluations, reports, explanations, argument essays, instructions, and so on. Don't get bogged down with naming text types or categorisations: there are different ways of categorising genres (for example, Derewianka 1996; Wing Jan 1991), but what is more important is that you can identify the writing genres for your subject and that you can explain how they work. Each genre has its own characteristic text structure and language features, and there are some helpful accounts of different genres in Christie and Martin (2005). But you can analyse texts yourself using the questions below to guide you:

- How does this text begin?
- Is it written in the first person or the third person?
- Is it formal or informal?
- Does it use the passive voice?
- Do the sentences tend to be short or long, or have any typical characteristic?
- Are there particular conjunctions or adverbs used to link ideas?
- Is there a vocabulary associated with this kind of text?
- Is there an underlying structure?
- How does this end?
- Is there a particular visual layout of the text?

To help writers understand and master the genres of your subject, it is helpful for you, as a teacher, to model them for the pupils. Modelling is a scaffolding strategy (Wood *et al.* 1976) teachers use that gives additional assistance in the early stages of learning and that is later withdrawn.

Whittaker et al. (2006) describe the modelling of written genres as a three-step process of deconstruction, joint construction and independent construction:

> From the examination of the purpose, structure and grammatical features of genres (deconstruction), through a critical phase of guided interaction which provided a context in which the 'constructedness' of texts could be explicitly negotiated, and responsibility for the construction of a new text could be shared among peers and with teachers, through to a phase of independent construction and 'control' of the genre.
>
> (Whittaker *et al.* 2006: 86)

If you have access to a visualiser in your classroom, these are immensely useful for modelling: not only can you annotate a text as you discuss it with a class, but you can also use pupils' developing texts, produced in the lesson, for discussion. You can also use the visualiser to compose, or co-construct a text together before pupils try to write the genre independently.

The benefit of modelling how a genre is constructed is that it makes visible things that writers might not have noticed otherwise and allows them to have more choice and control in designing their writing (Myhill 2010). But one danger of modelling genres is teaching writers formulaic approaches to writing, rather like offering them a recipe for writing that they must dutifully follow. Encourage writers to appreciate that there are often a range of ways to fulfil the demands of the genre, and that sometimes being unconventional can be very successful. Now complete Task 5.8.4.

 Task 5.8.4 Deconstructing text in particular genres

Take an example of a written genre from your subject and annotate with the genre features you would want pupils to understand and be able to use.

Then create a teaching episode where you model this text, using the deconstruction, joint construction and independent construction approach.

Put the annotated text and the episode plan in your PDP.

SUMMARY AND KEY POINTS

■ This unit has addressed the primacy of language for learning, and has emphasised the importance of language in creating learning classrooms.

■ Drawing principally on Vygotsky's theory of the relationship between thought and language, the unit outlines how, through developing young people's language, we are simultaneously supporting their development as learners.

■ All three language modes – talking, reading and writing – play a part in this interrelationship between language and learning, and by addressing language issues in your subject, you are also increasing pupil achievement in your subject.

■ The idea of 'language across the curriculum' is not that everyone does the job of the English department, but rather that all teachers understand this integral partnership between language and learning and take seriously how they can strengthen subject-specific language use.

■ This unit, then, is fundamentally about creating language-rich classrooms. To do this, you need to be able to plan explicitly for language activities in the context of your subject.

■ We hope this unit enables you to establish classroom interaction patterns where pupils talk more than teachers, and engage in collaborative and constructive group work.

■ We hope you will offer pupils activities that help them to become active and critical readers of texts, and that you will identify and model the written genres used in your subject.

■ Finally, we hope that you become a teacher who understands the power of language and knows that language is the very heart of empowered learning.

Check which requirements for your ITE programme you have addressed through this unit.

Further reading

Alexander, R. (2004) *Towards Dialogic Teaching: Rethinking Classroom Talk*, Cambridge: Dialogos.
This short booklet is invaluable in providing a thorough overview of the principles of dialogic teaching, and in offering ways to think about transforming the patterns of classroom talk so that young people are given more dynamic and challenging opportunities to learn.

Coultas, V. (2007) *Constructive Talk in Challenging Classrooms*, London: Routledge.
This book is full of practical, but principled, guidance on how to develop collaborative group work in classrooms where many teachers would avoid it, including where pupils have low levels of literacy or have English as an additional language. Coultas argues that talk is essential for building positive relationships, especially in difficult classrooms.

Cremin, T. and Myhill, D.A. (2012) *Writing Voices: Creating Communities of Writers*, London: Routledge.
This book considers writing from a range of perspectives and covers both primary and secondary phases. It offers a sound theoretical review of research on writing in the opening chapter and goes on to consider, for example, the role of talk in writing, agency and ownership, and metacognition in writing. The book is interspersed with vignettes of writing from preschool writers to professional novelists and journalists.

Harrison, C. (2004) *Understanding Reading Development*, London: Sage.
Underpinned by a strong grasp of research in reading, this book looks at various elements of reading development in the reading process; comprehension; critical literacy; assessment. It takes a holistic view of reading, addressing issues of reading in both primary and secondary school.

Ross, A. (2006) *Language Knowledge for Secondary Teachers*, London: David Fulton.
Many teachers, including English teachers, are not confident with grammar because for many years grammar was not taught in our schools. This book is a practical text that can also act as a reference point if you need to brush up on your nouns or clauses!

Other resources and websites

Dialogic teaching

Alexander, R. (2015) *Dialogic Teaching*, University of Cambridge, UK: www.robinalexander.org.uk/dialogic-teaching/

University of Cambridge (2015a) *Dialogic Teaching*: www.educ.cam.ac.uk/research/projects/dialogic/whatis.html.

University of Cambridge (2015b) *Thinking Together*: https://thinkingtogether.educ.cam.ac.uk/

MESHGuides

The Mapping Educational Specialist knowHow initiative (MESH) is producing research summaries called MESHGuides to support teachers becoming an evidence-informed practitioners. The following MESHGuides relevant to this unit, which can be found on www.meshguides.org, are:

English as an additional language

Flynn, N. (2015) *Teaching English as an Additional Language MESHGuide*, University of Winchester/University of Reading, UK.

Grammar

Eames, K. (2016) *Teaching Grammar*, MESHGuide, Bath Spa University, UK.

Reluctant writers

Gardner, P. (2013) *English Writing: Reluctant Writers*, MESHGuide, University of Bedfordshire, UK.

Special educational needs and disabilities

Blamires, M. *et al.* (2014) *Special Educational Needs and Disability: Enabling Pupil Participation*, MESHGuide, RIDDLE consultancy, previously Canterbury Christ Church University. (Funded initially by the now closed UK government agency, the Training and Development Agency for Schools.)

Spelling

Harrison, C. and Brookes, G. (2014) *Teaching Spelling in English*, MESHGuide, Universities of Nottingham and Sheffield, UK.

Appendix 2 on pages 591–595 provides further examples of websites you may find useful.

Capel, S., Leask, M. and Turner, T. (eds) (2010) *Readings for Learning to Teach in the Secondary School: A Companion to M Level Study*, London: Routledge.
    This book brings together essential readings to support you in your critical engagement with key issues raised in this textbook.

The subject-specific books in the Routledge *Learning to Teach* series are also very useful.

Any additional resources and an editable version of any relevant tasks/tables in this unit are available on the companion website: www.routledge.com/cw/capel

6 Assessment

Assessment and its reporting is a central issue in teaching and learning throughout education. In England, since the 1988 Education Reform Act, national testing has taken central stage in monitoring standards in schools.

This chapter addresses the purposes of assessment, their relationships to teaching and learning, and recent changes in assessment practice and reporting. The importance of formative assessment in raising achievement is discussed. Formative assessment is contrasted with summative assessment as is 'low stakes' versus 'high stakes' testing. The concepts of validity and reliability in assessment are addressed, including the tensions between them. Learning objectives that are difficult to assess but educationally important are also considered.

Formative assessment provides information about an individual pupil's progress, helps you devise appropriate teaching and learning strategies, and gives parents helpful information about their child's progress. Summative assessments are used to compare pupils, schools and local authorities (LAs) across the country. This chapter also discusses the extent to which any one test can be used to assess pupil progress, the quality of teaching and teachers, and school effectiveness in raising standards.

Unit 6.1, 'Assessing pupil progress: what do we know about good practice?', gives an overview of the principles of assessment, of formative and summative assessment, diagnostic testing and ideas of validity and reliability. The differences between norm-referenced, criterion-referenced and ipsative assessment are introduced and the nationally set tests discussed in the light of these principles. This unit shows how assessment can be used to identify progress and diagnose problems. The dangers of inappropriate assessment are mentioned. The management of assessment is addressed. The unit compares what could be assessed with what is assessed, linking the issues to public accountability of teachers, school governing bodies, LAs, and national educational standards. The chapter also considers the implications of the Department for Education's decision to move away from a 'levels'-based system of assessment for National Curriculum subjects (DfE 2013a), and suggests some pragmatic ways of assessing pupil progress based on what is known about good practice in assessment.

Unit 6.2, 'External assessment and examinations', considers preparing pupils for public examinations, an important feature of a teacher's work; this unit considers assessment as exemplified by General Certificate of Secondary Education (GCSE) and General Certificate of Education (GCE)

Advanced level. This unit links national monitoring of standards with your classroom work, raising issues of accountability. Public examinations grade pupils on a nationally recognised scale and exercise control over both entry to jobs and higher education. This unit addresses how national standards are maintained and national grades are awarded. Recent national developments in vocational education are discussed and the status of vocational education in relation to academic education is highlighted. Contrasts are drawn between the assessment methods used for vocational courses and academic courses.

6.1 Assessing pupil progress

What do we know about good practice?

Terry Haydn

Introduction

Assessment covers all those activities that are undertaken by teachers and others to measure the effectiveness of their teaching and the extent to which the pupils learned what they were trying to teach. Assessment includes not only setting and marking pupils' work, tests and examinations, but also the recording and reporting of the results. The three main purposes of assessment are:

■ *Accountability*: to make schools and teachers accountable for their work (for example, in the form of league tables of school examination results).
■ *Certification*: to issue statements about pupil attainment (for example, General Certificate of Secondary Education (GCSE) and General Certificate of Education (GCE) Advanced (A) level qualifications), which can be used by prospective employers and those controlling access to higher levels of education.
■ *To advance pupil learning*: where the primary purpose of the assessment is to promote pupil learning and help them to improve (for example, comments written at the end of a pupil's essay in order to give the pupil advice how to do a better essay next time). This function has been termed 'assessment for learning' (AfL), and is sometimes termed 'formative assessment'.

(Torrance and Pryor 1998; Black *et al.* 2003)

This unit focuses mainly on the third of these functions, for reasons that are explained below.

OBJECTIVES

At the end of this unit, you should be able to:

■ identify the differing purposes of assessment and the tensions between them;
■ explain what is meant by 'assessment for learning';
■ use correctly some important assessment terminology;
■ identify assessment practices that may be ineffective or harmful;

■ select strategies for making assessment and evaluation purposeful and manageable;

■ use assessment data in various ways to help pupils to make progress in their learning;

■ understand the implications of the move away from a 'levels'-based system of assessment.

Check the requirements of your initial teacher education (ITE) programme to see which relate to this unit.

What is assessment for learning and why is it important?

AfL has been defined as 'any assessment for which the first priority is to serve the purpose of promoting students' learning' (Black *et al.* 2003: 2). An important element of AfL is that the information derived from the assessment is used, by both teacher and pupils. In other words:

> An assessment functions formatively to the extent that evidence about student achievement is elicited, interpreted and used, by teachers, learners or their peers to make decisions about the next steps in instruction that are likely to be better, or better founded, than the decisions they would have made in the absence of that evidence.

(Wiliam 2011: 43)

Some general principles involved in using assessment to improve learning outcomes include:

■ the provision of *helpful and constructive* feedback to pupils;

■ an attempt to actively involve pupils in their own learning, including some use of self- and peer assessment;

■ teacher adjustments to future instruction based on the outcomes of the assessment;

■ taking into account the influence of assessment on learner motivation and self-esteem;

■ making learners aware of the success criteria needed to do well in the assessment activity.

Assessment for learning (AfL) is important because a substantial body of recent research suggests that intelligent, thoughtful and well-informed assessment practice is one of the most important factors in ensuring that pupils achieve their educational potential (ARG 2002; Swaffield 2008; Hattie 2012). Several research studies have shown that the use of assessment *to develop pupils' future learning* makes a substantial difference, not just to pupils' attainment, but to their attitude to learning, their engagement with school subjects and their motivation to do well in these subjects (Black and Wiliam 1998; Murphy 1999; Black *et al.* 2003; Hattie 2012). Procter's (2013) and Newton and Bowler's (2016) MESHGuides provide more detail on AfL (see the MESHGuides website).

When you are at Stage 1 of this cycle, part of your thinking should be about how you will go about finding out whether pupils have learned what you were trying to teach (see also Unit 5.4 on assessing the effectiveness of your teaching).

Assessment is not just a way of finding out about the extent to which pupils have learned what you were trying to teach; it is also a means of finding out which elements of your teaching were

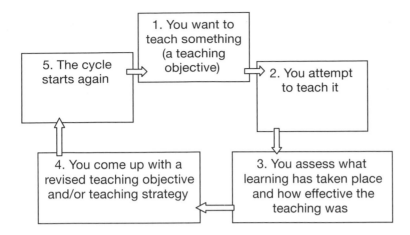

When you are at Stage 1 of this cycle, part of your thinking should be about how you will go about finding out whether pupils have learned what you were trying to teach.

Figure 6.1.1 The planning/teaching/assessment/planning loop

effective, and which elements were less successful, and might require rethinking in order to teach a topic more effectively next time (see Figure 6.1.1).

Teachers have to spend many hours assessing, recording and reporting pupils' work. You want to make sure that this investment in time spent marking pupils' work and giving feedback on their progress justifies the time and effort you spend on it. It is not a question of how much assessment of pupils' work you do, or even how *much* feedback you provide, but how *intelligently* you use assessment to inform your future teaching, and your feedback to pupils. Teachers who can use assessment to promote pupils' learning 'come to enjoy their work more and to find it more satisfying because it resonates with their professional values. They also see that their students come to enjoy, understand and value their learning more as a result of the innovations' (Black *et al.* 2003: 3).

However, assessment is a complex area of educational policy and practice. It has a complicated and sprawling agenda, making it difficult to gain a comprehensive grasp of assessment issues. It takes time; you need to work at it, both in terms of reading, and reflecting on your classroom practice. This unit provides an introduction to assessment issues and carries suggestions that should provide 'a grounding' in assessment. As in other areas of teaching, it requires initiative, application and thoughtfulness to use assessment effectively.

Understanding the vocabulary of assessment

Assessment has a technical vocabulary that you need to know in order to understand the importance of assessment both for your teaching and your pupils. This vocabulary includes:

- *Criterion-referenced assessment*: a process in which performance is measured by relating candidates' responses to predetermined criteria.
- *Formative assessment*: AfL, linked to teaching when the evidence from assessment is used to adapt teaching to meet pupils' learning needs.

- *Ipsative assessment*: assessing a learner's achievements in relation to their own previous performance. This is an important consideration in AfL, as it promotes the idea that all learners can make progress in a subject, even if they are not as accomplished as some of their peers.
- *Norm-referenced assessment*: a process in which performance is measured by comparing candidates' responses. Individual success is relative to the performance of all other candidates.
- *Reliable assessment – or reliability*: a measure of the consistency of the assessment or test item (that is, the extent to which the test gives repeatable results).
- *Summative assessment*: assessment linked to the end of a course of study; it sums up achievement in aggregate terms and is used to rank, grade or compare pupils.
- *Valid assessment or validity*: a measure of whether the assessment measures what it is meant to measure – often determined by consensus. Certain kinds of skills and abilities are extremely difficult to assess with validity via simple pencil and paper tests.
- *Value added*: the extent to which the school has raised the pupil's achievement beyond a predicted level.

Further explanation of these terms can be found online at https://terryhaydn.wordpress.com/pgce-history-at-uea/assessment/ based on previous achievement.

Context: assessment in uncertain and challenging times

In 2013, the Department for Education (DfE) in England announced that 'As part of our reforms to the National Curriculum, the current system of "levels", used to report children's attainment and progress will be removed. It will not be replaced' (DfE 2013a: 1). The system of 'levels' had dominated assessment policy in English schools since the inception of the National Curriculum in 1991 (see DfEE/QCA 1999a for a description and explanation of the levels system). In terms of assessment policy and practice, the new National Curriculum, which was introduced in schools in September 2014, simply stated that 'by the end of each key stage, pupils are expected to know, apply and understand the matters, skills and processes specified in the relevant programmes of study' (DfE 2013b). Although the move away from the 'levels' system was couched in terms of 'setting schools free' in terms of how they assessed pupil progress, it has introduced a degree of uncertainty about what, if anything, would replace the levels system. In the words of Fordham, the new National Curriculum 'has scrapped the level descriptors and put nothing in their place' (Fordham 2013: 16).

In spite of severe criticisms of the levels (see, for instance, Fordham 2013), Ford makes the point that 'many state-school teachers, trained in the last 20 years are unlikely ever to have used another means of assessment at Key Stage 3 (pupils aged 11–14)', pointing out that 'many teachers are unsure about how assessment . . . might be conceived once these "ladders" are removed' (Ford 2014: 28).

The 'abolition' of levels has therefore left something of a vacuum in terms of the provision of some form of model for assessing pupil attainment and progress. For both new teachers entering the profession and for experienced teachers moving between schools, there is a degree of uncertainty about what methods and systems should be used to assess pupil progress. A survey of 866 school leaders revealed very differing responses to the 'end of levels'. It is clear that many schools will continue to use the levels in some form, others are unsure about how they will adjust to a post-levels system, some are waiting for the development of new exemplar models of non-levels-based assessment to be published on the DfE website (Key Survey for School Leaders 2013). The National Association of Head Teachers (NAHT) Commission of enquiry into school assessment has also undertaken research on 'assessment after the end of levels' (NAHT 2014), but its findings were unpublished at the time of writing. An Internet search for 'NAHT Assessment Report' should locate the final report when it emerges.

It is therefore possible for you to be working in schools with very different models and systems for assessing pupil progress, from those that have retained the levels system in some form, to those who have completely abandoned it. How should student teachers respond to these variations in practice, both as students working within departments and in their first year of teaching?

It is helpful to be aware of the tensions that have influenced the ways in which levels have been used in schools in recent years. Senior management teams are under pressure to demonstrate to parents and to Office for Standards in Education (Ofsted) inspection teams that pupils are making good progress at school. The levels have sometimes been split into artificially constructed 'sublevels' in order to make it easier to demonstrate some form of improvement in pupil attainment, rather than using them as 'end of Key Stage, best fit descriptors' as originally intended (Wiliam 2001; Fordham 2014). Classroom teachers, immersed in the integrity of their subject, and with a deeply instilled curiosity about 'what it means to get better' at English/maths/science or whatever, have often been concerned about the uses to which levels assessment have been put in the name of 'pupil progress', and the validity of some of the 'sublevels' that have been constructed. Even the levels themselves – the idea of a simple ladder – like a set of linear steps to paint an accurate picture of pupil progression in every subject – have been described as 'woefully simplistic' (Fordham 2014). It could be argued that the strong concern to use assessment to make schools and teachers accountable (DES 1989b), meant that, to at least some extent, the validity of assessment judgments and the potential of assessment for advancing pupil learning were sacrificed on the altar of 'accountability'.

The current Teachers' Standards for Qualified Teacher Status in England explicitly make the point that those learning to teach must be able to make 'accurate and productive use of assessment' (DfE 2011i: 12).Given that you do not know what sort of assessment regime you will be working in, and what systems for recording pupil progress will emerge in the post-levels era, a pragmatic way forward is to prepare yourself for the challenges of making 'accurate and productive use of assessment' and become familiar with what is known about good practice in assessment, and attempt to assimilate this into your assessment practice. Of course, you are not 'a free agent', able to do whatever you want in terms of assessing pupil progress. Teachers have to work within an institutional framework, and 'fit in' to school systems. However, within school systems and senior management team policies, there is scope to assess pupil progress and guide pupils to better learning outcomes as intelligently and effectively as the school system makes possible.

It can also be helpful to develop an understanding of assessment policy and practice outside the schools you are working in. Even within the UK, countries are moving in different directions in terms of exactly what is to be assessed. In England in 2011, education ministers called for more emphasis to be placed on the assessment of pupils' grasp of a body of substantive content knowledge, sometimes spoken of in 'shorthand' terms as knowledge of 'facts' (Gove 2011). In Scotland, more emphasis has been placed on trying to ensure that assessment:

■ 'promotes learner engagement';
■ ensures that pupils 'can apply what they have learned in new and unfamiliar situations';
■ is used 'to inform planning for improvement'.

These statements are facets of 'AfL' principles (Scottish Government 2010).

Outside the UK, there has been a move in several countries towards attempting to assess high-order skills and dispositions towards learning, and away from assessment of the ability to recall factual information. The Organisation for Economic Co-operation and Development (OECD) has suggested that educational assessment should attempt to measure and promote what are called 'key competencies', such as the ability to communicate well, managing oneself and one's relation to others, and the assessment of learners, 'openness to learning', and disposition to contribute and participate in educational processes (OECD 2003). The move in some countries towards allowing learners to have access to the Internet in formal examinations also has implications for the way that learners are to be assessed in preparation for such examinations, and what sort of questions are posed of learners, with 'why and how' questions replacing 'what and when' questions. A British Broadcasting Corporation (BBC) report on these developments in 2009 suggested that in countries that have adapted this approach, 'Students are no longer required to regurgitate facts and figures. Instead, the emphasis is on their ability to sift through and analyse information' (BBC 2009) (see p. 465).

Assessment practice in some countries is moving towards measuring pupils' dispositions and attitudes towards learning rather than focusing primarily on cognitive attainment: their motivation to learn and do well in school subjects; their willingness to persevere with a difficult enquiry, their resourcefulness and sense of self-efficacy, and even their self-control. This is because there is some evidence to suggest that the cultivation and development of these qualities can have a major influence on pupil attainment (Goleman 2005; Carr 2008; Baumeister and Tierney 2012). See also Table 6.1.4 on marking and motivation.

'First do no harm'

'First do no harm' is a precept that all medical students are taught and is a fundamental principle in medicine. It is the idea that it may be better not to do something, or even to do nothing, than to do something that risks doing more harm than good.

It is useful to keep this phrase in mind when you are thinking about how to assess your pupils' learning. Assessment is an aspect of teaching that has come to be thought of as 'a good thing', with its connotations of 'rigour', close attention, checking that what has been taught has been learned (and making teachers accountable for their work). However, research on assessment in recent years has suggested that assessment practice does not necessarily have helpful or positive outcomes for either the assessor or the assessed. Desforges (2003) has argued that 'most assessment practice has no effect on learning whatsoever'. Gipps points out that a lot of the time and effort that is devoted to assessment does not help to move pupils forward in their learning:

> There's an awful lot of giving smiley faces at the bottom of children's work and very elaborate praise and stars and so on. They are fine for maintaining pupils' motivation and making children feel good about it, but unless it's accompanied by more direct specific advice about what to do to make the piece of work better it's actually of very little help to pupils as a learning activity.
>
> (Gipps 1997: 5)

It has also been argued that assessment activities can be harmful because they may result in spending too much time trying to measure increments in learning rather than getting more learning done; that is, 'spending too much time weighing the pig rather than fattening it'. It has even been argued that assessment activities can actually be harmful to pupil learning. There is now a substantial body of research evidence that suggests that the increased emphasis on testing of pupils has had harmful effects on pupils' self-esteem, well-being and attitudes towards school and learning (see, for example, ARG 2002; Bawden 2007; Crace 2007; Russell 2007; Wiliam 2011). Other evidence suggests that test results can influence friendship groups, with high achievers rejecting less successful pupils at primary school level (Bloom 2007). Assessment can be valid and reliable and yet have a profoundly dispiriting influence on pupils' attitude to a subject and to school in general. It has been argued that the ways in which some assessment has been developed in recent years has contributed to disaffection and disengagement in schools (Willingham 2009; Swann 2013). Others have indicated that there is a danger that 'pupils who see themselves as unable to learn usually cease to take school seriously, many are disruptive within school, others resort to truancy' (Black and Wiliam 1998: 4). Holt makes the point that pupils 'at the bottom of the pile' often do not respond by exhibiting determination to get to the top – they stop trying:

> Most people . . . understand it [education] as being made to go to a place called school, and there being made to learn something that they don't much want to learn, under the threat that bad things will be done to them if they don't. Needless to say, most people don't much like this game and stop playing as soon as they can.
>
> (Holt 1984: 34)

It is therefore important that you keep in mind the effect that your assessment activity has on the pupils in your care and that you develop a sound understanding of the ways in which assessment can impact on pupil attainment and pupils' *attitude* towards learning.

Other 'dangers' in the field of assessment include:

■ the temptation to assess what is easy to assess rather than learning experiences that are valuable and worthwhile, but difficult to assess;
■ the danger of 'teaching to the test' in order to optimise outcomes in external examinations;
■ distorting assessment procedures and measurements in order to improve departmental or school standing;
■ lack of challenge in assessment instruments, underestimating what pupils are capable of achieving.

(Torrance and Pryor 1998; Black *et al.* 2003; Swaffield 2008; Wiliam 2011)

Most teachers and many schools wrestle with the problem of how to make best use of assessment, how to ensure that the time and effort involved in assessing teaching and learning is not wasted, or even counterproductive. There is research evidence available to teachers and student teachers to inform their practice in assessment and to help improve pupil attainment, and help teachers avoid some of the pitfalls and 'collateral damage' that poor assessment practice can cause (see later in this unit).

The next section addresses some common misconceptions about learning and assessment.

Common misconceptions and problems relating to assessment and learning

Understanding and taking account of the limits of teaching effectiveness

People who have never been teachers sometimes underestimate how difficult it can be to try to teach something to a group of learners. There is a tendency to assume that if the teacher explains the idea competently, and the learners are reasonably intelligent, the learners will absorb and understand all that the teacher has tried to convey. It is quite common for student teachers to write in their lesson evaluations that all the learning outcomes for the lesson were achieved. And yet, in how many lessons do all the pupils learn everything that the teacher is trying to teach? What percentage of what is taught is learned in classrooms, in the sense of being understood, retained and, where appropriate, applied after the lesson? As Fullan points out, 'Even when people are sincerely motivated to learn from you, they have a devil of a time doing so. Transferability of ideas is a complex problem of the highest order' (Fullan 1999: 63).

The tendency to overestimate the extent to which teaching has been effective is not limited to student teachers. Research has explored experienced teachers' views on what proportion of pupils understood the concepts that they were trying to teach before their lessons and what proportion understood these concepts after the series of lessons (Sadler 1994). Some outcomes of this research are given in Tables 6.1.1 and 6.1.2.

Sadler suggests that teachers often disturb pupils' ideas without decisively changing them, with the result that they are often confused by the lessons, with teachers then moving quickly on, in order to cover an overloaded curriculum. Teachers do sometimes ask the class whether everyone has understood what they have just talked about, but how many pupils are confident enough to put their hand up to say they do not understand something?

Table 6.1.1 Percentage of pupils with a basic understanding of the concept of gravity before and after teaching

Before teaching		After teaching	
Teachers' predictions	Actual	Teachers' predictions	Actual
25%	30%	60%	15%

Source: Sadler (1994)

Table 6.1.2 Percentage of pupils with a basic understanding of the concept of planetary motion before and after teaching

Before teaching		After teaching	
Teachers' predictions	Actual	Teachers' predictions	Actual
25%	18%	70%	8%

Source: Sadler (1994)

It is because of these 'learning deficits' that assessment is so important. It is helpful for you to know which pupils know and understand what you were trying to teach, and those who do not. In short, you should beware of thinking that 'because you've taught it, they've learned it'.

The problem of retention

A second major issue in assessment is *when to assess*. Sometimes learners forget what we have taught them; the learning often 'slips away' (Greene and Miller 1996; Willingham 2009). As Fontana noted, 'we each of us receive a constant and varied stream of experiences throughout our waking moments, each one of which can potentially give rise to learning, yet most of which apparently vanish without trace from our mental lives' (Fontana 1993: 125). We all are subject to forgetting.

If you assess something directly after teaching it, a good proportion of the pupils may remember and understand it. If you assess it several weeks later, a different picture may emerge. We suggest you now try Task 6.1.1.

 Task 6.1.1 Delaying the timing of an assessment to check for retention

Find out the proportion of pupils who have remembered and understood something you taught them several weeks ago. At some point in your teaching, use a simple test to check recall of material you taught much earlier. Use, for example, a short written test, or 'put your hands up if you remember . . .'

Compare these results with your assessment made shortly after teaching the material. Store the results in your professional development portfolio (PDP).

Teaching for lasting understanding is a complex process and raises the issue of the importance of reinforcement, recap and returning to the material from time to time to check for recall and understanding. Didau (2015a) advises 'spacing' in terms of the teaching and assessing of topics. Read 'Why do students remember everything that's on television and forget everything I say?' (Willingham 2009a), which gives ideas about how to teach for retention.

The problem of knowledge application

Many student teachers are unfamiliar with the problem of knowledge application, even though it is a very important issue in education. In the words of Desforges:

> Schools worldwide are relatively successful at teaching bodies of knowledge, but they are much less good at getting pupils to be able to use and apply this knowledge in new settings or in problem solving . . . This failure to apply acquired skills is evident in all areas of the curriculum. It is a long-standing challenge to educational systems everywhere.
>
> (Desforges 2002: 4)

The practical problem facing teachers is how to assess learner understanding in a way that makes it clear whether or not learners have grasped the concept being taught, rather than learners only being able to regurgitate the information.

Learning should involve understanding that can be demonstrated by *using* new knowledge; as one writer has put it, 'It is the chasm between knowing X and using X to think about Y' (Wineburg 1997: 256).

The way that you formulate a question for pupils can have a significant influence on the chances of pupils responding with a correct answer. Several examples of this are provided in Unit 3.1. How useful is it if pupils only answer the question correctly if you ask them in a particular way? If you test pupils using the same questions in the same context in which it was taught, they may give you back just what you taught them. This approach may not test understanding, only recall. If you include in your testing application of the material in a new context, you may gain information about pupils' understanding of the topic, as well as details of partial understanding or misconceptions. Only if you have an accurate idea about pupils' current understanding of the topic can you make intelligent decisions about what to teach next. What is important is not just 'covering content', but to place learning in a wider context. In other words, 'helping pupils to make sense of what they are learning is the most important thing' (Clough 2001: para. 8). Assessment is part of pupils' learning, rather than just a check that they have recalled the material. Assessment should test real learning rather than simply regurgitation of information (Harlen 1995: 14).

John Holt gives some helpful pointers of ways of assessing genuine understanding that might lead to a greater likelihood of pupils being able to apply the knowledge they have gained to solve problems and use in other contexts (see Table 6.1.3).

Understanding progression in your subject

To improve your assessment of pupils, you need to have a clear grasp of progression in your subject; that is, to know what it means 'to get better at geography' (or whatever). There is more to getting better in school subjects than simply acquiring more factual knowledge. For example, in history, there is more to progression than simply 'knowing more stuff'. As well as developing the depth and breadth of their historical understanding, pupils should make progress in their understanding of the discipline of history, their ability to make intelligent historical enquiries themselves, and their ability to communicate their understanding orally and in writing. We are not just filling up pupils' 'hard disk' space with facts; we are helping to develop their ability to acquire, process and communicate subject-related information effectively.

Understanding progression in your subject is an important and essential prerequisite for a teacher in order to use assessment in a focused and appropriate way in your teaching.

Now consider Task 6.1.2.

Thinking that assessment comes 'at the end' of a topic or unit of work

Some student teachers tend to think (perhaps not unreasonably) that assessment comes *after* teaching. This seems a common-sense assumption; after all, it would not seem sensible to assess pupils' understanding before you had taught a topic. The problem here is that assessment at the end of teaching a topic can be a sort of 'bolt-on' activity, and can be mainly summative in purpose.

Table 6.1.3 What it means to understand something

Holt writes:

It may help to have in our minds a picture of what we mean by understanding. I feel I understand something if I can do some, at least, of the following:

- ■ state it in my own words
- ■ give examples of it
- ■ recognise it in various guises and circumstances
- ■ see connections between it and other facts or ideas
- ■ make use of it in various ways
- ■ foresee some of its consequences
- ■ state its opposite or converse.

The list is only a beginning, but it may help us in the future to find out what our students really know as opposed to what they can give the appearance of knowing, their real learning as opposed to their apparent learning.

(Holt 1964: 176)

 Task 6.1.2 Developing an understanding of progression in your subject

If you were asked at interview what it means to get better at history, geography or whatever your subject is, how well would you be able to answer this question? If you are not confident that you have a sound understanding of progression in your subject, read the specifications for your subject in the syllabus. In addition, identify research and inspection evidence related to progression in your subject, using government reports and other journal articles. Unit 4.1 also provides detailed advice on progression. In England, reports from Ofsted and the Standards Testing Agency (STA) (formerly QCA) are useful. Give examples of progression from two or more topics you expect to teach or have taught, indicating, for example, development across Key Stages 3 and 4. Store this information in your PDP.

If you give an 'end of unit' test to pupils, when are the deficits in learning to be addressed if you are going to move on to a new topic (Wiliam 2011). Providing a test around three-quarters of the way through the teaching of a topic leaves some lessons for 'filling the gaps' in pupils' understanding of the topic.

AfL is not a special event that takes place after several lessons. Rather, it is 'the process used by teachers and students to recognise and respond to student learning in order to enhance that learning *during the learning*' (emphasis added, Cowie and Bell 1999: 32). Furthermore, the statement that 'minute by minute and day-to-day formative assessment is likely to have the biggest impact on student outcomes' is a key assertion of AfL (Wiliam 2011: 27). Another way of looking at AfL is the idea that 'in every lesson, a teacher should aim to observe, listen, engage with and respond to pupil learning' (Philpott 2011: 264). This process might be termed assessment at the 'micro level' in the sense that it is not a formal 'set-piece' test or major event, just the idea that whenever a teacher has tried to explain something, they try to get a feel for how much of it pupils have understood, and which pupils have understood, which have not, and which pupils have only a partial understanding. This is done by talking to pupils, asking them questions, looking at their books as they write, discussing the ideas around the class, asking them to hold up a mini-whiteboard with a red, amber or green symbol on it to indicate levels of understanding, using an 'exit pass' system (see next section) as they leave the room, or getting pupils who have grasped the idea to explain it to those who are less certain in their understanding, or even just looking at the expressions on pupils' faces.

So, it is not just *at the end of lessons* that you try to gauge the extent of pupils' learning; it is all the way through lessons, but in a quick, 'light-touch' and unobtrusive way. This process should not entirely replace more conventional assessment activities, but should complement them. Ofsted stress the importance of regular 'within lesson' assessment: 'In the most effective schools, teachers and pupils often review learning against precise objectives regularly during lessons ... Where assessment is ineffective, teachers do not routinely check pupils' understanding as the lesson progresses' (Ofsted 2007: 66).

Understanding that not all feedback to pupils has a positive effect on their learning

As with the general idea of assessment itself, 'feedback' is generally thought of as being 'a good thing'. Feedback from assessment activities is essential so that pupils know how they have done, where they did well, where they made mistakes and what they might do to learn from their errors. Feedback 'is one of the most powerful influences on learning and achievement' (Hattie and Timperley 2007: 57). However, in a meta-analysis of the impact of feedback on learning, it was found that in two out of five instances, the effects of feedback on learners were negative (Kluger and DeNisi 1996). We also suggest that you keep a watching brief on the Education Endowment Foundation (EEF) blog on assessment (2015).

Pupils' *attitude* to learning has a big influence on how successful they are at learning. Feedback influences not just the chances of them getting it right, or doing better next time, but their attitude to learning and the amount of effort and thought that they are willing to put into learning. Thus, 'a number of pupils do not aspire to learn as much as possible, but are content "to get by", to get through the period, the day or the year without any major disaster, having made time for activities other than school work' (Perrenoud 1991: 2). See also Unit 3.2 on motivating pupils.

The danger is not just that learners may be indifferent to feedback, but that feedback might serve to discourage them from trying to do well in the future if it is consistently pointing out the serious weaknesses of the pupil in a particular subject. This problem is particularly acute in the case of less able pupils. How can you provide feedback that is honest but not dispiriting for such pupils? (A later section of the unit provides some suggestions; also see Figure 6.1.4.) Didau, citing Hattie and Timperly (2007), makes the point that the timing of feedback needs careful consideration, pointing out that there is not much use providing feedback on imperfectly understood material and that teachers' time would be better spent in developing pupil understanding through further elaboration, modelling or instruction (Didau 2015a).

Understanding that assessment information needs to be acted on, in order to be useful

Teachers spend many hours marking pupils' work. It can be chastening to think about what proportion of that work is actively used, by the teacher, pupils or both, to improve future learning outcomes. Gipps argues that the most common use of assessment outcomes is that they are recorded in the teacher's markbook and that 'often, that's all that happens to assessment results' (Gipps 1997: 4). The recording of a mark or grade for the work, and the comments that the teacher might have made on the pupil's work, are 'proof' that the work was done, and that the teacher has marked the work, but do not ensure that the assessment has what Gipps terms 'consequential validity' (Gipps 1997); that is, that either the teacher or the pupil acts on the information that the assessment provides, in order to improve subsequent performance. Several studies have suggested that where grades and comments have been given to pupils, the comments are not read and acted on (see, for example, Butler 1987; Black et al. 2003). Wiliam (2011) argues for trying to ensure that the overall processes involved in assessment oblige learners to do more work on the feedback from the assessment than the teachers have spent marking the work, but this requires careful thought on the part of the teacher.

It is not, therefore, a question of how much time or how often you assess pupils' work; it is about how much benefit derives from this work – for you and for your pupils.

How to make assessment useful

Having attempted to point out some of the tensions, problems and unintended consequences of assessment, the next section of this unit suggests ways of ensuring that your assessment practice helps you to teach more effectively, and that it helps your pupils to learn and improve.

(a) Being clear about the purposes and benefits of your assessment activities

Assessment can take a wide range of forms, from essay work, a quick 'pencil and paper' test on recall and comprehension of work covered, an end-of-lesson question-and-answer session (sometimes termed a 'QUAD' activity – question, answer and discussion), a 'quiz' activity, such as 'Blockbusters' or 'Who Wants to Be a Millionaire?', a group presentation, getting pupils to do a group activity where they (hopefully) learn from each other, or simply asking individual pupils questions as you walk round the room.

Assessments serve a variety of purposes, and sometimes tensions arise because of this. It is difficult to devise 'all-purpose' assessment instruments that serve all these purposes. One common tension is whether the assessment is more useful for supporting pupil learning ('formative' assessment)' or for making judgements ('summative' assessment), but there are others.

One purpose of assessment is to show pupils that you take an interest in their work; this can help to motivate pupils, but does not necessarily have this effect (see the section in this unit on feedback to pupils). Assessing pupils' work can also give you some idea about how well the pupils are doing, monitoring their progress. It can sometimes ascertain whether pupils have particular difficulties in their learning that might be alleviated with specifically targeted interventions and assistance once diagnosed (see also Unit 4.1 on differentiation). Assessment data on a pupil's prior attainment can also help to detect pupil underachievement, where a pupil may be 'coasting', or going through 'a bad patch' for some reason, which can then be investigated. Under the terms of the 1988 Education Reform Act for England and Wales (ERA 1988), schools also have a statutory responsibility to report to parents about pupils' progress at least once a year, and more regular communication between the school and parents (for example, through a weekly diary system) can be a valuable way of safeguarding pupils' academic and social well-being. As well as reporting on achievement, many schools also use assessment data to make comparisons between pupils or to 'group' pupils into particular teaching sets. Some pupils are motivated by competition, and try harder to do well and 'come top'; however, some commentators suggest that 'we should spend less time ranking children and more time helping them to identify their natural competences and gifts and cultivate these' (Gardner 1986). Assessment is not just about gaining information about pupil performance: teachers can use assessment data to reflect on and evaluate *their own* performance, to gauge which elements of learning they taught effectively, and which less so. Assessment data also make it possible for teachers, schools and local authorities (LAs) to be held to account for their performance.

Part of the challenge of becoming an effective teacher is devising appropriate and helpful learning experiences for pupils. In most lessons, at some stage, the pupils are 'doing something' other than simply listening to the teacher. Some benefits to pupils undertaking a lesson task include:

1   enthusing the pupils, making them keen to learn and find out more about the learning problem;
2   moving pupils forward in their learning;
3   providing information for the teacher on what the pupils have learned (which bits of the topic they understood and which they didn't fully grasp);
4   providing information to the teacher about *why* the pupils failed to understand aspects of the topic, the mistakes they made or the misconceptions they hold;
5   enabling the teacher to know which pupils have understood the topic, and which have not;
6   enabling pupils to take a particular move forward in their learning; the activity has made a particular point in a powerful way, changing pupils' ideas about the topic;
7   providing information for parents about how their child is progressing, and how well the pupils are likely to do in an external examination.

Use this list of benefits to address Task 6.1.3.

(b) The integration of a variety of assessment instruments into day-to-day classroom activities

An assessment should be a learning experience for pupils as well as measuring what they have learned. In Gardner's words:

> It is extremely desirable to have assessments occur in the context of students working on problems, projects or products which genuinely engage them, which hold their interest and which motivate them to do well. Such exercises may not be as easy to design . . . but they are far more likely to elicit a student's full repertoire of skills and to yield information that is useful for subsequent advice and placement.
>
> (Gardner 1999: 103)

Task 6.1.3 Understanding the benefits to pupils of assessment tasks

Select one class you teach and then some tasks you have given pupils to do in recent lessons.

1   Which of the benefits described above have been a feature of the tasks? (You may wish to identify other benefits.) Was there a task that delivered all these benefits or was it difficult to devise a task that incorporated all the benefits described?
2   Over a period of several lessons with a class, do your tasks address all the points described above or do they tend to fall into a limited band within the list?
3   Write brief notes summarising your analysis and the implications this may have for planning future tasks for your class.
4   Use your analysis and discussion to plan and execute a short unit of work that includes all or most of the benefits you have identified.

Finally, review the success or otherwise of your planned work, identifying the ideas and/or theories that have influenced your thinking about how you assess pupils' work and progress. Store in your PDP.

Another advantage of assessment tasks that are seen as routine and low-key classroom activities is that this avoids the negative effects that 'high-stakes' testing has on some learners. High-stakes assessments are those assessments for which the outcome is significant for the pupil (for example, the GCSE) or the school (for example, National Assessments Tests (NATs)). It has been suggested that pupils are most likely to engage with learning tasks if they are a combination of 'low stress' and high challenge – difficult enough to be interesting and worth exploring, but not accompanied by anxiety of being formally tested, with associations of judgement, possible failure and comparison to other pupils.

You should also employ a wide range of strategies to gain insights into pupils' understanding of their learning. As well as using written tasks, you can ask pupils, in small groups, to draw mind maps or spider diagrams (see Unit 5.2) expressing their ideas about the topic, or to give a short oral presentation or present a poster summarising the main points of their task. In terms of time-effective assessment, the use of closed questioning and multiple-choice questions to quickly explore pupil understanding has sometimes been underestimated in recent years. Christodoulou (2013) and Van Sledright (2014) have both pointed to the potential of multiple-choice questions, thoughtfully devised, to check pupil misconceptions. Employing a wide range of assessment instruments also guards against the danger of over-reliance on one form of testing, such as pupils' written work.

(c) Sharing learning goals

Recent research suggests that it is helpful if teachers are explicit about their learning outcomes and share them with pupils in a way that pupils can understand (ARG 2002; Black *et al.* 2003; Clarke 2005; Wiliam 2011).

This approach can include 'modelling' or showing them what a good response might look like and involving them in an active dialogue, talking to them and getting them to talk about their learning. This is not easy: 'How to draw the concept of excellence out of the heads of teachers, give it some external formulation and make it available to the learner is a non-trivial problem' (Sadler, in Gipps 1997). Some ways forward include:

■ 'Model' examples that might help pupils to grasp what it is you are looking for. Using (anonymised) 'good' and 'flawed' examples from a previous cohort of learners can be helpful here.
■ When pupils are doing presentations, give them explicit performance indicators that show them the criteria on which you judge their performance, such as quality of preparation and research, marshalling of information, structure, delivery, eye contact, answering of questions, and so on.
■ Discuss with pupils what constitutes a good essay.
■ Describe effective ways of working in a group.

An assessment instrument for pupils designed to help them think about what is involved in working successfully in groups is shown in Figure 6.1.2.

An editable version of Figure 6.1.2 is available on the companion website (www.routledge.com/cw/capel).

(d) Involving pupils in their learning: self- and peer assessment

Involving pupils in their learning and their understanding of the processes, issues and problems involved in learning is considered to be effective practice. For example, you could ask pupils to:

■ make their own judgement on the extent to which they have learned something;
■ mark each others' work;
■ give 'critical friend' advice to their peers;
■ draw up a mark scheme and performance criteria.

All these strategies shift assessment responsibilities towards the pupil and help the pupil to take responsibility for their own learning. In particular, you need to convey to pupils the nature of the 'gap' that exists between their current level of performance and what is desirable, and what it takes for them to bridge that gap (Clarke 2001). You can't do the learning for the pupils; they have to do it for themselves, and your job is to show them how to do this. Unless pupils are involved in working things out, learning may become memorisation without real understanding, and be soon forgotten. Having said this, Clarke also makes the point that pupils need to be given guidance on how to approach self- and peer assessment if it is to be helpful; teachers need to show pupils examples of 'constructive' marking; you could use examples from previous cohorts to show pupils. Another example is to suggest that pupils are asked to give 'two stars and a wish' (two positive comments and a constructive suggestion for improvement) when assessing a fellow pupil's work (Wiliam 2011).

(e) Questioning with and between pupils

This aspect of a teacher's work is central to checking what pupils can recall and have understood. Unit 3.1 has a section on this topic, and we have placed additional support and guidelines on the companion website, headed Unit 6.1 'Additional material: questioning with and between pupils'.

Name of pupil:	
People in my group:	
Task:	

Did I …?

Make sure I knew what we were supposed to do?	
Make a contribution to discussions?	
Listen to other people's ideas?	
Make suggestions to improve other people's ideas?	
Encourage other people to share their ideas?	
Give people good reasons when I did not agree with them?	
Avoid putting other people down?	
Avoid getting cross with other people?	
Talk to someone I don't usually talk to?	
Develop my understanding of the task by working with others?	

As a group, did we …?

Make sure that everyone had something to do and joined in?	
Keep on task?	
Come to agreements on what to do?	
Make compromises about what to do?	
Finish the task on time?	
Feedback our ideas clearly to the rest of the class?	

Figure 6.1.2 Helping pupils understand what is involved in working successfully in groups

(f) The art of giving feedback that has a positive effect on pupil motivation and learning

As noted earlier in this unit, feedback does not necessarily have a positive effect on pupils' learning. It can discourage them and make them feel that 'it is not worth the effort' to work hard to improve. Another limitation on the effectiveness of feedback is that pupils don't pay any heed to it and just carry on as before. This has occasioned an extensive debate on the comparative merits of giving grades and comments or just 'comments-only' marking (see, for example, Black *et al.* 2003). One should perhaps beware of generalisations and orthodoxies here. Perhaps some pupils like getting grades and marks for their work? This is something that you could helpfully explore with the teachers you work with.

But are there some underpinning principles about what constitutes good practice in giving feedback to pupils? The following points are an attempt to distil some of the suggestions for good practice where there appears to be a degree of consensus among researchers who have explored this area (see, for instance, Torrance and Pryor 1998; Black *et al.* 2003; Swaffield 2008; Wiliam 2011):

- Try to be precise in specifying what might be improved and how to go about doing this. As Gipps points out, 'It actually helps the pupil to be told directly but kindly, what it is they are not doing very well so that they know how to do it better' (Gipps 1997: 5).
- Where possible, try to make assessment activities interesting and challenging, so that pupils are made to think about and engage with the intellectual challenge involved. Wiliam goes as far as to suggest that 'If I had to reduce all the research on feedback into one simple overarching idea, it would be this: feedback should cause thinking' (Wiliam 2011: 127).
- Focus on how pupils can improve their own individual performance (sometimes termed 'ipsative assessment') rather than couching feedback in terms of comparison with other pupils.
- Try to ensure that pupils have to do something in response to the feedback you give them, some form of response, or action, even if this is simply at the level of being obliged to think about what you have said. One possibility here is to routinely dedicate some time for pupils to work on improvement points.

It is not simply a matter of showering extravagant, insincere and indiscriminate praise on pupil performance. Pupils are often aware when they are being patronised (Haydn 2012). However, it can be helpful to keep in mind the *breadth* of things that you can provide feedback on. This can make it easier to provide encouragement for less able pupils who are struggling with the cognitive demands of a subject (see section (j) later in this unit for more detail on this).

The overarching idea behind these suggestions is the idea of the teacher acting as a 'coach' and critical advisor to pupils, helping them achieve their 'personal best' in the way that an athletics coach might work with an athlete. Talk to teachers with whom you work about how they handle the challenge of providing feedback to pupils who are trying to do well in the subject, but whose progress is limited by lack of ability rather than lack of effort. How do experienced teachers engage pupils who are reluctant to learn?

(g) Using assessment feedback to improve your teaching

Lesson evaluation is an important part of planning future lessons and for ensuring progression in pupils' learning. Unit 2.2 addresses 'schemes of work and lesson planning', and we have placed additional support and guidelines on the companion website, headed Unit 6.1 'Additional material: using assessment feedback to improve your teaching'.

(h) Using assessment data

Teachers have access to a wide range of data about their pupils' prior academic achievement, including reports and tests taken in primary school. Some secondary schools also use the National Foundation for Educational Research (NFER) Cognitive Ability Tests (CATs), usually taken by pupils at the start of Year 7. CATs test pupils' abilities in spatial, numerical and verbal reasoning, and are a guide to pupils' cognitive abilities. These abilities are thought to be relevant to pupils' ability to achieve in a wide range of school subjects.

Schools also use other large data sets recording pupil performance over time, including MIDYIS (Middle Years Information System) and YELLIS (Year Eleven Information System) (CEM 2008). Other schools use the Fischer Family Trust data set (Schagen 2008). In addition, there is the RAISE (Reporting and Analysis for Improvement through School Self-Evaluation) data set published by the government in England.

These data sets allow teachers and schools to compare their own cohort of pupils in relation to the national cohort. The FFT data set makes it possible to disaggregate the relative performance of different groups of pupils, such as boys, pupils on free school meals, pupils for whom English is an additional language, and so on. In addition, comparisons can be made between pupils in one school and all other schools of a similar type or composition. The data set enables teachers to discern whether particular pupils are coasting or generally underachieving, or explore the performance of individual teachers, departments, schools and LAs.

The data set a parameter or expectation on future pupil attainment; for example, to predict future examination grades. These data can be used by the teacher, in negotiation with the pupil to discuss progress and try to boost performance beyond the predicted grade. The teacher (school, department or LA) has the challenge of trying to get the pupil to surpass the predicted grade to show that they have 'added value' beyond what might be expected for that pupil. Schools can use the data to see how they compare to similar institutions, how well they are performing with different types of pupils and where their strengths and weaknesses lie in terms of pupil attainment.

Teachers or departments who have been particularly successful in terms of the 'value' they have added to their pupils' performance can be invited to talk to other teachers and departments and share good practice. Conversely, where teacher or departmental 'residuals' are lower than those for pupils in other subjects or cohorts, a degree of anxiety and concern is created. Assessment data are used not just for formative purposes, but also for accountability and comparison.

Table 6.1.4 Marking and motivation: helping pupils understand feedback

Marking to encourage learning Includes:

■ helping pupils to take responsibility for their learning;
■ discussing the purpose of learning with pupils;
■ encouraging pupils to judge their work by how much they have learned and how much progress they have made;
■ helping pupils to understand the criteria by which their learning is assessed and to assess their own work;
■ giving feedback that enables pupils to know the next steps and how to succeed in taking them;
■ encouraging pupils to value effort and a wide range of attainments;
■ encouraging collaboration among pupils and a positive view of each other's achievements.

Some teachers welcome the use of such assessment data as it takes into account pupils' prior accomplishments in ways that raw examination results and league tables do not. Others feel that the imprecision of such testing and its susceptibility to manipulation make it inappropriate for such 'high-stakes' testing.

Because schools use different combinations of these data resources, a pragmatic way forward would be for you to first familiarise yourself with the assessment data in your placement school and, at a later stage, try to develop an understanding of other assessment data that you may encounter. A lucid and more developed explanation of the assessment instruments described above is in Husbands (2012).

An example of pupil assessment data given in Figure 6.1.3 provides information on the prior attainment of three Year 8 pupils, in terms of their performance in the cognitive ability tests taken at the start of Year 7, their performance in mathematics and reading tests, their spelling and reading 'ages', and their performance in Key Stage 2 NCTs for English, maths and science (see Figure 6.1.3).

This information was provided for all class teachers at an English secondary school, so the teachers would have this data 'at their fingertips' as they were teaching their classes. Such information may also be helpful to the teacher in arranging pupil groupings for collaborative work. The information gained can help teachers to plan their teaching to match pupils' individual needs.

(i) Keeping assessment manageable

One problem that has afflicted teachers in recent years is that marking regimes and policies have been put in place, mandated or encouraged by people who do not have to teach a full timetable of classes week in, week out. This has led to a substantial increase in teacher workload, and a reduction in the time available for planning for learning. A recent workload survey of teachers commissioned by the DfE (which elicited 44,000 responses from teachers) found that marking regimes were thought to be a major cause of 'overload' by 32 per cent of respondents (DfE 2015c).

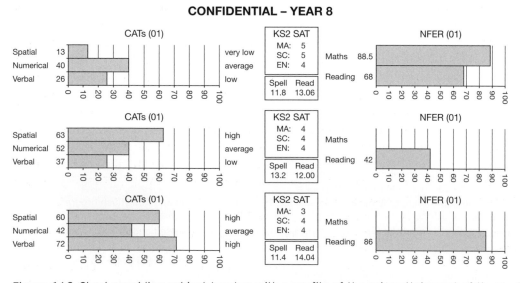

Figure 6.1.3 Chart providing subject teacher with a profile of the prior attainment of three of the pupils in a teaching group

You need to think about how to manage your time, so that assessment does not detract from the rest of your teaching (see Unit 1.3). Commentators who operate at some distance from the classroom sometimes bemoan the fact that not all weaknesses and mistakes in pupils' work are systematically and comprehensively corrected, including every error of spelling, punctuation and grammar. You may agree with this view. Measure how long it takes to do a comprehensive, all-embracing diagnostic dissection of a full set of 30 exercise books for a piece of extended writing and then review your position.

Teachers have to manage their time effectively; it is not practical to mark every piece of pupils' work in the same way without compromising the time available for lesson planning, and so on. There are no magic answers to make assessment burdens disappear, but there are ways to improve your time management. Table 6.1.5 explains these.

The list in Table 6.1.5 is not intended to suggest that you leave yourself without marking, but to make room, on occasions, for you to conduct a rigorous diagnosis of your pupils' written work and provide your pupils with constructive advice. These occasions allow you to give detailed and helpful comments that encourage your pupils and improve their learning. All marking should let your pupils feel that you care about their progress in your subject.

(j) Thinking about the breadth of what you are assessing

You need to be aware of the full breadth of benefits that pupils might derive from the study of your subject and from being in your classroom. Curriculum guidance in recent years has stressed that all subjects provide opportunities to promote pupil learning in a range of areas beyond subject specific learning; for example, to contribute to the development of pupils' 'key skills', such as communication, application of number, use of information and communications technology (ICT), the ability to work with others, the ability to problem-solve, and the ability to improve their own learning performance.

Keep in mind the question 'What is the full breadth of benefits that this pupil might derive from the study of my subject and being in my classroom?' and try to ensure that your assessment practices reflect this breadth.

In an effort to draw attention to the wider dimensions of learning, the Education Committee of the Inner London Education Authority (abolished in the 1980s) drafted a broad set of aims for schools called *Aspects of Achievement* (Hargreaves 1984). The aims were published in an attempt to counter the emphasis placed on examination success to the exclusion of other important pupil achievements. Hargreaves' idea should be a strong reminder to teachers that there should be more to assessment than just measuring the cognitive development of pupils. Hargreaves argued that assessment should also attempt to measure the development of pupils' personal and social skills: 'The capacity to work with others . . . to work cooperatively in the interests of a wider group; initiative, self-reliance and skills of leadership;' and also, pupils' motivation and commitment to learning: 'The willingness to accept failure without destructive consequences; readiness to persevere and the self-confidence to learn despite the difficulty of the task' (Hargreaves 1984: 2). Hargreaves makes the point that application and willingness to learn are considered to be valuable qualities in most spheres of public life, and have an important influence on other aspects of attainment. Keeping in mind these broader aspects of achievement in our assessment practice can also be very helpful in providing positive and encouraging feedback to pupils who are not 'high-fliers' in a subject, so that they maintain their commitment to learning rather than giving up.

Table 6.1.5 Managing your marking

Learn to mark flexibly
Some pieces of work require detailed attention and diagnosis; sometimes light touch monitoring is more appropriate.
Plan marking time
When you are planning lessons, think about setting fewer written tasks that require you to mark them in a time-intensive way. Student teachers sometimes set written tasks to take the pressure off themselves in the early stages of first placement or for class management purposes. Student teachers tend to set more written tasks than experienced teachers, and this produces a heavy marking load. Since lesson planning takes a long time, extra pressure builds. In your planning, try to prepare some lessons that have as one of the outcomes not requiring marking to be done in their aftermath; for example, by pupils marking their own work, or that of their peers.
Marking codes
Develop a shorthand code for signalling marking corrections, such as symbols for omissions, development, non sequitur, irrelevant, spelling errors or clumsy phrasing.
Common errors
Make brief notes on common errors as you are marking pupils' work so that you can report on them orally to the group as a whole, rather than writing the same comment in many books.
Pupil marking
On occasions, it is appropriate and helpful for pupils to mark each others' work, or their own work. You can use this strategy to help pupils understand the criteria for marking.
Oral feedback
It takes more than five times as long to write something down compared to saying it so sometimes prepare detailed oral feedback to pupils.
Pupil response to tasks
Structure tasks so that sometimes pupils present their work as a poster, a group ICT task or display work. This response may not require you to mark their books although you need to keep records of their performance.
Using ICT
Consider ways in which ICT might help to reduce the administration involved in assessment, recording and reporting. The facility to 'copy', 'cut' and 'paste' and build up an archive of models and exemplars of good and bad responses can save considerable amounts of time.

What will the be the effect of assessment on the motivation and attitude of pupils who are very weak in my subject if assessment focuses entirely on pupil attainment in my subject?

Figure 6.1.4 The influence of restricted assessment practice on the motivation of less able pupils

SUMMARY AND KEY POINTS

■ Although teachers and schools do have to be accountable for their work, the most valuable and important function of assessment is to move pupils forward in their learning.

■ Assessment needs to be built into your planning for teaching and learning, not tacked on as an afterthought.

■ You should be familiar with the idea of assessment as part of the cycle of planning, teaching and assessing, leading into revised planning and teaching.

■ A key facet of your ability as a teacher is your ability to devise and execute activities that help to move pupils forward in their learning, and that enable you to gain insight into the extent to which the pupils have learned what you were trying to teach.

■ You need to create a climate and culture in your classroom where 'making an effort, finding something difficult and learning from mistakes are all accepted and celebrated', and where 'pupils are more likely to respond to feedback in ways that help their learning rather than giving up or going into denial' (Swaffield 2008: 69).

■ You should make sure that you are familiar with the key features of formative assessment as outlined in this unit. These might be summarised as:

   ■ making learning goals and success criteria clear to learners;

   ■ designing a range of engaging activities that relate to the learning goals;

   ■ providing feedback that motivates learners to improve and that gives clear advice on how to do this;

   ■ getting learners to take some responsibility for their own learning;

   ■ engineering situations where learners can learn from each other.

■ You need to learn what constitutes effective practice in assessment, irrespective of what assessment 'frameworks' are in place in the schools you work in. There is a body of knowledge about what constitutes good assessment practice, and student teachers should be aware of this and should attempt to incorporate it into their practice.

■ Ascribing levels, marks or grades to pupils' work is not unproblematic, but it is not the most difficult part of assessment. The most challenging and important part of assessment is saying and doing things that help pupils to make progress in their learning.

Some of the issues raised in this unit can be developed further through the further reading. Check which requirements for your ITE programme you have addressed through this unit.

Further reading

Didau, D. (2015b) *What If Everything You Knew about Learning Was Wrong: Tackling the Myth of Progress*, Carmarthen: Independent Thinking Press.
  Interesting critique of some AfL 'orthodoxies'.

Knowles, C. (in press) *Achievement for All 3As MESHGuide*, London: Achievement for All.

Miller, D. and Lavin, F. (2007) '"But now I feel I want to give it a try": formative assessment, self-esteem and a sense of competence', *The Curriculum Journal*, 18(1): 3–25.
  Helpful for giving pupils' views on AfL in practice.

Newton, A. and Bowler, M. (2016) *Assessment in Physical Education*, MESHGuide, University of Bedfordshire, UK.

Powley, R. (2015) *Meaningful, Manageable Assessment: 26 Strategies*, available at: www.lovelearningideas.com (accessed 2 March 2015).

Procter, R. (2013) *Assessment for Learning*, MESHGuide, University of Bedfordshire, UK.

Swaffield, S. (2008) *Unlocking Assessment: Understanding for Reflection and Application*, London: David Fulton.
  Provides practical ideas for implementing the key principles of AfL.

Wiliam, D. (2011) *Embedded Formative Assessment*, Bloomington, IN: Solution Tree Press.
  Perhaps the most authoritative guide to embedding AfL into your classroom practice. Very lucidly explained and many good, practical ideas.

Other resources and websites

Some Twitter feeds on assessment issues: @assessment, @dtwillingham, @dylanwiliam
  Twitter is now an important mode of teacher professional development and a good way of keeping up with recent developments and controversies in the field of assessment of pupil progess.

Dylan Wiliam's website: www.dylanwiliam.org/Dylan_Wiliams_website/Welcome.html

Daisy Christodoulou's blog posts on issues in assessment: https://thewingtoheaven.wordpress.com/

Education Endowment Foundation (EEF) *BLOG: Feedback Matters! Putting Formative Assessment into Practice*, 2 April 2015: https://educationendowmentfoundation.org.uk/. . ./eef-blog-feedback-matters-putting-formative-assessment-into-practice/

MESHGuides (Mapping Education Specialist knowHow): www.meshguides.org
  This website provides specific guides on assessment, including Procter's (2013) and Newton and Bowler's (2015) MESHGuides which outline research informed practice and approaches to assessment.

Appendix 2 on pages 591–595 provides further examples of websites you may find useful.

Capel, S., Leask, M. and Turner, T. (eds) (2010) *Readings for Learning to Teach in the Secondary School: A Companion to M Level Study*, London: Routledge.
  This book brings together essential readings to support you in your critical engagement with key issues raised in this textbook.

The subject-specific books in the Routledge *Learning to Teach* series are also very useful.

Any additional resources and an editable version of any relevant tasks/tables in this unit are available on the companion website: www.routledge.com/cw/capel

6.2 External assessment and examinations

Bernadette Youens

Introduction

Principles of assessment were introduced in Unit 6.1. This unit looks at the particular role, function and nature of external assessment and examinations. We suggest you read Unit 6.1 before studying this unit. The public examination system at 16 is likely to reflect closely the content and principles of the national curriculum in force in the home countries of the UK, and you may need to refer to the units in Chapter 7 that relate to the country in which you wish to work, which are available on the companion website.

This unit aims to provide you with an overview of the framework for external assessment and examinations in secondary schools with a particular focus on England. Issues relevant to Northern Ireland, Scotland and Wales are covered in units in Chapter 7 on the companion website. Although you are familiar with the public examinations that you took in school, there are regular changes and significant developments in assessment methods and in the range of external examinations taken by pupils in secondary schools. In England, each phase of schooling has been the subject of various policy initiatives in recent years. This can mean that the national qualifications can be introduced and withdrawn within a relatively short timescale. As an example, new vocationally focused examination courses called diplomas were introduced in September 2008 but most were already withdrawn by September 2011, following a change of government in May 2010, having only ever been studied by a tiny proportion of pupils. The publication of the Wolf Report on vocational education has had a significant influence on national education policy, and is discussed later in this unit (Wolf 2011).

As well as knowing how pupils are assessed throughout their secondary education, it is important to be aware of the many purposes of external assessment and examinations. These purposes can be usefully divided into those associated with candidates and those that have more to do with educational establishments and public accountability (see Unit 6.1). Two important, recurrent themes that arise when discussing external assessment and examinations are validity and reliability. These two concepts, together with the agencies, regulations and processes involved in ensuring consistency in these two areas, are defined in Unit 6.1. Teaching externally examined classes is a challenge for any teacher and demands particular teaching skills and strategies, in addition to the routine elements of good lesson planning and teaching. This aspect of teaching, and the constraints and influence of the accountability agenda on the work of schools, is discussed in the final part of this unit.

OBJECTIVES

At the end of this unit, you should be able to:

- identify the range of external assessments in secondary schools and access the national qualifications and credit framework;
- understand the relationship between the national curriculum in a home country and external examinations;
- explain the main purposes of assessment;
- recall the processes involved in the setting of external examinations and the institutions involved;
- start addressing the issues relating to teaching examination classes;
- understand the impact of external accountability measures on schools and teaching.

Check the requirements of your initial teacher education (ITE) programme to see which relate to this unit.

Your own experience

A good starting point for this unit is your own experience of external assessment and examinations. Think back to your time at school. What did you think was the purpose of sitting examinations, and did preparing for examinations impact on your motivation as a learner? Did the teaching strategies of examination classes differ from non-examination classes? Recalling these impressions may provide a good starting point from which to develop your understanding of the issues pertaining to external assessment and examinations.

Types of assessment

In Unit 6.1, we discussed formative and summative assessment and we remind you of those terms. Formative assessment can be defined as assessment for learning, and summative assessment as assessment of learning (Stobart and Gipps 1997). External assessment and examinations are generally considered to be forms of summative assessment. There are two important methods used extensively in summative assessment that you need to be familiar with, namely norm-referenced assessment and criterion-referenced assessment.

Norm-referenced assessment has been used extensively throughout the British education system. In norm-referenced assessment, the value of, or grade related to, any mark awarded depends on how it compares with the marks of other candidates sitting the same assessment. The basis for this form of assessment is the assumption that the marks are normally distributed; that is, if you plot the marks awarded against the number of candidates, a bell-shaped curve is produced, providing the sample is big enough. This curve is then used to assign grade boundaries based on predetermined conditions; for example, that 80 per cent of all those sitting the examination pass and 20 per cent fail. In this way, an element of failure is built into the examination. The system of reporting by grades is essentially norm-referenced. For example, if you are awarded the highest grade in a subject in a public examination, this grade does not give any specific information about what you can do in that subject, simply that you were placed within the top group of candidates.

Criterion-referenced assessment, on the other hand, is concerned with what a candidate can do without reference to the performance of others, and so provides an alternative method to address the limitations of norm-referencing. A simple example of criterion-referenced assessment is that of a swimming test. If someone is entered for a 100-metre swimming award, and swims 100 metres, then they are awarded that certificate irrespective of how many other people also reach this standard. Academic courses, such as General Certificate of Secondary Education (GCSE) science, use criterion-referencing when assessing practical skills as part of the coursework element of the course, but the grades are awarded and the results are reported by comparing pupils with other pupils; that is, norm-referenced. Thus, the overall assessment in most examinations is a mixture of criterion-referenced marking together with norm-referenced grading and reporting of the level of achievement.

The framework of external assessment in secondary schools

External assessment in secondary schools is an area that has seen considerable change over a relatively short period of time. We consider in turn Key Stage 3 (KS3), GCSE and post-16 education in England. Different arrangements are in place in Northern Ireland, Scotland and Wales. We suggest you ensure you gather the information relevant to the context in which you are learning to teach. For example, in England, four assessment stages are referred to in this section; that is, Key Stage 2 (KS2), Years 3–6; Key Stage 3, Years 7–9; Key Stage 4 (KS4) (that is, GCSE); and post-16 assessment.

Key Stage 3 assessment

On transfer to secondary school, pupils bring with them information obtained from the end of Key Stage 2 assessment. This information has historically been reported as teacher-assessed and externally assessed National Curriculum (NC) levels. The introduction of a new National Curriculum in September 2014 saw the removal of levels and no intention to replace them (DfE 2014n). Since the introduction of a National Curriculum following the Education Reform Act of 1988, levels have underpinned assessment and reporting progress, particularly across Key Stages 1–3. The stated purposes of the current reform includes to 'allow teachers greater flexibility in the way that they plan and assess pupils' learning' and a commitment to 'curriculum freedom' (DfE 2014n). In practice, this means that summer 2015 was the final year that an end of Key Stage 'level' will be reported. New National Curriculum tests for Key Stages 1 and 2 were introduced in summer 2016, two years after the start of a new National Curriculum. One purpose of the new Key Stage 2 tests is to test that pupils are 'secondary-ready' by reporting: a scaled score, which will show whether a pupil has met the expected standard and is 'secondary-ready'; ranking in the national cohort (by decile); and the rate of progress from a baseline (DfE 2014n).

In England, until 2008, assessment at the end of Key Stage 3 took the form of internal teacher assessment for all NC subjects and external written tests, called Standard Assessment Tasks (SATs), for the core NC subjects of English, mathematics and science. The SATs were written with reference to the subject Programmes of Study of the NC; the questions in the tests were designed so that the demand on the pupil links closely to the level descriptions. Papers were set for each of the core subjects and tiered assessment was used to allow pupils to be entered for the paper most suited to their achievement. However, the written SATs were limited in what they tested and so had reduced validity in relation to the overall aims of NC subject specifications.

There are no longer external tests set at the end of Key Stage 3 and no public reporting of Key Stage 3 data, the last published tables being in 2007. Since 2014, schools no longer have a statutory requirement to report teacher-assessed levels for each of the core and non-core subjects.

Key Stage 4 assessment (Years 10-11) GCSE

The GCSE examination was introduced in 1986 to be taken at the end of Key Stage 4 to replace the General Certificate of Education (GCE) Ordinary (O) level and Certificate of Secondary Education (CSE), and to provide certification for about 90 per cent of candidates. Similar examinations are in place in Northern Ireland and Wales. The Scottish system has a different structure (see Unit 7.4 on the companion website).

At the time of writing, the GCSE examination offers eight pass grades, A* to G; the A* grade recognises exceptional performance. The GCSE examinations are designed to test recall, understanding and skills. The current GCSE has a tiered assessment pattern, to enable pupils to be entered for the paper most appropriate for their current achievement. Teachers assess pupils' progress and potential, and advise pupils on which tier of the examination to enter. Tiered papers carry grade limits, thus narrowing the opportunities of pupils. For example, a higher paper may enable pupils to be awarded grades A*-D, while a foundation paper may allow only the award of grades C-G. Furthermore, if pupils fail to achieve the marks required for the lowest grade in their tier, then they receive an unclassified grade.

In the *Importance of Teaching* White Paper (DfE 2010a), the government of the day signaled changes to 'restore confidence in GCSEs'. This statement heralded significant changes to the existing GCSE qualifications. The first change, introduced in September 2012, means that all GCSE courses are assessed by summer terminal examination only; the only exception to this rule is the opportunity to retake examinations in English, English language and mathematics GCSEs in November. The practice of pupils taking GCSE examinations by module, sometimes over a period of three years, and retaking individual modules on multiple occasions was withdrawn. Alongside these changes has been a return to the compulsory inclusion of marks for spelling, punctuation and grammar in GCSE examinations.

Further changes to the content and grading of GCSEs are being planned and introduced at the time of writing. From September 2015, new specifications in English language, English literature and mathematics were introduced followed by new specifications in science, history, geography, languages and the remaining National Curriculum subjects in September 2016. As well as new subject content, there are further changes to how GCSEs are graded, the use of tiered papers and controlled assessments and coursework; we will consider each of these points in turn. The grading has been changed from letters to numbers; 1-9, with 9 being the top mark; marks that fall below grade 1 will be classified as 'U' as in the current system. The use of tiered papers will be reduced. Decisions about the inclusion of tiered papers continue to be taken at a subject level and depend on how effectively a single paper allows all pupils opportunities to demonstrate what they know and can do. In the first three new specifications, mathematics has a foundation tier (grades 1-5) and a higher tier (grades 4-9), whereas English has a single paper.

Teacher-assessed coursework was introduced with the GCSE, and in the early days of GCSE some courses offered were entirely coursework-based. However, coursework has become progressively restricted by government legislation through the subject specifications and the amount allowed depends on the subject. In the more practically based subjects (for example, music, physical education), a larger proportion of teacher-based assessment contributes to the final mark than in other subjects. In music, for example, the upper limit in practice is about 60 per cent, whereas in geography a maximum of 25 per cent of the total mark is commonly awarded for coursework. No subject can be assessed only by teacher-assessed coursework, and in some subjects (for example, mathematics) there is no coursework.

Although a good motivator for pupils, coursework has also attracted significant criticism, focusing on plagiarism issues, principally the practice of some pupils buying ready-made answers from the Internet, and also the amount of parental contribution to the coursework. In response to these criticisms, significant changes to coursework have been introduced. From September 2009, coursework and tasks were replaced by 'controlled assessment' tasks in England and Wales. In practice, this means that pupils can undertake research and investigations outside the classroom in preparation for a task, but all written work must be completed in a classroom under supervised conditions. 'Controlled assessments will increase public confidence in the GCSE and allow the integration of new sources of data and information, including the Internet, under supervision' (Boston 2007). The latest reforms go even further with the expectation that all assessment will be by terminal examination only, unless essential skills need to be tested. At the time of writing for the three new specifications available (English language, English literature and mathematics), all assessment is by terminal examination. English language does have a non-examination assessment of spoken English but it will not contribute to the overall GCSE assessment.

Thus, the innovative approaches introduced with the GCSEs have been systematically removed to leave mainly single-tier, linear written examinations taken at the end of two years' study. It could be argued that the new structure and format of GCCSs share many features of the 'O' level qualifications that the GCSEs replaced some 30 years ago. It is important that you have a clear understanding of how and why GCSEs have changed; Task 6.2.1 asks you to address this issue.

Post-16 assessment

Of all of the changes that have followed the Education Reform Act (ERA 1988), the area that has continued to undergo reorganisation is the provision of post-16 courses and their assessment: General Certificate of Education (GCE) Advanced (A) level courses.

GCE A level courses were first introduced in 1951 and since then have been regarded as the academic 'gold standard' by successive governments. Substantial changes were made to the framework of the 16–19 qualifications following a review, and implemented in September 2000 (Dearing 1996), with further revisions introduced in 2007 (Ofqual 2007).

Alongside the GCSE reforms outlined above, new AS and A levels were introduced in schools in England from September 2015. At the time of writing, each GCE A level examination subject is composed of four discrete units of approximately the same size. The first two units make up an Advanced Subsidiary (AS) course, representing the first half of an advanced level course of study. The other two units, which make up the second part of the GCE A level, are known as A2. One of the aims underpinning the introduction of the AS qualification was to provide a more appropriate and manageable 'bridge' between GCSE and GCE A level. The A2 specifications include the setting of a broad range of question types to ensure that a wide range of skills is assessed, a requirement for extended writing to give candidates the opportunity to demonstrate the depth and breadth of their knowledge and understanding, and synoptic assessment (assessment across several modules

Task 6.2.1 GCSE examinations

Working with another student teacher in your own subject specialism, obtain copies of GCSE specifications from before and after the reforms introduced in 2015. For each specification, read the general introduction and familiarise yourself with the aims, assessment objectives and assessment patterns of the specification. Now turn to the assessment section and compare for each specification:

- how the subject content differs;
- how the structure of the qualification differs;
- what form the assessment takes in each of the specifications;
- whether there is any assessment outside the final examinations.

Discuss your findings with an experienced teacher in your placement school and find out:

- their perceptions of how the GCSE assessment has changed in recent years;
- what impact the changes have had on workload;
- any impact the changes have had on pupils' motivation, engagement, achievement and attainment.

Check the requirements for your ITE programme to see which relate to public examinations. A record of your work could be placed in your professional development portfolio (PDP).

---

or whole course). The AS course may be taken as a qualification in itself or it may be used as a foundation to study the A2 section of the course. Although for many years GCE A levels could be assessed in stages, as in a modular course, or terminally, this practice has now been stopped. For candidates embarking on AS courses starting in September 2013, all AS and A level assessment has been terminal. The introduction of modular assessment had proved to be very popular with candidates. The main advantages of modularity were:

- motivating pupils to maintain a high, constant commitment throughout their course;
- providing valuable diagnostic information from early results;
- providing the opportunity to have achievement recognised (Dearing 1996).

All GCE A2 courses must include an element of synoptic assessment designed to test a candidate's ability to make connections between different aspects of the course. There is no synoptic assessment at AS level. The synoptic element must normally contribute 20 per cent to the full GCE A level and take the form of external assessment at the end of the course. GCE A level pass grades range from A* to E, with A* the highest grade. The A* grade was introduced in response to concerns about the standard of GCE A level and the increase in the number of candidates achieving Grade A. An A* grade is awarded to candidates who achieve 90 per cent or more on the uniform mark scale across A2 units. The first A* grades were awarded in 2010. (A uniform mark scale, or UMS, is a way of standardising the marking of papers across different examination boards, allowing someone to compare two marks marked by two different examination boards. Grades are then calculated using grade boundaries set at particular UMS scores. For further information go to www.aqa.com and search for 'uniform mark scale'.)

A level qualifications are subject to the same drivers for reform that were described in the section on GCSE qualifications above. New A level specifications were introduced for first teaching in September 2015. Again, assessment was simplified and, wherever possible, is by written examination only at the end of two years of study. The AS qualification will become 'stand-alone' and will not contribute to the assessment of the full A level. It remains to be seen how schools respond to these reforms and whether the AS qualification will survive or whether schools will revert to a traditional 'three A level' curriculum diet at post-16.

Concern over the high number of A grades awarded at GCE A level and the challenge this presented to universities in being able to differentiate between the most able candidates has led to a number of initiatives. A successful recent development is the Extended Project Qualification, first taught in 2008. This is a separate qualification that pupils may add to their study course and is designed to be distinctive from GCE A level coursework, and is a stand-alone qualification that is deemed to be equivalent to an AS level.

Vocational courses post-16

The main vocational qualifications traditionally encountered in secondary schools in England have been the General National Vocational Qualifications (GNVQs) that were introduced into schools in 1992 and developed from National Vocational Qualifications (NVQs).

The NVQs are work-related, competence-based qualifications, and the courses were designed for people in work or undertaking work-based training. NVQ courses provide job-specific training, the assessment of which takes place in the work environment and is criterion-referenced. Central to the NVQ model is the idea of competence to perform a particular job, where competence is defined as the mastery of identified performance skills.

GNVQs were introduced to provide pupils with an introduction to occupational sectors through school- or college-based courses. Indeed, one of the principal aims of the GNVQ was to provide a middle road between the general academic route and occupational courses, such as the NVQs described above.

One of the main stumbling blocks to the uptake of vocational qualifications by schools was the difference in assessment practice and terminology between academic and vocational courses identified in the report on 16–19 qualifications (Dearing 1996). The report identified as well the need for a coherent qualifications framework encompassing all national qualifications and one that provides a status for vocational qualifications equivalent to the academic subjects at GCE A level. Following that report, vocational GCSE and vocational GCE A levels were introduced, accompanied by a timetable for the phased withdrawal of GNVQ courses. The vocational GCSE and GCE qualifications have been renamed and are known as GCSE and GCE in applied subjects with pupils at both levels maintaining their study of core curriculum subjects. The purpose of these developments, together with the other reforms outlined, is to encourage Key Stage 4 pupils and post-16 pupils to broaden their course of study to include vocational courses. The National Qualifications framework in Table 6.2.1 shows how the three qualification strands discussed are intended to overlap.

The framework for national qualifications has a total of nine separate levels of qualification (entry level to level 8) and shows progression across academic and vocational qualifications.

GCSE qualifications in vocational subjects were first introduced in September 2002 and are offered in eight subjects; for example, leisure and tourism, applied science. Each course consists of three common, compulsory and normally equally weighted units in each subject. The qualification is equivalent to two GCSEs and is graded, like GCSEs, from A* to U, covering both level 1 and level 2 of the national qualifications framework (Table 6.2.1).

Table 6.2.1 Framework of national qualifications (entry level to level 3 only)

Level of qualification	General qualifications
3	GCE A level grades A–E
2	GCSE grades A*–C
1	GCSE grades D–G
Entry	Certificate of (educational) achievement

The vocational sector of qualifications is also subject to significant change at the time of writing. The intention is that at Key Stage 4, the only qualifications that will be recognised in performance tables will be technical awards that are 'broad, high quality level 1 and level 2 qualifications in non EBacc subjects that equip pupils with applied knowledge and associated practical skills not usually acquired through general education' (DfE 2015e: 3). For post-16 pupils, the intention is that they follow one of three routes: an academic route, a vocational route or a combined route. Within the vocational route, there are three main types of qualification: applied general qualifications, technical levels and substantial vocational qualifications at level 2. As with other reforms, there is the expectation that there will be a significant level of external assessment.

Further discussion of vocational (applied) courses can be found in Brooks and Lucas (2004) and Wolf (2011).

The purposes of external assessment

There is a long-standing history in the United Kingdom of externally examining pupils at particular stages in their education, which is quite different from the practice in some other countries (QCA 2008c; Wolf 2011). In recent years in England, this practice has extended to the external assessment of pupils at the end of Key Stage 2. If the time and resources spent on this form of assessment are to be justified, then it is important that the purposes of external assessment are fully understood. The purposes of external, summative assessment can be thought of in terms of certificating candidates and the public accountability of teachers and schools. Another purpose is to categorise candidates in order to select people for higher education, employment, or to recognise achievement. The outcome of national examinations provides pupils with a grade so that they and other people can compare them with other candidates.

One recognised function of external assessment is that of certification. If you hold a certificate, then it is evidence that competence in particular skills or a level of knowledge has been achieved.

For example, if you hold a driving licence, this is evidence that in a driving test you successfully performed a hill start, completed a three-point turn, and so on. The significance to pupils, of both the categorising and certification purposes, is evidenced by the fact that an impending examination provides an incentive for pupils to concentrate on their studies and to acquire the relevant knowledge and skills required by the examination for which they are entered. Thus, a consequence of external examinations is to provide motivation for both pupils and teachers. Motivation is discussed in greater detail in Unit 3.2.

Public accountability

Assessment is high on the political agenda at present because it is inextricably linked with the notion of raising standards, narrowing the attainment gap between different groups of pupils, school improvement and making schools publicly accountable. Schools are statutorily required to publish information on public examination results and school statistics (for example, number on roll, gender balance, uptake of free school meals) each year in what are now known as the performance tables, often referred to simply as the 'league tables' (see Unit 6.1). In 2011, the data reported on KS4 and GCE A level attainment were expanded further to include significantly more data on a school's performance. The tables now include:

- how well disadvantaged pupils perform in each school;
- whether previous high-, middle- and low-achieving pupils continue to make progress;
- how many pupils at each school are entered into the core academic subjects that make up the English baccalaureate.

The English baccalaureate is not a qualification in its own right, but was introduced in the 2010 performance tables as a measure of the number of pupils securing a grade C or better in a selected core of academic subjects (DfE 2010b). The core subjects are closely prescribed, and at the time of writing include English, mathematics, science, a language (modern or classical) and either geography or history. The reasons behind the introduction of this measure are discussed below.

There is a variety of statistical information published each year; currently, schools in England are placed in rank order based on just one variable, the percentage of pupils gaining five or more GCSE passes at grades A*–C, including English and mathematics. The high profile given to the performance tables by the different stakeholders in the education process has led schools to implement strategies to increase the percentage of their pupils achieving five or more A*–C grades. For example, schools often target pupils predicted to achieve grade Ds at GCSE for additional tutoring and academic support as part of the school's strategy to increase the number of pupils achieving grade Cs in their GCSE exams.

There is also evidence that schools are selecting particular qualifications that make it easier for pupils to reach the key target of five GCSEs at A*–C. Recently, there has been a proposal to stop awarding bodies (ABs) preparing their own syllabuses and every subject would have just one subject syllabus. The subject syllabuses would be shared out between the three ABs (Vasagar 2012).

There has been a dramatic increase in the number of non-academic qualifications taken each year from about 15,000 in 2004 to 575,000 in 2010 (DfE 2015d). The Wolf Report explains how this shift was a consequence of two factors: the accountability regime becoming more rigorous and the simultaneous relaxing of National Curriculum requirements at Key Stage 4 (Wolf 2011). One quotation from the report aptly summarises concerns expressed by the education community for some time:

> For young people, which vocational courses, qualification or institution they choose really can be life-determining. 14–19 education is funded and provided for their sakes, not for the sakes of the institutions who provide it. This may be a truism; but it is one which policy too often seems to ignore.

(Wolf 2011: 8)

It is against this backdrop that the English Baccalaureate was introduced and the government announced a series of measures further tightening up the qualifications eligible to be included in the tables. Significant changes to the performance tables took effect from 2016 when schools are required to report four key measures on their website: pupils' progress across eight subjects from Key Stage 2 to Key Stage 4 to be known as Progress 8; an Attainment 8 measure; percentage of pupils achieving a grade C or higher in English and mathematics; and the percentage of pupils gaining an English Baccalaureate. The Progress 8 and the Attainment 8 measures can include up to three recognised vocational qualifications.

The introduction of external assessment of pupils at the end of Key Stage 2 also had a significant impact on the teaching of pupils in this age range, providing further evidence of the effect that so-called 'high stakes' external assessment has on classroom practice. This impact is reported as a concentration on the curriculum to be assessed through SATs or GCSE at the expense of a broader curriculum (Jozefkowicz 2006; Ofsted 2006a).

The term 'high stakes' is used to describe assessment that has significant consequences for either the candidate or the school (see Unit 6.1). Although no longer required to set and publish targets for all pupils aged 11–16 in order to demonstrate year-on-year improvements, in practice, target setting on many different levels has become a feature of school culture. To assist schools in setting targets, from 2007 all schools in England have been able to access the programme RAISEonline (DfE/Ofsted 2015). This programme provides interactive analysis of school and pupil performance data across the four Key Stages of the National Curriculum. This package contains benchmark data so that schools can compare whole-school performance with that of schools with similar intakes and profiles: also contextual value added (CVA) data, which aims to take into account a wide range of variables that may affect a school's performance; for example, number of pupils with SEN or number of pupils entitled to free school meals.

Validity and reliability

The concepts of validity and reliability are central to understanding an assessment process and are also discussed in Unit 6.1. For all external assessments and examinations, frameworks of regulations have been developed to ensure that the examination process and the results produced are both valid and reliable. To understand this framework, you need to be aware of the institutions and processes involved in this regulation.

Since October 2011, Ofqual is the government agency that approves all course specifications, as well as monitoring examinations through a programme of scrutinies, comparability exercises and probes, and is accountable to the DfE. There are three awarding organisations in England authorised by the government to offer GCSE, GCE A and AS and vocational courses. These are:

■ Assessment and Qualifications Alliance (AQA): www.aqa.org.uk
■ Edexcel: www.edexcel.com/
■ Oxford Cambridge and RSA Examinations (OCR): www.ocr.org.uk/index.html

Following the *Guaranteeing Standards* consultation (DfEE 1997), the formation of a single awarding body was considered, but a group of three was thought useful to retain a measure of competition. The key recommendations of the standards' consultation report were:

■ that for each externally examined course, there is a specification for the core material;
■ the publication of a detailed code of practice designed to ensure that grading standards are consistent across subjects and across the three awarding bodies, in the same subject, and from year to year;
■ that this code of practice should also set out the roles and responsibilities of those involved in the examining process and the key procedures for setting papers, standardising marking and grading.

The processes employed by the awarding bodies to address the recommendations above and to ensure that the examinations are valid and reliable are outlined in Figure 6.2.1.

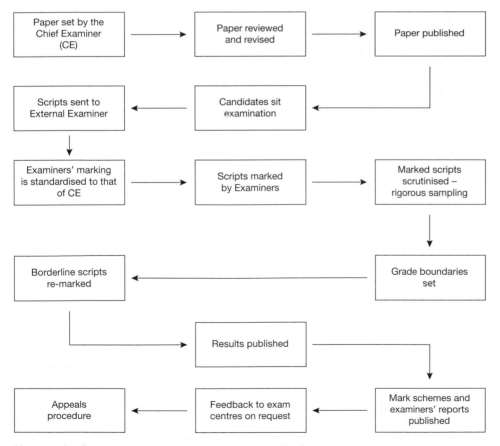

Figure 6.2.1 Processes involved in external examinations

Teaching externally assessed courses

All teachers have to think beyond the particular lesson they are teaching to the end of the unit of work, to ensure that pupils can respond successfully to any assessment scheduled to take place. When pupils are assessed externally the same considerations apply; that is, how to maximise pupils' achievement. However, you do need to be fully aware of the nature of the external assessment for which you are preparing your pupils. It is important not just to teach to the examination, but to hold on to the principles of good classroom practice.

In preparing your pupils for external assessment, you need to be familiar not only with the subject content, but also with the particular demands of the assessment process, such as the types of questions set and the language used in setting questions. Questions are set that often employ words with a specific meaning; for example, they ask candidates to describe, or explain, or use short notes or summarise. Candidates need to know what these words mean in examination conditions. Task 6.2.2 is designed to help you become familiar with types of questions currently set in examination papers in your own subject and the corresponding reports of examiners.

Once you are familiar with the structure and language used in past papers, you can then integrate this information into your teaching throughout the course. Another important aspect to consider is the development of study skills both in your lessons and throughout the school (see Task 6.2.3). Finally, we ask you to review the influence of public assessment on the way pupils are grouped and taught (see Task 6.2.4).

 Task 6.2.2 Using examination papers in your teaching

Collect a number of examination papers (for example, GCSE or the equivalent in other countries) for your subject together with the mark schemes and specification. Where possible, obtain the relevant examiners' reports, which are sent to schools entering candidates to that awarding body. Read through the specification for the examination arrangements. Then address the questions in the paper in the following way:

■ Answer the questions on the paper yourself.
■ Mark your answers using the mark scheme.
■ Evaluate your answers and marking and identify the key knowledge and concepts needed to gain maximum marks. Look back at the examination questions, identify the key words and phrases most often used in the questions.
■ Use the examiners' report to review and refine your findings.
■ Identify any ideas that might be useful to consider in your day-to-day teaching.
■ Repeat the exercise for another year of the same paper, or repeat the exercise using papers from a different level (for example, post-16 course).

The completed task should be placed in your PDP. Check the requirements for your initial teacher education (ITE) programme related to preparing pupils for public examinations.

Task 6.2.3 Study skills

Discuss with your tutor or other experienced teacher in your placement school the whole-school and departmental approaches available to support the development of pupils' study skills. These skills include, for example, planning and supporting revision, and time management. Use the information you gain to integrate the teaching of study skills in your own teaching.

Check the requirements for your initial teacher education that relate to developing study skills. File your notes in your PDP.

  Task 6.2.4 League tables and pupil grouping

Performance tables ('league tables') have been said to influence not only what is taught in a school, but also how pupils are grouped and subjects they are offered for study, thus influencing their final qualifications. Investigate whether pupil grouping in the school is affected by the league tables; that is, if teaching and learning is being driven by public accountability. You may find sharing this work with another student teacher helpful.

Check first your understanding of setting, banding, streaming and mixed-ability grouping (see Unit 4.1).

In your placement school (see Unit 4.1 on pupil grouping):

1   For each year cohort 7-11, identify how tutor groups are formed for pastoral purposes and the criteria used to do this.
2   Identify in broad terms which subjects teach tutor groups and those that reorganise the tutor groups for teaching purposes.
3   For your teaching subject and either English, mathematics or science in Year 7, find out how pupils new to the school are assessed and placed into teaching groups. Compare the criteria used for each subject.
4   How flexible is the placement? Can pupils move between groups? If so, how is this movement managed in practice?
5   For your teaching subject and either English, mathematics or science in Year 10, identify how pupils are grouped for teaching, and which courses the different groups are offered, and the criteria used to do this.

With the information gained from tasks 1-5 above, arrange to interview a number of pupils in Year 10 to elicit their views about subject and course choice and grouping. Choose your subject area and, if time, one other subject. How do pupils make their subject/course choices at the end of Year 9? Are pupils:

1   provided with information to help make choices?
2   guided towards particular courses by teachers at the school?
3   aware of the long-term consequences of the courses they select?
4   encouraged to choose courses that help them to achieve five 'good' GCSE passes in English baccalaureate subjects?

Within the same subject areas, find out what pupils think about the groups they are taught in. Are pupils aware of:

1   the reasons they were allocated to a group in that subject?
2   any advantages to the grouping system?
3   any limitations to their particular group, such as limit on grade at end of their course (for example, GCSE)?

Finally, interview a head of department for one or more subject areas chosen to find out their views about pupil choice of subject in Year 9 and how pupils are grouped for teaching purposes in their subject. You could use the questions you have put to the pupils.

Write a summary of your findings for discussion with your tutors, indicating whether the importance of league tables has had any effect on the way pupils are grouped. Evidence should be kept anonymous. The final document can be filed in your PDP.

SUMMARY AND KEY POINTS

■   In this unit, we have linked the framework for external assessment and examinations with the nature and purposes of summative assessment.

■   In England, the external examinations utilise aspects of both norm-referenced and criterion-referenced methods, and this is an important feature of assessment of which you need to be aware and understand.

■   Norm-referencing and criterion-referencing are factors used in discussions seeking to explain the steady increase in the proportion of candidates achieving A*–C grades.

■   The changes recently introduced to all sectors of education aim to promote the academic attainment of all pupils.

■   There are likely to be further innovations in approaches to assessment and, as long as there remains a political focus on raising standards in our schools, external assessment and examinations will maintain their present high profile and powerful influence in educational practice.

Check which requirements for your ITE programme you have addressed through this unit.

 ## Further reading

Bew, Lord (2011) *Independent Review of Key Stage 2 Testing, Assessment and Accountability: Final Report*, London: DfE.

Black, P. (1998) *Testing: Friend or Foe? Theory and Practice of Assessment and Testing (Master Classes in Education)*, London: RoutledgeFalmer.
    The author was deeply involved in the development of assessment practices for the National Curriculum. This text provides a review of the different issues surrounding assessment. An early text but important in the development of assessment practices.

Brooks, V. (2002) *Assessment in Secondary Schools: The New Teacher's Guide to Monitoring, Assessment, Recording, Reporting and Accountability*, Buckingham: Open University Press.
  Written specifically for new teachers, this is a comprehensive introduction to all aspects of assessment in the secondary school.

DfE (Department for Education) (2014n) *National Curriculum and Assessment from September 2014: Information for Schools*, London: DfE.

DfE (Department for Education) (2015d) *School and College Performance Tables*, available at: www.education.gov.uk/schools/performance/
  An informative website that is particularly useful for looking at school and college performance tables.

DfES (Department for Education and Skills) (2006b) *National Strategies: Grouping Pupils for Success*, available at: http://webarchive.nationalarchives.gov.uk/20110809101133/nsonline.org.uk/node/84974
  A report of a research project describing the policy and practice of grouping pupils in schools and identifies effective ways to improve learning.

Fautley, M. and Savage, J. (2008) *Assessment for Learning and Teaching in Secondary Schools*, Exeter: Learning Matters.
  Targeted specifically at student teachers, this text links explicitly to the new qualified teacher status (QTS) Standards, and the tasks provide opportunities for reflection and for practising the range of skills involved in assessing pupils.

Isaacs, T. (2010) 'Educational assessment in England', *Assessment in Education: Principles, Policy and Practice*, 17(3): 315–34.
  This article discusses assessment issues that highlight the role of government in the development, implementation and monitoring of national curriculum tests and 14–19 qualifications.

Stobart, G. (2008) *Testing Times: The Uses and Abuses of Assessment*, London: Routledge.
  A critical review of aspects of current assessment practice; addresses five issues that currently have high-profile status: intelligence, testing, learning skills, accountability and formative assessment.

Wiliam, D. and Bartholomew, H. (2004) 'It's not which school but which set you're in that matters: the influence on ability-grouping practices on student progress in mathematics', *British Educational Research Journal*, 30(2): 279–94.
  The report of a research project into the effect of setting in schools and the effect on pupil achievement in national assessments.

Wolf, A. (2011) *Review of Vocational Education: The Wolf Report*, DFE-00031-2011, available at: www.education.gov.uk/publications/standard/publicationDetail/Page1/DFE-00031-2011
  The review considers how vocational education for 14–19 year olds can be improved to promote successful progression and gives practical recommendations to inform policy.

Other resources and websites

Boston, K. (2007) Quoted in BBC news broadcast, June 17, 'GCSE home coursework scrapped': http://news.bbc.co.uk/1/hi/education/6747973.stm

BTEC (Business and Technology Education Council) *First*: http://qualifications.pearson.com/en/about-us/qualification-brands/btec.html

OCR (Oxford and Cambridge Regional Awarding Body) *Nationals*, available at: www.ocr.org.uk/

Appendix 2 on pages 591–595 provides further examples of websites you may find useful.

Capel, S., Leask, M. and Turner, T. (eds) (2010) *Readings for Learning to Teach in the Secondary School: A Companion to M Level Study*, London: Routledge.
  This book brings together essential readings to support you in your critical engagement with key issues raised in this textbook.

The subject-specific books in the Routledge *Learning to Teach* series are also very useful.

Any additional resources and an editable version of any relevant tasks/tables in this unit are available on the companion website: www.routledge.com/cw/capel

7 The school, curriculum and society

This chapter takes you away from the immediacy of teaching to consider the aims of education, how those aims might be identified and, more importantly perhaps, how the curriculum reflects those aims. In the day-to-day urgency of teaching the given curriculum, it is easy to push the 'why' into the background and simply get on with the 'how'. As a prospective teacher, you need to be able to explain to pupils and parents what the personal benefit to them is from learning your subject; and for yourself to understand why your country does things one way and that other countries offer a different and successful approach to educating their young people.

The chapter addresses the ways in which some other countries organise their education system and the different emphasis placed on various aspects of education by them; for example, the types of schools and the grouping of pupils, on assessment and the role of public examinations in promoting standards, and inspection and accountability. We include a unit considering international comparisons, and on the companion website we include units that focus on the education systems of the home countries of Northern Ireland, Scotland and Wales. The first units in the chapter focus on England.

In Unit 7.1, 'Aims of education', a comparative and analytical approach is taken to examine assumptions about education and a consideration of the different purposes of schooling. It discusses the origin of national aims and their translation into school aims and contrasts the aims of society with those of the individual. Unit 7.2, 'The school curriculum', examines the school curriculum in terms of aims and purposes. The unit draws attention to the formal and the informal, or hidden, curriculum, and discusses how the formal curriculum of subjects might develop from the broad aims of education and asks 'Who decides?'

Unit 7.3 offers a comparison between education in Finland and that in England, drawing attention to the striking differences in philosophy and organisation of schools and schooling. The unit also offers comparisons in the performance of pupils across a wider range of countries arising from, for example, the Programme for International Student Assessment (PISA) and the TIMMS project (Trends in International Mathematics and Science Study, carried out since 1995), as well as other data sources that provide international comparisons.

The following three units are available on the companion website and examine the education systems of the home countries, with Unit 7.4 on Northern Ireland, Unit 7.5 on Scotland and Unit 7.6 on Wales. Each unit focuses on the 'distinctive' nature of each country's education system, which includes the structure and governance of education in each country, alongside their school curriculum, the requirements of the teaching profession in each country and the future.

If education is 'what is left after most of what you have learned in school is forgotten', then what is education for and who decides? Young people, between the ages of 5 and 16, spend a substantial part of the formative period of their lives in school, and a significant slice of the national budget is channelled into education, so you can expect to be held accountable for what you teach. In meeting the demand for accountability, an understanding of one's own education system and its comparison with those of other countries may help frame your response.

7.1 Aims of education

Graham Haydon and Ruth Heilbronn

Introduction

In a busy schedule of preparation for life in the classroom, it is easy to become absorbed in the technicalities of how to teach, and there is an abundance of advice and guidance on important matters that need to be grasped, for which you need to be professionally prepared and effective. Most teachers come into teaching with wider aims and wider values than just implementing decisions of a technical and pedagogical nature. It is good to step further back from this busy and responsible daily work to reflect on a range of matters, and this unit aims to show how reflection on the aims of education is important.

We may well ask ourselves 'What is education for?' 'What should education prepare people to do?' In fact, teachers are often challenged to justify their aims on a deeper level than just stating a learning outcome for a particular lesson. For example, when a pupil asks 'What's the point of all this studying?', if you ask yourself what above all you are trying to achieve as a teacher, if the staff in your school collectively consider whether they are offering anything distinctive that other schools are not, if a politician complains that schools are not getting good enough exam grades or not doing as well as schools in some other countries, then the question of the aims of education is *implicitly* being raised. This unit asks you to consider the question explicitly, and in conjunction with the following unit it tries to show that the question is not an abstract theoretical one that can be put on one side while you get on with the job; it is an unavoidable part of the context in which you do the job.

OBJECTIVES

At the end of this unit, you should be able to:

- list a variety of actual and possible aims for education;
- reflect on and formulate your own aims in being a teacher;
- discuss aims of education with other teachers and with parents.

Check the requirements of your initial teacher education (ITE) programme to see which relate to this unit.

The social and political context of aims

Whether they are explicitly stated or not, all education systems are governed by underlying aims. These may be decided at different political or administrative levels. Many countries today have a national education system, at least partly state-funded and state-controlled. In some cases, as once in the Soviet Union, a clearly defined ideology sets aims that the whole education system is meant to promote. Even in a more decentralised system in which many decisions are taken at a local level, there may be a widely shared sense of what the aims of education should be. In the early twentieth century in the US, for example, there was a shared understanding that a primary aim of the national education system was to forge a single nation out of diverse communities. This was expressed most famously by John Dewey, and came to be known as the idea of the common school (Dewey 1916).

In Britain, the aim to promote common values is exemplified in the current requirement that schools create and publish a statement about how they demonstrate and promote 'British values'. Much comment has been generated over the phrase 'British values' on the grounds that the values promoted seem not to be exclusively those of one nation, but rather general values concerning democracy and 'the rule of law'. The requirement to make a statement of this kind illustrates how, at certain times, some fundamental values might be seen to be in need of reiteration and reinforcement. Reflecting on these statements and the way in which they are developed, promoted and exemplified in the school is a useful undertaking. A typical statement might make reference to preparing children for life in modern Britain, managing the curriculum to provide a vehicle for furthering understanding of the values related to democracy and the rule of law, and giving children a range of out-of-school activities where these values are implicit, such as sporting events and out-of-school visits.

Earlier and through much of the twentieth century in Britain, schools had a good deal of autonomy, from a legal point of view, in setting and pursuing their aims, though in many cases the aims of a particular school were not made explicit. There was also room for some variation at local authority (LA)[1] level. Currently, changes are occurring in the English education system allowing a diverse form of school management and organisation, with less national control (for example, the academy programme, on the model of charter schools in the US and Sweden). These changes have renewed a debate about the aims underlying the education system and what they should be (for example, Pring 2012; Reiss and White 2013). Significantly, in England, schools compete for a place in the national league tables. Governments also look to international comparison of results. On the one hand, this may lead to schools being less governed by a national imposition of aims and more focused on making their own aims clear to parents and prospective pupils, in order to present themselves as in some way distinctive from other schools. On the other hand, some have claimed that by focusing intensively on examination results, we may loose sight of other aims of education. They have pointed out that examination results are important for individuals and for the wider economy, but questioned whether a focus on targets and results might overwhelm any wider aims of education, such as preparing young people to take their place as future citizens (Pring 2012; Watkins 2012; Ravitch 2013).

Politicians do not often explicitly express their views on what the aims of education should be, but when they say that schools should enable Britain to compete economically with other nations, or that schools should inculcate 'British values' or should promote active citizenship, they are in effect recommending certain aims for schools. At this broad level, it is generally assumed that the same aims are shared by all schools. So there is potential tension between the possibility of a diversity of aims in different schools (perhaps because they are serving rather different communities) and the promotion of common aims across the school system as a whole.

You can see then that as a student teacher, you are working in a context in which many expectations about aims are already in place, explicitly or implicitly. You do not have a free hand to pursue any aims you like. You might wonder, then, whether there is much point in your doing your own thinking about the aims of education. It is a premise of this unit that good teachers will consider the aims of education and know what they endorse. We suggest two reasons why your own thinking about aims is relevant and you may well think of others. First, within the constraints of your individual school, curriculum and circumstances, your own thinking about aims influences the way you approach your task as a teacher of a particular subject (this aspect of aims of education is discussed further in Unit 7.2). Second, as a citizen, you have the same right as any other citizen to form and express your own view about the aims of education in general, but being a teacher with a duty of care towards young people, you are in a better position than the average citizen to make your views clear and be prepared to argue for them.

Thinking about aims

Tasks 7.1.1 and 7.1.2 are intended to give you some insight into the nature and variety of aims in education, as well as some experience in thinking about aims and their implications and discussing this with others.

 Task 7.1.1 School aims: a comparison

(a) What do you consider the aims of education to be? Some other ways into this reflection might be to consider other questions, such as:

■ 'What is education for?'
■ 'Who is education for?'
■ 'What kind of person do we wish to develop and why?'

(b) Think about two schools with which you are familiar; for example, the school in which you received your own secondary education (or the majority of it, if you changed schools) and your current placement school.

For the first school, your data will be wholly or largely from your own memory. Answer the following questions as far as you can:

■ Did your school have an explicit statement of its aims?
■ Were you, as a pupil, aware of the school's aims?
■ In what ways did the particular aims of your school impinge on your experience as a pupil?

For your placement school, ask:

■ Does your school have an explicit statement of aims - if so, what does it say?
■ Are the pupils you are teaching aware of the school's aims?

■ Does the existence of these aims appear to make any difference to the pupils' experience in the school?

If you are a parent, you could also identify the aims of your child's school, using the school's documentation and, perhaps, discussion with staff.

Compare your findings for the two schools. Do you find that aims have a higher profile in one school or the other? Is there any evidence that the existence of an explicit policy on aims enhances the education the school is providing?

(c) Go back to your own reflection in (a) and relate the answers you have given for the two schools to these thoughts. You could discuss your findings and your views with other student teachers.

(d) Answering these questions in the case of your present placement school gives scope for some small-scale empirical research. Depending on your subject, you may be able to incorporate some research into your teaching; for example, in a discussion about school aims or through pupils themselves conducting a survey into how far their fellow pupils are aware of the school aims. You should discuss first with your school tutor any enquiry you plan.

Keep your notes from this task in your professional development portfolio (PDP) for use when you are considering what schools to apply to work in and to prepare for an interview for a teaching post (see Unit 8.1).

Task 7.1.2 The governing body: aims for a new school

This task is suitable for a group of student teachers in the same school, or for a tutorial session with student teachers from several schools. It involves taking roles of people who might be governors of a school under the remit of the LA. In LA schools, governing bodies have a specified representation including parents, teachers and community representatives. (Other kinds of schools have different rules of who may be represented on the governing bodies.)

The intended outcome of the governors' meeting is to draft a statement of aims for a new school that is going to be set up under the auspices of your school. (Imagining a new school for the purposes of the role play allows you to start with a relatively clean sheet.) Within the allotted time (say, one hour), you must try to produce a statement of aims to be included in the prospectus, to help show prospective pupils and their parents what is distinctive about the new school and its educational priorities.

Before you start the role play, you should agree on any special characteristics of the area in which the school is located. It may be best to make it a school that has to serve a wide range of interests; that is, a comprehensive school with a socially and ethnically varied intake.

Depending on the number in your group, you can assign individuals to some of the following roles as governors. (You may think there is some stereotyping in the brief descriptions of these roles. If you have experience of role play, you should be able to distance yourself from the stereotypes.)

- a Conservative-voting company director;
- a Labour-voting trade union leader;
- a Church of England vicar;
- a spokesperson for the main local ethnic community;
- a parent of a bright child, with high academic ambitions for their child;
- a teacher-governor;
- the head teacher.

One of you should be elected to chair the meeting and another to take notes on the points made and record anything that is agreed.

After the role play, if you have not arrived at an agreed statement, talk about what it was that prevented agreement. In what ways does the disagreement within your group reflect the actual diversity of interests and cultures within our society?

Keep your notes in your PDP.

Recognising the diversity of aims

Education as such has no aims. Only persons, parents and teachers, etc., have aims, not an abstract idea like education.

(Dewey 1916: Chapter 8, 'Aims of education')

We have been talking about the aims of education in this unit. By now, your experience in doing the tasks may have backed up Dewey's point. Different people can have different ideas about the aims of education, and these differences may be quite legitimate. These are not matters on which there is a 'right' answer. At the same time, a school, and even a national education system, needs some coherent sense of direction. We might reflect on just how much overall coherence and agreement is needed and how far there is room for internal variation, yet some coherence and agreement seems to be necessary, because of the ways in which conceptions of aims can make a practical difference. They can make a difference, for instance, to:

- how a whole school system is organised (For example, the movement towards comprehensive education which began in the 1960s was driven at least partly by explicit aims of breaking down class barriers and distributing opportunities for education more widely.);
- how an individual school is run (For example, various aspects of a school's ethos and organisation may be motivated by the aim that pupils should respect and tolerate each other's differences.);
- how curriculum content is selected and taught (There is more on this aspect of aims in Unit 7.2.).

Given that aims in education can make a practical difference, it is important not just that the diversity of possible aims can be recognised, but also that there can be some prospect of reasoned debate over the importance of certain aims rather than others.

Comparing and justifying aims

Philosophers of education of an earlier generation sometimes argued in quite sophisticated ways that certain aims are inherent in the very *concept* of education, taking 'education' to be contrasted with 'training'. On this view, training someone to perform certain tasks or to think a certain way might be a form of *conditioning* or *indoctrination*, but not *education*. This is an interesting distinction and one that is still generating discussion on what actually goes on in schools. The question is worth putting – what *should* teachers and schools be aiming at? Perhaps there are certain beliefs or habits or skills that they should be trying to inculcate in an unquestioning way. If not, why not? Conversely, perhaps teachers should, above all, be aiming to turn pupils into autonomous adults, who can think critically about everything they are told and make up their own minds about what to think and what to do in their lives. Again, why should this be the aim?

Given that the actual diversity of views about what teachers and schools should be aiming at can be quite wide, it may help to identify some common ground as far as this is possible. A fundamental and common view of education is that it should in some way be improving the quality of life of individuals or of society in general. Otherwise, why bother with it? There is still room for discussion over the priority to put on aiming at what may be best for each individual, or aiming through education to improve the society as a whole, and it hardly needs saying that different people may have different views about what is good for individuals and about the nature of a good society. (We come back below to the question of whether societal and individual aims necessarily conflict.)

So how can the debate be taken further? What follows is intended more to stimulate your own thinking than to give any definitive answers. One starting point could be to focus first on a set of aims that are always likely to be very influential in determining what actually happens in education: the aims of government in setting educational policy. Then we can broaden the picture by looking at different people who have aims for education, and at a broader range of possible aims.

Societal and individual aims

Government education policies are inevitably influenced by political priorities, which may be largely driven by a concern to promote economic stability and growth. Parents too may think about the aims of education in a similar way, and so may pupils themselves. Most parents and pupils would not argue that the primary point of going to school is to get a job that will pay well. Taking into account overall societal aims together with individual aims, such jobs could be seen to contribute to the national economy. But this does not mean that there is no room for other conceptions of the aims of education.

Let's continue, then, with a provisional distinction between aims for a whole society – which are the kind of aims we mostly expect from government – and aims for individuals. The idea that governments should aim, above all, at economic growth is not unquestionable, since it appears increasingly unlikely that continued economic growth is a realistic possibility, especially if we take a global perspective. It may well be that governments' responsibilities towards their citizens have to extend beyond material conditions. For one thing, there is evidence that, above some level of minimal provision, increasing affluence does not produce increasing satisfaction with life. People's aspirations for their own lives may not be purely material, and governments may have a responsibility to protect and promote the well-being of their citizens in a broader than economic sense. Government policy, if it is explicit about aims at all rather than taking certain aims for granted, tends to sketch aims with a broad brush. Teachers (and perhaps parents and pupils themselves) need to be able to think about aims in more detail; and while they may see the point of education partly in terms of the good of society, their focus is likely to be aims for individuals: ways in which education can make the lives of individuals better than they would otherwise be. Governments need to take into account the ways, both positive and negative, that people's lives impinge on each other, and this consideration can lead to an explicit concern with values education in schools (see Unit 4.5).

With such a concern, we might say that education should do more than enable people to gain qualifications and 'transferable skills' for the global economy, because qualifications are only part of the preparation for becoming an adult in any society. It could also be argued that technological changes are bringing about social changes to the extent that we cannot predict what kind of employment and challenges young people might face as adults. On this view, the future labour market, the kinds of jobs that will exist, is not completely predictable. It follows that education might need to be broadly based, enabling people to adapt what they know, and enjoy what they are able to do, as preparation for life in uncertain times. As well as a core of skills, a deep familiarity with the arts and humanities and a critical and curious approach to problem-solving and discussion might be valuable aspects of education.

One way of approaching the question of aims is to start not from the idea of skills and knowledge that needs to be taught in order to get a job and contribute to society, but to start differently by asking 'what should count as an educated young person in this day and age?', which is to ask questions about which human qualities we wish to nurture and develop and how education may foster them. These might cover the knowledge and understanding required for work, but also for managing one's life and relationships. It is important too that people develop a practical capacity and an ability to make sensible and grounded decisions, given changing economic and social conditions. 'Moral seriousness' (Pring 2012) is a quality that has been highlighted as important for the individual and for society. This might involve having a sense of responsibility for the community, which might include kindness and respect towards others. This takes us into thinking not only about the knowledge and the skills that schools should aim to inculcate, but also about the kinds of qualities and dispositions we think pupils need to develop. Often, and perhaps increasingly, the language of 'skills' and knowledge tends to dominate. It is not controversial that education should lead pupils towards having certain skills and subject knowledge. Indeed, there is pragmatic reason for gaining certain knowledge and skills, which may be individual purposes (including earning a living) or societal purposes (including the filling of occupational roles that the society needs). There is also an intrinsic value to some knowledge and skills: it may just be interesting to know about certain things, or satisfying to be able to do certain things, regardless of any practical benefit. It's arguable that education should be at least partly about giving people access to such intrinsic sources of satisfaction.

To think further and beyond knowledge and skills as the end of education, it is questionable whether all the capacities and qualities we might want pupils to develop can be captured by the idea of skills and knowledge alone. Up to this point, a number of possible aims for education have been mentioned. Some, called here individual aims, are aims characterised by individual achievements or qualities that contribute towards making the lives of individuals better than they would otherwise be. Others, called here societal aims, are aims characterised by some possible state of society that is seen as desirable (such as an affluent society, or a free society, or a society with a strong sense of community).

Anyone is likely to have views about what makes a society a good society, and about what factors contribute to a good life for individuals: how far is a good life a matter of material prosperity, of job satisfaction, of richness of interests outside of work, of good relationships, of taking control autonomously of one's own life, and so on? Thinking about the aims of education is partly an attempt to get some coherent sense of priorities among such factors, but also crucially it will be a matter of thinking through how far and in what ways the kind of teaching and learning that we associate with school education has a special role to play in realising these positive factors in life (and in avoiding negative factors). What sort of society a person lives in may be largely outside the individual's control, but education may influence how far a person fits into that society or seeks to change it. Life opens up opportunities and risks that may be unforeseen and unavoidable, but education can influence an individual's capacity to take advantage of the opportunities and cope with the risks. Health, for instance, is an important factor in a good life; in relation to health, teachers and schools do not have the same role as doctors and nurses, but there is a lot that schools can do to influence a person's chances of having a healthy life.

Two further points before turning to issues about the curriculum and its relationship to aims: first, there is more to be considered about the relationship between aims for individuals and aims for society. This is the topic of Task 7.1.3. Then there is an assumption to be brought out and considered: that the fundamental aims of education are the same for everyone. This is the topic of the next section.

 Task 7.1.3 Individual and societal aims

This is a task for your individual reflection and group discussion.

There are some combinations of individual and societal aims that seem to fit neatly together; for example, the societal aim of a society of full employment and the individual aim of giving each individual the knowledge and skills to equip them to do one of the jobs available. There are other combinations where the relationship between societal and individual aims may be problematic: consider, for instance, the societal aim of maintaining a society characterised by traditional ways of doing things, and the individual aim of equipping and encouraging young people to be independent and critical in their thinking.

■ Can you think of other combinations of societal and individual aims that seem to be 'made for each other'?
■ And other ways in which there may be conflicts between societal and individual aims?
■ Do you think societal aims should always have priority over individual ones? Or vice versa?
■ Do you think that it is easier for societal and individual aims to fit together in some kinds of society than in others? (You could think, for instance, about how authoritarian or democratic a society is.)

Make notes of your discussion and summarise your views about aims. Keep your notes in your PDP.

Equal aims for everyone?

Through much of the history of education, it would have been an unquestioned assumption that the aims of education should be different for different people. Plato built his conception of an ideal state (The Republic) on the argument that the people in power would need a much more thorough education than anyone else. A similar position was apparent in Victorian Britain, where the expansion of education was driven in part by the aim that the mass of the population should be sufficiently well educated to form a productive workforce, but not so well educated that they might rebel against the (differently educated) ruling classes. Until quite recent times, it was usual for the education of boys to have different aims – implicitly and sometimes explicitly – from the education of girls: boys might be educated to acquire the abilities necessary for certain sorts of occupation (which might in turn depend on their social position); girls would often be educated on the assumption that professions needing an extensive education were not for them. In the mid-twentieth century in England, within a system selecting by ability, there were different aims behind the education offered in different types of schools: secondary modern, technical and grammar. An example that is still pertinent is that the aims of religious schools and the aims of secular schools are unlikely to coincide entirely (see below).

Despite these examples, today the unquestioned assumption is often that the basic aims of education are the same for everyone, even if different methods have to be used with different people in pursuing the same aims, and even if some people go further in the process than others. This assumption underlies many important developments in the promotion of equal opportunities. One of the basic reasons for being concerned with equal opportunities is that if what you are aiming at is worthwhile, no one should be excluded from it because of factors, such as race or gender, that ought to be irrelevant to achieving these worthwhile aims. But this basic assumption is still not without its problems.

In the area of special educational needs (SEN) in England and Wales, for instance, the Warnock Committee, which was set up in the late 1970s to look into the education of pupils with physical and mental disabilities, argued that the fundamental aims of education are the same for everyone (DES 1978). This was part of the thinking that led, in the 1980s, to the integration of an increasing proportion of pupils with SEN into mainstream schools, rather than their segregation in special schools. There has been debate ever since over how far integration can be taken and whether there is still a case for some degree of separation in provision. But the debate is still usually conducted on the assumption that there are underlying aims of education that are the same for all. (See Unit 4.6 for the current position on SEN.)

As regards gender, few people would now suggest that the aim of education for girls should be to produce wives and mothers while the aim of education for boys should be to produce breadwinners. When people today argue for single-sex schooling or for dividing teaching groups according to gender, it is usually not because they think there are separate aims for the education of boys and of girls, but because they recognise that giving boys and girls an equal opportunity to achieve those aims requires attention to practical conditions, and this may make a difference to the means though not to the ends. So, for instance, the teaching of boys and girls may be more effective if they are taught without the distractions or pressures present in mixed-sex groups (whether this actually is so is a matter for research). Even so, some might argue that a degree of differentiation in aims is needed; perhaps, for instance, there should be an attempt to develop assertiveness in girls and sensitivity in boys. (See Unit 4.4 for further discussion of gender issues).

Turning to different cultural, religious or ethnic groups, it is not surprising if governments expect the same aims to be pursued for all groups; anything else would seem grossly discriminatory. But at the same time, the members of particular groups may have special aims they would like to see pursued for their own children. To some religious believers, it may be more important that their children are brought up within the faith of their community than that they are brought up as citizens of a secular society. This illustrates the point made in the previous section, that conceptions of the aims of education turn in the end on views about what matters in life: to committed religious believers, there is a dimension to what matters in life that is absent for purely secular thinkers.

These examples illustrate that while, at one level, statements of the aims of education can appear rather platitudinous and bland, there is the potential for controversy when aims are considered in more detail, and an attempt is made to see how the pursuit of certain aims can be implemented in practice. (Unit 7.2 raises several questions about the relationship between stated aims and curriculum content.)

To conclude the present unit, we suggest you address Task 7.1.4, which asks you to reflect on any single published statement of aims.

 Task 7.1.4 Aims and education: a statement of aims

You need a statement of educational aims as a prompt for reflection that you can share with fellow student teachers. It does not have to be one that is currently in use. You might use one taken from another country, or your school, or one of the National Curriculum for England documents, in previous or current forms.

Analyse and evaluate the statement of aims, addressing questions such as the following:

■ Does the statement comprise a list of discrete aims in no order of priority, or does it convey that some aims have priority over others?
■ Where there are subordinate aims under a broader aim, is there a clear rationale for the particular subordinate aims listed?
■ Do the aims listed seem to you to fit together into a coherent idea of what education is about?

If the answer to the last question is 'Yes', can you write one sentence summarising this conception of education?

Finally, consider whether there is anything in this statement of aims that you would not have expected to see there. Is there anything that is likely to prove controversial? Is there anything you think should be mentioned that is not mentioned?

Discuss your responses with other student teachers, or with your tutor. Keep these notes together with those from Tasks 7.1.1, 7.1.2 and 7.1.3 in your PDP.

SUMMARY AND KEY POINTS

■ In working as a teacher, you necessarily have some aims, and these are more likely to be coherent and defensible if you have thought them through.

■ At the same time, you are operating within the context of aims set by others.

■ Aims can exist at different levels, local or national.

■ In England in 2014, there was a revision of the National Curriculum that enabled schools to plan much of their own curricula. The question of aims is therefore open to discussion where planning occurs, and this leaves room for you to form your own view on the most important priorities for education, and to discuss with others how these aims can best be realised.

■ It is always possible to raise questions about the justification of educational aims. Ultimately, our aims for education rest on our values – our conceptions of what makes for a good life both for individuals and for our society as a whole.

■ Because we do not share all of our values with each other, there is always room for debate about the aims of education.

Check which requirements for your ITE programme you have addressed through this unit.

Further reading

Brighouse, H. (2006) *On Education*, London: Routledge.
> Part One, 'Educational aims', argues for four aims: educating for self-government; educating for economic participation; educating for human flourishing; and educating for citizenship.

Dewey, J. (1916) *Democracy and Education*, New York: Free Press.
> A classic book (often reprinted) that is still well worth reading. It is downloadable as an open source document. Though Dewey is often thought of simply as an advocate of child-centred education, his educational theory is part of a well-worked-out theory of the relation between individual and society and of the nature of knowledge and thought. See especially Chapters 1–4, 8 and 9.

Haydon, G. (2007) *Values for Educational Leadership*, London: Sage.
> Of relevance also to those who are not in leadership roles, Chapter 2, 'Educational aims and moral purpose', goes in more detail into some of the issues raised in this unit.

Reiss, M. and White, J. (2013) *An Aims Based Curriculum*, London: IoE Press.
> A book relevant to this unit and the following one. It argues that curriculum design should start from a consideration of aims and not from subject divisions. The book starts with some overarching aims that will equip each learner to lead a personally fulfilling life and help others do so too. From these more specific aims are derived, covering the personal qualities, skills and understanding needed for a life of personal, civic and vocational well-being. The second half of the book focuses on the implementation of educational policy based on this view of aims and curriculum.

Other resources and websites

What is Education? Paul Standish: www.philosophy-of-education.org/resources/students/video-listing.html

See also other videos on the website of the Philosophy of Education Society of Great Britain: www.philosophy-of-education.org/resources/students/video-listing.html

National Curriculum in England: www.gov.uk/government/publications/national-curriculum-in-england-framework-for-key-stages-1-to-4/the-national-curriculum-in-england-framework-for-key-stages-1-to-4

Scottish National Curriculum: www.educationscotland.gov.uk/learningandteaching/thecurriculum/whatis curriculumforexcellence/

Welsh National Curriculum: wales.gov.uk/topics/educationandskills/schoolshome/curriculuminwales/arevised curriculumforwales/?lang=en

National Curriculum in Northern Ireland: www.nicurriculum.org.uk/

Daisy Christodoulou's blog posts on issues in assessment: https://thewingtoheaven.wordpress.com/

Dylan Wiliam's website: www.dylanwiliam.org/Dylan_Wiliams_website/Welcome.html

Education Endowment Foundation (EEF) blog on feedback and assessment: https://educationendowment foundation.org.uk/. . ./eef-blog-feedback-matters-putting-formative-assessment-into-practice/

Appendix 2 on pages 591–595 provides further examples of websites you may find useful.

Capel, S., Leask, M. and Turner, T. (eds) (2010) *Readings for Learning to Teach in the Secondary School: A Companion to M Level Study*, London: Routledge.
This book brings together essential readings to support you in your critical engagement with key issues raised in this textbook.

The subject-specific books in the Routledge *Learning to Teach* series are also very useful.

Any additional resources and an editable version of any relevant tasks/tables in this unit are available on the companion website: www.routledge.com/cw/capel

Note

1   The term LA replaced LEA (local education authorities) in 2004 in England when social care and education departments within councils were merged.

7.2 The school curriculum

Graham Haydon and Ruth Heilbronn

Introduction

This unit discusses the curriculum as one of the most important 'tools' through which educational aims can be realised; it is best read in conjunction with Unit 7.1.

We need first to be clearer about what the term 'the curriculum' refers to. The planned or formal curriculum is the intended content of an educational programme set out in advance. We refer later to the informal and hidden curriculum. Like other aspects of the context of your work (the school buildings, say, or the administrative organisation of the school), the curriculum (whether formal or not) forms a 'frame' to what you are doing, even when you are not explicitly thinking about it. But often you find that you do refer to the curriculum, in your everyday conversations with colleagues, and less frequently perhaps in meetings with parents or in talking to pupils in a pastoral role. It might seem that the curriculum is so clearly part of the context of your work that it must be obvious what the curriculum is. In which case, why does a book of this nature need units on the curriculum?

The purpose of this unit is to show you that once you think about it, it is not so obvious what the curriculum is and that it is not something you should, as a teacher take for granted. Rather than relying on implicit assumptions about the curriculum, you should be able and willing, as part of your professional role, to think about the curriculum, about its role in education and about ways in which it is controversial and might be open to challenge. In doing this, you will, of course, need to keep in mind the relevant legislation and government documentation for the country within which you are working. National curricula undergo revisions and sometimes radical changes are made, and you need to refer to the latest version for your school's jurisdiction, using the relevant websites. In England, the National Curriculum underwent a major review recently. At the time of writing, the latest version was published in September 2013 and updated in July 2014. You should bear in mind also that the education systems, including curricula, of Northern Ireland, Scotland and Wales are, in varying ways, different from that of England (see the other units for Chapter 7 on the companion website).

OBJECTIVES

At the end of this unit, you should be able to:

■ distinguish a number of different conceptions of the curriculum;
■ discuss ways in which the curriculum may or may not help to realise educational aims;
■ see why the content of the curriculum, even if often taken for granted, is potentially controversial;
■ discuss the place of your particular teaching subject within the broader curriculum.

Check the requirements of your initial teacher education (ITE) programme to see which relate to this unit.

The curriculum in general and within particular subjects

It helps to avoid confusion in the rest of this unit (and hopefully in your thinking more generally) if we distinguish between the curriculum of a school (or even of schools in general) and the curriculum within a particular subject. Sometimes, this distinction is marked by speaking of the 'syllabus', rather than curriculum, of a particular subject. The term 'syllabus' usually refers to a specific course of study in a specific subject set out in detail in advance, possibly designed by a particular teacher, but often laid down by an examination board or other body external to the school. But it is common now to speak of, say, 'the science curriculum' or 'the arts curriculum'. In the official documentation for the *current* National Curriculum (NC) for England (DfE 2013i), the term 'curriculum' is used throughout the document: 'syllabus' is not used.

For most of this unit, the focus is on the broad curriculum. Questions are raised about the role of particular subjects within the curriculum in general, more than about what goes on within the teaching of particular subjects. But we shall have to say something about the latter point as well, because the role of a subject within the curriculum partly depends on what is done within that subject (see the subject-specific and practical books that are a part of this *Learning to Teach* series, p. ii). (So far, the term 'the whole curriculum' has been avoided because that too may carry some ambiguity.) In Task 7.2.1, we ask you to compare two curricula.

The formal curriculum

There *could* be considerable variety in what you and other student teachers have written for Task 7.2.1, because the term 'curriculum' can be used in various ways. But it is likely that what you have written down, for both schools in the comparison, is a list of subjects. What this illustrates is that when people refer to 'the curriculum' without qualification, most often they think of what we can usefully label 'the formal curriculum'. This is the intended content of an educational programme, set out in advance.

At a minimal level of detail, the formal curriculum can be stated as a list of names of subjects. At this level, it is likely that there is considerable overlap between the lists for the two schools that you compared in the task, and in the lists that you and other student teachers have compiled. Indeed, at this level, the list of named subjects in the typical curriculum of an English school has changed relatively little over a long period. When the National Curriculum in England was first introduced in 1988, a historian of education pointed out its similarity to the curriculum in the secondary school regulations in England of 1904 (Aldrich 1988: 48). There are even recognisable overlaps with the curriculum parodied by Lewis Carroll in *Alice in Wonderland* (published 1865) when Alice and the Mock Turtle compare their respective curricula.

 Task 7.2.1 School curricula: a comparison

(This task is deliberately parallel to Task 7.1.1 on aims in Unit 7.1.)

When you have carried out this task by yourself, try to compare your findings with those of other student teachers.

Select two schools with which you are familiar; for example:

- the school in which you received your own secondary education (or the majority of it, if you changed schools);
- your current placement school.

From memory, write down briefly what was in the curriculum of the school you attended as a pupil. Then (without referring to documentation at this stage) write down what is in the curriculum of your placement school. Compare the two accounts. Store your comparison in your professional development portfolio (PDP).

While the formal curriculum can be listed simply as a set of subjects, it is always possible to set out in more detail the content that is supposed to be taught and learned. Even when the curriculum is stated simply as a list of subjects, those who write it and those who read it have some implicit understanding of what goes into each subject. It is important to keep this in mind when comparing the curriculum offered in schools at different times. So far as named subjects are concerned, the typical curriculum of English schools has *not* gone through revolutionary changes, though some new subjects, including ICT/computing and citizenship, have been added. But it would be a mistake to conclude from the similarity of the lists that the curriculum has hardly changed at all. Even if we could set aside all changes in teaching method and concentrate solely on the content of the subjects, what is taught under the heading of history or science in the early twenty-first century is obviously going to be very different in many ways from what was taught under the same headings in the early twentieth century.

Another point to note under 'formal curriculum' is that the curriculum may contain parts that are optional. Even before the introduction of a NC in England and Wales in 1988 made certain subjects compulsory, it was normal for most of the curriculum in a secondary school to consist of subjects that all pupils were expected to take. But there may also be options within the curriculum, particularly in the later years of secondary school.

Related to the idea of a compulsory curriculum are the notions of a 'common curriculum'; that is, one taken by everyone in practice, whether or not it is actually compulsory, and a 'core curriculum', the part of a formal curriculum that everyone takes, around which there is scope for variations.

The informal curriculum and the hidden curriculum

The notion of the *formal curriculum* refers to the content that is, quite deliberately, taught by teachers in a school, usually in periods structured by a timetable and labelled according to subject. So the fact that something is on the curriculum means that it is taught (or at least that the intention of the curriculum planners or of the school management is that it shall be taught). But since some pupils may fail to learn what teachers are intending to teach, the fact that something is a non-optional part of the formal curriculum does not guarantee that pupils learn it.

On the other hand, pupils may learn things in school that are not taught as part of the formal curriculum. Many of the possible aims of a school, which you were thinking about in Unit 7.1, involve matters of this kind. If a school wants, for instance, to promote cooperation and consideration for others, then (if these are to be more than pious aspirations) it needs to do something to try to bring about cooperation and to encourage pupils to behave in considerate ways (see also Unit 4.5 for further discussion of promoting common values). Teachers might agree to build cooperative work into their lessons, whatever the subject; teachers and pupils might draw up a code of behaviour; there may be some system of rewards and sanctions; the school management may pay attention to the way that pupils move around the school during break times, and so on. All such arrangements can be counted as part of the *informal curriculum* of the school. The *curriculum* can be defined taking into account both the formal and informal curriculum in some way such as this: 'The school curriculum comprises all learning and other experiences that each school plans for its pupils' (DfE 2014o).

But pupils may also learn things at school that the school does not intend them to learn. For several decades, sociologists have pointed out that many pupils at school were learning, for instance, to accept passively what they were told or to see themselves as failures, while some were learning to identify with and follow the mores of a rebellious subculture, and some were learning racist and sexist attitudes, and so on. Such learning was not normally part of what the school was intending its pupils to learn, and the school may not have been aware of many of the things that its pupils were learning; from the school's point of view, these outcomes were side effects of the pupils' time in school. The term 'hidden curriculum' is often used to cover such learning.

The side effects just mentioned are undesirable ones, but side effects could also be desirable ones; for instance, a side effect of pupils of different ethnic backgrounds learning and playing together might be the development of understanding and respect. The point about the idea of the hidden curriculum is not that its content is necessarily bad, but that the school is not aware of it. Today, teachers are far more likely to be aware of the likely side effects of all aspects of the school's activity. In that way, what might once have been part of a hidden curriculum comes to be hidden no longer. This does not mean that schools today have no hidden curriculum; it means that a school has to try consciously to uncover and become aware of side effects of what it does in its teaching and its organisation.

If these side effects are unwelcome – if, say, they work against the school achieving its intended aims – then the school may make deliberate attempts to counteract them. Often a school does this by paying attention to aspects of its teaching and organisation outside the formal curriculum. So where the learning of racist or sexist attitudes might once have been part of the *hidden curriculum* in some schools, it is more likely today that the *informal* curriculum includes anti-racist and anti-sexist policies. And it may also be that such policies alter what is done within the *formal* curriculum; for example, within personal, social and health education (PSHE) or citizenship.

Mention of the informal curriculum shows that the curriculum as a whole is not, for any teacher, a rigid framework within which there is no room for flexibility or planning. Even when the formal curriculum is determined largely in advance, as in the NC for England, there is still scope open to the school to design the details of the curriculum and the way that links between curriculum subjects are (or are not) made, and there is some space outside the NC, since it is not supposed to occupy the whole timetable.

You should, then, see it as part of your professional role as a teacher that you can take an overview of the curriculum, have a sense of 'where it comes from' and be able to engage in discussion on whether it could be improved and, if so, in what ways.

Curriculum as a selection from culture

A number of writers have referred to the curriculum as a selection from the culture of a society. 'Culture' here refers to 'everything that is created by human beings themselves: tools and technology, language and literature, music and art, science and mathematics – in effect, the whole way of life of a society' (Lawton 1989: 27). Any society passes on its culture to the next generation, and in modern societies schooling is one of the ways in which this is done. But obviously no school curriculum can accommodate the whole of human culture, so a selection has to be made.

A natural question to ask next is how do we make that selection? Different curriculum theories give different answers.

A first move is to recognise that since some aspects of culture are passed on or picked up independently of schools, it may make sense for schools in general to concentrate on matters that will not be learned if they are not included in the school curriculum, and secondary schools in particular have to try to build on, but not to duplicate, what pupils have learned by the end of primary school. Even these points give rise to many questions. For example, many young people of secondary age pick up much of what they know about computers, sport or popular music independently of school. Does this mean there is no point in including study of these areas in the curriculum?

After putting on one side things that pupils learn independently of school (if we can identify such things), there are principles by which we might try to make a selection from culture. In this unit, there is space to mention just three: to select what is *best*, or what is *distinctive* of a particular culture, or what is in some way *fundamental*.

The idea of selecting, and enabling people to appreciate, what is *best* goes back at least to Matthew Arnold (1822-1888). Arnold was not only a Victorian poet and a commentator on the culture of his day, but also a school inspector. Historically, this principle has been linked with the idea of whole areas of culture – 'high culture', centred on arts and literature, being thought of in this view to be of greater value than the rest of culture, and also perhaps being accessible only to a minority of society. The principle does not have to be interpreted in that way (see Gingell and Brandon 2000 for an updated interpretation). Whatever area of culture we are dealing with, including popular culture, we may well want people to be able to appreciate what is good rather than what is mediocre. It does not follow, though, that the school curriculum should always be focused on what is best in any area. If we suppose, for instance, that the greatest science is that of Einstein or Stephen Hawking, it does not mean we place this science at the centre of the school curriculum. In many areas, if people are ever to be able to appreciate the best, they need to start by understanding something more basic.

Another principle of selection that is sometimes favoured is to pick from the whole of human culture what is *distinctive* of a particular culture – the way of life of a particular nation, or ethnic group, or religion. This may apply more to the detailed content within areas of the curriculum than to the selection of the broad areas. We do not just learn language; we learn a particular language; and while it is possible to study historical method, any content of history is that of particular people in a particular part of the world. One question for curriculum planning, then, is how far to select from what we see as 'our' culture, and how to interpret what is 'our' culture. That question, in England, has to be resolved in a context of a multicultural society, within a world in which there is increasing interaction between different cultures.

Rather than looking to what is best, or what is distinctive, we may try to look to what is *fundamental*. This idea may apply both across the curriculum and within subject areas of the curriculum. Within the sciences and mathematics, for instance, the idea of what is culturally distinctive may have little application (which is not to say that these subjects as actually taught are culture-free), and the idea of teaching the best may be inappropriate. We need to think about what is fundamental in the educational sense of 'foundational': not what is fundamental in the whole structure of human knowledge, but what people need to learn if they are to have a foundation on which further knowledge or skills can be built.

Thinking about the curriculum in general, we can also try to ask what is fundamental in the whole human culture in which people are living. But this question depends, in turn, on some particular understanding of what is important in human life. Is it the development of the capacities for rational thought and judgement? Then we might argue, as the philosopher of education Paul Hirst (1974) once did, that there are certain basic forms of human understanding – science, mathematics, interpersonal understanding and so on – that are not interchangeable and each of which is necessary in its own way to the development of rational understanding.

Or is human life more fundamentally about providing the material necessities of life? Then we might stress what can be economically useful, and our curriculum might be primarily a vocational one. Or is the essential aspect of human life, so far as education is concerned, the fact that people live together in groups and have to organise their affairs together? Then preparing people to be citizens might turn out to be most fundamental.

So far, none of these approaches looks as if it takes us very far, by itself, in selecting which aspects of culture should make up a school curriculum. Besides, we do not *have to* transmit culture, or any aspect of culture, just as it stands (and in any case, it is constantly changing). So it looks as if making any selection from the available culture requires us to ask just the sorts of question that Unit 7.1 suggested we need to ask when deciding on aims of education: what is it that matters most in life, and how can teachers and schools best contribute to promoting that?

Relating curriculum to aims

The curriculum of a school is one of the major factors determining what actually goes on in the school. So the curriculum should be a major way through which we try to realise whatever we think the aims of education should be; we could say, in brief, that the curriculum is a tool for realising educational aims. So, rationally, the planning of a curriculum should depend on how the overall aims of education are conceived. Historically, this does not appear to have been always what has happened. A brief survey of some of the references to aims in the developing documentation of the National Curriculum for England will illustrate this point.

There have been several changes in the National Curriculum (NC) since it was first introduced for England (and at that time also Wales) in 1988; however, this does not necessarily mean that the curriculum designers have changed their conception of the aims of education during that time. It could be that the changes have come about through cumulative attempts to find a better way of realising the underlying aims. But, in fact, it is not easy to see how far the actual content of the NC has been determined, either originally or in later versions, by reference to underlying aims. The NC documentation *has* contained some reference to aims from the beginning. (Actually, the reference to aims usually refers to the aims *of the curriculum*; there is very little reference to the aims of education as such.) In the earliest version, in 1988, reference to aims was limited to stating merely that schools should promote the spiritual, moral, cultural, mental and physical development of pupils and prepare them to take their place in society as responsible adults. As a statement of aims, this was not very controversial (with the possible exception of the idea of spiritual development). Its problem was that it was so broad and general that it gave very little guidance. And in fact, there was no indication in the rest of the original documentation of the NC for England and Wales that its content had been influenced at all by the statement of aims. That statement seemed to be an example of an error that it is easy for government agencies, and also schools, to slip into: setting out a statement of aims that looks good but that makes no apparent difference to what actually happens.

In the 1999 revision of the NC for England, there were again two overall aims: to provide opportunities for all to learn and achieve, and to promote pupils' spiritual, moral, social, cultural and emotional well-being. But there were also two more significant changes. First, it was explicitly said that the aims of the curriculum were rooted in certain values that were held to be widely shared in the society; an outline list of values was given, based on the findings of the National Forum for Values in Education and the Community (see Unit 4.5). Second, a listing of more specific aims was given under each of the two overall aims.

By the time of the 2008 NC revision, three aims were explicitly stated to be the starting point for curriculum design:

> The curriculum should enable all young people to become:
> ■ successful learners who enjoy learning, make progress and achieve;
> ■ confident individuals who are able to live safe, healthy and fulfilling lives;
> ■ responsible citizens who make a positive contribution to society.
>
> (DfE 2012a)

These broad aims were broken down into 29 specific aims on an accompanying document on the Department for Education website. The website also provided a list of values underlying the aims and the purposes of the National Curriculum. In many ways, the relationship between values, aims, purposes and curriculum design was left vague. There was no explicit explanation of how the stated aims might be derived from the values. The section on purposes gave reasons for having a statutory National Curriculum, and included a list of some particular aims to be realised through this statutory curriculum, but there was overlap between 'Aims' and 'Purposes' in the document that seem to echo the individual/societal distinction used in Unit 7.1. (Under 'Aims' were the qualities and capacities to be developed in the learners. Under 'Purposes' were what society as a whole hoped to achieve through the statutory curriculum.) The detailed account in the 2008 National Curriculum of the relations between the curriculum aims, purposes and values does not appear in later versions, but is a useful reminder of their underlying relations and connections, even with its limitations in terms of precision.

It is important to think about how a particular curriculum might be derived from stated aims, and how a statement of aims might serve as a practical guide to what is done in schools. Here, we can usefully contrast the 1988 version and the 2008 version of the NC. The 1988 version was so broad and open-ended that it left almost all discussion about the actual content of the curriculum still to be carried out (in principle; in practice it seems likely that an almost ready-made list of subjects was taken over from what had already been normal practice in schools). In contrast, the 2008 version, in listing as many as 29 aims (divided between three broader aims), gave a series of reference points that *potentially* could be used almost as a checklist in seeing how far a school was actually doing something concrete towards realising the aims.

To illustrate, within the broad aim that pupils should become 'successful learners who enjoy learning, make progress and achieve', we could take the specific aim that schools should enable pupils to be 'creative, resourceful and able to identify and solve problems', and then ask what a specific school is doing in practice towards achieving this aim. Similarly, within the broad aim that pupils should become 'confident individuals who are able to live safe, happy and fulfilling lives', we can ask whether a school is paying enough attention to helping pupils to 'have a sense of self-worth and personal identity'. Within the broad aim that pupils should become 'responsible citizens who make a positive contribution to society', we can ask what the school is doing to ensure that they become people who 'challenge injustice, are committed to human rights and strive to live peaceably with others'. And so on through the remaining 26 specific aims. In principle, such a list seems to offer a level of detail that could be used for detailed curriculum planning. The same would be true of any reasonably detailed list of aims, whether it is some future revised list of aims from government or a school's own list.

Cross-matching and cross-planning at such detail as above is not without its difficulties and drawbacks, and this may have informed current practice to slim down such guidance. Indeed, the introduction to the current NC has a short section of two sentences entitled 'Aims' (DfE 2014o: S3), and more detailed elaboration of the aims to be achieved in specific NC curriculum subject areas. Also, official statements about the curriculum are not necessarily intended to apply to the *whole* curriculum of a school. In the case at least of England, while government agencies are setting out the aims to be pursued through a statutory curriculum, they are also reducing the extent to which the whole curriculum of a school has to be determined by the *statutory* National Curriculum: 'The national curriculum is just one element in the education of every child. There is time and space in the school day and in each week, term and year to range beyond the national curriculum specifications' (DfE 2014o: S3).

Schools may increasingly need to do their own thinking about the topic of Unit 7.1 above, namely the aims of *education*, rather than following official guidance about the aims of the National Curriculum. Now complete Task 7.2.2.

When you have tried this task both individually and in discussion, move on to the next section of this unit.

Task 7.2.2 Realising aims through the curriculum

(This is a task for individual reflection and group discussion.)

Taking as your reference point the most recent detailed list of NC aims to which you have access (or, if you prefer, any other detailed list of aims to which you and your fellow student teachers have access), consider how far these aims could be realised through aspects of the *formal* curriculum. For reasons of time, you will probably be able to concentrate on only a limited number of the aims listed. For each aim you consider, ask which (if any) subject on the formal curriculum would be relevant to the realisation of this aim.

For each subject you consider to be relevant, ask which particular aspects of that subject would help to realise the aim in question. Is there something in the subject content that would need to be emphasised, or something that would need to be specially added, if the subject is to help towards the realisation of this aim? Or would some part of the content have to be approached in a particular way?

If it is hard to see how the aim in question could be pursued through subjects in the formal curriculum, what about the informal curriculum?

Store your findings in your PDP.

Relating curriculum subjects to wider aims

In the task you have just carried out, you may well have identified some aims to which the teaching of traditional curriculum subjects clearly is relevant: promoting pupils' intellectual development, for instance, and promoting their learning and achievement (at any rate, achievement within those subjects, although there are other kinds of achievement as well). But we saw above, some other sorts of aims. Here are a few more: that pupils should 'relate well to others and form good relationships', be 'willing to try new things and make the most of opportunities' or 'appreciate the benefits of diversity'. We may think of these as broader aims of an emotional, moral and social kind. Such aims have always been recognised in NC documents since 1988 and have gained greater prominence in later versions. It seems likely that a school that gave its attention *only* to the teaching of traditional subjects as discrete entities might fail to be addressing such aims at all.

The first version of the NC in England and Wales, brought in by the Education Reform Act 1988, attempted to address such aims within the curriculum by incorporating a number of cross-curricular themes: health education, citizenship education, careers education and guidance, environmental education, and education for economic and industrial understanding. These themes did not have the statutory force of the core and foundation subjects, and it was left largely to individual schools (with limited published guidance) to decide how to teach them. In fact, in many schools, the cross-curricular themes were not systematically taken up at all. Of the original cross-curricular themes, only citizenship has gained the status of a statutory subject, and the other areas are no longer there as distinct themes. Health was taken up within the broader area of personal, social and health education (PSHE), which became a recognised part of the NC for England in 2008.

It remains true that the content of the National Curriculum very much revolves around a list of subjects, and that these subjects, to a large extent, were ones that had been in the curricula of schools for a long time. How far can the inclusion of these subjects be justified, not just because they have traditionally been in the curriculum, but because they can actually be shown to contribute to the stated aims of the curriculum? Questions can be raised about the contribution of individual subjects to the overall aims of the curriculum. How such questions are answered not only bears on the justification of particular subjects being in a compulsory curriculum at all, but can also make a difference to the aims of a teacher of a particular subject. In science and mathematics, what is the balance between equipping pupils with skills that they can put to practical use (thus furthering training and employment opportunities) and trying to show pupils something of the sheer fascination that science and mathematics can hold quite apart from their applications? In English, what is the balance to studying a canon of classical literature and exploring the writings and culture of a variety of writers using English as a world language? Similar questions can be raised about other subjects. The book *Rethinking the School Curriculum: Values, Aims and Purposes* (White 2004) devotes a chapter to each subject of the National Curriculum, with the exception of PSHE, citizenship, and information and communications technology (ICT), and also to religious education. The discussions and further references in that book help you in thinking about the role of your own subject within the whole curriculum (see also Task 7.2.3).

M

 Task 7.2.3 Justifying your subject in the school curriculum

This can be a two-part task, with an individual stage followed by a group stage.

The task is to contribute to a school prospectus (it might be for the same imaginary school that you used in Task 7.1.2.). Suppose now that the school is trying to follow the statement of aims from a specific national curriculum. At the same time, remember that the national curriculum you are referring to does not necessarily attempt to prescribe the *whole* curriculum for the school (see the section above on relating curriculum to aims).

Your individual task is to write a paragraph of not more than 100 words setting out for prospective parents the ways in which your teaching subject fits into the whole curriculum, and thus contributes to realising the overall aims of the curriculum. (Remember that some parents – and pupils – may wonder what the point of studying certain subjects is at all.)

The group task for you and your fellow student teachers, representing different subjects, is to make sure that the individual subject statements fit together into a coherent description of a curriculum, complementing and not competing with each other. In addition to your individual subjects, you may add any elements you consider necessary to complete the whole curriculum of the school. Then, cooperatively, draft in not more than 200 words a statement for the prospectus outlining and promoting the whole curriculum of the school.

Reflect on this task and check your development against the standards for your ITE programme. File your statement in your PDP.

SUMMARY AND KEY POINTS

■ The curriculum is perhaps the most important means through which educational aims can be pursued.

■ Any curriculum is a selection from the culture of a society. The attempt to select what is best or distinctive or fundamental may not be adequate without a view of the overall aims of education.

■ The curriculum includes both the *formal curriculum*, which sets out in detail the subjects to be taught; the *informal curriculum*, which covers the variety of ways in which a school can attempt to achieve the kinds of aims that cannot be captured in the content of timetabled subjects; and the *hidden curriculum*, which is the way the school relates to pupils and parents, sometimes referred to as the ethos of a school.

■ You should get the opportunity to contribute to discussion and planning about the curriculum, and should be able to take and argue a view, both on the whole curriculum and on the place of your own subject within it.

■ 'Curriculum studies' is a subject area in its own right within educational research and theory and has a large literature. Some of this is in the further reading below.

■ Finally, a reminder that Unit 7.1 should be read in conjunction with this unit.

Check which requirements for your ITE programme you have addressed through this unit.

Further reading

Reiss, M. and White, J. (2013) *An Aims Based Curriculum*, London: IoE Press.
  This book sets out an alternative to a subjects-based curriculum having as its starting point not subjects, but a question about what schools should be for, which Reiss and White state as to equip each learner to lead a personally fulfilling life and help others do so too. From these, they derive more specific aims covering the personal qualities, skills and understanding needed for a life of personal, civic and vocational well-being, and from this a discussion about how curricula could be designed in different ways, in different schools, starting with aims and not subjects.

Aldrich, R. and White, J. (1998) *The National Curriculum beyond 2000: The QCA and the Aims of Education*, London: Institute of Education, University of London.
  With contributions from a historian and a philosopher, this argues for basing the curriculum on an explicit consideration of aims, and for deriving these aims from democratic values.

Lawton, D. (1996) *Beyond the National Curriculum: Teacher Professionalism and Empowerment*, Sevenoaks: Hodder & Stoughton.
  From one of the major British contributors to curriculum studies, this, as the title implies, considers not just the National Curriculum, but how the curriculum impinges on teachers and how teachers can be involved in curriculum planning.

Other resources and websites

Note: With changing government policies on education, URLs for the relevant documentation on the National Curriculum have also changed from time to time. It should not be difficult for you to find the most recent official documentation from the relevant government department or agency. Your tutor will be able to guide you.

National Curriculum in England: www.gov.uk/government/publications/national-curriculum-in-england-framework-for-key-stages-1-to-4/the-national-curriculum-in-england-framework-for-key-stages-1-to-4

Scottish National Curriculum: www.ltscotland.org.uk/5to14/guidelines/

Welsh National Curriculum: http://wales.gov.uk/topics/educationandskills/schoolshome/curriculuminwales/arevisedcurriculumforwales/?lang=en

National Curriculum in Northern Ireland: www.nicurriculum.org.uk/

Appendix 2 on pages 591–595 provides examples of further websites you may find useful.

Capel, S., Leask, M. and Turner, T. (eds) (2010) *Readings for Learning to Teach in the Secondary School: A Companion to M Level Study*, London: Routledge.
This book brings together essential readings to support you in your critical engagement with key issues raised in this textbook.

The subject-specific books in the Routledge *Learning to Teach* series are also very useful.

Any additional resources and an editable version of any relevant tasks/tables in this unit are available on the companion website: www.routledge.com/cw/capel

7.3 International education comparisons

Understanding UK education in an international context

Andrea Raiker and Matti Rautiainen

Introduction

This unit challenges you to consider viewpoints and practices from other cultures. You may find that others in your group or school have been educated or taught in other countries, so this unit provides an opportunity to draw on these resources too. We suggest it is difficult to gain insights into the social and cultural constructs of what teachers do and are in your own country until you consider teaching and learning approaches in other countries, approaches that have arisen from differing historical, socio-economic and political processes and events. In your own country, you may 'not be able to see the wood for the trees'.

Gaining such insights is important for your development as an educator. While learning to be a teacher, you are encouraged to be reflective and critical of your reading and your practice. This is essential for your professionalism. Freire, an influential Brazilian educator (cited in Leach and Moon 1999: 53), suggests teachers should be critical of what is taught and why. It is not enough, for example, to uphold learner-centred teaching or group work because that is what other teachers do in school. Teachers must question and reflect on their personal understandings of the nature of knowledge and its acquisition. You should expect over time to develop your professional knowledge base. This includes finding out about education systems and practices other than your own. By questioning and reflecting upon your knowledge, you gain insights on your identity as a teacher, your understanding of why you teach as you do, and the possibilities for positive change to benefit learners. You also come to have a greater understanding not only of issues in your own system, but also of how countries address similar or emerging problems.

OBJECTIVES

At the end of this unit, you should be able to:

- demonstrate an awareness of how educational practices can vary between countries;
- identify aspects of good practice from another country that could be tried out in schools in your country;

■ identify aspects of good practice in your country that could be adopted by another country;

■ find databases and literature to gain insights on the United Kingdom (UK) and other education systems;

■ understand and apply theories that explore the complexity of relationships between individuals in schools.

Check the requirements of your initial teacher education (ITE) programme to see which relate to this unit.

International comparisons

International comparisons in education are becoming increasingly important. Governments throughout the world are using them to identify nations that are high-achieving. The most recent Organisation for Economic Co-operation and Development (OECD) Programme for International Student Assessment (PISA) survey of 65 countries (OECD 2014) shows that UK pupils' performance compared with other countries continues to cause concern. Since the 2000 survey, the UK has slipped from seventh to twenty-third in reading, although this shows improvement over the 2009 PISA position of twenty-fifth. In mathematics, the UK has fallen from eighth to twenty-sixth and from fourth to twenty-first in science. Assumptions in the UK that the education system had maintained excellence and high standards were undermined by these results. In comparison, in the 2012 PISA (OECD 2014) exercise, Finland came sixth in reading, twelfth overall in mathematics and fifth in science. These results are not as good as in the 2009 PISA exercise (third in reading, fifth in mathematics and second in science); nevertheless, Finland's results are considerably better than the UK's. As Finland is a Western European country, the attainment of their pupils has been the focus of direct interest to politicians with educational responsibilities in the UK for some years. For this reason, this unit refers particularly to educational practices in Finland.

Issues arising from comparing statistical data from the UK and Finland

The drawbacks of tests such as PISA (for example, issues with eradication of cultural bias, decontextualisation and the secrecy behind the whole process) (Sjøberg 2007) do not appear in government documentation and discussion.

In considering the Finnish success in PISA, it must also be remembered that Finland has a small population of just over 5.47 million (density 17.94/km^2) (Statistics Finland 2015) compared with approximately 64.1 million in the UK and 53.9 million living in England (density 413/km^2) (ONS 2014). Only 5 per cent of Finnish citizens do not have Finnish as mother tongue, and most of these are Finnish born but live in the Swedish-speaking south and south-west or in the Sami-speaking north (Statistics Finland 2011). In comparison, 80.5 per cent of the UK population is white British, meaning that 19.5 per cent, or 3,100,000 people, are from other ethnic groups (ONS 2011).

The Office for Standards in Education (Ofsted), in its 2014 report, does not mention ethnicity impacting adversely on achievement. Its focus of concern is on low achievement by pupils from impoverished backgrounds and by white boys eligible for free school meals (see also Unit 4.4 for further information related to cultural diversity). Although PISA 2012 (OECD 2014) established that there continued to be significant differences in performance between UK schools but not between Finnish schools, both countries have similar reading performance and economic profiles. However, there is a marked difference in income inequality, with Finland having below OECD average income inequality and the UK above, though decreasing since 2009.

Despite the differences in population size, average class size is about the same at 20 pupils (DfE 2011h; Statistics Finland 2015).

The next section provides a summary of the Finnish system, and in order to help you articulate your educational philosophy you are asked to compare this system with your own and other systems you know well.

Education in Finland

The statutory age for starting school in England is 5; in Finland, children begin school the year they celebrate their seventh birthday (see Figure 7.3.1). Compulsory basic education then has nine grades compared with 11 in the English system. In Finnish schools the borderline between primary and secondary school traditionally lies between class 6 and class 7 (see Figure 7.3.1). In present-day schools in Finland, it is not at all unusual for a class teacher (a generalist) to take lessons in the lower secondary school (classes 7–9) and a subject specialist teacher to take lessons in the primary school (classes 1–6). School begins without subject differentiation; by the end of lower secondary school, it has already become tightly segmented around subjects.

In Finnish schools, pupils up to age 12 study two or three languages (mother tongue and foreign languages, mainly English), mathematics, biology, geography, chemistry, physics, history, religion, music, crafts, visual arts and physical education. Primary school teachers are required to be able to teach all these subjects except foreign languages. (In England, primary schools (that is, pupils up to age 11) have sessions devoted to number; language, including speaking, listening and writing; mathematics, science, arts, including singing, playing, drawing, painting; games/physical education (PE) as well as integrated studies. These have a soft subject focus. Primary teachers in the UK have a wide range of backgrounds, with some being specialists and others generalists.) The teaching of a foreign language in the primary school was introduced by the government in England in around 2003, education for primary teachers was established and then the requirement to teach a language was dropped in about 2011. Education through politicians' fads rather than any educational principle appears to be a feature of the English system. Scotland, Wales and Northern Ireland run their own education systems (for more information on the differences between the UK countries, see the companion website).

Schools are very similar all around Finland. There are only a few private schools, based on alternative pedagogical principles; for example, Steiner schools. This situation can be compared with the extensive English independent or private school system running parallel to the state system, which educates about 7 per cent of pupils. In Finland, children normally go to the nearest school regardless of social status. Schools are organised by municipality but are partly financed by the national government.

Curriculum guidelines are given by the national administration (www.oph.fi/english). A new curriculum for basic education is to be introduced on 1 August 2016. Schools and munincipalities are

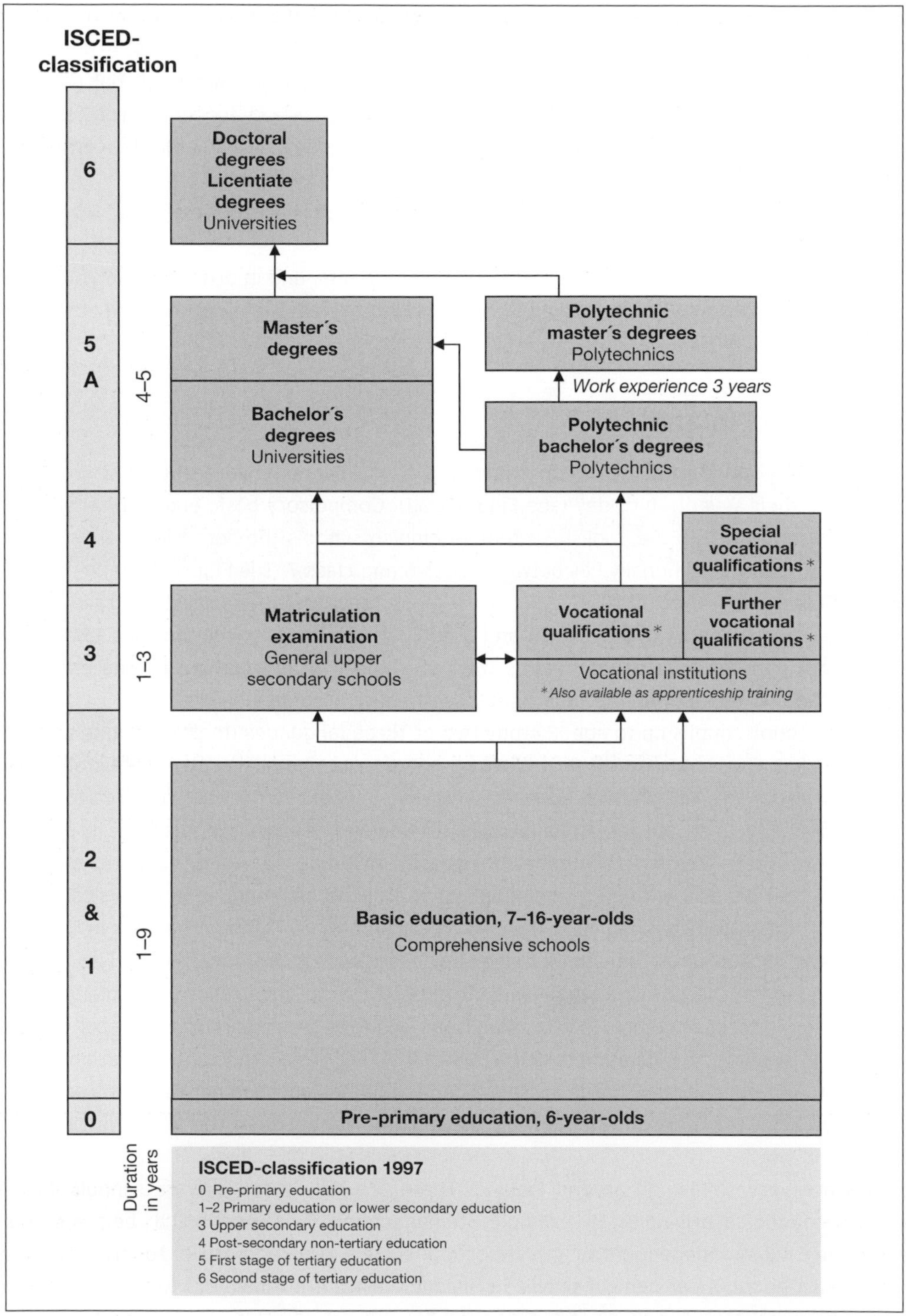

Figure 7.3.1 The Finnish education system 2015

Source: Ministry of Education and Culture, Finland (www.oph.fi/english)

Note: ISCED is 'International Standard Classification of Education'

in the process of adapting the new national core curriculum for the local context to include the following changes:

1   The learning culture should be based more on inquiry-oriented learning.
2   The learning culture in schools should be based more on action focused on democracy and pupils' participation.
3   There should be closer interaction between schools and other stakeholders in society.

In addition, the preschool year that is, at present, optional will become compulsory from 1 August 2016 for all children.

Autonomy and pedagogical freedom are crucial aspects of teacher identity in Finland. Parents appear to have confidence that their children receive the same quality of education regardless of the school. This confidence is placed, above all, in the system and in teachers, whose professional skill is trusted. In the school culture itself, this trust is manifested as the considerable pedagogical autonomy of teachers, with their work not subject to any supervisory or control mechanism.

At the level of the basic school, there is no nationwide system of evaluation that applies to all schools. Assessment is done by the teacher following final-assessment criteria defined in the National Core Curriculum for Basic Education. The system has its critics. Since assessment is in the hands of the teacher, some people regard the system as unfair because it is open to the potential of bias or discrimination; for example, from the viewpoint of applying for further studies. Task 7.3.1 asks you to compare accountability systems in Finland with those in your own country.

 Task 7.3.1 Comparing accountability systems in your country with those in Finland

Compare the Finnish system of trust in the schools and the teachers with the inspection systems in your context. What might be the implications of there being no national check that the curriculum is being followed? Or how good or poor teachers are? Or how weak teachers are given support? Or how weaker-performing schools are recognised and given support? Unit 8.3 sets out the expectations of professional accountability for a teacher and provides information to help you with this task.

Discuss these issues with other student teachers and record the results in your professional development portfolio (PDP).

The international assessment studies show that the differences in levels of achievement between Finnish schools are small; in other words, the basic school's principle of equality has been realised well, but the most recent results also show a trend towards inequality. Although teachers in the basic school enjoy a high social status and university class teacher courses are oversubscribed, it has occasionally been difficult to find qualified teachers for remote areas or the capital region. Both the population of cities becoming more multicultural and the continuing rural depopulation confront schools with huge challenges. In the inner cities, the school population is changing from a homogeneous one to a more mixed one, and in the rural areas schools are closing.

All secondary school teachers – called subject teachers – qualify through successfully completing a course in pedagogical studies (60 European credit transfer and accumulation system (ECTS), which is equal to 120 UK credits) as part of, or in addition to, their master's degree. Student teachers have to pass aptitude tests to assess their suitability as prospective teachers before they can start their studies. Universities have the autonomy to make decisions concerning these aptitude tests, which usually include an interview, group exercise, psychological tests and different types of written tests. Pedagogical studies contain educational theory and practice, which is mainly done in the teacher training school (*normaalikoulu*). All universities having departments of teacher education have their own *normaalikoulu*. There have always been tensions between theory and practice in teacher education and the teaching profession in Finland. When teacher education took place in training colleges, the skills of teaching were emphasised. Today, all teacher education takes place in universities and the teacher education curriculum has become more theoretical. Student teachers must acquire knowledge and understanding of the theoretic underpinnings of both teaching and learning.

A case study from a Finnish classroom

While statistical data are useful in identifying trends that might indicate causal relationships and correlations, qualitative data can provide depth and richness when considering classroom practice. In this section, an extract from a field diary entry from qualitative research undertaken in Finnish municipal and teacher training schools is used as the basis for comparing the English and Finnish methods of educating teachers and teaching pupils (Raiker 2011). The mathematics lesson recounted below was delivered in the junior secondary school at Jyväskylä *normaalikoulu* (the seventh largest city in Finland) to 17 pupils aged 13/14 years (Grade 7, first year of lower secondary school). Typically, lesson periods in Finnish schools in grades 1–9 are 45 minutes long, separated by 15-minute breaks. There is some research (Goverover *et al.* 2009) that suggests breaks allow time for neural connections to be strengthened, thus supporting learning (see Unit 5.6).

The lesson was led by two student teachers in the second year of their five-year course. The student teachers did not have formal lesson plans as they based their lesson on the Grade 7 mathematics textbook. The textbook is seen as a way of providing a common learning environment, in this case for mathematics. It is seen as a way of ensuring inclusion. Views on the use of textbooks vary between countries. In England, it is not uncommon to find teachers with views that textbooks are a constraint on teacher initiative and freedom to interpret the curriculum and that novice teachers need to learn how to construct their own lessons to meet new situations and the needs of the pupil.

The pupils waited outside the door until Student Teacher A brought them into class. The pupils in the class were of mixed ability, as are all classes in Finland. In this class was a Japanese boy who was having difficulty learning Finnish. A message giving general information on school matters was broadcast through loudspeakers in all classrooms followed by music. This approach is used to normalise behaviour. A pupil late for class knocked to be admitted after the music stopped.

The lesson was 'teaching from the front' with no peer-to-peer interaction and the pace was slow in comparison with English classroom practice. The Finnish method is to develop understanding slowly by working steadily through the grade's textbook. All subjects (apart from art, craft, PE and, to some extent, music) are taught with reference to textbooks so student teachers have to become familiar with them. Teachers' handbooks that suggest practical activities and pedagogy for complete lessons accompany the textbooks. Textbooks have homework sections, practice sections and problem-solving sections. They begin with recapping key aspects of the previous year's work, but after this there is little repetition. In England, teachers complain at times about teaching to the test. Here, teachers may be teaching to the textbook. You may like to consider the differences between the two approaches.

Student Teacher A asked the pupils to get out their textbooks, which they own. These were of the write-on format so that pupils could have both questions and answers clearly recorded in the same book. Student Teacher A used a visualiser to show the textbook page. He picked a pupil to come to the visualiser, show the class her work and explain her answer. Her answer was incorrect, so Student Teacher A laid a sheet of paper on her book under the visualiser, and explained with workings how to reach the right answer. The pupil showed no anxiety. Getting answers wrong is considered an essential part of learning and developing self-efficacy, not an indication of weakness or inability.

Student Teacher A began the main lesson on algebra by displaying a textbook page on the interactive whiteboard, but he demonstrated through worked examples on the blackboard. He questioned pupils and asked them to come to the board to complete parts of the task. Then four examples were set. As the pupils worked in their textbooks, the student teachers went round the class to each pupil. The Japanese boy was visited more frequently than the other pupils. It should be noted that all support was by the student teachers and not other pupils. Peer and group work is infrequently used to support learning. Early-finishing pupils are not given any further work to do. Lack of stretching able pupils has been noted as a downside of the Finnish system (Ofsted 2010d; Heikkinen *et al.* 2011). Student Teacher B then took over and taught in a similar fashion. There was no marking of work, or collection of work to be marked. Marking is not a feature of the Finnish system. Formative assessment on individual pupil progress by the teacher is a mental, inwardly recorded process, communicated to the pupil on the spot, either during shared homework discussion time or as the teacher circulates while the pupils are engaged with in-class tasks. There is no formal teacher record-keeping, but all teachers have a record system of their own. There is also at least one meeting with parents every year, when the teacher deals with pupils' progress and behaviour in the school.

Assessment and SEND (special educational needs and disability)

Summative teacher assessment occurs through testing at the end of each topic of work within the textbook, again to inform on individual progress. Teacher responsibilities include identifying and addressing individual pupils' needs as soon as they arise; the pupil's responsibility is to work to the best of their ability and to make the most of the activities and support offered. Unlike the UK, Finland does not have a statutory code directing the identification of and procedures related to special education needs and disability (SEND). It is the professional role of the teacher to identify areas where individual pupils fall behind and to address them immediately. Unlike in the UK, there are relatively few SEND teachers and fewer teaching assistants to support pupils in class (Raiker 2011).

Teacher education

In Finland, the number of student teachers educated per year per head of population is similar to that in the UK, but the system is different, with training schools attached to universities. Training schools attached to universities were in fashion in the UK about 50 years ago and have been reintroduced in England by the UK government elected in 2010. There are advantages and disadvantages to the approach. For example, student teachers may not gain as much experience controlling a class alone as they might where there are only a few student teachers in a school, as in much of the UK system, but there are advantages in being part of a group of student teachers who are at similar stages in their learning and who can learn from, challenge and support each other. Teaching assistants in Finland are expected to have degrees.

Values

According to Finland's National Board of Education (www.oph.fi/english), the key words in their educational policy are quality, efficiency, equity and internationalisation. Education is seen as necessary for global competitiveness. There are also specific issues that have to be addressed. For example, in 2010, Finland took top place in the International Civic and Citizenship Education Study, which looked at the civic knowledge, skills, values and attitudes of young people. The results showed that the civic knowledge of young Finns in the eighth class of comprehensive education (Year 10 in the UK) ranked among the highest in the world. However, when attention was shifted from knowledge to attitudes, and particularly to participatory culture, Finland came out near the bottom. Only a small minority of young people are interested in politics, or even indeed in civic activity; that is, participating in the activities of the community (Kerr *et al.* 2010). A further International Civic and Citizenship Education Study will be carried out in 2015, with results published in 2017. Finnish educators are hopeful that the results will show improvement in this area. Aspects of the education system in Finland are discussed in the following section as politicians in European countries often use Finland as an example of an effective education system because of its high PISA scores.

Considering the advantages and disadvantages of the Finnish model

Finland has been named in English educational policy documents as one of the countries that has managed to close the socio-economic gap and increase attainment at the same time (for example, DfE 2010a). It has been suggested that applying key aspects of Finnish education to the English system would be beneficial. However Ofsted, in its report on Finnish pupils' success in mathematics, has advised that 'aspects of the current Finnish approach might not be transferred easily to the current English context' (Ofsted 2010e: 6). The question immediately arises: why not? Many points of difference can be identified through the information above and the case study. Table 7.3.1 summarises key points of comparison between the Finnish and English education systems (Raiker 2011), and Task 7.3.2 asks you to consider these, identify what you consider the advantages and disadvantages, and discuss these with your tutor or other student teachers.

As is clear from Table 7.3.1 and the other information provided, there are many other points of difference between the Finnish and the English systems. Task 7.3.2 is intended to help you be clear about your own values and what you consider good practice in education.

Should you wish to find out more information about international comparisons, we suggest you start by consulting the major databases listed in Table 7.3.2, which can be easily found on the Web.

Table 7.3.1 Selected points of comparison between the Finnish and English education systems

	Finland	England
Teacher qualifications	A qualified teacher has to have an internationally recognised master's-level qualification in education (following five years study) (Hobson *et al.* 2010). Criteria for qualified teacher status vary across Finnish universities but there is cooperation between them (FTTS 2011).	A qualified teacher has to attain the government initiated national standard of qualified teacher status (QTS), which does not have international recognition.
Initial teacher education (ITE)	Five years ITE is required, theory is seen as equally important as practice.	ITE for those with a subject degree varies from on the job entirely, from six-week courses to three- or four-year undergraduate courses, with four-year undergraduate degrees being phased out and replaced by three-year degrees. There are diverse views in England about the role of universities in ITE, with a Parliamentary Select Committee for Education saying universities should have a role and government policy supporting ITE organisations with no links with universities.*
Teacher status	Highly regarded. Teaching is considered as a profession to be comparable with medicine and law.	Respected by parents. Regarded as a lower-level profession than medicine and law.
Teacher autonomy	Finnish teachers' professional competence is trusted by stakeholders such as parents and politicians (Sahlberg 2011; Ofsted 2010e). In Finland, practising teachers are considered to be the experts in teaching and learning.	Politicians and Ofsted inspectors consider themselves the experts.
Accountability	In Finland, there is no equivalent to the UK's inspection regimes. Teachers are accountable to parents and the community.	Inspection is high-stakes in England, with schools and teachers labelled from outstanding to failing. In the UK, inspection is undertaken by the Office for Standards in Education (Ofsted) in England, Education and Training Inspectorate (ESTYN) in Wales, Her Majesty's Inspectorate (HMI) in Scotland, and Education and Training Inspectorate (ETINI) in Northern Ireland. In England, Ofsted is a centralised inspection system with no responsibility for teacher or school advice and support.

Table 7.3.1 continued

	Finland	England
Assessment	In Finland, there are no national examinations similar to Standard Assessment Tests (SATs). The first national examination taken by Finnish pupils is the Matriculation Examination at the end of upper secondary education when pupils are approximately 18 or 19 years old. Tests in schools are devised and marked by teachers to inform themselves and parents of individual progress.	There are teacher assessments, SATs, General Certificate of Secondary Education (GCSE), Advanced (A) level exams, and so on. Assessment of individual pupils introduces competitiveness and categorises pupils into ability groups, allowing parents and pupils to make comparisons. This is possibly an unintended consequence.
Use of data	There is no emphasis on the production of data for internal or external use, and there are no league tables. Finland, in contrast to England, is not driven by private sector performance criteria (Sahlberg 2011).	Government produces benchmarking data that are used by each school to compare school and individual pupil performance. Data about performance in SATS, GCSE, A level, and so on is public. Schools gather and use a considerable amount of data on a wide range of issues.
Class organisation	There are no ability groupings or class streaming; all classes are of mixed ability in Finland.	Class streaming and ability groups are common. Mixed-ability teaching is not acceptable to many influential politicians, the press and some teachers.
Types of school	There is just one type of school, comprehensive. There is little class difference.	There is increasing diversity in schools, including academies, free schools and independent schools. Independent schools perpetuate class differences. In England, the comprehensive school system (with pupils of all abilities in the same school) has been labelled a failure by some politicians.
Pupil diversity	The population is 95 per cent Finnish and speaks Finnish as a first language.	High diversity in urban areas.
Curriculum	Common textbooks, co-authored by teachers, direct teaching. The teacher's role is to ensure that no pupil is left behind and every pupil achieves standards set by teachers representing the community.	In England, the National Curriculum is centrally directed and has been changed five times in 25 years. The teacher's role is to deliver the curriculum to government-prescribed standards. Whether pupils have textbooks depends on whether the school decides to spend money on textbooks. These are not usually owned by the individual and have to be returned to the school.

	Finland	England
Teaching assistants	Teaching assistants are expected to have a vocational qualification in an appropriate area of study, usually through a one-year course.	There is no standard qualification. The qualifications of teaching assistants vary considerably, even though it is common practice that they work with the least able pupils.
School starting age	Formal schooling starts at age 7.	Formal schooling starts at age 5.
School structure	Change of schools occurs around 13 years but some primary and secondary schools are on the same site.	Change of schools can be at 8 or 9 and again at 13 for middle school systems or at 11 for primary and secondary systems. Independent schools are typically all-age schools. Research in England shows that the least able pupils regress in their learning when they change schools.**
Structure of the day	There is a 15-minute break between lessons where pupils can talk with teachers if necessary.	There is a mid-morning 15-minute break between usually four lessons. Afternoon often two or three consecutive lessons. Neuroscience research indicates that 'spaced learning' with very short intense learning periods followed by a break can promote effective learning, but this is not widely applied.>

* Parliamentary Select Committee for Education (2012)

** See Galton *et al.* (1999)

🖊 **Task 7.3.2 Identifying good practice transferable from one country to another**

Using the information in Table 7.3.1 and in the case study and other information provided, consider what aspects of the Finnish educational model you would like to see adopted in the system in which you work. If you have knowledge of other systems, include an analysis of these in this task as well.

What aspects of the Finnish educational model or other models with which you are familiar would you not like to see adopted in the system in which you work?

Record the reasons for your choices and why a government would be likely or unlikely to adopt the aspects you identify.

Discuss your ideas with your tutor or with other student teachers. Record the outcomes of the discussions in your PDP.

Table 7.3.2 Data sources for international comparisons of educational systems and pupil attainment

- ■ Your own country's government education website and statistics department; for example, the UK's Department for Education (www.education.gov.uk/) and the Office for National Statistics (www.ons.gov.uk/)
- ■ United Nations Educational, Scientific and Cultural Organisation (UNESCO)
- ■ The UNESCO Institute for National Statistics
- ■ The UNESCO Centre for Comparative Education Research
- ■ PISA
- ■ Key Data on Education in Europe 2012: http://eacea.ec.europa.eu/education/eurydice/documents/key_data_series/134EN.pdf
- ■ The Institute of Education Science at the US Department of Education National Centre for Education Statistics, includes The Trends in International Mathematics and Science Study (TIMSS) data
- ■ The Finnish National Board for Education (www.oph.fi/english)
- ■ The International Association for the Evaluation of Educational Achievement (IEA)
- ■ The Finnish Institute for Educational Research (https://ktl.jyu.fi/en)
- ■ The Organisation for Economic Co-operation and Development (OECD) – the Progress International Reading Literacy Study (PIRLS)
- ■ Websites of universities educating teachers; for example, in Finland www.jyu.fi/edu/en (University of Jyväskylä; www.helsinki.fi/teachereducation/ (University of Helsinki); www.oulu.fi/edu/ (University of Oulu).

Internationalisation of classrooms

Knowing and understanding aspects of teaching and learning in other countries is not simply an academic exercise. Globalisation and mobility have resulted in the populations in many countries, including those in the UK, becoming multicultural and multi-ethnic. You can expect to have pupils in your classes who have experience of very different education systems and who have been taught in ways you yourself may not recognise; for example, in mathematical operations. Gaining insights into the heritages and the diverse experiences of the pupils you teach not only enables you to adopt a personalised approach to their learning (see also Unit 5.5 on personalising learning), but your insights help you create a classroom environment that supports greater levels of trust, tolerance, respect and understanding of national and global citizenship (see also Unit 4.4 on diversity in the classroom). These are crucial traits to develop in pupils as the interdependence of societies and cultures is becoming increasingly evident.

Using Bourdieu's theory to analyse the complex relationships existing in multicultural classrooms

In this unit, you have been introduced to some of the differences that occur in the European educational context. Your classroom is likely to include pupils from many countries. Your responsibility as a teacher is to understand how the backgrounds of your pupils may affect their approach and that of their parents to schooling (see also Unit 4.4).

Some educators find a useful framework for exploring the complexity of a multicultural classroom is provided by the work of French educationalist and anthropologist Pierre Bourdieu (1930–2002). To help you understand key elements of Bourdieu's work, we invite you to consider your own situation at this moment. You are in the process of learning how to be a secondary school teacher. You are becoming an expert in your subject and now you are learning how to infuse your young people with your knowledge, understanding and passion for your discipline. Whatever learning environment you are in, your learning is bounded by the lecturers and teachers who are educating you, your university and/or school, by the local authority in which you are experiencing teaching, and by the documentation and legal requirements emanating from national government. A theoretical perspective on this boundedness is given by Bourdieu's work. The key elements of his theory are *habitus*, *field* and *cultural capital*. Bourdieu's ideas have also been briefly mentioned in Unit 4.4.

Habitus is everything that you have learned and experienced in the past that has resulted in 'you' at this present time. This includes the learning you are undertaking to become a teacher. The environment in which you are learning and practising Bourdieu would term 'field'. A field has its own particular perceptions of orthodoxy or conformity – of place, language, dress, behaviour, activities, hierarchies of power, and so on.

Pupils come from different backgrounds (fields) with, for example, different experiences, personalities, abilities, motivations, expectations and attitudes (habitus). Somehow or other, you, as a secondary teacher, must create a learning environment or field where all pupils feel comfortable and ready to learn. The result of your endeavours will be that each pupil leaves your class with cultural capital, learning that can be traded for something else. For example, the cultural capital gained could be knowledge and skills that could be traded for a paid job, or examination results that could be traded for a university place. Providing the right experiences for pupils to maximise their cultural capital at secondary school is of great importance (see also Unit 4.4).

Education systems are the result of complex political, socio-economic, historical and cultural factors. So the classroom learning environment, a field, in one country has significant differences to a classroom in another. These same complex factors influence the backgrounds or habitus of all teachers and all pupils, whether they teach and learn in Shanghai (China), Korea or Finland. Yet, in spite of these differences, surveys are undertaken that aim to compare the attainment of pupils in these very differing countries and others throughout the world (over 60 in each survey). These surveys include PISA or TIMSS (see Table 7.3.1). Pupils in Shanghai, Korea and Finland attain more highly than those in the UK. Does this mean schools and teachers in the UK are not as good as these high-achieving countries? Are there other factors at play?

Importantly, can we learn what these factors might be from looking at another country's practices? This unit is intended to help you gain perspective by looking at practice in another country (for example, Finland) and to help you to teach pupils from diverse cultural and social backgrounds (fields) more empathetically and effectively. Pupils in your multicultural classroom may have many expectations of you and the education system. These expectations are derived from quite different education systems with quite different practices and values. As a teacher, you need to be aware of, and accommodate through your teaching, this diversity of background and expectation.

Task 7.3.3 is intended to help you to identify and analyse the complex relationships you find in classrooms – applying Bourdieu's theory.

M

Task 7.3.3 Identifying and analysing the complex relationships you encounter in classrooms – applying Bourdieu's theory

Think about your classroom. Every pupil has a different background (habitus), which is brought to the learning environment in the classroom (field). What are the implications of this for teaching and learning? Does an understanding of habitus and field explain why some students are particularly diligent in their studies and why there could be behaviour problems for some pupils?

The term cultural capital implies aspects of learning that a culture finds valuable as they are worthy of trade. What aspects of what you teach are considered valuable by your culture, and why? What cultural capital does a pupil receive in the course of a school year? For what can they trade that cultural capital?

Discuss these issues with other student teachers and record the outcomes of your discussions in your PDP.

SUMMARY AND KEY POINTS

■ The aims of an education system reflect the value system of the people who determine what is taught and how it is taught. In England, those people are politicians.

■ The value system politicians hold is reflected in how the curriculum in England is set up, its aims and how it is to be taught. In that sense, what is taught and how it is taught is socially and culturally determined.

■ It is in our interests as teachers and in the interests of the pupils we teach to know and understand different ways of educating and the historical, socio-economic and cultural constructs from which they emanate.

■ Because of the interconnectedness caused by globalisation, problems of one nation's education system today become the problems of another tomorrow.

■ How individual countries tackle these problems varies because of local and regional differences.

■ Your role as a teacher now includes a responsibility to learn about other countries' practices and outcomes. In doing so, your awareness of these global problems will grow so that you can 'see the wood for the trees' and take action in your own classroom.

Check which requirements for your ITE programme you have addressed through this unit.

 Further reading

Arnove, R.F. and Torres, C.A. (eds) (2007) *Comparative Education: The Dialectic of the Global and the Local*, Lanham, MA: Rowman & Littlefield.
  An introduction to the problems caused to education systems around the world by social interconnectedness and globalisation of economies.

Grenfell, M. and James, D. (1998) *Bourdieu and Education*, London: Falmer Press.
  Bourdieu's theories applied to pedagogy, with particular reference to gender, language, career decision-making and higher education. Bourdieu's interest in the position of the researcher in research and the implications of this for methodology are analysed and evaluated.

Hobson, A.J., Ashby, P., McIntyre, J. and Malderez, A. (2010) *International Approaches to Teacher Selection and Recruitment*, OECD Education Working Papers No. 47, OECD Publishing.
  A review of the literature describing how different countries select and recruit teachers, and in particular focusing on assessment of teacher readiness to take up teaching posts.

Sahlberg, P. (2011) *'Finnish Lessons'. What Can the World Learn from Educational Change in Finland?* New York: Teachers College Press.
  An investigation into how a small country has managed to achieve in international tests, plus an evaluation of why various strategies might or might not translate to other less successful countries.

 Other resources and websites

Appendix 2 on pages 591–595 provides examples of websites you may find useful.

Capel, S., Leask, M. and Turner, T. (eds) (2010) *Readings for Learning to Teach in the Secondary School: A Companion to M Level Study*, London: Routledge.
  This book brings together essential readings to support you in your critical engagement with key issues raised in this textbook.

The subject-specific books in the Routledge *Learning to Teach* series are also very useful.

 Any additional resources and an editable version of any relevant tasks/tables in this unit are available on the companion website: www.routledge.com/cw/capel

8 Your professional development

In this chapter, we consider life beyond your student teaching experience. The chapter is designed to prepare you for applying for your first post and to make you aware of the opportunities available to continue your professional development as a teacher after you have completed your initial teacher education (ITE) programme. Society is constantly changing, and so the demands society places on teachers change. Consequently, as your career progresses, you will find you need new skills and knowledge about teaching and learning (pedagogy), so you can expect to continue to learn through your career. Professional development is therefore a lifelong process that is aided by regular reflection on practice and continuing education. The chapter also provides an overview of accountability, and contractual and statutory duties. It contains three units.

Getting a job at the end of your initial teacher education is important, time-consuming and a high priority for student teachers. Unit 8.1 is designed to help you at every stage of the process of getting your first post. It takes you through the stages of considering, once again, why you want to enter the teaching profession; deciding where, and in what type of school, you want to teach; looking for suitable vacancies; sending for further details of posts that interest you; making an application – asking referees, different methods of application – an application form, letter of application and a curriculum vitae; preparing for and attending an interview – including teaching a lesson as part of an interview; and accepting a post.

The success of any school depends on its staff. However, although you have successfully met the requirements to qualify as a teacher at the end of your ITE programme, you still have a lot to learn about teaching to increase your effectiveness. Unit 8.2 considers your further development as a teacher. It looks at planning your professional development, and the transition from student teacher to newly qualified teacher, focusing on five specific times – before you start the job, starting the job, after the first few weeks, over the course of the first year, and continuing professional development beyond the first year. It then focuses on your professional development to help you continue to learn and develop professionally throughout your career.

Unit 8.3 is designed to give you an insight into the system in which many of you will be working as teachers and your accountability, contractual and statutory duties. We look briefly at where teachers fit within the education system in the structure of the state education system in England and then at teachers' accountability: organisational, legal, professional and moral. This leads into a slightly fuller consideration of the legal duties and responsibilities, highlighting important legislation – including rights and responsibilities, child protection, safeguarding children and young people, the welfare of children and young people, special educational and physical needs, managing pupils' behaviour, and recruitment of teachers and other staff. Finally, the unit considers contractual requirements and statutory duties that govern the work of teachers.

8.1 Getting your first post

Julia Lawrence and Susan Capel

Introduction

Applying for and obtaining your first post is one of the most important decisions you make; therefore, it needs to be thought through and considered carefully. The process itself is more than just completing an application form. It involves a number of stages, each of which is equally important. You need to be clear about why you want to enter the teaching profession, as well as about where and in what type of school you want to teach. You need to look for suitable vacancies, select a post that interests you and request further details. You need to prepare your curriculum vitae (CV), write a letter of application and contact potential referees. Once these have been completed, you need to complete your application, prepare for and attend an interview in order to secure a full-time post.

There is a lot to do, and being organised and prepared are key elements to a successful outcome. There is usually a session or two in an initial teacher education (ITE) programme on applying for jobs. This may include support for writing your CV and letters of application and opportunities for mock interviews. You may be able to access further support from your careers advisors, and many schools now contact universities to come to speak to student teachers to share teaching opportunities within their school or across the alliances they may work with. You should make every effort to attend these. The aim of this unit is to offer advice and guidance to support you with the process of getting your first post.

OBJECTIVES

At the end of this unit, you should be able to:

- articulate why you want to enter the teaching profession;
- follow the procedure for, and the process of, applying for your first teaching post;
- make a written application;
- prepare for an interview for a teaching post.

Check the requirements of your ITE programme to see which relate to this unit.

Consider why you want to enter the teaching profession

In many respects, you have already joined the profession in undertaking your ITE programme. However, the type of ITE programme you have undertaken may now start to influence your future career aspirations. Having undertaken substantial periods of school experience, and being aware of the demanding nature of the profession that you are entering, now is the time to reaffirm the reasons for your decision to pursue a career in teaching, in preparation for questions you may be posed at interview.

Teaching is an attractive choice of career for many reasons, and different people have different reasons for wanting to become a teacher. For many, it is altruistic and intrinsic reasons that motivate them to enter the profession rather than the extrinsic rewards they might get. Your reasons might also influence your choice of post and the type of school in which you wish to teach.

Deciding where, and in what type of school, you want to teach

There are complexities involved in getting your first post; thus, it is best to consider the whole picture before you start applying, rather than finding things out once you have accepted a post. Deciding on the location in which you wish to teach is one of the first major decisions. You may be committed to teaching in a specific area because of family commitments or because you wish to stay close to where you have undertaken your ITE programme, where you have set up and established social networks, or because you would like to work in the school where you have undertaken school experience.

If you are committed to a specific area, you may need to consider the cost of renting or buying in the area. Whether you are renting, buying or already have accommodation, you need to consider the distance and the amount of time it may take to travel to and from work in order to determine the radius in which you can look for a post. The travel time to and from school is important, as you probably will not want a long journey in your first year of teaching when you are likely to be tired at the end of each day or when you have had a school commitment in the evening.

You also need to recognise that if you are limiting your search to a small and specific location, it may be difficult to find a post, and hence your employment opportunities may be limited. Popular areas may have few schools, low turnover of staff, or have a large number of applicants, especially if they are located close to a higher education institution (HEI) offering ITE programmes. Conversely, areas with no HEIs offering ITE programmes normally have fewer applications for posts.

Ask yourself, are your preferred areas popular and, if so, can you be flexible as to where you teach? The more flexible you can be increases the number of posts for which you might apply.

A number of student teachers look to teach abroad as a first teaching post. International schools offer many benefits, although you do need to understand the implication of taking this type of employment in terms of completing any induction period required, contributions to pensions, payment of taxes, and so on. Further, many countries require experience prior to appointment. You may also want to consider organisations such as Voluntary Service Overseas (VSO).

You should now spend some time thinking about where you want to teach by completing Task 8.1.1.

As well as location, consider the type of school in which you wish to work. Over recent years, the range of schools has increased. During your ITE programme, you should have been placed in different

Task 8.1.1 Where do you want to teach?

Think about where you would like to teach and how flexible you can be in where you can look for a post. List all areas in which you would consider working and find out as much information about these areas as you can; for example, transport networks, travelling time, local facilities, house rent or purchase prices. Talk to anyone you know who lives in these areas. If possible, visit the area so that you can get a 'general feel of the place'. You can find a list of schools in the area; for example, in the Education Authorities Directory and Annual. Store the information in your professional development portfolio (PDP) for later reference.

types of school. These might have varied in, for example, the general location (for example, rural or inner-city school), size, ethnic make-up, the general philosophy of the school, and independent as well as state sector. You may have surprised yourself by enjoying teaching in a type of school that you have not previously considered (for example, if you have an experience based in a special school). You may also have heard about other types of school from others. These will have provided you with an insight into different types of school and helped you to identify those in which you would prefer to teach.

Task 8.1.2 engages you in considering what type of school you might wish to work in.

 Task 8.1.2 What type of school do you want to teach in?

Think back to the types of school that you have experienced on school placement during your ITE programme. List positive aspects about working in the different types of school, opportunities you are/were able/not able to experience in these different types of school, and identify any experiences you felt you would like to focus on in your first teaching post.

From this, identify the types of school you would be happy to teach in (for example, state, independent, specialist school, academy, free school, sixth form college). Identify why you want to teach in that type of school.

Store this information in your PDP for use in planning applications.

Looking for suitable vacancies

The majority of advertisements for teaching posts in the UK are for specific posts in specific schools. Teaching posts are advertised in a number of places: the *Times Educational Supplement* (www.tes.co.uk), national press, local press/other local publications, school websites, employment websites (for example, www.eteach.com, www.jobsgopublic.com). Some local authorities operate newly qualified teacher (NQT) pools. On some occasions, schools contact ITE providers directly. You may also hear details of vacancies via your placement school. Many organisations, including schools, allow you to sign up for 'alerts', which means that you can receive regular updates on posts becoming available.

Advertisements occur year round. Traditionally, the majority of posts are for a September start, so the bulk of advertisements are published between March and May because teachers who are leaving at the end of the academic year are required to hand in their notice by the end of May. Try to set aside time each week to check vacancies. Apply for as many jobs as you want but do not apply for a job you do not want because you are panicking that you won't have a job for September. You should not be disheartened if you are unsuccessful for a post for a September start as January start dates are also common. Maternity cover is also worthwhile as you can still undertake your induction. Also, opportunities for work through a teaching supply agency may be available as a short-term solution to gain experience while you wait until opportunities arise within your chosen location. You may find that if you get a long-term supply post, you may be able to use some of this time against any induction period you may need to undertake.

Getting a job is not easy. You should therefore not close your mind to the range of options available to you. Try to be as flexible as you can.

Check your online professional identity

Throughout your ITE programme, issues around appropriate use of social media and safeguarding will have been highlighted. It is not uncommon for potential employers to check your online identity (for example, through Twitter, Facebook and LinkedIn). At this point, you should review all information about yourself that is on the Web and consider whether the way you present yourself online is appropriate for the professional you wish to be. Remember, your online identity is visible to potential employers, as well as the press, other teachers, pupils, parents and governors.

Selecting a post that interests you

You cannot start early enough in looking for appropriate posts. If an advertisement interests you, contact the school for further details. You can phone or email the school (the school secretary is a good starting point if the advertisement does not specify a point of contact); for example:

Dear Sir/Madam (or name if given in the advertisement)

I am interested in the vacancy for a (subject) teacher (quote reference number if one is given) at ABC school, advertised in (publication; for example, *Times Educational Supplement*) of (date) and would be grateful to receive further details of this post.

Yours faithfully (if you use Sir/Madam) or sincerely (if you use a name)

Making an application

Your application is the first formal contact you have with the school, and first impressions count. If you decide to apply, remember that applications are an early stage in the selection process, and the decision to call you for interview is based on the quality of this application. Hence, the importance of presenting yourself effectively in your application cannot be overestimated. You need to make sure that you have as much information available to you as possible – both about the school and the particular post – so you can develop a better understanding about the school (for example, its philosophy and organisation). The school website will provide information about the general activities of the school. The latest school inspection report is on the relevant website (see websites for England, Northern Ireland, Scotland and Wales in Further reading at the end of this unit). Accessing the most recent inspection report allows you to develop an impression of how the school is performing. If possible, organise a visit to the school; this allows you to get a better feel for the school and the area and to personalise your application.

Any job advertisement will include a description of the post (job description) and in some cases an overview of what they are looking for in the person applying (sometimes referred to as a person specification), which focuses on the main knowledge, skills and experiences the school are looking for and any presentation/teaching activity you are asked to do if called for interview.

Highlight key words and phrases contained in the job description and the requirements of the post. You need to consider whether you have the knowledge, skills, experience and qualities the school is looking for and whether the school meets some or all of your requirements. You need to make sure you highlight your strengths in your application, providing, where possible, examples where you have demonstrated the skills and experience they are looking for. For example, if the advertisement identifies strong behaviour management as a requirement, you should include examples of when you have demonstrated this in your teaching: state what you did and why and how you knew it was successful. You should also demonstrate other qualities you have that would contribute to the school's vision (which is why it is important to access as much information about the school as you can) and what makes you distinct from other applicants.

Plan the content of your application before you complete the application form or write a covering letter for a specific post and finalise your CV. You may want to store the relevant information in the form of a Word document, from which you take relevant information, especially if you are completing an online application. If you are making multiple applications, do not be tempted to use the same form, letter or CV. While many applications require the same basic information (for example, previous experience, prior employment), you cannot have a standard application form, letter of application or CV that you use for every application. Each application needs to match your experience and qualifications to the specific requirements of the post, highlighting different points and varying the amount of detail you provide, according to the specific requirements of the post and the school. If you use some of the same information, make sure you have changed all references that are specific to other applications.

As well as demonstrating why you want the job, a customised application also shows that you have taken the effort to find out about a specific post in a specific school, which should help your application to stand out from the others. An application that fails to explain why you are interested in the specific post in the specific school is unlikely to be considered further. Being proactive is a good quality to demonstrate.

Hopefully, you have started to see that the application process is more than just form filling. To do it properly takes time. Two hours is probably the minimum time to complete an application properly without rushing it if you have prepared beforehand and have all the information available. Most applications have a closing date about two weeks after the original advertisement is placed. Getting yourself organised is therefore important, as is starting the application early. Do not leave it to the last minute, otherwise you might have to rush it – it is usually clear when you have rushed an application. Much of the information you need to include on an application can be prepared in advance. The next section provides examples.

Referees

You are normally asked to supply the names and contact details of at least two people who are willing to act as referees. These are people who have a good knowledge of you as an individual as well as your teaching ability and academic work. Check whether there is one particular person within your ITE provider whom you should name as the first referee and, if not, ask someone who has knowledge of your teaching abilities. Examples might include a tutor from your teaching placement school, a member of staff from your ITE provider or a previous employer. Your second referee should be someone who knows you well and is able to comment on your character, qualities, achievements and commitment to teaching as a career. You should not include family members.

You should contact your referees before any application is made to check that they are willing to act for you. You should confirm the contact details of your referees are accurate, including telephone contact details as well as email address, and whether there are any dates when they are away and unable to respond should a request arrive. Many schools require references to be taken up prior to interviews, and in some instances an offer of employment may be withheld until these have been received.

You will have selected your referees because you feel they will be supportive of your application, so try to give them as much information as possible about you that might be included in the reference; for example, other activities in which you have been involved. It is often helpful for the referee to have a copy of your CV. Also provide them with as much information about the post as you can. While most schools send out such information to referees about the post to which you have applied, this tends to be very close to the interview date. It is therefore useful when sending in your application to remember to send through the job description so that your referee has time to complete their reference.

Some schools have a policy of open references; that is, the reference is shown to the applicant in certain circumstances. The referee knows this at the time of writing the reference.

Methods of application

Schools normally require job applicants to submit a completed application form or letter of application and CV. Most frequently, you complete a form plus a letter or a personal statement. In these cases, the form acts as your CV.

Modern technology means that many applications are now made online, rather than either sending hard copy by post or attaching a letter to an email, although some still require you to send an application by post. You need to check what process is expected for the post for which you are applying. If postal applications are required, you need to build time into the process (including getting access to the post office) so that it arrives before, or on, the due date.

An application form

The information required on an application form closely matches that identified for a letter of application and CV (see the companion website, www.routledge.com/cw/capel).

It is likely that one page of the form will be blank for you to explain why you are applying for the post, add additional information and elaborate on the skills and experience that equip you for it. As with the letter of application (see below), unless otherwise stated, this should focus on the specific job you are applying for, on the experience, skills and qualities you have to be able to do the job, and any additional skills you might bring to the post. This section should be written in continuous prose as if it is a section of a letter, following the suggested format and containing the type of information in a letter of application. Adding headings related to the person specification and job description before the relevant text can help those who are shortlisting candidates to see easily that you meet the specification for the post.

When you submit the application, you may need to include a covering letter (this may be included in an email if appropriate) indicating the post you have applied for and where you accessed information about it. This will generally be very short, but will be written formally, indicating that you have included your application for the post of (subject) teacher as advertised in (publication).

Letter of application

Some schools require you to write a letter of application. This should state clearly your reasons for applying for the post, matching your qualifications, experiences, particular skills and personal qualities to the post as described in the information sent to you from the school. The letter should normally be no more than two sides of A4 in length. A suggested format is given in Figure 8.1.1 on the companion website (www.routledge.com/cw/capel).

Your curriculum vitae (CV)

A CV summarises your educational background, qualifications, teaching and other work experience and any other relevant information (for example, interests and activities that you enjoy outside of school), as well as any other relevant qualifications (for example a clean driving licence) or any course you might have attended as part of your development as a teacher (for example, coaching qualifications, first aid). It should always accompany a letter of application and provides detail and further information to support your application. Remember, it is a supportive tool. Figure 8.1.2 (on the companion website, www.routledge.com/cw/capel) provides an editable version of a sample template for a CV.

To consolidate your learning from this section, Task 8.1.3 provides you with an opportunity to compile both a CV and letter of application.

 Task 8.1.3 Your curriculum vitae

Draft a specimen letter of application and CV, and obtain and complete an application form.

Ask your tutor to check these for you and give formative feedback on any changes they feel are appropriate. Store these in your PDP to use as the basis for all your job applications.

Notes and reminders about applications

With any completed application, indicate clearly (if appropriate) any dates that you are unable to attend for interview; for example, because you have an examination. Most advertisements will identify the proposed date for interview so you will have some indication of whether clashes are likely to occur. Examinations must normally take precedence over interviews. If you are concerned, you should contact your ITE tutors immediately to see if there are any alternatives. Holidays do not take precedence over interviews and most schools do not wait until you return from holiday to interview you; therefore, do not book holidays at times when you are likely to be called for interview. Other than for examinations, most ITE providers release student teachers to attend interviews without penalties. If you attend a lot of interviews during one of your school placements, you may be expected to complete additional days in school to ensure that you have completed the required number of days in school for your ITE programme.

Remember that you are not the only person applying for a post. In some cases, there may be more than 50 applications for one post. It is therefore important to make sure that your application is laid out and presented well, without using jargon. Most of your applications will be typed but some (although very few) require applications to be handwritten. Electronic forms are now widely used, some of which enable you to complete individual sections and save and return to them prior to submitting the form - rather than having to complete the whole form at one time. Check your application to make sure there are no basic errors such as typing errors, mistakes in spelling, grammar or punctuation, and that the information is accurate and consistent. If the form does not allow you to spellcheck, or does not allow you to use more than a specific number of words, complete the information in another format so that you can spellcheck or count the number of words - and then cut and paste it into the file. This also allows you to spend time focusing on exactly what you want to say, and the words you want to use.

It is also important that you make your application stand out. Consider how you can do this in what and how you write your application. For example, try to use phrases that show your good qualities. For example, 'I successfully led an initiative to introduce a new monitoring system to check pupils' homework' is better than 'I checked pupils' homework'. However, do not exaggerate claims. Make sure you sell yourself - if you do not have a strong letter of application or statement, the school are unlikely to be interested; however, do not sound too arrogant. They do not want you to tell them what they already know about their school (for example, it does this, that or the other). Remember that if you put down additional skills and experiences (for example, that you sing in a local choir), you may be invited to use those skills in school. Also, clearly demonstrate that you have read and understood some of the school policies. Do not use jargon in an application.

Do ensure all relevant information is included. Check there is no missing information, dates or other details, or questions that you have not answered. Do not leave any sections of the form blank. If there are sections that you cannot complete (for example, you have had no previous teaching posts), then just put not applicable (N/A). Remember, you only have one chance to get this right.

Ask someone to read through any application to check for spelling and grammatical errors. Tutors will usually look through your application before you send it off but build this time into the process.

Bear in mind that the turnaround time for the receipt of applications, shortlisting (that is, the selection of candidates to be called for interview) and confirmation of an interview is usually quick.

Keep a copy of each application with details of the post. If you are called for interview, you will need this information to prepare.

The interview

If you are invited to interview, confirm that you will attend, confirming the post, date and time of interview and the requirements for any lessons you are asked to teach and/or presentations. If your situation changes (for example, if you are unable to attend the interview because of a clash - you might have another interview on the same day - or you have had another interview and been offered that post and therefore decide to withdraw), let the school know as soon as possible. This will allow them to invite another candidate if they wish. If you are offered two interviews on the same day, you might be able to attend at a different time. Sometimes, though, you will have to decide which one you will attend. Write and decline the interview you decide not to attend as they could invite another person to interview.

For any change, where possible, speak directly to the school contact rather than leave an answerphone message or email, and be honest and explain the situation. Try to avoid ringing on the day of interview unless your problem is illness-related.

Preparing for the interview

Prepare for an interview in advance by refreshing your memory about your application and the school itself and considering the points below.

You might find it helpful to reflect on why you applied for this particular post, so that you can put across the relevant information convincingly at the interview. Read through the advertisement, job description, any other information about the post and school, and your application again so you can communicate effectively the information and evidence you consider to be relevant to the post. It also helps to avoid any contradictions between what you say and what you wrote in your application, as each member of the interview panel has a copy of your application so can compare answers. It may be that someone you know has knowledge of the school or the area; if so, talk to them. Access recent reports on the school (see Further reading for relevant websites).

If you are asked to deliver a lesson on the day of interview, make sure you have all the information you need before you teach any class (see teaching a lesson as part of the interview, below). You should be told this in the letter of invitation to interview, but if not, contact the school and ask. If you have not already done so, you might wish to visit the school (always organise an appointment) or at least travel to it so that you know where you are going on the actual day.

Write down any questions you have about the post or the school. While many might be answered during the course of the day, it is always useful to have one or two to ask in the interview.

As a professional, you are expected to keep as up to date as possible on your subject and education generally. Read around the subject you are hoping to be employed to teach, as well as about education more generally, so that you can discuss the latest educational issues and debates, as well as changes in your subject area. If appropriate, prepare a portfolio of your resources, or attainment against the teaching standards for qualified teacher status or teaching related activities; for example, good lesson plans, examples of pupils' assessed work, worksheets, evaluations, photographs of displays or trips, review of resources, information and communications (ICT) skills. This is derived from the PDP you are keeping throughout your ITE programme. Many institutions encourage student teachers to complete e-portfolios that allow you to showcase your work and progress over the duration of your ITE programme. On the interview day, you may not have time to show these, but reflecting on them prior to the day may well help relax you and give you good examples of practice to use during the interview itself. Plan what you are going to wear at the interview. Appearance is important. You should dress professionally, smartly and conservatively, but with appropriate clothing for teaching your lesson. Prepare any resources you might need for your lesson in advance and remember to take them with you! If you are giving a presentation, offer to send it through prior to the interview so that it can be uploaded on to the school system (also, this will mean that you have it in your emails should you forget your memory stick).

Attending the interview

The interview starts as soon as you walk into the school and does not finish until you leave the school at the end of the day. Hence, the initial impact you make is very important as interviewers tend to form an overall impression early. You are assessed throughout the day, so your performance, including your verbal and non-verbal communication in each activity, is important and could make the difference between being offered the job or not.

An interview is a two-way affair. The fact you have been called for an interview demonstrates you have the qualifications to do the job. By attending, the school is identifying whether you are what they are looking for, but you are being given the opportunity to identify whether you want to teach at that school. Thus, at the same time as being interviewed, you are, in effect, interviewing the school and deciding whether this is a school in which you could work and therefore whether this is a post for you. Take the opportunity to learn as much as you can about the post, the school and the working environment. This requires you to be alert to what is being said and to be prepared to ask as well as answer questions. If at any stage during the day you feel this is not the right post/school for you, you can withdraw, and it is fair to do so.

It is difficult to generalise about interviews because they vary considerably. When you are offered an interview, you should expect to be given information about the format of the day. This might include a tour of the school, a teaching episode (a lesson/part of a lesson), an informal talk or interview with the head of department, a senior teacher or other staff in the department, group interview, individual interview, and interview/talk with pupils. It might also include a group discussion or an activity such as an 'in-tray' exercise or drafting a letter to parents.

For many interviews, all interviewees are required to attend at the same time, while others specify a time for your interview so you do not meet the other candidates. In some interviews, there is a sifting process, whereby some interviewees are sent home part way through the day while the others remain for a formal interview. In some interviews, where there are a number of people, some teach in the morning and some are interviewed in the morning – then vice versa in the afternoon. You need to understand the processes for the day, and if you are in any doubt you should contact the school for clarification. Because of these variations, the format and length of an interview day varies.

Teaching a lesson as part of the interview

It is regular practice for candidates to be asked to teach a lesson or section of a lesson as part of the interviewing process. You should be notified of this when you are called for interview and be given specific information about the age and size of the class, what you are expected to teach and the pupils' ability and prior knowledge, the length of the lesson, what facilities, resources and equipment are available (that is, all the information you require before teaching any class). If you require further information (for example, the prior learning of the pupils, what level of attainment they are working at, where the lesson fits in to the wider unit of work), then you should contact the school as soon as you receive your initial information. You might also want to do some research on how the school currently delivers lessons (for example, how do they share learning outcomes, how do they assess progress?) so that you can reflect aspects of this in your own delivery, or offer activities that develop these principles further.

Plan the lesson carefully, giving attention to learning outcomes, purpose and content of activities, teaching strategies including questioning technique, resources and using as many of the principles you have developed during your ITE programme as possible. It is useful to have copies of the lesson plan available to give to those observing you. This is an opportunity to show the quality of your preparation and planning. Lessons taught as part of the interview process also provide you with the opportunity to demonstrate the level of your subject content knowledge and implementation of appropriate pedagogy so, again, prepare well, particularly if you have been asked to teach a topic with which you are not totally familiar. It is probably best to try to base your interview lesson on something that has been successful on a previous occasion with similar classes. The lesson is also an opportunity for you to show your enthusiasm for teaching, pupils' learning and your subject. This is your opportunity to demonstrate how you develop a rapport with your classes, as well as how you organise and progress lessons. Try to appear confident and relaxed, although those observing you understand that you probably feel a little nervous!

If possible, practise the lesson before you deliver it. This allows you the opportunity to evaluate and modify your plan based on feedback.

Be prepared to discuss your lesson during your formal interview, but if not it is a good idea to talk with relevant staff about the lesson; for example, how you feel it went, what the pupils learned, how you know they learned this, and what you might change. It might be worth making a few notes about the lesson once you have taught it to help you with this. Be honest and do not be anxious about mentioning it if some things have not gone to plan. For example, your timing might have gone astray or your instructions were not as clear as you had anticipated. Where this is the case, offer examples of developments/improvements you might make. In essence, you are providing a verbal evaluation of the lesson itself. In doing so, you demonstrate your ability to analyse why it happened and how you might change this in the future. This demonstrates your level of reflexivity, but also that you have given serious thought to what you have just done, and hence about your practice.

The interview

As the format of interviews varies across schools, so do the composition and size of interview panels. In some interviews, you are faced by a panel comprising anything between two to three and six to seven people; in others, you have a series of interviews with different people. In either case, these people normally include the following: the head teacher, a (parent) governor, another senior member of the school staff, head of subject department. The length of the panel interview also varies, from about half an hour to one and a half hours. Commonly, interviews are scheduled to last for about 45 minutes, with time for you to ask questions yourself.

In the formal interview, the initial impression you make is very important. For example, how will you greet the panel when you arrive? Do not sit down until you are invited to do so. Think about your body language; for example, how you sit (sit comfortably on your chair looking alert – do not sit on the edge of your chair looking anxious or slouch in your chair looking too relaxed). Look and sound calm, relaxed and confident (even if you are not). Try to be yourself. Try to smile and direct your answers to the person who has asked the specific question, as well as the panel, during discussion. You may want to change your body position slightly to face the person asking the question so that you maintain eye contact when answering questions. Do try not to speak too quickly and try to keep your answers to the question posed. If you are unsure about how much information to give when answering questions, it is probably better to keep an answer brief and then ask the panel if they would like further information. If you are not sure what the question means, do not hesitate to ask for clarification. If your mind goes blank, ask them to repeat the question. Avoid repetition, but do not worry if you repeat information included in your application, as long as you do not contradict what you wrote.

Interviewers have various degrees of specialist knowledge and understanding. Avoid jargon in explanations but assume interviewers have some knowledge and understanding of your subject area. Aim to provide a balanced picture of yourself, being on the whole positive and emphasising your strengths, while acknowledging areas of potential development. Interviewers are trying to form an impression of you as a future teacher and as a person, and so have a number of things they are looking for. These include:

■ *Your knowledge and understanding of your subject and your ability to teach it.* Interviewers assess your ability to discuss, analyse, appraise and make critical comment about ideas, issues and developments in your subject and subject curriculum, your personal philosophy about and commitment to the teaching of your subject(s).

■ *Your professional development as a teacher.* This is based partly on your school experiences. Interviewers assess your ability to analyse observations of pupils' behaviour and development, your own development and your involvement in the whole life of the school on school experiences, and your ability to discuss, analyse, appraise and make critical comment about educational issues.

■ *Your ability to cope with the post.* Interviewers assess how you would approach your teaching (for example, your understanding of the different roles you are required to undertake as a teacher, how you have coped or would cope, in a number of different situations, such as disciplining a pupil or class experiencing difficulties, dealing with a concerned parent or with teaching another subject).

■ *Your ability to fit into the school and the staffroom and to make contact with and relate to colleagues and pupils.* Interviewers assess your interpersonal skills, verbal and non-verbal communication skills (your written communication skills have been assessed from your application).

■ *Your commitment to the specific post.* Interviewers assess the interest and enthusiasm you show for the post to try to find out whether this is a post you really want or whether you see this post as a short-term stop-gap before you can find a post in an area or school where you really want to teach.

After introductions and preliminaries, interviewers normally ask why you have applied for this specific post. They then focus on the information in your application, including your personal experiences, your education, qualifications, teaching skills gained from teaching experience and other teaching and/or work experience, your interest and activities and other qualifications. Throughout your ITE programme, you should have been encouraged to gain as much wider experience as you can; it is now that you can demonstrate how this has contributed to your own personal development as well as how it will benefit the school as a whole. In addition, you are normally also asked what you feel you can contribute to the school and general questions about professional or personal interests, ideas, issues or attitudes.

Remember that the interview provides you with an opportunity to expand upon information contained in your original application. Consequently, you can predict some of the questions that are likely to be asked based on the job description or person specification. Look back at the initial information you received to identify the parts of the job on which they expect to get information at the formal interview. Try to give practical examples to support your answers. If asked about your approaches to teaching, give examples of how you have used different approaches in your own practice. Talking through an example tends to allow you to demonstrate a deeper level of understanding than writing it down. However, try to remain focused. Make your point as clearly and succinctly as possible and then stop. If the panel want more information, they will probe further.

Therefore, think about areas you want to emphasise or any additional evidence of your suitability for the post that you did not have room to include in your application. Draw on both the university-based part of your ITE programme and school experience and on other experience; for example, other work with young people such as work in a youth club or voluntary work. This demonstrates your commitment to working with young people.

You also need to show you realise you still have things to learn and that you are committed to continuing your development as a teacher. You should come prepared with examples of potential short-term and longer-term targets for development. For example, you need to consolidate your learning in your first year, perhaps gain further experience of other areas, such as teaching Years 12 and 13 or taking on a tutor group. As you come to the end of your ITE programme, you are expected to develop some form of early professional development planning, so use this to support your answers. You might also wish to consider undertaking an additional academic qualification; for example, studying at master's level (see also Unit 8.2 on continuing professional development). It is helpful to have a career plan, but not to appear so ambitious that you give the school the impression that you will leave at the first opportunity.

Possible interview questions

Questions asked at interview vary considerably; therefore, it is not possible for you to prepare precisely for an interview. However, it is helpful if you identify possible questions in your preparation and prepare some possible outline responses to such questions. It is useful to give a general response to the question to show you are aware of some of the principles and issues and also to refer to examples of your own practice. For example:

Interviewer: How did you set about planning differentiated learning for a class you have taught recently?

Candidate: This is an important way of enabling all pupils to have equal access to the curriculum so that they learn as much as possible and fulfil their individual potential. There are a number of strategies that can be used; for example, differentiation by outcome, by task or by rate of work. During my last school experience, I was teaching a Year 7 class about religious festivals. I did not want to give out several different worksheets as this might have embarrassed some pupils, so I made one worksheet that had some core tasks for all pupils and also some option tasks, which involved different levels of work and different types of activities. I also developed differentiation through my use of questioning . . .

Some possible interview questions are included in Figure 8.1.3 on the companion website (www. routledge.com/cw/capel).

Other questions

At the end of the interview, you may be asked: if you were to be offered this post, would you be in a position to accept it? In addition, you may be asked whether you have any questions. Asking one or two questions shows a genuine interest in the post and the school. You are likely to forget the questions you wanted to ask if you are nervous; therefore, do not be afraid to prepare a list of questions and take this with you to interview. It is quite acceptable to refer to this at this stage of the interview. You may also wish, at this stage, to seek clarification on some issues that might have arisen during the day; for example, whether you would be expected to have a tutor group or deliver across subject areas. You should enquire what arrangements there are for induction of NQTs in the school and what you might expect. You may also want to ask questions about the contract; for example, to check about the type of contract (such as fixed term or temporary contract) that is being offered and whether this is what you were expecting, when would you be expected to start (some schools employ staff during the summer term or offer part-time work once you have finished your commitments to your ITE programme).

At some point, you may want to ask about your starting salary. If you are an NQT, there may be little room for negotiation unless you have something the school really needs/wants; for example, if you have been a cover supervisor previously and have specialist behaviour management training above and beyond what you would have covered in an ITE programme. How you describe experience in an application and at interview, therefore, is very important as it may be used to support any claim for increments above the starting salary.

Avoid asking questions just because you think you should; do not ask questions just to impress. If all your questions have been answered during the course of the day and you do not have any questions, just say politely that all the questions you wanted to ask have been answered during the day (or in the interview).

Earlier, we identified the benefits of practising your lesson prior to delivering it at interview. Many ITE providers provide opportunities for you to experience a mock interview. You are encouraged to take up any such opportunity (see also Task 8.1.4).

 Task 8.1.4 Mock interviews

Arrange for a mock interview with your tutor. If possible, either have an observer or video the interview so that you and the interviewer can use this to analyse your verbal and non-verbal communication after the interview. Identify ways you could improve and practise these. If possible, organise another mock interview.

Accepting a post

The process of being notified about the outcome of the interview should be explained to you at the end of the interview. If you are not going to be told prior to leaving the school, confirm the best form of contact; for example, your mobile number or landline. You may have to wait several days before being told whether or not you have been successful.

Where all candidates are invited for interview at the same time, you may be offered the post on the same day as the interview. You are normally expected to verbally accept or reject the offer at this time. Schools rarely give you time to think about an offer; therefore, it is important that you consider all the implications of accepting the post before you attend for interview. On rare occasions, it may be that you feel you really need some time to think about the offer. You may want to ask whether you can think about the offer – in which case, be clear about when you will inform the school of your decision (for example, you want to think about it overnight and telephone first thing in the morning). Be prepared for such a request to be rejected. If your request is refused, you have to make the decision there and then or be prepared for the post to be offered to another candidate. Your decision depends on how much you want a particular job and how strong a position you think you are in.

If you are offered a post verbally at or following the interview, the offer of a post must be followed by a written confirmation and a contract. Also, it is normal practice for you to be asked to confirm your verbal acceptance of a post in writing. This might be via the completion of a letter issued by the school, or in a formal letter written by yourself.

Do check carefully your contract, your salary and the induction programme. Offers of a post are made on certain conditions, therefore may be conditional until those conditions are met (for example, until you have passed a medical, in which case the school or the local authority (LA) sends you details), until references have been received or until you have met legal requirements (for example, undertaken an enhanced check with the Disclosure and Barring Service (DBS) – you will have completed one of these as part of your ITE programme).

Once you have signed your contract, you are tied to it, so spending time seeking clarity is important. It is unprofessional to continue to apply for other teaching posts after you have verbally accepted a post, even if you see one advertised that you prefer.

The transition from student teacher to teacher is not easy. Being a teacher involves you coming to terms with your new role within a new institutional context and an awareness of the complexities of its organisation, structures and routines, as well as ethos and expectations. This transition may be easier if you have gained employment in one of the schools in which you completed your school placement. If not, make arrangements (with your future mentor, for example) to visit the school again to make preparations to start your post. This is not dissimilar to the preparations you make when you go on school experience. You are able to meet members of the department and find out about facilities in the school. You also need to collect information about classes you will be teaching and what you will be teaching, as well as your teaching timetable. You may find it useful to make a few visits to get to know the school culture. For example, you may become involved in some school activities such as sports day or perhaps observe some classes or teach some lessons before you start your post.

If you are not offered a post

It is disappointing when a post is offered to another candidate. However, try not to think of this in terms of failure on your part. There may be many legitimate reasons why the post was offered to the other candidate in preference to you. For example, the other candidate might have relevant teaching experience (which you did not have) in an aspect of the curriculum required for the post. Try to be reflective about the decision and acknowledge where you might need to make improvements next time. For example, can you gain any further experiences to strengthen your application? Can you take up any further opportunities to practise your interview technique? If you are not successful, build this into your learning experience. Most interview panels routinely offer feedback to candidates. If not, you can ask if this is possible as it helps you identify strengths and areas to develop in preparation for your next interview.

Also, if you are still looking for a job in September, do not be too disappointed and give up. Ask yourself whether you have been too set on obtaining your ideal job and need to reassess your search criteria; for example, in terms of area, type of school or age range. You may also want to consider other options; for example, part-time work, a job-share, temporary post or supply work. These can give you valuable experience while you continue to search for a permanent full-time post, and can sometimes lead to permanent work in a school. You can find out details about supply work in your chosen area from the LA, schools and teaching supply agencies. If you decide to take such a route, you should check carefully the implications in terms of contracts, pay, implications for your formal induction period and your further professional development. It is also worth maintaining contact with your ITE provider to see whether they are aware of any opportunities. You might even start to consider other teaching-related opportunities. Tasks 8.1.5 and 8.1.6 are designed to help you to reflect on the change from student to newly qualified teacher.

 Task 8.1.5 Moving from student to newly qualified teacher

How do student teachers learn to become teachers? Consider this critically in relation to the literature.

Identify similarities and differences between being a student teacher and being an NQT. Discuss your perceptions with a small number of NQTs. Critically compare their biographical stories with your own considerations for entry into the teaching profession. Store this information in your PDP.

 Task 8.1.6 Entering and staying in the profession

Design and conduct a piece of empirical research with selected established teachers in your placement school about the factors that: (a) influenced them to become teachers; and (b) make them stay in the teaching profession. Report critically on your analysis, identifying issues related to the philosophical assumptions underlying the methods of data collection and analysis. Give a critical evaluation of their choice, design and effective use, as well as a critical analysis of the factors identified and comparison with your own personal circumstances. Store this information in your PDP.

SUMMARY AND KEY POINTS

This unit is designed to help you realise that, just as with your teaching, you must prepare for obtaining your first teaching post; you cannot leave it to chance or rely on your innate ability to perform well at interview. In this unit, we tried to lead you through the steps, skills and techniques you need to prepare actively for obtaining your first post; that is:

- why you want to enter the teaching profession, as well as about where and in what type of school you want to teach;
- looking for suitable vacancies;
- selecting a post that interests you and requesting further details;
- preparing your CV, writing a letter of application and contacting potential referees;
- completing your application, preparing for and attending an interview in order to secure a full-time post.

To be successful, you need to:

- be proactive;
- be prepared;
- practise your techniques;
- be confident.

Check which requirements for your ITE programme you have addressed through this unit.

Further reading

Eggert, M. (2008) *The Perfect Interview: All You Need to Know to Get It Right First Time*, London: Random House.
  This book has excellent succinct advice about preparing for an interview.

English, P. (2004) *Succeeding at Interviews Pocketbook*, Alresford: Management Pocketbooks.
  While potentially dated, this easy read provides relevant advice and guidance on all aspects of an interview.

Other resources and websites

Teaching jobs are advertised on the following websites:

Guardian Education: http://jobs.guardian.co.uk/jobs/education/schools/

Jobsgopublic: www.jobsgopublic.com/

Local government: www.lgjobs.com/

http://jobsearch.about.com/od/jobsearchglossary/g/letterofapplication.htm
  This site provides guidance on writing letters of application. It is quite Americanised but gives some useful tips.

www.tes.co.uk/article.aspx?storycode=6000318
  This article focuses on how to produce a covering letter when applying for a job. It is probably best read in conjunction with the article below.

www.tes.co.uk/article.aspx?storycode=6008055
> Provides guidance on how to get shortlisted for a job. It provides clear practical guidance on how to complete an application.

Times Educational Supplement: www.tes.co.uk/jobs/

Information about obtaining your first post is available from teaching unions; for example:

Association of Teachers and Lecturers, England, Wales and Northern Ireland (ATL): www.atl.org.uk/

Irish National Teachers' Organisation, Northern Ireland: www.into.ie/NI/

National Association of Schoolmasters/Union of Women Teachers, England, Wales, Scotland and Northern Ireland: NASUWT www.nasuwt.org.uk/

National Union of Teachers, England and Wales (NUT): www.teachers.org.uk/

Scottish Secondary Teachers' Association, Scotland: www.ssta.org.uk

The Educational Institute of Scotland (EIS), Scotland: www.eis.org.uk/

Ulster Teachers Union, Northern Ireland: www.utu.edu/

Voice, previously the Professional Association of Teachers, England, Wales and Northern Ireland: www.voicetheunion.org.uk/

School inspection reports and further information about education can be obtained from:

England: Ofsted: www.ofsted.gov.uk; and Department for Education: www.education.gov.uk/

Scotland: Education Scotland: www.educationscotland.gov.uk/scottishschoolsonline/; and the Scottish Government: www.scotland.gov.uk/Topics/Statistics/Browse/School-Education

Wales: Estyn – The Office of Her Majesty's Inspectorate for Education and Training in Wales: www.estyn.gov.uk/; and the Welsh Government: http://wales.gov.uk/topics/educationandskills/?lang=en

Northern Ireland: The Education and Training Inspectorate Northern Ireland: www.etini.gov.uk/index/inspection-reports.htm; and the Department of Education Northern Ireland: www.deni.gov.uk/

Starting Out Guide for Newly Qualified and Trainee Teachers: www.teachersupport.info/starting-out-guide-new-teachers
> This is published by the Teacher Support Network, which provides a 24-hour information, support and counselling service (www.teachersupport.info/); Tel. England 08000 562 561, Scotland 0800 564 2270; Wales 08000 855 088.

Appendix 2 on pages 591–595 provides further examples of websites you may find useful.

Capel, S., Leask, M. and Turner, T. (eds) (2010) *Readings for Learning to Teach in the Secondary School: A Companion to M Level Study*, London: Routledge.
> This book brings together essential readings to support you in your critical engagement with key issues raised in this textbook.

The subject-specific books in the Routledge *Learning to Teach* series are also very useful.

Any additional resources and an editable version of any relevant tasks/tables in this unit are available on the companion website: www.routledge.com/cw/capel

8.2 Developing further as a teacher

Jeanne Keay

Introduction

> The main driver of the variation in pupil learning at school is the quality of the teachers.
>
> (Barber and Mourshed 2007: 15)

Successfully completing the initial phase of teacher education is a big achievement. It is, however, only the beginning of a continuous process of professional learning. You have a responsibility as a teacher to ensure that you are developing in ways that will not only help you to further your career, but will also help you to meet the learning needs of your pupils. Barber and Mourshed (2007), in their review of the best-performing school systems, found that it was teachers who made the difference and that getting the right teachers into the profession and developing them were two of the most important elements of a high-performing system. In a follow-up to this review, they looked at how the world's most improved school systems keep getting better and found that improving system performance essentially comes down to improving pupils' learning experiences (Mourshed *et al.* 2010). As a teacher, you provide those learning experiences and you are therefore central to the success of your pupils. You must be aware of your weaknesses, understand what best practice is and must be motivated to improve (Barber and Mourshed 2007). These elements are reflected in the focus for this unit. However, I would like to promote a positive approach to professional development that not only recognises the need to be aware of weaknesses, but also demands that you know your strengths and can build on them. This entails taking a reflective approach to your teaching, taking responsibility for planning and undertaking professional development, and understanding your professional role as a teacher. These expectations are not meant to scare you, but to encourage you to ask questions that will help you make a successful transition from your initial teacher education (ITE) programme into your induction year. You are not expected to be a perfect teacher at the end of this initial stage of teacher education, but you should have a clear view of your strengths and areas for development.

OBJECTIVES

At the end of this unit, you should be able to:

■   plan your professional development and keep a record of professional learning;
■   plan a successful transition into your first teaching post;
■   understand and make best use of the range of professional development opportunities available to you during induction;
■   better understand your role as a professional.

Check the requirements of your ITE programme to see which relate to this unit.

Developing further as a teacher

Your professional development as a teacher began when you were at school; as a pupil, you experienced good, and sometimes perhaps not so good, teaching and you entered your ITE programme with professional knowledge gained through this experience, having served what Lortie (1975) called 'an apprenticeship of observation'. You are now progressing through a professional learning process that is enabling you to meet the standards required to embark on a career in teaching, but this is not the end of your development; it is the beginning of a continuous career-long process. A teaching career is sometimes described as four key stages of professional development: initial; induction (the first year of teaching); early professional development (the second and third years of teaching); and continuing professional development. However, while this ensures that we think of a teaching career as a long process of development, it does present the stages as discrete elements, which may be problematic. A review of literature in teacher education in Scotland highlights this point and criticises the compartmentalised nature of teacher education. The review suggests that teacher education should be seen to operate as a continuum, spanning a career, and the authors suggest that there is a need for much better alignment between schools, local authorities, universities and national organisations in order to achieve coherent and progressive professional development throughout a teacher's career (Menter *et al.* 2010).

   Much will be expected of you as a teacher and the quality of your teaching must be high, but you will only achieve this through a professional, organised and committed approach to development. You are not expected to achieve this alone and, in the same way as you are supported through your ITE programme, there will be specific support for you from more experienced teachers during your induction year. Having met the requirements to become a teacher at the end of your ITE programme, during your induction period you will work towards meeting a further set of expectations. Although arrangements will be slightly different depending on the country in which you are teaching, most governments want to be assured that, through induction, you are on the way to becoming a good teacher. A recent Organisation for Economic Co-operation and Development (OECD) report found that formal induction programmes are mandatory in half the countries surveyed and that more experienced teaching staff were responsible for supporting new teachers in their first year (OECD 2014). Each school has different support systems but each should provide you with an induction tutor and protected development time; in addition, you should also expect to be observed and to have your performance assessed.

Beyond induction, schools have appraisal and performance management arrangements that continue to provide support.

The main purpose of this unit is to help you to prepare for the responsibility you have to support pupils' learning through adopting, from the start of your career, a planned approach to professional development. This unit considers professional development beyond your ITE programme and, in particular, focuses on the period of transition from your ITE programme into your first post and the early years of your teaching career.

Planning your professional development

As suggested in the introduction to this unit, planning and keeping a record of professional learning is central to your development as a teacher. During your ITE programme, you are encouraged, and in some places required, to maintain what might be called a professional development profile (PDP). There are different names for this document, and it might simply be a profile in which you record evidence to demonstrate that you are meeting the requirements for becoming a teacher. Some student teachers find this process easy to follow and others find it tedious; however, profiling your learning helps you to celebrate achievements and identify areas for development. You may also find it useful to keep a diary of reflective practice, which helps you to consider the impact of your professional development on your pupils' learning and to plan for future learning. Your PDP is a useful record not only in providing evidence during your ITE programme, but also when preparing for job interviews and in professional, subject and career planning.

Whatever method you choose to use to record achievement and development, the process should be realistic and achievable. You are expected to take control of, and responsibility for, your professional development, which is an expectation in performance management arrangements for all teachers. A practical approach to planning and recording achievement necessitates thinking about the sort of evidence of learning you will collect, as simply undertaking professional development activities is, in itself, not enough. You should record:

■ your learning objectives;
■ why you decided to focus on a particular area of learning, based on your reflections and other evidence;
■ how you will know you have met your objectives;
■ what professional development you undertook to meet those objectives.

This process requires you to engage in a cyclical process of reflective practice (see Unit 5.4 for a detailed overview of reflective practice), involving planning, implementation and gathering evidence of success. Task 8.2.1 is designed to help you with this.

Transition into your first teaching post

Moving from your ITE programme into your first teaching post is an exciting but possibly daunting prospect. However, you will not be expected to demonstrate the attributes of an experienced teacher in one year and your school should provide you with a support programme. Inevitably, you will be

---

  Task 8.2.1 Planning your professional development

Start to gather evidence of professional development as a basis for your planning, using either the form of portfolio suggested by your tutors or a PDP that you have designed yourself.

Gathering evidence

■ If you are at the beginning of your ITE programme, start to plan how you will gather evidence of professional progress.

■ If you are at the end of your ITE programme and have not started this process, begin to gather as much evidence of professional progression as possible.

Action planning

■ Whatever stage of your ITE programme you are at, develop and start to implement an action plan to extend strengths and address areas identified for development.

■ When you are near the end of your ITE programme, review the evidence you have gathered and reflect on what this tells you about your current strengths and areas for development and start to plan your future development.

Use this action plan to initiate discussions about your professional needs with your tutors and fellow teachers.

---

anxious about this phase of your career and you will have expectations based on your current and past experiences in schools. All of this is very normal, and most new teachers embark on induction with concerns that are varied but often include behaviour management issues (Hobson *et al.* 2009). You must be realistic about what you can achieve and recognise that each school is different, and that the difficulties you have experienced in one school may not be present in another school. Of course, the reverse is also true, and when you start your induction period, circumstances in a different school may present new challenges. Over several decades, teachers' concerns have been, and continue to be, the subject of much research (for example, Veenman 1984; Mawer 1995; Conway and Clarke 2003). We know that teachers go through a cycle of concerns (Fuller 1969) that not only occur when beginning induction, but are also present when beginning a new job in a different school or a new role in the same school. More recently, research has been undertaken to explore the resilience of teachers; Gu and Day (2013: 39) define this as 'the capacity to manage the unavoidable uncertainties inherent in the realities of teaching'. They identify personal, relational and organisational settings as influences on teachers' capacities to cope with the everyday demands of the job. Beltman *et al.* (2011), in their review of literature on teacher resilience, suggest that self-efficacy and intrinsic motivation, together with collegial and mentor support, are key protective factors. The ability to sustain an approach to teaching that ensures you successfully meet induction requirements and at the same time maintain a proactive and planned approach to development should be your goal. However, you are more likely to achieve this goal if you adopt a reflective approach to teaching, seek support from more experienced teachers and, most importantly, take responsibility for identifying your own development needs.

As you may have experienced during your ITE programme, challenges not only come in the form of pupils, but they also occur in your relationships with other staff. As a new member of a subject department, you may be expected to understand the department ethos and work in particular ways before you are accepted as a valued member of the team. Lave and Wenger (1991) called this *legitimate peripheral participation*; that is, as a new member of the community, you are expected to watch from the sidelines and learn the rules before making an effective contribution to the community. This concept can be seen as both problematic and productive. Working collaboratively as a member of a professional learning community, such as a subject group, is a very useful form of professional development. However, if membership of that community simply means adopting community practices instead of contributing to their development, it can be problematic. When you are a qualified teacher, you will need to consider how to balance independence with collaborative working, and how to fit into the department while at the same time making a contribution to practice.

The following sections present some practical considerations that may help you to deal with these challenges.

Before starting the job

A good induction programme will ease you into a career in teaching; however, although induction support is mandatory in most countries, sometimes it is not well organised. While it is a school's responsibility to provide support, it is also your responsibility to ensure that recommended induction processes are in place and used. You need to start preparing for undertaking induction while you are in your ITE programme and you must have a realistic understanding of what can be achieved during this period. A professional development action plan in your PDP will help you to achieve this. Task 8.2.2 is designed to help you with that planning.

 Task 8.2.2 Your induction

Check the expectations of an induction programme for the country in which you are learning to teach. What should be provided? Is this what you expected?

Now you are aware of induction programme expectations, how can you prepare for induction? Discuss this with your tutor and store it in your PDP.

Starting the job

In the first few days and weeks of any job, you will need to focus on familiarising yourself with the school and building on the information you have gained during the job application process and interview. Initially, you need information that will help you to operate successfully in the school, and this may cover a range of practical issues, such as:

■ management, administrative arrangements and school policies (for example, staff responsibilities, sickness policy, accessing school buildings);

- structures and departments (for example, staff responsibilities, line managers, meeting other members of staff);
- rules, regulations and procedures within the school and your department (for example, behaviour policy, equal opportunities policies, lesson planning and assessment policies);
- health and safety requirements (for example, fire drill, pupil medical information).

During the first term in your new post, you will probably find that you concentrate mainly on becoming confident and competent in your teaching in order to establish yourself in the school. You are busy getting to know your classes, planning units of teaching from the school's schemes of work, preparing lesson plans, teaching, setting and marking homework, undertaking pastoral activities with your form and getting to know the rules, routines and procedures of the school. Task 8.2.3 is designed to help you prepare for your first week in school.

 Task 8.2.3 Gathering information during induction

Make a list of the information you will need to gather at specific points during induction:

- before starting your new post;
- during the first week;
- during the first month;
- during the first term.

Check this list with a teacher who has recently completed induction in your school and use it to inform your professional development planning.

After the first few weeks

Induction must be linked to and develop from your ITE programme. You need to use your induction action plan, which has identified strengths and areas for development, as the starting point for a discussion about professional development priorities, targets and support with your induction tutor (or line manager). This set of priorities should be revisited regularly throughout your induction year and used to help you to identify and evidence development, as well as to inform future planning.

Starting a career in teaching is very demanding, more so than your ITE programme, because you have to sustain your practice over a whole year. Many new teachers experience what has been termed *reality shock* (Veenman 1984) because while your ITE programme gives you some experience of teaching, it is not until you are employed as a teacher that you realise the enormity of the role and the scope of responsibility. You will feel tired and it will be a stressful period; however, it is also a time when you can form strong relationships with other members of staff and your pupils, when you can try different teaching approaches and really see the impact of your work with pupils. You will be observed and evaluated, but this will be in relation to the whole year of induction and in the context of managing and supporting your performance.

While you will have the responsibility of being a 'real' teacher, you will be supported on your journey through this period. It is inevitable that you will feel unprepared for some aspects of the role, but remember, your ITE programme is only the start of your professional development; it does not cover all eventualities. In your first year of teaching, you undertake a greater range of responsibilities; for example, you have your own groups and classes and can establish your own procedures and rules for classroom management right from the beginning of the school year. However, while as a newly qualified teacher (NQT) you contribute to long-term planning such as developing schemes of work, you are not be expected to undertake the full range of a teacher's roles and responsibilities; for example, you may not be expected to deal with some of the more serious pastoral problems or to undertake the full range of administrative demands.

Over the course of the first year

During induction, you face situations and challenges that you did not experience as a student teacher. This includes undertaking activities for the first time such as setting questions for examinations, undertaking supervisory duties, or sustaining activities over a long period of time; for example:

- planning and preparing for a year to incorporate different material, teaching and assessment strategies and approaches to sustain pupil interest and motivation;
- setting targets to maintain progress in learning over the period of a year;
- maintaining discipline over a whole year, which is very different to maintaining discipline over a short period of time on school experience. You cannot accept poor behaviour that you may have been able to put up with for a relatively short period of time during school experience.

Although providing extracurricular activities may be expected of you, and indeed you can gain a great deal from involvement in such activities, you should be careful not to take on too many.

At some points, you may feel that teaching is more difficult than you first thought, and inevitably you may become frustrated and have doubts about whether you can teach and question what you are achieving with the pupils. You may need help from other members of staff to overcome these doubts and continue to develop as a teacher. Although some support may be informal, your induction tutor (or head of department) should provide structured support. You can draw on your tutor's experience to help you to answer the numerous questions you have as new situations arise, and to overcome problems with aspects of your teaching. Your tutor can help you to learn as part of your daily routine, by identifying and using opportunities available in your everyday work to develop your knowledge, skills and/or understanding. In an ideal world a tutor is proactive, making a conscious effort to look for opportunities for development. However, your tutor is likely to be busy and you will spend much of your time in a classroom on your own with pupils; therefore, there may be limited opportunities to work with your tutor.

Most staff are helpful and understanding, especially if you establish good relationships with them, but relationships take time to develop and you need to be sensitive to the environment you are in. Be aware of how you behave (for example, do not try to change something immediately because you think things you have seen in other schools could work better), learn procedures and policies, and operate within the organisational rules. If you do not, for example, enforce school rules, you undermine the system and create tensions between pupils and teachers, and between yourself and other members of staff.

Alternatively, as you settle into the job and work with your classes and learn the procedures, rules and routines, some staff may forget that you are new, and this is also a problem. As the term and year progress, they may treat you as any other member of staff and not offer help and advice. Initially, this might be flattering, but if you need support you must approach staff and talk to them about your concerns and ask for help. You may also find it helpful to form a support group with other NQTs in the school or within the local subject community, through which you can share your concerns and problems, and support and learn from each other. Task 8.2.4 is designed to help you identify experiences of NQTs.

M

✎ Task 8.2.4 NQT experience

While you are on school experience during your ITE programme, undertake a small-scale research project (see Unit 5.4 for detailed support in undertaking practitioner research) with NQTs in your school. Find out what their experiences of induction have been.

How can you use this information to help you prepare for induction? Store the information in your PDP.

Continuing professional development (CPD) beyond the first year

Induction should lead seamlessly into your second year of teaching and your professional development planning should involve consideration, not only of your teaching, but also of how you may want to develop; for example, some new teachers take on posts of responsibility very early in their careers. Is this something you are ready for? Would you like to take responsibility for part of the subject or undertake a pastoral role or to be involved in supporting new teachers? You should also consider further qualifications, especially completing a master's course, if you have not already done so. You may decide to undertake other qualifications; for example, some teachers find they need further support in relation to pupils' special educational needs. Towards the end of induction, you should find out about the process for appraisal and performance management in your school, as you will now participate in these processes.

Professional development

Professional development can be aimed at achieving career progression (for example, focusing on issues such as development to undertake posts of responsibility through undertaking a middle management programme), but it can also be seen as a way to overcome professional challenges encountered in your daily work. Both aspects of professional development are important and should be included in your planning.

There are several challenges to be considered when planning professional development; for example:

■ What counts as professional development?
■ Are planned learning activities relevant to your needs?
■ Does identified development meet your needs or your institution's needs?
■ Do you have access to high-quality learning experiences?

■ How will you measure the impact of your professional learning?

■ What evidence of the impact of your professional learning on pupils' learning will you collect?

Teachers interpret and undertake professional development in different ways but it is often defined in a very narrow way, a common definition being 'going on a course' (Bolam and Weindling 2006). When planning professional development, activities should not only match your needs, but should be relevant to your pupils' needs and the school context. A further problem lies in the questionable quality of some professional development activities and the lack of evaluation undertaken by providers (Keay and Lloyd 2009). A good venue and a take-home pack are not always indicative of a good professional development activity. You should be aware of these issues as you plan professional development activities.

One of the most challenging issues you will have to address relates to providing evidence of the impact of your professional development on pupils' learning (Burchell *et al.* 2002). Development needs must be identified effectively and meeting them must be planned carefully. One way to consider this is to use a process model that links pupils' learning and professional learning. Such a model, developed by Keay and Lloyd (2011), has been used with teachers in a range of schools. As an integral part of the process, the model demands reflective practice from those using it. As Figure 8.2.1 shows, you are asked to consider the culture and organisation of professional development

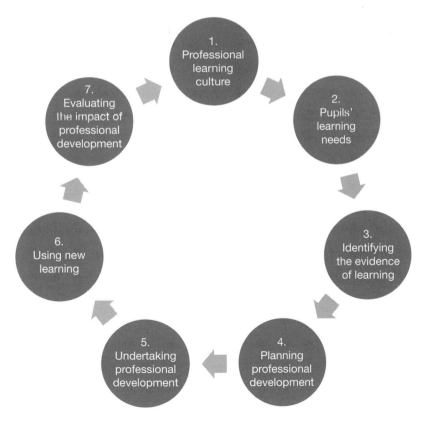

Figure 8.2.1 Professional development process model

Source: Keay and Lloyd (2011: 99)

in your school. This is part of the planning described in the sections above; for example, induction support and learning from different members of staff. You are then asked to locate your professional learning in the everyday process of teaching and link your professional development with your pupils' learning by identifying learning outcomes and the evidence of meeting those learning outcomes. It is at this point you ask yourself whether you have the knowledge, skills and understanding to meet your pupils' needs and, if not, you identify those professional development needs.

Stages 4, 5 and 6 are similar to the professional development planning process suggested earlier in this unit; the difference lies in the clear link you make to your pupils' learning and the identification of evidence of impact identified early in the process, and consequently easily gathered in stage 7 of the process (for a more detailed explanation of this process and the contributing research, see Keay and Lloyd 2011). Task 8.2.5 is designed to help you link your learning with pupils' learning.

✎ Task 8.2.5 Linking your learning with your pupils' learning

During school experience, try the process suggested in the model, focusing on linking the learning of one pupil with your professional learning. Reflect on the process and whether it might be useful to incorporate in your daily teaching practice. Write notes on what you have learned and store it in your PDP.

Teaching: a professional role

Teaching is a professional role, with professional demands and professional values and a specialised knowledge base that is embedded in the standards and demands of the role. However, the way the demands of the role are played out through the adoption of different forms of professionalism in schools affects the way teachers are viewed as professionals.

Menter *et al.* (2010) identified four models of teacher professionalism emerging from policy and research literature. They found that the *effective* teacher was the dominant model emphasising technical accomplishment, which relates to a practical interpretation of professional knowledge. The *reflective* teacher model, which emphasises the need for continuing and collaborative professional development, has been influential for over 20 years and remains popular; it has already been promoted in this and previous units. A third model, which is also highlighted in this book, is the *enquiring* teacher model, which promotes a research orientation within teachers' work. The final model could be linked to the intention behind the process model presented in Figure 8.2.1 as it positions teaching as a transformative activity. However, professionalism has also been considered as *managerial* or *democratic*, and the adoption of each one has an impact on how professional development is enacted in schools; that is, teacher professionalism in action. *Managerial* professionalism values effectiveness, efficiency and compliance, in contrast to a *democratic* form of professionalism, which values a collaborative and inclusive approach within a self-regulating environment. Table 8.2.1 summarises the work of Evetts (2009), Kennedy (2007) and Sachs (2001, 2003), and applies their views of professionalism to professional development.

A collaborative approach to learning, as suggested within *democratic* professionalism, provides you with opportunities not only to learn with colleagues, but also to participate in 'group learning'.

Table 8.2.1 Professionalism and professional development

Managerial professionalism	Aspects of professional development	Democratic professionalism
External regulation	Control	Self-regulation
Compliance with policy	Authority	Decisions taken by school
Slow to change, reactive, conservative practices	Decision-making	Collaborative, collegial, within an ethical code of practice
External assessment	Performance review	Critically reflective practice
Self-interest of the organisation and individual	Motivation	Pupil-centred
Efficiency, effectiveness	Focus	Inclusive, enquiry-driven, knowledge building

Source: Developed from Keay and Lloyd (2011)

It also provides opportunities to develop networking skills within the school and within the subject community. As a teacher, you are a member of a community, and learning in that community has its advantages and challenges depending on the culture of professionalism adopted within the school. Now complete Task 8.2.6.

M

    Task 8.2.6 Professionalism and CPD

Use Table 8.2.1 to consider the form of professionalism prevalent in your department while on school experience. Reflect on how this might affect your professional development planning. Record this in your PDP.

SUMMARY AND KEY POINTS

This unit highlights the importance of professional development in providing high-quality learning and teaching in schools. In particular, it emphasises the following points:

■ The process of professional learning is continuous and it is important for you to take responsibility for and control of planning your development.

■ Using a portfolio, through which you gather evidence to use in subsequent planning will be a practical way of ensuring that you continuously develop.

■ In order to make a successful transition into teaching, you need to be knowledgeable about induction expectations and school systems, so preparation for this period during your ITE programme is important.

■ Once in your first job, you should expect challenges and prepare to overcome them, which will ensure that you enjoy making a contribution to the learning of the pupils in your classes.

■ Your professional development should be relevant not only to your career needs, but also to meeting the needs of your pupils. In order to achieve this, you will need formal support from an induction tutor and will need to participate in a range of development activities. However, you will also need to use the opportunities to learn in everyday teaching practice.

■ Finally, being a teacher means being a member of a community of practice that has both pupils' and teachers' learning at its heart. Understanding the culture of the community and participating and contributing to it is an important element of your teaching role and one that supports your development.

Check which requirements for your ITE programme you have addressed throughout this unit.

Further reading

Hobson, A.J., Malderez, A., Tracey, L., Homer, M.S., Tomlinson, P.D., Ashby, P., Mitchell, N., McIntyre, J, Cooper, D., Roper, T., Chambers, G.N. and Tomlinson, P.D. (2009) *Becoming a Teacher: Teachers' Experiences of Initial Teacher Training, Induction and Early Professional Development: Research Report*, DCSF Research Report No. RR115.
This publication provides a report on a large-scale longitudinal research project that examined the experiences of teachers during their ITE programme, induction and their early career professional development.

Other resources and websites

The Teacher Education Observatory: http://teachereducationobservatory.org
This website provides a network which can monitor developments across teacher education and provides signposts to resources.

The teaching and learning research programme (TLRP) webwww.tlrp.org/)
This website provides access to a large range of material relating to teaching.

The Stanford Center for Opportunity Policy in Education (SCOPE): https://edpolicy.stanford.edu
This website offers links to a range of education literature and project overviews relating to teaching.

Wenger-Trayner: www.ewenger.com
Look at Wenger's website and consider your school as a community of learning and you as a member of that community. This website provides an overview of communities of practice and presents a brief introduction to the concept and the characteristics of such communities.

Appendix 2 on pages 591–595 provides further examples of websites you may find useful.

Capel, S., Leask, M. and Turner, T. (eds) (2010) *Readings for Learning to Teach in the Secondary School: A Companion to M Level Study*, London: Routledge.
This book brings together essential readings to support you in your critical engagement with key issues raised in this textbook.

The subject-specific books in the Routledge *Learning to Teach* series are also very useful.

Any additional resources and an editable version of any relevant tasks/tables in this unit are available on the companion website: www.routledge.com/cw/capel

8.3 Accountability, contractual and statutory duties

Sue Collins and Dawn Leslie

Introduction

The work of teachers is guided and regulated in different ways and by different agencies (for example, by national and local government, academy trusts, the school, school governors, parents and pupils), so you are potentially accountable to a whole range of interested parties for the quality of your work.

This unit is designed to help you understand how the education system in state schools in England functions in relation to the accountability of teachers for their work, including the care and welfare of pupils. Although the details will be different in different countries, many of the principles in this unit will be relevant wherever you are teaching.

OBJECTIVES

At the end of this unit, you should be able to:

- understand the structure of the state education system in England;
- be aware of the different types of accountability of teachers;
- be aware of the legal and contractual requirements that govern the work of the teacher.

Check the requirements of your initial teacher education (ITE) programme to see which relate to this unit.

Where do teachers fit within the education system?

The structure of the education system across the developed world is based on common principles, though variations inevitably occur and should be explored. As an example, the relationships between the education system and teachers in England is set out in Figure 8.3.1. The Secretary of State, ministers and staff at the Department for Education (DfE) are not required to have teaching experience: they are provided with professional advice by advisory bodies such as the National College for Teaching and Leadership (NCTL). In early 2013, the National College for School Leadership and the Teaching Agency were merged to form the NCTL, which has the broad remit of improving the quality of the education workforce and helping schools to help each other to improve, bringing under one umbrella all aspects of teacher training, continuing professional development (CPD), special educational needs provision and the regulation of teachers' professional conduct in England. Members of advisory bodies usually begin their careers as student teachers like you, and so are likely to have been classroom teachers for some time before taking on these other roles.

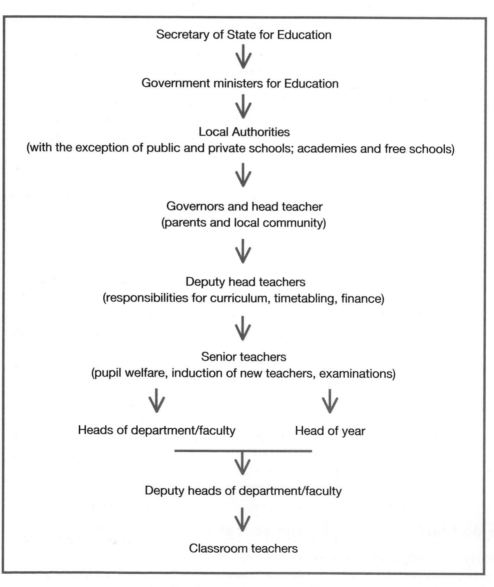

Figure 8.3.1 Common structure of aspects of the education system in England (excluding the further education (FE) sector)

While the responsibilities within the school, listed in Figure 8.3.1, may vary across schools and the terminology used is likely to differ, the general structure will be very similar. However, not included here are the numerous support staff whose contribution to school life is essential to the smooth running of the school; for example, teaching assistants, school's premises' officer, nurse, administrative staff, technical staff, cleaners, lunchtime supervisors, and the bursar.

People from other professions are also linked with the school (for example, the education welfare officer and school psychologists); some pupils also have social workers who are responsible for overseeing their progress. Parents and members of local communities will often have roles in schools – as governors or in providing support in a wide range of ways.

Task 8.3.1 asks you to map out the system in which you work.

 Task 8.3.1 The structure of the education system

Draw and label your own version of Figure 8.3.1 as appropriate to the school and context in which you are working. Check you are aware of any documents produced by government agencies that are relevant to your work by asking your tutor and checking key national websites and those referred to in Unit 7.3. Store this in your professional development portfolio (PDP).

Accountability

Accountability in education is a broad concept that is addressed in many ways, such as using political processes to ensure democratic accountability, introducing reforms to increase accountability to parents and pupils, or developing peer-based accountability systems to increase the professional accountability of teachers. Sometimes described as 'an ethical concept' (Levitt *et al.* 2008), accountability permeates education systems across the world, focusing on the distribution of responsibility for managing all aspects of pupils' education and producing results and measures devised principally by government agencies, to determine the extent to which the processes and products of education meet given criteria and attain set targets. The key purpose of school and teacher accountability is to improve the education system, and responsibility for monitoring improvements is commonly given to semi-independent bodies; for instance, the Office for Standards in Education (Ofsted) in England (Brundrett and Rhodes 2011). For you as a teacher, accountability involves both *responsibility* towards and *accounting* to:

- pupils – the intrinsic sense of responsibility for the individual pupils in your care (moral accountability);
- colleagues – including all members of your school community (professional accountability);
- employers and the government (contractual accountability);
- the market – where parents and pupils have a choice of school (market accountability).

(Mongon and Chapman 2012; Earley and Weindling 2004)

Types of accountability

The types of accountability applicable to you as a beginning teacher will fall into four broad categories as follows:

1   *Organisational accountability*: refers to the responsibility of all members of the school community to work collaboratively in ensuring compliance with relevant government targets, policies and standards. However, the development, implementation and regular revision of a school improvement plan (SIP) is first and foremost the responsibility of individual schools – the school's governing body holds head teachers and senior members of staff accountable for the success of SIP initiatives. Teachers and other members of the school community are, in turn, held accountable for the effective implementation of school improvement initiatives. Teachers are responsible for providing feedback to inform continuing improvements in the school.

2   *Legal accountability*: as a teacher, you have a responsibility to do all that is reasonable to protect the health, safety and welfare of pupils. For teachers in England, *The Bristol Guide* (2014) provides you with detailed information and guidance about relevant aspects of the law and general advice relating to your professional responsibilities and duties. You may wish to consider becoming a member of a teaching union, which would provide you with access to a range of services, both legal and professional.

3   *Professional accountability*: your professional behaviour is monitored and appraised by your peers and by external bodies such as Ofsted. You are bound by codes of practice laid down by professional bodies and the government, which are now encompassed by the Teachers' Standards (DfE 2013g). The standards define the minimum level of practice expected of trainees and teachers from the point of being awarded qualified teacher status (QTS). Teachers are expected to make the education and welfare of pupils their first concern and are accountable for achieving the highest possible standards in work and professional conduct. Teachers act with honesty and integrity; have strong subject knowledge; keep their knowledge and skills as teachers up to date and are self-critical; forge positive professional relationships; and work with parents in the best interests of their pupils (DfE 2013g).

4   *Moral accountability*: refers to the sometimes competing demands of your own values and beliefs and the requirements of the school in which you are working. You will have your own values and your own code of conduct and these should be adapted in response to the requirements of the school. As a teacher, you have a responsibility to act, at all times, in the best interest of the pupils you teach, their parents/carers and other stakeholders. In 2009, the General Teaching Council (GTCE) proposed a new code of conduct for teachers in which they were required to act as role models, both in and out of school. 'Role modelling' was made obligatory because teachers, as members of a profession, were expected to maintain high standards of personal and professional behaviour. Because the well-being of pupils depends on the teachers' moral behaviour, and since parents place a high degree of trust in teachers, teachers are expected to honour this confidence (GTCE 2009). The code of conduct has been subsumed into the Teachers' Standards Part Two: Personal and Professional Conduct (DfE 2013g).

Task 8.3.2 focuses on moral and professional accountability, the importance of role models in particular.

Task 8.3.2 Moral and professional accountability

There are many ways in which a teacher can act as a role model for their pupils. Consider how this might be, with particular reference to pupils in your school. Discuss this with other student teachers or your tutor and record these in your PDP.

The next section sets out in a little more detail your legal duties, both contractual and statutory. However, it does not pretend to contain a complete or exhaustive account, but to indicate some of the areas that you will benefit from investigating further.

Legal duties and responsibilities

Teachers have a number of legally binding contractual responsibilities and statutory duties. In addition, you also have, as do all citizens, common law duties (NUT 2013), which means, among other things, that you have a duty of care towards pupils. The standard of care expected of you as a teacher is 'that of a reasonable person in the circumstance of a class teacher' (NUT 2013: 2). There is a recognition of the fact that your duty of care to individual pupils will inevitably be influenced by the subject or activity being taught, the age of the children, the available resources and the size of the class.

Teachers, again as citizens, are subject to criminal law. One aspect of criminal law you should note is that if you hit a pupil, this may fall within the definition of corporal punishment, which is illegal in England and many other countries (DfE 2013j). Any deliberate application of unlawful force is an assault. It will be unlawful if it is not in self-defence, for example. Further to this, the government regularly updates guidelines for teachers designed to improve discipline in schools in England (DfE 2013j). The 2013 guidance clarifies the authority of teachers, making it clear that:

■ Schools should no longer adopt a 'no touch' policy. There is recognition that it is sometimes necessary for a teacher to touch a pupil; for example, when attending to an accident or teaching a musical instrument.

■ Teachers have been advised that it is not unlawful to use *reasonable* force in certain circumstances to control or restrain a pupil. This can range from guiding a pupil to safety by the arm through to more extreme circumstances such as breaking up a fight or where a student needs to be restrained to prevent violence or injury. It is important to note that *reasonable* in this context means using no more force than is needed (DfE 2013j: 4).

■ Head teachers have the authority to search pupils for an extended list of items, including alcohol, illegal drugs and stolen property.

■ Head teachers have been given the power to discipline pupils who misbehave outside the school premises and outside school hours.

On the issue of teachers' legal rights, guidance has been issued to protect teachers from malicious allegations, further details of which may be found at DfE (2013j). However, as a student teacher, you should always follow the policies of the school in which you are placed.

Important legislation

Rights and responsibilities

Teachers also have important rights and responsibilities under the Equality Act 2010 and the Human Rights Act 1998 (incorporating the European Convention on Human Rights and Fundamental Freedoms). For example, under the heading 'Right to Education', Article 2 of the First Protocol to the Convention states that:

> No person shall be denied the right to education. In the exercise of any functions which it assumes in relation to education and to teaching, the State shall respect the right of parents to ensure such education and teaching is in conformity with their own religious and philosophical convictions.

Child protection

Teachers in schools in England should be familiar with the general principles of the Children Act 1989, which put in place the first significant child protection structures that have considerable relevance to teachers today. Guidance for teachers, governors and schools in England is provided by the publication *Keeping Children Safe in Education* (DfE 2014g). Other countries have similar guidance for teachers, and you should explore these for your particular context.

Child protection training is a mandatory requirement for all student teachers. In order to be awarded qualified teacher status, student teachers have to demonstrate a sound understanding of their contractual, administrative and pastoral responsibilities. Newly qualified teachers are expected to be able to identify pupils with special educational needs and demonstrate a sound understanding of the procedures for seeking advice and support from appropriate agencies; for example, social workers and healthcare professionals (Singh 2011).

Safeguarding children and young people

The document *Working Together to Safeguard Children* (DCSF 2010) was revised in response to the findings of the Laming Report *The Protection of Children in England: A Progress Report* (DCSF 2009b), which contained 58 recommendations designed to improve safeguarding procedures for children and young people in schools and the wider community. The revised *Working Together to Safeguard Children* (HMG 2013) document reiterates the key tenets of the Children Acts of 1989 and 2004 in stressing the need for organisations and individuals to work collaboratively to:

■ protect children from maltreatment;
■ prevent impairment of children's health or development;
■ ensure that children grow up in circumstance consistent with the provision of safe and effective care;
■ take action to enable all children to have the best outcomes.

As a teacher, part of your professional responsibility is to help your school create and maintain a safe learning environment for every pupil. What does this mean for you as the class teacher?

Your role is to be fully conversant with the policies and procedures in place in your school that address issues of children protection, health and safety, and bullying (including cyberbullying).

The welfare of children and young people

As a member of the school community, you have a responsibility for the arrangements made to meet the health and safety needs of pupils. Most pupils at school with medical conditions should be properly supported so that they have full access to education, including school trips and physical education (DfE 2014l). However, you and your colleagues may need to take extra care in supervising some activities to make sure that these children and others are not put at risk. It should be noted that there is no legal duty for you to administer medicines to pupils: after discussion with parents, pupils who are competent should be encouraged to take responsibility for managing their own medicines and procedures; wherever possible, pupils should be allowed to carry their own medicines and relevant devices or should be able to access their medicines for self-medication, quickly and easily; pupils who can take their medicines themselves or manage procedures may require a level of supervision; if it is not appropriate for a pupil to self-manage, then relevant staff should administer medicines and manage procedures for them (DfE 2014l: 12).

As a member of your school community, you have a responsibility to tackle issues of drug taking and substance misuse. Schools are strongly advised to have a written drugs policy (DfE/ACPO 2012), and it is your responsibility to follow closely the policy and guidelines of your school. You share responsibility with colleagues for school security and for following procedures in place to safeguard pupils and promote their welfare during periods of vocational work experience.

Teachers have a crucially important role to play in helping with the earliest possible identification of welfare concerns, including signs of possible abuse or neglect. You should not take it upon yourself to investigate possible abuse or neglect, but you are expected to familiarise yourself with your school's procedures for referral of concerns to the appropriate organisation; for example, the local authority social services department whose role it is to carry out an assessment of the pupil's needs and to act on this as appropriate. As a student teacher, you should share any concerns you might have about any pupil with the relevant colleague in school.

Special educational and physical needs

In some instances, your school will be very well equipped to address the needs of the individual pupil; for instance, a pupil with special educational and/or physical needs will move into secondary school with detailed information about their ongoing needs and the most effective means of meeting those needs. Your responsibility is to familiarise yourself with all documentation about the needs of the individual and to ensure that these needs are met through planning and your teaching and learning strategies. As a student teacher, you need to follow school procedures and talk to/seek guidance from the class teacher and/or special educational needs coordinator (SENCO) about any pupil with special educational needs in any of your classes. Unit 4.6 covers special education needs.

Managing pupil behaviour

As stated earlier, corporal punishment is illegal in any school in England and in the majority of developed countries across the world. The law forbids a teacher, or any member of staff, from using any form of physical contact with a pupil that is deliberately designed to punish or cause pain, injury or humiliation (DfE 2013j). However, recent advice from the government makes it clear that teachers have power to discipline pupils for misbehaviour that occurs in school and, in some circumstances, outside school (DfE 2014e: 3). Head teachers of maintained schools in England are required by law to set out measures in the behaviour policy that aim to:

■ promote good behaviour, self-discipline and respect;
■ prevent bullying;
■ ensure that pupils complete assigned work;
■ regulate the conduct of pupils.

It is your responsibility as a student teacher to familiarise yourself with the details of your school policy on behaviour. Unit 3.3 covers behaviour for learning that takes a positive approach to managing pupil behaviour.

Recruitment of teachers and other school staff

Every school in England has responsibility for safeguarding children and young people. You will first encounter legislation and school policies on safeguarding during your ITE programme and when applying for your first post. You will need to familiarise yourself with the publication *Keeping Children Safe in Education* (DfE 2014g), particularly 'Part 3: Safer Recruitment', which sets out the procedures for selection and pre-employment vetting for schools that will provide the framework for all schools' recruitment policies. Schools will have explicit employment policies that take account of national and local safeguarding requirements. It is vital that you familiarise yourself with these before writing and submitting your application, to ensure you comply with all requirements. The school to which you are applying will require you to provide evidence of an enhanced Disclosure and Barring Service (DBS) check at the level appropriate to the post. Your prospective employer will seek references, usually once you are a shortlisted candidate, and will approach your previous employer or your ITE provider for clarification of points made in your reference and/or to verify your qualifications and experience before your interview. You need to take great care in completing your application form because providing false information is an offence and could result in your application being rejected or could be the basis for dismissing you subsequently.

The importance of the implementation of safer recruitment procedures was reflected in the introduction, in January 2010, of mandatory safer recruitment training for head teachers, members of the school governing body and any other staff involved in recruitment to ensure that the policies and principles of safeguarding children and young people are respected and applied consistently across schools. However, since the beginning of September 2014, safer recruitment training no longer needs to be approved by the Secretary of State, although schools will continue to be required to ensure that at least one member of any recruitment panel has received appropriate training in line with safeguarding guidance. In January 2015, the National Society for the Prevention of Cruelty to Children (NSPCC) opened the online *Safer Recruitment in Education Course* designed for teachers, head teachers, governors and anyone responsible for recruitment in schools (NSPCC 2015). All recruitment panels must have at least one member who has completed training.

Having read the above, move on to complete Task 8.3.3.

Task 8.3.3 Safeguarding and the class teacher

Consider safeguarding and promoting the welfare of every pupil in your class. What are your main responsibilities? What challenges might these present for you as a teacher? What support would you seek in addressing these challenges? Make notes in your PDP and discuss this with other student teachers, your tutor and/or your school-based tutor to ensure that you fully understand your responsibilities when you become a qualified teacher.

Contractual and statutory duties

Contractual rights and duties are negotiated between teachers and their employer, while statutory duties are those that the government has established through legislation.

In the case of teachers employed in state schools in England, the document that sets out teachers' contractual rights and duties is *School Teachers' Pay and Conditions*, which is produced by the DfE and updated annually (DfE 2014i). This document outlines the statutory requirements for teachers' pay and conditions by which maintained schools in England must abide. The guidelines for you as a beginning teacher are laid down for the exercise of your professional responsibilities under the headings of teaching; contribution to whole school organisation, strategy and development; health, safety and discipline; management of staff (that is, support staff) and resources; professional development; communication (with pupils, parents and carers); and working with colleagues and other relevant professionals.

To learn more about your legal liabilities, see Berry (2013), and for clear guidance on issues related to child protection, see Singh (2011).

Additional conditions may apply in individual schools. There may also be implied terms to your contract; that is, terms that are not written down. All employment contracts contain the following implied terms: to maintain trust and confidence through cooperation; to act in good faith towards each other; and to take reasonable care to ensure health and safety in the workplace, but there may be implied terms specific to your school.

The *Head's Legal Guide* (Croner, updated annually) is recommended further reading for those with a particular interest in this area.

Specific advice on teaching contracts is available from the teaching unions; for example, the National Union of Teachers (NUT) (www.teachers.org.uk/) and the National Association of Schoolmasters/Union of Women Teachers (NASUWT) (www.nasuwt.org.uk/).

Task 8.3.4 looks at your contractual and statutory duties.

 Task 8.3.4 Your contractual and statutory duties

Obtain a copy of the conditions likely to govern your employment as a teacher. In England, the *School Teacher's Pay and Conditions Document* contains this information. Discuss this with other student teachers or your tutor and ensure that you understand what is required of you when you become a qualified teacher. Keep this in your PDP.

SUMMARY AND KEY POINTS

▤ As a student teacher, you need to be aware of the full range of a teacher's duties.

▤ Whenever you are working in a school, you are acting with the agreement and support of qualified teachers.

▤ When you take over their classes, you are accountable for the work in the classroom in the same ways they are.

▤ You are responsible for safeguarding and promoting the welfare and health and safety of every pupil and need to be aware of the requirements in any school in which you teach.

Check which requirements for your ITE programme you have addressed through this completing this unit.

Further reading

Berry, J. (2013) *Teachers' Legal Rights and Responsibilities: A Guide for Trainee Teachers and Those New to the Profession*, 3rd edn, Hatfield: University of Hertfordshire Press.
This guide provides an overview of the legal issues relevant to teachers to help them understand their rights, responsibilities and professional duties.

Brundrett, M. and Rhodes, C. (2011) *Leadership for Quality and Accountability Education*, London: Routledge.
This book addresses issues of quality and accountability in the education system and provides a framework within which these issues can be analysed. The authors outline the significance of promoting quality in all educational establishments and go on to discuss *why* quality and accountability have become so essential to the framework of leadership in education, *how* quality and accountability have been utilised on a national and international scale and *what* the defining characteristics of these terms are.

Croner (updated annually) *Head's Guide to the Law*, New Malden: Croner.
Essential legal and education management information for head teachers, with regularly updated guidance on legislation and good practice for schools in England and Wales.

Levitt, R., Janta, B. and Wegrich, K. (2008) *Accountability of Teachers: Literature Review* (Prepared for the GTCE), London: General Teaching Council for England.
This is a useful review of selected literature that explores issues of teacher accountability and professional autonomy and responsibility. This is an important publication as many changes have taken place over the past 20 years that have implications for school policies and practices, management and changes to external monitoring of schools. The document makes the point that 'these changes have both reflected and altered perceptions of teachers' professionalism' (p. 9).

Singh, J. (2011) *Child Protection: A Manual for School Teachers*, USA: LAP.
These texts provide invaluable and up-to-date information for teachers on legal liabilities and responsibilities for child protection in schools in England and Wales. However, the issues discussed are relevant to schools and teachers working elsewhere in the UK.

The Bristol Guide (2014 edn, updated regularly) *Professional Responsibilities and Statutory Frameworks for Teachers and Others in Schools*, Bristol: University of Bristol, School of Education, available at: www.bristol.ac.uk/education/expertiseandresources/bristolguide.
Updated regularly, *The Bristol Guide* is crucial reading for everyone who works with children and young people in school settings. It provides up-to-date guidance on teachers' statutory frameworks and the law that governs professional responsibilities and duties.

Other resources and websites

Appendix 2 on pages 591-595 provides examples of websites you may find useful.

Capel, S., Leask, M. and Turner, T. (eds) (2010) *Readings for Learning to Teach in the Secondary School: A Companion to M Level Study*, London: Routledge.
This book brings together essential readings to support you in your critical engagement with key issues raised in this textbook.

The subject-specific books in the Routledge *Learning to Teach* series are also very useful.

Any additional resources and an editable version of any relevant tasks/tables in this unit are available on the companion website: www.routledge.com/cw/capel

9 And finally

Marilyn Leask and Andrew Green

Introduction

The introduction to this text sets you the challenge of considering what you want to achieve by becoming a teacher and what it means to be a teacher. Each unit has been designed to help you understand the different elements of teaching. This 'whole-part-whole approach' to introducing you to teaching through this text mirrors best practice in teaching – introducing the whole, undertaking work on the parts, then returning to review the learning in the context of the whole.

Here, in the last unit, we return to the issue of how your values and beliefs shape your work as a teacher. Unit 7.1 challenged you to think about the aims of education. Units 1.1 and 4.5 asked you to consider your values to adopt a code of conduct to guide your work as a professional. Over your teaching career, you can expect demands on teachers to be able to demonstrate evidence-informed practice to become the norm. We do not expect doctors to practice without reference to the latest evidence, and learners and their parents and carers too can expect evidence-informed practice from you. (In Unit 5.4, we made the point that evidence-informed practice = professional judgement + evidence: research is never adopted without reference to the learner and the environment and subject context.) The list of websites on pages 591–595 provides information to enable you to keep up to date.

This text has drawn on the evidence base for educational practice in providing information and background then exploring these through linked tasks. Some tasks provide opportunities to reflect on and examine the practice of other teachers, of yourself and the organisation of schools; others are enquiry-based and generate data or ideas for reflective thinking upon which an understanding of, and an explanation for, the complex world of teaching and learning in schools are built.

The relationship between explanation and practice is a dynamic one; explanations are needed to make sense of experience and inform developing practice. Some explanations will be your own, to be tried and tested against the theories of others, often more experienced teachers. At other times, you may use others' explanations directly. Explanations in turn generate working theories, responsive to practice and experience. Theory is important, as it provides a variety of ways of thinking about the complex world of the classroom and directs further personal research into improving the quality of teaching and learning. It also provides a basis for judging both personal and institutional change. The interplay of theory and practice develops your professional judgement and underpins the notion of the reflective and evidence-informed practitioner.

What values will you pass on?

To teach young people is to contribute directly to shaping the society of tomorrow. What values will you pass on to the young people you teach? As a last task, we ask you to consider the messages in the letter and poem in Tables 9.1 and 9.2.

The letter 'Dear Teacher' (Table 9.1) was written by a US high school principal, a World War II concentration camp survivor who was separated from her sister and mother whom she never saw again. She gives the letter to all new staff at her school (Pring 2004). The poem 'Children learn what they live' (Table 9.2, Dorothy Law Nolte) is often displayed on staffroom walls. Read the letter and the poem and then complete Task 9.1.

Table 9.1 'Dear teacher'

Dear teacher,
I am the survivor of a concentration camp. My eyes saw what no man should witness.
Gas chambers built by learned engineers,
Children poisoned by educated physicians,
Infants killed by trained nurses,
Women and babies shot and burned by high school and college graduates.
So I am suspicious of education.
My request is: Help your students become human.
Your efforts must never produce learned monsters, skilled psychopaths, educated Eichmanns.
Reading writing and arithmetic are important only if they serve to make our children more human.

Table 9.2 'Children learn what they live'

If a child lives with criticism,
he learns to condemn,
If a child lives with hostility,
he learns to fight,
If a child lives with ridicule,
he learns to be shy,
If a child lives with shame,
he learns to feel guilty,
If a child lives with tolerance,
he learns to be patient,
If a child lives with encouragement,
he learns confidence,
If a child lives with praise,
he learns to appreciate,
If a child lives with fairness,
he learns justice,
If a child lives with security,
he learns to have faith,
If a child lives with approval,
he learns to like himself,
If a child lives with acceptance and friendship,
he learns to find love in the world.

Source: Dorothy Law Nolte

Task 9.1 What will your pupils learn from you?

Read the poems in table 9.1 and table 9.2. Consider the values that you as a teacher will pass on for your teaching and through the relationships you develop with your pupils. Write a note to yourself about what you hope to achieve and revisit and review your aspirations for yourself as a teacher at the beginning of each term of your teaching.

SUMMARY AND KEY POINTS

■ As a teacher, you will have more impact than you will ever know – on the lives of the pupils you teach, their parents and carers, and the communities and societies within which they live.

■ We hope that you will help pupils to build the personal self-confidence and skills to cope with adult life and to become autonomous learners and caring members of society.

■ We hope too that what your pupils learn from you will help them make positive contributions to their world.

■ To achieve these goals, you should expect to carry on learning throughout your professional life.

■ As a first step, joining your subject association will ensure you receive publications outlining good practice, and attending your annual subject conference will introduce you to the network of educators taking thinking in your subject forward. You can find your subject association by asking colleagues and tutors or through the Council for Subject Associations (www.subjectassociation.org.uk).

■ Teachers are expected to continue to undertake reflective practice and learning beyond their ITE. Teachers in some countries have to have master's-level qualifications; in those countries where this is not required, many teachers study part-time to achieve this level of qualification.

■ The issues raised in this unit about the purpose of education and how children learn are areas you may wish to follow up through engaging with networks of other educators to develop and share the evidence base for professional practice in education.

Check which requirements for your ITE programme you have addressed through this unit.

 Further reading

The texts below provide an introduction to some of the debates and thinking that have shaped educational practice in the UK over more than 100 years. The Masterclass texts (www.bloomsbury.com/uk/series/masterclass/) provide materials giving an in-depth examination of issues in particular subject areas.

Aldrich, R. (2006) *Lessons from History of Education: The Selected Works of Richard Aldrich*, London: Routledge.
This text provides a useful introduction to recurrent issues in education.

Bruner, J.S. (2006a) *In Search of Pedagogy Volume 1: The Selected Works of Jerome S. Bruner*, London: Routledge.

Bruner, J.S. (2006b) *In Search of Pedagogy Volume 2: The Selected Works of Jerome S. Bruner*, London: Routledge.
  Bruner's work on pedagogy is seminal – changing thinking and practice.

Dewey, J. (1933) *How We Think*, Boston, MA: Houghton Mifflin.
  Dewey's ideas endure. This text will challenge you to think to what extent these ideas are now spread across the education system.

Gardner, H. (2006b) *The Development and Education of the Mind: The Selected Works of Howard Gardner*, London: Routledge.
  This is just one of Gardner's challenging and informative publications.

Marples, R. (2012) *The Aims of Education*, London: Routledge.
  This provides a useful introduction and overview of aims of education.

Other resources and websites

Council for Subject Associations: www.subjectassociation.org.uk/members_links.aspx
  This site provides contact details of the major professional associations.

Teaching Councils: Membership is by subscription and confirmation of qualifications. Normally, Councils have a code of conduct members are expected to adhere to.
  At the time of writing, a Teaching Council for England is under development. The previous Council, the General Teaching Council for England, was not independently run by the profession as other councils are and was closed by Michael Gove, the Secretary of State for Education in the UK government, in 2011. For information about resources, see: http://webarchive.nationalarchives.gov.uk/20111213132132/http:/www.gtce.org.uk.

For Scotland, see: www.gtcs.org.uk/home/home.aspx.
  This council has been in existence for over 50 years and a benefit of membership is open access to academic journals, which is covered by the fee.

For Northern Ireland, see: www.gtcni.org.uk/.

For Wales, see: www.teachertrainingcymru.org/node/26.

To become engaged in developing the evidence base for practice, see the 'Get Involved' tab on www.meshguides.org.

Appendix 2 on pages 591–595 provides examples of further websites you may find useful.

Any additional resources and an editable version of any relevant tasks/tables in this unit are available on the companion website: www.routledge.com/cw/capel

Appendix 1
Glossary of terms

Terms shown in bold within a definition have their own entry in the glossary.

A level See **GCE**.

A2 level See **GCE**.

Academies In England, all-ability schools established by sponsors from business, faith or voluntary groups in partnership with central government and **LAs**. Often, so-called 'failing' state schools taken out of LA control but any school can apply for academy status. See also **state-maintained schools in England** and **other state schools in England**.

ACCAC (Awdurdod Cymwysterau, Cwricwlwm ac Asesu Cymru) Formerly the Qualifications, Curriculum and Assessment Authority for Wales. Merged with **DCELLS** in 2006.

AEB See **AQA**.

Annual review The review of a statement of special educational needs (**SEN**) that an **LA** must make within 12 months of making the statement or from a previous review.

AQA Assessment and Qualifications Alliance. An **awarding body** for **GCSE**, **GCE A** and **AS levels** and **diplomas** (www.aqa.org.uk). Formed in 2000 by a merger of City and Guilds GNVQ, Associated Examining Board (AEB), Southern Examining Group (SEG) and Northern Examination and Assessment Board (NEAB).

AS level See **GCE**.

Assessment Assessment covers all those activities that are undertaken by teachers and others to measure the effectiveness of their teaching and of pupils learning. See also **assessment for learning**, **assessment of learning**, **criterion-referenced assessment**, **formative assessment**, **ipsative assessment**, **norm-referenced assessment** and **summative assessment**.

Assessment for learning Assessment for which the first priority is to promote pupils' learning. It allows teachers and pupils to decide where the learners are in their learning and encourages pupils to take ownership of their learning. See also **assessment**, **assessment of learning**, **formative assessment**, **ipsative assessment**, **norm-referenced assessment** and **summative assessment**.

Assessment of learning The summative assessment of pupils' attainment and progress periodically in a variety of ways and for a variety of purposes. See also **assessment**, **assessment for learning**, **criterion-referenced assessment**, **formative assessment**, **ipsative assessment**, **norm-referenced assessment** and **summative assessment**.

Attainment targets (ATs) of **NC** for England The knowledge, skills and understanding that pupils of different abilities and maturities are expected to have by the end of each **Key Stage**. Attainment targets consist of eight **level descriptions** of increasing difficulty, plus a description for exceptional performance above level 8. The latest **National Curriculum** (2014) has removed all level descriptions. See also **programmes of study**.

Awarding body There are three awarding bodies that set public examinations in England: the Assessment and Qualifications Alliance (**AQA**), **EdExcel** (Pearson), and Oxford and Cambridge Regional (**OCR**).

BA/BSc (QTS) bachelor of arts/bachelor of science with **QTS** A teaching qualification awarded in England – a combined course with route to QTS. *Note*: Your teaching qualification may not be recognised in other countries, including in others of the four countries in the UK.

Banding The structuring of a year group into divisions, each usually containing two or three classes, on grounds of general ability. Pupils are taught within the band for virtually all the curriculum. See also **mixed ability grouping**, **setting** and **streaming**.

Baseline testing Any process that sets out to find out what the learner can do now in relation to the next stage of learning. For example, the assessment of practical skills and familiarity of pupils with equipment and tools prior to a **D and T** course. Or the assessment of pupils in Year 1 and reception classes for speaking, listening, reading, writing, mathematics and social skills. See also **benchmarking**.

Basic curriculum for England The requirements of the **National Curriculum** as at 2012:

- ■ **Key Stage 3** comprises 12 statutory subjects, which are art and design, citizenship, design and technology, English, geography, history, ICT/computing, mathematics, modern foreign languages, music, physical education and science. Careers education, sex education and religious education are also statutory.
- ■ At **Key Stage 4**, pupils study a mix of compulsory subjects and, if they so elect, a course of study in a subject within each of four 'entitlement' areas. The compulsory subjects are English, mathematics, science, ICT/computing, PE, RE and citizenship. The entitlement areas are arts (five subjects), design and technology, humanities (two subjects) and a modern foreign language (unspecified).

BEd bachelor of education A teacher training qualification in England leading to **QTS**.

Benchmarking A term used to describe a standard against which comparisons can be made. Can be used by schools; for example, to measure success of the school in public examinations relative to a national norm.

BESD (behavioural, emotional and social difficulties) A group of pupils with special educational needs. The term is often applied to pupils whose behaviour is consistently poor and not obviously related to the circumstances and environment in which pupils find themselves. Pupils who are withdrawn also fit into this category. See also **SEN** and **SEND**.

BTEC (Business and Technician Education Council) Part of **EdExcel Foundation**, which offers courses called BTEC Nationals.

C and G (City and Guilds) See **AQA**.

Career entry and development profile (CEDP) All **ITE** providers in England are required to provide newly qualified teachers with a **CEDP** to help newly qualified teachers in their first teaching post schools and support **induction**. Details available at: www.education.gov.uk/publications/eOrderingDownload/cepd_2011-12_tda0876.pdf.

Careers education Designed to help pupils to choose and prepare for opportunities, responsibilities and experiences in education, training and employment.

CEDP See **career entry and development profile**.

CEHR Commission for Equality and Human Rights; also referred to as Equality and Human Rights Commission (www.equalityhumanrights.com/).

Certificate of achievement (COA) An examination designed to give a qualification to pupils who may not gain a GCSE grade, offered by the **awarding bodies**. Also called **entry-level certificate**; see Directgov website.

Church and faith schools A faith school is a British school teaching a general curriculum but with a particular religious character or having formal links with a religious organisation. Regulations differ in detail among constituent countries of Britain. In England, the curriculum, admissions criteria and staffing policies may reflect their religious foundation. See also **state-maintained schools in England** and **other state schools in England**.

Citizenship A statutory subject of the English **NC** at **Key Stages** 3 and 4. See also **cross-curricular elements**.

Collaborative group A way of working in which groups of children are assigned to groups or engage spontaneously in working together to solve problems; sometimes called cooperative group work. See the now archived DCFS Standards website *Grouping Pupils for Success* (http://web archive.nationalarchives.gov.uk/20110809101133/nsonline.org.uk/node/84974).

Combined course A course to which several subjects contribute while retaining their distinct identity (for example, history, geography and RE within humanities). See also **integrated course**.

Community and foundation special schools For children with specific special educational needs, such as physical or learning difficulties. See also **state-maintained schools in England** and **other state schools in England**.

Community of practice Groups of people who share a concern for something or have knowledge and skills to share. For example, a subject association network or a network of teachers working on solving a particular problem.

Community school A school run by the **LA**, which employs the staff, owns the land and buildings and decides admission criteria. Develops links with community. See also **state-maintained schools in England** and **other state schools in England**.

Comprehensive school A type of state-maintained secondary school that admits pupils of age 11 to 16 or 19 from a given catchment area, regardless of their ability. See also **state-maintained schools in England** and **other state schools in England**.

Computer science In England, a proposal in 2012 by the Secretary of State for Education to replace ICT by a new course, 'computer science'. See **ICT**.

Continuity A feature of a curriculum and of lesson plans that ensure that learning builds on what has already been taught and experienced and prepares pupils for what is to come. See also **progression**.

Core skills Skills required by all students following 14–19 courses. See **functional skills** and **personal learning and thinking skills**.

Core standards The professional standards that teachers must meet to confirm their qualified teacher status. See **induction**.

Core subjects Foundation subjects that are taught at both KS3 and KS4 comprising English, mathematics and science in the **National Curriculum** for England. See also **entitlement subjects**.

Coursework Work carried out by pupils during a course of study marked by teachers and contributing to the final examination mark. Usually externally moderated.

CPD Continuing professional development.

CRE Commission for Racial Equality; now part of **CEHR**.

Criterion-referenced assessment A process in which performance is measured by relating candidates' responses to predetermined criteria. See also **assessment, assessment for learning, assessment of learning, formative assessment, ipsative assessment, norm-referenced assessment** and **summative assessment**.

Cross-curricular elements Additional elements of a curriculum beyond statutory subjects, which includes careers, **citizenship**, economic education, **key skills**, **personal learning and thinking skills (PLTS)** and personal, social and health education (**PSHE**).

Curriculum A course of study followed by a pupil.

Curriculum guidelines Written guidance for organising and teaching a particular subject or area of the curriculum. See also **programmes of study**.

D and T Design and technology in **NC** for England.

DCELLS Department for Children, Education, Lifelong Learning and Skills of the Welsh Assembly (www.accreditedqualifications.org.uk/department-for-children-education-lifelong-learning-and-skills-dcells.html).

Department Section of the curriculum/administrative structure of a (secondary) school, usually based on a subject.

DES, **DfE**, **DfEE**, **DfES**, **DCSF** Various names for the ministry of education in England. See **government education departments and chronology**.

DfE circular Advice issued by the DfE (Department for Education) to **LAs**. Circulars do not have the status of law.

Differentiation The matching of work to the differing capabilities and learning needs of individuals or groups of pupils in order to extend their learning.

Diploma A 14–19 qualification involving academic qualifications, vocational qualifications and key skills. In England 14 diplomas are available.

Disapplication Arrangement for lifting part or all of the **NC** in England requirements for individuals or for any other grouping specified by the Secretary of State.

DRC Disability Rights Commission; now part of **CEHR**.

EAL English as an additional language.

EBDD Emotional and behavioural difficulties and disorders. Used with reference to pupils with such difficulties or schools/units that cater for such pupils.

EdExcel Foundation An **awarding body** (www.edexcel.org.uk).

Education welfare officer (EWO) An official of the **LA** concerned with pupils' attendance and with liaison between the school, the parents and the authority.

Entitlement subjects (in NC) Non-statutory subjects in four curriculum areas, arts, design and technology, humanities and modern foreign languages (see 'About the school curriculum: what is statutory?' on DfE website).

Entry level See **certificate of achievement**.

EOC Equal Opportunities Commission; now **CEHR**.

ERA Education Reform Act (1988) for England and Wales.

ESL English as a second language.

Exclusion Head teachers of **state-maintained schools** and **other state schools** in England are empowered to exclude pupils temporarily or permanently when faced with a serious breach of their disciplinary code. The exclusions are either a fixed term or permanent. Schools may send pupils to a **pupil referral unit (PRU)**.

EYFS Early Years Foundation Stage (of the **NC** for England).

Faculty Grouping of subjects for administrative and curricular purposes.

Formative assessment Or assessment for learning, linked to teaching when the evidence from assessment is used to adapt teaching to meet pupils' learning needs. See also **assessment**, **assessment for learning**, **assessment of learning**, **criterion-referenced assessment**, **ipsative assessment**, **norm-referenced assessment** and **summative assessment**.

Forms of entry (FE) The number of forms (for example, of 30 pupils) that a school takes into its intake year. From this can be estimated the size of the intake year and the size of the school.

Foundation schools The governing body of these schools employs the staff and sets the admissions criteria. The school land and buildings are owned by the governing body or a charitable foundation. See **state-maintained schools** and **other state schools in England**.

Foundation subjects Subjects that **state-maintained schools** are required by law to teach. In England, four **foundation subjects** are designated **core subjects**. Different subjects are compulsory at different **Key Stages** in England. See **basic curriculum**, **core subjects** and **entitlement subjects**.

Free schools In England, all ability, independent, state-funded schools, non-selective and outside **LA** control, set up in 2010 under the **Academies Act**. Free schools are set up by parents, teachers, charities or businesses. Grants are available to support the initial setting up process. They are subject to the Schools Admissions Code of Practice but priority is given to founders' children. Subject to **Ofsted** inspection. See also **state-maintained schools in England** and **other state schools in England**.

Functional skills Functional skills in the **NC** for England are those core elements of English, mathematics and **ICT** that provide individuals with the skills and abilities they need to operate confidently, effectively and independently in life, their communities and work. They can be examined individually. See Directgov website.

GCE General Certificate of Education – also called Advanced level of the GCE. An award after two years' study usually post **GCSE**. Comprises two awards; an AS level taken after one year of study and A2 level after two years of study.

GCSE General Certificate of Secondary Education.

GNVQ General National Vocational Qualifications.

Government education department titles and chronology For England and Wales to 2006, then England:

- ■ **DCSF** (Department for Children, Schools and Families) 2007–2010
- ■ **DES** (Department of Education and Science) Pre-1992
- ■ **DfE** (Department for Education) 1992–1995; title reappeared 2010–present
- ■ **DfEE** (Department for Education and Employment) 1995–2001
- ■ **DfES** (Department for Education and Skills) 2001–2007

Grade-related criteria The identification of criteria, the achievement of which are related to different levels of performance by the candidate.

Grammar schools State-maintained or independent schools that select all or almost all of their pupils based on academic ability. See also **state-maintained schools in England** and **other state schools in England**.

Group work A way of organising pupils where the teacher assigns tasks to groups of pupils, to be undertaken collectively although the work is completed on an individual basis.

GTCE General Teaching Council for England. Closed 2010 and duties taken over by **National College of Teaching and Leadership (NCTL)**. Northern Ireland, Scotland and Wales have their own teaching councils.

HEI Higher Education Institution.

HMCI Her Majesty's Chief Inspector of Schools in England.

HMI Her Majesty's Inspectors of Schools in England.

HOD Head of department.

House system A structure for pastoral care/pupil welfare within a school in which pupils are grouped in vertical units; that is, sections of the school that include pupils from all year groups. Alternative to the **year system**.

HOY Head of year.

IB International baccalaureate. A post-16 qualification designed for university entrance.

ICT See **information and communications technology**.

In-class support Support within a lesson provided by an additional teacher, often with expertise in teaching pupils with special educational, disability or language needs. See also **learning support**, **learning support assistant**, **partnership teaching** and **withdrawal**.

Inclusion Inclusion involves the processes of increasing the participation of pupils in, and reducing their exclusion from, schools. Inclusion is concerned with the learning participation of all pupils vulnerable to exclusionary pressures, not only those with impairments or categorised as having special educational needs.

Independent school A private school that receives no state assistance but is financed by fees. Often registered as a charity. See also **public school**.

Induction For teachers, the first stage of **continuing professional development (CPD)**. A statutory requirement for newly qualified teachers (**NQTs**) in England in the first year of teaching. Successful completion of induction requires NQTs to meet the **National Induction Standards (Core Standards)** set by the Training and Development Agency (**TDA 2007**). Head teachers are responsible for ensuring statutory requirements are met.

Information and communications technology (ICT) Computer hardware and software that extend beyond the usual word processing, databases, graphics and spreadsheet applications to include hardware and software that allow computers to be networked across the world through the World Wide Web, to access information on the Internet, and which supports other communication activities such as email and video conferencing. ICT was a compulsory subject in the **NC** for England but has been replaced by **computer science** post 2012 (DfE 2012c).

Integrated course A course, usually in a secondary school, to which several subjects contribute without retaining their distinct identity (for example, integrated humanities, which explores themes that include aspects of geography, history and RE). See also **combined course**.

Integration Educating children with special educational needs together with children without special educational needs in mainstream schools. See **inclusion**.

Ipsative assessment A process in which performance is measured against previous performance by the same person. See also **assessment**, **assessment for learning**, **assessment of learning**, criterion-referenced assessment, formative assessment, norm-referenced assessment and summative assessment.

ITE Initial teacher education.

ITT Initial teacher training.

ITTE Initial teacher training and education.

Key skills See functional skills and personal learning and thinking skills.

Key Stages (KS) The periods in each pupil's education to which the elements of the NC for England apply. There are four Key Stages, normally related to the age of the majority of the pupils in a teaching group. They are: Key Stage 1, beginning of compulsory education to age 7 (Years R (Reception), 1 and 2); Key Stage 2, ages 7-11 (Years 3-6); Key Stage 3, ages 11-14 (Years 7-9); Key Stage 4, 14 to end of compulsory education (Years 10 and 11). Post-16 is a further Key Stage.

LA See local authority.

Language support teacher A teacher provided by the LA or school to enhance language work with particular groups of pupils.

Learning objectives What pupils are expected to have learned as a result of an activity, lesson or topic.

Learning outcomes Assessable learning objectives; the action or behaviour of pupils that provides evidence that they have met the learning objectives.

Learning support A means of providing extra help for pupils, usually those with learning difficulties; for example, through a specialist teacher or specially designed materials. See also learning support assistants, in-class support, partnership teaching and withdrawal.

Learning support assistants Teachers who give additional support for a variety of purposes; for example, general learning support for pupils with SEND or ESL; most support is given in-class although sometimes pupils are withdrawn from class. See also learning support, in-class support, partnership teaching and withdrawal.

Lesson plan The detailed planning of work to be undertaken in a lesson. This follows a particular structure, appropriate to the demands of a particular lesson. An individual lesson plan is usually part of a series of lessons in a unit of work.

Level description (NC for England) A statement describing the types and range of performance that pupils working at a particular level should characteristically demonstrate. Level descriptions provide the basis for making judgements about pupils' performance at the end of Key Stages 1, 2 and 3. At Key Stage 4, national qualifications are the main means of assessing attainment in National Curriculum subjects. These level descriptions have been removed in the latest version of the NC (2014).

Levels of attainment in England Eight levels of attainment, plus exceptional performance, are defined within the National Curriculum attainment targets in England. These stop at Key Stage 3; see level description. In deciding a pupil's level of attainment, teachers should judge which description best fits the pupil's performance (considering each description alongside descriptions of adjacent levels).

Local authority (LA) An LA has responsibility for local services, including education, libraries and social services. It has a statutory duty to provide education in their area. Many schools have opted out of LA control; see, for example, academies, free schools.

Maintained boarding schools State-funded schools that offer free tuition but charge fees for board and lodging. See also state-maintained schools in England and other state schools in England.

Middle school A school that caters for pupils aged 8–12 or 9–13. They are classified legally as either primary or secondary schools depending on whether the preponderance of pupils in the school is under or over 11 years of age.

Minority ethnic groups Pupils, many of whom have been born in the United Kingdom, from other ethnic heritages; for example, those of Asian heritage from Bangladesh, China, Pakistan, India or East Africa, and those of African or Caribbean heritage or from countries in the European Union.

Mixed-ability grouping Teaching group containing pupils representative of the range of ability within the school. See also **banding**, **setting** and **streaming**.

Moderation An exercise involving teachers representing an **awarding body** external to the school whose purpose is to check that standards are comparable across schools and teachers. Usually carried out by sampling coursework or examination papers.

Moderator An examiner who monitors marking and examining to ensure that standards are consistent in a number of schools and colleges.

Module A definable section of work of fixed length with specific learning objectives and usually with some form of terminal assessment. Several such units may constitute a modular course.

National Assessment Agency (NAA) Set up as a separate body by QCA in 2004 to deliver and administer **National Curriculum Tests**. Closed 2008 and functions subsumed into **QCA**. Later **QCDA** and **STA**.

National College of Teaching and Leadership (NCTL) The National College for Teaching and Leadership is an executive agency of the UK's Department for Education (DfE) that offers head teachers, school leaders, senior children's services leaders and teachers' opportunities for professional development.

NC (National Curriculum) The core and other foundation subjects and their associated attainment targets, programmes of study and assessment arrangements of the curriculum.

National Curriculum Tests Formerly **Standard Assessment Tasks (q.v.)**.

National Induction Standards See **induction**.

National Qualifications Framework (NQF) A framework that links academic and vocational qualifications and shows their equivalence at several levels of attainment. See also **awarding bodies**, **vocational courses**, **GNVQ** and **NVQ**. See Directgov website at: www.direct.gov.uk/en/educationandlearning/qualificationsexplained/dg_10039017.

NEAB See **AQA**.

NFER National Foundation for Educational Research. Carries out research and produces educational diagnostic tests.

Non-contact time Time provided by a school for a teacher to prepare work or carry out assigned responsibilities other than direct teaching.

Norm-referenced assessment A process in which performance is measured by comparing candidates' responses. Individual success is relative to the performance of all other candidates. See also **assessment**, **assessment for learning**, **assessment of learning**, **criterion-referenced assessment**, **formative assessment**, **ipsative assessment** and **summative assessment**.

NQT Newly qualified teacher.

NSG Non-statutory guidance (**NC** in England). Additional subject guidance that is not mandatory; to be found attached to National Curriculum Subject Orders such as **PSHE**, **citizenship**.

NVQ National Vocational Qualifications.

OCR Oxford and Cambridge Regional **awarding body** (www.ocr.org.uk).

OFQUAL Set up in 2008. Regulator of examinations and tests in England, taking over that aspect of **QCA**. Independent (of **DfE** ministers) and responsible directly to parliament (www.gov.uk/government/organisations/ofqual).

Ofsted Office for Standards in Education. Non-ministerial government department established under the Education (Schools) Act (1992) to take responsibility for the inspection of schools in England. Ofsted inspects preschool provision, further education, teacher education institutions and **local authorities**. **Her Majesty's Inspectors (HMI)** form the professional arm of **Ofsted**. See also **OHMCI**.

OHMCI Office of Her Majesty's Chief Inspector (Wales). Non-ministerial government department established under the Education (Schools) Act (1992) to take responsibility for the inspection of schools in Wales. **Her Majesty's Inspectors (HMI)** form the professional arm of OHMCI. See also **Ofsted**.

Other state schools in England These include **academies**, **community and foundation special schools**, **church and faith schools** (see **voluntary schools**), **free schools**, **grammar schools**, **maintained boarding schools**, **specialist schools** and **pupil referral units**. See Directgov website. See also **state-maintained schools in England**.

PANDA See **RAISEonline**.

Parent Under section 576 of the Education Act 1996, a parent includes any person who is not a parent of the child, but has parental responsibility (see **parental responsibility**), or who cares for him.

Parental responsibility Under section 2 of the Children Act 1989, parental responsibility falls upon:

- All mothers and fathers who were married to each other at the time of the child's birth (including those who have since separated or divorced).
- Mothers who were not married to the father at the time of the child's birth;
- Fathers who were not married to the mother at the time of the child's birth, but who have obtained parental responsibility either by agreement with the child's mother or through a court order. Under section 12 of the Children Act 1989, where a court makes a residence order in favour of any person who is not the parent or guardian of the child, that person has parental responsibility for the child while the residence order remains in force. See *Code of Practice on the Identification and Assessment of Special Educational Needs* (DfES 2001b) and *Support and Aspiration: A New Approach to Special Educational Needs and Disability* (DfE 2011f) for further details.

Partnership teaching An increasingly common means of meeting the language needs of bilingual pupils in which support and class teachers plan and implement together a specially devised programme of in-class teaching and learning. See also **learning support**, **learning support assistants**, **in-class support** and **withdrawal**.

Pastoral care Those aspects of a school's work and structures concerned to promote the general welfare of all pupils, particularly their academic, personal and social development, their attendance and behaviour.

PAT Pupil achievement tracker; now part of **RAISEonline**.

Pedagogic content knowledge (PCK) The skills to transform subject knowledge into suitable learning activities for a particular group of pupils.

Personal learning and thinking skills (PLTS) In the National Curriculum for England related to the development of pupils as independent enquirers, creative thinkers, reflective learners, team workers, self-managers and effective participants.

PGCE Post Graduate Certificate in Education. The main qualification for secondary school teachers in England and Wales recognised by the **DfE** for **QTS**.

PLTS See **Personal, learning and thinking skills**.

Policy An agreed school statement relating to a particular area of its life and work.

PoS See **programmes of study**.

Pre-vocational courses Courses specifically designed and taught to help pupils to prepare for employment.

Profile Samples of work of pupils, used to illustrate progress, with or without added comments by teachers and/or pupils.

Programme of study (PoS) for NC in England The subject matter, skills and processes that must be taught to pupils during each **Key Stage** in order that they may meet the objectives set out in **attainment targets**. They provide the basis for planning **schemes of work**.

Progression The planned development of pupils' knowledge, skills, understanding and attitudes over time. See also **continuity**.

Project An investigation with a particular focus undertaken by individuals or small groups of pupils leading to a written, oral or graphic presentation of the outcome.

PSE Personal and social education.

PSHCE **PSHE** with a specific additional **citizenship** component.

PSHE Personal, social and health education, a non-statutory subject in the English National Curriculum. See also **PSHCE**.

PSHEE **PSHE** with a specific additional economic component.

PTA Parent-teacher association. Voluntary grouping of parents and school staff to support the school in a variety of ways.

PTR Pupil:teacher ratio. The ratio of pupils to teachers within a school or group of schools (for example, 17.4:1).

Public school **Independent school** not state-funded. So-called because at their inception, they were funded by public charity.

Pupil achievement tracker (PAT) See **RAISEonline**.

Pupil referral units (PRUs) For children of compulsory school age who may otherwise not receive suitable education, focusing on getting them back into a mainstream school.

QCA The Qualifications and Curriculum Authority. Initiated in 1997 by the merger of **SCAA** and National Council for Vocational Qualifications (**NCVQ**). Was responsible for overview of the curriculum, assessment and qualifications across the whole of education and training, from preschool to higher vocational levels. QCA advised the Secretary of State for education on such matters. Aspects of assessment were delegated by QCA to the **NAA**. Dissolved in 2010, with the responsibilities shared between **QCDA** and **Ofqual**. The Welsh equivalent of QCA was **ACCAC**, later **DCELLS**.

QCDA Qualification, Curriculum and Development Agency. Formerly **QCA**. Set up 2008. Responsible for the **National Curriculum** and associated assessments, tests examinations. Dissolved in 2012, its functions taken over by the **Standards and Testing Agency (STA)**.

QTS Qualified teacher status. This is usually attained by completion of a Post Graduate Certificate in Education (**PGCE**) or a bachelor of education (**BED**) degree or a bachelor of arts/science degree with qualified teacher status (**BA/BSc** (**QTS**)). There are other routes into teaching.

RAISEonline Reporting and Analysis for Improvement through School Self-Evaluation. In England, it provides interactive analysis of school and pupil performance data. It replaces the Ofsted Performance and Assessment (**PANDA**) reports and the pupil achievement tracker (**PAT**). See DfE website at: www.raiseonline.org/login.aspx?ReturnUrl=%2f.

Record of achievement (ROA) Cumulative record of a pupil's academic, personal and social progress over a stage of education.

Reliability A measure of the consistency of the assessment or test item; that is, the extent to which the test gives repeatable results. See also **validity**.

RSA Royal Society of Arts.

SACRE The Standing Advisory Council on Religious Education in each LA to advise the LA on matters connected with religious education and collective worship, particularly methods of teaching, the choice of teaching materials and the provision of teacher training.

SATs See **Standard Assessment Tasks**.

Scheme of work (SoW) A planned course of study over a period of time (for example, a **Key Stage** or a Year). In England, it contains knowledge, skills and processes derived from the **programmes of study** and **attainment targets** together with **units of work** and **lesson plans**.

School development plan (SDP) A coherent plan, required to be made by a school, identifying improvements needed in curriculum, organisation, staffing and resources, and setting out action needed to make those improvements.

SEG See **AQA**.

SEN (special educational needs) Children have special educational needs if they have a *learning difficulty*. Children have a *learning difficulty* if they:

(a) have a significantly greater difficulty in learning than the majority of children of the same age;

(b) have a disability that prevents or hinders them from making use of educational facilities of a kind generally provided for children of the same age in schools within the area of the local authority; or

(c) are under compulsory school age and fall within the definition at (a) or (b) above or would so do if special educational provision was not made for them. Very able or gifted pupils are not included in **SEN**. See also **SEND** and **SENCO**.

SEN Code of Practice Act of Parliament describing and prescribing the regulations for the support of pupils with SEN.

SENCO Special educational needs coordinator in schools. See also **SEN** and **SEND**.

SEND Special educational needs and/or disability. In England, a widening of the scope of **SEN** (Ofsted 2010b).

Setting The grouping of pupils according to their ability in a subject for lessons in that subject. See also **banding**, **mixed-ability grouping** and **streaming**.

Short course A course in a National Curriculum foundation subject in **Key Stage** 4 that, by itself, does not lead to a full **GCSE** or equivalent qualification. Two short courses in different subjects may be combined to form one full GCSE or equivalent course.**Sixth form college** A post-16 institution for 16-19 year olds. It offers **GCSE**, **GCE A level** and **vocational courses**.

SLD Specific learning difficulties.

SOA Statements of attainment (of **NC** subjects).

Special school See **community and foundation special schools**.

Specialist schools Teach the whole curriculum but with a focus on one subject area such as: arts; business and enterprise; engineering; humanities; language; mathematics and computing; music; science; sports; technology. See **other state schools in England**.

STA (Standards and Testing Agency) An executive agency of the **DfE** set up in 2011. It is responsible for the development and delivery of all statutory assessments from early years to the end of Key Stage 3, which formerly were carried out by **QCDA** (dissolved in March 2012).

Standard Assessment Tasks (SATs) Externally prescribed **National Curriculum for England** assessments that incorporate a variety of assessment methods depending on the subject and **Key Stage**. The term SAT is not now widely used, having been replaced by '**National Curriculum Tests**', overseen by **STA**.

State-maintained schools In England, there are four main types of schools, **community** schools, **foundation and trust** schools, **voluntary-aided** and **voluntary controlled** schools. All are funded by **LA** and/or central government. Many of these schools admit pupils from a wide range of ability; see **comprehensive schools**. Within the four categories are schools with special characteristics; see **other state-maintained schools in England**.

Statements of special educational needs Provided under the 1981 Education Act and subsequent Acts to ensure appropriate provision for pupils formally assessed as having **SEN**. See **SEN code of practice** and **SEND**.

Statutory order A statutory instrument that is regarded as an extension of an Act, enabling provisions of the Act to be augmented or updated.

Streaming The organisation of pupils according to general ability into classes in which they are taught for all subjects and courses. See also **banding**, **mixed-ability grouping** and **setting**.

Summative assessment Assessment linked to the end of a course of study; it sums up achievement in aggregate terms and is used to rank, grade or compare pupils, groups or schools. It uses a narrow range of methods that are efficient and reliable, normally formal; that is, under examination conditions. See also **assessment**, **assessment for learning**, **assessment of learning**, **formative assessment**, **ipsative assessment** and **norm-referenced assessment**.

Supply teacher Teachers appointed temporarily to fill vacancies.

Support teacher See **in-class support** and **learning support**.

TA Teaching assistant. An individual who assists a teacher with classroom responsibilities, mainly focused on providing learning support to pupils. Or, Teaching Agency. Set up in 2012. Responsible for the initial and in-service training of teachers and other school staff in England. Comprises the former bodies **TDA**, **General Teaching Council for England** and **QCDA**.

TDA Training and Development Agency. Set up in 2005. Formerly the **TTA**, now **TA**. The TDA had a remit for overseeing standards and qualifications across the school workforce.

Teacher assessments **Assessments** made by teachers alongside **National Curriculum Tests** at some **Key Stages** in England.

Teacher's record book A book in which teachers plan and record teaching and learning for their classes on a regular basis.

Team-teaching The teaching of a number of classes simultaneously by teachers acting as a team. They usually divide the work between them, allowing those with particular expertise to lead different parts of the work, the others supporting the follow-up work with groups or individuals. See also **in-class support**, **learning support** and **partnership teaching**.

Thinking skills Additional skills to be promoted across the **NC**. See also **cross-curricular elements** and **personal learning and thinking skills**.

Traveller education The development of policy and provision that provides traveller children with unhindered access to, and full integration in, mainstream education.

Travellers A term used to cover those communities, some of which have minority ethnic status, and either are or have been traditionally associated with a nomadic lifestyle, and include gypsy travellers, fairground or show people, circus families, New Age travellers, and bargees.

Trust schools A **foundation school** supported by a charitable foundation or trust that appoints school governors. A trust school employs its own staff, manages its own land and assets, and sets its own admissions criteria.

TTA Teacher Training Agency. Established in 1994 and responsible for the quality of teacher education in England and the supply of teachers. Later (2005) the **TDA**, then the **TA** in 2012.

Tutor group Grouping of secondary pupils for registration and pastoral care purposes.

Unit of work Medium-term planning of work for pupils over half a term or a number of weeks. The number of lessons in a unit of work may vary according to each school's organisation. A unit of work usually introduces a new aspect of learning. Units of work derive from **schemes of work** and are the basis for **lesson plans**.

Validity A measure of whether the assessment measures what it is meant to measure – often determined by consensus. Certain kinds of skills and abilities are extremely difficult to assess with validity via simple pencil and paper tests. See also **reliability**.

Vocational courses Are programmes of study leading to vocational qualifications that are work-related preparing learners for employment. **Awarding bodies** offer vocational courses. See also **NVQ**, **GNVQ**, **BTEC** and **national qualifications**.

Voluntary-aided school Often religious schools. The governing body, often a religious organisation, employs the staff and sets admissions criteria. The school land and buildings are also owned by a charitable foundation. See also **state-maintained schools in England** and **other state schools in England**.

Voluntary-controlled school Mainly religious or 'faith' schools, but run by the LA. The land and buildings are often owned by a charitable foundation, but the LA employs the staff and has primary responsibility for admission arrangements. See also **state-maintained schools in England** and **other state schools in England**.

Voluntary school School that receives financial assistance from the **LA**, but owned by a voluntary body, usually religious. See **state-maintained Schools in England** and **other state schools in England**.

Withdrawal Removal of pupils with particular needs from class teaching in primary schools and from specified subjects in secondary schools for extra help individually or in small groups. In-class support is increasingly provided in preference to withdrawal. See also **learning support**, **learning support assistants**, **in-class support** and **partnership teaching**.

WJEC Welsh Joint Education Committee. Provides examinations, assessment, professional development, educational resources, support for adults who wish to learn Welsh and access to youth arts activities. It also provides examinations throughout England.

Work experience The opportunity for secondary pupils to have experience of a work environment for one or two weeks, usually within school time, during which a pupil carries out a particular job or range of jobs more or less as would regular employees, although with emphasis on the educational aspects of the experience.

World class tests Tests for high-achieving 9 and 13 year olds in 'mathematics' and in 'problem-solving in mathematics, science and technology', sponsored by government (see www.nottingham.ac.uk/education/MARS/services/wct.htm).

Year system A structure for pastoral care/pupil welfare within a school in which pupils are grouped according to years; that is, in groups spanning an age range of only one year. An alternative grouping is the **house system**.

Years 1–11 Year of schooling in England. Five year olds start at Year 1 (Y1) and progress through to Year 11 (Y11) at 16 years old. See **Key Stages** for details.

Appendix 2

Examples of relevant websites

Providers of Web resources for teachers do so for a range of purposes. Some sites are professional, such as subject associations sharing knowledge between professionals; others explicitly support government policy, so advice may be changed or withdrawn on ideological grounds; and others are designed to sell you products. The list below includes websites from:

- professional associations, teaching councils and unions;
- charities and university research centres and social enterprises;
- government-funded organisations;
- private companies.

For the most part, we have excluded websites apparently linked with just one individual. Exceptions are where the individuals have clearly researched and published widely in the area.

There are formal and informal networks on various social media sites, including: Facebook, LinkedIn and Twitter.

You are advised to check the reliability of any advice – on the Web or in print. For teaching to be an evidence-informed profession, teachers need to know the strength of evidence for any pedagogical intervention. By strength of evidence, we mean:

- Methods and ethics: Has the advice been gathered by ethical (see the BERA ethical code, www.bera.ac.uk) and reliable research methods (see Unit 5.4 and Patterson's MESHGuides) Usual research instruments are interviews, questionnaires, documentary analysis and observation, but there is huge variation of options within each instrument.
- Independence: Were the researchers independent? Who funded the research? Were researchers free to publish adverse findings?
- Quality assurance: Has the advice been independently peer-reviewed? Peer review, by an independent panel of educators, is the normal form of quality assurance used for professional association and professional journal sites. Materials from other sites may or may not be peer reviewed.
- Sample: What is the size and type of the sample used to provide the evidence? What confidence does this give you in the results?

■ Transferability: How transferable is the advice likely to be? How similar is the research context to your context. This is not at all to say you reject research and evidence from contexts different to your own but just that you need to bring your professional judgement to bear in applying the findings. Teachers in many countries face similar challenges in maximising the learning of young people and there is a lot to learn from solutions elsewhere.

For an up-to-date list, see www.meshguides.org/website_list/. To submit websites for inclusion, email enquiries@meshguides.org. The MESHGuides initiative is run by an educational charity and teacher volunteers to give teachers quick access to research summaries and tools and resources to support teaching becoming an evidence-informed profession. To become involved, see the 'Get Involved' tab on www.meshguides.org.

All websites listed here were accessed on 10 August 2015.

Further information is given only where it is not obvious what the website offers.

The list starts with generic websites followed by a list of sites grouped alphabetically by theme (for example, behaviour, neuroscience, subject associations, unions).

Generic websites: covering a wide range of areas

British Education Research Tool in Education (BERTIE): www.bathspa.ac.uk/static/bertie/bertie.html
Ed Talks: www.edtalks.org/
Education Endowment Foundation: see EEF
Education Evidence Portal: www.eep.ac.uk
      (This is a search tool for specific sites but has not been updated since the 2012 decisions of the UK coalition government to close online services for teachers in England. It is useful for historical documents.)
Education-line: www.leeds.ac.uk/bei/COLN/COLN_default.html
      (Repository of British Education Research Association conferences research papers: www.bera.ac.uk)
EEF (Education Endowment Foundation): https://educationendowmentfoundation.org.uk /
ERIC - USA Government Education Resources Information Center: http://eric.ed.gov/
European SchoolNet: www.eun.org
Evidence for Policy and Practice Information Centre: www.eppi.ioe.ac.uk
      (This has a list of systematic reviews of practice in education.)
Khan academy - Teaching Videos: www.khanacademy.org/
MESHGuides (Mapping Education Specialist knowHow): www.meshguides.org
National STEM Centre: www.nationalstemcentre.org.uk/elibrary/resource/1482/
Open University, Open Learn: www.open.edu/openlearnworks/course/view.php?id=1490%3F
Stanford University Teaching Commons - Resources tab: https://teachingcommons.stanford.edu/
Teacher Education Observatory: http://teachereducationobservatory.org
TED-Ed Lessons Worth Sharing: http://ed.ted.com/
Times Educational Supplement: www.tes.co.uk/
TLRP, major UK research project on teaching and learning: www.tlrp.org/

UK Government:
England: Department for Education: www.education.gov.uk/ and inspection: Office for Standards in Education (Ofsted): www.ofsted.gov.uk
Northern Ireland: Department of Education Northern Ireland: www.deni.gov.uk and inspection: The Education and Training Inspectorate Northern Ireland: www.etini.gov.uk/index/inspection-reports.htm
Scotland: Education Scotland: www.educationscotland.gov.uk/index.asp and The Scottish Government: www.gov.scot/Topics/Statistics/Browse/School-Education
Wales: Welsh Government: http://gov.wales/topics/educationandskills/%20?lang=en and inspection: Estyn - The Office of Her Majesty's Inspectorate for Education and Training in Wales: www.estyn.gov.uk/
You Tube: Teaching Channel and Teachers: www.youtube.com/user/teachers; www.youtube.com/user/TeachingChannel

Additional websites by theme

Assessment for learning: see specialist MESHGuides (www.meshguides.org) and, for example, Wiliam, D.: www.dylanwiliam.org/Dylan_Wiliams_website/Welcome.html

Autism: National Autistic Society: www.nas.org.uk

Behaviour:
Behaviour2Learn: www.behaviour2learn.co.uk
See also DFE advice
(September 2014): www.gov.uk/government/policies/improving-behaviour-and-attendance-in-schools
(April 2012): www.gov.uk/government/publications/behaviour-and-discipline-in-schools; behaviour checklists: www.education.gov.uk/schools/pupilsupport/behaviour/a00199342/getting-the-simple-thingsright-charlie-taylors-behaviour-checklists
(July 2013) Guidance for governing bodies: www.gov.uk/government/publications/behaviour-and-discipline-in-schools-guidance-for-governing-bodies
(July 2013) Use of reasonable force: www.gov.uk/government/publications/use-of-reasonable-force-in-schools
(February 2014) Screening, searching and confiscation: www.gov.uk/government/publications/searching-screening-and-confiscation

Preventing and tackling bullying
www.gov.uk/government/publications/preventing-and-tackling-bullying

Citizenship:
British Humanist Association: www.humanism.org.uk/education/education-policy
Citizenship Foundation: www.citizenshipfoundation.org.uk
CitizED subject resource bank: www.citized.info
Jubilee Centre for Character and Virtues: www.jubileecentre.ac.uk

Code of practice for teaching – see Teaching Councils

Curriculum – national requirements:
England: www.gov.uk/government/publications/national-curriculum-in-england-framework-for-key-stages-1-to-4/the-national-curriculum-in-england-framework-for-key-stages-1-to-4
Northern Ireland: www.nicurriculum.org.uk/
Scotland: www.educationscotland.gov.uk/learningandteaching/thecurriculum/whatiscurriculumforexcellence/
Wales: http://wales.gov.uk/topics/educationandskills/schoolshome/curriculuminwales/arevisedcurriculum forwales/?lang=en

Deaf and hearing impaired:
National Deaf Children's Society: www.ndcs.org.uk
BATOD Foundation: www.batodfoundation.org.uk /

Dialogic teaching:
Alexander, R. (2015) www.robinalexander.org.uk/dialogic-teaching/
University of Cambridge: www.educ.cam.ac.uk/research/projects/dialogic/whatis.html

English as an additional language:
Flynn, N. (2015) *Teaching English as an Additional Language MESHGuide*, University of Winchester, UK www.meshguides.org/category/general-pedagogy/english-as-an-additional-language-general-pedagogy/.

Equal and Human Rights Commission (EHRC): www.equalityhumanrights.com
Joseph Rowntree Foundation (focus: poverty and injustice): www.jrf.org.uk

Ethics:
Professional – see Teaching Councils
Research – see research ethics.

Europe: European Schoolnet (EUN): www.eun.org

Gifted and talented:
National Association for Able Children in Education: www.nace.co.uk

Handwriting: National Handwriting Association: www.nha-handwriting.org.uk

Health:
British Nutrition Foundation: www.nutrition.org.uk
Food Standards Agency: www.eatwell.gov.uk
NICE (National Institute for Health and Care Excellence): www.nice.org.uk/guidance

Intelligences: Gardner, H. http://howardgardner.com/multiple-intelligences

Lesson study:
Dudley, P. http://lessonstudy.co.uk/about-us-pete-dudley/

Learning theories – see the specialist sites in this list
Claxton, G. (2015) *Building Learning Power*: www.buildinglearningpower.co.uk/

Names (remembering):
Buzan: www.open.edu/openlearn/body-mind/psychology/buzan-on-how-remember-names-and-faces
TeacherVision: www.teachervision.com/teaching-methods/classroom-management/6708.html

Neuroscience:
Blakemore, S. www.ted.com/talks/sarah_jayne_blakemore_the_mysterious_workings_of_the_adolescent_
    brain?language=en
Centre for Neuroscience in Education led by Professor Usha Goswami: www.cne.psychol.cam.ac.uk/
    people/ucg10@cam.ac.uk
Neuroscience for Kids: http://faculty.washington.edu/chudler/neurok.html
Royal Society: http://royalsociety.org/policy/projects/brain-waves/education-lifelong-learning
The Brain from Top to Bottom: http://thebrain.mcgill.ca
The International Mind, Brain and Education Society: www.imbes.org

Philosophy: Philosophy of Education: www.philosophy-of-education.org/resources/students/video-listing.html

Projects:
Collaborative projects across Europe – E-twinning: www.etwinning.net/en/pub/index.htm
WebQuests UK: www.webquestuk.org.uk/

Risk:
CLEAPSS: www.cleapss.org.uk/attachments/article/0/L196.pdf?Secondary/Science/Guides/
Eaton Vale Schools Activity Centre: www.eatonvale.co.uk/schools/riskassessments.aspx
Health and Safety Executive: www.hse.gov.uk/risk/classroom-checklist.htm

Research methods/research ethics:
British Educational Research Association: www.bera.ac.uk
Patterson, E. (2016) *Research Methods 1: How to Get Started on a Literature Review*, MESHGuide, University
    of Winchester. www.meshguides.org/category/research-methods/literature-reviews/
Patterson, E. (2016) *Research Methods 2: Developing Your Research Design*, MESHGuide, University of
    Winchester. http://www.meshguides.org/category/research-methods/research-design/
Patterson, E. (2016) *Research Methods 3: Considering Ethics in Your Research*, MESHGuide, University of
    Winchester. http://www.meshguides.org/category/research-methods/ethics/

SEND – see also deaf, hearing impaired: NASEN (National Association for Special Educational Needs):
    www.nasen.org.uk/ and www.nasen.org.uk/onlinesendcpd/
Blamires, M. and others (2014) *Special Educational Needs and Disability: Enabling Pupil Participation*,
    MESHGuide: www.meshguides.org/category/special-needs-2/enabling-pupil-participation-special-needs-
    2/
The Professional Association of Teachers of Students with Specific Learning Difficulties (PATOSS):
    www.patoss-dyslexia.org
Royal National Institute for the Blind: www.rnib.org.uk

Subject Associations: are represented by the Council for Subject Associations www.subjectassociation.
    org.uk/. Here is the list of subject associations: www.subjectassociation.org.uk/members_links.aspx

Teacher Support Network: www.teachersupport.info (24-hour confidential counselling)

Teacher Training Resource Bank:
www.ttrb3.org.uk/, maintained by Mike Blamires
http://webarchive.nationalarchives.gov.uk/20101021152907/ www.ttrb.ac.uk/

Teachers' councils:

England (GTCE, closed by UK government 2011), College of Teaching now being developed (2016)
    http://webarchive.nationalarchives.gov.uk/20111213132132/http:/www.gtce.org.uk
Northern Ireland: www.gtcni.org.uk/
Scotland: www.gtcs.org.uk/home/home.aspx
Wales: www.teachertrainingcymru.org/node/26

Teacher Standards:

England: www.legislation.gov.uk/uksi/2003/1662/schedule/2/made
Northern Ireland: www.deni.gov.uk/index/school-staff/teachers-teachinginnorthernireland_pg.htm
Scotland: www.gtcs.org.uk/standards/
Wales: http://gov.wales/topics/educationandskills/publications/circulars/becomingateacher/?lang=en

Teaching and learning: as well as MESHGuides (www.meshguides.org) and Education Endowment Foundation
    and EPPI Centre above, see the specialist sites listed here and:
British Council/British Broadcasting Corporation Learning Styles and Teaching: www.teachingenglish.
    org.uk/articles/learning-styles-teaching

Thinking – see also dialogic teaching:

Education Scotland (2015) *Skills in Practice: Thinking Skills*: www.educationscotland.gov.uk/resources/s/
    skillsinpracticethinkingskills/knowing.asp
University of Cambridge, *Thinking Together*: https://thinkingtogether.educ.cam.ac.uk/ University of
    Cambridge/Professor Neil Mercer (2015) *Thinking Together*: http://thinkingtogether.educ.cam.ac.uk/
    resources/

Transitions: www.dundee.ac.uk/eswce/research/resources/

Unions: some professional associations listed on the CfSA site (www.subjectassociation.org.uk) are also
    unions and some invest in research.
Association of Teachers and Lecturers, England, Wales and Northern Ireland (ATL): www.atl.org.uk/
Irish National Teachers' Organisation, Northern Ireland: www.into.ie/NI/
National Association of Schoolmasters/Union of Women Teachers, England, Wales, Scotland and Northern
    Ireland (NASUWT): www.nasuwt.org.uk/
National Union of Teachers, England and Wales (NUT): www.teachers.org.uk/
Scottish Secondary Teachers' Association, Scotland: www.ssta.org.uk
The Educational Institute of Scotland (EIS), Scotland: www.eis.org.uk/
Ulster Teachers Union, Northern Ireland: www.utu.edu/
Voice, previously the Professional Association of Teachers, England, Wales and Northern Ireland:
    www.voicetheunion.org.uk/

Values – see Citizenship

References

Abercrombie, M.L. (1985) *The Anatomy of Judgement*, Harmondsworth: Pelican Books.

Adams, J., Tyrekll, R., Adamson, A.J. and White, M. (2012) 'Effects of restrictions on television food advertising to children on exposure to adverts for 'less healthy foods': Repeat cross sectional study', *PLoS ONE Journal*, available at: www.plosone.org (accessed 20 March 2012).

Addison, N. and Burgess, L. (eds) (2007) *Learning to Teach Art and Design in the Secondary School: A Companion to School Experience*, 2nd edn, London: Routledge.

Adey, P. (1992) 'The CASE results: implications for science teaching', *International Journal of Science Education*, 14: 137–46.

Adey, P. (2008) *Let's Think Handbook: Cognitive Acceleration in the Primary School*, London: NFER Nelson.

Adey, P. and Serret, N. (2010) 'Science teaching and cognitive acceleration', in J. Osborne and J. Dillon (eds) *Good Practice in Science Teaching: What Research Has to Say*, Buckingham: Open University Press, pp. 82–107.

Adey, P., Shayer, M. and Yates, C. (1989) *Thinking Science*, London: Macmillan.

Adey, P., Shayer, M. and Yates, C. (2001) *Thinking Science: The Curriculum Materials of the CASE Project*, 3rd edn, London: Nelson Thornes.

Adeyemo, D.A. (2005) 'The buffering effect of emotional intelligence on the adjustment of secondary school students in transition', *Electronic Journal of Research in Educational Psychology*, 3(2): 79–90.

Adeyemo, D.A. (2010) 'Educational transition and emotional intelligence', in D. Jindal-Snape (ed.) *Educational Transitions: Moving Stories from around the World*, New York: Routledge, pp. 33–47.

Akhlaq, M., Amjadz, M. and Mehmoda, K. (2010) 'An evaluation of the effects of stress on the job performance of secondary school teachers', *Journal of Law and Psychology*, September: 43–54.

Akos, P. (2004) 'Advice and student agency in the transition to middle school', *Research in Middle Level Education*, 27: 1–11.

Aldrich, R. (1988) 'The National Curriculum: an historical perspective', in D. Lawton and C. Chitty (eds) *The National Curriculum*, Bedford Way Papers No. 33, London: Institute of Education, University of London.

Aldrich, R. (2006) *Lessons from History of Education: The Selected Works of Richard Aldrich*, London: Routledge.

Aldrich, R. and White, J. (1998) *The National Curriculum beyond 2000: The QCA and the Aims of Education*, London: Institute of Education, University of London.

Aldridge, H., Parekh, A., MacInnes, T. and Kenway, P. (2011) *Monitoring Poverty and Social Exclusion*, York: Joseph Rowntree Foundation.

Alexander, R. (2001) *Culture and Pedagogy: International Comparisons in Primary Education*, Oxford: Blackwell.

Alexander, R. (2004) *Towards Dialogic Teaching: Rethinking Classroom Talk*, Cambridge: Dialogos.

Alexander, R. (2008) *Essays on Pedagogy*, London: Routledge.

Alexander, R. (2015) *Dialogic Teaching*, available at: www.robinalexander.org.uk/dialogic-teaching/ (accessed 19 July 2015).

Alliance for Excellent Education (2004) *Tapping the Potential: Retaining and Developing High Quality New Teachers*, Washington, DC: Alliance for Excellent Education.

Alloway, T.P. and Alloway, R.G. (2015) *Understanding Working Memory*, 2nd edn, London: Sage.

Altrichter, H., Feldman, A., Posch, P. and Somekh, B. (2008) *Teachers Investigate Their Work: An Introduction to Action Research across the Professions*, 2nd edn, London: Routledge.

Ames, C. (1992a) 'Achievement goals and the classroom motivational climate', in D.H. Schunk and J.L. Meece (eds) *Student Perception in the Classroom*, Hillsdale, NJ: Erlbaum, pp. 327–48.

Ames, C. (1992b) 'Classrooms: goals, structures and student motivation', *Journal of Educational Psychology*, 84: 261–71.

Amos, J-A. (1998) *Managing Your Time: What to Do and How to Do It in Order to Do More*, Oxford: How To Books.

Anderson, J.R., Reder, L.M. and Simon, H.A. (1996) 'Situated learning and education', *Educational Researcher*, 25: 5–11.

Anderson, L. and Krathwohl, D.A. (2001) *Taxonomy for Learning, Teaching and Assessing: A Revision of Bloom's Taxonomy of Educational Objectives*, New York: Longman.

Anderson, M. (1992) *Intelligence and Development: A Cognitive Theory*, London: Blackwell.

Archer, L. (2008) 'The impossibility of minority ethnic educational "success"? An examination of the discourses of teachers and pupils in British secondary schools', *European Educational Research Journal*, 7(1): 89–107.

Archer, L. and Francis, B. (2007) *Understanding Minority Ethnic Achievement in Schools*, London: Routledge.

ARG (Assessment Reform Group) (2002) *Testing, Motivation and Learning*, Cambridge: University of Cambridge Faculty of Education.

Arikewuyo, M.O. (2004) 'Stress management strategies of secondary school teachers in Nigeria', *Educational Research*, 46(2): 196–207.

Arnove, R.F. and Torres, C.A. (eds) (2007) *Comparative Education: The Dialectic of the Global and the Local*, Lanham, MA: Rowman & Littlefield.

Arter, J.A. and Jenkins, J.R. (1979) 'Differential diagnosis – prescriptive teaching: a critical appraisal', *Review of Educational Research*, 49: 517–55.

Association of American Educators (2015) *Code of Conduct for Educators*, available at: www.aaeteachers.org/index.php/about-us/aae-code-of-ethics (accessed 29 July 2015).

Atherton, J.S. (2011) *Learning and Teaching: Piaget's Developmental Theory*, available at: www.learningandteaching.info/learning/piaget.htm (accessed 31 December 2011).

Atkinson, J.W. (1964) *An Introduction to Motivation*, Princeton, NJ: Van Nostrand.

Atkinson, R.C. and Shiffrin, R.M. (1968) 'Human memory: a proposed system and its control processes', in K.W. Spence and J.T. Spence (eds) *The Psychology of Learning and Motivation: Advances in Research and Theory*, Volume 2, New York: Academic Press, pp. 742–75.

Ausubel, D. P. (1968) *Educational Psychology: A Cognitive View*, New York: Holt, Rinehart & Winston.

Axup, T. and Gersh, I. (2008) 'The impact of challenging student behaviour upon teachers' lives in a secondary school: teachers' perceptions', *British Journal of Special Education*, 35(3): 144–51.

Ayers, H. and Prytys, C. (2002) *An A–Z Practical Guide to Emotional and Behavioural Difficulties*, London: David Fulton.

Ball, S. (2003) *Class Strategies and the Education Market: The Middle Classes and Social Advantage*, London: RoutledgeFalmer.

Bandura, A. (1969) *Social Learning and Personality Development*, London: Holt, Rinehart & Winston.

Banks, F., Leach, J. and Moon, B. (1999) 'New understandings of teachers' pedagogic knowledge', in J. Leach and B. Moon (eds) *Learners and Pedagogy*, London: Paul Chapman, pp. 89–110.

Barber, M. and Mourshed, M. (2007) *How the World's Best Performing School Systems Come Out on Top*, available at: www.closingtheachievementgap.org/cs/ctag/view/resources/111 (accessed 18 December 2011).

Bar-David, Y., Urkin, J. and Kozminsky, E. (2005) 'The effect of voluntary dehydration on cognitive functions of elementary school children', *Acta Paediatrica*, 94: 1667–73.

Barnes, B. (1987) *Learning Styles in TVEI: Evaluation Report No. 3*, Leeds: Manpower Service Commission.

Barnes, I. and Harris, S. (2006) *Special Series on Personalised Learning: An Overview of the Summary Report Findings*, Nottingham: NCSL.

Barnett, R. (1994) *The Limits of Competence*, Buckingham: SRHE/OUP.

Barnett, R. (1997) *Higher Education, a Critical Business*, Buckingham: SRHE/OUP.

Bar-Or, O., Dotan, R., Inbar, O., Rotshstein, A. and Zonder, H. (1980) 'Voluntary hypohydration in 10 to 12 year old boys', *Journal of Applied Physiology*, 48: 104–8.

Bartlett, S.J. and Burton, D.M. (2016) *Introduction to Education Studies*, 4th edn, London: Sage.

Barton, G. (2010) *Grammar Survival: A Teacher's Toolkit*, London: Routledge.

Batchford, R. (1992) *Values: Assemblies for the 1990s*, Cheltenham: Stanley Thornes.

Battisch, V., Solomon, D. and Watson, M. (1998) 'Sense of community as a mediating factor in promoting children's social and ethical development', Developmental Studies Center Paper presented at the meeting of the American Educational Research Association, San Diego, CA, April 1998, available at: http://tigger.uic.edu/~lnucci/MoralEd/articles/battistich.html (accessed 31 December 2011).

Baumeister, R. and Tierney, J. (2012) *Willpower: Rediscovering Our Greatest Strength*, London: Allen Lane.

Bawden, A. (2007) 'Walking back to happiness', *Education Guardian*, 20 March: 8.

BBC (British Broadcasting Corporation) (2009) 'Danish pupils use web in exams', *BBC News*, 4 November.

Beauchamp, G. and Kennewell, S. (2010) 'Interactivity in the classroom and its impact on learning', *Computers and Education*, 54(3): 759-66.

Bee, H. and Boyd, D. (2013) *The Developing Child*, 13th edn, Boston, MA: Pearson Education.

Bell, J. and Waters, S. (2014) *Doing Your Research Project: A Guide for First Time Researchers*, 6th edn, Berkshire: McGraw-Hill.

Beltman, S., Mansfield, C. and Price, A. (2011) 'Thriving not just surviving: a review of research on teacher resilience', *Educational Research Review*, 6(3): 185-207.

Berger, J. (1972) *Ways of Seeing*, London: Penguin.

Berkeley, S. Scruggs, T.E. and Mastropieri, M.A. (2010) 'Reading comprehension instruction for students with learning disabilities, 1995-2006: a meta-analysis', *Remedial and Special Education*, 31(6): 423-36.

Berkowitz, M., Gibbs, J. and Broughton, J. (1980) 'The relation of moral judgment stage disparity to developmental effects of peer dialogues', *Merrill-Palmer Quarterly*, 26: 341-57.

Bernstein, B. (1977) *Class, Codes and Control, Volume 3: Towards a Theory of Educational Transmissions*, 2nd edn, London: Routledge & Kegan Paul.

Berry, J. (2013) *Teachers' Legal Rights and Responsibilities: A Guide for Trainee Teachers and Those New to the Profession*, 3rd edn, Hatfield: University of Hertfordshire Press.

Best, B. and O'Donnell, G. (2011) *Learning to Learn Toolkit*, London: Optimus Education Bookshop.

Bew, Lord (2011) *Independent Review of Key Stage 2 Testing, Assessment and Accountability: Final Report*, London: DfE.

Bhatti, A.J. (2015) *Curriculum Alignment MESHGuide*, Islamabad, International Islamic University.

BHF (British Heart Foundation) (2011) *The 21st Century Gingerbread House: How Companies Are Marketing Junk Food to Children On Line*, available at: www.bhf.org.uk.the_21st_century_gingerbread_house.pdf (accessed 20 March 2012).

Biggam, J. (2015) *Succeeding With Your Master's Dissertation: A Step by Step Handbook*, 3rd edn, Maidenhead: Open University Press.

Biggs, J.B. (1978) 'Individual and group differences in study processes', *British Journal of Educational Psychology*, 48: 266-79.

Biggs, J.B. (1987) *Student Approaches to Learning and Studying*, Hawthorne, Victoria: Australian Council for Educational Research.

Biggs, J.B. (1993) 'What do inventories of students' learning processes really measure? A theoretical review and clarification', *British Journal of Educational Psychology*, 63: 3-19.

Biggs, J. (1996) 'Enhancing teaching through constructive alignment', *Higher Education*, 347-64.

Biggs, J.B. (2001) 'Enhancing learning: a matter of style or approach?', in R.J. Sternberg and L.F. Zhang (eds) *Perspectives on Thinking, Learning and Cognitive Styles*, Mahwah, NJ: Lawrence Erlbaum Associates.

Biggs, J.B. (2003) *Teaching for Quality Learning at University*, 2nd edn, Buckingham: Open University Press/Society for Research into Higher Education.

Bjork, R.A., Dunlosky, J. and Kornell, N. (2013) 'Self-regulated learning: beliefs, techniques and illusions', *Annual Review of Psychology*, 64: 417-444.

Black, P. (1998) *Testing: Friend or Foe? Theory and Practice of Assessment and Testing (Master Classes in Education)*, London: RoutledgeFalmer.

Black, P. and Wiliam, D. (1998) *Inside the Black Box: Raising Standards through Classroom Assessment*, London: King's College, University of London.

Black, P. and Wiliam, D. (2002) *Working Inside the Black Box: Assessment for Learning in the Classroom*, London: King's College.

Black, P., Harrison, C., Lee, C., Marshall, B. and Wiliam, D. (2002) *Working Inside the Black Box: Assessment for Learning in the Classroom*, London: King's College, University of London.

Black, P., Harrison, C., Lee, C., Marshall, B. and Wiliam, D. (2003) *Assessment for Learning: Putting it into Practice*, Maidenhead: Open University Press.

Black, P., McCormick, R., James, M. and Pedder, D. (2006) 'Learning how to learn and assessment for learning: a theoretical inquiry', *Research Papers in Education*, 21(2): 119-32.

Blakemore, S. and Frith, U. (2005) *The Learning Brain: Lessons for Education*, Oxford: Blackwell.

Blamires, M. (ed.) (2014) *Special Educational Needs and Disability: Enabling Pupil Participation MESHGuide*, RIDDLE Consultancy, previously Canterbury Christ Church University, available at: www.meshguides.org/category/special-needs-2/enabling-pupil-participation-special-needs-2/ (accessed 18 July 2015).

Blatchford, P., Bassett, P., Brown, P., Koutsoubou, M., Martin, P., Russell, A. and Webster, R. with Rubie-Davies, C. (2009) *Deployment and Impact of Support Staff in Schools: The Impact of Support Staff in Schools. Results from Strand 2, Wave 2*, Department for Children, Schools and Families (DCSF) Research Report DCSF RR148, available at: www.ioe.ac.uk/DISS_Strand_2_Wave_2_Report.pdf (accessed 10 November 2015).

Bloom, A. (2007) 'Me level 4, you level 2 = end of friendship', *Times Educational Supplement*, 9 February: 13.

Bloom, B.S. (ed.) (1956) *Taxonomy of Educational Objectives: Handbook 1 – Cognitive Domain*, New York: Longmans Green.

BMA (British Medical Association) (2003) *Adolescent Health*, London: BMA, available at: www.bma.org.uk (go to 'Health and Well being', then search title) (accessed 20 March 2012).

BNF (British Nutrition Foundation) (2011a) *Factsheet: Nutrition, Health and Schoolchildren – Overweight and Obesity*, available at: www.nutrition.org.uk/nutritionscience/life/schoolchildren-factsheets (accessed 20 March 2012).

BNF (British Nutrition Foundation) (2011b) *Factsheet: Nutrition, Health and Schoolchildren – Food Provision in Schools*, available at: www.nutrition.org.uk/nutritionscience/life/schoolchildren-factsheets (accessed 20 March 2012).

Boaler, J. (1997) *Experiencing School Mathematics: Teaching Style, Sex and Setting*, Buckingham: Open University Press.

Bobek, B.L. (2002) 'Teacher resiliency: a key to career longevity', *Clearing House*, 75(4): 202–5.

Bochner, S. (1978) 'Ayres, sensory integration and learning disorders: a question of theory and practice', *Australian Journal of Mental Retardation*, 5(2): 41–5.

Bolam, R. and Weindling, D. (2006) *Synthesis of Research and Evaluation Projects Concerned with Capacity Building Through Teachers' Professional Development*, Report for General Teaching Council for England.

Bolton, G. (2005) *Reflective Practice: Writing and Professional Development*, London: Sage.

Boston, K. (2007) Quoted in BBC news broadcast, June 17, 'GCSE home coursework scrapped', available at: http://news.bbc.co.uk/1/hi/education/6747973.stm (accessed 2 June 2012).

Bourdieu, P. (1974) 'The school as a conservative force: scholastic and cultural inequalities', in J. Egglestone (ed.) *Contemporary Research in the Sociology of Education*, London: Methuen & Co, pp. 32–46.

Bourdieu, P. (1986) 'The forms of capital', in J.G. Richardson (ed.) *Handbook of Theory and Research for the Sociology of Education*, New York: Greenwood Press, pp. 241–60.

Brandreth, G. (1981) *The Puzzle Mountain*, Harmondsworth: Penguin Books.

Bransford, J.D., Brown, A. and Cocking, R.C. (eds) (1999) *How People Learn: Brain, Mind, Experience and School*, Washington, DC: National Academy Press.

Branzi, A. (2004) Keynote Lecture at the Crossing Boundaries Conference, Reggio Emilia, Italy.

Briggs, A. (1983) *A Social History of England*, London: Book Club Associates.

Brighouse, H. (2006) *On Education*, London: Routledge.

Brindley, S. (ed.) (2015) *Masterclass* series of texts, London: Bloomsbury, available at: www.bloomsbury.com/uk/education/series/masterclass/ (accessed 15 July 2015).

Brody, L. (ed.) (2004) *Grouping and Acceleration Practices in Gifted Education*, Newbury Park, CA: Corwin Press and National Association for Gifted Children.

Bronfenbrenner, U. (1979) *The Ecology of Human Development*, Cambridge, MA: Harvard University Press.

Brookfield, S. (1993) *Developing Critical Thinkers*, Oxford: Oxford University Press.

Brookfield, S. (1995) *Becoming a Critically Reflective Teacher*, San Francisco, CA: Jossey-Bass.

Brooks, J. and Lucas, N. (2004) 'The school sixth form and the growth of vocational qualifications', in S. Capel, R. Heilbronn, M. Leask and T. Turner (eds) *Starting to Teach in the Secondary School: A Companion for the Newly Qualified Teacher*, 2nd edn, London: RoutledgeFalmer, pp. 205–17.

Brooks, V. (2002) *Assessment in Secondary Schools: The New Teacher's Guide to Monitoring, Assessment, Recording, Reporting and Accountability*, Buckingham: Open University Press.

Brown, A.L. (1994) 'The advancement of learning', *Educational Researcher*, 23: 4–12.

Brown, M. and Ralph, S. (2002) 'Teacher stress and school improvement', *Improving Schools*, 5(2): 55–65.

Brown, T. and Summerbell, C. (2009) 'Systematic review of school-based interventions that focus on changing dietary intake and physical activity levels to prevent childhood obesity: an update to the obesity guidance produced by the national institute for health and clinical excellence', *Obesity Research*, 10: 110–41.

Brundrett, M. and Rhodes, C. (2011) *Leadership for Quality and Accountability Education*, London: Routledge.

Bruner, J. (1966) *Towards a Theory of Instruction*, New York: W.W. Norton.

Bruner, J. (1976) *On Knowing: Essays for the Left Hand*, Cambridge, MA: Harvard University Press.

Bruner, J. (1983) *Child's Talk: Learning to Use Language*, Oxford: Oxford University Press.

Bruner, J.S. (2006a) *In Search of Pedagogy Volume 1: The Selected Works of Jerome S. Bruner*, London: Routledge.

Bruner, J.S. (2006b) *In Search of Pedagogy Volume 2: The Selected Works of Jerome S. Bruner*, London: Routledge.

Bryan, H., Carpenter, C. and Hoult, S. (2010) *Learning and Teaching at M Level: A Guide for Student Teachers*, London: Sage.

Bubb, S. and Earley, P. (2004) *Managing Teacher Workload: Work-Life Balance and Wellbeing*, London: Paul Chapman.

Bull, S. and Solity, J. (1987) *Classroom Management: Principles to Practice*, London: Croom Helm.

Burchell, H., Dyson, J. and Rees, M. (2002) 'Making a difference: a study of the impact of continuing professional development on professional practice', *Journal of In-Service Education*, 28(2): 219-29.

Burden, K. and Younie, S. (2014) *Using iPads Effectively to Enhance Learning in Schools MESHGuide*, University of Hull and De Montfort University, UK, available at: www.meshguides.org/category/icttechnology/tabletsipad-pedagogy/ (accessed 18 July 2015).

Burgess, T. (2004) 'Language in the classroom and curriculum', in S. Capel, R. Heilbronn, M. Leask and T. Turner (eds) *Starting to Teach in the Secondary School: A Companion for the Newly Qualified Teacher*, 2nd edn, London: RoutledgeFalmer, pp. 117-138.

Bullock Report (1975) *A Language for Life*, London: HMSO.

Burnett, P. (2002) 'Teacher praise and feedback and students' perception of the classroom environment', *Educational Psychology*, 22(1): 5-16.

Burton, D.M. (2007) 'Psychopedagogy and personalised learning', *Journal of Education for Teaching*, 33(1): 5-17.

Burton, D. and Bartlett, S. (2004) *Practitioner Research for Teachers*, London: Paul Chapman.

Burton, N., Brundrett, M. and Jones, M. (2008) *Doing Your Education Research Project*, London: Sage.

Buscemi (date unknown) in P. Reeve, 'The Average Child', unpublished dissertation, De Montfort University, Bedford, 1992.

Busch, C.R., Taylor, H.A., Kanarek, R.B. and Holcomb, P.J. (2002) 'The effects of a confectionery snack on attention in young boys', *Physiology and Behavior*, 77(2-3): 333-340.

Butler, R. (1987) 'Task-involving and ego-involving properties of evaluation: effects of different feedback conditions on motivational perceptions, interest and performance', *Journal of Educational Psychology*, 79(4): 474-82.

Butt, G. (2006) *Lesson Planning*, 3rd edn, London: Continuum.

Buzan, T. (2008) *How to Remember Names and Faces*, available at: www.open.edu/openlearn/body-mind/psychology/buzan-on-how-remember-names-and-faces (accessed 17 July 2015).

Cain, T., Holmes, M., Larrett, A. and Mattock, J. (2007) 'Literature-informed, one-turn action research: three cases and a commentary', *British Educational Research Journal*, 33(1): 91-106.

Calderhead, J. and Shorrock, S.B. (1997) *Understanding Teacher Education: Case Studies in the Professional Development of Beginning Teachers*, London: Falmer Press.

Capel, S., Heilbronn, R., Leask, M. and Turner, T. (2004) *Starting to Teach in the Secondary School: A Companion for the Newly-Qualified Teacher*, 2nd edn, London: RoutledgeFalmer.

Capel, S., Leask, M. and Turner, T. (eds) (2010) *Readings for Learning to Teach in the Secondary School: A Companion to M Level Study*, London: Routledge.

Carr, D. (1993) 'Questions of competence', *British Journal of Educational Studies*, 41: 253-71.

Carr, M. (2008) 'Can assessment unlock the doors to resourcefulness and agency?', in S. Swaffield (ed.) *Unlocking Assessment: Understanding for Reflection and Application*, London: David Fulton, pp. 36-54.

CASH (Consensus Action on Salt and Health) (2010) *Children's Takeaways Survey 2010*, available at: www.actiononsalt.org.uk/news/surveys/2010/takeaways/index/html (accessed 4 June 2012).

Catterall, J. (1998) 'Risk and resilience in student transitions to high school', *American Journal of Education*, 10(2): 302-33.

CEM (Curriculum, Evaluation and Management Centre) (2008) *University of Durham*, available at: www.cemcentre.org (accessed 30 May 2012).

Centre for Neuroscience in Education led by Professor Usha Goswami, available at: www.cne.psychol.cam.ac.uk/people/ucg10@cam.ac.uk (accessed 19 July 2015).

Centre for Studies on Inclusive Education (2011) *Index for Inclusion: Developing Learning and Participation in Schools*, available at: www.csie.org.uk/resources/inclusion-index-explained.shtml (accessed 9 July 2015).

Chalabi, M (2013) 'Gay Britain: what do the statistics say?' The Guardian 3 October, available at: www.theguardian.com/politics/reality-check/2013/oct/03/gay-britain-what-do-statistics-say (accessed 21 January 2016).

Changying, W. (2007) 'Analysis of teacher attrition', *Chinese Education and Society*, 40(5): 6–10.

Chaplain, R.P. (2008) 'Stress and psychological distress among trainee secondary teachers in England', *Educational Psychology*, 28(2): 195–209.

Cherniss, C. (2000) *Emotional Intelligence: What It Is and Why It Matters*, available at: www.eiconsortium.org/reports/what_is_emotional_intelligence.html (accessed 4 June 2012).

Child, D. (2007) *Psychology and the Teacher*, 8th edn, London: Continuum.

Christie, F. and Martin, J.R. (2005) *Genre and Institutions: Social Processes in the Workplace and School*, London: Continuum.

Christodoulou, D. (2013) *Closed Questions and Higher Order Thinking*, available at: http://thewingtoheaven.wordpress.com/2013/10/06/closed-questions-and-higher-order-thinking/ (accessed 2 March 2015).

Cian, C., Koulman, N., Barraud, P.A., Raphel, C., Jimnez, C. and Melin, B. (2000) 'Influence of variations in body hydration on cognitive function: effect of hyperhydration, heat stress and exercise-induced dehydration', *Journal of Psychophysiology*, 14: 29–36.

Clarke, S. (2001) *Unlocking Formative Assessment*, London: King's College.

Clarke, S. (2005) *Formative Assessment in Action*, London: Hodder Murray.

Claxton, C. (2001) *Wise Up*, Stafford: Network Educational Press.

Claxton, G. (2002) *Building Learning Power: Helping Young People Become Better Learners*, Bristol: TLO.

Claxton, G. (2007) 'Expanding young people's capacity to learn', *British Journal of Educational Studies*, 5(2): 115–34.

Claxton, G (2015) *Building Learning Power*, available at: www.buildinglearningpower.co.uk/ (accessed 19 July 2015).

Claxton, G., Chambers, M., Powell, G. and Lucas, B. (2011) *The Learning Powered School: Pioneering 21st Century Education*, Bristol: TLO.

CLEAPSS (2005) *Managing Risk Assessment in Science Classrooms*, available at: www.cleapss.org.uk/attachments/article/0/L196.pdf?Secondary/Science/Guides/ (accessed 17 July 2015).

Clough, J. (2001) Quoted in Duffy, M. 'How many strings to your bow?', *Times Educational Supplement*, 19 October.

Clough, P. and Nutbrown C. (2007) *A Student's Guide to Methodology: Justifying Enquiry*, London: Sage.

Clucas, B. and O'Donnell, K. (2002) 'Conjoined twins: the cutting edge', *Web Journal of Current Legal Issues*, 5, available at: http://webjcli.ncl.ac.uk/2002/issue5/clucas5.html (accessed 17 November 2011).

Clunies-Ross, P., Little, E. and Kienhuis, M. (2008) 'Self-reported and actual use of proactive and reactive classroom management strategies and their relationship with teacher stress and student behaviour', *Educational Psychology: An International Journal of Experimental Educational Psychology*, 28(6): 693–710.

Coe, R., Aloisi, C., Higgins, S. and Elliot, L. (2014) 'What makes great teaching? Review of the underpinning research', *The Sutton Trust*, available at: www.suttontrust.com/wp-content/uploads/2014/10/What-makes-great-teaching-FINAL-4.11.14.pdf (accessed 18 December 2014).

Coffield, F. (2008) *Just Suppose Teaching and Learning Became the First Priority*, London: Learning and Skills Network.

Coffield, F., Moseley, D., Hall, E. and Ecclestone, K. (2004a) *Learning Styles and Pedagogy in Post-16 Learning: A Systematic and Critical Review*, Report no. 041543, London: Learning and Skills Research Centre, Learning and Skills Development Agency.

Coffield, F., Moseley, D., Hall, E. and Ecclestone, K. (2004b) *Should We Be Using Learning Styles? What Research Has to Say to Practice*, London: Learning and Skills Research Centre, Learning and Skills Development Agency.

Cohen, L., Manion, L., Morrison, K. and Wyse, D. (2010) *A Guide to Teaching Practice*, 5th edn, London: Routledge.

Cohen, S.A. (1969) 'Studies in visual perception and reading in disadvantaged children', *Journal of Learning Disabilities*, 2: 498–507.

Connolly, P. (2006) 'The effects of social class and ethnicity on gender differences in GCSE attainment: a secondary analysis of the Youth Cohort Study of England and Wales 1997–2001', *British Educational Research Journal*, 32(1): 3–21.

Conway, P.F. and Clarke, C. (2003) 'The journey inward and outward: a re-examination of Fuller's concerns-based model of teacher development', *Teaching and Teacher Education*, 19(5): 466–82.

Costello, P.J.M. (2011) *Effective Action Research: Developing Reflective Thinking and Practice*, London: Continuum.

Coultas, V. (2007) *Constructive Talk in Challenging Classrooms*, London: Routledge.

Covington, M.V. (2000) 'Goal theory, motivation and school achievement: an integrative review', *Annual Review of Psychology*, 51: 171–200.

Cowie, B. and Bell, B. (1999) 'A model of formative assessment in science education', *Assessment in Education: Principles, Policy and Practice*, 6(1): 32–42.

Crace, J. (2007) 'Is this the end of SATS?', *Education Guardian*, 6 December: 1.

Cremin, T. and Myhill, D.A. (2012) *Writing Voices: Creating Communities of Writers*, London: Routledge.

Croner (updated annually) *Head's Guide to the Law*, New Malden: Croner.

Crothers, L.M., Kanyongo, G.Y., Kolbert, J.B., Lipinski, J., Kachmar, S.P. and Koch, G.D. (2010) 'Job stress and locus of control in teachers: comparisons between samples from the United States and Zimbabwe', *International Review of Education*, 56: 651–69.

Darling-Hammond, L. (1999) *Solving the Dilemmas of Teacher Supply, Demand and Standards: How We Can Ensure a Competent, Caring and Qualified Teacher for Every Child*, New York: National Commission on Teaching and America's Future.

Das, S., Dewhurst, Y. and Gray, D. (2011) 'A teacher's repertoire: developing creative pedagogy', *International Journal of Education and the Arts*, 12(15), available at: www.ijea.org/v12n15/v12n15.pdf (accessed 19 December 2014).

Dave, R.H. (1975) 'Psychomotor levels', in R.J. Armstrong (ed.) *Developing and Writing Behavioral Objectives*, Tucson, AZ: Educational Innovators Press, pp. 20–1.

Davies, D., Jindal-Snape, D., Collier, C., Digby, R., Hay, P. and Howe, A. (2013). 'Creative learning environments in education: a systematic literature review', *Thinking Skills and Creativity*, 8: 80–91.

Davies, J. and Brember, I. (1999) 'Standards in mathematics in Years 2 and 6: a nine year crosssectional study', *Educational Review*, 51(3): 243.

Davies, F. and Greene, T. (1984) *Reading for Learning in Science*, Edinburgh: Oliver & Boyd.

Davies, N. (2000) *The School Report: Why Britain's Schools are Failing*, London: Vintage Books.

Davis, B. and Sumara, D.J. (1997) 'Cognition, complexity and teacher education', *Harvard Educational Review*, 67: 105–21.

Davison, J. and Dowson, J. (eds) (2003) *Learning to Teach English in the Secondary School: A Companion to School Experience*, 2nd edn, London: Routledge.

Day, C. (1999) *Developing Teachers: The Challenges of Lifelong Learning*, London: Falmer Press.

Day, C. (2008) 'Committed for life? Variations in teachers' work, lives and effectiveness', *Journal of Educational Change*, 9(3): 243–60.

Day, C., Edwards, A., Griffiths, A. and Gu, Q. (2011) *Beyond Survival: Teachers and Resilience*, Nottingham: University of Nottingham.

Day, J.J. and Sweatt, J.D. (2011) 'Epigenetic mechanisms in cognition', *Neuron*, 70(5): 813–29, available at: http://ac.els-cdn.com/S0896627311004338/1-s2.0-S0896627311004338-main.pdf?_ (accessed 15 November 2015).

DCSF (Department for Children, Schools and Families) (2008a) *Guidance on Preventing Underachievement: A Focus on Exceptionally Able Pupils*, London: DCSF.

DCSF (Department for Children, Schools and Families) (2008b) *Key Stage 3 National Strategy Materials*, London: DCSF, available at: http://webarchive.nationalarchives.gov.uk/20110809091832/www.teaching andlearningresources.org.uk (accessed 7 December 2014).

DCSF (Department for Children, Schools and Families) (2008c) *The National Strategies 1997–2011: A Brief Summary of the Impact and Effectiveness of the National Strategies*, London: DCSF, available at: www.gov.uk/government/uploads/system/uploads/attachment_data/file/175408/DFE-00032-2011.pdf (accessed 2 November 2014).

DCSF (Department for Children, Schools and Families) (2008d) *Pedagogy and practice: Teaching and Learning in Secondary Schools*, London: DCSF.

DCSF (Department for Children, Schools and Families) (2009a) *Lamb Inquiry: Special Educational Needs and Parental Confidence*, London: DCSF, available at: www.dcsf.gov.uk/lambinquiry/downloads/8553-lamb-inquiry.pdf (accessed 22 March 2012).

DCSF (Department for Children, Schools and Families) (2009b) *The Protection of Children in England: A Progress Report, The Lord Laming*, London: DCSF, available at: www.education.gov.uk/publications/eOrderingDownload/HC-330.pdf (accessed 16 November 2015).

DCSF (Department for Children, Schools and Families) (2010) *Working Together to Safeguard Children*, London: DCSF.

de Bono, E. (1972) *Children Solve Problems*, London: Penguin Education.

De Geest, E. (2013) *Mathematics: Reading and Writing Mathematics MESHGuide*, Open University, UK.

Dearing, R. (1996) *Review of Qualifications for 16–19 Year Olds* (full report), London: School Curriculum and Assessment Authority.

Deci, E.L. and Ryan, R.M. (1985) *Intrinsic Motivation and Self-Determination in Human Behavior*, New York: Plenum.

Deci, E.L., Nezlek, J. and Sheinman, L. (1981) 'Characteristics of the rewarder and intrinsic motivation of the rewardee', *Journal of Personality and Social Psychology*, 40: 1–10.

Delamont, S. (1991) 'The hit list and other horror stories', *Sociological Review*, 39(2): 238–59.

Delazer, M., Domahs, F., Bartha, L., Brenneis, C., Lochy, A., Trieb, T. and Benke, T. (2003) 'Learning complex arithmetic: an fMRI study', *Cognitive Brain Research*, 18: 76–88.

Derewianka, B. (1996) *Exploring the Writing of Genres*, Royston, Hertfordshire: UKRA.

DES (Department of Education and Science) (1978) *Special Educational Needs*, London: HMSO.

DES (Department of Education and Science) (1985) *Education for All: The Final Report of the Committee of Inquiry into the Education of Children from Ethnic Minority Groups, Cmnd. 9469* (The Swann Report), London: HMSO.

DES (Department of Education and Science) (1989a) *Discipline in Schools (The Elton Report)*, London: HMSD, available at: www.dg.dial.pipex.com/documents/docs1/elton.shtml (accessed 27 October 2014).

DES (Department of Education and Science) (1989b) *Memo to National Curriculum Working Groups*, para 4.1, London: DES.

Des Fountain, J. (1994) 'Planning for learning through talk', in S. Brindley (ed.) *Teaching English*, London: Routledge, pp. 55–63.

Desforges, C. (2002) *On Teaching and Learning*, Cranfield: NCSL.

Desforges, C. (2003) 'Leading change through collaborative learning', Address to Networked Learning Community Conference, Daventry, 15 October.

DeWert, M.H., Babinski, L.M. and Jones, B.D. (2003) 'Safe passages: providing online support to beginning teachers', *Journal of Teacher Education*, 54(4): 311–20.

Dewey, J. (1909) *The Moral Principles in Education: The Middle Works of John Dewey, 1899–1924. Volume 4: 1907–1909, Essays*, Carbondale and Edwardsville, IL: Southern Illinois University Press.

Dewey, J. (1916) *Democracy and Education*, New York: Free Press.

Dewey, J. (1933) *How We Think*, Boston, MA: Houghton Mifflin.

DfE (Department for Education) (updated annually) *School Teachers' Pay and Conditions*, London: HMSO, available at: www.teachernet.gov.uk/paysite/ (accessed 16 November 2015).

DfE (Department for Education) (1994a) *Code of Practice on the Identification and Assessment of Pupils with Special Educational Needs*, London: DfE.

DfE (Department for Education) (1994b) *The Education of Children with Emotional and Behavioural Difficulties*, Circular 9/94, London: DfE.

DfE (Department for Education) (2006) *Grouping Pupils for Success: National Literacy and Numeracy Strategies*, London: DfE, available at: http://webarchive.nationalarchives.gov.uk/20110809101133/http://wsassets.s3.amazonaws.com/ws/nso/pdf/bbd59a99cf4ad4a66ac8a25069a72063.pdf (accessed 19 July 2015).

DfE (Department for Education) (2010a) *Importance of Teaching*, White Paper, London: DfE.

DfE (Department for Education) (2010b) *Statement of Intent*, available at: www.education.gov.uk/performancetables/Statement-of-Intent-2010 Addendum.pdf (accessed 10 June 2012).

DfE (Department for Education) (2011a) *About the School Curriculum*, available at: www.education.gov.uk/schools/teachingandlearning/curriculum/b00200366/about-the-school-curriculum (accessed 30 May 2012).

DfE (Department for Education) (2011b) *Achievement for All: National Evaluation*, London: DfE, available at: www.education.gov.uk/schools/leadership/schoolperformance/a00199926/achievement-forall (accessed 7 January 2016).

DfE (Department for Education) (2011c) *Aims, Values and Purposes of the National Curriculum*, available at: www.education.gov.uk/schools/teachingandlearning/curriculum/b00199676/aims-values-and-purposes/values (accessed 9 June 2012).

DfE (Department for Education) (2011d) *Getting the Simple Things Right: Charlie Taylor's Behaviour Checklists*, available at: www.education.gov.uk/schools/pupilsupport/behaviour/a00199342/getting-the-simple-things-right-charlie-taylors-behaviour-checklists (accessed 23 April 2015).

DfE (Department for Education) (2011e) *School Achievement and Attainment Tables*, available at: www.education.gov.uk/search/results?q=Schools+achievement+and+Attainment+tablesandpage=2 (accessed 3 June 2012).

DfE (Department for Education) (2011f) *Support and Aspiration: A New Approach to Special Educational Needs and Disability*, London: DfE, available at: www.education.gov.uk/publications/standard/publication Detail/Page1/CM%208027 (accessed 22 March 2012).

DfE (Department for Education) (2011g) *The Overall Aims of the National Curriculum*, London: DfE, available at: www.education.gov.uk/publications/eOrderingDownload/QCA-99-457.pdf (accessed 1 June 2012).

DfE (Department for Education (2011h) *Class Size and Education in England Evidence Report*, London: DfE, available at: www.gov.uk/government/uploads/system/uploads/attachment_data/file/183364/DFE-RR169.pdf (accessed 13 November 2015).

DfE (Department for Education) (2011i) *Teachers Standards in England from September 2012*, London: HMSO, available at: www.gov.uk/government/uploads/system/uploads/attachment_data/file/301107/Teachers__ Standards.pdf (accessed 3 December 2014).

DfE (Department for Education) (2012a) *Aims, Values and Purposes of the National Curriculum for England (2012)*, available at: www.education.gov.uk/schools/teachingandlearning/curriculum/b00199676/aims-values-and-purposes (accessed 1 April 2012).

DfE (Department for Education) (2012b) *Assessment and Reporting Arrangements*, available at: www. education.gov.uk/schools/teachingandlearning/assessment/a00197251/assessment-and-reporting-arrangements (accessed 10 June 2012).

DfE (Department for Education) (2012c) *National Curriculum for England (2012)*, available at: www. education.gov.uk/schools/teachingandlearning/curriculum (accessed 1 April 2012).

DfE (Department for Education) (2012d) *Teachers' Standards*, available at: http://www.education. gov.uk/publications/eOrderingDownload/DFE-00066-2011.pdf (accessed 9 April 2015).

DfE (Department for Education) (2012e) *The GCSE and Equivalent Attainment by Pupil Characteristics in England8.2.1 2010/11*, available at: www.education.gov.uk/researchandstatistics/datasets/a00202462/ gcse-equivalent-attainment-pupil-characteristics (accessed 28 February 2012).

DfE (Department for Education) (2012f) *Literacy and Numeracy Catch-up Strategies*, London: DfE, available at www.gov.uk/government/uploads/system/uploads/attachment_data/file/268031/literacy_ and_numeracy_catch_up_strategies_in_secondary_schools.pdf (accessed 13 January 2016).

DfE (Department for Education) (2013a) *Assessing Without Levels*, London: DfE, available at: www.education. gov.uk/a00225864 (accessed 2 March 2015).

DfE (Department for Education) (2013b) *Computing Programmes of Study: Key Stages 3 and 4*, London: DfE.

DfE (Department for Education) (2013c) *Design and Technology Programmes of Study: Key Stage 3*, London: DfE, available at: www.gov.uk/government/uploads/system/uploads/attachment_data/file/ 239089/SECONDARY_national_curriculum_-_Design_and_technology.pdf (accessed 29 March 2015).

DfE (Department for Education) (2013d) *Guidance for Governing Bodies on Behaviour and Discipline*, available at: www.gov.uk/government/publications/behaviour-and-discipline-in-schools-guidance-for-governing-bodies (accessed 23 April 2015).

DfE (Department for Education) (2013e) *Statutory Guidance National Curriculum in England: Framework for Key Stages 1 to 4*, available at: www.gov.uk/government/publications/national-curriculum-in-england-framework-for-key-stages-1-to-4 (accessed 5 January 2014).

DfE (Department for Education) (2013f) *Statutory Guidance National Curriculum in England: Computing Programmes of Study*, London: DfE, available at: www.gov.uk/government/publications/national-curriculum-in-england-computing-programmes-of-study (accessed 18 November 2014).

DfE (Department for Education) (2013g) *Teachers Standards, Department for Education*, available at: www.gov.uk/government/publications/teachers-standards (accessed 3 January 2016).

DfE (Department for Education) (2013h) *The National Curriculum in England: Key Stages 3 and 4 Framework Document*, London: DfE, Reference: DFE-00183-2013.

DfE (Department for Education) (2013i) *The National Curriculum*, London: DfE, available at: www.gov.uk/ national-curriculum (accessed 3 March 2015).

DfE (Department for Education) (2013j) *Use of Reasonable Force: Advice for Headteachers, Staff and Governing Bodies*, available at: www.gov.uk/government/publications/use-of-reasonable-force-in-schools (accessed 23 April 2015).

DfE (Department for Education) (2013k) *Statutory Guidance National Curriculum in England: Design and Technology Programme of Study Key Stage 3*, London: DfE, available at: www.gov.uk/government/ uploads/system/uploads/attachment_data/file/239089/SECONDARY_national_curriculum_- Design_ and_technology.pdf (accessed 13 November 2015).

DfE (Department for Education) (2013l) *Statutory Guidance National Curriculum in England: Physical Education programmes of study*, London: DfE, available at: www.gov.uk/government/publications/national-curriculum-in-england-physical-education-programmes-of-study.

DfE (Department for Education) (2014a) *Behaviour and Discipline in Schools: Advice to Headteachers and School Staff*, available at: www.gov.uk/government/publications/behaviour-and-discipline-in-schools (accessed 23 April 2015).

DfE (Department for Education) (2014b) *Child Poverty Strategy 2014–17*, London: HMSO.

DfE (Department for Education) (2014c) *First Statistical Release: Special Educational Needs in England, January 2014*, London: DfE.

DfE (Department for Education) (2014d) *Guidance for Schools to Prevent and Respond to Bullying as Part of their Overall Behaviour Policy*, available at: www.education.gov.uk/schools/pupilsupport/behaviour/bullying/f0076899/preventing-and-tackling-bullying (accessed 16 November 2015).

DfE (Department for Education) (2014e) *Guide for Heads and School Staff on Behaviour and Discipline*, London: DfE, available at: www.gov.uk/government/publications/behaviour-and-discipline-in-schools (accessed 3 January 2016).

DfE (Department for Education) (2014f) *Improving Behaviour and Attendance in Schools*, available at: www.gov.uk/government/policies/improving-behaviour-and-attendance-in-schools (accessed 23 April 2015).

DfE (Department for Education) (2014g) *Keeping Children Safe in Education: Statutory Guidance for Schools and Colleges*, available at: www.gov.uk/government/publications/keeping-children-safe-in-education (accessed 16 November 2015).

DfE (Department for Education) (2014h) *Preventing and Tackling Bullying: Advice for Headteachers, Staff and Governing Bodies*, available at: www.gov.uk/government/uploads/system/uploads/attachment_data/file/368340/preventing_and_tackling_bullying_october14.pdf (accessed 29 October 2014).

DfE (Department for Education) (2014i) *School Teachers' Pay and Conditions: Document and Guidance on School Teachers' Pay and Conditions 2014*, available at: www.gov.uk/government/publications/school-teachers-pay-and-conditions-2014 (accessed 16 November 2015).

DfE (Department for Education) (2014j) *Screening, Searching and Confiscation*, available at: www.gov.uk/government/publications/searching-screening-and-confiscation (accessed 23 April 2015).

DfE (Department for Education) (2014k) *SEND Code of Practice: 0–25 Years*, London: DfE, available at: www.gov.uk/government/uploads/system/attachment_data/file/484418/send-code-of-practice-0-to-25 (accessed 1 November 2014).

DfE (Department for Education) (2014l) *Supporting Pupils at School with Medical Conditions: Statutory Guidance for Governing Bodies of Maintained Schools and Proprietors of Academies in England*, available at: www.gov.uk/government/uploads/system/attachment_data/file/484418/supporting-pupils-at-school-with-medical-conditions.pdf (accessed 3 January 2016).

DfE (Department for Education) (2014m) *The GCSE and Equivalent Attainment by Pupil Characteristics in England, 2012/13*, available at: www.gov.uk/government/statistics/gcse-and-equivalent-attainment-by-pupil-characteristics-2012-to-2013 (accessed 1 February 2015).

DFE (Department for Education) (2014n) *National Curriculum and Assessment from September 2014: Information for Schools*, London: DfE.

DfE (Department for Education) (2014o) *Statutory Guidance National Curriculum in England: Framework for Key Stages 1 to 4*, available at: www.gov.uk/government/publications/national-curriculum-in-england-framework-for-key-stages-1-to-4 (accessed 13 November 2015).

DfE (Department for Education) (2015a) *Government Response to the Carter Review of Initial Teacher Training*, London: Crown.

DfE (Department for Education) (2015b) *Government Response to the Workload Challenge*, London: Crown.

DfE (Department for Education) (2015c) *Workload Challenge: Analysis of Teacher Consultation Responses*, London: DfE, available at: www.gov.uk/government/publications/workload-challenge-analysis-of-teacher-responses (accessed 3 March 2015).

DfE (Department for Education) (2015d) *School and College Performance Tables*, available at: www.education.gov.uk/schools/performance/ (accessed 24 April 2015).

DfE (Department for Education) (2015e) *2017 Key Stage 4 Performance Tables: Qualifications in the Technical Award Category*, available at: www.gov.uk/government/uploads/system/uploads/attachment_data/file/448760/Technical_Awards_2017_list_July_2015.pdf (accessed 14 November 2015).

DfE (Department for Education) (2015f) *Carter Review of Initial Teacher Training*, London: DfE, available at: www.gov.uk/government/uploads/system/uploads/attachment_data/file/399957/Carter_Review.pdf (accessed 14 November 2015).

DfE (Department for Education) (2015g) *Government Response to the Workload Challenge*, London: Department for Education, www.gov.uk/government/uploads/system/uploads/attachment_data/file/415874/Government_Response_to_the_Workload_Challenge.pdf (accessed 14 November 2015).

DfE (Department for Education) www.gov.uk/topic/schools-colleges-childrens-services/curriculum-qualifications (accessed 15 November 2015).

DfE/ACPO (Department for Education/Association of Chief Police Officers) (2012) *Drug Advice for Schools*, London: DfE.

DfE/DoH (2015) *Special educational needs and disability code of practice 0–25 Years*, available at: www.gov.uk/government/uploads/system/uploads/attachment_data/file/398815/SEND_Code_of_Practice_January_2015.pdf (accessed 10 November 2015).

DfE/Ofsted (Department for Education/Office for Standards in Education) (2012) *About Raiseonline*, available at: www.raiseonline.org/About.aspx (accessed 10 June 2012).

DfE/Ofsted (Department for Education/Office for Standards in Education) (2015) *About Raiseonline*, available at: www.raiseonline.org/login.aspx?ReturnUrl=%2f (accessed 14 November 2015).

DfEE (Department for Education and Employment) (1995) *Disability Discrimination Act (1995): A Consultation on the Employment Code of Practice, Guidance on the Definition of Disability and Related Regulations*, London: DfEE.

DfEE (Department for Education and Employment) (1997) *Guaranteeing Standards: A Consultation Paper on the Structure of Awarding Bodies*, London: DfEE.

DfEE (Department for Education and Employment) (1999) *Social Inclusion: Pupil Support*, Circular 10/99, London: DfEE.

DfEE/QCA (Department for Education and Employment/Qualifications and Curriculum Authority) (1999a) *The National Curriculum*, London: DfE/QCA.

DfEE/QCA (Department for Education and Employment/Qualifications and Curriculum Authority) (1999b) *The National Curriculum for England. Handbook for Secondary Teachers: Key Stages 3 and 4*, London: DfEE/QCA.

DfEE/QCA (Department for Education and Employment/Qualifications and Curriculum Authority) (2001) *Guidelines for Teaching Pupils with Learning Difficulties*, London: QCA.

DfES/QCA (Department for Education and Skills/Qualifications and Curriculum Authority) (2004) *The National Curriculum Handbook for Secondary Teachers in England*, London: QCA, p.32, available online at http://webarchive.nationalarchives.gov.uk/20130401151715/http://www.education.gov.uk/publications/eOrderingDownload/QCA-04-1374.pdf (accessed 22 January 2016)

DfES (Department for Education and Skills) (2001a) *Inclusive Schooling*, London: DfES.

DfES (Department for Education and Skills) (2001b) *Special Educational Needs Code of Practice on the Identification and Assessment of Pupils with Special Educational Needs*, London: DfES.

DfES (Department for Education and Skills) (2002) *Guided Reading in English at Key Stage 3*, Ref. DfES 0044/2002, London: DfES.

DfES (Department for Education and Skills) (2003a) *Every Child Matters*, London: DfES.

DfES (Department for Education and Skills) (2003b) *Key Stage 3 Strategy: Key Messages about Assessment and Learning*, London: DfES.

DfES (Department for Education and Skills) (2004a) *Every Child Matters; Change for Children*, London: DfES, available at: www.education.gov.uk/consultations/downloadableDocs/EveryChildMatters.pdf (accessed 11 June 2012).

DfES (Department for Education and Skills) (2004b) *Group Work Pedagogy and Practice: Teaching and Learning in Secondary Schools. Unit 10 Group Work*, available at: http://webarchive.nationalarchives.gov.uk/20110202093118/HTTP:/nationalstrategies.standards.dcsf.gov.uk/node/96255 (accessed 7 December 2014).

DfES (Department for Education and Skills) (2004c) *Pedagogy and Practice: Teaching and Learning in the Secondary School, Unit 18 Improving the Climate for Learning*, London: DfES.

DfES (Department for Education and Skills) (2004d) *Pedagogy and Practice: Teaching and Learning in the Secondary School, Unit 8 Explaining*, London: DfES.

DfES (Department for Education and Skills) (2004e) *Pedagogy and Practice: Teaching and Learning in the Secondary School, Unit 6 Modelling*, London: DfES.

DfES (Department for Education and Skills) (2004f) *Pedagogy and Practice: Teaching and Learning in the Secondary School, Unit 7 Questioning*, London: DfES.

DfES (Department for Education and Skills) (2004g) *Pedagogy and Practice: Teaching and Learning in Secondary Schools: Unit 19 Learning Styles*, London: DfES.

DfES (Department for Education and Skills) (2004h) *Removing Barriers to Achievement: The Government's Strategy for SEN*, London: DfES.

DfES (Department for Education and Skills) (2005a) *Implementing the Disability Discrimination Act in Schools and Early Years Settings*, available at: www.education.gov.uk/publications/standard/publicationdetail/page1/DfES%200160%202006 (accessed 11 June 2012).

DfES (Department for Education and Skills) (2005b) *Key Stage 3 National Strategy: Leading in Learning: Developing Thinking Skills at Key Stage 3*, DfES 0036-2205G.

DfES (Department for Education and Skills) (2005c) *National Curriculum Schemes of Work*, London: Crown, available at: http://webarchive.nationalarchives.gov.uk/20090608182316/standards.dfes.gov.uk/schemes3/ (accessed 7 December 2014).

DfES (Department for Education and Skills) (2005d) *Statistics of Education: School Workforce in England*, 2004 edn, London: DfES.

DfES (Department for Education and Skills) (2006a) *Highlights: Personalised Learning*, London: DfES.

DfES (Department for Education and Skills) (2006b) *National Strategies: Grouping Pupils for Success*, London: DfES, available at: http://webarchive.nationalarchives.gov.uk/20130401151715/http://www.education.gov.uk/publications/eOrderingDownload/00844-2008DOM-EN.pdf (accessed 7 December 2014).

DfT (Department for Transport) (2010) *National Travel Survey 2010*, available at: www.dft.gov.uk/statistics/releases/nation-travel-survey-2010/nts2010-06.pdf (accessed 20 March 2012).

Didau, D. (2015a) *Learning Is Invisible: Slides from the London Festival of Education Presentation*, available at: www.learningspy.co.uk/featured/learning-is-invisible-my-slides-from-lef15/ (accessed 2 March 2015).

Didau, D. (2015b) *What If Everything You Knew about Learning Was Wrong: Tackling the Myth of Progress*, Carmarthen: Independent Thinking Press.

Dillon, J. and Maguire, M. (eds) (2001) *Becoming a Teacher: Issues in Secondary Teaching*, 3rd edn, Buckingham: Open University Press.

Dimbleby, H. and Vincent, J. (2013) *The School Food Plan*, London: DfE, available at www.gov.uk/government/uploads/system/uploads/attachment_data/file/251020/The_School_Food_Plan.pdf (accessed 12 November 2015).

Dix, P. (2007) *Taking Care of Behaviour: Practical Skills for Teachers*, Harlow: Pearson Education.

DoH (Department of Health) (2007) *Department of Health Food in Schools: Pilot Project 'Dining Room Environment'*, available at: www.dh.gov.uk/en/policyandguidance/healthandsocialcaretopics/foodinschoolsprogramme (accessed 20 March 2012).

DoH (Department of Health) (2011a) *National Diet and Nutrition Survey. Headline Results from Years 1 and 2 (Combined) of the Rolling Programme (2008/2009-2009/2010)*, London: DoH, available at: www.dh.gov.uk/en/Publicationsandstatistics (accessed 20 March 2012).

DoH (Department of Health) (2011b) *Physical Activity Guidelines for Children and Young People (5-18 years)*, London: DoH, available at: www.dh.gov.uk/health/2011/07/physical-activityguidelines/ (accessed 23 July 2012).

Donaldson, M. (1978) *Children's Minds*, Glasgow: Fonanta/Colllns.

Donaldson, M. (1992) *Human Minds: An Exploration*, London: Allen Lane.

Draganski, B., Gaser, C., Busch, V., Schuierer, G., Bogdahn, U. and May, A. (2004) 'Changes in grey matter induced by training', *Nature*, 427: 311-12.

Driver, R. (1983) *The Pupil as Scientist*, Milton Keynes: Open University Press.

Driver, R. and Bell, J. (1986) 'Students' thinking and learning of science: a constructivist view', *School Science Review*, 67(240): 443-56.

Dryden, G. and Vos, J. (2001) *The Learning Revolution: To Change the Way the World Learns*, Stafford: Network Educational Press in association with Learning Web.

Dudek, M. (2000) *Architecture of Schools: The New Learning Environments*, Boston, MA: Architectural Press.

Dudley, P. (2014) *Lesson Study: Professional Learning for Our Time*, London: Routledge; see also: http://lessonstudy.co.uk/about-us-pete-dudley/ (accessed 21 July 2015).

Dunne, J. (2003) 'Arguing for teaching as a practice: a reply to Alasdair MacIntyre', *Journal of Philosophy of Education*, 37(2): 353-69.

Dweck, C. (1986) 'Motivational processes affecting learning', *American Psychologist*, 41: 1040-8.

Dweck, C.S. (1999) *Self Theories: Their Role in Motivation, Personality and Development*, Philadelphia, PA: Psychology Press.

Dweck, C.S. (2007) *Mindset: The New Psychology of Success*, New York: Ballantine Books.

Dweck, C.S. (2012) *Mindset: How You Can Fulfill Your Potential*, London: Constable & Robinson.

Dweck, C.S. and Leggett, E. (1988) 'A social-cognitive approach to motivation and personality', *Psychological Review*, 95: 256-73.

DWP (Department for Work and Pensions) (2013) Free School Meal Entitlement and Child Poverty in England, available at: www.gov.uk/government/uploads/system/uploads/attachment_data/file/266587/free-school-meals-and-poverty.pdf (assessed 12 November 2015).

DWP (Department for Work and Pensions) (2014) *Labour Market Status by Ethnic Group*, available at: www.gov.uk/government/uploads/system/uploads/attachment_data/file/269689/labour-market-status-by-ethnic-group.pdf (accessed 12 November 2015).

Dyson, A. (2001) 'Special needs in the twenty-first century: where we've been and where we're going', *British Journal of Special Education*, 28(1): 24-9.

Eames, K. (2016) *Teaching Grammar in the English Language MESHGuide*, Bath Spa University, UK.

Earley, P. and Weindling, D. (2004) *Understanding School Leadership*, London: Sage.

Eaton Vale Schools Activity Centre (2015) *Risk Assessments*, available at: www.eatonvale.co.uk/schools/riskassessments.aspx (accessed 17 July 2015).

Eccles, J.S. and Midgley, C. (1989) 'Stage-environment fit: developmentally appropriate classrooms for young adolescents', in C. Ames and R. Ames (eds) *Research on Motivation in Education: Goals and Cognitions*, Volume 3, New York: Academic Press, pp. 139-86.

Education Scotland (2015) *Skills in Practice: Thinking Skills*, available at: www.educationscotland.gov.uk/resources/s/skillsinpracticethinkingskills/knowing.asp (accessed 18 July 2015).

Edwards, A.D. and Westgate, D.P.G. (1994) *Investigating Classroom Talk*, 2nd edn, London: Falmer.

Eggert, M. (2008) *The Perfect Interview: All You Need to Know to Get It Right First Time*, London: Random House.

EHRC (Equality and Human Rights Commission) (2010) *How Fair is Britain? Equality, Human Rights and Good Relations in 2010*, available at: www.equalityhumanrights.com/key-projects/how-fair-is-britain/full-report-and-evidence-downloads (accessed 28 February 2012).

EHRC (Equality and Human Rights Commission) (2013) *Gender Pay Gaps 2012*, London: Government Equalities Office.

Elliot, A.J. and McGregor, H.A. (2001) 'A 2 × 2 achievement goal framework', *Journal of Personality and Social Psychology*, 80: 501-19.

Elliott, J. (1991) *Action Research for Educational Change*, Milton Keynes: Open University Press.

Ellis, S. and Tod, J. (2009) *Behaviour for Learning: Proactive Approaches to Behaviour Management*, London: Routledge.

Ellis, S. and Tod, J. (2014) *Promoting Behaviour for Learning in the Classroom*, London: Routledge.

English, P. (2004) *Succeeding at Interviews Pocketbook*, Alresford, Hants: Management Pocketbooks.

Entwistle, N.J. (1981) *Styles of Learning and Teaching*, Chichester: Wiley.

Entwistle, N. (1990) *Handbook of Educational Ideas and Practices*, London: Routledge.

Entwistle, N.J. (1993) *Styles of Learning and Teaching*, 3rd edn, London: David Fulton.

Entwistle, N., McCune, V. and Walker, P. (2001) 'Conceptions, styles and approaches within higher education: analytic abstractions and everyday experience', in R.J. Sternberg and L.F. Zhang (eds) *Perspectives on Thinking, Learning and Cognitive Styles*, Mahwah, NJ: Lawrence Erlbaum Associates.

ERA (Education Reform Act) (1988) *Education Reform Act, 29 July 1988; Section 1, 2 Aims of the School Curriculum*, London: HMSO.

Erikson, E.H. (1980) *Identity and the Life Cycle*, New York: W.W. Norton.

ESRC (Economic and Social Research Council) (1997) *What Pupils Tell Us about Teachers and Lessons*, available at: www.consultingpupils.co.uk/Resources/.../Jean%20nov%201.htm (accessed 28 December 2011).

Evans, C. (2004) 'Exploring the relationship between cognitive style and teaching style', *Educational Psychology*, 24(4): 509-30.

Evans, J. and Lunt, I. (2002) 'Inclusive education: are there limits?', *European Journal of Special Needs Education*, 17: 1-14.

Evetts, J. (2009) 'The management of professionalism: a contemporary paradox', in S. Gewirtz, P. Mahony, I. Hextall and A. Cribb (eds) *Changing Teacher Professionalism: International Trends, Challenges and Ways Forward*, London: Routledge, pp. 19-30.

Fairclough, S., Hackett, A., Davies, I., Gobbi, R., Mackintosh, K., Warburton, G., Stratton, G., Sluijs, E. and Boddy, L. (2013) 'Promoting healthy weight in primary school children through physical activity and nutrition education: a pragmatic evaluation of the CHANGE! randomised intervention study', *BMC Public Health*, 13: 626.

Fantilli, R.D. and McDougall, D.E. (2009) 'A study of novice teachers: challenges and supports in the first years', *Teaching and Teacher Education*, 25: 814-25.

Farrell, M. (2009) *The Special Education Handbook: An A-Z Guide for Students and Professionals*, 4th edn, London: Routledge.

Fautley, M. and Savage, J. (2008) *Assessment for Learning and Teaching in Secondary Schools*, Exeter: Learning Matters.

Fernet, C., Guay, F., Senécal, C. and Austin, S. (2012) 'Predicting intraindividual changes in teacher burnout: the role of perceived school environment and motivational factors', *Teaching and Teacher Education*, 28: 514-25.

Fielding, M. (1996) 'Why and how learning styles matter: valuing difference in teachers and learners', in S. Hart (ed.) *Differentiation and the Secondary Curriculum: Debates and Dilemmas*, London: Routledge.

Fisher, R. (2009) *Creative Dialogue: Talk for Thinking in the Classroom*, London: Routledge.

Fitzgerald, R., Finch, S. and Nove, A. (2000) *Black Caribbean Young Men's Experiences of Education and Employment, Report No. RR186*, London: DfEE.

Flavell, J.H. (1979) 'Metacognition and cognitive monitoring', *American Psychologist*, 34: 906–11.

Flavell, J.H. (1982) 'Structures, stages, and sequences in cognitive development', in W.A. Collins (ed.) *The Concept of Development: The Minnesota Symposia on Child Psychology*, 15: 1–28.

Fleet, A., Kitson, R., Cassady, B. and Hughes, R. (2007) 'University-qualified indigenous early childhood teachers: voices of resilience', *Australian Journal of Early Childhood*, 32(3): 17–25.

Fleming, M. and Stevens, D. (1998) *English Teaching in the Secondary School*, London: David Fulton.

Fletcher-Campbell, F. (2004a) 'Pupils with moderate learning difficulties', in A. Lewis and B. Norwich (eds) *How Specialist Is Teaching Children with Difficulties and Disabilities?* Buckingham: Open University Press.

Fletcher-Campbell, F. (2004) 'Moderate "Learning difficulties"', in A. Lewis and B. Norwich (eds) *Special Teaching for Special Children? Pedagogies for Inclusion*, Maidenhead: Open University Press.

Flores, M.A. (2006) 'Being a novice teacher in two different settings: struggles, continuities and discontinuities', *Teachers College Record*, 108(10): 2021–52.

Florian, L. and Black-Hawkins, K. (2011) 'Exploring inclusive pedagogy', *British Educational Research Journal*, 37(5): 813–28.

Flynn, N. (2015) *Teaching English as an Additional Language MESHGuide*, University of Winchester/University of Reading, UK.

Fontana, D. (1993) *Psychology for Teachers*, London: Macmillan.

Ford, A. (2014) 'Setting us free? Building meaningful models of progression for a "post-levels" world', *Teaching History*, 157: 28–41.

Fordham, M. (2013) 'O brave new world without those levels in't', *Teaching History*, 16: 16–23.

Fordham, M. (2014) *Beyond Levels Part 1: Knowledge-Rich and Task-Specific Mark Schemes*, available at: http://clioetcetera.com/2014/02/17/beyond-levels-knowledge-rich-and-task-specific-mark-schemes/ (accessed 2 March 2015).

Freakley M., Burgh G. and MacSporran, M.T. (2008) *Values Education in Schools: A Resource Book for Student Inquiry*, Camberwell: Australian Council Educational Research (ACER).

Freeman, N.H. and Parsons, M.J. (2001) 'Children's intuitive understanding of pictures', in B. Torff and R.J. Sternberg (eds) *Understanding and Teaching the Intuitive Mind: Student and Teacher Learning*, London: Lawrence Erlbaum Associates.

Freire, P. (1992) *Pedagogy of Hope*, London: Continuum.

Freud, S. (1901) *The Psychopathology of Everyday Life*, republished 1953 in J. Strachey (ed.) *The Standard Edition of the Complete Psychological Works of Sigmund Freud Vol. 6*, London: Hogarth.

Frost, J. (2010) *Learning to Teach Science in the Secondary School: A Companion to School Experience*, 3rd edn, London: Routledge.

Frost, J. and Turner, T. (2005) *Learning to Teach Science in the Secondary School: A Companion to School Experience*, 2nd edn, London: RoutledgeFalmer.

Fullan, M. (1999) *Change Forces: The Sequel*, London: Falmer Press.

Fuller, F. (1969) 'Concerns of teachers: a developmental conceptualisation', *American Educational Research Journal*, 6(2): 207–26.

Fuller, F.F. and Brown, O.H. (1975) 'Becoming a teacher', in K. Ryan (ed.) *Teacher Education (Seventy-Fourth Yearbook of the National Society of Education)*, Chicago, IL: University of Chicago Press, pp. 25–52.

Furlong, J. and Maynard, T. (1995) *Mentoring Student Teachers: The Growth of Professional Knowledge*, London: Routledge.

Gagné, R.M. (1977) *The Conditions of Learning*, New York: Holt International.

Galton, M. (2010) 'Moving to secondary school: what do pupils in England say about the experience?', in D. Jindal-Snape (ed.) *Educational Transitions: Moving Stories from around the World*, New York: Routledge, pp. 107–24.

Galton, M. and MacBeath, J. (2008) *Teachers under Pressure*, London: Sage with the National Union of Teachers (NUT).

Galton, M. Gray, J. and Rudduck, M. (1999) *The Impact of School Transitions and Transfers on Pupil Progress and Attainment*, available at: www.cumbria.gov.uk/elibrary/Content/Internet/537/40696142430.pdf (accessed 20 November 2015).

Galton, M., Hargreaves, L., Comber, C., Wall, D. and Pell, T. (1999b) 'Changes in patterns of classroom interaction in primary classrooms: 1976-1996', *British Educational Research Journal*, 25(1): 23–37.

Gardner, H. (1983) *Frames of Mind: The Theory of Multiple Intelligences*, New York: Basic Books.

Gardner, H. (1986) Quoted in the *New York Times Educational Supplement*, 19 November.

Gardner, H. (1991) *The Unschooled Mind*, London: HarperCollins.

Gardner, H. (1993a) *Frames of Mind: The Theory of Multiple Intelligences*, 2nd edn, London: Fontana.

Gardner, H. (1993b) *Multiple Intelligences: The Theory in Practice*, New York: Basic Books.

Gardner, H. (1995) 'Reflections on multiple intelligences: myths and messages', *Phi Delta Kappan*, 77: 200–3, 206–9.

Gardner, H. (1999) *Intelligence Reframed: Multiple Intelligences for the 21st Century*, New York: Basic Books.

Gardner, H. (2006a) *Multiple Intelligences: New Horizons*, New York: Basic Books.

Gardner, H. (2006b) *The Development and Education of the Mind: The Selected Works of Howard Gardner*, London: Routledge.

Gardner, H. (2011) *Frames of Mind: The Theory of Multiple Intelligences*, New York: Basic Books.

Gardner, H. (2015) *Multiple Intelligences*, available at: http://howardgardner.com/multiple-intelligences/ (accessed 19 July 2015).

Gardner, H., Kornhaber, M. and Wake, W. (1996) *Intelligence: Multiple Perspectives*, Fort Worth, TX: Harcourt Brace.

Gardner, P. (2013) *English Writing: Reluctant Writers*, MESHGuide, University of Bedfordshire, UK.

Gardner, P., Kauffman, J. and Elliott, J. (2014) *The Handbook of Emotional and Behavioural Difficulties*, London: Sage.

Gathercole, S. (2008) 'Working memory in the classroom: the President's Award lecture to the Annual Conference of the British Psychological Society', *The Psychologist*, 21(5): 382–5.

Geake, J.G. (2009) *The Brain at School*, Milton Keynes: Open University Press.

Gessell, A. (1925) *The Mental Growth of the Preschool Child*, New York: Macmillan.

Giallo, R. and Little, E. (2003) 'Classroom behaviour problems: the relationship between preparedness, classroom experiences and self-efficacy in graduate and student teachers', *Australian Journal of Educational and Developmental Psychology*, 3(2): 21–34.

Gilbert, I. (2002) *Essential Motivation in the Classroom*, London: RoutledgeFalmer.

Gilham, B. (ed.) (1986) *The Language of School Subjects*, London: Heinemann.

Gillard, D. (2008) 'A history of pupil grouping policies in England's schools up to 2008', *Education in England: The History of our Schools, History Docs Articles*, available at: www.educationengland.org.uk/articles/27grouping.html (accessed 7 December 2014).

Gillborn, D. and Gipps, C. (1996) *Recent Research on the Achievements of Ethnic Minority Pupils, Ofsted Reviews of Research*, London: HMSO.

Gillborn, D. and Mirza, H.S. (2000) *Educational Inequality: Mapping Race, Class and Gender; A Synthesis of Research Evidence*, London: Ofsted.

Gingell, J. and Brandon, E.P. (2000) *In Defence of High Culture*, Oxford: Blackwell.

Gipps, C. (1997) 'Principles of assessment', unpublished lecture, Institute of Education, University of London, 7 February.

Gipps, C. and Stobart, G. (1997) *Assessment: A Teacher's Guide to the Issues*, 3rd edn, London: Hodder & Stoughton.

Giroux, H. (2011) *On Critical Pedagogy*, London: Continuum.

Glinkowski, P. and Bamford, A. (2009) *Insight and Exchange: An Evaluation of the Wellcome Trust's Sciart Programme*, London: Wellcome Trust, available at: www.wellcome.ac.uk/sciartevaluation (accessed 1 November 2011).

Gold, Y. and Roth, R.A. (1993) *Teachers Managing Stress and Preventing Burnout*, London: Falmer Press.

Goleman, D. (1995) *Emotional Intelligence: Why It Can Matter More Than IQ for Character, Health and Lifelong Achievement*, New York: Bantam Press.

Goleman, D. (2005) *Emotional Intelligence*, 2nd edn, New York: Bantam.

Goleman, D. (2006) *Emotional Intelligence: Why It Can Matter More Than IQ*, 10th anniversary edn, New York: Bantam Books.

Goleman, D. (2011) *The Brain and Emotional Intelligence: New Insights*, More Than Sound (e-book).

Good, T. and Brophy, J. (2000) *Looking in Classrooms*, 8th edn, New York: Addison-Wesley Longman.

Good, T. and Brophy, J. (2007) *Looking in Classrooms*, 10th edn, New York: Addison-Wesley Longman.

Goswami, U. (2008) *Cognitive Development: The Learning Brain*, Hove and New York: Psychology Press.

Gough, P.B. and Tunmer, W.E. (1986) 'Decoding, reading and reading disability', *Remedial and Special Education*, 7: 6–10.

Gould, S.J. (1981) *The Mismeasure of Man*, New York: Norton.

Goulding, M. (2005) 'Pupils learning mathematics', in S. Johnston-Wilder, P. Johnston-Wilder, D. Pimm and J. Westwell (eds) *Learning to Teach Mathematics in the Secondary School: A Companion to School Experience*, 2nd edn, London: Routledge.

Gove, M. (2011) Quoted in 'Gove stresses "facts" in school curriculum revamp', *BBC News*, 20 January.

Goverover, Y., Hillary, F.G., Chiaravalloti, N., Arango-Lasprilla, J.C. and DeLuca, J. (2009) 'A functional application of the spacing effect to improve learning and memory in persons with multiple sclerosis', *Journal of Clinical and Experimental Neuropsychology*, 31(5): 513–22.

Greene, B. and Miller, R. (1996) 'Influences on achievement: goals, perceived ability and cognitive engagement', *Contemporary Educational Psychology*, 22(2): 181–92.

Greenhalgh, P. (1994) *Emotional Growth and Learning*, London: Routledge.

Grenfell, M. and James, D. (1998) *Bourdieu and Education*, London: Falmer Press.

Griebel, W. and Niesel, R. (2001) 'Transition to school child: what children tell us about school and what they teach us', Paper presented at the 11th European Conference on Quality of Early Childhood Education, Alkmaar, the Netherlands, 29 August–1 September 2001.

Grossman, P.L. (1990) *The Making of a Teacher: Teacher Knowledge and Teacher Education*, New York: Teachers College Press.

Grossman, P.L., Wilson, S.M. and Shulman, L.S. (1989) 'Teachers of substance: subject matter knowledge for teaching', in M.C. Reynolds (ed.) *Knowledge Base for the Beginning Teacher*, Oxford: Pergamon Press, pp. 23–36.

GTCE (General Teaching Council for England) (2009) *Code of Conduct and Practice for Registered Teachers: Consultation and Engagement on the Revised Draft*, Report for the General Teaching Council for England (GTCE), available at: www.bury.gov.uk/CHTTP:Handler.ashx?id=5348&p=0 (accessed 16 November 2015).

GTCS (General Teaching Council for Scotland) (2012) *Code of Professionalism and Conduct*, available at: www.gtcs.org.uk/web/FILES/teacher-regulation/copac-0412.pdf (accessed 21 July 2015).

GTCS (General Teaching Council for Scotland) (2015) *Code of Professionalism and Conduct*, available at: www.gtcs.org.uk/standards/copac.aspx (accessed 29 July 2015).

Gu, Q. and Day, C. (2007) 'Teachers' resilience: a necessary condition for effectiveness', *Teaching and Teacher Education*, 23(8): 1302–16.

Gu, Q. and Day, C. (2013) 'Challenges to teacher resilience: conditions count', *British Educational Journal*, 39(1): 22–44.

Habermas, J. (1971) *Knowledge and Human Interests*, London: Heineman.

Hall, D. (1996) *Assessing the Needs of Bilingual Pupils*, London: David Fulton.

Hall, E., Leat, D., Wall, K., Higgins, S. and Edwards, G. (2006) 'Learning to learn: teacher research in the zone of proximal development', *Teacher Development*, 10(2): 149–66.

Hallam, S. (2002) *Ability Grouping Schools: A Literature Review*, London: Institute of Education, University of London, in the series *Perspectives on Education*.

Halpern, D. (1998) 'Teaching critical thinking for transfer across domains', *American Psychologist*, 53: 449–55.

Halstead, M. and Taylor, M. (2000) 'Learning and teaching about values: a review of recent research', *Cambridge Journal of Education*, 30(2): 169–202.

Hammill, D., Goodman, L. and Wiederholt, J.L. (1974) 'Visual-motor processes: what success have we had in training them?', *The Reading Teacher*, 27: 469–78.

Hand, M. (2003) 'The meaning of spiritual education', *Oxford Review of Education*, 29(3): 391–401.

Hand, M. and Levinson, R. (2011) 'Discussing controversial issues in the classroom', *Educational Philosophy and Theory*, 44(6): 614–29.

Handscomb, G. (2013) 'Empowering teachers . . . through practitioner research', *Education Today*, 63(3): 3–11.

Hansen, D. (1995) 'Teaching and the moral life of classrooms', *Journal for a Just and Caring Education*, 2, available at: http://tigger.uic.edu/~lnucci/MoralEd/articles/hansen.html (accessed 8 June 2012).

Hara, N. (2009) *Communities of Practice: Fostering Peer to Peer Learning and Informal Knowledge Sharing in the Workplace*, Berlin: Springer.

Hargreaves, A. (1984) *Improving Secondary Schools: Report of the Committee on the Curriculum and Organisation of Secondary Schools*, London: Inner London Education Authority (ILEA).

Hargreaves, A. and Fullan, M. (2012) *Professional Capital: Transforming Teaching in Every School*, New York: Teachers College Press and Toronto: Ontario Principals' Council.

Hargreaves, D. (2005) *About Learning: Report of the Learning Working Group*, London: Demos.

Harlen, W. (1995) 'To the rescue of formative assessment', *Primary Science Review*, 37 (April): 14–15.

Harlen, W. (1997) *Making Sense of the Research on Ability Grouping*, Newsletter No. 60 (Spring), Scottish Council for Research in Education (SCRE).

Harrison, C. (2004) *Understanding Reading Development*, London: Sage.

Harrison, C., Brookes, G. *et al.* (2014) *Spelling in English MESHGuide*, Universities of Nottingham and Sheffield, UK.

Hart, K. (1981) *Children's Understanding of Mathematics*, London: Murray.

Hartley, B. and Sutton, R. (2010) 'Children's development of stereotypical gender-related expectations about academic engagement and consequences for performance', Poster presented at the British Educational Research Association (BERA) Annual Conference, University of Warwick, 1–4 September 2010.

Hartley, B. and Sutton, R. (2013) 'A stereotype threat account of boys' academic underachievement', *Child Development*, 84: 1716–33.

Hatcher, R. (1998) 'Class differentiation in education: rational choices?', *British Journal of Sociology of Education*, 19(1): 5–24.

Hattie, J. (2009) *Visible Learning: A Synthesis of Over 800 Meta-Analyses Relating to Achievement*, London: and New York: Routledge.

Hattie, J. (2012) *Visible Learning for Teachers: Maximising Impact on Learning*, London: Routledge.

Hattie, J. and Timperley, H. (2007) 'The power of feedback', *Review of Educational Research*, 77(1): 81–102, available at: http://growthmindseteaz.org/files/Power_of_Feedback_JHattie.pdf (accessed 2 March 2015).

Hayden, S. and Jordan, E. (2012) *Language for Learning in the Secondary School: A Practical Guide for Supporting Students with Speech, Language and Communication Needs*, London: Routledge.

Haydn, T. (2008) *Managing Pupil Behaviour*, London: Routledge.

Haydn, T. (2012) *Managing Pupil Behaviour: Improving the Classroom Atmosphere*, 2nd edn, London: Routledge.

Haydn, T., Arthur, J., Hunt. M. and Stephen, A. (2008) *Learning to Teach History in the Secondary School*. 3rd edition, London: Routledge.

Haydon, G. (2006a) *Values in Education*, London: Continuum.

Haydon, G. (2006b) *Education, Philosophy and the Ethical Environment*, London: Faber & Faber.

Haydon, G. (2007) *Values for Educational Leadership*, London: Sage.

Haydon, G. and Hayward, J. (2004) 'Values and citizenship education', in S. Capel, R. Heilbronn, M. Leask and T. Tutner (eds) *Starting to Teach in the Secondary School: A Companion for the Newly Qualified Teacher*, 2nd edn, London: RoutledgeFalmer, pp. 161–75.

Hayes, C. (2006) *Stress Relief for Teachers: The 'Coping Triangle'*, London: Routledge.

Heatherley, S.V., Hancock, K.M.F. and Rogers, P.J. (2006) 'Psychostimulant and other effects of caffeine in 9- to 11-year-old children', *Journal of Child Psychology and Psychiatry*, 4(2): 135–42.

Heikkinen, H., Tynjäla. P. and Kiviniemi, U. (2011) 'Interactive pedagogy in practicum', in M. Mattsson, T.V. Ellertson and D. Rorrison (eds) *A Practicum Turn in Teacher Education*, Rotterdam: Sense.

Heilbronn, R. (2008) *Teacher Education and the Development of Practical Judgement*, London: Continuum.

Heilbronn, R., Jones, C. Bubb, S. and Totterdell, M. (2002) 'School based induction tutors: a challenging role', *School Leadership and Management*, 22(4): 372–87.

Hennessy, S., Ruthven, K. and Brindley, S. (2005) 'Teacher perspectives on integrating ICT into subject teaching: commitment, constraints, caution and change', *Journal of Curriculum Studies*, 37(2): 155–92, available at: www.educ.cam.ac.uk/research/projects/istl/WP042.pdf (accessed 16 October 2015).

Henry, J. (2007) 'Twice as many teachers retiring early', *The Daily Telegraph*, 14 January 2007.

Higgins, S. (2015) *Fact Check: Is the Pupil Premium Narrowing the Attainment Gap?*, available at: http://theconversation.com/fact-check-is-the-pupil-premium-narrowing-the-attainment-gap-39601 (accessed 3 April 2015).

Higgins, S., Katsipataki, M., Kokotsaki, D., Coleman, R., Major, L.E. and Coe, R. (2013) *The Sutton Trust-Education Endowment Foundation Teaching and Learning Toolkit*, London: Education Endowment Foundation, available at: www.educationendowmentfoundation.org.uk/toolkit/ (accessed 18 December 2014).

Hillman, C.H., Erickson, K.I. and Framer, A.F. (2008) 'Be smart, exercise your heart: exercise effects on brain and cognition', *Nature Reviews Neuroscience*, 9: 58–65.

Hirst, P. (1974) *Knowledge and the Curriculum*, London: Routledge.

HMG (Her Majesty's Government) (2011) *Prevent Strategy* co8092, available at: www.gov.uk/government/uploads/system/uploads/attachment_data/file/97976/prevent-strategy-review.pdf (accessed 10 November 2015)

HMG (Her Majesty's Government) (2013) *Working Together to Safeguard Children: A Guide to Inter-Agency Working to Safeguard and Promote the Welfare of Children*, available at: www.gov.uk/government/uploads/system/uploads/attachment_data/file/281368/Working_together_to_safeguard_children.pdf (accessed 16 November 2015).

Hobson, A.J., Malderez, A., Tracey, L., Homer, M.S., Tomlinson, P.D., Ashby, P., Mitchell, N., McIntyre, J, Cooper, D., Roper, T., Chambers, G.N. and Tomlinson, P.D. (2009) *Becoming a Teacher: Teachers' Experiences of Initial Teacher Training, Induction and Early Professional Development: Research Report*, DCSF Research Report No. RR115.

Hobson, A.J., Ashby, P., McIntyre, J. and Malderez, A. (2010) *International Approaches to Teacher Selection and Recruitment*, OECD Education Working Papers No. 47, OECD Publishing.

Holliday, A. (2007) *Doing and Writing Qualitative Research*, London: Sage.

Holmes, E. (2009) *The Newly Qualified Teacher's Handbook*, 2nd edn, London: Routledge.

Holt, J. (1964) *How children fail*, London: Penguin.

Holt, J. (1984) *How Children Learn*, London: Penguin.

Hong, J.Y. (2010) 'Pre-service and beginning teachers' professional identity and its relation to dropping out of the profession', *Teaching and Teacher Education*, 26: 1530–43.

Hook, P. and Vass, A. (2000) *Confident Classroom Leadership*, London: David Fulton.

Hopkins, D. (2008) *A Teacher's Guide to Classroom Research*, 4th edn, Milton Keynes: Open University Press.

Howard, S. and Johnson, B. (2004) 'Resilient teachers: resisting stress and burnout', *Social Psychology of Education*, 7(4): 399–420.

Howard-Jones, P.A. (2010) *Introducing Neuroeducational Research*, London: Routledge.

Howard-Jones, P. (2013) *Neuroscience and Education: A Review of Educational Interventions and Approaches Informed by Neuroscience*, London: Educational Endowment Foundation, available at: http://educationendowmentfoundation.org.uk.

Howard-Jones, P.A. (2014) 'Neuroscience and education: myths and messages', *Nature Reviews Neuroscience*, 15: 817–24.

Howard-Jones, P.A., Franey, L., Mashmoushi, R. and Liao, Y.-C. (2009) 'The neuroscience literacy of trainee teachers', Paper presented at the British Educational Research Association Annual Conference, available at: www.leedsac.uk/educol/documents/185140.pdf (accessed 16 November 2015).

Howard-Jones, P.A., Bogacz, R., Yoo, J.H., Leonards, U. and Demetriou, S. (2010) 'The neural mechanisms of learning from competitors', *Neuroimage*, 53(2): 790–9.

Howard-Jones, P.A., Demetriou, S., Bogacz, R., Yoo, J.H. and Leonards, U. (2011) 'Toward a science of learning games', *Mind, Brain and Education*, 5(1): 33–41.

Howard-Jones, P. *et al.* (2014) 'Neuroeducational research in the design and use of a learning technology', *Learning, Media and Technology*, 1–20.

Howe, A. (1992) *Making Talk Work*, London: Hodder & Stoughton.

Hoyle, E. (1974) 'Professionality, professionalism and control in teaching', *London Educational Review*, 3: 13–19.

Hoyle, E. and John, P. (1995) *Professional Knowledge and Professional Practice*, London: Cassell.

Hromek, R. and Roffey, S. (2009) 'Promoting social and emotional learning with games: "it's fun and we learn things"', *Simulation and Gaming*, 40(5): 626–44.

HSE (Health and Safety Executive) (2013) *Labour Force Survey*, available at: www.hse.gov.uk/Statistics/lfs/index.htm (accessed 16 March 2015).

HSE (Health and Safety Executive) (2015) *Health and Safety Checklist for Classrooms*, available at: www.hse.gov.uk/risk/classroom-checklist.htm (accessed 17 July 2015).

Hughes, H. and Vass, A. (2001) *Strategies for Closing the Learning Gap*, Stafford: Network Educational Press.

Huitt, W. and Hummel, J. (2003) 'Piaget's theory of cognitive development', *Educational Psychology Interactive*, available at: www.edpsycinteractive.org/topics/cognition/piaget.html (accessed 31 December 2011).

Husbands, C. (2012) 'Using assessment data to support pupil achievement', in V. Brooks, I. Abbott and P. Huddleston (eds) *Preparing to Teach in the Secondary School*, Maidenhead: Open University Press, pp. 132–44.

Hyatt, K.J. (2007) 'Brain gym: building stronger brains or wishful thinking?', *Remedial and Special Education*, 28(2): 117–24.

Imbeau, M.B. and Tomlinson, C.A. (2010) *Leading and Managing a Differentiated Classroom*, Alexandria, VA: Association for Supervision and Curriculum Development (ASCD).

Ingersoll, R.M. (2003) 'Turnover and shortages among science and mathematics teachers in the United States', in J. Rhoton and P. Bowers (eds) *Science Teachers Retention: Mentoring and Renewal*, Arlington, VA: National Science Education Leadership Association and National Science Teachers Association Press, pp. 1–12.

IOP (Institute of Physics) (2013) *Closing Doors: Exploring Gender and Subject Choice in Schools*, London: IOP.

Ireson, J. and Hallam, S. (2001) *Ability Grouping in Education*, London: Paul Chapman.

Ireson, J., Hallam, S. and Hurley, C. (2005) 'What are the effects of ability grouping on GCSE attainment?', *British Educational Research Journal*, 31: 443–58.

Ireson, J., Hallam, S., Hack, S., Clark, H. and Plewis, I. (2002) 'Ability grouping in English secondary schools: effects on attainment in English, mathematics and science', *Educational Research and Evaluation*, 8(3): 299–318.

Isaacs, T. (2010) 'Educational assessment in England', *Assessment in Education: Principles, Policy and Practice*, 17(3): 315–34.

Jackson, C. and Warin, J. (2000) 'The importance of gender as an aspect of identity at key transition points in compulsory education', *British Educational Research Journal*, 26(3): 375–91.

Jackson, P. (1968) *Life in Classrooms*, New York: Holt, Rinehart & Winston.

Jackson, C.A., Henderson, M., Frank, J.W. and Haw, S.J. (2012) 'An overview of prevention of multiple risk behaviour in adolescence and young adulthood', *Journal of Public Health*, 34(1): 31–40.

Jenkins, K., Smith, H. and Maxwell, T. (2009) 'Challenging experiences faced by beginning casual teachers: here one day and gone the next!', *Asia-Pacific Journal of Teacher Education*, 37(1): 63–78.

Jensen, E. (2009) *Super Teaching*, 4th edn, San Diego, CA: The Brain Store.

Jerome, L. and Bhargava, M. (2015) *Effective Medium-Term Planning for Teachers*, London: Sage.

Jindal-Snape, D. (2010a) 'Setting the scene: educational transitions and moving', in D. Jindal-Snape (ed.) *Educational Transitions: Moving Stories from around the World*, New York: Routledge, pp. 1–8.

Jindal-Snape, D. (2010b) *Moving to Secondary School: Board Game for Facilitating Primary-Secondary School Transition*, available at: www.dundee.ac.uk/eswce/people/djindalsnape/transitions/ (accessed 5 February 2012).

Jindal-Snape, D. (2010c) 'Moving on: integrating the lessons learnt and the way ahead', in D. Jindal-Snape (ed.) *Educational Transitions: Moving Stories from around the World*, New York: Routledge, pp. 223–44.

Jindal-Snape, D. (ed.) (2010d) *Educational Transitions: Moving Stories from around the World*, New York: Routledge.

Jindal-Snape, D. (2011) 'Understanding transitions across educational stages: implications for children/young people who are visually or/and hearing impaired', Invited Keynote speaker at Empowerment of Sensory Impaired Young People Getting ready for the World of Work, Berkshire Sensory Consortium Service, 15 February 2011, Wokingham, England.

Jindal-Snape, D. (2012) 'Lost – and found – in transition', Discovery Day Lectures, 12–13 January 2012, University of Dundee, available at: www.youtube.com/watch?v=v79I43eh5Xg (accessed 4 April 2012)

Jindal-Snape, D. and Foggie, J. (2006) *Moving Stories: A Research Study Exploring Children/Young People, Parents and Practitioners' Perceptions of Primary-Secondary Transitions*, Report for Transitions Partnership Project, Dundee: University of Dundee.

Jindal-Snape, D. and Foggie, J. (2008) 'A holistic approach to primary-secondary transitions', *Improving Schools*, 11: 5–18.

Jindal-Snape, D. and Hannah, E.F.S. (2014) 'Promoting resilience for primary-secondary transitions: supporting children, parents and professionals', in A.B. Liegmann, I. Mammes and K. Racherbäumer (eds) *Facetten von übergängen im bildungssystem: nationale und internationale ergebnisse empirischer forschung*, Munster: Waxmann, pp. 265–77.

Jindal-Snape, D. and Ingram, R. (2013) 'Understanding and supporting triple transitions of international doctoral students: ELT and SuReCom models', *Journal of Perspectives in Applied Academic Practice*, 1(1): 17–24.

Jindal-Snape, D. and Miller, D.J. (2008) 'A challenge of living? Understanding the psycho-social processes of the child during primary-secondary transition through resilience and self-esteem theories', *Educational Psychology Review*, 20: 217–36.

Jindal-Snape, D., Douglas, W., Topping, K.J., Kerr, C. and Smith, E.F. (2006) 'Autistic spectrum disorders and primary-secondary transition', *International Journal of Special Education*, 21(2): 18–31, available at: www.internationalsped.com/documents/03Jindalsnape.doc (accessed 5 February 2012).

Jindal-Snape, D., Vettraino, E., Lowson, A. and McDuff, W. (2011) 'Using creative drama to facilitate primary-secondary transition', *Education*, 3-13(4): 383–94.

Jindal-Snape, D., Roberts, G. and Venditozzi, D. (2012) 'Parental involvement, participation and home-school partnership: using the Scottish lens to explore parental participation in the context of transitions', in M. Soininen and T. Merisuo-Storm (eds) *Home-School Partnership in a Multicultural Society*, Turku, Finland: Turku University Faculty of Education B: 80, pp. 73–101.

Johnson, S., Cooper, C., Cartwright, S., Donald, I., Taylor, P. and Millet, C. (2005) 'The experience of work-related stress across occupations', *Journal of Managerial Psychology*, 20: 178–87.

Johnston-Wilder, S. and Lee, C. (2010) 'Developing mathematical resilience', BERA Annual Conference 2010, 1–4 September 2010, University of Warwick, available at: http://oro.open.ac.uk/24261/2/3C23606C.pdf (accessed 18 July 2015).

Jones, M.V., Meijen, C., McCarthy, P.J. and Sheffield, D. (2009) 'A theory of challenge and threat states in athletes', *International Review of Sport and Exercise Psychology*, 2(2): 161–80.

Joyce, B., Weil, M. and Cahoun, E. (2009) *Models of Teaching*, 8th edn, Boston, MA: Allyn & Bacon.

Jozefkowicz, E. (2006) 'Too many teachers "teaching to the test"', *Education Guardian*, 20 July 2006.

Kavale, K.A. and Forness, S.R. (1987) 'Substance over style: assessing the efficacy of modality testing and teaching', *Exceptional Children*, 54: 228–39.

Kayes, D. (2005) 'Internal validity and reliability of Kolb's learning style inventory, Version 3 (1999)', *Journal of Business and Psychology*, 20(2): 249–57.

Kayser, C. (2007) 'Listening with your eyes', *Scientific American Mind*, 18(2): 24–9.

Keay, J. and Lloyd, C. (2009) 'High quality professional development in physical education: the role of a subject association', *Professional Development in Education* (previously *Journal of In-Service Education*), 35(4): 655–76.

Keay, J. and Lloyd, C. (2011) *Linking Children's Learning with Professional Learning: Impact, Evidence and Inclusive Practice*, Rotterdam: Sense.

Kellogg, R.T. (2008) 'Training writing skills: a cognitive developmental perspective', *Journal of Writing Research*, 1(1): 1–26.

Kelly, G.A. (1955) *The Psychology of Personal Constructs*, New York: Norton.

Kemmis, S. and McTaggert, R. (1988) *The Action Research Planner*, 3rd edn, Geelong: Deakin University Press.

Kennedy, A. (2007) 'Continuing professional development (CPD) policy and the discourse of teacher professionalism in Scotland', *Research Papers in Education*, 22(1): 95–111.

Kennewell, S., Parkinson, S. and Tanner, H. (2002) *Learning to Teach ICT in the Secondary School: A Companion to School Experience*, London: Routledge.

Kerr, D., Sturman, L. and Friedman, T. (2010) *Priorities for Civic and Citizenship Education in Europe*, available at: http://research.acer.edu.au/cgi/viewcontent.cgi?article=1020&context=civics (accessed 16 November 2015).

Kerry, T. (2002) *Learning Objectives, Task-Setting and Differentiation*, London: Nelson-Thornes.

Kerry, T. (2004) *Explaining and Questioning*, Cheltenham: Nelson Thornes.

Keuchel, T. and Beaudry, J. (2015) *Visual Literacy MESHGuide*, Senior Mirandanet Fellow, NAACE Fellow, UK; University of Southern Maine, USA, available at: www.meshguides.org/meshguides-full-list/. (accessed 3 January 2016)

Key for School Leaders (2013) *The Key Survey of School Leaders: National Curriculum Challenges*, November 2013, available at: www.thekeysupport.com/media/cms_page_media/23/The%20Key%20Survey%2 0results%20%20-%20Curriculum%20-%20Nov%202013.pdf (accessed 2 March 2015).

Keys, W., Harris, S. and Fernandes, C. (1996) *Third International Mathematics and Science Study – First National Report – Part 1: Achievement in Mathematics and Science at Age 13 in England*, London: National Foundation for Educational Research.

King, P. and Kitchener, K. (1994) *Developing Reflective Judgement*, San Francisco, CA: Jossey-Bass.

Kingdon, G. and Cassen, C. (2007) *Understanding Low Achievement in English Schools*, London: Centre for the Economics of Education, LSE.

Kintsch, W. (2009) 'Learning and constructivism', in S. Tobias and T. Duffy (2009) (eds) *Constructivist Instruction: Success or Failure*, New York: Routledge.

Kitching, K., Morgan, M. and O'Leary, M. (2009) 'It's the little things: exploring the importance of commonplace events for early-career teachers' motivation', *Teachers and Teaching: Theory and Practice*, 15(1): 43–58.

Kizlik, R. (2015) *Characteristics of a Profession*, Florida: AdPrima, available at: www.adprima.com/profession.htm (accessed 19 October 2015).

Klaasen, R.M. (2010) 'Teacher stress: the mediating role of collective efficacy beliefs', *The Journal of Educational Research*, 103: 342–50.

Klaasen, R.M. and Chui, M.M. (2010) 'Effects on teachers' self efficacy and job satisfaction: teacher gender, years of experience and job stress', *Journal of Educational Psychology*, 102(3): 741–56.

Kluger, A. and DeNisi, A. (1996) 'The historical effects of feedback interventions on performance: a historical review', *Psychological Bulletin*, 119(2): 254–84.

Knapp, M. and Hall, J. (2010) *Non-Verbal Communication in Human Interaction*, 7th edn, Boston, MA: Wadsworth/Cengage Learning.

Knowles, C. (2016) *Achievement for All 3As MESHGuide*, London: Achievement for All.

Kohlberg, L. (1976) 'Moral stages and moralization: the cognitive-developmental approach', in T. Lickona (ed.) *Moral Development and Behaviour: Theory, Research, and Social Issues*, New York: Holt, Rinehart & Winston.

Kohlberg, L. (1985) 'The just community: approach to moral education in theory and practice', in M. Berkowitz and F. Oser (eds) *Moral Education: Theory and Application*, Hillsdale, NJ: Lawrence Erlbaum Associates, pp. 27–87.

Kolb, D.A. (1976) *The Learning Style Inventory: Technical Manual*, Boston, MA: McBer.

Kolb, D. (1984a) *Experience as the Source of Learning and Development*, London: Financial Times/Prentice Hall.

Kolb, D. (1984b) *Experiential Learning*, New York: Prentice Hall.

Kolb, D.A. (1985) *The Learning Style Inventory: Technical Manual*, revised edn, Boston, MA: McBer.

Koshy, V. (2005) *Action Research for Improving Practice: A Practical Guide*, London: Paul Chapman.

Kozulin, A. (1998) *Psychological Tools: A Sociocultural Approach to Education*, Cambridge, MA: Harvard University Press.

Krathwohl, D.R., Bloom, B.S. and Masia, B.B. (1973) *Taxonomy of Educational Objectives: The Classification of Educational Goals*, Handbook II: Affective Domain. New York: David McKay.

Kratzig, G.P. and Arbuthnott, K.D. (2006) 'Perceptual learning style and learning proficiency: a test of the hypothesis', *Journal of Educational Psychology*, 98(1): 238–46.

Kutnick, P., Blatchford, P. and Baines, E. (2002) 'Pupil groupings in primary school classrooms: sites for learning and social pedagogy?', *British Educational Research Journal*, 28(2): 187–206.

Kutnick, P., Sebba, J., Blatchford, P., Galton, M. and Thorp, J. (2005) *The Effect of Pupil Grouping: A Literature Review*, London: DfES Research Report RR 688.

Kutnick, P., Hodgkinson, S., Sebba, J., Humphreys, S., Galton, M., Steward, S., Blatchford, P. and Baines, E. (2006) *Pupil Grouping Strategies at Key Stage 2 and 3: Case Studies of 24 Schools in England*, DFES Research Report RR796, London: DfES.

Kyriacou, C. (2000) *Stress-Busting for Teachers*, Cheltenham: Stanley Thornes.

Kyriacou, C. (2001) 'Teacher stress: directions for future research', *Educational Review*, 53(1): 27–35.

Kyriacou, C. (2007) *Essential Teaching Skills*, 3rd edn, Cheltenham: Stanley Thornes.

Kyriacou, C. (2009) *Effective Teaching in Schools*, 3rd edn, Cheltenham: Stanley Thornes.

Kyriacou, C. (2014) *Essential Teaching Skills*, 4th edn, Cheltenham: Nelson Thornes.

Kyriacou, C. and Coulthard, M. (2000) 'Undergraduates' views of teaching as a career choice', *Journal of Education for Teaching: International Research and Pedagogy*, 26: 117–26.

Kyriacou, C. and Kunc, R. (2007) 'Beginning teachers' expectations of teaching', *Teaching and Teacher Education*, 23: 1246–57.

Kyriacou, C., Kunc, R., Stephens, P. and Hultgren, A. (2003) 'Student teachers' expectations of teaching as a career in England and Norway', *Educational Review*, 55(3): 255–63.

Lam, S.F., Yim, P.S., Law, J.S.F. and Cheung, R.W.Y. (2004) 'The effects of competition on achievement motivation in Chinese classrooms', *British Journal of Educational Psychology*, 74: 281–96.

Lamb, B. (2009) *The Lamb Inquiry: Special Educational Needs and Parental Confidence*, London: DCSF.

Lambert, D. and Balderstone, D. (2009) *Learning to Teach Geography in the Secondary School: A Companion to School Experience*, 2nd edn, London: RoutledgeFalmer.

Langford, P. (1995) *Approaches to the Development of Moral Reasoning*, Hove: Erlbaum.

Lapinoja, K. and Heikkinen, H. (2006) 'Autonomy and teacher professionalism', in A. Teokessa and J. Onnismaa (eds) *Professionalism and Professional Growth*, Adult Education 46, Yearbook, New York: Public Awareness Society and the Adult Education Research Society.

Lave, J. and Wenger, E. (1991) *Situated Learning: Legitimate Peripheral Participation*, Cambridge: Cambridge University Press.

Lawton, D. (1989) *Education, Culture and the National Curriculum*, Sevenoaks: Hodder & Stoughton.

Lawton, D. (1996) *Beyond the National Curriculum: Teacher Professionalism and Empowerment*, Sevenoaks: Hodder & Stoughton.

Leach, J. and Moon, B. (1999) *Learners and Pedagogy*, London: Paul Chapman.

Leask, M. (1988) *Teachers as evaluators: a grounded approach to project evaluation*, MPhil Thesis, Cambridge: Cambridge Institute of Education (now available in the Homerton College library, University of Cambridge).

Leask, M. (2004) *Using research and evidence to improve teaching and learning in the training of professionals - an example from teacher training in England*. Paper presented at the British Educational Research Association Annual Conference, University of Manchester, UK. 16–18 September 2004, available at: http://www.leeds.ac.uk/educol/documents/00003666.htm

Leask, M. (2011) 'Improving the Professional Knowledge base for Education: Using knowledge management and Web 2.0 tools', *Policy Futures in Education*, 9(5): 644–660

Leask, M. and Moorehouse, C. (2005) 'The student teacher's role and responsibilities', in S. Capel, M. Leask and T. Turner (eds) *Learning to Teach in the Secondary School*, 4th edn, London: Routledge, pp. 18–31.

Leask, M. and Pachler, N. (eds) (2013) *Teaching and Learning Using ICT in the Secondary School*, 3rd edn, London: Routledge.

Leask, M. and Pachler, N. (eds) (2014) *Learning to Teach Using ICT in the Classroom: A Companion to School Experience*, 4th edn, London: Routledge.

Leask, M. and Younie, S. (2014) 'National models for CPD: the challenges of 21st C knowledge management', *Professional Development in Education*, 39(2): 273–287.

Leat, D. (1998) *Thinking Through Geography*, Cambridge: Chris Kington.

Lee, C. (2013) *Mathematics: Assessment for Learning: The Four Operations MESHGuide*, Open University, UK, available at: www.meshguides.org/assessment-for-learning-the-four-operations/ (accessed 24 July 2015).

Leung, S.S.K., Chiang, V.C.L., Chui, Y-Y., Lee, A.C.K. and Mak, Y-W. (2011) 'Feasibility and potentials of online support for stress management among secondary school teachers', *Stress and Health*, 27: e282–6.

Levinson, R. (2005a) 'Planning for progression in science', in J. Frost and T. Turner (eds) *Learning to Teach Science in the Secondary School: A Companion to School Experience*, 2nd edn, London: RoutledgeFalmer.

Levinson, R. (2005b) 'Science for citizenship', in J. Frost and T. Turner (eds) *Learning to Teach Science in the Secondary School: A Companion to School Experience*, 2nd edn, London: RoutledgeFalmer.

Levitt, R., Janta, B. and Wegrich, K. (2008) *Accountability of Teachers: Literature Review* (Prepared for the GTCE), London: General Teaching Council for England.

Liang, L. and Gabel, D. (2005) 'Effectiveness of a constructivist approach to science instruction for prospective elementary teachers', *International Journal of Science Education*, 27(10): 1143–62.

Lickona, T. (1983) *Raising Good Children*, New York: Bantam Books.

Lindsay, G., Cullen, M.A., Cullen, S., Dockrell, J., Strand, S., Arweck, E., Hegarty, S. and Goodlad, S. (2011) *Evaluation of Impact of DfE Investment in Initiatives Designed to Improve Teacher Workforce Skills in Relation to SEN and Disabilities*, London: DfE RR115.

Liu, S. and Meng, L., (2009) 'Perceptions of teachers, students and parents of the characteristics of good teachers: a cross-cultural comparison of China and the United States', *Educational Assessment, Evaluation and Accountability*, 21(4): 313–28.

Long, M., Wood, C., Littleton, K., Passenger, T. and Sheehy, K. (2010) *Psychology of Education*, London: Routledge.

Long, M., Wood, C., Littleton, K., Passenger, T. and Sheehy, K. (2011) *The Psychology of Education*, 2nd edn, London: Routledge.

Lortie, D. (1975) *Schoolteacher*, Chicago, IL: University of Chicago Press.

Lu, M-L. (1998) *English-Only Movement: Its Consequences for the Education of Language Minority Children*, Bloomington, IN: University of Indiana, an ERIC Clearinghouse Digest No 139 (EDO-CS-98-12 Nov 1998), available at: www.ericdigests.org/1999-4/english.htm (accessed 15 November 2015).

Lucey, H. and Reay, R. (2000) 'Identities in transition: anxiety and excitement in the move to secondary school', *Oxford Review of Education*, 26: 191–205.

Lunzer, E.A. and Gardner, K. (1979) *The Effective Use of Reading*, London: Heinemann.

Luthar, S.S. (2006) 'Resilience in development: a synthesis of research across five decades', in D. Cicchetti and D.J. Cohen (eds) *Developmental Psychopathology: Risk, Disorder and Adaptation*, New York: Wiley, pp. 739–50.

Lymperopoulou, K. and Parameshwaran, M. (2014) *How Are Ethnic Inequalities in Education Changing? Dynamics of Diversity: Evidence from the 2011 Census*, Manchester: Centre on Dynamics of Ethnicity.

Machino, T. and Yoshizawa, T. (2006) 'Brain shrinkage due to acute hypernatremia', *Neurology*, 67(5): 878–80.

MacInnes, T., Aldridge, H., Bushe, S., Tinson, A. and Born, T. (2014) *Monitoring Poverty and Social Exclusion 2014*, York: Joseph Rowntree Foundation.

Mager, R. (2005) *Preparing Instructional Objectives*, 3rd edn, Atlanta, GA: Center for Effective Performance.

Maker, C.J. and Nielson, A.B. (1995) *Teaching/Learning Models in Education of the Gifted*, 2nd edn, Austin, TX: Pro-Ed.

Malina, R.M., Bouchard, C. and Bar-or, O. (2004) *Growth, Maturation and Physical Activity*, Champaign, IL: Human Kinetics.

Malloy, W.W. and Allen, T. (2007) 'Teacher retention in a teacher resiliency-building rural school', *Rural Educator*, 28(2): 19–27.

Manouchehri, A. (2004) 'Implementing mathematics reform in urban schools: a study of the effect of teachers' motivational style', *Urban Education*, 39(5): 472–508.

Marples, R. (2012) *The Aims of Education*, London: Routledge.

Marsden, E. (2009) 'Observing in the classroom', in S. Younie, S. Capel and M. Leask (eds) *Supporting Teaching and Learning in Schools: A Handbook for Higher Level Teaching Assistants*, London: Routledge, pp. 133–46.

Martin, J. (1985) *Factual Writing*, Geelong, Victoria: Deakin University Press.

Martin, J.R. (1976) 'What should we do with a hidden curriculum when we find one?', *Curriculum Inquiry*, 6: 131-51.

Maslow, A.H. (1970) *Motivation and Personality*, 2nd edn, New York: Harper & Row.

Mawer, M. (1995) *The Effective Teaching of Physical Education*, London: Longman.

Mayer, J.D. and Salovey, P. (1997) 'What is emotional intelligence?', in P. Salovey and D. Sluyter (eds) *Emotional Development and Emotional Intelligence: Implications for Educators*, New York: Basic Books, pp. 3-31.

Mayer, J.D., Salovey, P. and Caruso, D.R. (2004) 'Emotional intelligence: theory, findings and implications', *Psychological Inquiry*, 15(3): 197-215.

McClelland, D.C. (1961) *The Achieving Society*, Princeton, NJ: Van Norstrand.

McCormack, A. and Gore, J. (2008) '"If only I could just teach": early career teachers, their colleagues and the operation of power', paper presented at the annual conference of the Australian Association for Research in Education, Brisbane, November-December.

McDonagh, C., Roche, M., Sullivan, B. and Glenn, M. (2012) *Enhancing Practice through Classroom Research: A Teacher's Guide to Professional Development*, London: Routledge.

McGregor, D. (1960) *The Human Side of Enterprise*, New York: McGraw-Hill.

McGregor, D. and Cartwright, L. (2011) *Developing Reflective Practice: a Guide for Beginner Teachers*, Berkshire: Open University Press.

McIntyre, D., Pedder, D. and Rudduck, J. (2005) 'Pupil voice: comfortable and uncomfortable learnings for teachers', *Research Papers in Education*, 20(2): 149-68.

McLaughlin, T. (2004) 'Philosophy, values and schooling: principles and predicaments of teacher example', in W. Aiken and J. Haldanne (eds) *Philosophy and Its Public Role: Essays in Ethics, Politics, Society and Culture*, Exeter and Charlottesville, VA: Imprint Academic.

McNiff, J. and Whitehead, J. (2002) *Action Research: Principles and Practice*, London: Routledge.

McNiff, J. and Whitehead, J. (2009) *You and Your Action Research Project*, 3rd edn, London: Routledge.

Mead, G.H. (1934) *Mind, Self and Society*, Chicago, IL: University of Chicago Press.

Mehrabian, A. (1972) *Non-Verbal Communication*, New York: Aldine Atherton.

Menter, I., Hulme, M., Elliot, D. and Lewin, J. (2010) *Literature Review on Teacher Education in the 21st Century*, Edinburgh: Scottish Government, Schools Research, Education Analytical Services.

Menter, I., Elliot, D., Hulme, M., Lewin, J. and Lowden, K. (2011) *A Guide to Practitioner Research in Education*, London: Sage.

Mercer, N. (1995) *The Guided Construction of Knowledge*, Clevedon: Multilingual Matters.

Mercer, N. (2000) *Words and Minds: How We Use Language to Think Together*, London: Routledge.

Mercer, N. (2015) *Thinking Together Project Materials*, University of Cambridge Faculty of Education, available at: http://thinkingtogether.educ.cam.ac.uk/ (accessed 15 July 2015).

Mercer, N. (2015) *The Educational Value of Dialogic Talk in Whole-Class Dialogue*, available on http://oer.educ.cam.ac.uk/wiki/The-educational-value-of-dialogic-talk-in-whole-class-dialogue (accessed 4 January 2016).

Mercer, N. and Littleton, K. (2007) *Dialogue and the Development of Children's Thinking: A Socio-Cultural Approach*, London: Routledge.

Mersh, R. and Fairclough, S. (2010) 'Physical activity, lesson context and teacher behaviours within the revised English National Curriculum for Physical Education: a case study of one school'. *European Physical Education Review*, 16(1): 29-45.

Mezirow, J. (1997) 'Transformative learning: theory to practice', *New Directions for Adult and Continuing Education*, 74: 5-12.

Miles, M. and Huberman, M. (1994) *Qualitative Data Analysis: A Sourcebook of New Methods*, Thousand Oaks, CA: Sage.

Millar, R., Leach, J., Osborne, J. and Ratcliffe, M. (2006) *Improving Subject Teaching*, London: RoutledgeFalmer.

Miller, D. and Lavin, F. (2007) '"But now I feel I want to give it a try": formative assessment, self-esteem and a sense of competence', *The Curriculum Journal*, 18(1): 3-25.

Miller, D.J. and Moran, T.R. (2012) *Self Esteem: A Guide for Teachers*, London: Sage.

Miller, N. and Boud, D. (1996) 'Animating learning from experience', in D. Boud and N. Miller (eds) *Working with Experience*, London: Routledge.

Mills, S. (1995) *Stress Management for the Individual Teacher*, Lancaster: Framework Press.

Mongon, D. and Chapman, C. (2012) *High-Leverage Leadership: Improving Outcomes in Educational Settings*, London: Routledge.

Monk, J. and Silman, C. (2011) *Active Learning in Primary Classrooms: A Case Study Approach*, Harlow: Longman.

Moon, J. (2005) *Reflection in Learning and Professional Development*, London: RoutledgeFalmer.

Moon, J. (2008) *Critical Thinking: An Exploration of Theory and Practice*, London: Routledge.

Moore, A. (2004) *The Good Teacher: Dominant Discourses in Teaching and Teacher Education*, London: RoutledgeFalmer.

Moore, A. (2012) *Teaching and Learning: Pedagogy, Curriculum and Culture*, London: Routledge.

Morgan, N. and Saxton, J. (1991) *Teaching Questioning and Learning*, London: Routledge.

Morris, C. (2004) 'Towards an evidence-based approach to quality enhancement: a modest proposal', discussion paper for the Higher Education Academy.

Mosston, M. and Ashworth, S. (1990). *The Spectrum of Teaching Styles*. From command to discovery. White Plains, NY: Longman.

Mosston, M. and Ashworth, S. (2002) *Teaching Physical Education*, 5th edn, New York: Macmillan College.

Mourshed, M., Chijioke, C. and Barber, M. (2010) *How the World's Most Improved School Systems Keep Getting Better*, London: McKinsey & Company.

Mruk, C. (1999) *Self-Esteem: Research, Theory and Practice*, London: Free Association Books.

Muijs, D. and Reynolds, D. (2005) *Effective Teaching: Evidence and Practice*, 2nd edn, London: Paul Chapman.

Muijs, D. and Reynolds, D. (2011) *Effective Teaching: Evidence and Practice*, 3rd edn, London: Sage.

Murdock, T.B. (1999) 'The social context of risk: social and motivational predictors of alienation in middle school', *Journal of Educational Psychology*, 91: 1-14.

Murphy, P. (ed.) (1999) *Learners, Learning and Assessment*, Buckingham: Open University Press.

Murray-Harvey, R., Slee, P.T., Lawson, M.J., Silins, H., Banfield, G. and Russell, A. (2000) 'Under stress: the concerns and coping strategies of teacher education students', *European Journal of Teacher Education*, 23: 19-35.

Myhill, D. (2002) 'Bad boys and good girls? Patterns of interaction and response in whole class teaching', *British Educational Research Journal*, 28(3): 339-52.

Myhill, D.A. (2006) 'Talk, talk, talk: teaching and learning in whole class discourse', *Research Papers in Education*, 21(1): 19-41.

Myhill, D.A. (2009) 'Becoming a designer: trajectories of linguistic development', in R. Beard, D. Myhill, J. Riley and M. Nystrand (eds) *The Sage Handbook of Writing Development*, London: Sage, pp. 402-14.

Myhill, D.A. (2010) 'Ways of knowing: grammar as a tool for developing writing', in T. Locke (ed.) *Beyond the Grammar Wars: A Resource for Teachers and Students on Developing Language Knowledge in the English/Literacy Classroom*, London: Routledge, pp. 129-48.

Myhill, D. and Jones, S. (2006) '"She doesn't shout at no girls": pupils' perceptions of gender equity in the classroom', *Cambridge Journal of Education*, 36(1): 99-113.

Myhill, D.A. and Warren, P. (2005) 'Scaffolds or straitjackets? Critical moments in classroom discourse', *Educational Review*, 57(1): 55-69.

Namrouti, A. and Alshannag, Q. (2004) 'Effect of using a metacognitive teaching strategy on seventh grade students' achievement in science', *Dirasat*, 31(1): 1-13.

National Association of Head Teachers (NAHT) (2014) *Report of the NAHT on Assessment – February 2014*, available at: www.thekeysupport.com/media/cms_page_media/23/The%20Key%20Survey%20results%20%20-%20Curriculum%20-%20Nov%202013.pdf (accessed 2 March 2015).

National STEM Centre (2015) *Concept Cartoons*, available at: www.nationalstemcentre.org.uk/elibrary/resource/1482/concept-cartoons (accessed 19 July 2015).

Naylor, S. and Keogh, B. (1999) 'Constructivism in the classroom: theory into practice', *Journal of Science Teacher Education*, 10(2): 93-106.

Nazroo, J. and Kapadia, D. (2013) 'Ethnic inequalities in labour market participation', *Dynamics of Diversity: Evidence from the 2011 Census*, Manchester: Centre on Dynamics of Ethnicity.

Newman, T. and Blackburn, S. (2002) *Transitions in the Lives of Children and Young People: Resilience Factors*, Edinburgh: Scottish Executive Education Department.

Newton, A. and Bowler, M. (2016) *Assessment in Physical Education MESHGuide*, University of Bedfordshire, UK.

NHS (National Health Service) (2009) *Health Survey for England 2008: Physical Activity and Fitness*, Information Centre for Health and Social Care, available at: www.ic.nhs.uk/webfiles/publications/HSE/HSE08_Summary_of_key_findings (accessed 20 March 2012).

NHS (National Health Service) (2010) *Health Survey for England 2009*, Information Centre for Health and Social Care, available at: www.ic.nhs.uk/webfiles/publications/003_health_lifestyles/hse09report (accessed 20 March 2012).

NHS (National Health Service) (2012) *Statistics on Obesity, Physical Activity and Diet 2012*, Information Centre for Health and Social Care, Lifestyles Statistics, available at: www.ic.nhs.uk/webfiles/publications/003_healthy_lifestyles> (accessed 20 March 2012).

Nicholls, J.G. (1984) 'Achievement motivation: conceptions of ability, subjective experience, task choice and performance', *Psychological Review*, 91: 328–46.

Nicholls, J.G. (1989) *The Competitive Ethos and Democratic Education*, Cambridge, MA: Harvard University Press.

Nicholson, N. (1987) 'The transition cycle: a conceptual framework for the analysis of change and human resources management', *Research in Personnel and Human Resources Management*, 5: 167–222.

Noble, T. (2004) 'Integrating the revised Bloom's taxonomy with multiple intelligences: a planning tool for curriculum differentiation', *Teachers College Record*, 106(1): 193–211.

Noble, T. (n.d.) *Integrating the Revised Bloom's Taxonomy with Multiple Intelligences: A Planning Tool for Curriculum Differentiation*, National Australian Catholic University, available at: www.bounceback.com.au/sites/default/files/Integrating%20the%20Revised%20Bloom%E2%80%99s%20Taxonomy%20With%20Multiple%20Intelligences_0.pdf (accessed 19 July 2015).

NOO (National Obesity Observatory) (2011) *Childhood Obesity*, available at: www.noo.org.uk/NOO_about_obesity/ (accessed 31 March 2012).

Norman, K. (ed.) (1992) *Thinking Voices: The Work of the National Oracy Project*, London: Hodder & Stoughton.

Norwich, B. (1993) 'Ideological dilemmas in special needs education: practitioners' views', *Oxford Review of Education*, 19(4): 527–45.

Noyes, A. (2003) 'Moving schools and social relocation', *International Studies in Sociology of Education*, 13(3): 261–80.

NSPCC (National Society for the Prevention of Cruelty to Children) (2015) *Safer Recruitment in Education Course: Online Safeguarding Training to Help You Recruit Staff or Volunteers in Schools, Academies or Colleges*, available at: www.nspcc.org.uk/what-you-can-do/get-expert-training/safer-recruitment-education-course/ (accessed 16 November 2015).

Nucci, L. (1987) 'Synthesis of research on moral development', *Educational Leadership*, February, available at: http://tigger.uic.edu/~lnucci/MoralEd/articles/nuccisynthesis.html (accessed 28 November 2011).

Nucci, L. (2007) *Moral Development and Moral Education: An Overview/Kohlberg's Theory*, available at: http://tigger.uic.edu/~lnucci/MoralEd/overview.html kohlberg (accessed 29 November 2011).

NUT (National Union of Teachers) (2013) *NUT Notes 2013–2014: Education, the Law and You*, available at: www.teachers.org.uk (accessed 16 November 2015).

OECD (Organisation for Economic Co-operation and Development) (2003) *Key Competencies for a Successful and Well Functioning Society*, Paris: OECD.

OECD (Organisation for Economic Co-operation and Development) (2011) *Divided We Stand: Why Inequality Keeps Rising*, Paris: OECD, available at: http://dx.doi.org/10.1787/9789264119536-en (accessed 28 February 2012).

OECD (Organisation for Economic Co-operation and Development) (2014) *Education at a Glance 2014, OECD Indicators*, Paris: OECD.

OECD TALIS (2015) *The Teaching and Learning International Survey*, Paris: OECD, available at: www.oecd.org/edu/school/talis.htm (accessed 15 July 2015).

Ofqual (Office for Qualifications and Examination Regulation) (2007) *Changes to A Levels*, available at: www.ofqual.gov.uk/files/Changes_to_A_Levels_Factsheet_-_October_2007.pdf (accessed 10 June 2012).

Ofsted (Office for Standards in Education) (1993) *The New Teacher in School: A Survey by Her Majesty's Inspectorate in England and Wales, 1992*, London: HMSO.

Ofsted (Office for Standards in Education) (1996) *The Annual Report of Her Majesty's Chief Inspector of Schools*, London: HMSO.

Ofsted (Office for Standards in Education) (2002) *Good Teaching: Effective Departments*, London: Ofsted.

Ofsted (Office for Standards in Education) (2004) *Promoting and Evaluating Pupils' Spiritual, Moral, Social and Cultural Development*, available at: www.ofsted.gov.uk/resources/promoting-and-evaluating-pupils-spiritual-moral-social-and-cultural-development (accessed 31 December 2011).

Ofsted (Office for Standards in Education) (2006a) *Evaluating Mathematics Provision for 14–19 Year Olds*, London: Ofsted.

Ofsted (Office for Standards in Education) (2006b) *Inclusion: Does It Matter Where Pupils Are Taught? An Ofsted Report on the Provision and Outcomes in Different Settings for Pupils with Learning Difficulties and Disabilities*, London: Ofsted

Ofsted (Office for Standards in Education) (2007) *The Annual Report of Her Majesty's Chief Inspector of Education, Children's Services and Skills 2006/07*, London: The Stationery Office, Available at: www.ofsted.gov.uk/ (accessed 30 May 2012).

Ofsted (Office for Standards in Education) (2008) *Assessment for Learning: The Impact of National Strategy Support*, available at: http://dera.ioe.ac.uk/9309/1/Assessment%20for%20learning%20-%20the%20impact%20of%20National%20Strategy%20support.pdf (accessed 21 July 2015).

Ofsted (Office for Standards in Education) (2010a) *Food in Schools: Progress in Implementing the New Food Standards*, Ref/No 090230, available at: www.ofsted.gov.uk (accessed 20 March 2012).

Ofsted (Office for Standards in Education) (2010b) *The Special Educational Needs and Disability Review: A Statement Is Not Enough*, London: Ofsted.

Ofsted (Office for Standards in Education) (2010c) *The Special Educational Needs and Disabilities Review*, available at: www.ofsted.gov.uk/resources/special-educational-needs-and-disability-review (accessed 20 March 2012).

Ofsted (Office for Standards in Education) (2010d) *Learning: Creative Approaches to Raise Standards*, Manchester: Ofsted.

Ofsted (Office for Standards in Education) (2010e) *Finnish Pupils' Success in Mathematics*, London: Ofsted.

Ofsted (Office for Standards in Education) (2011a) *ICT in Schools 2008–11*, Reference no: 110134, Manchester: Ofsted.

Ofsted (Office for Standards in Education) (2011b) *The Annual Report of Her Majesty's Chief Inspector of Education, Children's Services and Skills 2010/11*, available at: www.gov.uk/government/uploads/system/uploads/attachment_data/file/379294/Ofsted_20Annual_20Report_2010-11_20-_20full.pdf (accessed 18 March 2015).

Ofsted (Office for Standards in Education) (2012a) *Questioning to Promote Learning*, available at: www.fromgoodtooutstanding.com/2012/05/ofsted-2012-questioning-to-promote-learning (accessed 20 March 2015).

Ofsted (Office for Standards in Education) (2012b) *The Shape of School Inspection from 2012*, London: Ofsted, available at: www.ofsted.gov.uk/news/shape-of-school-inspection-2012-0 (accessed 3 January 2016).

Ofsted (Office for Standards in Education) (2013) *Unseen Children: Access and Achievement 20 Years On*, London: Ofsted.

Ofsted (Office for Standards in Education) (2014a) *Inspecting Safeguarding in Maintained Schools and Academies: Briefing for Section 5 Inspections*, Children's Services and Skills Ref: 140143, London: Ofsted, available at: www.ofsted.gov.uk/resources/inspecting-safeguarding-maintained-schools-and-academies-briefing-for-section-5-inspections (accessed 18 November 2014).

Ofsted (Office for Standards in Education) (2014b) *Note for Inspectors: Use of Assessment Information during Inspections in 2014/15*, available at: www.gov.uk/government/uploads/system/uploads/attachment_data/file/379630/Note_20for_20inspectors_20-_20use_20of_20assessment_20information_20during_20inspections_20in_202014-15.doc (accessed 21 July 2015).

Ofsted (Office for Standards in Education) (2014c) *The Framework for School Inspection*, available at: www.gov.uk/government/publications/the-framework-for-school-inspection (accessed 8 April 2015).

Ofsted (Office for Standards in Education) (2014d) *Inspection Framework*, available at: www.ofsted.gov.uk/resources/framework-for-school-inspection (accessed 18 July 2015).

Ofsted (Office for Standards in Education) (2015) *School Inspection Handbook*, available at: www.gov.uk.government/publicationsschool-inspection-handbook-from-september-2015 (accessed 10 November 2015)

O'Leary, M. (2014) *Classroom Observation: A Guide to the Effective Observation of Teaching and Learning*, London: Routledge.

Olweus, D. (1993) *Bullying at School*, Oxford: Blackwell.

ONS (Office for National Statistics) (2011) *Divorces in England and Wales 2010*, available at: www.ons.gov.uk/ons/dcp171776_290558.pdf (accessed 22 January 2016).

ONS (Office for National Statistics) (2012a) *2011 Census: Key Statistics for England and Wales*, March 2011, available at: http://www.ons.gov.uk/ons/dcp171778_290685.pdf (accessed 21 January 16).

ONS (Office for National Statistics) (2012b) *Integrated Household Survey* April 2011 to March 2012, available at http://www.ons.gov.uk/ons/rel/integrated-household-survey/integrated-household-survey/april-2011-to-march-2012/stb-integrated-household-survey-april-2011-to-march-2012.html (accessed 21 January 2016).

ONS (Office for National Statistics) (2014) *Divorces in England and Wales 2012*, available at: www.ons.gov.uk/ons/dcp171778_367167.pdf (accessed 22 January 2016)

Oversby, J. (2012) 'Science education research: a critical appraisal of its contribution to education', in J. Oversby (ed.) *ASE Guide to Research in Science Education*, Herts: ASE.

Owen-Jackson, G. (ed.) (2008) *Learning to Teach Design and Technology in the Secondary School: A Companion to School Experience*, 2nd edn, London: Routledge.

Oxfam (2012) *The Perfect Storm: Economic Stagnation, the Rising Cost of Living, Public Spending Cuts and the Impact on UK Poverty*, Oxford: Oxfam GB.

Paechter, C. (2000) *Changing School Subjects: Power, Gender and Curriculum*, Buckingham: Open University Press.

Palmer, S. (2011) *Speaking Frames: How to Teach Talk for Writing*, London: Routledge.

Parliamentary Select Committee for Education (20112) *Education Committee – Ninth Report Great Teachers: Attracting, Training and Retaining the Best*, available at: www.publications.parliament.uk/pa/cm201213/cmselect/cmeduc/524/524.pdf (accessed 13 November 2015)

Patterson, E. (2016a) *Research Methods 1: How to Get Started on a Literature Review MESHGuide*, University of Winchester.

Patterson, E. (2016b) *Research Methods 2: Developing Your Research Design*, MESHGuide, University of Winchester.

Patterson, E. (2016c) *Research Methods 3: Considering Ethics in Your Research*, MESHGuide, University of Winchester.

Pearce, S. (2005) *You Wouldn't Understand: White Teachers in the Multiethnic Classroom*, Stoke-on-Trent: Trentham.

Pease, A. and Pease, B. (2011) *Body Language in the Workplace*, London: Orion.

Perera, K. (1987) *Understanding Language*, Sheffield: NAAE.

Perrenoud, P. (1991) 'Towards a pragmatic approach to formative evaluation', in P. Weston (ed.) *Assessment of Pupils' Achievement, Motivation and School Success*, Amsterdam: Swets & Zeitlinger, pp. 79–101.

Peters, S. (2010) *Literature Review: Transition from Early Childhood Education to School*, Report commissioned by the Ministry of Education, Wellington: Ministry of Education.

Petrides, K.V. (2009) *Technical Manual for the Trait Emotional Intelligence Questionnaires (TEIQue)*, London: London Psychometric Laboratory.

Petrides, K.V., Vernon, P.A., Aitken Schermer, J. and Veselka, L. (2011) 'Trait emotional intelligence and the dark triad traits of personality', *Twin Research and Human Genetics*, 14(1): 35–41.

Phan, H.P. and Deo, B. (2007) 'The revised learning processing questionnaire: a validation of a Western model of students' study approaches to the South Pacific context using confirmatory factor analysis', *British Journal of Educational Psychology*, 77: 719–39.

Phillips, D.K. and Carr, K. (2010) *Becoming a Teacher through Action Research: Process, Context and Self-Study*, 2nd edn, New York and London: Routledge.

Philpott, J. (2011) 'Assessment', in I. Davies (ed.) *Debates in History Teaching*, London: Routledge, pp. 261–72.

Piaget, J. (1932) *The Moral Judgement of the Child*, New York: Harcourt, Brace Jovanovich.

Piaget, J. (1954) *The Construction of Reality in the Child*, New York: Basic Books.

Pickering, J., Daly, C. and Pachler, N. (2007) *New Designs for Teachers' Professional Learning*, London: Institute of Education.

Pietarinen, J., Pyhältö, K. and Soini, T. (2010a) 'A horizontal approach to school transitions: a lesson learned from Finnish 15-year-olds', *Cambridge Journal of Education*, 40(3): 229–45.

Pietarinen, J., Soini, T. and Pyhältö, K. (2010b) 'Learning and well-being in transitions: how to promote pupils' active learning agency?', in D. Jindal-Snape (ed.) *Educational Transitions: Moving Stories from Around the World*, New York: Routledge, pp. 143–58.

Pintrich, P.R. (2004) 'A conceptual framework for assessing motivation and self-regulated learning in college students', *Educational Psychology Review*, 16(4): 385–407.

Plowden, B. (1967) *Children and Their Primary Schools*, London: HMSO.

Postlethwaite, K. (1993) *Differentiated Science Teaching: Responding to Individual Differences and Special Educational Needs*, Milton Keynes: Open University Press.

Poulson, L. and Wallace, M. (eds) (2004) *Learning to Read Critically in Learning and Teaching*, London: Sage.

Powell, E. (2005) 'Conceptualising and facilitating active learning: teachers' video-stimulated reflective dialogues', *Reflective Practice*, 6(3): 407–18.

Power, S., Edwards, T., Whitty, G. and Wigfall, V. (2003) *Education and Middle Class*, Buckingham: Open University Press.

Powley, R. (2015) *Meaningful, Manageable Assessment: 26 Strategies*, available at: www/lovelearning ideas.com (accessed 2 March 2015).

Pressley, M. (2000) 'What should comprehension instruction be the instruction of?', in M.L. Kamil, P.B. Mosenthal, P.D. Pearson and R. Barr (eds) *Handbook of Reading Research, Volume 3*, Mahwah, NJ: Erlbaum, pp. 545–61.

Pring, R. (2004) *A Comprehensive Curriculum for Comprehensive Schools: The Fourth Caroline Benn Memorial Lecture*, London: Socialist Educational Association.

Pring, R. (2012) *The Life and Death of Secondary Education for All*, London: Continuum.

Procter, R. (2013) *Assessment for Learning MESHGuide*, University of Bedfordshire, UK.

Prosser, M. and Trigwell, K. (1999) *Understanding Teaching and Learning: The Experience in Higher Education, The Society for Research into Higher Education*, Buckingham: Open University Press.

QCA (Qualifications and Curriculum Authority) (2001a) *Planning, Teaching and Assessing Pupils with Learning Difficulties*, Sudbury: QCA, available at: http://webarchive.nationalarchives.gov.uk/20110223175304/http://www.qcda.gov.uk/curriculum/sen/3605.aspx (accessed 3 April 2012).

QCA (Qualifications and Curriculum Authority) (2001b) *Supporting School Improvement: Emotional and Behavioural Development*, London: QCA.

QCA (Qualifications and Curriculum Authority) (2005) *The National Curriculum Handbook for Secondary Teachers in England*, London: QCA.

QCA (Qualifications and Curriculum Authority) (2007a) *Framework for Personal Learning and Thinking Skills*, London: QCA.

QCA (Qualifications and Curriculum Authority) (2007b) *Geography Programme of Study and Attainment Target*, London: QCA, available at: http://media.education.gov.uk/assets/files/pdf/g/geography%202007%20programme%20of%20study%20for%20key%20stage%203.pdf (accessed 5 April 2012).

QCA (Qualifications and Curriculum Authority) (2008a) *International Review of Curriculum and Assessment Frameworks Internet Archive; Table 9 National Assessment and Public Examinations*, available at: www.inca.org.uk/pdf/table_9.pdf (accessed 2 June 2012).

QCA (Qualifications and Curriculum Authority) (2008b) *National Curriculum for England: General Teaching Requirements: Inclusion*, available at: www.education.gov.uk/schools/teachingandlearning/curriculum/b00199686/inclusion (accessed 6 April 2012).

QCA (Qualifications and Curriculum Authority) (2008c) *National Curriculum Key Stages 3 and 4*, available at: www.education.gov.uk/schools/teachingandlearning/curriculum/secondary (accessed 6 April 2012).

Quality Counts (2000) 'Who should teach?', *Education Week*, 19 (31 January).

Quartz, K.H. (2003) '"Too angry to leave": supporting new teachers' commitment to transform urban schools', *Journal of Teacher Education*, 54(2): 99–111.

Queensland Government (2015) *Attributes of a Good Teacher*, available at: http://education.qld.gov.au/hr/recruitment/teaching/qualities-good-teacher.html (accessed 18 July 2015).

Raiker, A. (2011) *Finnish University Training Schools: Principles and Pedagogy*, available at: www.beds.ac.uk/__data/assets/pdf_file/0003/83433/finnishmodel-110713-finland-v2.pdf (accessed 13 November 2015).

Ravitch, D. (2013) *Reign of Error: The Hoax of the Privatization Movement and the Danger to Americas Public Schools*, New York: Alfred A. Knopf.

Reardon, S. (2011) 'The widening academic achievement gap between the rich and the poor: new evidence and possible explanations', in G. Duncan and R. Murnane (eds) *Whither Opportunity? Rising Inequality, Schools and Children's Life Chances*, New York: Russell Sage Foundation.

Redpath, R. and Harker, M. (1999) 'Becoming solution-focused in practice', *Educational Psychology in Practice*, 15(2): 116–21.

Reiss, M. and White, J. (2013) *An Aims Based Curriculum*, London: IoE Press.

Riding, R. (2002) *School Learning and Cognitive Styles*, London: David Fulton.

Riding, R.J. and Cheema, I. (1991) 'Cognitive styles: an overview and integration', *Educational Psychology*, 11: 193–215.

Riding, R.J. and Rayner, S. (1998) *Learning Styles and Strategies*, London: David Fulton.

Robertson, J. (1996) *Effective Classroom Control: Understanding Teacher-Student Relationships*, 3rd edn, London: Hodder & Stoughton.

Roffey, S (2010) *Changing Behaviour in Schools*, London: Sage.

Rogers, B. (2002) *Classroom Behaviour*, London: Paul Chapman.

Rogers, B. (2011) *Classroom Behaviour: A Practical Guide to Effective Teaching, Behaviour Management and Colleague Support*, 3rd edn, London: Sage.

Rogers, P.J., Kainth, A. and Smit, H.J. (2001) 'A drink of water can improve or impair mental performance depending on small differences in thirst', *Appetite*, 36: 57–8.

Rogers, W. (2011) *Classroom Behaviour: A Practical Guide to Effective Teaching, Behaviour Management and Colleague Support*, London: Sage.

Rogoff, B. (1990) *Apprenticeship in Thinking: Cognitive Development in Social Context*, Oxford: Oxford University Press.

Roosevelt, F. (1933) Inaugural Address, 4 March 1933, as published in S. Rosenman (ed.) (1938) *The Public Papers of Franklin D. Roosevelt, Volume Two: The Year of Crisis, 1933*, New York: Random House, pp. 11–16.

Rose, R. (2004) 'Towards a better understanding of the needs of pupils who have difficulties accessing learning', in S. Capel, R. Heilbronn, M. Leask and T. Turner (eds) (2004) *Starting to Teach in the Secondary School: A Companion for the Newly Qualified Teacher*, 2nd edn, London: RoutledgeFalmer, pp. 139–48.

Rosenthal, R. and Jacobson, L. (1968) *Pygmalion in the Classroom*, New York: Holt, Rinehart & Winston.

Ross, A. (2006) *Language Knowledge for Secondary Teachers*, London: David Fulton.

Rowland, T. (2004) 'The childhood obesity epidemic: putting the dynamics into thermodynamics', *Ped Exerc Sci*, 16: 86–93.

Royal Society (2011) *Brain Waves Module 2: Neuroscience: Implications for Education and Lifelong Learning*, available at: http://royalsociety.org/policy/projects/brain-waves/education-lifelong-learning/ (accessed 16 November 2015).

Rudduck, J. (2004) *Developing a Gender Policy for Secondary Schools*, Buckingham: Open University Press.

Rudduck, J., Brown, N. and Hendy, L. (2006) *Personalised Learning and Pupil Voice: The East Sussex Project*, London: DfES.

Russell, J. (2007) 'The folly of our text fixation is plain to all. Except ministers', *The Guardian*, 7 February: 36.

Ryan, R.M. and Deci, E.L. (2000a) 'Intrinsic and extrinsic motivations: classic definitions and new directions', *Contemporary Educational Psychology*, 25: 54–67.

Ryan, R.M. and Deci, E.L. (2000b) 'Self-determination theory and the facilitation of intrinsic motivation, social development and well-being', *American Psychologist*, 55: 68–78.

Ryan, R.M. and Stiller, J. (1991) 'The social contexts of internalization: parent and teacher influences on autonomy, motivation and learning', in P.R. Pintrich and M.L. Maehr (eds) *Advances in Motivation and Achievement, Volume 7*, Greenwich, CT: JAI Press, pp. 115–49.

Sachs, J. (2001) 'Teacher professional identity: competing discourses, competing outcomes', *Journal of Education Policy*, 16(2): 149–61.

Sachs, J. (2003) *The Activist Teaching Profession*, Buckingham: Open University Press.

Sadler, P. (1994) *Simple Minds*, BBC 2 television broadcast, 19 September.

Sage, R. (2000) *Class Talk*, Stafford: Network Educational Press.

Sahlberg, P. (2011) *'Finnish Lessons'. What Can the World Learn from Educational Change in Finland?* New York: Teachers College Press.

Säljö, R. (1979) 'Learning in the learner's perspective. 1: Some commonplace misconceptions', *Reports from the Institute of Education*, Sweden: University of Gothenburg.

Salmon, P. (1988) *Psychology for Teachers: An Alternative Approach*, London: Hutchinson.

Salmon, P. (1995) *Psychology in the Classroom: Reconstructing Teachers and Learners*, London: Cassell.

Salovey, P. and Mayer, J.D. (1990) 'Emotional intelligence', *Imagination, Cognition and Personality*, 9: 185–211.

Sammons, P., Day, C., Kington, A., Gu, Q., Stobart, G. and Smees, R. (2007) 'Exploring variations in teachers' work, lives and their effects on pupils: key findings and implications from a longitudinal mixed-method study', *British Educational Research Journal*, 33(5): 681–701.

Savage, M., Devine, F., Cunningham, N., Taylor, M., Li, Y., Hjellbrekke, J., Le Roux, B., Friedman, S. and Miles, A. (2013) 'A new model of social class? Findings from the BBC's Great British Class Survey experiment', *Sociology*, 47(2): 219–50.

Sawyer, S.M., Afifi, R.A., Bearinger, L.H., Blakemore, S-J., Dick, B., Ezeh, A.C. and Patton, G.C. (2012) 'Adolescence: a foundation for future health', *The Lancet*, 379: 1630–40.

Schagen, I. (2008) 'Understanding Fischer Family Trust output', *Practical Research for Education*, (40): 46–51. Available at: https://www.nfer.ac.uk/nfer/PRE_PDF_Files/08_40_08.pdf (accessed 22 January 2016).

Schön, D. (1983) *The Reflective Practitioner*, Aldershot: Arena.

Schwab, J.J. (1964) 'The structure of the disciplines: meanings and significance', in G. Ford and L. Purgo (eds) *The Structure of Knowledge and the Curriculum*, Chicago, IL: Rand McNally.

Scott, D. (2000) *Reading Educational Research and Policy*, London: RoutledgeFalmer.

Scottish Government (2009) *The Education (Additional Support for Learning) (Scotland) Acts 2004 and 2009*, available at: www.scotland.gov.uk/Publications/2009/11/03140104/4 (accessed 22 March 2012).

Scottish Government (2010) *Assessment for Curriculum for Excellence: Strategic Vision, Key Principles*, Edinburgh: Scottish Government.

SEED (Scottish Executive Education Department) (1999) *Review of Assessment in Pre-School and 5–14*, Edinburgh: HMSO.

Seker, H. (2008) 'Will the constructivist approach employed in science teaching change the "grammar" of schooling?', *Journal of Baltic Science Education*, 7(3): 175–84.

Sellers, M. (2014) *Reflective Practice for Teachers*, London: Sage.

Selman, R.L. (1980) *The Growth of Interpersonal Understanding*, New York: Academic Press.

SFT (School Food Trust) (2009) *School Lunch and Learning Behaviour in Secondary Schools: An Intervention Study*, available at: www.schoolfoodtrust.org.uk/school-cooks-caterers/reports (accessed 20 March 2012).

SFT (School Food Trust) (2011) *Parent Voice: School Meals and Packed Lunches*, available at: www.schoolfood trust.org.uk/partners/reports/parent-voice-school-meals-and-packed-lunches (accessed 4 June 2012).

Sharp, J.G. (2009) *Success with Your Education Research Project*, Exeter: Learning Matters.

Sharples, J., Webster, R. and Blatchford, P. (2015) *Making Best Use of Teaching Assistants*, London: Education Endowment Foundation.

Shayer, M. (2008) 'Intelligence for education: as described by Piaget and measured by psychometrics', *British Journal of Educational Psychology*, 78(1): 1–29.

Shayer, M. and Adey, P. (eds) (2002) *Learning Intelligence: Cognitive Acceleration across the Curriculum from 5 to 15 Years*, Buckingham: Open University Press.

Shea, J. and Stockford, A. (2014) *Inspiring the Secondary Curriculum with Technology: Let the Students Do the Work!* London: Routledge.

Short, G. (1986) 'Teacher expectation and West Indian underachievement', *Educational Research*, 27(2): 95–101.

Shulman, L. (1986) 'Those who understand: knowledge growth in teaching', *Educational Researcher*, 15: 4–14.

Shulman, L. (1987) 'Knowledge and teaching: foundation of a new reform', *Harvard Review*, 57: 1–22.

Sifft, J.M. and Khalsa, G.C.K. (1991) 'Effect of educational kinesiology upon simple response-times and choice response-times', *Perceptual and Motor Skills*, 73(3): 1011–15.

Singh, J. (2011) *Child Protection: A Manual for School Teachers*, USA: LAP.

Sjøberg, S. (2007) 'PISA and "real live challenges": mission impossible?', in *PISA According to PISA Revised Version Oct 8 2007*, available at: http://folk.uio.no/sveinsj/Sjoberg-PISA-book-2007.pdf (accessed 13 November 2015).

Skidmore, D. (2000) 'From pedagogical dialogue to dialogic pedagogy', *Language and Education*, 14: 4.

Skinner, B.F. (1953) *Science and Human Behavior*, New York: Macmillan.

Smith, A. and Call, N. (2002) *The ALPS (Accelerated Learning in Primary School) Approach*, London: Accelerated Learning in Training and Education (ALITE).

Smith, E. (2005) *Analysing Underachievement in Schools*, London: Continuum.

Smith, R. and Standish, P. (eds) (1997) *Teaching Right and Wrong: Moral Education in the Balance*, Stoke-on-Trent: Trentham.

Smithers, A. and Robinson, P. (2011) *The Good Teacher Training Guide 2011*, University of Buckingham, available at: www.buckingham.ac.uk/wp-content/uploads/2010/11/GTTG2011.pdf (accessed 15 April 2015).

Smyth, J. (1989) *Rationale for Teachers' Critical Pedagogy: A Handbook*, Geelong: Deakin University Press.

Snow, C.P. (1960) *The Two Cultures and the Scientific Revolution* (The Rede Lecture, 1959), Cambridge: Cambridge University Press.

Spada, M., Nikvecic, I., Moneta, G. and Ireson, J. (2006) 'Metacognition as a mediator of the effect of test anxiety on a surface approach to studying', *Educational Psychology*, 26(5): 615–24.

Stanford University (2015) *Teaching Commons: Bloom's Taxonomy of Educational Objectives*, available at: http://teachingcommons.stanford.edu/resources/course-preparation-resources/course-design-aids/bloom%E2%80%99s-taxonomy-educational-objectives (accessed 19 July 2015).

Statistics Finland (2015) *Population*, available at: www.stat.fi (accessed 12 November 2015).

Stenhouse, L. (1975) *An Introduction to Curriculum Research and Development*, London: Heinemann.

Stenhouse, L. (1983) *Authority, Education and Emancipation*, London: Heinemann.

Stern, D.N. (1985) *The Interpersonal World of the Infant*, New York: Basic Books.

Steuer, N. and Marks, N. (2008) *Local Wellbeing: Can We Measure It?* London: The Young Foundation, in collaboration with the New Economics Foundation (NEF).

Stobart, G. (2008) *Testing Times: The Uses and Abuses of Assessment*, London: Routledge.

Stobart, G. and Gipps, C. (1997) *Assessment: A Teacher's Guide to the Issues*, London: Hodder & Stoughton.

Stokking, K., Leenders, F., De Jong, J. and Van Tartwijk, J. (2003) 'From student to teacher: reducing practice shock and early dropout in the teaching profession', *European Journal of Teacher Education*, 26(3): 329–50.

Stoten, D. (2014) 'Are we there yet? Progress in promoting independent learning in a Sixth Form College', *Educational Studies*, 40(4): 452–5.

Strand, S. (2008) *Minority Ethnic Pupils in the Longitudinal Study of Young People in England*, Report DCSF-RR029, London: DCSF.

Street, P. (2004) 'Those who can teach: deconstructing the teacher's personal presence and impact in the classroom', *Triangle Journals*.

Struppert, A. (2010) '"It's a whole new fun different way to learn": students' perceptions of learning with an electronic simulation: selected results from three case studies in an Australian, an American and a Swiss middle school', *The International Journal of Learning*, 17(9): 363–75.

Stuart, M., Stainthorp, R. and Snowling, M. (2008) 'Literacy as a complex activity: deconstructing the simple view of reading', *Literacy*, 42: 59–66.

Sullivan, J. (1972) 'The effects of Kephart's perceptual motor-training on a reading clinic sample', *Journal of Learning Disabilities*, 5(10): 32–8.

Sumsion, J. (2003) '"Bad days don't kill you: they just make you stronger": a case study of an early childhood educator's resilience', *International Journal of Early Years Education*, 11(2): 141–54.

Sutton, C. (1981) *Communicating in the Classroom*, London: Hodder & Stoughton.

Swaffield, S. (2008) *Unlocking Assessment: Understanding for Reflection and Application*, London: David Fulton.

Swales, J. (1990) *Genre Analysis*, Cambridge: Cambridge University Press.

Swann, M. (1985) *Education for All*, London: HMSO.

Swann, S. (2013) *Pupil Disaffection in Schools*, Farnham: Ashgate.

TA (Teaching Agency) (2008) *Professional Standards for Qualified Teacher Status and Requirements for Initial Teacher Training (Revised 2008)*, London: TA, available at: www.education.gov.uk/publications/standard/publicationDetail/Page1/TDA0600 (accessed 5 April 2012).

Tackey, N., Barnes, H. and Khambhaita, P. (2011) *Poverty, Ethnicity and Education*, York: Joseph Rowntree Foundation.

Tafarodi, R.W. and Vu, C. (1997) 'Two-dimensional self-esteem and reactions to success and failure', *Personality and Social Psychology Bulletin*, 23: 626–35.

Tait, M. (2008) 'Resilience as a contributor to novice teacher success, commitment and retention', *Teacher Education Quarterly*, 35(4): 57–75.

Taylor, C. (2011) *Getting the Simple Things Right: Charlie Taylor's Behaviour Checklists*, available at: www.gov.uk/government/uploads/system/uploads/attachment_data/file/283997/charlie_taylor_checklist.pdf (accessed 18 July 2015).

Teacher Support Network (n.d.) *Starting Out Guide for Newly Qualified and Trainee Teachers*, available at: www.teachersupport.info/search/node/starting%20out%20guide%20for%20newly%20qualified%20teachers (accessed 23 April 2015).

TeacherVision (2015) *Learning Students' Names Quickly*, available at: www.teachervision.com/teaching-methods/classroom-management/6708.html (accessed 17 July 2015).

Teaching College New Jersey (2015) *Anti-Violence Measures*, available at: http://oavi.tcnj.edu/tools-for-everyone/assertiveness/assertive-nonassertive-and-aggressive-behaviors/ (accessed 21 July 2015).

Terzi, L. (2008) 'Beyond the dilemma of difference: the capability approach to disability and special educational needs', in L. Florian and M. McLaughlin (eds) *Disability Classification in Education: Issues and Perspectives*, Thousand Oaks, CA: Corwin Press, pp. 244–62.

The Bristol Guide (2014 edn, updated regularly) *Professional Responsibilities and Statutory Frameworks for Teachers and Others in Schools*, Bristol: University of Bristol, School of Education, available at: www.bristol.ac.uk/education/expertiseandresources/bristolguide (accessed 16 November 2015).

The Children's Society (2012) *The Good Childhood Report: A Review of Our Children's Well-Being*, available at: www.childrenssociety.org.uk/what-we-do/research/well-being/good-childhood-report-2012 (accessed 3 February 2012).

The Marmot Review (2010) *Fair Society, Healthy Lives: A Strategic Review of Health Inequalities in England*, available at: www.instituteofhealthequity.org/projects/fair-society-healthy-lives-the-marmot-review (accessed 20 March 2012).

The Teaching Council (for Ireland) (2012) *Code of Professional Conduct for Educators*, available at: www.teachingcouncil.ie/_fileupload/Professional%20Standards/code_of_conduct_2012_web%2019June2012.pdf (accessed 21 July 2015).

Thomas, G. (2009) *How to Do Your Research Project: A Guide for Students in Education and Applied Social Sciences*, London: Sage.

Titchmarsh, A. (2012) Personal communication.

TLRP (Teaching and Learning Research Programme) (2006) *Learning How to Learn – in Classrooms, Schools and Networks*, available at: www.tlrp.org/pub/documents/no17_james.pdf (accessed 19 July 2015).

TLRP/ESRC (Teaching and Learning Research Project/Economic and Social Research Council) (2006) 'A commentary on the teaching and research programme', in P. Howard-Jones (ed.) *Neuroscience in Education Issues and Opportunities*, available at: www.tlrp.org/pub/documents/Neuroscience%20Commentary%20FINAL.pdf (accessed 6 August 2012).

Tobin, K. (1987) 'The role of wait time in higher cognitive functioning', *Review of Higher Education Research*, 57(1): 69–75.

Tod, J. and Powell, S. (2004) *A Systematic Review of How Theories Explain Learning Behaviour in School Contexts*, London: EPPI.

Tokuhama-Espinosa, T. (2014) *Making Classrooms Better: 50 Practical Applications of Mind, Brain and Education Science*, New York: Norton.

Tomlinson, C. (1999) *The Differentiated Classroom: Responding to the Needs of All Learners*, Alexandria, VA: Association for Supervision and Curriculum.

Torrance, H. and Pryor, J. (1998) *Investigating Formative Assessment*, Buckingham: Open University Press.

Turner, S. (1995) 'Simulations', in J. Frost (ed.) *Teaching Science*, London: The Woburn Press, pp. 181-2.

UK government (2014) *Children and Families Act 2014*, London: The Stationery Office, available at: www.legislation.gov.uk/ukpga/2014/6/pdfs/ukpga_20140006_en.pdf (accessed 22 January 2016).

Underwood, A., Turner, R., Whyte, S. and Rosenberg, J. (2015) *Acoustic Accessibility MESHGuide*, BATOD Foundation, available at: www.meshguides.org/category/general-pedagogy/acoustics-listening-and-learning/ (accessed 18 July 2015).

University of Cambridge (2015a) *Dialogic Teaching*, available at: www.educ.cam.ac.uk/research/projects/dialogic/whatis.html (accessed 15 July 2015).

University of Cambridge (2015b) *Thinking Together*, available at: https://thinkingtogether.educ.cam.ac.uk/ (accessed 15 July 2015).

University of Cambridge/Professor Neil Mercer (2015) *Thinking Together*, available at: http://thinking together.educ.cam.ac.uk/resources/ (accessed 19 July 2015).

Van Der Horst, K., Paw, M.J.C.A., Twisk, J.W.R. and Van Mechelen, W. (2007) 'A brief review on correlates of physical activity and sedentariness in youth', *Medicine and Science in Sports and Exercise*, 39: 1241-50.

Van Manen, M. (1991) *The Tact of Teaching*, Alberta: The Althouse Press.

Van Sledright, B. (2014) *Assessing Historical Thinking and Understanding*, London, Routledge.

Vanes, R. (2012) *Tricks of the Writer's Trade and How to Teach Them to Children Aged 8-14*, London: Routledge.

Vasagar, J. (2012) 'Exam boards should not set their own syllabuses, say MPs', *Education Guardian*, 3 July, available at: www.guardian.co.uk/education/2012/jul/03/exam-boards-set-syllabuses-mps (accessed 21 November 2012).

Veenman, S. (1984) 'Perceived problems of beginning teachers', *Review of Educational Research*, 54: 143-78.

Verenikina, n. (n.d.) *Understanding Scaffolding and the ZPD in Educational Research*, University of Wollongong, NSW, Australia, available at: http://ro.uow.edu.au/cgi/viewcontent.cgi?article=1695andcontext=edupaper (accessed 19 July 2015).

Vernon-Feagans, L., Odom, E., Panscofar, N. and Kainz, K. (2008) 'Comments on Farkas and Hibel: a transactional/ecological model of readiness and inequality', In A. Booth and A.C. Crouter (eds) *Disparities in School Readiness*, New York: Lawrence Earlbaum Associates, pp. 61-78.

Volante, L. (2004) 'Teaching to the test: what every educator and policy-maker should know', *Canadian Journal of Educational Administration and Policy*, 35, available at: http://eric.ed.gov/?id=EJ848235 (accessed 29 July 2015).

Vygotsky, L.S. (1962) *Thought and Language*, Cambridge, MA: MIT Press.

Vygotsky, L.S. (1978) *Mind and Society: The Development of Higher Psychological Processes*, Cambridge, MA: Harvard University Press.

Vygotsky, L.S. (1986) *Thought and Language*, trans. and ed. A. Kozulin, Cambridge, MA: MIT Press.

Walker, S. (2004) 'Interprofessional work in child and adolescent mental health services', *Emotional and Behavioural Difficulties*, 9(1): 189-204.

Wallace, B. (2000) *Teaching the Very Able Child*, London: NACE/David Fulton.

Wallace, B., Leyden, S., Montgomery, D., Winstanley, C., Pomerantz, M. and Fitton, S. (2009) *Raising the Achievement of All Pupils within an Inclusive Setting: Practical Strategies for Developing Best Practice*, London: Routledge.

Walsh, J. (n.d) *How Can Quality Questioning Transform Classrooms?*, available at: www.sagepub.com/upm-data/6605_walsh_ch_1.pdf (accessed 20 March 2015).

Wang, M-T. and Holcombe, R. (2010) 'Adolescents' perceptions of school environment, engagement and academic achievement in middle school', *American Educational Research Journal*, 47: 63, available at: http://aer.sagepub.com/content/47/3/633 (accessed 28 December 2011).

Wasserman, D. (2001) 'Killing Mary to save Jodie: conjoined twins and individual rights', *Philosophy and Public Policy Quarterly*, 21(1): 9-14.

Waters, E., De Silva-Sanigorski, A., Hall, B.J., Brown, T., Campbell, K.J., Gao, Y., Armstrong, R., Prosser, L. and Summerbell, C. (2011) *Interventions for Preventing Obesity in Children*, Cochrane Database Sys Rev.

Watkins, C., Carnell, E. and Lodge, C. (2007) *Effective Learning in Classrooms*, London: Paul Chapman.

Watkins, W. (2012) *The Assault on Public Education*, Columbia, NY: Teachers College Press.

Weare, K. (2004) *Developing the Emotionally Literate School*, London: Paul Chapman.

Webb, N., Ing, M., Kersting, N. and Nemer, K.M. (2009) 'Help seeking in co-operative learning groups', in S.A. Karabenick and S. Newman (eds) *Help-Seeking in Academic Settings*, Mahwah, NJ: Lawrence Erlbaum, pp. 45–72.

Wegerif, R. and Dawes, L. (2004) *Thinking and Learning with ICT: Raising Achievement in Primary Classrooms*, London: Routledge.

Wegerif, R., Li, L. and Kaufman, J.C. (eds) (2015) *The Routledge International Handbook of Research on Teaching Thinking*, London and New York: Routledge.

Weiner, B.J. (1972) *Theories of Motivation*, Chicago, IL: Markham.

Weiten, W. (1992) *Psychology: Themes and Variations*, 2nd edn, Belmont, CA: Brooks/Cole.

Wellings, C. and Wood, A. (2012) *Closing the Achievement Gap in England's Secondary Schools*, London: Save the Children.

Wentzel, K. (1997) 'Student motivation in middle school: the role of perceived pedagogical caring', *Journal of Educational Psychology*, 89: 411–17.

West-Burnham, J. and Coates, M. (2007) *Personalizing Learning: Transforming Learning for Every Child*, London: Network Educational Press.

Westwood, P. (2007) *Commonsense Methods for Children with Special Educational Needs*, 5th edn, London: RoutledgeFalmer.

White, J. (1998) *Do Howard Gardner's Multiple Intelligences Add Up?* London: The Institute of Education, University of London, in the series *Perspectives on Education Policy*.

White, J. (ed.) (2004) *Rethinking the School Curriculum: Values, Aims and Purposes*, London: RoutledgeFalmer.

White, J. (2005) *Howard Gardner: The Myth of Multiple Intelligences*, London: The Institute of Education, University of London, Viewpoint Number 16 (October).

Whittaker, R., O'Donnell, M. and McCabe, A. (eds) (2006) *Language and Literacy: Functional Approaches*, London: Continuum.

WHO (World Health Organization) (2010) *Set of Recommendations on the Marketing of Food and Non-Alcoholic Beverages to Children*, available at: www.who.int/dietphysicalactivity/publications/recsmarketing/en (accessed 20 March 2012).

Whylam, H. and Shayer, M. (1978) *CSMS Reasoning Tasks: General Guide*, Windsor: National Foundation for Educational Research.

Wiedmaier, D., Moore, C., Onwuegbuzie, A., Witcher, A., Collins, J. and Filer, C. (2007) 'Students' perceptions of characteristics of effective college teachers', *American Educational Research Journal*, 44(1): 113–60, available at: http://aer.sagepub.com/content/44/1/113 (accessed 28 December 2011).

Wigfield, A., Eccles, J.S., MacIver, D., Redman, D.A. and Midgley, C. (1991) 'Transitions during early adolescence: changes in children's domain-specific self-perceptions and general self-esteem across the transition to junior high school', *Developmental Psychology*, 27: 552–65.

Wiliam, D. (2001) *Level Best? Levels of Attainment in National Curriculum Assessment*, London: ATL.

Wiliam, D. (2011) *Embedded Formative Assessment*, Bloomington, IN: Solution Tree Press.

Wiliam, D. and Bartholomew, H. (2004) 'It's not which school but which set you're in that matters: the influence on ability-grouping practices on student progress in mathematics', *British Educational Research Journal*, 30(2): 279–94.

Willingham, D. (2009a) 'Why do students remember everything they see on television and forget everything I say?', in D. Willingham (ed.) *Why Don't Students Like School?* San Francisco, CA: Jossey-Bass, pp. 53–86.

Willingham, D. (2009b) *Why Don't Students Like School?* San Francisco, CA: Jossey-Bass.

Willis, P. (1977) *Learning to Labour: How Working Class Kids Get Working Class Jobs*, Aldershot: Gower.

Wilson, E. (2009) *School-Based Research: A Guide for Education Students*, London: Sage.

Wilson, H., Pianta, R. and Stuhlman, M. (2007) 'Typical classroom experiences in first grade: the role of classroom climate and functional risk in the development of social competencies', *The Elementary School Journal*, 108(2): 81–96.

Wilson, V. (2002) *Feeling the Strain: An Overview of the Literature on Teacher Stress* (Research Report 109), Edinburgh: Scottish Council for Research in Education.

Wineburg, S. (1997) 'Beyond breadth and depth: subject matter knowledge and assessment', *Theory into Practice*, 36(4): 255–61.

Wing Jan, L. (1991) *Write Ways: Modelling Writing Forms*, Melbourne: Oxford University Press.

Winstanley, C. (2010) *The Ingredients of Challenge*, Staffs: Trentham Books.

Winter, B., Breitenstein, C., Mooren, F.C., Voelker, K., Fobker, M., Lechtermann, A., *et al.* (2007) 'High impact running improves learning', *Neurobiology of Learning and Memory*, 87: 597–609.

Wittgenstein, L. (1961) *Tractatus Logico-Philosophicus*, trans. D.F. Pears and B.F. McGuinnes, London: Routledge & Kegan Paul.

Wolf, A. (2011) *Review of Vocational Education: The Wolf Report*, DFE-00031-2011, available at: www.education. gov.uk/publications/standard/publicationDetail/Page1/DFE-00031-2011 (accessed 10 June 2012).

Wood, D. (1988) *How Children Think and Learn*, Oxford: Blackwell Press.

Wood, D., Bruner, J. and Ross, G. (1976) 'The role of tutoring in problem-solving', *Journal of Child Psychology*, 17: 89–100.

Woodward, W. (2003) 'Poverty hits exam scores', *The Guardian*, 21 April, available at: www.guardian.co.uk/uk/ 2003/apr/21/politics.schools (accessed 4 March 2012).

Wragg, E.C. (ed.) (1984) *Classroom Teaching Skills*, London: Croom Helm.

Wragg, E.C. (ed.) (2004) *The RoutledgeFalmer Reader in Teaching and Learning*, London: RoutledgeFalmer.

Wragg, E.C. and Brown, G. (2001) *Questioning in the Secondary School*, London: RoutledgeFalmer.

Wright, T. (2008) *How to Be a Brilliant Trainee Teacher*, London: Routledge.

Younger, M., Warrington, M. and Williams, J. (1999) 'The gender gap and classroom interactions: reality and rhetoric?', *British Journal of Sociology of Education*, 20(3): 325–41.

Younie, S. and Leask, M. (2013) *Teaching with Technologies: The Essential Guide*, Buckingham: Open University Press.

Younie, S., Leask, M. and Burden, K. (2015) *Learning to Teach Using ICT in the Primary School*, London: Routledge.

Yuill, N. and Oakhill, J. (2010) *Children's Problems in Text Comprehension: An Experimental Investigation*, Cambridge: Cambridge University Press.

Zimmerman, B.J. (2002) 'Becoming a self-regulated learner: An overview', *Theory Into Practice*, 41(2): 64–70.

Zimmerman, B.J. (1989) 'A social cognitive view of self-regulated academic learning', *Journal of Educational Psychology*, 81(3): 329–39.

Zimmerman, B.J. and Schunk, D.H. (1989/2001) *Self-Regulated Learning and Academic Achievement: Theoretical Perspectives*, London: Routledge.

Zwozdiak-Myers, P. (2009) 'An enquiry into how reflective practice influenced the professional development of teachers as they engaged in action research to study their own teaching', London: Brunel University, unpublished PhD thesis.

Zwozdiak-Myers, P. (2012) *The Teacher's Reflective Practice Handbook: Becoming an Extended Professional through Capturing Evidence-Informed Practice*, London: Routledge.

Author index

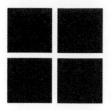

Subject index